THE NATURE
OF SACRIFICE

THE NATURE OF SACRIFICE

A Biography of

Charles Russell Lowell, Jr.,

1835–64

CAROL BUNDY

Farrar, Straus and Giroux / New York

Farrar, Straus and Giroux
19 Union Square West, New York 10003

Library of Congress Cataloging-in-Publication Data
Bundy, Carol, 1958–
    The nature of sacrifice : a biography of Charles Russell Lowell, Jr., 1835–64 /
Carol Bundy.— 1st ed.
        p.   cm.
    Includes bibliographical references (p.) and index.
    ISBN-13: 978-0-374-12077-1
    ISBN-10: 0-374-12077-3
    1. Lowell, Charles Russell, 1835–1864.   2. Generals—United States—Biography.
3. United States. Army—Biography.   4. United States—History—Civil War,
1861–1865—Campaigns.   I. Title.

E467.1.L6B86 2005
973.7´41´092—dc22
[B]

                                                        2004047130

Photographs that appear without a credit line come from the author's collection.

Designed by Jonathan D. Lippincott

www.fsgbooks.com

1   3   5   7   9   10   8   6   4   2

This book is dedicated to my two sons,
Percy and Sam,
and to the memory of my father,
W.L.P.B.,
1917–2000

CONTENTS

A family tree can be found on pages 22–23. Illustrations follow page 278.

INTRODUCTION

THE FUNERAL

October 28, 1864

No nation, of course, can view its young men with indifference: the nurse of
Krishna, when she looked in the infant's mouth, beheld whole kingdoms; so
each nation sees in its young men the means of fulfilling its wishes.
— Charles Russell Lowell, Commencement Day oration, 1854

Colonel Charles Russell Lowell died on October 19, 1864, in the Shenandoah Valley, at the Battle of Cedar Creek, which ended in the decisive and
long-awaited victory that President Lincoln needed to protect his reelection,
only two weeks away. The North, so weary of war, was poised for a choice
between electing the Copperhead Democrat Major General George B.
McClellan, and suing for peace, or continuing the war under Abraham
Lincoln. In this mood of uncertainty and division, the city of Boston found
a hero. Newspaper editorial headlines trumpeted NOBLE DEATH and LAMENT
FOR A TRUE KNIGHT as reporters indulged in an orgy of grief extolling Lowell's excellent ancestry, brilliant mind, military skills, and heroic death. In
the suffering of his family, Bostonians recognized the horror of war: of fourteen cousins who had gone to fight, now the seventh and best was dead.
Mourning this man so universally admired, they found a unity beyond political differences. The same quality that had made Lowell's men believe him
invulnerable had convinced many in Massachusetts that he would survive
the war. Some had even begun to imagine his postwar career: running their
railroad, or seeking political office, or (for the idealists) rebuilding the recovered nation.[1]

"Never . . . within your knowledge or mine has such a funeral as this
been seen," wrote Caroline Healey Dall (a social reformer and, in 1865, co-
founder of the American Social Science Association), who arrived early on
the damp morning of October 28 to help decorate the Harvard College

chapel. She and other bonneted women carrying baskets of floral cuttings scurried across the Harvard Yard, weaving around black-robed scholars. Inside Harvard's new Appleton Chapel, the women decorated the chancel, the reading desk, and the pulpit with sprays of pine boughs and fern fronds, trailing vines of variegated ivies and myrtle, and blasts of chrysanthemums — both the button "Soleil d'Or" and the giant "Emperor of China."[2]

For the altar, cartloads of flowers had been sent into town from the greenhouses of various gentleman horticulturalists in Waltham, Roxbury, and Brookline: orchids, camelias, miniature orange and lemon, scented geraniums, pelargoniums, Cape jasmine. The altar soon disappeared under a profusion of blossoms. Beside the pulpit hung the American flag, representing both "the stars of Heaven in their field of blue" and the "bloody stripes of this cruel war." Mourners entering the chapel were immediately struck not only by the drama of the floral displays but also by the scent. The entire chapel was heavy with the fragrance of hothouse flowers and pine boughs.

An observant eye would have spotted many of Boston's most famous figures: Longfellow's great white mane, Emerson's hawklike profile, James Russell Lowell's ginger curls, and the elfin Dr. Oliver Wendell Holmes. Also a bevy of small, plump, tousle-haired, bespectacled professors, among them the owl-eyed aesthete Charles Eliot Norton and the charismatic Swiss geologist Louis Agassiz, with his squat wealthy wife and lovely daughters.

The lieutenant-governor of Massachusetts and most of the governor's staff arrived from Boston, flushed with self-importance. The governor himself was in Washington, but his hand was evident in this display of state power. A mass of state officials drew like magnets a variety of men, young and old: cronies, members of the Bird Club, and Radical Republicans like Dr. Samuel G. Howe, Frank Sanborn, and Thomas Wentworth Higginson, who had been co-conspirators with John Brown. The leonine head of the belligerent Senator Charles Sumner towered over the others. It was with his help that Lowell had received his commission in the regular army. Also present were members of the governor's war cabinet, valuable for their moderation and their impeccable social credentials untainted by liberal politics: the elegant Colonel Henry Lee and Lowell's Latin School friends Albert G. Browne and John Quincy Adams, Jr.

Others pointedly avoided this group, splendidly got-up members of Boston's Cotton Aristocracy, among them Appletons, Bootts, Lawrences, and the John Amory Lowells. They all loathed the Radical Republicans as fanatics and social inferiors. Yet to some degree they had all been coopted into the war effort. Particularly splendid would have been the industrialist and philanthropist Amos Adams Lawrence. His wealth had spread well beyond textiles, but he continued to represent the quintessence of Cotton over Conscience, the partnership between the slave owners of the South and the textile magnates of New England. Paradoxically, Lawrence had underwritten the Second Massachusetts Cavalry, Lowell's regiment, just as he had bankrolled Yankee emigration into Kansas, even supplying weapons.

Another official party added weight and pomp to the occasion: the overseers of Harvard University and members of the Harvard Corporation, dressed in ceremonial robes and broad collars, serious, sober men standing together, inscrutable, recognizing no one, appearing almost oblivious to their surroundings—literally pillars of the community, reminders of an authority older than the nation and the Commonwealth, when the college, like the Province, had bowed to the clerical mandate.

Rumbling up in a large but worn carriage came a man Lowell had greatly admired and to whom he had owed much: John Murray Forbes, a diminutive, bald dynamo of enterprise made rich by the China trade. More than any figure present, Forbes had pushed forward the Massachusetts war effort, drawing into action Boston's wealth and its radical political leaders. Although he had attempted to find "safe" places for his favorites, his son had become a prisoner of war five months previously; and now Lowell had died, Forbes's greatest personal loss of the war. A crowd of young people accompanied him—his own children with their friends and spouses, fresh-faced girls, boys with hair wetted down. All had idolized Lowell; all now wept for him.

One would have seen clumps of Lowell's former classmates and friends, some on crutches, some maimed, others gaunt and frail. Quite a few, like the "Boy General," Major-General Francis C. Barlow, had been, like Lowell, acolytes of Emerson. Barlow's military talents had exceeded Lowell's, and his collapse, just months before, was not from war but from the sudden death of his wife. The emaciated Lieutenant-Colonel Oliver Wendell Holmes, Jr., Lowell's cousin, had been mustered out of service in July after three years of grueling duty in the Twentieth Massachusetts Infantry. These two were regarded and greeted with admiration by all, with envy by some, with shame by others. Classmates—now businessmen, lawyers, and merchants, members of the Somerset Club, married to the daughters of Boston's elite—they had profited in the war economy and were now poised to become mainstays of Boston civic life. The old acquaintances greeted one another stiffly. Their speech fell into embarrassed pleasantries or, worse, silence, their grief commingled with guilt.

One would have seen a swath of cousins, almost exclusively female—a sea of Jackson faces, long, grave, handsome, and reassuring on a man but severe and plain on the women, and Lowell girls, with small heart-shaped faces culminating in sharp, pointed chins. Their men either were dead or were standing with the institutions they represented, the university or the state. Lowell's great-uncle Dr. James Jackson, the last of the famous three Jackson brothers, was there, his white head bobbing above the crowd, his kindly face clouded by age. Shepherding him was Lizzie Putnam, his favorite grandchild, carrying her own private grief for another dead soldier, James Savage. As one of Boston's preeminent physicians, Dr. Jackson, now ninety, had been present at the birth of many of the people gathered there. Now his sweet face wore a look of confusion, as if instinctively understanding the deeper currents: had he come for a birth or a death?

A stone's throw away, the coffin waited on the Quincy Street edge of the Harvard Yard, in front of a small gingerbread house, the Lowell residence. The Independent Corps of Cadets massed outside. Shortly before noon their commanding officer raised his sword and at noon sharp, with military precision, gave the signal. The band on the chapel steps struck up Pleyel's Hymn. The cadets started their procession. Stragglers made a last dash for the now-overflowing pews. The pallbearers raised the coffin onto their shoulders and carried it down the steps of Mrs. Lowell's porch, through the now-driving rain, diagonally along the familiar college paths, under the elms and up the steps of the chapel. As the coffin crossed the threshold, the band ceased. In silence the soldiers and pallbearers made their way among the mourners.

As the coffin passed, the congregation rose row by row. Although it had been only a short walk, the pallbearers were breathing hard, especially Henry Lee Higginson, Lowell's oldest and most devoted friend. Wounded in the spine at Aldie the year before, Higginson was now out of the war; his back was permanently weakened. In the silence, he stumbled. As his sword struck a pew, the sharp thud and ring sent a jolt and murmur through the congregation. The other pallbearers were officers of Lowell's regiment, notably Lowell's adjutant, Lieutenant Henry E. Alvord, an abolitionist, into whose arms Lowell had fallen from his horse. It was he who had brought Lowell's body back to Massachusetts from the Shenandoah Valley.

The cadets in their gleaming dress uniforms led the way to the altar and turned to form a line across the width of the choir, a half-ring around the coffin. The pallbearers, having set down their burden, joined them. Only then could the congregation recognize the sixth pallbearer. Dressed in civilian clothes, John Chandler Bancroft stood with, but apart from, the military ceremony. Son of the great American historian and Democratic diplomat George Bancroft, scion of the powerful Dwight family clan, Johnny Bancroft, an artist, had not joined the Union cause, having found a substitute, an immigrant, to take his place. It was expressive of the power of Lowell's friendships that Bancroft had found the courage to honor the request that he serve as a pallbearer.

On the communion table, where the pallbearers had placed it, lay the regulation army coffin, flag-draped and wreathed in flowers. On it were Lowell's sword, the hilt worn, the scabbard battered; his cap, dirty, torn, dull, shabby; and his campaign-soiled gauntlets.

The elderly Reverend Dr. James Walker, former president of Harvard, rose and declaimed: "The beauty of Israel is slain upon thy high places: how are the mighty fallen! . . . From the blood of the slain, from the fat of the mighty, the bow of Jonathan turned not back." These familiar words had been used often in the past three years. The congregation knew them by heart. Even so, they listened as if hearing them for the first time. "Saul and Jonathan were lovely and . . . in their death they were not divided. They were swifter than eagles, they were stronger than lions. Ye daughters of Israel, weep."

The amiable, stone-deaf old man, who had watched the youthful Lowell (and all the Harvard war dead) in their college years, paused to catch his breath. Then, as he continued the lamentation of King David, his voice rasped. It was too loud, too insistent, as he concluded: "How are the mighty fallen in the midst of the battle! O Jonathan . . . thy love to me was wonderful . . . How are the mighty fallen and the weapons of war perished."

The congregation sat like stones, watching the old man before them, his own head bowed. And then, with a shuffle of feet and a swish of robes, Reverend Cyrus Augustus Bartol came forward, and Reverend Walker resumed his seat.

Bartol had been Lowell's grandfather's assistant at the West Church in Boston for twenty-five years, inheriting the pulpit on the old man's death only three years before. A Transcendentalist of Italian origin (Bartol was shortened from Bartoldi), he was an enthusiast. In his own church the previous Sunday, he had preached a fiery sermon entitled "The Purchase of

Blood: A Tribute to Brigadier-General Charles Russell Lowell, Jr." He had begun by saying that "blood has in it a certain price or power to purchase. Any thing in the world is worth what you can buy with it; and blood is incomparable treasure, by this rule. So I claim to-day the blood nowhere more copious or pure than has marked your lintels and these church-doors." Then he declared, "Blood, shed in testimony to any truth or principle, is the chief riches of mankind. It is not money, or what we commonly mean by value . . ." And on he went, weighing and gauging what had been bought and paid for, discussing various forms of specie, referring at a certain point to the "Almighty Dealer," and calling at the end for "more blood, if more for our great purchase be required!"[3]

The family agreed that Reverend Bartol had gone too far. They had never much liked him. In fact, Charles Russell Lowell himself had on numerous occasions ridiculed the man. In the rush toward great and divine truths, this eager and ambitious preacher strove for an originality that succeeded only in introducing elements of the absurd. For this occasion, he confined himself to offering a prayer for the country, for the parish, and for the college "with its proud expectation baffled."

And then Reverend George Putnam rose to give the address. Minister of the First Church of Roxbury, Putnam was a Unitarian and a conservative. He provided a manly, compassionate, thoughtful but businesslike ministry, and for the past twenty years he had done all he could to suppress the slavery controversy. "Religion and practical goodness are one and the same thing," Putnam believed, and he was filled with practical goodness, or at least a pragmatic goodness. His son, Lowell's Harvard classmate, had married Lowell's sister Harriet, so Lowell's death was a personal loss for Putnam. As he reached the pulpit, he paused momentarily, running his hand over his face, and then he began. He paid tribute to Lowell's breeding, his good blood, his good education, his popularity, his genius, his great promise, and his decision, at the start of the war, to throw all this aside.[4]

Some things Putnam could not possibly say. Yet because most of the older people present knew at least a few of them, he felt compelled to bow to this unspoken knowledge. He paused, allowing minds to wander and recall that illness, insanity, and wrecked fortunes had cut deeply into the Lowell family. They had known the sort of failure that destroys, but, like an answer to a prayer, this son had come and gracefully taken up the burden of rescuing his family. It was bad enough that at twenty-two he had fallen prey to seemingly terminal tuberculosis. Fighting his way back to health, taking up his burden afresh, Lowell had only improved with adversity. And now this.

When Putnam resumed, he spoke of the war, cataloguing those whom "the present sojourner into God's eternal embrace" had outlived: his younger brother, James Jackson Lowell, whose body lay behind enemy lines beneath a tree near a farm in Virginia; his cousin William Lowell Putnam, whose guts had been shot away in the fiasco of Ball's Bluff; another cousin, Cabot Jackson Russel, and a brother-in-law, Robert Gould Shaw, both buried in a mass grave at Fort Wagner; and two more cousins: Warren Dutton Russell, killed at Second Bull Run, and Sumner Paine, who fell at Gettysburg. Putnam, recognizing the bonds of childhood, also mentioned Lowell's close friends Stephen Perkins, James Savage, Richard Goodwin, Paul Revere, William Sedgwick, and Wilder Dwight. On and on the list went, mercilessly.[5]

To this host now came Charles Russell Lowell, killed at Cedar Creek two weeks short of his first wedding anniversary, one month short of the birth of his first child, and less than three months before his thirtieth birthday. This was a man who in the Shenandoah Valley campaign alone had had thirteen horses shot from under him, a man whom, in three and a half years of battle, no bullet had touched. And so when the spent minié bullet hit him high in the chest, knocking him from his horse and reducing his voice to a whisper, he had refused to leave the field. At the summons to attack, he had been strapped back into his saddle, and with sword drawn he had led the charge, his red officer's sash making him an irresistible target for the rebel sharpshooters on the rooftops of Middletown. When he was shot the second time, the bullet passed from shoulder to shoulder, severing his spinal cord. Thus he had received his fatal wounds.

News of his death traveled fast. General George Custer, his fellow brigade leader, cried. General Wesley Merritt, his division commander, mumbled that he would give up his command if only Lowell were there to receive it. General Philip H. Sheridan, who owed to Lowell the rescue of his reputation on that day, said, "He was the perfection of a man and a soldier." He went on in his report to insist that if Lowell had lived, he would have commanded all his cavalry.[6]

Instead, Lowell's body was brought by train back to Boston, leaving behind the battlefields of the war-ravaged Shenandoah Valley and the strange and difficult alliances that he, a "Black Republican," had forged with his fellow officers, most of them West Point Democrats; leaving behind the rough and varied group of men he had patched together and drilled into his regiment, the Second Massachusetts Cavalry; leaving behind the regular troops of the Reserve Brigade, whom he had been proud to command; leaving behind his most formidable foe, Colonel John Singleton Mosby, the Gray Ghost. Leaving all this behind, his body had now returned to its beginnings: to Quincy Street, his parents' home; to Harvard, his alma mater; to the West Church, his grandfather's pulpit; to Boston, to family, to friends; to Mount Auburn Cemetery, final resting place of his forebears.

And he was returned to those who loved him best. A group of faces clustered in the illustrious crowd: his mother, Anna Cabot Jackson Lowell, worn from years of overwork, as she grimly confronted the adversity from which she would never recover, the death of her oldest, last living, and, truth be told, favorite son; his father, Charles Russell Lowell, Sr., pale from ill health, already dying from grief for his namesake, who he had believed would redeem his own failed life; his pregnant wife, Josephine Shaw Lowell, who "bore it like a hero's wife, staggered at first, she soon recovered her composure";[7] his tubercular sister, Harriet, who had been his favorite; and then the aunts and grandmothers and female cousins who made up his extended family and lived on into the next century, brotherless and husbandless. These women had taken him to school, nursed him through childhood diseases, bragged about his college successes, and, once the war came, provided the boxes of food and clothing and letters, the clucking and worrying and pampering that were every soldier's due. Only his older sister, Anna, was not there. As a nurse in Washington, where the wards were overflowing with casualties, she could not be spared. Anna had marked his passing on October 22, when she first learned of it in a long talk with Custer, who told her of her brother's last days.

Reverend Putnam moved to his conclusion:

> This mighty mother of us all, our country, . . . steeps her soil in her children's most precious blood. She tears her brightest jewels from her own forehead, and flings them in the dust. She sends daily her swift messengers of grief and desolation from heart to heart, and from house to house, throughout her borders. She does all this; but she does it not in cruelty, but in love, that she may preserve her own glorious life, her own imperial sovereignty, and her benignant power to bless her children, and fold them under her brooding wings, to nour-

ish and keep them, as she only can, in freedom, in honor, and in peace. And thus she pays the stupendous debt she owes to her afflicted people.[8]

To many in the congregation, the good reverend seemed to have read their minds. Gathered to commemorate the life of Charles Russell Lowell were men who represented almost all positions on the political map, men who could influence the votes of countless others. They had put aside their arguments to unite in grief and respect. But in a week's time they would go to the polls to vote either for continued war, for more of the same stumbling costly leadership that had been provided by the rough, hedging Abraham Lincoln; or for peace, for an end to madness, for an end to the folly of good men dying for slaves, for the fine words and arrogant assurance of George McClellan.

Turning toward the coffin with outstretched arms, Reverend Putnam asked: "Are we paying too heavy a price for our country's freedom?"[9]

What had been the price? A generation of men—a generation of mothers now sonless, sisters brotherless, wives husbandless, children fatherless. And now, today, Lowell. Lowell had been different. He had had a curious power over people. Certainly his charm, his naturally jubilant spirit, and his wit had been attractive. His photographic memory and impressive intellect had inspired, awed, and impressed. He was much trusted for his fairness, for being a moral anchor. Lowell's power over people was such that he "drew their wills to him, as a lodestone attracts iron." He possessed an irresistible magnetism. And yet Lowell himself remained an enigma, known only in parts, rarely speaking of himself. He had what one friend described as "the impersonality of genius."[10]

Turning back to face the mourners, Reverend Putnam concluded, "Here if ever we might be permitted to say so, but here, beside these precious remains, our full hearts answer—no—not too much—not too much."[11]

Then, as if it had caught a voice of triumph from his magnificent exordium, the choir burst out like trumpets: "The Lord hath triumphed, triumphed, gloriously triumphed, gloriously the horse and his rider hath he thrown into the sea."[12] The song from Exodus of Moses, of praise, of victory. And that, of course, was the point. Lowell had fallen at the head of his men, he had fallen leading the charge, but the battle had been won. Without Lowell's decisive leadership, there would have been no army left for Sheridan to rally after he made his famous ride from Winchester. The battle had

decided the Shenandoah Valley campaign and begun the ruin of the Confederate cavalry. It had given Lincoln the victory he needed for reelection.
Lowell had triumphed, even in death.

The blessing was spoken. The guard re-formed its escort. The drumbeat
sounded, and the congregation rose again as the body passed for the last
time among them. Out into the pouring rain the coffin was carried. The
congregation followed. The rain continued to fall. The wind blew it at a
harsh slant and swept what was left of the yellow leaves from the trees and
drove them swirling to the ground. As the coffin was loaded onto a cart, the
grandees and political figures peeled away. Most of the congregation hurried
out of the harsh weather. Only the most intimate of family and friends now
followed the riderless horse, Lowell's boots slung over the saddle pommel, as
it led the procession—the coffin, then the cadets, then mourners—on the
long march from the chapel, out of the village of Cambridge and west along
Brattle Street. It was a walk Lowell had made countless times, but he had always stopped at Elmwood, the Lowell family house. Now the procession
passed the house and continued on down the road to Mount Auburn Cemetery, where Lowell would join his grandfather and his cousin. As the band
played the "Dead March" from Handel's *Saul*, the coffin was lowered. A
prayer was given. Clumps of dirt were thrown in. Charles Russell Lowell was
consigned to the hearts and memories of those who had known him.

PART I

TOO YOUNG
TO BE TAUGHT

—◦◦◦—

The old men, the men of the last generation, *cannot* teach us of the present what should be, for we know as well as they, or better; they should not tell us what *can* be, for the world always advances by impossibilities achieved, and if life has taught them what *cannot* be, such knowledge in the world's march is only *impedimenta*. In short, though men are often too old to learn, they are often too young to be taught.
                    —Charles Russell Lowell, Commencement Day oration, 1854

The Lowell-Jackson Family

THE LOWELL-JACKSON FAMILY

The clan into which Charles Russell Lowell was born had its origins in a vow of "eternal celibacy"[1] taken in the late 1750s by two young scholars, Jonathan Jackson, an orphan of considerable means, and John Lowell, the only son of a respectable family. Such was their "romantic attachment" (as it was called within the family) that on their graduation from Harvard, Jackson followed Lowell to Newburyport, where they built identical houses, side by side, on the High Street overlooking the town's harbor—its bay, mudflats, marshes, and beaches—and the sea. Lowell, whose father was the leading minister of Newburyport, became a lawyer. Jackson entered the employ of the richest merchant-ship owner, Patrick Tracy, soon becoming his partner.

Neither Tracy nor Lowell resembled Jackson. Patrick Tracy was an Irishman who had made his fortune in the shipping business. A swarthy man and a bit of a scrapper, even in a full-length portrait he could not be made to look elegant, let alone refined. His broad red cheeks, bulbous nose, and calculating eyes suggest a man with little patience. One hand rests on a rather lethal-looking anchor. He stands on the shore as if ready to pounce, seashells at his feet, a barrel on its side, and the sails of his ships behind him. Tracy, Tracy & Jackson specialized in the flax trade, shipping flax grown in the Merrimack Valley to Philadelphia, shipping Pennsylvania linen to the West Indies, shipping molasses and rum to Britain, and returning to Newburyport with finished textiles. It was a trade sufficiently lucrative to make Tracy a benefactor of Newburyport and a property owner throughout Massachusetts.[2]

John Lowell was a tall man, "inclined to corpulence,"[3] with plain features made plainer by his fleshiness: cheeks that dissolved into jowls and double chins, wispy hair rather vaguely curled. There was no vanity in either his dress or his self-esteem. In his portrait he rather smartly meets his portraitist's gaze and, with mouth set firmly shut, appears barely able to suppress his impatience. Lowell was in all things rapid: gait, conversation, success. His friendship with Jonathan Jackson secured him the legal representation of the Tracy shipping empire and of the partners' extensive personal business, launching a distinguished career in maritime law. Lowell also argued what would today be called "civil rights" or "human rights" cases: the liberation of a slave, the exoneration of an alleged witch. To Lowell the law was an instrument of progress and reason, as well as an opportunity to exercise his forensic agility and his rhetorical skill.

Jonathan Jackson, having money of his own and marrying into it, lived the life of a wealthy merchant. He was a vain man, "a slave to his black barber" and "careful of his dress." Long after fashion and his fortunes changed, Jackson continued to dress in the colonial style, with a gilt-buttoned deep blue coat over a broadly striped waistcoat. Each of Jackson's five portraits by John Singleton Copley depicts a gentleman with precise lips, an aquiline nose, delicate skin, and hair immaculately coiffed and powdered. In those pre-Revolutionary days the Jackson house had been grandeur itself. Jackson preferred formality and courtly courtesy. A black servant stood attendance behind Jackson at table; his coachmen wore livery. He named his slave Pomp, after the fashion established by his father-in-law, Patrick Tracy, who owned a slave called Apropos.[4]

"Eternal celibacy" had lasted only until 1767, when both men married. Between them they had five wives and eighteen children. It is hardly surprising that the lives of the Lowell and Jackson children, growing up in the twin houses, soon became intertwined. Jackson's daughter Hannah married one of Lowell's sons, Francis. Hannah's brother Charles married Francis's cousin Amelia Lee and, after her early death, another Lowell cousin, Frances Cabot. Another Jackson brother, James, married yet another Lowell cousin, Elizabeth Cabot; after her death he married her sister Sarah. The youngest Jackson brother, Patrick, married Elizabeth's sister Lydia. And the youngest Jackson of all, Mary, married the younger brother of Amelia, Henry Lee.

Both intermarriage and clannishness typified New England family behavior, and the Lowell-Jackson "system of seclusion,"[5] as one cousin described the arrangement, survived the Revolution, the transplanting of its members fifty miles south to the bigger and deeper port of Boston, the death of the family business in the maritime trade, the rise of industrialization, and civil war.

The Townshend Act of 1767 began the political partnership of Jonathan Jackson and John Lowell. This general import tax on British goods (one of the many taxes that precipitated the Revolution) particularly affected New-buryport's leading merchants, chief among them Tracy, Tracy & Jackson. When Boston responded to the tax with a boycott of British goods, urging other Massachusetts towns to do likewise, the firm and the town were placed in a difficult position. Newburyport's chief product was ships built for firms like Tracy, Tracy & Jackson, which paid for the ships with British goods.

For nearly a decade the seven-member Newburyport non-importation committee, with John Lowell giving legal advice and Jonathan Jackson and Patrick Tracy as members, straddled the growing divergence between colony and king, treading a fine line between flouting the tax on the one hand, and on the other preserving the right to continue trading with Britain. By 1774 that position had become untenable. Signing a declaration defying King George III, Lowell and Jackson spent the next fifteen years serving on various local and continental committees and congresses that established the laws and constitutions of the nascent American nation. They were Federalists—George Washington's party—urging stability, a strong central government, and the swiftest possible return to prewar commercial life. Liberty and democracy they regarded as but two among many ingredients that, when balanced, might create a harmony that could be called good government and provide social stability. Their overriding concern was fear that the particular constellation of new institutions created by the Constitution would reward demagogues and that the masses, still largely illiterate and easily manipulated, would fall prey to a "strong man."[6]

Equally mistrustful and disapproving of aristocratic rule, with its inherent corruption and decadence, they embraced the virtues of an oligarchic, meritocratic republic dominated by a mercantile class: independent, self-reliant, educated, cultured. They believed themselves, individually and collectively, an ideal balance of social virtues, enjoying sufficient stability and inherited wealth to create culture and refinement, sufficient instability and drive to work hard, and sufficient wisdom to retain a virile, creative, energetic practicality. They were religious liberals and prodigious in their civic activities. Founders of libraries, societies, banks, and orphanages, they held views that were exclusive and paternalistic, but by their actions they demonstrated sincere commitment to the commonweal. That their political philosophy should reinforce their own high opinion of themselves is not surprising. The high tone with which they expressed their self-satisfaction led even their supporters to declare that they wished "to establish a nobility of opinion" of which Boston would be the "Headquarters of Good Principles."[7]

Shortly after the end of the Revolutionary War, both men were living in

Boston. Lowell had relocated as early as 1776, the better to serve his clients and potential clients. The confusion of war had created innumerable legal questions and cases: legislation, personal debt, privateering, and the disposal of Loyalist property. His moderation, which in 1774 had been so dangerous, was now an asset. Lowell was entrusted with the management of a large number of Loyalists' property and business. Making many trips to Philadelphia, Lowell argued seven hundred of the eleven hundred cases concerning privateering brought before the national government. He rapidly became the leading admiralty lawyer in Boston.

Meanwhile, Jackson's fortune had vanished. His commitment to American independence had been wholehearted, and he had put Tracy, Tracy & Jackson's entire fleet at the service of the revolutionary forces, fitting out the first privateer of the war, a twenty-gun brig called, appropriately, the *Yankee Hero*. During the war, the firm's huge fleet captured some 120 enemy vessels, which together with their cargoes were sold by the provisional government for some $4 million. Nevertheless, in 1783, at the end of the war, the company fleet, once valued at more than $3 million, had been reduced to thirteen merchant vessels and one cruiser. The new United States, burdened by some $20 million in war debts, could not repay Jackson; the old trade with Britain was now impossible, and it was difficult to develop a trade with France. By 1789, when the French Revolution disrupted even that trade, the elder Tracy was dead, the younger Tracy was bankrupt, and Jackson had secured a sinecure from the president as United States Marshal for Massachusetts.

Jackson strove, in his reduced circumstances, to preserve his dignity, decorum, and standing as a gentleman within the community. He expected of his sons what he would maintain for himself: "to act well his part; to act it gracefully if he could, but first of all to act it well." At the nadir of his father's fortunes, thirteen-year-old Patrick Tracy Jackson—Charlie Lowell's grandfather—was apprenticed to the richest merchant in Newburyport, a position his father and grandfather once held. William Bartlett, a man of humble origins, hesitated before accepting the boy. Was young Patrick a Tracy or a Jackson? Did he have his grandfather's drive to work or his father's more courtly habits? Determined to give Bartlett no grounds for complaint, young Patrick applied himself to his tasks, however tedious and menial, and declared that "he should not feel disgraced by anything which it was his duty to do." This experience undoubtedly gave him one of his distinctive qualities: he had the common touch. His relations with his workmen were always good, and although at times he would find himself under suspicion from his colleagues, he was known to those he employed as a rarity among his class, inspiring trust so firm that a written contract was never needed.[8]

After serving out his apprenticeship in 1801, Patrick went into partnership with two of his brothers-in-law, Francis Cabot Lowell and Henry Lee, sailing the world as supercargo. He often faced moments of potential disaster, most notably in 1805 when the British, in the midst of taking control of the strategic port of Cape Town, impounded his ship and cargo and detained Jackson for a year. By means unknown Jackson managed to exchange his cargo of perishables for the sweet Constantia wine that was produced locally and highly prized in Europe. (It was Napoleon's favorite.) This experience, and the death of his two eldest brothers at sea, helped to confirm Jackson's desire for a life on land, particularly as New England maritime trade over the next seven years was slowly strangled by the Francophile policy of the Jefferson and Madison administrations.

Caught in the Napoleonic Wars between France and Britain, and siding with America's first ally, France, Jefferson imposed the ineffective and soon notorious Embargo of 1807 banning trade with Britain. The election of James Madison as president in 1808 brought New England a small reprieve: in exchange for Federalist support, Madison lifted the embargo, but he could not steer off a course toward war with Britain. When it came, Yankee shipowners returned to privateering, but by 1814 the British blockade of New England was almost completely effective. As shipyards stood empty, as ships rotted at the docks, as not a sail was to be seen in Boston Harbor, invective and tirades poured from the pens of Jackson's friends and relations in the Essex Junto (a conservative faction of Federalists from Essex County on Massachusetts's North Shore). So dire was the effect of war on New England that in 1814 these men met to discuss whether New England should secede from the Union. Nothing so decisive occurred. The leaders of the Essex Junto had gone to their meeting full of wrath and indignation, but they returned more sober. They were stained, however, by reports of their treasonable thoughts, and this was not lost on their political opponents. In the volatile political atmosphere, the Junto members were showered with abuse—at once "British bootlickers," "monarchial aristocrats," and "Lobster princes."[9]

Francis Cabot Lowell and Patrick Tracy Jackson forwent political action and responded in their own way to the maritime crisis and the vicissitudes of European conflict. They abandoned their trade in Bengali coarse cotton cloth, procured from the British port of Calcutta, and in 1813 established the

Lowell/Jackson Family Tree

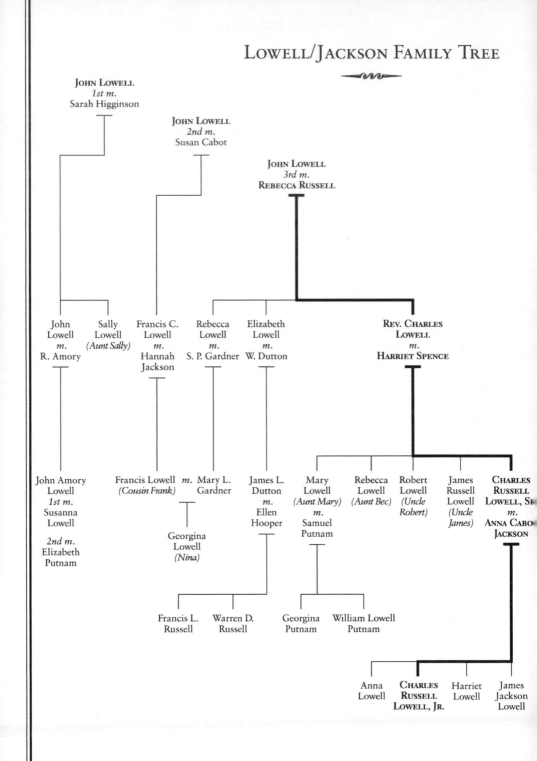

John Lowell
1st m.
Sarah Higginson

John Lowell
2nd m.
Susan Cabot

John Lowell
3rd m.
Rebecca Russell

John
Lowell
m.
R. Amory

Sally
Lowell
(Aunt Sally)

Francis C.
Lowell
m.
Hannah
Jackson

Rebecca
Lowell
m.
S. P. Gardner

Elizabeth
Lowell
m.
W. Dutton

**Rev. Charles
Lowell**
m.
Harriet Spence

John Amory
Lowell
1st m.
Susanna
Lowell

2nd m.
Elizabeth
Putnam

Francis Lowell   *m.*   Mary L.
(Cousin Frank)   Gardner

Georgina
Lowell
(Nina)

James L.
Dutton
m.
Ellen
Hooper

Mary
Lowell
(Aunt Mary)
m.
Samuel
Putnam

Rebecca
Lowell
(Aunt Bec)

Robert
Lowell
*(Uncle
Robert)*

James
Russell
Lowell
*(Uncle
James)*

**Charles
Russell
Lowell, Sr**
m.
**Anna Cabot
Jackson**

Francis L.
Russell

Warren D.
Russell

Georgina
Putnam

William Lowell
Putnam

Anna
Lowell

**Charles
Russell
Lowell, Jr.**

Harriet
Lowell

James
Jackson
Lowell

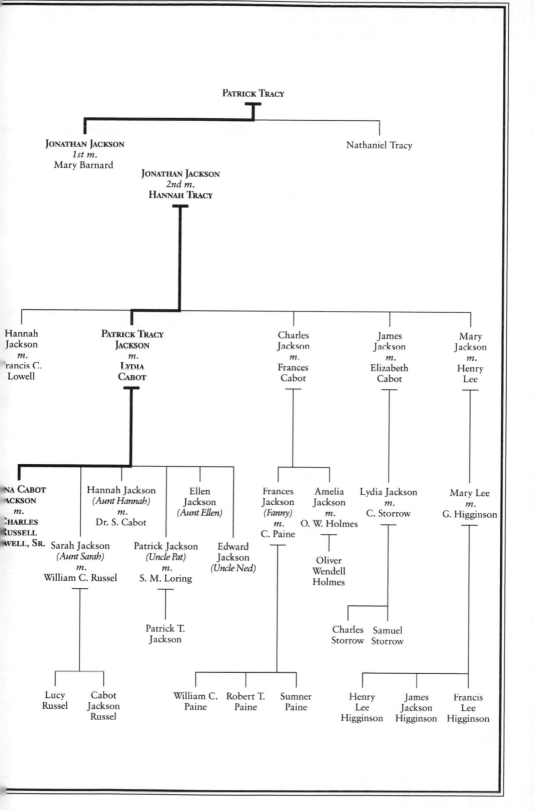

Boston Manufacturing Company on a bend in the Charles River a few miles north of Boston, at Waltham. They brought together under one roof all the processes of textile production: pounds of raw cotton entered at one end and in sequence were washed, combed, carded, spun, and woven; the fabric emerged at the other end, ready for market. The plant, which claimed to be the first integrated factory in the United States, was an almost instant success. The corporate structure was also pioneering in its separation of the stockholders, who knew nothing of cotton or power looms, from the managers who ran the factory and maintained the equipment. Thus the cupolaed five-story brick building, situated between the small town and the river, surrounded by clapboard boardinghouses and grazing cows, was in at the beginning of America's industrialization and corporatization.[10]

Ironically, raising funds had been difficult. While many of their associates were interested, virtually no one was ready to risk money. In the end, the Lowell-Jackson family owned 70 out of 100 shares, the largest investor being Jackson himself, who saw it as his duty to take the largest risk. The success of the company brought enormous wealth to the Lowell-Jackson family and to Patrick Tracy Jackson in particular, a success he compounded by buying the water rights to the Pawtucket Falls on the Merrimack River. In 1823 he renamed this portion of Chelmsford after his dead partner and brother-in-law, Francis Cabot Lowell. As proprietor of the Merrimack Locks & Canals Company, Jackson controlled the energy source for this new industrial city. The company harnessed, channeled, and regulated the flow of water by manipulating holding tanks, locks, and canals, and thus the development of the city. Nothing could be built or expanded without Jackson's cooperation and approval. His position was strong: the pressure to erect new cotton mills intensified as the nation's demand for cotton cloth soared.

The Lowell mills were only the start of Jackson's intended empire. True, they had made him rich enough to retire in 1827, at the age of forty-seven; he bought an estate in Waltham and set about leading a leisured, gracious existence like other wealthy Bostonians who were establishing their own country seats, experimenting in agriculture, hybridizing plants in large greenhouses, and going on long tours of Europe. But after his triumph at Lowell, developing a mere estate failed to satisfy. He found himself depressed and dyspeptic. Visits to various spas did not help. Finally his medical brother, Dr. James Jackson, prescribed a return to work, and within the year Patrick Tracy Jackson had launched several new ventures.

Taking an interest in the Boston Gas Works, another technologically advanced business, Jackson also started to develop both commercial and residential properties in Boston. But his pet project was the Lycoming Coal Company, which he bought in 1828 along with three other investors: Thomas Handasyd Perkins, Edmund Dwight, and George William Lyman. Perkins, called "the Colonel," was a man of the old school. He had made a fortune in the China trade and had investments throughout the state. Perkins and Jackson were old friends, and Perkins always bought a stake in Jackson's enterprises. Dwight, from western Massachusetts, owned controlling interests in most of the major industrial projects there. He was also an investor in the Worcester-to-Albany railroad. Lyman, six years Jackson's junior, had made most of his money in the fur trade before selling out to Perkins. He had married first a daughter of the Boston Federalist Harrison Gray Otis; then a daughter of William Pratt, another man of considerable wealth, whose business association with Jackson dated back to 1811. In addition, Lyman's brother was mayor of Boston.

The Lycoming Coal Company consisted of three thousand acres in a remote, virtually unpopulated, and mountainous region of central Pennsylvania. One William Farrand had undertaken the initial explorations of the area, traveling up the Susquehanna River into what had until quite recently been Indian land—its few white inhabitants were descendants of outcasts and outlaws. In this unpromising region Farrand explored fast-moving creeks and dense woods and eventually found coal and iron-ore deposits running in parallel veins high up on the eastern slopes of the Alleghenies. He began to mine for coal at a location he named Farrandsville.

At the time of its purchase, Lycoming was producing only firebricks. Expansion began almost immediately. Jackson led the way, personally investing in adjoining lands. The partners proceeded with what they hoped was great secrecy, for they were not alone in their interest in iron; other ventures were developing sites north, south, and west of theirs. The next advance for American industry was waiting for the development of a domestic supply of coal and iron as well as for smelting technology. Jackson's initial grasp of this reality had come from his mills at Lowell. Once iron gears replaced leather belting systems, looms became stronger, capable of tolerating greater pressure and operating faster. Then more powerful steam engines could replace waterwheels, and coal would replace water as the energy source. Owning water rights, Jackson understood the value of owning coal.[11]

Jackson was also well-placed to understand how waterpower put one at the inconveniences of geography: Lowell was some twenty-five miles from Boston, and its goods reached the city via the Middlesex Canal, which froze in winter and was drought-prone in summer, and which seriously hampered both the procurement of raw cotton and the delivery of finished cloth to markets. To remedy this problem, in 1830 Jackson began construction of a railroad. Jackson sought the best advice but encountered many delays during construction that prevented his from being the first American railroad. Certain farmers had resisted selling their land, forcing the tracks to be rerouted. Making hard ground out of the marshes on the Cambridge side of the Charles River proved more difficult than anticipated. Most damagingly, Jackson had miscalculated the size of the train yards the new line would require. The only way to produce the needed acreage was to fill the Boston Mill Pond. To acquire gravel for this purpose, Jackson bought Pemberton Hill, just behind Beacon Hill, the last of the three hills that had formed Boston's original topography. On it stood the estate of Gardiner Greene (father-in-law to the painter John Singleton Copley). One of the last from pre-Revolutionary days to survive, it retained the gentility and grace of the colonial era. Many were sad to see it disappear.

Jackson heretofore had situated his projects well beyond the view of his fellow Bostonians. But using Pemberton Hill as a gravel quarry opened his operation to close inspection. First, he cannibalized the gardens, sending many of the plants to his Waltham estate. Then he pulled down one house, using another as a workmen's bunkhouse. Jackson brought in an ox team and a horde of Irish immigrants to dig, cart, shore, and plug. He often dined with the men, using the lunch hour to consult with his foremen. Many in Boston found this habit a trifle too democratic for polite society. Aboard ship, in foreign parts, all sorts of behavior might pass; but at home Boston maintained a rigid idea of social propriety.

Residents who bordered the new gravel pit waited anxiously for their houses to collapse or be wrenched free of their foundations. Worse, all of Boston lay in a perpetual coating of gravel dust. Although people kept their windows closed, it settled indoors. To control the problem, the city required Jackson to hose down the streets twice a day. Still, the unwieldy carts careened down the steep streets spilling their loads, leaving trails of dust and dirt, and coming to rest in inconvenient places. Even before a single locomotive appeared, the railroad rumbled over Boston's domestic and commercial life.

By the 1820s the entire Lowell-Jackson family had transplanted itself to Boston. Most of them lived in neighboring houses built by Thomas Lee (brother to the one-eyed sea captain Henry Lee, whom Patrick Jackson's sister Mary had married), creating a family enclave within the city. The result was a gaggle of female cousins migrating in and out of each other's houses when a baby was due, or to avoid illness, or to lighten the embarrassment of a poor relation. The friendships formed under these circumstances bonded them for life.

Under the influence of the Jacksons' minister, William Ellery Channing, known as the "morning star" of the Transcendentalist movement, the family had established one of the first schools for girls, hiring George Barrell Emerson (cousin of Ralph Waldo) as their teacher. From the beginning, Anna Cabot Jackson, the eldest of Patrick Tracy Jackson's nine children, and his favorite, had outshone the others and became their recognized leader. Friends, cousins, and younger sisters regarded her as an arbiter of good taste and wisdom. "Anna is my oracle,"[12] wrote her earnest, adoring sibling Hannah. All the cousins watched and reported on Anna's activities in detail. Although other girls were shy, uncertain, and tentative, Anna Cabot Jackson was confident, sparkling with an individuality that the others tried to imitate. She did not do the expected thing, but she behaved as if she had.

When the girls entered Boston society, Anna was to be found at social occasions with a flower in her hair and surrounded by young men. Not particularly beautiful, she was charming and witty and an excellent dancer. She mixed with what was called the "best society," her father's wealth and social position making her an attractive prospect. Anna was of the opinion that in the case of her own family it was not wise to marry a cousin of "any degree." However, she ignored her own advice and most of her cousins did as well. As she was the first to marry, her choice of a husband was unexpected. Charles Russell Lowell was the nephew of her father's business partner, and the cousin of her cousin John Lowell, Jr. But in the scheme of things this was a fairly distant connection. A handsome young man, Charles was fond of children and somewhat uncomfortable in society and, while scholarly, lacked enterprise. No one doubted that Anna might have made a more brilliant match. It was, however, a love match. The two were besotted with each other. "Nothing can equal their intense devotion,"[13] wrote one cousin.

They were married in the spring of 1832. Shortly after the wedding Anna's father gave the newlyweds a house on Winter Street. In addition, he brought his new son-in-law into the Jackson empire, setting him up as the treasurer and Boston agent of the Lycoming Coal Company, having stock in the company and being placed to receive a commission from all sales. In 1833 Anna gave birth to a daughter, Anna.

Fast on her heels her cousins Fanny and Lydia Jackson married Charles Storrow and Charles Paine, both young men attached to Anna's father's business enterprises. Her favorite cousin, Mary Lee, married George Higginson (like Charles Lowell, a cousin of sorts), and her closest sister married William Russel, a young Transcendentalist and lawyer. Her first cousins Susan and Charles Jackson married each other. Amelia Jackson married the doctor and poet Oliver Wendell Holmes. And they all had babies, mostly boys. The family enclave resembled a small day-care center as these young women entertained themselves and their new babies. The progression from their own infancy to motherhood was seamlessly in step, perpetuating into the next generation "our system of seclusion."

It was into this world that, on the second day of 1835, Charles Russell Lowell, Jr., was born in his grandfather Jackson's house in Boston. Almost immediately this large, lively baby, who ate or tried to eat whatever came within his grasp, was effortlessly folded into the Jackson household. (His grandmother Lydia Cabot Jackson's youngest child, Ned, was only five.) Named after his father, in the traditional manner of New England families, he was quickly nicknamed "Chargy." The nickname is explained by an episode that occurred shortly after his birth. His fifteen-year-old uncle Patrick, having bundled the baby into his arms, carried him out onto the portico of the family's country house in Waltham and was strolling amid the hampers and blankets and paraphernalia deposited there, awaiting the arrival of the cart that was to take the family on a picnic, when, suddenly, "Chargy" threw back his head, gave a wriggle, and, to Uncle Patrick's horror, slipped from his grasp, plunging headfirst toward the marble steps. Fortunately Patrick's ten-year-old sister, Ellen, was sitting on the steps below and caught the baby.[14]

As the first grandson, Charlie gave great pleasure and earned a princely place in the esteem of his grandfather, who was now at the height of his powers, fifty-five years old and very rich. Patrick Tracy Jackson was a lanky man with a jaunty grin, lively eyes, and the slightly disheveled hair of an enthusiast. He was also impatient, relentless, confident, and charming. In May he had inaugurated his latest project, the Boston & Lowell Railroad. Its completion in 1835 was a great achievement. It ran from Boston to the mills

at Lowell, twenty-five miles away, in an hour and fifteen minutes and rendered the Middlesex Canal obsolete. The booming mills at Lowell soon felt
the benefit of the year-round transportation that the railroad promised. Later
in the summer Jackson paid a visit to Farrandsville, where Lycoming, having
just completed construction of a hot-blast furnace, was ready to make its first
essay at smelting. Jackson was in the enviable position of having one fortune
in Lowell and a second coming to fruition in Pennsylvania.

In 1836 Anna gave birth to another daughter, Harriet, and in 1837 James,
the last child, was born. Anna and James were united in their essentially vir-
tuous and loving, if slightly uninspiring, personalities. They always played
"in the safest possible way." Charlie, on the other hand, used every stick he
found to whack something. His sister Harriet, nicknamed Patsy, enjoyed
Charlie's rough play, and her stubbornness often exceeded his own. But
Charlie had the edge: older by a year and nine months, he took whatever he
wanted from her simply by unfolding her fingers from around the desired
object and saying, "Dear little Patsy, or poor little Patsy, give it to Charlie."
He ignored her howls of frustration and rage, and it galled their mother that
he was "perfectly unconscious" of his sister's rights "and even her existence."[15]

Yet Charlie adored Harriet, who was at times as imperious as a princess,
at others mischievous in her pranks. When footprints in the wet soil gave
away who had plucked every single flower in the entire garden, Charlie
came to Patsy's defense, pleading with their mother, "Don't whip her. It will
make her cry more, I know it will."

When Charlie was two his parents moved into Elmwood, the Lowell
family house in Cambridge. Charlie's paternal grandfather, Reverend
Charles Lowell, his wife, and their eldest daughter, Rebecca, sailed for Europe, where they stayed for three years traveling in an attempt to restore Mrs.
Lowell's declining health. Harriet Spence Lowell was a woman of minute
proportions and birdlike manner. She was given to "second sight," to bursts
of poetic recitation, and to manic enthusiasms. She had red hair. Her absentmindedness was legendary. These peculiarities were attributed to her
"Orkney blood"—the Spences were from the northern Scottish isles of
Orkney.

Rebecca Lowell, Charlie's aunt, had her mother's lovely large eyes, delicate features, and reclusive nature. A contemporary portrait shows her
dressed charmingly with her shoulders exposed, a flower tucked in her
bodice, her shawl trimmed with embroidered flowers. "Little Bec" possessed

talents much admired in decorative painting and embroidery, but it remained unclear whether she shared her mother's debilities or was their prime casualty, as she became indispensable to her mother's equilibrium.[16]

While they were gone, Charlie's father was left in charge of the family house, Elmwood, the family finances, and his two younger brothers. Elmwood, the last of the grand Tory mansions dotting the westward road out of the village of Cambridge, sat on thirty-odd acres, surrounded by American and English elms on a knoll overlooking the Charles River and its marshland to the southeast, and to the east the fields and distant spires of the churches on the Cambridge Common. To the west sprawled farms, orchards, woodland, and Fresh Pond.

Built in 1767 for the lieutenant-governor of the colony, Thomas Oliver, and his bride, Elmwood was typical of its period: a clapboard adaptation of a center-hall Georgian manor house with a double staircase leading up to three floors, wainscoted ground-floor rooms with large fireplaces, and long, shuttered windows. In places the wainscoting was scarred and dented by bayonets, marks dating from the house's use as a hospital during the Revolution. "Libertas 1776" was scratched on a windowpane in an upstairs bedroom—perhaps the work of a wounded soldier or of someone right after the war, when the state constitutional convention had used the house as its headquarters. Family portraits dating back to the Elizabethan period lined the walls. In the drawing room hung a number of Washington Allston's paintings, particularly his Salvator Rosa landscapes. The library was extensive, focusing on classical literature and moral philosophy: Locke, Hume, and Pope. Atop the bookcases stood busts of classical giants and Enlightenment luminaries.[17]

But Elmwood was never a grand country house. It might, under different ownership, have had pretensions in that direction, despite being too near Cambridge. But in Boston parlance, the Charles Lowells were exceptionally "long-tailed." They had no taste for fashion and even wished to be known to have none. Although the Jackson houses in Boston acquired indoor plumbing and gas lighting, Elmwood continued oblivious of modern amenities. In December water froze in the washbasins. The drafts that blew through every chink of the old house created "a complete Temple of the Winds."[18]

Nor was Elmwood a proper working farm. Dogs, horses, chickens, orchards, and gardens came and went according to whim or infatuation. No system, no practical design governed the management of its thirty acres.

Fields were rented out to those who asked. The Lowells loved nature but only for its beauty—dinner might be hours late because someone became entranced by a particular birdsong—and they had no conscious intent to control or benefit from its bounty. With its ramshackle charm, old-fashioned, even timeless, Elmwood perfectly suited the Lowells' eccentric otherworldliness.

By the time Charlie was three, his mother felt it was time for him to learn that "life is not all play." She wanted her children to "reconcile themselves to the hard ring of necessity." With this in mind, she began to read, in French, *A Progressive Education: A Moral History of Life* by one Madame de Saussure, friend and cousin of the celebrated writer Germaine de Staël. With chapters entitled "Imagination at Three Years Old," "On the Conscience Before Four Years Old," and "Continuation of the Third Year—On Truth," it was in effect a treatise on child development. Since Anna regarded the moral education of her children as her primary task, she read attentively. Madame de Saussure explained that small boys needed to "brave emotions," to harden themselves against their feelings. A little boy's acts of violence and cruelty were his attempts to master his emotions. His naughtiness was inevitable and necessary.

Anna was not convinced. She believed in submitting to the control of others, and in self-control. She taught Charlie her "rules of duty," starting with the Golden Rule. More maxims were added depending on each child's particular faults. Charlie was expected to recite such formulas as "Speak the truth always and act the truth always. Do what you ought, not what you wish. Treat your elders with respect. Reverence all the world. Love your neighbors as yourself." His particular favorite was "Obey instantly, cheerfully and fully," which he pronounced, his mother said, in "a most emphatic manner; it evidently makes a deep impression on him, perhaps because it is peculiarly irksome."

Anna made a point of forcing her children to note the ill effects of their actions: how they had caused others pain or unhappiness. But when verbal chastisement, moral suasion, and banishment did not succeed in influencing Charlie, she resorted to slaps on the hand, the force varying with the severity of the crime. She was rigorous and consistent in her approach, hoping firmness would help her children see the futility of rebellion. "I have never yielded or felt inclined to yield to crying," she wrote.

Although Anna's consistency in discipline quickly taught Charlie what to expect, it did not tame him. Instead he became resigned to punishment. Often, when he failed to resist defying her interdiction, he would immediately present his mother, unbidden, his "outstretched palm." Willing to pay for his sins, he was not above trying to plead for mercy: he would cock his head and say as persuasively as possible "only one drop, one little drop." When on one occasion his mother hit him harder than he expected, he burst into tears of outrage.

He soon learned to parrot the virtues his mother valued. To his aunt he talked "sagely about not minding the cold & taking care of his playthings."[19] In front of company, he would ask his mother, "Mama, ain't I good boy?" These attempts appear to have fooled no one. Of his various dodges, he learned early that fibbing was an unsophisticated and not very successful maneuver, and that deception was equally futile. "Chiefly for Charlie's benefit," Anna added to the list of rules "Act in mamma's absence precisely as you would in her presence." From Charlie's point of view, temper tantrums were somewhat more successful. After he displayed a number of these, his mother learned that "he cannot bear the least personality in a reproof, I must find fault with the act apart from the actor if I intend to do any good." If Charlie had successfully trained his mother to preserve his self-respect when she criticized his actions, then she had succeeded in getting her son to accept the principle of self-improvement: "C is separating himself from his faults by observing how bad they are in H[arriet]." Another mother-son compromise was revealed six months later: "Charlie contradicts me very often and sometimes obeys while he is refusing."

But by far his greatest successes resulted from his irresistible boisterousness. Despite continual banishment to the kitchen or nursery, smacks to his hands, lecturing and explaining, and required recitation of the "rules of duty," Charlie remained uncowed. His mother's diary is sprinkled with comments such as "C is delightful but he has no conscience," and his good humor "overcame everyone."

By "everyone" Anna meant the larger extended family, and given their "system of seclusion," it is not surprising that at Elmwood, once the elder Lowells had departed for Europe, Anna ran what amounted to an extended house party for her siblings and those of her husband. Permanently resident were Charlie's two Lowell uncles. Robert, or Uncle "Robbo," had just graduated from Harvard in 1837. A handsome, gentle middle child, he was quiet, devoted, intensely earnest, and an excellent sailor. Harriet worshiped him and would run about the house performing errands on his behalf. These did not always work perfectly: Harriet would appear in the library commanding her mother to give Robbo a piece of twine when the requested object had in fact been *Oliver Twist.**

Charlie's favorite was his uncle James, who was still a student. Clever, with an excellent memory, he tended to speak before he thought. The adored youngest child, James Russell Lowell was too charming even at his most exasperating to get sufficient chastisement; one contemporary described him as having "the coaxin'est eyes."[20] He was all enthusiasm. Anna listened, fascinated, as he recited his "pottery," as they jokingly called it, or expounded on everything from the latest political developments to the nature of life. She willingly played the foil in debates over Carlyle or the merits of Shelley, Byron, and Keats.

Uncle James never lost an infantile delight in nonsense and rough play. He was charmed by Charlie's good humor and vitality. James admired Charlie's early drawings, always the same: a big round face with three huge eggs representing eyes and nose—"the very proto-type of a Jack Falstaff."[21] It was Uncle James who persuaded Charlie's mother to take him a mile over a perfect sheet of clear black ice at Fresh Pond, from which deep booms echoed in a "solemn subdued tone," so that Charlie could watch the ice-cutters at work: marking the huge blocks, sawing them, and then hoisting them onto carts. It was Uncle James who held him up to look inside the huge, dark, dank buildings smelling of sawdust where the ice was stored. And it was Uncle James who explained that this activity led to the ice carts coming to the house or passing in the street with their glittering cargo headed for the docks to be loaded for shipment to distant parts.

There were simple pleasures, too: the utter thrill of his uncle, on his skates, swooping down and plucking the boy from the shoreline, tucking him in his arms, and carrying him over the ice, faster and faster. Then with a quick twist, they were dashing back, ending with the harsh sound of the skates' edges scraping as they ground to a halt inches from the grass edge and Charlie's mother. Uncle James could gratify Charlie's love of action. The best his mother could do was to have "an heirloom of a carryall" hitched to September, the aged pony. They rode around the countryside, while Anna held the reins and Charlie "with all his might wields his whip, and Sep. good soul, jogs along as if it were all meant to put him to sleep."

---

*Robert Trail Spence Lowell was a fine but unrecognized author, an ardent minister who nearly starved with his congregation in Newfoundland, and the great-grandfather of the poet of the same name.

Charlie's various Jackson aunts came to live with his family at Elmwood, and the young enjoyed it as a place to escape the watchful eye of the older generation. Charlie became a pet to his many teenage aunts—not only to his aunt Ellen, who had saved him from a miserable early death and who thought him "a very droll little boy, full of spirits . . . with a keen sense . . . of the ludicrous,"[22] but also to his aunt Hannah and his favorite, Aunt Catherine, who indulged him. In early September 1838 Aunt Catherine took him to his first day at the local preschool, or dame school, as they were then called. Once there he was overcome at the thought of being left in a strange place and cried inconsolably, refusing to let his aunt leave. Catherine and the teacher agreed to suspend the rules, and Catherine stayed all day as Charlie adjusted to his new environment. His transition thus eased, Charlie quickly flourished. When his mother next brought him to school, she noticed that "as soon as he appears at the door half a dozen girls fly at him to secure him to sit with them. His good humor is so irresistible, he soon makes friends everywhere."

For Charlie and his siblings, the strong socializing force of so many adoring aunts and uncles provided a groundswell of affection that leavened Anna Lowell's daunting moral education. By her estimation happiness in life was best achieved by not expecting too much: "I am contented with life: nothing could befall me which I could not meet with equanimity." This was the key to her own cheerfulness, she believed. She admiringly noted that her husband and his family "demand[ed] less of life than any persons I ever saw." And yet they did give love unstintingly, encouraging self-control in Charlie by bestowing the reward of fun and the gratification of their affection.

Anna was also attached to the new health theory of "air at all seasons." Elmwood suited perfectly. She dressed her children warmly but lightly, gave them a cold bath every morning, and in the evening put them to bed in a room without a fire. The children were allowed outside in all weather for as long as they pleased and were expected to amuse themselves. She wanted them to be familiar with the natural world. If they got dirty in the process, then so be it. In the spring the children were given their own gardens to dig, and they reveled in the small mysteries of farm life. The white hens would barely settle onto their nests when Charlie would appear to check again for eggs. A litter of piglets was irresistible. Cows needed milking, and the peacock was worthy of deep study. Charlie went off with the local farmer to dig and haul. During the summer months all the children harvested vegetables and fruit to aid in preserving, canning, and jam-making. At the end of the day, when her children stank of the barnyard and were splattered with mud, stained with berry juice, and scraped and cut and bruised by their adventures, Anna regarded "the soil and stains on their faces [as] badges of effort, and of something won." On coming in, they were warmed and dried out thoroughly but not cleaned. This she considered too much trouble. A good proper cleaning once a day was sufficient; after that she merely took off "the worst of the dirt." She declared that notions of dirt and the dirty had varied "extremely in different ages and nations, we call many things dirty, which are really only out of place."

What was it about "nature" that she wished her children to grasp? Certainly the general health of her children was important to her; she preferred some dirt on the face to yet another round of croup or influenza, both potential killers. But more profoundly, she wished to make her children "love beauty." And yet she was out of her depth. Anna was quite confident she was teaching them the "hard virtues" of self-control: submission, courage, fortitude, perseverance, and the will to labor. Of this she was proud. Her instinct led her to toughen her children, to wish them to be "independent." She was "afraid of doing too much for them . . . I fear I shall be tempted to learn their lessons and conquer their battle-fields for them." However deeply she valued self-control and her husband's "contentment" with life, neither was a cure-all. Yet Anna was not sure what was. "I do not myself know the value of beauty even in the material universe." It was this she wanted them to learn from nature. Through their senses her children would come to know their world, to apprehend its order and interrelatedness, and to feel at one with it. She encouraged them to observe the natural world, pointing out plants, small animals, and birds. "We cannot tell why nature soothes us," she wrote. "Life draws us, and we call our feelings instinctive." The closest she could come to acknowledging her own very real happiness was to describe how each evening she and the children walked with their father through the fields: "They see the sun set, and the stars and sometimes the moon come gently out, and when we reach our house, sheltered by those noble elms, and resting as it were against the soft western sky, it seems an abode worthy of the angels."

TWO

MRS. LOWELL TAKES OVER

1840–50

All this came to an abrupt end on Valentine's Day 1840, when news of Charles Lowell's bankruptcy was published in the Boston papers. The disgrace was immediate. Several days before, Anna Lowell and her children had gone to live with her father, where they were safely isolated, but the fall from grace could not be hidden. Gossip and rumor, mixed with truth, swirled about the streets of Boston. The Lowells' house was seized and sold, as was their furniture and silver. Throughout the spring Charles appeared at Patrick Tracy Jackson's front door, looking wretched and wanting to see his wife and children. They ran to him, expecting to be held, and to play, and their expectations were fulfilled. He was an indulgent father, never denying or disciplining his children. With no responsibilities any longer, he now had all the time in the world for his children. The Jackson women could not but pity the bedraggled and sorrowful man. They knew that whenever his absent father's name was mentioned Charlie burst into tears and wistfully told them he hoped "it won't be many years before papa comes."[1] But Patrick Tracy Jackson would have nothing to do with his son-in-law.

Perhaps he understood Lowell's failure better than anyone. In 1832 he had appointed his new son-in-law treasurer and Boston agent of Lycoming Coal, responsible for managing the funds and directing the company's development. Now Lowell was being forced to resign under the accusation of "lavish expenditures" and "inefficient management."[2] Patrick Tracy Jackson felt his own integrity was at stake.

In the halcyon days of the early 1830s money had poured into the coal company. By 1835 its four-pronged development in Farrandsville, Pennsylvania, had impressed visitors as an industrial city rising in the wilderness. High on the mountain, three chutes loaded coal onto railcars that traveled down the mountain on two miles of winding track. The coal was sorted, some to be shipped to Philadelphia for domestic use, and a cruder grade to be coked for railroad use and to fuel the company's iron projects. A nail works—complete with mill, furnace, and workmen's cottages—was located halfway down the mountain, and on the banks of the Susquehanna River stood the beginnings of a commercial town: more cottages, and an extensive port with docks and basins in which barges loaded with coal awaited transport. A blast furnace was under construction, planned to the most modern specifications and intended to smelt iron of English quality. But beneath all the activity and optimism lay problems for which no solution could be found, the most obvious being that the blast furnace failed in its maiden attempt.

Before this disappointment could be absorbed, an economic downturn hit with the Panic of 1837. A run on banks throughout the country, particularly the Second Bank of the United States, resulted in loans called in, banks closed, and credit dried up. The once-abundant funds of Lycoming Coal were sharply reduced. Rather than retrench, Lowell chose to forge ahead with the ambitious plan of rebuilding the hot-blast furnace. It is most likely at this point that Lowell turned to his father's capital for liquidity. But the furnace failed on its second attempt to smelt iron in 1838. Jackson, who had traveled to Farrandsville to witness its success, was shocked by what he saw. What in 1835 had seemed a budding industrial city was now a desolate place filled with ruffian workmen. Jackson immediately closed down all those activities of the company that did not center on the blast furnace and returned to Boston with detailed proposals. But when Jackson explained that householders in Philadelphia rejected their coal when it clogged ovens, that the coke was also rejected as being too light for railroads, and, worse, that the nails were returned as defective, his fellow proprietors lost faith in the enterprise.

In late 1839, with the Franklin Nail Works on the verge of collapse, the Boston proprietors sent a "shrewd Yankee iron master" to investigate. After a thorough examination and much calculation, he delivered his opinion: "there was no money to be made, and [he] advised them to cease operations and pocket their loss." Lycoming's iron ore had a high nonferrous metal content, making it extremely brittle; its coal was of equally poor quality. The "scientific gentlemen" who had made the initial analyses when the property was acquired had been wrong about the quality of both the coal and iron ore, a gross miscalculation due partly to greed and partly to ignorance. The early 1830s had been a time of expansion and optimism, when the entire country was developing with great speed; local and foreign investors had been keen to open western territories, to build roads, canals, and railroads, to develop industry, to find coalfields that would fuel the new industries, and most of all, to build ironworks. "Iron fever," as it was called, arose from the certainty that the future of everything from the plow to the railroad would be transformed when high-quality iron was produced in America.[3]

Nor had anyone reckoned on the superiority of anthracite over bituminous coal. Called "stone coal," anthracite was so dense that initially it was thought useless because it had been impossible to ignite. Once this difficulty was overcome, however, the advantages of the cleaner, long-burning fuel were obvious. Pittsburgh's abundant anthracite fields on the western slopes of the Alleghenies rapidly developed, while the eastern slopes with their mediocre bituminous coal were abandoned. In hindsight it is clear that Lycoming would have failed whoever ran it. But at the time such a philosophic perspective was not possible.[4]

An examination of the treasurer's books revealed that long after the coal operation was evidently unprofitable, Charles Lowell had permitted it to continue. When questioned, he confessed that he had had suspicions and doubts but had pushed them to the back of his mind. The proprietors were apoplectic. In his defense Lowell could only say that others had been enthusiastic and had dismissed his tentative doubts. His failings were kindly described as "inefficient management." The proprietors then demanded that Lowell buy up a considerable portion of the company stock by way of compensation. Lowell's failure to do so was the first inkling of the precariousness of his personal finances: he had used all his own money to buy stock in Lycoming Coal. Worse, he had also invested family money. This was perhaps the greater sin or moral failure: reckless mismanagement of family money betrayed disregard for the welfare of those dearest to him. Patrick Tracy Jackson, considering himself responsible for his son-in-law's position at Lycoming, paid his debts. In all roughly $700,000 had been sunk into the enterprise, without a penny's profit or dividend. In January 1840 Lycoming Coal borrowed $20,000, paid its debts, and closed down, unable to sell.[5]

Although Jackson understood the circumstances, he could not fathom the weaknesses of character that had led Lowell to his ostrichlike behavior. It was both inexcusable and inconceivable. Jackson's own life and his own family had accustomed him to adversity and taught him different lessons. Since Jackson had trusted Lowell, the fiasco rankled all the more. Bostonians were sympathetic to business reverses, understood the vicissitudes of a capricious economic world, and even had an admiration for genteel poverty, but they regarded bankruptcy, very rare among their class, as disgraceful. In most instances, if money was lost, another family member honored the debt, shored up the failing member, and found him a position in a family business that suited his skills. This often led to a brutally frank assessment of individuals' talents within a family and a clearly defined hierarchy, which may not have always improved family relations but preserved the family reputation: debts were internal affairs; publicly, the family presented a united front.

In this case, Charles Lowell had lost not only his own money but also his father's, entrusted to him in 1837. Four-fifths of Reverend Lowell's estate had disappeared, leaving him only the farmland of Elmwood for capital and forcing him to live off his salary from the West Church, just recently reduced because he had taken on an assistant minister. Although the reverend was "tender in finding excuses" for his eldest son, the effect on the family was grim. Robert and James Lowell, who were just leaving school, were now brothers of a bankrupt man, and without capital of their own to start their careers. Under a cloud of shame they were forced to reappraise their ambitions. Robert left Boston to emigrate to the West. (He got only as far as Albany.) James Russell Lowell, his dreams of being a poet dispelled, stormed out of Elmwood and took lodgings in town. He tried to study law, but it did not interest him. Like Robert, he thought of emigrating, but he knew he was unsuited. His sarcasm turned in on himself, and he "lost his reverence for the human mind." He confessed in later years that he had held a loaded pistol to his head, lacking the courage to fire it.[6]

Their mother, Harriet Spence Lowell, found the shame too great to bear. Her grasp on sanity had been tenuous for some time. Now, what had once been an amusing habit of free association took on a strangely disoriented, discordant note. Her old dreamy absentmindedness became alarming, and her ebullient enthusiasms turned into an uncontainable torrent of ranting. She would compulsively wring her hands. Alternatively, she sank into depressions from which she could not be roused. Often whole days were spent sitting by the fire; her once-red hair turned pure white. On good days Charlie would come upon his grandmother in the pantry holding a cup and dishrag, staring into space. On seeing him, she would jump, startled, and stare at him with her huge eyes, looking frightened.

The running of the household now fell squarely on the eldest Lowell daughter, Rebecca. But "Little Bec" had neither the physical nor the emotional strength for her job. Already reclusive, she withdrew entirely to her bedroom and refused to speak. To help his father, Uncle James moved back into the family house, but he found the stress of his mother's disintegration hard to bear and began to suffer from periodic episodes of blindness. Soon Harriet Lowell's manic fits turned psychotic. She became completely unmanageable, violent toward others and perhaps toward herself. Her illness had become so unpleasant that her son could write: "Not as much of thee is left among us / As the hum outliving the hushed bell."[7] In 1845 she was committed to the MacLean Hospital for the Insane.

Before her own troubles began, Anna Lowell had followed the effects of the Panic of 1837, noting the "hopeless poverty" of one family, watching as the wife of another acquaintance was "returned to her father" and yet another was forced to migrate west. To her sister she confided that "we will avoid their errors." Now, with her husband bankrupt and her father in straitened circumstances, she convinced herself that she was "glad we are likely to be the poorest of the L[owell] family because we shall have the advantages of their acquirement and refinement without their evils. I would far rather be the poorest of a rich family than the richest of a poor one."[8]

Reverend Charles Lowell had always been "the poorest" of old John Lowell's three sons, but before 1840 the difference had not been noticeable among them. The first son, called John Lowell after his father, was a lawyer; the second, Francis Cabot Lowell, had a textile fortune. John's eldest son, John Amory Lowell, married Francis's daughter, Susannah Cabot Lowell, uniting the two senior branches of the family. By a quirk of fate, both Francis Cabot Lowell, his wife, and two of their three children (including Susannah) died prematurely, so the bulk of the textile fortune devolved on the family of this half-cousin and son-in-law, John Amory Lowell. Meanwhile the third son, Reverend Charles Lowell, faced the ignominy of learning that his more modest inheritance had evaporated. The disparities among the branches of the Lowell family became acute.

The vast wealth of John Amory Lowell was now used to shore up Reverend Lowell and his younger children, principally Mary, the Lowells' second daughter. She was married to Samuel Putnam, the elder brother of John Amory Lowell's second wife, Elizabeth Putnam. John and Elizabeth now took Mary Lowell Putnam's family under their wing. Even so Mary, too, had attacks of temporary blindness. Entirely devoted to her father, she was a prodigy who spoke some twenty modern languages, among them French, German, Italian, Polish, Swedish, and Hungarian. She was fluent in classical languages as well—Greek, Latin, Hebrew, Persian, and Arabic. She wrote novels, plays, and articles and translated many books. For several years she passed her days in a pitch-dark library, shades, curtains, shutters drawn, swinging in a hammock that she had slung from the bookcases. There she held language tutorials, from the gloom of her hammock, correcting her students' errors in their recitations.[9]

Most direly affected was Aunt Sally, who, at seventy-two, was now destitute. She found lodgings with Henry Wadsworth Longfellow, a young poet, recently widowed. The two became great friends, their living arrangement being "a mutual life-insurance company," as he put it. To Longfellow, Aunt Sally confessed that she considered her nephew guilty of "moral delinquencies" and declared that his bankruptcy was "the first stain on the Lowell escutcheon."[10]

Aunt Sally was referring to the fact that the Lowells were an armigerous family. Back in the fifteenth century the English king had given them the right to bear arms and to have a coat of arms. In 1639 a small signet ring had come to America on the hand of Percival Lowell, formerly a rich merchant of Bristol and the Lowell family partriarch. In 1774, when John Lowell of Newburyport signed his public declaration of disloyalty to King George III, he had worn Percival's ring. Aunt Sally, who was but a girl at the time, later passed on the family legend that the kinship he felt with the first Lowell to come to America had never been stronger. For a family with such self-pride, the humiliation of Charles Lowell's bankruptcy was acute. It was, as she explained, "a stain." Among the Lowells it was too painful to mention, and under the weight of this humiliation Charles Lowell himself crumpled, developing physical maladies that made him unable to search for work.[11]

Virtually every element of Patrick Tracy Jackson's many ventures was now overextended, putting him in a particularly vulnerable position. A drought in 1836 had halted the water-powered textile mills, which at considerable capital outlay were then converted to steam. The railroad was not yet returning a profit. His vast holdings in Boston were in the midst of development, huge sums having been borrowed for that purpose. To cover his debts and those of his son-in-law, he was forced to sell property at vastly diminished prices, and his taxable wealth was reduced to one-tenth of its original value. While most Boston businessmen were damaged by the Panic of 1837, of the top forty only Patrick Tracy Jackson did not recover. Compounding his problems, his second daughter, also married, was not only in financial need but ill. His other daughters remained unmarried, his sons were still young, and he had in his care the children of his dead sisters. To meet these responsibilities, he went back to work managing the Merrimack Locks & Canals Company at Lowell.[12]

Anna Lowell refused to fade into a discreet and listless poverty, however genteel. She was also reluctant to become any more of a burden to her father than was absolutely necessary. A woman of great intelligence and enormous intellectual curiosity, Anna expressed even self-doubt with philosophical vigor and confidence. After hearing a lecture by William Emerson, elder brother of Ralph Waldo Emerson, in which he described his own frugal upbringing and how the four Emerson boys had derived pleasure and strength from their poverty, she decided to "forget that we have culminated and put on the vigor and assume the attitudes of those who have never known better days."[13] Few women would have struck out with such independence, but Anna's decision was made under the influence of watching her father, age sixty, return to work.

There were few professions that a respectable woman might pursue. Teaching was one, and Anna decided to open a school. She sent out a prospectus offering "Instruction . . . in all the branches of a good English Education, and particular attention will be given to reading English. Latin and French will be taught to those under twelve, and Italian and German to all over twelve who desire it." To attract students she wrote a book, *Theory of Teaching with a few Practical Illustrations*, which was published in 1841. When Elizabeth Peabody reviewed it in the Transcendentalist journal *The Dial*, she recommended it "to the attention of all whose minds are engaged in ascertaining the best way not to injure children." Miss Peabody's support was invaluable in dissipating the suspicion and distrust that had arisen among Boston parents as a result of a recent scandal at Bronson Alcott's Temple School, which had hitherto attracted the children of many of the liberally inclined of Boston's wealthy families. The visionary Alcott had stretched liberality too far: some said because he admitted a child of color, while others complained that when the children inquired into the practical details of Jesus' birth, he took the opportunity to discuss human sexuality; most of the children were withdrawn, and the school was closed. Anna Lowell promised to hold a high regard for the individual development of children, and she made clear that she had a proper regard for their innocence.[14]

Originally advertised as to be held in the vestry of King's Chapel, by the time the school actually opened Anna Lowell had enough pupils to warrant renting a small house in Winter Place, where she fixed up the parlor as a classroom. She procured a separate desk for each child and for herself a high-backed black chair. Her bell was a little bronze lady. The youngest of the children were given their lessons in the china closet, and their privilege was to play with the "lady-bell." In her first year she made $3,000.[15]

By the winter of 1843 the success of the school and the rising number of pupils required that the school move to a larger house in Winter Place; the top floor was converted into a giant schoolroom, while Anna and her family lived in the lower part of the house. These early years of the school were difficult, and success only increased the pressure on her. She ran the school, taught in it, did all the preparatory work, wrote innovative schoolbooks, tended her husband during his frequent bouts of ill health, and looked after her four children. In holding her world together, she demanded of herself extraordinary discipline and sacrifice—hard virtues she had thoroughly mastered.

Years before, Anna Lowell had noted "something hard in my philosophy." Expressing a curious ambivalence about herself, she was proud to be determined, earnest, strong, and resolved, yet recognized that she lacked whim, caprice, and spontaneity and found it hard to share her children's pleasures. Before her husband's failures, her confidence in her own fortitude had seemed arrogant and limited by privilege and naïveté. But after disaster struck and Anna learned those lessons that she had once imagined would be good for her soul, her prediction proved accurate.

What she grasped less clearly was the sacrifice she was asking of her children. There was little time in that busy household to attend to the ubiquitous cares of children, their silliness and shyness and need for reassurance. There was little time for fumbling awkwardness, for inarticulacy. A thousand moments arose in which the busy mother accused the children of wasting her time. "Don't be silly," they were told, or, "What nonsense." When her children came rushing home, wounded from play or tearful from an insult, she, busy preparing for the next day's lesson, was as apt to greet them with a maxim as with a hug or sympathy. While her children were discovering just how heartless, cruel, and capricious the ways of the world were, she took these truths as her premise and seemed vaguely annoyed that her children did not as well.

No longer did she have to teach them the "hard ring of necessity." She was in fact barely capable of providing the comforts they needed to endure its overwhelming truth. Perhaps it was not just shortsightedness at work in her. Comfort might have caused collapse. She cleaved to hard truth as if she feared self-delusion, as if the slightest departure would wing her (or her husband) up into a fantasy world from which the only escape would be a fall.

Whatever dreams her husband had indulged in were now dead, and Anna was no dreamer. One suspects that she wanted to make sure her children were not, either.

Charlie received the greater part of his early education at home, from his family. Until he was nine, he attended his mother's school and was given various tasks in maintaining it. His first job was to open the shutters every morning and close them each night. In the evenings the family parlor was silent, everyone with a book. Anna had always encouraged her children, from an early age, to read from her large and serendipitously acquired collection of books. Charlie started with alphabet books that opened like accordions; books illustrating Bible stories; and a small book of the kings of England, each page containing a colorful portrait and a jingle describing the monarch. There were abundant volumes of Maria Edgeworth and Reverend Jacob Abbott, who specialized in moralizing primers, as well as Mother Goose, Aesop's Fables in French, Hans Christian Andersen's Danish stories, German tales, and *The Arabian Nights*.[16]

Reading quickly became an escape from, and a substitute for, family life. Charlie early developed a multifarious and broad knowledge base. By the time he was five, he was interested in science and nature, initially encouraged by such books as *Charlie's Discoveries: or A Good Use for Eyes and Ears*, which explained various natural phenomena such as caterpillars, starfish, otters, and hummingbirds. Soon he was reading from a variety of newly published multivolume sets of "entertaining knowledge" that offered snippets of information on such subjects as the interior of the earth, the nature of serpents, the history of factories, and the distinctions among the various religious sects. Then he graduated to Leonhard Euler's *Letters to a German Princess*, in which diagrams and charts described the solar system, the effects of gravitation on tides, velocity, rays of light, the effects of compressed air, and the alchemy of gunpowder.

Charlie had great powers of concentration as well as a near-to-photographic memory. He read voraciously and eclectically: the myths of the Hindu gods and the life of Buddha; books of action and adventure; *Robinson Crusoe*; *True Stories from Ancient History*; *Tales of the Saxons*; and countless books on the history of ancient Rome and Greece. He also read English Romantic writers—Alfred Tennyson and Walter Scott—who specialized in making the distant past vivid and real. Charlie particularly liked one of the most popular historical novels, Edward Bulwer-Lytton's *The Last Days of Pompeii*, which begins, "Ho, Diomed, well met—do you sup with Glaucus to-night?"

In this regard, his mother's neglect was a boon: Anna pointed Charlie toward a rewarding life of the mind. He learned to live in books. She established the perfect environment for self-directed study, providing a rich collection of books and setting a model example. While the children read, their mother prepared her lessons, corrected students' work, and wrote books, at least one book a year over the next ten years, all of them concerning education—textbooks, anthologies, treatises. Three volumes came out in 1843: *Edward's First Lessons in Grammar, An Introduction to Geometry and the Science of Form,* and *Poetry for Home and School: An Anthology.* In 1844 Edward had his *First Lessons in Geometry,* and in 1845 came *Olympic Games: A Gift for the Holidays.* In quick succession followed *Elements of Astronomy, The World As It Is and As It Appears,* and *Gleanings from the Poets.*

By Christmas 1843, when Charlie was almost nine, Anna could write to her sister, "This last year I have looked on as a little haven of calm for myself and the children . . . They are old enough to be companions, their minds are unfolding, their characters forming but without having yet lost the charm of childhood . . . It would be difficult to find a happier family, everything goes on regularly, there is no hurry, no interruption. To be sure there is not much play. Each one as he comes in takes a book, and there is not a sound heard till Jem with a loud clear voice spells r e c r i m i n a t e."[17]

It can hardly be coincidental that she should have recalled the word her youngest son spelled, for recrimination was forbidden in the household: a Pandora's box that dared not be opened. Once Anna could afford to rent a house and no longer lived upon her father's largesse, Charles Lowell had rejoined his family, but he was incapable of bearing the weight of recrimination; his own shame had destroyed him. Never physically strong, he had fallen prey since his business failure to a variety of ailments of an unspecified nature: stomach problems, strange paralyses, a peculiar vulnerability to the east wind. His illnesses became such that even if he had found work, he could not have done it. Eventually in 1844 he and a partner set up as "commercial agents," with a shop on Utica Street, in the southernmost part of Boston. The shop, within easy access of the docks, the neck, and the Boylston Market, was less advantageously poised to dispose of goods. Lowell & Hinckley sold a variety of New England products: cheddar, apples, dried beans, grains, and cider. But the neighborhood was rapidly filling with Irish immigrants pouring into Boston. Although some Yankees fleeced these new immigrants of what little they had, this shop did not do business that way. Lowell's ability to make a bad investment and then stick by it to the bitter end once again proved itself unerring. As his paying customers fled the encroaching slums, he extended credit without hope of being paid. (Not until 1856 did the shop close, when Charles became assistant librarian at the Boston Athenaeum, where he helped prepare the first card catalog of its collection: a fastidious, time-consuming occupation for which he was well suited and where he could do no damage).[18]

The demands placed on Anna Lowell were so heavy that little energy remained for acrimony. Nor could she have sustained her workload hobbled by bitterness. Nor would vituperation have accorded with her sense of herself: her self-control, her submission to necessity, her belief that happiness came from not expecting "too much." Yet however well she sublimated and repressed, however well she conquered her obstacles, however much she pretended that she "had never known better days," in truth she had. Inevitably, strong emotions were associated with the loss. And if neither she nor her husband could confront them, her children could not avoid them.

Often her children were fractious and rebellious. The anger and resentment that might more justifiably have been leveled against their father were directed at the school—ironically, the very thing that was their salvation. "You don't know how I have hated the school," Harriet wrote years later. "Three of us it has almost ruined." Charlie felt "a burning rage and indignation at the school," at their mother's working so hard for them, at the sacrifice of her health and her pleasure. He wanted to do something to remove the burden, but there was nothing he could do. Instead he presented to the world a tough facade, seemingly impervious to emotion or feeling. He was recognized as having a "hardness of heart." Few understood its source. He became a surly little boy full of bluster and wild doings, proud, sulky, teaming up with older boys, putting his head down, taking the punches, earning respect.[19]

The house on Winter Place was within the Lowell-Jackson enclave centered on Temple Court. The Court, as the children knew it, stood in a dead end off Winter Street, just behind the Perkins and Jackson houses—and was the hub of the neighborhood as far as the children were concerned. The crowd that met at the Court in the afternoons included boys and girls alike, almost all of them cousins in some degree. The children played games in the Court, ran in and out of one another's houses, and put on plays organized and masterminded by Charlie's aunt Mary Lowell Putnam.[20]

Henry Lee Higginson, "Higgy," the son of Anna's dearest friend and cousin, Mary Lee Higginson (now dying of tuberculosis), was Charlie's earliest and most intimate friend. The two boys complemented each other:

Charlie was "as bright as I was stupid," Higgy recalled.[21] Charlie's next closest friends were James Savage and Stephen Perkins, a cousin of Higgy's. None of these three was good at school, although Perkins was highly original in his ideas. Each had lost his mother. All were large, athletic boys, slightly older and more robust than Charlie, who was wiry, small for his age, and slow to mature.

The boys explored their neighborhood by traversing it atop the many walls that separated the yards and outhouses. As they got older, they went onto the Boston Common and from there ran all over the city. Often their destination was Charles Street, on Beacon Hill, between Chestnut and Mount Vernon Streets, where a small shop sold the best pickled limes in Boston and black molasses candy, which, at a penny a stick, was thought an exceptionally good deal. Henry and Charlie "cut up all sorts of pranks," his uncle reported. They broke windows, hooted, robbed hen roosts or market gardens, and collected signs and numbers from shops and houses. But it was the Common that became Charlie Lowell's favorite stomping ground.

A great expanse of grassy hillside in the midst of the city, the Common was a source of infinite pleasure for small boys. A variety of sport was played, including cricket. But the sport that really mattered to small boys (and whence they derived their status) was coasting, not the genteel sleighing typified by Cleopatra's Barge, a very long sleigh curved up in the front into a "swan's neck" that arched back over the passengers and thus made a great cave lined with fur. At four or five o'clock in the afternoon this sleigh went from house to house, picking up children. It then whisked them out over the Cambridge Bridge to Watertown on a moonlit ride.

But Cleopatra's Barge was far too tame for Charlie Lowell, who was known for having "surpassed all his companions in invention and daring," a dubious honor from a parental point of view. When the family went to Elmwood for New Year's Day and everyone else sat properly in the sleigh, Charlie insisted on standing on the runners at the back, causing terrible anxiety to his mother and to the driver. To Charlie, a proper sled was akin to a racehorse: the issue was not comfort but speed. Serious and deeply considered negotiations went on within his gang concerning the acquisition of sleds named Eagle or Comet. The boys watched the weather with calculating eyes, prayed for snowstorms, and reported religiously to friends not present who had, with which sled, performed what feat.

One particular hill on the Common was known as the "long coast." It began at the top of the hill just below the State House, known in those days as

"Nigger Hill" and now the site of the Saint-Gaudens monument to the Fifty-fourth Regiment. It was so popular that at both the head and the foot Irish women stationed themselves selling apples and nuts from large baskets. They would sit shrouded in their "brave blue Kerry hoods and cloaks," beating their hands, their cheeks wrinkled, puffing on short black pipes as they waited for the boys to tire and buy their snacks. In addition to coasting, the boys skated and played hockey. Charlie was particularly fond of hockey, a sport that could easily degenerate—cracking ice, wobbly ankles, sticks flying. The boys often came home with sore backsides, cut-up shins, lumps about their bodies, and the occasional black eye. To Charlie, it was all in a day's play. If within his mother's house he had to master prodigious self-control, his boisterousness elsewhere may well have released him from that discipline and ensured him his share of childhood. His afternoons of freedom earned him a reputation in the larger family as a difficult boy, but not to his mother. They were extremely close, cast from the same mold: Anna Jackson Lowell, too proud to be a burden to her own father, had a son who was determined not to be a burden to her.[22]

When Charlie was eight, Anna confessed that she did not prefer her "good children"; rather, "that great coarse rough bonnie boy lies nearer to my heart." She admitted that in public he "always acts badly . . . and shows the very worst parts of his character, and I am obliged to check him," but in the privacy of home "we are the best of friends." He was an intense boy, granting few access to his deeper self. Jealous and distrustful but profoundly loyal, he was capable of deep affection. "It will be everything to him to feel very near to one person," his mother observed, and she had great sympathy for this aspect of his character, for she promised, "He always shall feel it."[23]

When he was nine, Charlie began attending the Boston Latin School, which gave boys the fundamental education of a gentleman and fitted them for college, a mission that distinguished the school from the common public schools, where not all boys were expected to go on to further education or to become "gentlemen." It was the oldest educational institution in the country, and its alumni included many celebrated and revered citizens. While its reputation did much to persuade parents that their children would benefit from attending, none of Charlie's contemporaries had anything good to say about the experience. The building was of brick, but with "a cold, dreary, granite edifice, of the stone-mason style of architecture in vogue about 1840." Charlie's attendance there overlapped with that of two of the Adams boys, John and Charles, grandsons of the sixth president. Never known for their ebullience, they too loathed the school. "John loathed it worse than I," Charles reported. "Not one single cheerful or satisfactory memory is with me associated therewith. Its methods were bad, its standards low, its rooms unspeakably gloomy." Another classmate declared in his old age, "I wouldn't send a dog to the Latin School!" It cost nothing to attend, and many of the boys came and went casually from the school. In the intervals some were sent to boarding school; others were tutored at home. And some, like Charlie, spent four years there, day in, day out.[24]

The course of study was virtually the same as it had been for two hundred years. The boys studied Latin, Greek, mathematics, and "elements of Greek and Roman history." The education relied almost entirely on the boys' capacity to commit chunks of material to memory and to recite them on command. They were given six months in which to memorize their Latin grammar book, and only then were they taught anything about grammar, the headmaster believing that an understanding of the material distracted the boys from memorizing. For many children this was insufferably hard work. Higgy, who had trouble reading throughout his life, tried to work hard but seldom understood his lessons. "Our teachers explained nothing, and, as I see it, taught us nothing: they made us learn, and made us recite, and if we did not do it, we were punished."[25]

If the Latin School did nothing to open Charlie's mind, it did give him a place in the larger community beyond his extended family. Still a city of sea merchants, Boston was at once intensely provincial and very cosmopolitan: families lived in enclaves; private gardens still produced fruit and vegetables; women still bottled and preserved, and they still made their clothes at home. But the city's business was global: fancy linens came from Russia, tea from China, fur pelts from the Pacific Northwest, and exotic fruits from South America. Even the grandest of merchants still lived within easy walking distance of his office on the wharves that ringed Boston like the crenellation on a castle tower: men loaded and unloaded ships piled high with crated goods while other men from strange places lounged on barrels and shouted orders in foreign tongues.

But the Boston of Charlie's childhood was rapidly changing. Since the late 1830s immigration to Boston had risen swiftly. In increasingly large numbers, fleeing disease and hunger, the Irish arrived, often with little or no money, their passage paid by Irish landowners glad to be rid of them. By 1845 one-third of Boston's residents were immigrants. Many had lived for generations in a hopeless poverty in which bread cost more than whiskey.

Unskilled and penniless, in a city that had virtually no industry, they provided the cheap labor heretofore traditionally lacking in New England: they were the waiters, dockworkers, skivvies, stable boys, and hostlers; the women worked as servants and as seamstresses. And with such an influx, their numbers drove down the price of their labor. Nonetheless, the Irish stayed in Boston because the only land route out was across a thin neck connecting Boston to the mainland at Roxbury, where travelers had to pay a toll.

Living conditions deteriorated rapidly. Sometimes as many as fifteen people slept in one attic room, five or six to a bed. Cellars were the most popular dwellings, being cheap to heat, but they had no air, light, or plumbing and were given to flooding. The city became loud, crowded, noisy. As many as one hundred people used one privy, open sewers ran, and yards were filled with rotting excrement and garbage. The overcrowding led to fires and disease: smallpox, cholera, and tuberculosis revived.

Charlie and his gang, playing on the Boston Common, first encountered the newcomers in snowball fights. A seemingly innocent pleasure, snowballing became "a game of war . . . the Latin School against all comers," by which was meant the Yanks versus the Irish. The game would start in daylight, on the Common, with a full team of Latin School boys. Their leader was Henry Higginson or, as he was known on the street, "Bully Hig." Second in command was Jim Savage. These two were the biggest and toughest boys the school had to offer.

One particular battle became legendary: Higgy was struck in the head by a snowball into which a stone had been packed. Bleeding profusely, he was forced to leave the field. Darkness had sent many boys home cold and hungry. Meantime more "roughs" joined the other side, while the Latin School team, greatly diminished, retreated toward its own neighborhood. At this vulnerable moment "a swarm of blackguards from the slums, led by a grisly terror called Conky Daniels, with a club and a hideous reputation," came careening down upon the now-leaderless Latin School boys, one of its lesser members recalled. Conky Daniels yelled that he was "going to put an end to the Beacon Street cowards forever." And briefly it seemed that the prudent thing to do was to break and run for home. But Jim Savage refused to run away, and the depleted Latin School forces stood their ground, discovering that their solidarity was enough to temper the bluster of the menacing gang.[26]

The second thing the Latin School gave Charlie was to reinforce his dawning realization that the demands of society were onerous. Discipline, duty, self-control, and low expectations were all vital to survival. His prodigious memory was a great help in getting through a school whose curriculum focused exclusively on rote. Although he was always at the top of his class, the school did little to stimulate his mind or arouse his curiosity. When he came home every afternoon, he threw his school bags against the bend in the stairs with a loud thunk, and there they remained until the next morning. For Charlie, the rigor of the Latin School involved staving off ennui.

Boredom at school was counterbalanced by an increasingly interesting home life. After her husband's bankruptcy, Anna Lowell had made no effort to regain her former social position. She had been too busy, and her husband was unfit for society, his shame too complete; she understood the prejudices of Boston's upper crust too well to test the limits of its tolerance. So she turned to the intellectual companionship provided by Elizabeth Peabody's West Street Bookshop, around the corner from her house. She frequented it not only for the foreign books it specialized in, but also for the Transcendentalist Conversations that were held there in the evenings. These gatherings of progressive thinkers offered her companionship and the sort of intellectual stimulation she needed.

Universally admired for her intellect and for her ability to listen empathetically while retaining the skill to argue her own point, Anna Lowell was emerging from her years of hard work with a reputation as a courageous educator. She was famous for instilling "a love of literature that her students never lost." The success of her school and the adoration of her pupils did much to win her respectability. Even her less than brilliant pupils considered her "a bright star on this earth." Anna believed literature was there not simply to enjoy or edify but to stimulate, to challenge, and to inspire the reader to become and to do. She was not loath to mold the young minds in her charge. Ideas were real; words had the power to change people. She was recognized for "arousing her pupils to intense action."[27]

Her children felt this same influence. Charlie and his mother shared books the way others shared experiences. Their conversations about authors, characters, and the worlds created in them established their mutual belief in the deep reality of books. His mother may have failed to give him much emotional succor, but she more than made up for it with intellectual stimulation.

By the time Charlie was ten, he found Sunday lunches at Elmwood fascinating when voluble debates concerning religion, literature, revolution, and slavery absorbed his various relatives. Perhaps because unified by great mutual affection and a liberal reforming sensibility, the family's disagreements over fine points and distinctions became particularly vehement, more so than if their differences had been truly severe. Cambridge humor had it that when the Lowells started talking, they could be heard a mile away in Harvard Square. Certainly the family went at conversation as if it were sport. They argued to win and to entertain. They thrived on the friction, delighted in the working of one another's minds, and competed with one another to provide the most original intellectual route to their common convictions. They were an intimidating bunch, and even if Charlie failed to get a word in edgewise, he did not fail to take an interest.

His grandfather was inevitably the most cautious and conservative person at the table. Reverend Lowell's republicanism was qualified: like his father and elder brother, he had a respect for great men and a distrust of mobs. But his Christianity led him into more radical avenues, and his opposition to slavery was as old as the century. His commitment to improving the welfare of the poor during the great depression in Boston (the result of Madison's war with Britain in 1812) had exhausted him and put his own health at risk. With his recovery, he developed a measured caution. He now believed that the Christian struggle toward a greater humanity had been and would continue to be long and slow but, for those with faith, was inexorable. Neither brilliant nor witty in his remarks, he had a long memory, thought deeply, and had a broad understanding of human nature. His children marveled at his calm defense in the face of their passionate convictions.

In 1848, at the time of the liberal uprisings across Europe, Reverend Lowell gave Charlie, then thirteen, a first edition of *A Letter Concerning Toleration* by John Locke, the founder of philosophical liberalism. It was Locke, champion and codifier of liberal principles, who argued that as integral as a monarch's right to rule was the right of the people, possessed of a natural sense of justice and morality, to depose a government if it "offended against" them. The book had belonged to Thomas Hollis, an Englishman of ample fortune, a benefactor of Harvard College, but, most important to Lowell, a republican. Hollis had filled the margins of the opening pages, writing on the title page, "*scripta a Pacis amico, persecutionis osore, Johanne Lockio, Anglo*" (written by a friend of peace, a hater of persecution, John Locke, Englishman). He underlined Locke's statement that "Absolute Liberty, just and true Liberty, Equal and Impartial Liberty, is the thing we stand in need of." While the reverend gave Charlie many other books, this one summed up what he wished his grandson to know: that liberty and toleration were the basis of republican government and the foundation of a just world.

James Russell Lowell was finally finding his poetic voice and his place in the literary community. Like Charlie's mother, James believed in literature as action. Literature had not only an aesthetic but also a redemptive purpose, with the writer serving the rest of society as a sort of bushwhacker or path-clearer toward the greater development of humanity.

He had been active in the abolitionist cause since 1837, when angry mobs for the third time destroyed the presses of a small abolitionist press in Illinois and murdered the owner, Elijah P. Lovejoy, originally a New Englander. The Lovejoy murder had been particularly distressing because it united the issues of slavery and freedom of speech. Along with a few other young Bostonians, James Lowell publicly supported the antislavery movement by donating money to the American Anti-Slavery Society. In his first attempt as an editor of the literary magazine *The Pioneer*, Lowell published articles supporting William Lloyd Garrison, the controversial editor of the abolitionist paper *The Liberator*. He also supported his friend Lydia Maria Child, an editor of the *Anti-Slavery Standard* and the author of an early and influential treatise, "An Appeal in Favour of That Class of Americans Called Africans" (1833).

Lowell belonged to the radical wing of the abolitionist movement, calling not only for immediate emancipation but for a reform in the way the North treated free blacks. He did not believe in the inferiority of the African and argued that blacks' debased condition was a result of their predicament. Given the right opportunities, they were capable of intellectual, artistic, and political achievement. But Lowell never fit easily into abolitionist circles. He was too individualistic. He could not hate, his interests were too various, and his irrepressible humor—mocking, self-deprecating, ironic—was not appreciated by those who took their cause and themselves with utmost seriousness. Nor was he sufficiently exclusionary. Rather than scorning those who held moderate antislavery positions, he tried to establish common ground and to keep a dialogue alive, hoping to encourage greater radical action out of them. On policy issues his ideals were tempered by his desire to be not only right but effective, showing a realism that most of his colleagues lacked. But these qualities, so lacking in fanaticism, were often misinterpreted as insincerity, softness, and unreliability.

Nevertheless these qualities won Lowell great popularity when his scrial poem "The Bigelow Papers" was published in 1848. Expertly employing local dialect, Lowell created a cast of quintessential characters from New England village life as they debated the domestic politics of the times. Only Senator Daniel Webster equaled Lowell in characterizing the war with Mexico as one of southern imperialism acting at the behest of the "Slave Power"—oligarchic slaveholding southern Democratic despots. This unadulterated Yankee view had a long history going back to the early years of the century, when another war—the War of 1812, entered at the insistence of Virginians—had wrought havoc with New England's maritime interests. Antiwar sentiment asked the question: why had New England now twice fought and suffered the consequences of wars that it did not want, that served only the Slave Power? To the plain-spoken Yankee, the blame lay with the fatal compromises that the Founding Fathers had thought necessary to cement the Union. The Constitution included the slave population in its criteria for state representation in the political process: a plantation owner was worth more votes than the richest and most powerful of Boston's merchant princes. Every time a southern president was elected or a controversial bill passed by narrow margins, New Englanders blamed this original gerrymandering.

Massachusetts's Whig Party began to fracture over the war with Mexico. Stalwart industrialists and businessmen pragmatically followed the economic imperatives of "Cotton," wanting to cooperate with the southern states that were both the suppliers of raw cotton and the market for manufactured goods. "Conscience" Whigs did not. They believed that the lure of wealth and aggrandizement encouraged "Cotton Whigs" to postpone the inevitable confrontation over slavery. They made much of Cotton Whigs' being tainted with oligarchic tendencies themselves. It did not help that so many of them were descendants of the old Federalists, the "Lobster princes" of thirty years before. That this branch of the Lowell-Jackson family found itself in the Conscience camp was perhaps possible only because of their loss of fortune, which freed them from any financial connection to the cotton mills and cleared the way for a more principled stand. But the success of Lowell's poem was that it presented many points of view, permitting the reader to sympathize with a variety of characters and perspectives.

Uncle James regretted that Charlie was a city child, robbed of the easy intimacy with nature that he had enjoyed growing up at Elmwood and never lost. He exhorted Charlie to use the countryside as "the great school of the senses." Just as school enriched the intellect through study, so nature would teach as well: "Train your eyes and ears. Learn to know the trees by their bark and leaves, by their general shape and manner of growth . . . Learn also to know all the birds by sight, by their notes, by their manner of flying." This training in observation, Uncle James believed, would teach that "a person with eyes in his head cannot look even into a pigsty without learning something that will be useful to him." He wanted Charlie to know that knowledge was power, not because it made one superior but because "it enables us to benefit others and to pay our way honorably in life by being of use." Usefulness to Uncle James included being amusing: he reminded Charlie that "our company will be desired no longer than we honestly pay our proper share in the general reckoning of mutual entertainment." But he also believed that "a man who knows more than another, knows incalculably more."[28]

Charlie's Jackson grandparents gave him the opportunity to follow his Lowell uncle's instructions. In the mid-1840s Charlie's maternal grandmother, Lydia Cabot Jackson, used an inheritance from her mother to buy land in Beverly. The overcrowding of Boston and the gradual loss of its gardens and trees made the city less than attractive in the hot summer months, and many Bostonians were eager to find summer residences on the coast. The Jackson summerhouse was a simple but ample clapboard structure built on rocks surrounded by cedar, wild cherry, and barberry scrub, overlooking the sea. Charlie and his sisters called it "Aunt-Hill" because all summer their many aunts and cousins swarmed about the place.

The Jacksons' house sat on a point of rocky coast between two beaches, one of fine sand, the other of gravel. The second was called Mingo's Beach, after a freed slave whose home it had been. Opposite the house were thick woods that stretched inland to hilly country. The children explored these woods looking for wildflowers and the "witch's farm" they believed was hidden somewhere in the overgrowth. On a calm day the view from the house was of a sea crammed with boats of all descriptions. But foul weather would engulf the house in thick fog, the only indication of an outside world being the sound of the surf and the foghorns' warning to approaching ships.

For Charlie and his cousins, Aunt-Hill was where they rose in the small hours to see the circus pass on the old coach road to Gloucester, which ran in front of the house. In the half-light they sat on a low stone wall waiting until through the wet sea-mist loomed elephants, camels, and then caravans with dwarves, bearded ladies, and trapeze artists. Animals and humans alike were weary and silent as they plodded on their predawn journey. Aunt-Hill was also where Charlie and his cousins learned to sail, and where Charlie built a raft that did not float, spent days in unsuccessful attempts to trap muskrats, and sailed to rocky islands, then when the wind died, rowed home. It was where he learned to ride, and where, during a week of fog and rain, he lounged in an armchair passing the days in books or playing endless board games with his many cousins. A love of books, a communion with nature, and a devotion to family were the three legs on which Charlie's family education stood.[29]

In 1848, after four years, Charlie had exhausted the offerings of the Latin School and won the school's top honor, the Franklin Medal. He was thirteen years old, two or three years younger than his classmates. Charlie's mental powers far exceeded his emotional maturity. The question arose what to do with him. Most of Charlie's Latin School classmates went on to college, many to Harvard, while others were sent to the Phillips Academy at Andover for one or two terms and from there to college. But the Lowells could not afford Andover, where his father had gone; nor could Anna pay Harvard's tuition and meet the expense of boarding her son in Cambridge.

The Jackson family believed Charlie's distinguishing characteristics— enthusiasm, energy, and enterprise—were those he shared with his grandfather Jackson, who had died the year before, in 1847. Charlie was expected to follow in his footsteps and become an industrialist, not requiring a university education. His Lowell relatives, too, were more impressed by his qualities of character, which they saw as rare, while his mental skills were, by their standards, only average. Only when he helped Anna with her school paperwork did she notice his powers of concentration, so complete that he was oblivious of his surroundings and as serene as a Confucian scholar.

When Charlie discussed his future with his mother, he assumed he would pursue an "active life." At its most basic, that meant a career in business. For Charlie, it was an extension of his strong, precocious desire to provide for her, to rescue the women in the family from hard work, and to redeem his father's failure. He admired his grandfather Jackson for his verve, his power, his dominating position in the family, and the respect accorded him by others, particularly his mother. He was impatient with school, was eager to get out into the world, and wished for practical skills.

A stopgap solution was the English High School, a sort of technical school with premises in the same building as the Latin School. Established in 1821, the English High School offered a student courses in the sciences and the mechanical arts that would "fit him for active life . . . whether mercantile or mechanical."[30] Charlie learned about machines, industry, and technology, which pleased him, in the company of a few other boys from his circle whose families also needed to get an eldest son into the working world quickly.

In Charlie's second year at the English High School, the Lowells' circumstances altered somewhat and their finances improved. Charlie's younger brother, Jemie, finished at the Latin School and showed promise as a scholar. (A much gentler boy, Jemie was never thought of as a potential businessman: a college education would be crucial to his future.) At the same time, Anna, after ten years of hard work, felt she could turn over the day-to-day administration of her school to someone else. Meanwhile Aunt Sally Lowell, now very elderly and in declining health, could no longer live alone. (Since Longfellow's remarriage, her "mutual life-insurance" arrangement had collapsed.) Anna proposed that they combine incomes and find a house in Cambridge into which they could all move and where she could take care of Aunt Sally. They found a gingerbread cottage on Quincy Street, which bordered the Harvard Yard, and in the fall of 1850 Charlie went to Harvard.

THREE

HARVARD

1850–52

From the front porch of his parents' new house, Charlie Lowell could look across tree-lined Quincy Street to the Harvard Yard, an open and relatively empty expanse when the leaves were off the trees. He could easily see the new granite library that housed the university's eighty thousand volumes, and beyond it to the cluster of small eighteenth-century brick buildings that were the life of the college and into which were crammed classrooms, offices, and what student accommodations existed. Here he was to spend the next four years—and it was not clear to him for what purpose.

In 1850 a Harvard education gave students a general cultivation of "the faculties" and an elementary knowledge of many things preparatory to future "usefulness." This vague term was heatedly contested, but whatever it meant, it did not mean pure scholarship. This had never been Harvard's purpose. Specialized and narrow studies typical of European universities were seen as inappropriate to American needs. Knowledge was useful, but in many different ways. Here the debate became political.

Harvard's original mission had been the training of an enlightened clergy that ran the Massachusetts Bay Colony. This goal had long been abandoned, but no adequate substitute had been found. Since the theocratic state in Massachusetts had collapsed slowly, far more slowly than the independence of the new republic had arisen, it was only recently that the debate over Harvard's future had blossomed. Was it to democratize itself, as the state had? Or would it continue to train a ruling elite? The popular perspective was reflected in Harvard's Board of Overseers, appointed by the state legislature. They believed Harvard's exorbitant tuition and its admission test, requiring a knowledge of the classics, was exclusionary. They criticized its course of study for being antidemocratic because it provided an education that was of little use to the common man. Instead they demanded that Harvard become something approaching a giant lyceum, an open university where anyone might study anything at any intensity or depth. They wished to establish "a college for the education of the people."[1]

This popular vision of the college was opposed by the Corporation, the small committee that controlled Harvard's finances. The Fellows, as they were called, represented the merchant-industrialists who over the past twenty years had increasingly shaped Harvard's development. They had made large donations toward the development of the sciences—geology, chemistry, physics, and applied mathematics—a greater understanding of which would further the industrial expansion of the country, in which these wealthy men wished to play a profitable part. They aimed to cultivate and solidify an elite class which could enter the business world with sufficient education to understand and make use of the new advances in knowledge. Thus the young men's moral and character development was potentially of even greater "usefulness" than any expertise in the finer points of obscure subjects or even an ability to exploit knowledge. Throughout the 1850s, as the overseers fought with the Corporation, Harvard was besieged by conflicting notions of "usefulness," populist and elitist. This "age of transition," as it has been tactfully called, was marked by confusion, contradiction, and aimlessness.[2]

Part of this aimlessness was due to the college president, Jared Sparks, a handsome, remote man widely respected as an American historian. The papers of Benjamin Franklin and George Washington have been preserved, largely because Sparks tracked them down in abandoned attics. He had hoped that the presidency of Harvard would give him an easy salary and the time to write. To his disappointment, more was demanded of him than he had expected. His response was to delegate as much responsibility as he could and ignore the rest. When confronted by the overseers with the boys' waywardness, sloppy habits, and lack of discipline, President Sparks is said to have given an exasperated sigh: "Gentlemen, let the boys alone!" Sparks's benign neglect made him popular with "the boys."[3]

Of the sixty-five students in Charlie Lowell's freshman class, all were from northern states: most from New England, just under half from Massachusetts, and more than a third from the Boston Latin School. Two of them had been in Lowell's Latin School class; one was Richard Goodwin, whom Lowell mentioned only on his death at Cedar Mountain in 1862, and the other was his great friend Jim Savage, hero of the childhood encounter with Conky Daniels. The recent deaths of two of Savage's sisters from lingering and wasting disease had plunged Savage into a depression that outlasted his

Harvard days. He was a well-built young man whose natural shyness was ex-acerbated by grief and who in his solitude became increasingly earnest. Charlie, although part of the largest element in the class, was a relative un-known; at fifteen, he was its youngest member. Most of his classmates were two or three years older, and some as much as six years his senior. They sported mustaches, spectacles, shaved chins, fancy suits, and lanky limbs. Quite a few were young gentlemen who brought carpets and bathtubs to their college rooms and stabled their horses nearby. Their elegant dress, which included top hat, shooting jacket, and cane, cost as much as Har-vard's yearly tuition.

Lowell became known for his juvenile boisterousness, which "did not win him popularity at once." His "rosy-tinted complexion," delicate features, and expressive face still had a child's transparency, conveying the full intensity of his feelings. Some liked his contagious good humor and thought he had a "boyish beauty," but to others his schoolboy's haircut and "roundabout jacket" were only evidence that he was "unusually boyish in appearance."[4]

A college that valued highly the "future usefulness" of its students pro-vided virtually no structure for time spent out of class, and Harvard under-graduates had a reputation as "the most dissipated set of students in the Union."[5] A long history of rioting on campus, during which a surprisingly large amount of damage was done to the buildings, attests to the continuous mutual distrust and suspicion between the boys and the college authorities, each side regarding itself as David fighting Goliath. Charlie Lowell must have known something of this history, for his uncle James had been rusti-cated for drunkenness and disrupting evening prayers, and his illustrious great-uncle Francis Cabot Lowell for lighting a bonfire in his college room. It was deemed almost essential that a man of substance have some story of delinquency in college.

Most of the student unrest in Charlie Lowell's time centered on the last vestige of Harvard's original mission: the obligatory thrice-daily chapel atten-dance at morning, noon, and evening prayer. Charlie's sophomore class took it upon itself to prevent the ringing of the bells: the ropes were cut, the tower lock jammed, the bell stuffed. They went so far as to hang a rooster to a tree outside the administrative offices. On New Year's Eve and Washington's Birthday the boys stayed up late around bonfires drinking, singing, and ca-vorting. On various occasions "frail and fair ones" had to be escorted from the scene; it was not until 1860 that the college could announce that a lady might walk through the college grounds at any hour without "seeing or hearing anything to alarm or offend her."[6]

Nevertheless, during Charlie's four years relations between students and authority were relatively easy. Sparks's languid leadership may have given the students little to rebel against, but for Lowell and his friends the greatest factor contributing to the calm on campus was their interest in the contentious national politics surrounding the Compromise of 1850, which attempted to resolve the territorial, economic, and political questions that had arisen over the spoils of war with Mexico, specifically the status of its former territories: Texas, New Mexico, Utah, and California. The stakes in California were high—gold had been discovered in 1848—but they were even higher for control of the U.S. Senate, which was evenly balanced between free and slave states, a balance now threatened by these new territories. Any nonpartisan spirit evaporated from the Congress as the debate became rancorous and senators displayed their pistols on their desks.

Alarmed by the severity of the crisis, Senate leaders sought a compromise that would guarantee that the balance of power was maintained. In this effort Massachusetts's senior senator, Daniel Webster, gave his now-famous March 7 speech: "I wish to speak to-day, not as a Massachusetts man, nor as a Northern man, but as an American. I speak to-day for the preservation of the Union. Hear me for my cause."[7] The eloquence of Webster's speech was undeniable as he urged national reconciliation, and he gained the support of those conservative Cotton Whigs whom he had previously alienated. Some three hundred of them rushed to cement what they believed was a reunification of the Whig Party by publishing a letter of support in the Whig paper the *Boston Daily Advertiser*. But the controversy continued. Liberal state politics was in turmoil. Many Conscience Whigs, disgusted and disheartened, were chagrined to find that the new senator from New York, William H. Seward, best expressed their sentiments. In a speech that helped inflame the passions of the southerners and sent ripples of instability throughout the national Whig coalition, Seward declared, "You cannot roll back the tide of social progress." The choice facing the nation, he believed, was between gradual emancipation or civil war. As for the guarantees of slavery in the Constitution, Seward swept these aside, declaring, "There is a higher law than the Constitution." Although this deeply inflammatory remark expressed a conservative antislavery position based on religious scruples, it was nevertheless a radical statement for a politician and lawyer to make. It raised the hackles of the southern senators, and Cotton Whigs snorted in outrage and scorn. Meanwhile former Conscience Whigs broke irreparably with their party and began to articulate a position they called "Free Soil"—an allusion to their opposition to the expansion of slavery into new territories.[8]

Compounding national tensions was the sudden death in July 1850 of President Zachary Taylor, whose sympathies had been with the North. His vice president, Millard Fillmore, leaned toward the South. Ultimately, in August and September 1850, Senator Stephen Douglas from Illinois cobbled together a series of compromises passed as separate laws, each representing fragile trade-offs and separate majorities. This was the Compromise of 1850: northern money would pay off Texas debts; in exchange, Texas would not be broken into smaller states but would be admitted as only one slave state; to preserve the balance of power, California would be admitted as a free state; despite being below the latitude of the Mason-Dixon line, the territories of New Mexico and Utah would not automatically become slave states but could be settled with "no restrictions on slavery," meaning their status would be determined by those who settled there, or "popular sovereignty"; slave trade in the District of Columbia was prohibited, but in exchange a tough fugitive slave law was enacted.

Surprisingly, it was not the larger issues of territorial expansion and congressional power that caused trouble in Boston but the seemingly minor and barely debated Fugitive Slave Law, which passed on September 18, 1850. Nullifying all state laws to the contrary, it established as federal law the requirement that any state, free or slave, must assist a slave owner in the retrieval of his property: that is, the return of runaway slaves to bondage. The most alarming aspect of this new law was the absence of a statute of limitations: not only were recent fugitives vulnerable, but long-established Massachusetts residents, many of whom openly acknowledged their former slave status, were vulnerable as well, even more so as their relatively public existence made them the easiest to find. Put in immediate jeopardy were four to six hundred fugitives in Boston, forty of whom instantly fled the city. But the anxiety extended to the larger free black population of some two thousand. As long as fugitives lacked the protections of due process, nothing could prevent the old habits of slave catchers from resurfacing: in the pursuit of one fugitive, any black recaptured would suffice. Boston's small and hitherto stable African American community was on the verge of panic.

The emotional weight of the crisis had been brought home to Charlie even before 1850. A girl attending Anna Lowell's school turned out to be the mulatto child of her southern white owner; years earlier she had been sent north to be brought up with most of the privileges that a white daughter would have had. When her father died, she assumed that she was freed and went home for his funeral. There she discovered that, contrary to her assumption—for years she had passed for white—she was now the property of her uncle, an unsympathetic man. Precisely how he proposed to dispose of her is not revealed, but in despair at her predicament the young woman committed suicide.

The news of this tragedy, and the grief of her surviving sister who had remained in the North and was now in jeopardy, profoundly affected Anna Lowell's children and the students at her school. Young Anna and Harriet knew these girls well. Their mother quickly sought the help not only of James Russell Lowell but of her brothers, Ned and Pat Jackson, and her brother-in-law, Dr. Sam Cabot, all of whom were Free-Soilers and had been members of the Vigilance Committee in 1846. Swiftly the remaining sister was sent to Paris. This traumatic experience of the effects of the slave system galvanized Charlie's family to oppose the Fugitive Slave Law. For Charlie and his cousins, it set a clear example. Anna had thought only of protecting a vulnerable young woman. Charlie had run back and forth carrying messages between his mother and his various uncles and had been drawn into the antislavery and abolitionist network.[9]

To rally public support for the protection of Boston's vulnerable African American community, a small band of abolitionists, of whom Theodore Parker, Richard Henry Dana, and Wendell Phillips were the principals, organized an interracial rally to protest and defy federal law at Faneuil Hall on October 14. Parker, a minister now without a church thanks to his uncompromising abolitionist views, which he fearlessly pronounced, was well hated in established Boston circles. His wife, Lydia Dodge Parker, was a cousin of Charlie's mother. Wendell Phillips was the son of Boston's first mayor and a member of one of its wealthiest and most respectable families. Richard Henry Dana, the grandson of two signers of the Declaration of Independence, was a lawyer who had achieved early fame as the author of *Two Years Before the Mast*.

All three men recognized that in agreeing to organize this rally, they did not have an easy task. Boston in 1850 was "almost avowedly a pro-slavery community."[10] The city's dependence on cotton was obvious. Lowell, Lawrence, and other smaller textile centers required an inexhaustible supply of raw cotton; the southern states, lacking their own manufactures, were a huge market for northern goods of any description. Also, Boston ships transported southern cotton around the world, Boston capital financed southern banks, and Boston lenders accepted slaves as collateral against loans. The question of slavery was not just a hypothetical moral issue but an economic one that could be measured and argued, as freed slaves meant capital depleted, earnings lost, deals compromised. So long as the slave represented property, the Yankee merchant would ally himself with the owner of that property. Hundreds of respectable Bostonians came forward to assure the federal marshals that they would aid in the capture of fugitive slaves.

The challenge to the organizers of the October 14 rally was to puncture this seemingly impenetrable veneer of self-interest and prejudice. The main responsibility fell to Wendell Phillips, who ardently wanted to force the placid and powerful citizens of Boston to recognize their civic responsibilities. Only by effectively putting "the cotton power" on its guard could he hope to protect Boston's blacks. To this end, a preeminent cast was assembled. As the keynote speaker, Phillips enlisted the most celebrated runaway slave, Frederick Douglass, whose eloquence and gravitas were unparalleled: if anyone could bring across the humanity and the tragedy of the fugitive slave, it was this remarkable man. His account of his own escape to freedom, *Narrative of the Life of Frederick Douglass, an American Slave*, had been published in 1845 and read across the North. Presiding over the meeting, Phillips secured the leader of the Conscience Whigs and a longtime congressman, Charles Francis Adams, grandson of the nation's second president and son of John Quincy Adams, its sixth.

But even a roster of celebrities could not avert the danger of a riot. The African American community was jittery, nervous, and excitable. Abolitionists were burning with indignation and rage. It would take very little to start a riot, and abolitionist and antislavery rallies in Boston had a history of erupting in violence. In the 1830s Cotton Whigs had hired mobs from among Boston's Irish poor—crudely antiblack and available—to disrupt antislavery protest. These same forces, indeed many of the same men, did not want this rally to succeed. Any ensuing violence had the potential to do more damage to Boston's African American community than federal marshals, and the protest would be discredited.

Phillips wanted to open the meeting with a figure who commanded respect and was above the political fray, who would speak to the "higher law." He decided to open the meeting with a prayer, partly to force the issue on the recalcitrant Boston churches and partly to temper the evening's angry political edge. Phillips believed that there was only one Boston minister who would agree to associate with so radical an enterprise: Charlie's grandfather, Reverend Charles Lowell.

Lowell had a number of things to recommend him, most notably that he was the white minister best known to Boston's free black community. His involvement with it dated to Boston's depression during the War of 1812, when he had taken upon himself its pastoral care. Called by illness or birth or death, Reverend Lowell would come groping "his way by night through unlighted lanes and alleys, reeking with peril, alike from foul miasma and from human lawlessness."[11] His thirty years of association with African American Bostonians was solid, incontrovertible, and personal, long antedating the present antislavery agitation. It was hoped that the presence of this old and trusted figure would help to calm and reassure.

To white Bostonians, Reverend Lowell was a phenomenon. Since 1806 he had been the senior minister of the West Church, the largest of Boston's five leading churches. Lowell inspired universal affection among his parishioners for his piety, wisdom, compassion, and gentleness. The average tenure of a minister at any single parish was only five years, so his forty-four-year tenure was highly unusual. Earlier in 1850 the newspapers had reported with astonishment his baptizing a child whose mother and grandmother he had also christened.

And finally, blood was thicker than politics; the reverend's nephew, John Amory Lowell, was now running the Lowell mills. The Cotton Whigs would not send in bully mobs to break up a rally at which Reverend Lowell spoke.

For a number of reasons, Lowell might have chosen not to help, not the least being his nephew's position in the cotton textile business. But the reasons compelling him to engage were much stronger. His commitment to the African American community of West Boston demanded it, as did his own sentiments. His opposition to slavery was as old as the century, originating in his childhood with Philodlia, a family servant to whom he was devoted and who, when he was sent away to school, corresponded with him, writing in verse the news of the family. This childhood bond with an exceptional black woman had given him a human experience that defied the prejudices of the day. It had led to his searching out the great British abolitionist William Wilberforce (whose portrait hung in the dining room at Elmwood) while he was studying in England; the two had become personal friends.

Since 1821 Reverend Lowell had preached many sermons on the evils of slavery. His public prayers always remembered the slave and the fugitive.

These prayers were not unanimously appreciated. One parishioner grumbled that Lowell should be prosecuted for "mixing prayer with treason."[12] A few left the parish, but most indulged him more graciously, if without enthusiasm. His efforts to desegregate the West Church, which began sometime after 1837 and continued fitfully till the end of his ministry, also came to nothing. It galled the reverend that even his own church had failed him. Boston's churches were all run like joint-stock companies; the pewholders, like stockholders, hired and fired the ministers, approved or disapproved church policy. Phillips offered Lowell the opportunity to speak out independently of the West Church, and Lowell seized the chance.

On October 14 in Faneuil Hall he stood before a packed audience of some three thousand people, including his entire family and Charlie. Now sixty-eight, the reverend was still erect, of middling height and firm build. The sensuous beauty of his youth was long gone. His ruddy cheeks were craggy, his curling blond hair now lank and gray, his lips thin slits. But his manner was still confident and easy, and his eyes beautiful. The chin was noticeable from a distance, jutting forward with a pronounced underbite.

When it was time to speak, he began without notes. His prayer called for God's blessing, for calm and peace, and addressed God as "Thou who art no respecter of persons." To the Bible-literate, the allusion was clear: Acts 10:34 gives the words that Peter uses when, sent by visions from God, he first preaches to a non-Jew, a centurion who wishes to hear of the life of Christ. "God is no respecter of persons: but in every nation he that feareth him, and worketh righteousness, is accepted with him." With this Peter recognizes that God's chosen people are not solely the people of Israel but those of any nation or race who follow the teachings of Christ. Jesus is no longer king of the Jews but the leader of Christians. Lowell was reminding his audience that God had always challenged his followers to broaden their minds. The prayer continued by asking for the protection of "those of our brethren on whose behalf we are now assembled, fugitives from slavery." He called for the time to come when "we shall act in consistency with our profession as freemen and Christians. God of mercy, who hath made of one blood all nations, incline the hearts of all men, everywhere, to kindness and brotherly love."[13]

Amid the platitudes of piety, Lowell was refuting the claim made by many scientists (notably Samuel Morton) that African Americans were a different race from whites. A supposedly scientific theory that supported slavery, "polygenism" pointedly insisted that from the first, black and white had been distinct. Lowell cast aside this spurious notion and appealed to spiritual truth. His God had "made of one blood all nations." And he defined our common humanity not by the size of skulls and other pseudoscience but by three criteria—"intelligent, moral, immortal"—in themselves potentially controversial. He firmly aligned the true Christian kingdom with a radical humanity in which "without violence or bloodshed, every yoke shall be broken, and the oppressed go free." His peroration enjoined God to "forgive the sins of the nation against our brethren." Then he placed himself and everyone there in New England's favorite position, that of the humble sinner in a sinful world who must look to God for salvation and the forgiveness of sins: "Bring not down upon us the judgment we justly deserve."[14]

His prayer accomplished all that could have been hoped, placing the audience in the context of its broadest sense of humanity. After the prayer had finished, the meeting went on to the speeches of Frederick Douglass and others; the bully mobs stayed away. The result was an outpouring of support for the black community. The Boston Vigilance Committee was formed (a similar committee had flourished briefly in 1846). Fifty members signed up immediately, with membership growing to more than 250 in the next months. This loosely knit organization worked for the relief of refugees from slavery, providing funds, shelter, clothing, and medical treatment, helping some in their flight to Canada, and relocating many more in or around Boston. Charlie's uncles were active in the Vigilance Committee, notably Dr. Samuel Cabot, who offered free medical treatment and his house in Brookline as a way station for fugitives. Although few used Boston as a route to freedom (it was too far east), fugitives did appeal to the Vigilance Committee for material assistance, health care, and funds to buy family members out of slavery.

Throughout the winter of 1850–51 the Vigilance Committee appeared to be having its desired effect. As its members heckled and intimidated the few slave catchers who came to the city, the Boston establishment turned a blind eye. Fugitives were protected. In late February, however, a fugitive called Shadrach was captured and brought to court. Just as the session was breaking up, a band of black members of the Vigilance Committee led by Lewis Hayden, a fugitive himself, raided the courthouse and successfully made off with Shadrach, spiriting him to safety. This much-celebrated act of daring forced the hand of the city fathers. Senator Webster called the rescue of Shadrach "a case of treason." The New York *Journal of Commerce* reported it as a "negro insurrection in Boston." The Senate floor in Washington was pounded with the indignation of even moderate southerners like Henry Clay. Cotton Whigs were embarrassed, and Massachusetts became known throughout the country as a hotbed of "mad Abolitionism," where a handful of blacks had made a mockery of the courts.

When in April 1851 another fugitive, Thomas Sims, was apprehended, the full power of the state was brought to bear against him. Despite a massive legal effort on the part of the Vigilance Committee, and high drama— Sims declared in court, "Give me a knife, and when the Commissioner declares me a slave I will stab myself in the heart, and die before his eyes! I will not be a slave!"[15]—early one April morning Sims was marched down to a waiting boat that transported him to Georgia and his owner. It had cost Massachusetts some $20,000 to enforce the Fugitive Slave Act and restore its good image in the eyes of distrusting southerners.

Even so, Robert Barnwell Rhett, a South Carolina congressman of deep proslavery convictions, withdrew his son from Harvard because of the inhospitable "antislavery agitation" in the state. The Harvard Coporation, made up entirely of Cotton Whigs, was embarassed by the events and determined to show the goodwill of Harvard toward the South. They voted to give the boy his degree "as a special favor," which then raised the hackles of the liberal press: "What subservancy!" the *Massachusetts Spy* snorted.[16] But Harvard wanted to restore the flow of southern students; President Sparks had many connections and friends in the South (his work on the Founding Fathers had won him considerable respect there); and by his efforts, Lowell's Class of 1854, in the middle of its sophomore year, was increased by almost half again with the arrival of twenty-five new students from a South Carolina college that had closed. (Unfortunately, shortly after the new arrangements were made, Sparks was run over by a carriage, which had slipped in a snowstorm, and never fully recovered from his injuries. The acting president, James Walker, was, if anything, even more lackluster than Sparks. Hampered by almost complete deafness, the students dismissed him as "a lying old Jesuit.")[17]

Part of the effort to accommodate the twenty-five new southern students in the Class of 1854 was the announcement that they would, because of the credits given for their previous study, upset the ranking system. Five of the new students were ranked among the top ten in the class, and one was ranked first, displacing Charlie Lowell as first scholar. Harvard's draconian ranking system, called the Scale of Merit, established a student's rank and then monitored it, so that on any given day, from the first to the last in any specific course, term, and year or over his entire time at Harvard, it was known where he stood in the order of his class. The reward for being among the top ten was a speaking part in the class's Exhibition Day and ultimately at its commencement exercises. The first scholar of the class got the best speaking part. Public recognition was considerable, as these college events were community spectacles attended by large audiences. Fierce competition existed among the top twenty-five students to place well.

The Scale of Merit had a very broad range. At the end of the first term, Lowell had an aggregate score of 3092, giving him the rank of first scholar, while the lowest score was 942; with the exception of two half terms, he retained this position for four years. Undoubtedly his photographic memory had much to do with his success, but he worked hard to hold his rank: his course records show that his efforts were more deliberate than he admitted or than was generally recognized, for he led people to believe that he never studied and that he was indifferent to high rank.

Being first scholar was not just a matter of prestige. Financial scholarships as such did not exist until 1852, when the alumni began to organize funds to be awarded to one scholar per class, inevitably the first scholar, but in Charlie's first two years a "worthy student" found that the university would simply disregard his bill. Scholastic prizes—the Deturs and Bowdoin prizes in Latin and Greek, for example—were worth half to three-quarters of a term's tuition. Charlie won at least one, often both, at every opportunity presented. His scholarship ensured that his mother paid no or few fees for his Harvard years. Thus Charlie's apparent indifference to the prestige was due less to modesty than to a desire not to dwell on the need he felt to relieve his mother of a financial burden.[18]

His position as first scholar notwithstanding, Charlie loathed the ranking system, as did virtually everyone associated with it, both students and professors. It was disliked for its relentless drudgery and was blamed for the college's demoralized atmosphere. As a result, Charlie's formal studies did little to satisfy his intellectual curiosity. His love of literature was not indulged, his aptitude for languages not pursued, his devotion to philosophy stymied. The intellectual atmosphere was almost as stultifying as that of the Latin School. The one exception was mathematics, where Lowell found a professor who fired his imagination.

The brilliant and deeply eccentric Benjamin Peirce had great charisma. Tall, with a flowing beard and long hair, Peirce "taught mathematics as a kind of Pythagorean prayer," in which religious mysticism, influenced by

Emmanuel Swedenborg, could lead to philosophical truths. Peirce insisted that mathematics was pure philosophy: "Facts combined into formulae, and formulae organized into theory, penetrate the whole domain of physical science and ascend to the very throne of ideality," he explained. This was perfect for Charlie, whose attraction to the subject was due to its being both intensely practical *and* philosophical. As one of only three students studying analytical mechanics, he engaged in the early work of statistics and probability theory, which offered an entirely new way of regarding the material world.[19]

Charlie, believing that organized religion was the cause of most human misery and evil, wanted to supplant religion with a materialistic philosophy. He approached the challenge through mathematics and subscribed to Peirce's mystical belief that it revealed "a divine pattern or order" underlying perceived reality. Using Socrates' pupil Plato as a "guide-light,"[20] Lowell was determined to arrive at an apprehension of the truth, the ideal forms of Platonic reality behind the shadows on the wall mistaken for reality by Plato's prisoners in a cave.

Mathematics aside, the classroom was a mere formality. It was in the clubs, which were not then as exclusively social as they later became, that the students learned from one another. Watching Charlie study, his friends noted (as his mother had observed years before) his extraordinary powers of concentration and rapid analysis. He had a "genius for detecting in principles the key to facts."[21] Most of the clubs had rooms about Harvard Square offering a wide selection of periodicals to read, and members could join in organized debates and lectures. Rather than being made dour and serious by the effort of debate, Charlie gathered up ideas, facts, and quotations effortlessly, becoming increasingly animated when challenged. Scornful of conventional feeling or opinion, he enjoyed searching for the original and various; sometimes he took an extreme or provocative position simply for the mental exercise of defending it.

When his classmates learned that Charlie had been displaced as first scholar by one of the incoming southerners, they mutinied. Some lodged protests with the president. One of them wrote home, "It is the greatest outrage I ever heard of. I am sure if such is the case, if Lowell doesn't have the Valedictory at Commencement, there will be little short of rebellion. I for one won't speak on that day & I doubt whether another single fellow of the first thirty-five would."[22] The crisis passed when Charlie recovered his position in the next term, but the class's clannish fidelity to its leader is interesting. His classmates had turned a position based on merit into one based on consensus: on a footing if not democratic, then certainly consentient or ac-clamatory.

Southerners at Harvard stood out. They "generally spent much money, drank freely, and considered themselves better than the Northern mudsill; they were overbearing and quarrelsome, but brave and full of honor, al-though they often did not pay their debts." This judgment was made by Thomas Jefferson Coolidge, whose mother was a granddaughter of his namesake and who belonged to both regions. The southerners kept to them-selves or found a safe haven in the Porcellian Club. Few joined other clubs. Many, like the Johnston brothers from Louisville, Kentucky, planned to be-come plantation owners and saw their time at Harvard exclusively as an op-portunity to enjoy the Boston theater and attend dances.[23]

The northern and southern students had plenty of opportunities to dis-cover their differences. The deaths of Henry Clay and Daniel Webster in 1852 provided two such occasions, the publication of Harriet Beecher Stowe's *Uncle Tom's Cabin* that same year another. Anna considered it "a perfect picture of slavery . . . perfectly dispassionate and unprejudiced" and believed the book "will do more to free us from slavery than all that has ever been done." Needless to say, southerners found the book hateful, grossly dis-torted, and evil in intent. In club life, debates had a nasty habit of becom-ing angry shouting matches, although students tried to avoid the subject of slavery. The proposed annexation of Cuba (to the Yankees, an expansionist southern imperial fantasy) understandably could not be argued without dis-cussing slavery. But even tangential questions on seemingly unrelated sub-jects were fraught: the problems of an industrial society and the changes industry brought to social organization were just one example.[24]

The inherent dignity of labor was a New England truism that was rapidly dissolving in the new industrial order. Labor had had a quasi-sacramental status as a means of serving God, of finding one's calling. Virtually all New England students presumed that they would work. In addition, they all had some acquaintance with "manual labor," however slight. Confusion on the subject arose over the specifics of individual fulfillment, not over the con-cept of labor itself. The New Englanders were stunned by a southern class-mate, a tall, impulsive Floridian, who declared in one debate, "You don't believe in manual labor any more than I. You wouldn't black your own boots, you know." The southerner was equally stunned to learn that the northerner not only blacked his own boots but "should have held any one to be a snob, here, who should refuse to do it." Friendships were, of course, made across this divide of culture, but while Lowell came to know fairly well a number of his southern classmates, none became intimates.[25]

While the Lowell family had always gone to Elmwood for Sunday lunch, Charlie was now going there almost every afternoon. In January 1852 his grandfather, Reverend Lowell, suffered a stroke that left him semiparalyzed. The stroke could not have come at a more unfortunate time. Uncle James had taken his wife, whose health was poor, and their two surviving children (two had died in infancy) to Europe. Charlie's aunt Rebecca was deeply unstable and rarely left her room.

The lion's share of caring for his grandfather fell to Charlie, who coaxed him to eat and assisted him in various ways. But he was slow to regain the power of speech, and his digestion was ruined. Most of his few bright moments came during his grandson's visits. The old man became jovial in Charlie's company, made bad puns, and even composed a sonnet to his much-loathed mush.

Charlie read him the newspapers. As the debate over the Fugitive Slave Act intensified, the reverend was upset by the blanket condemnations of the Boston clergy, whose silence was the subject of slurs and bitter attacks. He was frustrated that his own efforts were ignored, and that even after complaint, published criticism had not been emended to exempt him. Although his stroke had him left with control over only three fingers, he wrote angry, barely legible letters of protest: "Your sermon will go abroad, and it will be handed down, and a stigma, a monstrous stigma upon my name, will go along with it." To his own parishioners he expressed his chagrin that the West Church had never been desegregated, saying that this was "the only thing which I remember as having been mortifying and painful to me in my communications."[26] After a lifetime of restraint and gentleness, he had found a new vehemence.

The reverend was quite deaf. Although he could understand Charlie, most others he could not; the grandson provided crucial assistance when visitors called. Most came away charmed by this relic from another era, with his hair now wild wisps, his body obviously damaged, but with a radiant smile and graceful antique manners. They did not know that he was in constant pain, ate little, and tired rapidly. It was Charlie who protected him, who regulated his time, and who helped him physically.

On May 4, 1852, Reverend Lowell once again found himself at the forefront of liberal Boston politics when the great Hungarian republican Louis Kossuth came to call after attending Harvard's Exhibition Day. No one stirred the American imagination as did Kossuth. In the nationalist and republican uprisings of 1848, which began in Paris with the overthrow of Louis Philippe and spread to Vienna, Bohemia, Milan, Venice, and Prussia, Kossuth had, for a brief spell in Hungary, wrested power from the mighty Habsburg Empire. Shortly his efforts collapsed and he was forced into a life of exile. Americans followed these events with much sympathy. Boston's own Dr. Samuel G. Howe had, as a young man, fought with the revolutionaries, winning their medal as a chevalier in the Légion d'Honneur (hence his nickname of "Chev"). The Italian struggle had been reported by Margaret Fuller, whose ties to Giuseppe Mazzini through her husband, Count Ossoli, had given her stories special power. (Her tragic death and the loss of the manuscript of her book on the subject when the boat on which she was traveling sank in a storm had helped to publicize Mazzini's efforts.) Through Boston had trooped a variety of exiles from Europe: the mad one-eyed Polish count Adam Gurowski; the Russian anarchist Michael Bakunin; and Harvard's own Professor Sophocles, a scholar-hermit bred in a monastery on Mount Athos and now a tutor in Greek. (And of course, significant numbers of immigrants entered the country as a result of these conflicts.)

Charlie's brilliant aunt Mary Lowell Putnam, one of the few Americans to speak and read Hungarian, used her astonishing skill at languages to befriend many of these European republicans, Kossuth in particular, and she became an advocate for his failed republican movement. As part of his extended and increasingly triumphant tour of America, Kossuth spent a week in Boston. He was surrounded by the state's various political figures, who lauded him as a freedom fighter visiting "the birthplace of liberty." In their speeches they refought the American Revolution, recasting Great Britain as the Habsburg Empire and the thirteen colonies as the Hungarian people. Expressing their fervent devotion to Hungarian independence, they reaffirmed their conviction that Kossuth himself was a great man committed to a noble cause. Kossuth made a point of stopping at Elmwood, even though Charlie's aunt Mary was abroad.

Kossuth thanked Reverend Lowell, who served as his daughter's proxy, for the "zeal, learning and ability" with which Mary had "vindicated" his country in many articles in the American press.[27] They then adjourned to tea at the Lowells' Quincy Street house, to which Anna had invited a great many luminaries. Hordes of students milled about outside. The tea she hosted for Louis Kossuth represented Anna Lowell's emergence as a Cambridge institution. She was already known for her "Saturday evenings," to which came a vast assortment of students, younger professors, and their families and friends, the conversation ranging from Platonic philosophy to politics to pure buffoonery. A German class met weekly. Private theatricals were organized. When the first installment of Dickens's serial novel *Bleak House* was published, Anna threw a party to which people came dressed as Dickensian characters. This party was talked of for years afterward. Charlie brought home his friends, his two sisters had their friends, many of Anna's former pupils visited, and friends on the Harvard faculty regularly stopped by. At the core of these faculty friends were Charles Eliot Norton; Francis James Child, a literature professor who was especially devoted to Anna; and of course James Russell Lowell. These three treated Anna's front parlor as a sort of private club to which they could go between classes.[28]

Accompanying Kossuth on his American tour were Ferencz and Theresa Pulszky, Hungarian exiles and writers whom Anna befriended. She agreed to write three letters to be published as appendices in their book *White, Red, Black: Sketches of American Society in the United States* (1853). These letters, the result of a lively conversation during Kossuth's visit in Boston, tried to explain the peculiar elements of American culture. Some of her comments express a nascent feminism: marriage made a woman's life "a defenseless territory," she said, arguing that "eight mothers to one child should be the rule . . . not one mother to eight children." Without servants, women were made "the slave of things": "Intellect in a woman is a foe to domestic comfort; but in America, at least a sensible woman makes the best housewife."

Anna had an equal sympathy for the expectations put on men to support themselves and their families financially. Anna believed that "a niggardly husband or father is almost unknown in America . . . he tries to keep from his household the naughty spirits of care with a plug of gold." This pursuit of money was necessary because financial autonomy was "the skeleton of independence." This forced men to live two lives, one of business, the other of pleasure. Beyond their power to earn, Anna believed, "to every man there is appointed a certain ministry and service, a path described of duty, a work to perform, and a race to run, an office in the economy of Providence, for usefulness is a necessary property of goodness." And she returned continually to the subject of young people — what must be done for them, what must be expected of them. "Children are monarchs: . . . on them hangs the destiny of the New World, and to each parent's heart they offer the possibility of living over again his own life free from past errors and privations." She freely recognized that training children for their own and the nation's future objectified their parents' regard for them.[29]

These letters give a strong sense of Anna's attitudes, and of her distinctive style — insightful, direct, radical, yet deeply sympathetic. Her critique was not in the end subversive. She did not want to undo the system in which she lived in. Instead, she was bent on perfecting it; she was a meliorist who believed that individuals served society, not the reverse.

Since he had been caring for his ill grandfather while his uncle was away, Charlie's relationship with James Russell Lowell had altered dramatically; now James treated him more like a friend than a nephew, and their letters assumed a tone of almost conspiratorial camaraderie. They began to have friends in common. One, Arthur Hugh Clough, midway in age between them, was a young English poet whom Emerson had persuaded to visit Cambridge in the hopes of receiving a teaching appointment. (Clough's closest friend was another English poet, Matthew Arnold.) Then James suffered the death of another child (his third), and in November 1853, shortly after returning to Cambridge from Europe, his wife died after a long and agonizing battle with tuberculosis. Her death devastated him. Throughout the winter and spring of 1854 he leaned heavily on the Lowell family, coming almost daily to the house, dining with them every other day. He was severely depressed, unable to express his grief except by scrawling his wife's initials in his diary day after day — sometimes small and neat, sometimes huge or in a quivering line, as if his hand could barely hold the pen. He contemplated suicide. He described his depression as "the drop of black blood I inherited from my dear mother and which is apt to spread itself over the pupil of my eye and darken everything."[30]

That summer James and Charlie went on a camping expedition in Maine, James's account of which became A *Moosehead Journal*, in which Charlie is called Telemachus. That James saw himself as Odysseus the wanderer, the hero lost at the wars, and that he cast Charlie as his son, the loyal Telemachus who searches for him, speaks to Charlie's role in caring for Reverend Lowell during James's misbegotten European venture, when his own son died. And it may speak to a spiritual kinship that had always existed between the two.[31]

At this time James wrote two poems, one of which, a sonnet to Anna, praised her fortitude and acknowledged how deeply he leaned on her in his grief and how he drew strength from her example: "Through suffering and sorrow thou hast passed / To show us what a woman true may be," it began, and ended, "Nor hast thy knowledge of adversity / Robbed thee of any faith in happiness, / But rather cleared thine inner eyes to see / How many simple ways there are to bless."[32] The second poem—longer, more complicated, and more melancholic—was written to Charlie. Using the imagery of the changing seasons to describe mortal life's various stages, the poem suggests that the tragedies of human life have some hidden inevitability, as regular as the seasons, part of the inevitable, melancholic progression from youth to adulthood to old age.

Recalling "we once were young . . . We trusted then, aspired, believed / That the earth could be re-made tomorrow," the poet lapses into a pained nostalgia: "why be ever undeceived? / Why give up faith for sorrow?" In the final verse, he addresses Charlie directly: "O thou, whose days are yet all spring, / Faith, blighted once, is past retrieving; / Experience is a dumb, dead thing; / The victory is in believing."[33] Was this curious poem an attempt to explain the disappointed lives of people surrounding Charlie? An attempt to free him from the bondage of association? Or an effort to bind him more closely to them, urging him to do for them what they could no longer do for themselves? Is he saying, Be young for us? Believe for us? Is it an envy-filled admonition to live fully while the chance exists?

At the beginning of his junior year at Harvard, after his most intense efforts of caring for his grandfather, Charlie wrote to a friend: "I feel a great deal older now than I did three years ago, or even two months ago."[34] The support his classmates had shown him over his loss of position as first scholar the previous spring had boosted his confidence, but now they noticed other changes in him as well. The experience of intimately watching an elderly man prepare for death is inevitably a maturing one. His grandfather's dependence on Charlie must have revealed to him his capacity for fulfilling responsibilities and also its rewards. Equally maturing was to watch his adored uncle James be almost broken by grief. His classmates began to seek him out for his advice, it being generally acknowledged that his sympathies were wide, his compassion strong, and his judgment sound.

Exuberant, at times bursting with energy, he had an intensity that attracted a large circle of friends and followers. He was surprisingly charismatic and strong. One of them explained that he drew "their wills to him, as a loadstone attracts iron." Soon he was "proudly acknowledged, without a dissenting voice," this classmate recalled, "as the foremost man of the Class." And yet Lowell himself remained reserved, revealing little of his inner self or feelings, so that casual observers often supposed him somewhat cold. Some found his manner brusque or chilly. Respecting him, they did not become intimate or even fond. Charlie let few behind his reserve, yet even these few continued to feel that he was somewhat unknowable.[35]

FOUR

THE AMERICAN SCHOLAR

1854

In his final year at Harvard, 1854, Lowell wrote in his class book, "I was not at all anxious to come to college and have been ready to leave at any moment." His classmate and close friend William James Potter even more bluntly declared that his time at Harvard had been the "four most wasted years of my life up to this time."[1] They were not alone in these sentiments. Charles Francis Adams condemned his Harvard years. Even such upright contemporaries as Charles William Eliot, the future president of Harvard, and Phillips Brooks, who became an eminent bishop, loathed their experience and into their old age argued over whether 1853 or 1855 was Harvard's lowest ebb.

The cause for this disaffection involved two struggles. The first, specific to the college, was its rudderless course as the powers behind the scene fought over a populist or elitist culture; the second was political, concerned slavery, and would have profound consequences for the country. Harvard had always allied itself with the most conservative forces in Boston society, but never more clearly so than in the early 1850s, when the power of the old Cotton Whig ascendancy was still dominant and its critics were freshly and ardently uniting in opposition to the Slave Power. Scholars have generally agreed that in the 1850s the question of slavery "drew a line of cleavage through all Boston society, leaving most of the more powerful or wealthy families on the conservative side."[2] Many of Lowell's friends experienced this as a generational issue. George Putnam's father, as John Amory Lowell's family minister, was a leader among the Unitarian ministers trying to suppress discussion of slavery and the Fugitive Slave Law. The premier dandy of the class was Robert Winthrop, Jr., son of Robert Winthrop, Sr., the multi-termed Boston Whig representative to Congress who, as Speaker of the House, had been a key player in preserving the proslavery Whig coalition of northern and southern members.

Lowell's friend Jim Savage, an abolitionist on the basis of his Christian beliefs, stood at the opposite end of the political spectrum from his father, one of the signatories to the letter published in the *Daily Advertiser* endorsing Daniel Webster's notorious March 7 speech. To one degree or another, the political situation forced fissures in the extended families of all of Lowell's oldest friends. Stephen Perkins's father was a Cotton Whig through and through, but Stephen had been tutored by his cousin Thomas Wentworth Higginson, a radical abolitionist minister just beginning his career in activism. Some old friends like Henry Higginson and Charlie Adams belonged to liberal but not radical families. Their parents were Conscience Whigs, Free-Soilers, supporters of Adams's father, Charles Francis Adams, who was founding the Republican Party in Massachusetts. Lowell's friends were impatient with their parents' cautious faith in half measures and symbolic protest. In Lowell's lucky family the early death of the conservative grandparent, Patrick Tracy Jackson, had liberalized all the members, sparing them the worst of the conflict. Even more unusual was the case of Reverend Charles Lowell, who despite his age and generation was surprisingly radical.

Yet the Lowells were not without their rifts and difficulties. James Russell Lowell, who had been a Garrisonian abolitionist since 1837, was in the compromised position, thrust upon him by financial need, of accepting a teaching position at Harvard—provided he did not speak out on the subject of slavery. This appointment was engineered by his second cousin, John Amory Lowell, one of the most influential of Harvard's private benefactors, a Fellow of the Corporation, and a conservative Cotton Whig. J. A. Lowell held critical positions on the boards of a variety of Boston cultural institutions and was an important player in the political activities of the Whig Party. Because Harvard was so identified with the Cotton Whig position, because its educational methods were outdated, because it had cravenly courted southern students, and because political opinion had created such a generational divide, students during Lowell's years at Harvard felt a "slow-burning rage"[3] that was not equaled among later generations of students until the late 1960s.

Increasingly Lowell was drawn to other students who, like him, were children of liberal intellectuals relatively free from the constraints of Boston convention. Horace Furness was one: he was the son of a committed abolitionist. Frank Barlow and John Bancroft both spent part of their childhood at Brook Farm and were literally products of the Transcendentalist experiment. Barlow's mother, Almira Penniman Barlow, had brought herself and her three sons to the tolerant atmosphere of Brook Farm after she had broken the bonds of social convention by deserting her husband, an alcoholic and unstable minister. An extremely good student, Barlow was devoted to Emerson, in whom he found a father figure. He was called "Crazy Barlow" because despite his tremendous self-containment, he occasionally let loose with a force that astounded. He was blunt-spoken. One friend explained he had no "veneration, imagination or poetic conception," which led to his "absolute honesty." Lowell, cherishing this ruthless honesty, found in Barlow a companion.[4]

Johnny Bancroft was very different in temperament. An attractive young man, fond of pleasures, with an irreverent sense of humor and a clever undisciplined mind, he was firm in his conviction that he would live an original life. The younger son of the eminent historian and diplomat George Bancroft, he and his brother George had been parked at Brook Farm after their mother's early death; they had lived with a few other children in the "phalanstery," educated there by the elderly, legendary Miss Ripley. This unconventional childhood, lacking in parental affection, was nevertheless filled with curiosities. Nathaniel Hawthorne had lived at Brook Farm for a short spell, for instance. The children adored him, for he joined in their pillow fights and games, even inventing some of his own. Johnny and Frank Barlow used to follow the shy writer on his walks. Deep in thought, head bowed, hands clasped meditatively behind him, Hawthorne would wander on no discernible route, struggling with some creative problem. Behind him, literally in his footsteps, the boys followed, stooping every now and then to scour the ground, only to rise all smiles and hurry after him. The children were in fact finding the pennies that occasionally dropped through a hole in Hawthorne's pocket.[5]

Two other new companions were William James Potter and Frank Sanborn. Potter, who came of Connecticut Quakers, was as bright as, and perhaps brighter than, Lowell, and like most Quakers he was a pacifist, imbued with egalitarian feelings. Highly principled and interested in philosophical and religious questions, he wanted to define a religious position devoted to improving the lives of the poor. He was a philosopher searching for an avenue of action. Frank Sanborn was the reverse: an activist in search of a philosophy. He was a New Hampshire boy from a respectable but poor family with good political connections whose father had died in his childhood. A very tall young man with aquiline good looks, he had a way of attaching himself to older mentors. He read to the abolitionist Theodore Parker, whose eyesight was poor. This served as his entry into abolitionist circles, which he quickly penetrated to the center.

It was these young men in particular whom Lowell brought home to the Blue Room, with its French doors opening out onto a wide porch at the front of his mother's house. Here they discussed everything—the inadequacies of their education, the failures of their society, and the meaning of Plato and Lucretius. They considered themselves "reformers," and intended to be activists, not simply critics. They believed in progress and were optimistic that society was improving. Utopian experiments like Brook Farm they regarded as forms of escapism and nostalgia. While some of these friends were financially well off (Perkins, Bancroft, Furness), most were not (Sanborn, Potter, Putnam, Barlow). All were increasingly aware that they would have to establish careers for themselves. Even those for whom wealth was assured or who could easily procure a position in a family business believed that they should do more than simply take these opportunities. They were earnest in their desire to find, in Anna Lowell's words, "their office in the economy of Providence." This included a need to change their world.

All these young men had experienced either financial or emotional hardship and the loss of a parent. Their desire for reform had not only an intellectual basis but a strong emotional component. In searching for their own truths, they were repelled by hypocrisies, and much of their discussion concerned the misguidedness of the adult world, Sanborn playing the role of political reformer, Potter that of social activist, Furness and Bancroft advocating a cultural or literary reformation, and Lowell developing a theory for "the improvement of the industrial classes,"[6] which his friends regarded as a radical form of socialism.

Ralph Waldo Emerson, aware of the inadequacies of the "Cambridge system of instruction" and the restrictions of society generally, was eager to discover students who "showed sympathy with his poetry or philosophy." His critique of society and his position as an outsider gave him an unusual degree of empathy with youthful discontent. But his appeal in the early 1850s was by no means universal. He was not invited to speak at Harvard—not only were his politics abhorrent, but his theology and even his oratorical style repelled many listeners. In 1851 he had given a speech in Cambridge at which a "detachment of Harvard students, practical defenders of slavery and some of the slaveholders,—to whom Webster and Clay were demigods, and Parker and Phillips were little better than two of the wicked"—had hissed and hooted. Harvard professors regularly mocked Emerson to win an easy laugh from their students. Some, more serious, "threatened him with prosecution for blasphemy."[7]

However, in late 1853 Moncure Conway, who was teaching at Harvard, arranged for Emerson to speak to a select group that included Anna Lowell, Uncle James, and Charlie Lowell, as well as Barlow, Bancroft, and Sanborn. This meeting convinced young Lowell, Sanborn, and Barlow to request another meeting, and Emerson responded by inviting four students—Lowell, Bancroft, Furness, and Sanborn—to lunch with him in Concord in April 1854. The conversation was stimulating, and Emerson resolved to open his study to occasional seminars at which he and his fellow Transcendentalist, Bronson Alcott, might speak to more students. To Anna, Emerson remarked on Charlie's "generous discontent with the conditions of society . . . I hope he will never get over it." Emerson had decided there was "a good crop of mystics at Harvard College."[8]

Emerson's appeal was largely the invigoration and stimulation offered in such essays as "Self-Reliance" and "Man, the Reformer," and in the example he set in "The American Scholar," when he rejected the compromises required of him to live within the conventions of the Boston clergy, gave up his pulpit, and set off on his uncertain course of thought and writing in Concord. As an unfettered man, Emerson embodied his ideas of "self-culture." His was a lone voice that urged the young to believe in themselves and their potentialities when all about them were adult expectations of conformity and conventionality.

On May 20, 1854, Lowell and his friends again went to Concord. The conversation ranged over many topics, but Lowell was most impressed by Emerson's admiration for the English philosopher, historian, and essayist Thomas Carlyle, the preeminent spokesman for mature English Romantic thought. Lowell had been reading Carlyle not only for his philosophy but for his historical interpretations. For Carlyle, history was infused with the spiritual impulses in human development that lay beneath facts, actions, and the surface of things. The French Revolution and the uprisings of 1848 were expressions of Europe's attempts to throw off a medieval world view and enter the modern age. Lowell was immediately drawn to these ideas and began to steep himself in Carlyle's writing.

Harvard naturally noticed a scholar of Lowell's caliber, and he was "strongly urged to devote himself to letters or science,"[9] but he had no wish to be a traditional scholar. Others expected that he would use his skill in the Lowell tradition of the law, but Charlie demurred. Emerson's interest encouraged him to consider yet a third future path. One of the changes occurring in American society was the growth of magazines, lectures, and public commentary generally. It was now possible for American intellectuals to live as Europeans did by their wit, their philosophy, their ideas. Emerson believed that Lowell could be valued chiefly for his opinions and ideas: he was a "thinker." This was a condition that Uncle James, Aunt Mary, and to a lesser degree his mother had already attained.

Lowell's ambitions, however, were complicated. Despite the celebrity of both Aunt Mary and Uncle James and the deep affection Charlie had for his relatives at Elmwood, he could see beyond their public success to their private failings: their ineptitude in practical matters, their susceptibility to physical and mental disease, and their antiquated habits. Grandmother Harriet Spence Lowell's "black blood," of which his uncle James felt tormented by only a "drop," was more liberally diffused in Aunt Rebecca and Aunt Mary but was perhaps most evident in his own father.

Lowell understood that after their financial debacle his family had survived by their wits, by the generosity of relations, and by slowly selling off the land that surrounded Elmwood. He had felt keenly the struggle for financial stability. The role of "reformer" or "thinker," he knew, promised scant security. Uncle James had recently found it necessary to accept a post at Harvard on condition that he moderate his abolitionist position: a serious, perhaps irretrievable compromise. "Thinkers" who were successful usually had independent means: a private income, a rich wife, or a benefactor. Was it a wise or responsible choice of career for a young man of no fortune?

Those who knew him and his circumstances well understood that Charlie's desire to restore the family finances had been formed early on, even before he attended the English High School. Much as he might have enjoyed the life of a "thinker," and to whatever degree he entertained ideas of struggling toward that life, Lowell considered it "a foregone decision of long standing" that he would have a career in business.[10] His most intimate friends understood that he wished to unite these two roles of "reformer" and businessman.*

By the time of his May visit to Emerson, Lowell had been selected to give the valedictory address at Harvard's commencement. He chose as his

---

*As if to reinforce this perspective, Anna's school was now failing. She had leased both her house in Boston and the school to one of her former teachers, who, it had been hoped, would carry on the venture. But Lucia Peabody quickly squandered her opportunity. By 1854 there were fewer than fifteen pupils, the yearly lease could not be paid, and the school was headed for failure. Worse than the loss of this steady source of income, Charlie's mother would have to renew her long years of hard work to rescue the school. If there had been any indecision on Charlie's part, this ended it.

topic "The Reverence Due from Old Age to Youth." Just what he intended to do with his speech no one knew; he showed no signs of writing it in advance. His mother became increasingly anxious that Charlie had put nothing on paper. He was in fact hardly ever home. He had become so engrossed in the political situation in Boston that he paid scant heed to his college obligations.

The political controversies of 1850, Lowell's freshman year, had been reignited in early 1854, when the Senate debated the Kansas-Nebraska Bill, which organized two new territories for settlement. Nebraska would be a free territory; Kansas, however, would follow the model of "popular sovereignty" used in New Mexico: the settlers would decide whether Kansas would be slave or free. Worse, the bill nullified the Missouri Compromise of 1820, which banned slavery north of the Mason-Dixon line; slavery might now expand northward unfettered. The propelling force behind the bill was the need to formalize as territories the land along which northern industrialists wanted to build a transcontinental railroad that would connect prosperous California with Chicago, the projected terminus of several railroads already under construction, originating in eastern port cities—Baltimore, New York, Boston. Passage of the legislation required the support of the president pro tem of the Senate, David R. Atchison of Missouri, and it was at his insistence that Kansas was being opened for settlement by slaveholders.

Normally an astute politician, Senator Stephen Douglas of Illinois, the bill's architect, had miscalculated. Righteous indignation at the bill's repeal of the Missouri Compromise poured from northern pens. They roundly denounced Douglas's argument that by allowing popular sovereignty in New Mexico in 1850, the Missouri Compromise had already been "superseded." As this debate carried on, it served to solidify Free Soil politics; antislavery forces opposed the new territories' becoming slave states both on populist grounds (free settlers did not want to compete with slave labor) and on economic and political grounds (adding more slave states to the Union would augment the power of slave states in the Congress). Even New England Cotton Whigs were sufficiently alarmed to oppose the bill. Yankee industrialists and bankers had been benefiting greatly from the South's failure to diversify. As southerners used their profits to acquire more land and more slaves to grow more cotton for yet more profit, Yankees made their own profits providing almost every other service; this knowledge confirmed to them that it would be disastrous to give southerners, with their shortsighted economic vision, greater power over the national economy.

Thus in February 1854 Lowell attended a protest at Faneuil Hall sponsored by confirmed conservatives such as Robert Winthrop, Samuel Eliot, and the younger Amos A. Lawrence (whom Wendell Phillips had denounced as one of the "snobbish sons of fathers lately rich"). Throughout the North, conservative and moderate Whigs deserted their southern associates, provoking a sectional split in the party that proved irreparable. (In Massachusetts the death of Daniel Webster in 1852 had left a vacuum at the moderate center of Massachusetts politics that undoubtedly hastened the Whig collapse.) A broad cross section of northerners now favored the free settlement of Kansas. In June, Lowell's uncle Patrick Jackson became treasurer of the newly formed Massachusetts Emigrant Aid Society, committed to raising money to underwrite the emigration of free farmers recruited throughout New England for Kansas.

Simultaneously with this national debate, slave hunters once again appeared in Boston. The Vigilance Committee, which for three years had quite successfully spirited fugitives away from Boston, now widely broadcast the presence of these slave hunters, who were after Anthony Burns, the property of one Colonel Suttle of Alexandria, Virginia. A tall, solidly built man, the literate Burns had a job in a clothing store. Despite the precautions he took, he was apprehended one evening while leaving work. The Vigilance Committee immediately set to work with handbills and posters advertising the facts. It called a meeting in Faneuil Hall on May 26 which Lowell and his friends attended. George R. Russell presided. The politically moderate ex-mayor of Roxbury, Russell was a man of wealth and respectability but also a Transcendentalist who had provided some of the funds for Brook Farm. With Russell moderation ceased: the key figures behind the meeting were Dr. Samuel G. Howe and the more radical activists within the Vigilance Committee. Theodore Parker's speech was particularly incendiary, beginning, "Fellow subjects of Virginia," and declaring, "There is no Boston to-day. There was a Boston once. Now there is a north suburb to the city of Alexandria," and finishing with the exhortation "To the Court House! To the Revere House for the slave catchers!" Men planted in the audience shouted that the raid on the courthouse had begun, and pandemonium broke out.[11]

Thomas Wentworth Higginson (Stephen Perkins's cousin and former tutor) had that very morning purchased a dozen hand axes and had sent for a gang of men. That evening an angry mass of blacks, including Lewis Hayden, the leader of the violent rescue that had freed Shadrach, filled the basement of a nearby meetinghouse, ready once again to attempt a similar liberation. Higginson gathered a band of them and appeared at Faneuil Hall; Howe, Parker, and Phillips let him recruit more volunteers from among their crowd and soon lost control altogether. Higginson headed for the courthouse to free Burns; others went to attack the slave catchers, who were lodged at the Revere House.

Lowell and Sanborn followed Higginson, but on approaching the courthouse, they hung back, daunted and lacking weapons. Higginson and his band attacked the courthouse guards, using a huge timber as a battering ram on the main door. On the street the mob surrounding Lowell shouted, threw stones, and even shot at the windows. As the courthouse doors gave way, Higginson, Hayden, and a few others succeeded in getting in, but they were confronted by guards armed with sabers and billy clubs. In the scuffle a gun went off, killing a guard. More guards rushed to defend the courthouse, and Higginson's band was beaten back. Meanwhile two companies of state militia arrived on the scene, effectively bringing the attack to an end. Some thirteen men were arrested, and Higginson, who had been slashed in the face, was spirited away. He went into hiding.

The assault, resulting from high emotion and poor planning, had been doomed from the start. Many members of the Vigilance Committee recognized this immediately, but to young men like Lowell, the boldness and audacity of the action was riveting. Only the obvious evidence of failure drove home the futility of the attempt. Afterward the courthouse was ringed with two companies of marines and two of artillery. Burns himself was guarded by 125 volunteer militia drawn from "the vilest sinks of scoundrelism, corruption and crime of the city."[12] The following day, Saturday, May 27, Boston was flooded with militia reinforcements. The courthouse was sealed off, and there was much concern for the homes of abolitionist leaders. Young men like Lowell and Sanborn were used as runners, lookouts, and guards protecting various Vigilance Committee members. But any hope of a violent rescue of Burns was now gone. His potential salvation lay with moderates of the Vigilance Committee, who undertook a massive publicity campaign, printing placards and posters calling upon the "yeomanry of New England" to attend Burns's trial—what they called his "Mock Trial"—to begin on Monday morning. This they did, traveling from rural areas and outlying towns until some seven to eight thousand people thronged the courthouse square.

Over the weekend rumors floated through Lowell's family house that relatively conservative Bostonians were attempting to purchase Burns from

Colonel Suttle to avert further conflict. They raised $785 and appeared to have worked out a deal, but it was scuttled after the district attorney declared that it was illegal to sell slaves in Massachusetts. On Sunday, May 28, Lowell attended a rally at the Music Hall at which Theodore Parker, preaching to a packed audience, attacked Judge Loring, who was to preside over Burns's trial. His eloquence further inflamed the abolitionists' suppressed rage. Lowell, convinced that Judge Loring did not understand the situation, persuaded Sanborn to call on the judge with him and try to explain it. Needless to say, Judge Loring, most likely in consultation with the city fathers over whether there was any way to permit the sale of Burns, was not at home.[13]

When the court convened on Monday morning, Burns was defended by a Vigilance Committee member, Richard Henry Dana, who made several attempts to postpone the hearing, all of which were denied. In fact, there were no legal arguments to raise in Burns's favor. Nevertheless, the mood of the crowd outside so violently supported release that the judgment remanding Burns into the custody of his owner came as a terrible shock. A reading of Loring's judgment suggests that he would very much have liked to free Burns but lacked the legal ground to do so.

Boston now faced the problem of getting Burns out of town without provoking yet another riot. There was no hope of spiriting him out at the crack of dawn, as had been done with Thomas Sims: the Vigilance Committee had organized a twenty-four-hour guard of the courthouse to prevent exactly that. The city authorities saw an overwhelming show of force as the only option. On June 2 troops assembled on the Common, each man carrying eleven rounds of ammunition. They loaded their guns in full view of the roughly twenty thousand people assembled there. Although the mayor had forbidden bell ringing, churches in Cambridge and the adjoining towns tolled theirs, and one Boston bell (with the belfry locked and the key misplaced) rang free. At this point, the captain of the police resigned his position. This delayed events for several hours, until three o'clock, when Burns was led out, surrounded by a square of 120 men carrying drawn swords and revolvers. Then, as the procession began down Court Street, the crowd hissed, groaned, and shouted, "Shame!" Black flags hung out of windows, and from one dangled a black coffin on which was written "the Funeral of Liberty." Shops were shut. Streets were closed. Some of the troops were drunk. Some in the crowd carried cutlasses and revolvers. At the head of State Street two cannons were aimed at the crowd. As the procession moved on, soldiers had to press back the throng. Occasionally the procession halted.

At the Customs House clouds of cayenne pepper were tossed from a window; a bottle of vitriol was hurled onto the street, smashing into fragments as it hit the pavement. The crowd surged forward, and lancers on horseback charged, as did the infantry with fixed bayonets. People "were driven like rats into cellar-ways and forced up flights of stairs and into passages." A number were injured. Turning onto Commercial Street, the procession ran into a long line of traffic headed by an ornery truckman who refused to budge. With a company of soldiers' guns trained on him, he "rose on his horse, bared his breast, snatched off his hat, and waving it above his head, cried: 'Fire! You cowards.' " The commanding officer ordered his men ready, but a local constable pulled the man off his cart and arrested him.

Finally the procession reached T Wharf, where a steamer waited. By now those of the troops who had been drinking to relieve their tension were truly drunk. They began to sing "Carry Me Back to Ol' Virginny," which incensed the protesters, but the bayonet charge had reduced the crowd as some were wounded and others scared off. Those who remained recognized that their protest had failed. The state had spent $30,000. As Burns boarded ship, many spectators burst into tears.[14]

Charlie Lowell and Henry Higginson, who had followed the procession, had never seen anything like what they encountered that day. As Burns's ship left Boston Harbor and the crowd dispersed, they were filled with shame at the disgrace to Boston. Although older and wiser men could have told them that the day was preordained, to their youthful minds the passions were momentous. They were shocked that popular moral protest had had no effect. But most fundamentally they felt betrayed. They had witnessed the power of the state to carry out federal law, a power that they thought "disarmed & emasculated us." They had seen the crowd cowed by fear of that power. People had been bayoneted and charged by horses—and had been powerless in the face of it. The indignation of the people and their moral right had meant nothing. This manifestation of absolute state power fostered in Lowell resentment and disrespect for the authority of the law: justice and the law, he believed, were two distinctly separate things. He and Higginson thought their parents' generation had failed to address the moral evil within the nation. Neither congressional means nor political suasion had brought results. Now the courts, too, were besmirched by the stain of slavery. As the two walked back to Cambridge that evening, Higginson declared, "Charlie, it will come to us to set this right."[15]

As Lowell wrote his Commencement Day oration, he could not fail to remark how his four years at Harvard had been framed by the Fugitive Slave Law. It was a point made at Class Day on June 23 by Robert Winthrop, Jr., who described how his class had arrived at Harvard at "a period of assured national peace,—we go, when the entire press teems with rumors of war."[16] (Due to excessive partying after giving this speech, Winthrop was not allowed to graduate with his class.) The initial protest in October 1850 had taught Lowell a great deal about how individuals responded to the demands of his time. He had seen his mother put her beliefs into action, his moderate grandfather rediscover the urgency, passion, and ideals of his youth, and his passionate uncle be silenced by circumstance. Even more startling, the Burns affair had galvanized a huge number of Bostonians from their complacency. Almost overnight men of a conservative and skeptical cast of mind, finally fed up with the ineffectiveness and humiliation of years of appeasement, turned against the Slave Power, and the Whig Party collapsed. For those already committed to the abolition of slavery, the experience with the legal process shredded their patience and engendered a cynical despair with the system generally.

The enforcement of the hated law showed Lowell that slavery was worked into the deepest fibers of the Constitution. A blind eye turned to it to ensure Union and generations of accommodation had bound it more tightly into the fabric of all political debate and economic development. Every avenue of reform appeared to have been tried and failed, and yet Lowell believed more profoundly than ever that slavery would have to end. How, he did not know. In many respects this was a terrifying if exciting conclusion. Work on his speech took on a whole new dimension, informed as it was by the passionate indignation aroused by what he had witnessed.

On a hot mid-July day nineteen-year-old Charles Lowell, in cap and gown, still boyish in his looks, stood before his Harvard class, the Board of Overseers, the Fellows of the Corporation, members of the government of the Commonwealth of Massachusetts, his entire family, and countless others to declaim on "The Reverence Due from Old Age to Youth."[17] He began by proposing that a nation's reverence for its youth should be the test of its civilization. He acknowledged that the United States had a better record than some European countries, but he believed that Americans were still "twenty millions of semi-barbarians." He set about defining what it was in youth that was of such value.

Alluding to Hinduism, Islam, and certain mathematical laws, Lowell cast aside the argument for youth's physical stamina and energy: its labor. Instead he promised its "fresher and purer ideals" and reforming spirit. Taking as its mission the transformation of its ideals into the "rational aim of the man," this spirit orients youth to the future, toward how life *should* be. The older generation must be ready to see its ideals transformed by newer ones, since this striving after new ideals is the primary engine of change, and "change is indeed the only constancy."[18]

Youthful ideals, Lowell warned, are delicate and fragile: they need nurture. To scoff at or scorn youthful dreaming was to destroy a creative process, for the real is a distillation of many ideals: "Out of the thousand fragile *chateaux in Spain* rises this one Gibraltar." In this way, "the world always advances by impossibilities achieved." He also warned against loving progress and seeing action as progress. Americans put too much emphasis on the quantity, not the quality, of their action. He feared that youth was used as the "tool" for action rather than as its "guide." Because of such shortsightedness, "Action, then, is the Minotaur which claims and devours our youths; Athens bewailed the seven who yearly left her shore; with us scarce seven remain, and we urge the victims to their fate."[19]

If the fate of the seven young Athenian men was to be sacrificed to the Minotaur, the fate that Boston, the Athens of America, was urging on Lowell and his classmates was sacrifice in the name of progress. Out of the same kind of desperation that had gripped Thebes, America was feeding its own Minotaur: a notion of progress that failed to recognize the corruption that lay at the heart of the American experience, slavery. Lowell never directly mentioned Burns or slavery in his speech, but in that charged atmosphere it would have been unnecessary to be explicit. The image of young men setting sail for enslavement and death was strong enough.

Each generation, he continued, began idealistically, but the natural corruption of living compromised its goals. Quoting Shakespeare's 111th sonnet, a strange, dark poem of inadequacy, corruption, and repentance, he noted that simultaneously, as the higher ideals are realized, so baser instincts are also at work; addressing Fortune, "the guilty goddess of my harmful deeds," the poet confessed that "my nature is subdued to what it works in, like the dyer's hand." Hence the need for yet unstained youth with fresh eyes and fresh ideals to revisit old problems.*

Lowell concluded with an image taken from the gospel of Apollonius of

---

*Shakespeare had been rediscovered by the Romantics and his texts restored. Both James Russell Lowell and Ralph Waldo Emerson had made thorough studies of Shakespeare.

Tyana, a genius who, according to Philostratus, traveled across the ancient world to India. On his travels Apollonius saw

> a youth, one of the blackest of the Indians, who had between his eyebrows a shining moon. Another youth, named Memnon, the pupil of [the Greek orator] Herodes, the sophist, had this moon when he was young, but as he approached to man's estate, its light grew fainter and fainter and finally vanished.

Lowell asked his audience to recognize that every youth wore his ideals on his brow like this shining moon.

> It should remember that he is already in the hands of a sophist more dangerous than Herodes, for that sophist is himself. It should watch lest, from too early or exclusive action, the moon on his brow, growing fainter and fainter, should finally vanish, and sadder than all, should leave in vanishing no sense of loss.

Youthful ideals, like youth itself, fade away with age. Emerson made this point in *The Transcendentalist*: "where are the old idealists? . . . Are they dead, taken in early ripeness to the gods,—as ancient wisdom foretold their fate? Or did the high idea die out of them and leave their unperfumed body as its tomb and tablet, announcing that all the celestial inhabitants, who once gave them beauty, had departed?"[20] Lowell's image also recalled his uncle's poem in its anguished feeling of sadness and fatedness for a man mourning his own youth, his own days of "believing."

The speech was a cry against cynicism, which Lowell feared might be a reaction to the Burns event; he hated the idea that he too might one day accept such patent injustice as the price that must be paid for the greater good. And it was a rejection of the various attempts—parental, societal, educational—to force upon him a "usefulness" that he did not embrace. Finally, it was a sort of manifesto. His ambiguities and tensions were still unresolved as he stood perched between a commitment to be of use to society and a temptation to remain a free spirit. This speech was his effort, after four years at Harvard, to define "usefulness" for himself.

The Making of a Young Man

FIVE

FINDING A CAREER

1854–56

Within a week of delivering his Commencement Day oration, Lowell was working in Boston for Larkin & Stackpole, a commissioned merchant firm with offices at 43 Commercial Wharf, the heart of Boston's waterfront. Each of the wharves that ringed Boston consisted of a row of warehouses flanked by two long cobbled streets, along which several ships could dock simultaneously and efficiently. To the grandest and largest wharves—India, T, Long, Commercial, and Lewis situated in the deepest part of the harbor and closest to the Customs House, came the richest and most distant cargoes. Alongside the warehouses were the counting houses and offices of merchant firms, railroad freight companies, fish-packing plants, and oyster bars. Ship-owners and grand merchants jostled with the Irish skivvies who hauled barrels, pushed barrows, and loaded holds and horse-drawn wagons. Larkin & Stackpole's goods came largely from the Caribbean and South America—wool, hides, hair, grease, and ostrich feathers from Buenos Aires; cigars, brown sugar, molasses, and honey from Cuba; cochineal from Guatemala; indigo from San Juan—but also rice from Savannah, salt from Cádiz, and champagne and brandy from La Rochelle.[1]

Lowell's position required him to do whatever came to hand, from sweeping out the shop floor to bookkeeping to seeing to the loading and unloading of goods. For generations such employment, amid the hustle and bustle of Boston's commercial life, had been the means by which young men were introduced to the world of business; it was the initiation rite of a future merchant. Many of his former classmates were employed in the same way at similar firms on neighboring wharves. Lowell's position was only marginally more exalted than that at which his grandfather Jackson had begun his working life at the age of thirteen.

The position did not fulfill Lowell's promise or expectations; nor were his ambitions satisfied. But two distinct needs were met: his old resolution not to have his mother support him longer than was necessary, and his mother's wish to see him safely launched. His experience on Commercial Wharf, however, confirmed his instinctive antipathy toward the merchant life. He was bored by mercantile transactions. What fascinated him was the actual production of goods, in particular "the mechanic arts," and like many young men he hoped to "found a manufacturing establishment."[2] All across New England, as industrialization spread, small manufacturing concerns sprang up and, around them, cities and towns. Lowell was but one among many: Lynn, Lawrence, Clinton, Fitchburg, Holyoke. New England manufacturers were also city founders.

Lowell's friends recognized that his ambitions were not small, but they felt they were appropriate to his gifts, his "capacity of ruling men,"[3] and they knew he wanted to be of "practical usefulness." Rather like his grandfather Jackson, Lowell's desire for financial success was linked to his need to accomplish, to build, to create. The challenge before him now was to place himself so he could seize an opportunity when one arose.

Early in 1855, after six months on the wharf, Lowell thought he had found it. He went "as a common workman . . . cleaning old chains or filing iron" to the Ames Company, in western Massachusetts, in the fledgling town of Chicopee, near Springfield, on the Connecticut River. This job was as atypical as a Harvard graduate could take, and it surprised his classmates even more than the rather mundane post at Larkin & Stackpole. Friends wrote him stern letters of advice: they knew that his manufacturing ambitions were complicated by ideas on the reorganization of the workplace, and they feared he was carrying his concern for social reform in the wrong direction, sacrificing himself without realizing those ideals.

At Harvard he had formulated a plan "in minute detail," his friends recalled, for improving workmen's living and working conditions. His ambition with his manufactory was to offer "both instruction and employment." Unfortunately the plan has been lost: all we know is that it involved some form of profit-sharing, in which a portion of the men's wages would depend on the company's profits. He hoped to create an interest in the success of the company and thereby introduce the entrepreneurial spirit among the workmen. Friends recalled that his attitude was neither sentimental nor patronizing. He "liked discipline, wished each person to do his part well, but his instincts and sympathies were . . . with the workers, and he cherished the hope of helping them to have richer and nobler lives." Sanborn described Lowell as approaching his business career with the "soul of a philosopher and philanthropist." Thus Lowell added an almost subversive idealism and social conscience to his ambitions to succeed where his father had failed, to rescue his mother and sisters from the discomforts of limited resources, and to realize some of the successes his grandfather Jackson had achieved.[4]

While his job was "common," Ames was no ordinary company, and Lowell arrived at his post by no ordinary means. He had explained that he wanted to learn about iron manufacture, and the company recommended that he get experience of the technology: the calibrating instruments, the special lathes, and the milling machines. He went to work on the shop floor, learning the minutiae of setting machines and operating jigs. The Ames technology, developed to fulfill a government contract for swords, carbines, cannons, and guns, was the reason the company had attracted international attention in the summer of 1854, when a small committee of British engineers and small arms experts visited the U.S. arsenal at Springfield. They were making an extensive study of the American arms industry for a parliamentary committee delegated to establish a state-of-the-art gun manufactory at Enfield. At the Great Exhibition of 1851 at the Crystal Palace in London, they had been impressed by the degree of mechanization in American manufacturing but were as yet unconvinced by the claims of American gun manufacturers that their weapons' parts were interchangeable.

The arsenal's superintendent, Colonel J. W. Ripley, asked them to pick out ten from among the collection of guns fabricated between 1844 and 1853. These were then dismantled, the parts thrown into a box, and the box shaken about. The various parts were then picked out at random and reassembled into ten working guns. This convincing demonstration drove home the enormous value of interchangeable parts for immediate repairs on the battlefield. The life of a gun could be extended, spare parts easily supplied, and the capacity of an army to fight better sustained.

"Unless the American example is followed at home," the committee reported, "it is feared that American manufacturers will before long become exporters . . . to England." It recommended buying the technology—a system of fine gauges, exact matrices, and calibrated measuring tools with which a properly trained workforce could measure parts at various critical stages of production—from American sources, namely, the Ames Company. The British signed a $40,000 contract in the autumn of 1854.[5]

Ames provided Lowell with an excellent perspective on metal fabrication, and he had intended to stay a full year, but within a few months Lowell decided that once the contract for the British government was completed, he would move on. He was picking up the business more quickly than he had imagined. Nor was Ames still at the forefront of the field. The innovations that had been peculiar to gun manufacture (for which it had such a reputation) were spreading rapidly into other fields, most notably clock and lock production.

In July 1855 Lowell went to New York City, principally to investigate a company called the Novelty Iron Works, judged by Ames to be "the best place of the sort in the country." Lowell hoped that working there would give him a "thorough knowledge of steam work, practical and scientific." The 1850s were the heyday of steam power in America, and Lowell imagined that a few years spent learning the business would provide him with an ever-marketable skill, "something to fall back upon."[6]

On this trip Lowell met Abram Hewitt, son-in-law of the New York industrialist Peter Cooper. Hewitt operated the Trenton Iron Works in New Jersey, on the Delaware River, the most successful iron-manufacturing company in America. One key to Trenton's success was that it controlled its product from beginning to end: the company mined its own superior ore, had developed its own smelting furnaces (the largest in the country), and puddled and rolled its own iron into finished goods.

Like most iron companies, the Trenton Iron Works had always been closely linked with railroads, in Trenton's case specializing in T rails, but Hewitt had quickly diversified. By 1853 his wire-making plant was one of the largest and best in the United States—making bridge wire, wire fencing, rivets, railroad spikes, and soon, most profitably, telegraph wire. Superior quality and great flexibility characterized Hewitt's operation.

Thirteen years older than Lowell, Hewitt was pleasantly surprised by his interview with young Lowell. Struck immediately by Charlie's intelligence and wide range of interests, Hewitt was attracted to him personally, and believed he had the qualities to rise in the company to a high position. He convinced Lowell of the future of iron manufacture, and offered him a job. Charlie immediately accepted, moving to Trenton in late August 1855 to take up a position in charge of puddling. This was a process in which pigs or ingots were heated in puddling furnaces, then passed through a rolling mill, which crushed them into blooms, or flat blocks. While white-hot and hissing from contact with moisture, these blooms were shot forward like phosphorous snakes and subjected to a series of other rolls, making them into rails or rods or beams, as required. Finally they were dumped onto cooling beds and put under presses to remove any irregular bends. For specialty work the blooms might be passed directly to a smaller foundry for special castings, or sent across to a machine shop.*

Within a little more than a year, by a mixture of luck, enterprise, and hard work Lowell had launched himself on a promising career at the forefront of iron manufacture, gaining the support of prominent men and finding a job in a thriving and expanding company. He also began his efforts with the working classes: he learned to speak German (the workforce in Trenton was largely German) and started several singing clubs. Still, this first year was not one of unalloyed optimism or even happiness.

His mother had remained a skeptical supporter, ambivalent about yet a third generation of the family being gripped by "iron fever." Her side of their correspondence is not preserved, but from her son's responses it seems clear she tried to warn him against the sins of his father: overconfidence, extravagance, too lavish an ambition, and an incapacity for pure hard work.

Lowell responded to this hectoring with much teasing and considerable firmness. Nevertheless his letters to his mother are slightly defensive and full of preemptive reassurances. His first from Chicopee began, "For your satisfaction I will say that my life here is just exactly what we all expected, neither better, nor worse." Chicopee, an industrial site at a bend and fall in the Connecticut River, "was not a place to pass one's life in," he conceded. Twice boredom drove him to church on Sunday, but he confessed the experience was unsatisfactory. After he moved to Trenton, he was pleased to discover a *"wonderfully* good little Town Library of about 1000 vols." He read the German and English Romantic poets and philosophers—Carlyle, Fichte, Coleridge, Jean Paul Richter, Schiller, Wordsworth—and the American Transcendentalists—Emerson, Thoreau, Henry James, Sr.—as well as Homer, Shakespeare, and the young Matthew Arnold. While his reading

---

*Hewitt's program was to expand continually: The T rail had started the company's success; wire cabling then became its boom trade, followed by the I beam. Twenty feet long and seven inches thick, I beams were first used to construct Peter Cooper's philanthropic institute the Cooper Union, in 1854, then to rebuild the fire-damaged Harper & Brothers building and to construct the federal assay office in New York. The reputation of the beams was made. Commissions rolled in, and the I beam saw the Trenton Iron Works through the crisis in railmaking that beset most American ironmakers in the 1850s. While Lowell was at the ironworks, Hewitt became interested in the work of the British experimentalist Henry Bessemer, who was trying to purify cast iron by passing a stream of air through the metal while it was still liquid. Although it would take years of experiments to refine the process, this was the beginning of Bessemer steel.

stimulated him, it often increased his sense of isolation as well. "Thoughts arise which I perfectly yearn to communicate with someone," he confessed. He was starved for the intellectual camaraderie that had been his daily experience in Cambridge. More ideas passed through his mother's Quincy Street house in one day than he encountered in all his time away. Trenton was "decidedly a 'one horse' city," he wrote.[7]

Attempting to make a virtue of necessity, he adopted a new devotion to silence. He wrote his friend Potter, "A silent man can ask himself enough questions in two hours to keep him thinking for a month, and to make him wiser for a lifetime." He tried to identify with James Brindley, the eighteenth-century English engineer and canal builder held up by Carlyle as the inarticulate but invaluable Practical Man, "the stupidest in speech, the wisest in action." The illiterate Brindley had tackled his engineering feats by going to bed for days at a time to think out the entire problem.[8]

As part of his exploration of silence, Lowell longed to acquire greater self-containment. The metaphor he used, that of "consuming his own smoke," was borrowed from Carlyle and from Emerson, who posited: "As a good chimney burns its smoke, so a philosopher converts the value of all his fortunes into his intellectual performances. There is no good in emitting smoke till you have made it into fire." Lowell set himself this goal. Yet after a scant month of silence, he missed his friends and did not quite feel whole. He proposed to them that they establish a club the purpose of which would be to aid "the ripening process"—by which he meant conversation, for however golden silence might be, it had led Lowell to decide that "Socrates was a wiser man than I ever supposed before." Dialogue was now of high value to him. Recognizing that a man's idiosyncrasies were peculiarly his own and rightfully so, Lowell wanted to explore and understand what men had in common, and "*exactly* where the universal within him terminates." Taking inspiration from Homer's *Odyssey*, he wrote to his friends: "The Gods know one another even though they dwell far apart,—not so men; but men should know one another, and must, if they wish to do good service in any common cause." Their friendships, he said, would "make an integer of me." For clubmates Lowell chose friends whose distinct qualities he most admired: Potter, Sanborn, and himself as reformers, Alexander Agassiz (son of Louis) as the earnest scientific man, Henry Higginson as a truly honest soul, Bancroft for his genius and taste, and Perkins as satirist.[9]

At the same time Charlie was engaged in a debate with his mother over the nature of work, a subject that preoccupied the whole family, the more so after Anna's school failed and, with it, a considerable portion of the Lowell income. His sister Harriet's letters reveal her sense of dependence, obligation, and guilt as she watched her mother trudging in to Boston to give lectures and run private study groups. She herself wanted to work, but her mother forbade it, desiring to protect her from the experiences of her own life. Ironically Harriet's "dream of happiness" was to live with her brother and "keep school."

Since early childhood the four Lowell children had paired off—Charlie and Harriet, Anna and Jim. Now, with Charlie gone, Harriet was unable to break in on the intimacy that her other two siblings had developed. This, along with her boredom and frustration with the inactive life of young womanhood, made her feel acutely the loss of her older brother. In her anguish all the old childhood wounds were revived. "You cannot imagine how I feel toward the school," she wrote, "though I try to think what a noble thing it was in Mother to renounce all the pleasures of society and companionship which she enjoyed, and to which she was accustomed, and to tie herself down to a very disagreeable task for our sakes; still I cannot, I feel the disadvantages too strongly the injuries it has done us."[10]

In response to Harriet's many letters venting her frustration, Charlie sent her a quotation he found helpful: "Infinite toil would not enable you to sweep away a mist; but, by ascending a little, you may often look over it altogether. So it is with our moral improvement; we wrestle fiercely with a vicious habit, which would have no hold upon us if we ascended into a higher moral atmosphere."[11]

In Cambridge Harriet struggled to sweep away her mist; in Trenton Charlie strove to convert his smoke into fire. Their mother badgered them both. She sarcastically accused Charlie of thinking it "necessary to exclude work" to make life "gracious as roses." Charlie responded, "For our family, work is absolutely necessary, but, by Plato! our lives need not for that cease to be poems," and criticized his mother for not being judicious in her own choice of work. "Roses work," Charlie explained to his mother. They put as much effort into producing their flower as beets or some other "useful" crop plant did. She did not understand poetry, and she could not distinguish between the poetic and the prosaic; between his poetic rose and her prosaic beet.

He told her to "sweep rooms—that you can do poetically." This was an allusion to George Herbert's poem "The Elixir"—"Teach me, my God and King, / In all things Thee to see, / And what I do in anything, / To do it as for

Thee . . . Who sweeps a room as for thy laws, / Makes that and th' action fine"—which was sung as a hymn throughout New England, well known to everyone. It well summed up his mother's industrious, faithful, prosaic godliness as well as that self-denying, almost crippling Puritan tradition of humility: faith in an uncomplaining commitment to dogged work, faith of such power that drudgery became divine. It was just this aspect of his mother and of his family life that he found unbearable. Even at a distance of several hundred miles, he did not find much relief. Nor was Harriet rising above her mist; rather, she was deepening her feelings of inadequacy because it was precisely this prosaic, dogged room-sweeping that she too found so deadly. She admired the saints and martyrs and tales of old in which heroes suffered out of "love of one's relations or for faith," but in her own life she could find no larger glory in the requirement of "little every day acts of self-denial," at which she believed she failed miserably.[12]

Lowell found inspiration from reading Carlyle and wrote home that "the need of work is a disease." Predictably, this raised the hackles of his strong-minded parent. Lowell was referring to Carlyle's "Life itself is a disease; a working incited by suffering." He meant that once man had, in biblical terms, eaten of the Tree of Knowledge and become self-conscious, he was banished from Eden and forced to labor. To have self-knowledge, he believed, was to know one's work. Thus work was a fundamental duty, a fundamental purpose and function of existence. The divine were touched with genius: entirely unselfconscious, remaining within the divine blessing, divine men had no "need" to work. Heroes, Lowell told his mother, "certainly needed work and had it and done it well, and it is Heroes that we must try to be."[13]

We should not dismiss Lowell's wish to be a hero as arrogant or vainglorious, for the rhetorical currency was a valid one in his day, when hero worship, or "infinite admiration," as it was called, was an accepted aspect of Romanticism. The heroic mode was one of earnestness and enthusiasm, fused with a desired power to transform the world. Heroes were men who changed the way others saw and thought. They were not rational but inspirational. In an age of science and the deflation of religion, hero worship offered a means by which to retain the powers of revelation, self-sacrifice, and the ideal. It served as a counterbalance to the forces of industrial society: anonymous, propelled by market forces, by commercial self-interest, by amoral realities. Many looked back to the Middle Ages, to the classical world, or to the myths and legends of the world's great cultures to rediscover an enthusiasm and energy with which to confront and combat a world beset with overwhelming and seemingly insoluble problems. Lowell's major influences—Emerson, Carlyle, Arnold, Clough—were all intensely committed to a post-Christian enthusiasm, to tapping some wellspring of faith and optimism. On reading Emerson's essays, Matthew Arnold wrote a poem that perhaps best sums up the appeal of heroism: "O monstrous, dead, unprofitable world, / That thou canst hear, and hearing, hold thy way! / A voice oracular hath peal'd to-day, / To-day a hero's banner is unfurl'd . . . the will is free; / Strong is the soul, and wise, and beautiful; / The seeds of god-like power are in us still; / Gods are we, bards, saints, heroes, if we will!"[14]

Stimulating as such a point of view might be, it left Charlie with little room for uncertainty as he faced the world, and it may also explain his unwillingness to notice or credit any weakness of his own. He could not shake a bad cold, so he simply ignored it. A tired, almost peevish tone entered his letters as he fended off his mother's concerns about his health. She sent pages filled with truisms about staying fit and nagged him into swallowing "two doses of laudanum and two lumps of sugar." He wrote back, trying to sound his old self, "Do you not know that I respect health and the healthy more even than I do morality?" (this to ruffle her feathers), and more tenderly, he observed that in an inversion of most people's experience, reading and writing came by nature but health did not. Good health required "a good fight with the climate, with society, with [one]self, and with [one's] business." He confessed, "I shall certainly feel a very great self-contempt, if at the age of thirty-five I have puddled myself down into a miserable nervous 'ball' of discomfort to self and friends."[15]

By October Charlie was no longer disguising his mood: "It was hard enough sometimes in Chicopee, scraping away at cast-iron, to believe, as Emerson says, that 'to-day is a Monarch in disguise' but after tea, when I got at Carlyle or Wordsworth or old Sir Thomas Browne, I generally found my faith grew stronger. Now, however, I haven't the spirit to touch a book; even Shakespeare is heavy, and Schiller flat." He was at a loss to explain his low spirits; the work was not too hard and he found it interesting; perhaps it was homesickness, he speculated. He preferred his malaise to be anything but a loss of "interest in things really high." Then, at the end of the month, Uncle Patrick found Charlie in his rooms "bleeding at the lungs and seriously changed." At almost exactly the same time, news arrived from Europe, where Aunt Mary's family was living, that Alfred Putnam, Charlie's contemporary, was dead.[16]

Consumption, endemic throughout New England, was responsible for one-fifth of all deaths. It had come to be known as the Romantic or Transcendentalist disease, but in fact it affected young and old, rich and poor, educated and illiterate, bohemian artist and conventional housewife. The consumptive death was an agonizing demise both for the sufferer—who wasted away, gasping for breath and choking on coughed-up blood—and for those who witnessed this terrible end. It was also extremely familiar. Virtually everyone had lost at least one family member or friend to tuberculosis.[17]

For all this familiarity, the early signs of consumption were seldom recognized. They closely resembled the symptoms of other lung ailments— frequent colds, persistent coughs, spitting, and wheezing. Only after consumption reached its more advanced and virulent phase did its symptoms become recognizable: fevers, night sweats, an unstable pulse, an alternation between extreme pallor and flushed cheeks, between lassitude and an almost manic mood. The coughing up of blood was widely recognized as an ominous sign of the coming end. Once in the bloodstream the tubercule bacilli quickly spread to every organ in the body, and death shortly followed. Only luck and prompt remedial action could prevent this end.

Lowell had waited for the irrefutable symptom before taking action, but Uncle Patrick moved swiftly. Within days Charlie was brought home and put under the care of his great-uncle, Dr. James Jackson, one of Boston's leading physicians. Now seventy-eight years old, he was no longer at the forefront of his field, but even the most advanced physicians understood little about consumption.

Most experts ascribed the cause of tuberculosis to a hereditary predisposition, a poor or "miasmic" climate, or the pursuit of an unhealthy profession. On all these counts Lowell was vulnerable. There appeared to be a distinct propensity for tuberculosis in the Lowell and Jackson families, New England was generally recognized as "miasmic," and Lowell's choice of profession was a high-risk one: the extreme temperatures caused by iron furnaces were not healthy, and the countless inhalable irritants in a metal shop were sure to endanger fragile lungs. Also, Lowell's practice of studying all night after a hard day's work undoubtedly wore him down: scholarly pursuits were notoriously deleterious to one's health. Long hours poring over books in overheated rooms, lack of fresh air, lack of stimulation to the body, and a tendency toward less-than-wholesome eating all contributed to poor health among scholars. While it was possible that Lowell's illness was not tuberculosis but rather some sort of lung poisoning, it was far more likely that he caught tuberculosis along with measles and chickenpox and all the other ill-nesses that the many children attending Anna's school had brought into the house; its heating system was based on the flow of air heated in the base-ment and circulated through the building by hot-air registers. (The Lowell children suffered from an especially high incidence of childhood diseases and a relentless round of colds.)

Once inhaled, the tubercule bacillus, a bacterium, settles on the edge of the lung. Because the germ reproduces itself very slowly, it may take a con-siderable time for the boil-like growth to develop; the body defends itself by building a fibrous shell around the growth to contain it. Inside the shell the bacterium will continue to grow, but because it is contained, the disease will appear to have vanished. If the disease is contained quickly, so that no obvi-ous symptoms present themselves, the patient will have no idea he carries it until, his immune system depleted, the bacterium bursts its containing shell and attacks the host body anew. With immediate attention, the disease can even then again be contained. But with every outbreak lung capacity is lost, until the lungs are so scarred that the patient can no longer inhale sufficient oxygen; hence the severe symptom of heart irregularities.

None of this was understood by physicians, though tuberculosis was spreading rapidly through an increasingly urbanized population. Not even the concept of contagion was fully understood. Dr. Jackson could only try to convince Lowell that, if the disease did not kill him outright, he would have to be reconciled to the life of an invalid. Invalidism, familiar enough to be not only a medical condition but a social position, was governed by one car-dinal tenet: the invalid was obliged to improve, to reverse the illness, to re-duce the influence of the disease. The new challenge facing Charlie was to reorder his life so as to accommodate his disease; this meant a change of ca-reer, a change of environment, and a change of ambition.

Dr. Jackson insisted that only complete rest would cure him. He recom-mended that Charlie give up all thought of work for ten years. His family, deeply alarmed, quickly developed a plan to send Charlie to southern Eu-rope, with Grandmother Jackson footing the bill: he was told to regard it as an early receipt of his inheritance. A milder, drier climate was believed to help an invalid stabilize his condition and strengthen his body to combat the disease or at least not grow worse. Charlie resisted the plan as too radical. Just after Thanksgiving he resumed the career his mother preferred for him by going to work for J. M. Forbes & Co.

———

John Murray Forbes and Charlie Lowell took an immediate liking to each other. Even at this low point in both his health and his confidence, Charlie retained his charismatic qualities. In later years, writing to another businessman with whom Charlie had dealings, Forbes recalled: "one of the strangest things has been how he magnetized you and me at first sight! We are both practical, unsentimental, and perhaps hard, at least externally, yet he captivated me just as he did you, and I came home and told my wife I had fallen in love."[18] Forbes was not a particularly gregarious man; he saved his affection for his large family and valued his privacy. Nevertheless, to his own surprise, he befriended Lowell.

Vanity did not trouble Forbes, a small, compact man with an enormous hooked nose and a long face with sad eyes. He had gone bald when young, but what he lacked in looks, he made up for in success. With little formal education but great character, he had made a fortune by the time he was twenty-five as the agent for Hou Qua, the greatest of all Hong merchants in Canton and said to be the richest man in the world, with a fortune estimated at £20 million in 1820. In addition to his legitimate and lucrative commerce, Forbes and, particularly, his brother Bennet engaged in the opium trade; Bennet commanded one of the "lintin" ships in what was known as the Boston Concern, a loose partnership of Boston traders with a monopoly on Turkish opium, which they sold in China at a vast profit. The trade was strictly illegal, and when the Chinese cracked down, the smaller traders (of whom John Jacob Astor was one) were driven from the market. But the Boston Concern anchored their lintin ships downriver from Whampoa, just outside Chinese jurisdiction, and from these stationary vessels sold the opium to Chinese smugglers.

Lowell's brief term at J. M. Forbes & Co. was devoted to assisting in the execution of a secret grain deal. Forbes had been approached in 1855 by Baring Brothers, the British bank, acting for Emperor Napoleon III, who feared famine in France due to a shortfall of wheat and flour. Forbes was directed to purchase more than $5 million in wheat and flour in America, as quietly as possible, so as to prevent a run on the market and a sharp rise in price.[19]

The deal went well but Lowell's health was not improving. On his twenty-first birthday, January 2, 1856, he received a letter from his father that helped reconcile him to his poor health. Charles Lowell explained that he had been offered the position of assistant librarian at the Boston Athenaeum and would be giving up his shop. He also offered his son an exoneration: exactly how he spoke of his own failure is lost to us, but it apparently released

Charlie from his sense of obligation and reinforced what had often been lost in his family life, a fount of parental love. Pride in accomplishment, a desire to see expectations fulfilled, and urgency of the moment can leave a child with the idea that parental love is earned by success and that one's value within the family is based on achievement. Anna Lowell, in her determination to escape failure, underscored this notion, but her husband had always offered his children unqualified love. Now, at a critical moment, he offered it again, and his son was moved to tears: "I never can read it now without crying."[20]

By mid-February 1856 John Murray Forbes recognized that Lowell's pride was all that prevented him from following medical advice, and he presented Lowell with a face-saving plan: he and his son Malcolm were planning a trip to Cuba; Malcolm needed a tutor along so that he would not fall behind in his studies; if Lowell agreed, Forbes would be grateful and willing to pay to have him accompany them as that tutor. With this dignified means of following his great-uncle's advice, Lowell agreed, and the three set sail at the end of February. They went first to Havana, where Forbes had business to do, and then to various plantations in Cuba. Afterward they sailed to Charleston, South Carolina, visiting various plantations there, then made their way through Georgia, northern Florida, and Alabama to New Orleans.

On the cruise the heat was oppressive, which Forbes found "intolerable," but Lowell thrived, stretching out on deck like a cat in the sun. The others were often seasick and closeted belowdecks, but Charlie enjoyed his hours spent looking at the blue of the Caribbean Sea, feeling the heat and the softness of the breezes. Arriving in Havana, he was immediately impressed by the Spanish influence. The streets—extremely narrow and always crowded—boasted shop signs that startled him, as "all the retail business of Havana is in the hands of saints, goddesses and heroes, of birds, beasts, and beauties." The shops were named after "the sun and moon and stars; after gods and goddesses, demi-gods and heroes; after fruits and flowers, gems and precious stones." Cuban women, dressed in "the most intense colors, fiery red, ultramarine blue, gamboge yellow, colours as vivid as the hues of the flamingo and the parrot, the cactus-flower and the jaquey," paraded themselves in front of their huge ground-floor windows. Behind them their "dowdy mammas" rocked slowly in huge *butacas*, or armchairs.

On the train route that took them to Cienfuegos and thence to a plantation, they passed stations where black slave children "offered oranges and cheese and strange fruits." Out the window they could see roads filled with naked slave children, "running about looking like so many monkeys," and Cubans with long machetes. They passed many wonderfully shaded coffee plantations, with their panoplies of trees, but as Forbes explained, they were on the decline: Brazilian coffee was flooding the international market, and the Cuban plantations were converting to sugarcane.[21]

Forbes, at the request of his contacts in the China trade, was investigating whether an orange plantation in Florida worked by coolie labor could be a viable venture. (Chinese indentured laborers were used in huge numbers in Cuba, where they served eight-year indentures that paid them each four hundred dollars. The coolies were poorly treated, and had an alarmingly high suicide rate.) Their host in Florida, James Hamilton Couper, was suspicious of and lacked interest in Forbes's proposal. Although indentured labor was used extensively in Cuba, Couper—whose Georgia and Florida plantations were worked by several thousand slaves—was convinced of its impracticalities, for he did not believe that free albeit indentured men were as productive as slaves. He thought that the more enterprising coolies would simply break their contracts and desert for greener pastures. Most fundamentally, he believed that "enlightened patriotism will revolt at the introduction of an inferior race of free men; and local prejudice will suspect an attempt to attack the institution of slavery."[22]

To avoid entanglement, and in an attempt to shelter his northern guests from the actualities of slavery (for both Forbes and Lowell, this was a first exposure to it), Couper offered them long days of hunting, and it is hard to see how Lowell had the opportunity to tutor young Malcolm. Provided with a flat-bottomed boat and a guide, they meandered along rivers oxbowing through the dense jungle of tangled vines, interlacing branches, and fragrant fruit trees filled with an abundance of wildlife. Lowell was struck by the beauty of the unfamiliar terrain, the voluptuousness of rampant nature. They found eagles, hawks, great white cranes, ducks, and wild turkeys. Alligators swam ahead and slithered up the sides of the river to bask on the sunlit banks. Occasionally they passed a simple log cabin in which a woodsman lived in pitiful poverty.

Back at the plantation house, they were assured that working conditions were "very humane," that the slaves were well fed and clothed and not generally overworked except during the harvest. The whip was seldom used. Nevertheless, Forbes, who was familiar with Chinese coolie labor practices, was shocked. The sharp contrasts baffled both Forbes and Lowell—between the almost prissy finery of the plantation house and the dirt and desolation of the slave quarters, between the idleness of the whites and the toil of the slaves. Forbes was disconcerted by the dirty courtyard, where jerked beef hung to dry in the sun much too close to the house, and by the proximity of slaves often without clothes.

A certain primness overcame Forbes as he was assaulted by the sensuousness of the hot, humid climate, the ripe fruits, the rampant nature, the nakedness and seminakedness of the slaves. Perhaps miscegenation, so distasteful to northerners, was in his thoughts. He noted again and again the "shiftless style," the "irresponsible idleness," and the "unemployed" lack of industry. His complaints were less those of a businessman dismayed by inefficiency and bad management than those of a person shocked at a world where his own values seemed so completely irrelevant. This was not an unusual reaction among New Englanders who visited the South. Moral and religious arguments against slavery were one thing, but this visceral dislike was more persuasive, playing on the fears, taboos, and basic assumptions of Yankee culture. Notions of work, purpose, improvement, and betterment were deeply woven into the New England psyche. To do nothing but enjoy one's comforts, as did the southern gentlemen, sent shivers down Forbes's spine. "The unemployed white gentleman slowly puffing his cigar and never seeing a book or moving out of a snail's pace from the hall to the piazza and back," with his plantation run by a mulatto agent, was an idle man with no purpose, object, or interest so far as Forbes could detect: "a walking oyster."[23]

The friendship between Forbes and Lowell deepened throughout their trip. They earnestly discussed plans to draw Lowell from the gloom of his thwarted ambitions into some interesting position for a clever young man within the growing web of Forbes's businesses. John Murray Forbes was singularly placed to understand the forces at work on the young Charles Lowell. When he returned from China in 1837, he had had to rescue from the cusp of bankruptcy his brother Bennet, who was heavily invested in the Franklin Nail Works, the subsidiary of Lycoming Coal, which was collapsing. It was John Murray Forbes's forthrightness and common sense that had brought Lycoming to its dismal end, which, to the end of his life, he remembered as the greatest folly with which he had ever been associated. If anyone could judge the conduct of Charlie Lowell's father at Lycoming, it was Forbes, but he did not divulge his analysis of its failure, and he may not have given Charlie Lowell any more than the briefest account.

Forbes's own father had also failed miserably when Forbes was young, becoming bankrupt and dying prematurely. His mother—sister of the wealthy Thomas Handasyd Perkins—had been too proud to turn to her family for direct help, so Forbes and his brothers, like the young Lowells, had known shame, poverty, and hard work. But Forbes's interest in Lowell was not solely charitable: he recognized that a man of Lowell's qualities could be useful to him, just as he and his brothers had been useful to their uncle in the China trade. On this trip the two men bonded for life. To his mother, Lowell wrote, "I *cannot* tell you how kind Mr. Forbes has been . . . Had not the bad management on Southern R.R.'s kept us for the last half hour dodging about after baggage, &c., I am certain we should not have separated without *one* cry." On April 7, 1856, they parted in New Orleans with the explicit agreement that Lowell would consider himself "engaged to him when I come back." Forbes then traveled by rail back to Boston, while Lowell boarded a steamer bound for the Mediterranean.[24]

SIX

EUROPE

1856–58

Well, my dear Mother, here I sit at the foot of Hercules' pillar, sucking oranges and fattening on British beer. I discovered my new world about two o'clock on Sunday. —Charles Russell Lowell, Jr., Gibraltar, May 27, 1856

On May 24, after eight weeks at sea, Lowell docked at Gibraltar. The British town poised on the Spanish side of the entrance to the Mediterranean, winding its way up the steep Rock, was full of soldiers. British Redcoats, standing guard, looked "as hot and uncomfortable as tiger-lilies" as they "sheltered like some delicate exotic from the sun" under grass mats on the city ramparts. The Treaty of Paris, which had ended the Crimean War and reinforced the Ottoman Empire, had been signed in March, and Lowell watched regiment after regiment arrive from the front on their way home. As these veterans marched to band music in the promenade, Lowell walked the steep narrow streets, passing donkeys loaded with water-casks, flocks of goats being led from door to door to be milked, and knots of solemn white-turbaned Moors.[1]

He was half-hoping for a letter from Uncle James or Uncle Ned (his mother's youngest brother), who were both ending European tours of their own. There was only the slimmest of chances for such a letter, but he wanted companionship. Then he met up with two Australians, and over dinner they agreed to tour Moorish Spain together. It proved, aptly, a quixotic journey, not least because of the quantities they drank of Valdepenas, "Don Quixote's favorite wine." They crossed from Gilbraltar to Málaga in a storm and then, finding no seat below in the diligence, rode on the top to Granada. The skeletal Lowell and his two robust, red-faced Australian friends in their huge brimmed hats reached Granada very tired and dusty but exhilarated. They tramped about the deserted palaces of the Alhambra, its extensive gardens fragrant with the scent of roses. Climbing higher and higher, they reached the Moorish tower in time to watch the sun set. The snow-capped Sierra Nevada to the east caught the last glint of sunlight while the bulk of the mountains basked in a pinkish-purple light. Below them lay the great *vega* across which Columbus had come to persuade Queen Isabella to support his voyage to the Indies.

The Australians were adamant that they reach Cádiz to meet a certain boat. Told they could get no seat on a diligence for a fortnight, they flagged down a stray coach that took the three of them to an unknown town along the way. They spent a miserable night attacked by fleas and mosquitoes in a dubious *posada*, only to find next morning that the horses they had hired arrived without stirrups. These, when finally procured, had to be tied on with string. The three got to Seville well after midnight, tired, dusty, and very irritated. The "constant *Io no se* of the officials," as Lowell put it, accompanied by a shrug and a complacent smile, sent the Australians into paroxysms of indignation. Their appearance and their impatience brought titters of amusement from the Spanish. Lowell would have willingly accepted the Spanish "want of method," but his companions insisted on sticking to their schedule.

The Australians continued on to Cádiz, but Lowell, feeling the effects of their fortnight's journey, stopped in Seville. He slept a good deal and went to a bullfight, which he found, as he told his mother, "cruel certainly, still I rather like it; it is very exciting, and requires great nerve, agility, courage and mind on the part of the torreros." But he could not enter a cathedral or dank building without a coughing fit coming on. "Hola, my dear Mother," he wrote, confessing that he was getting a little homesick in the finest city in Spain.[2]

When Lowell returned to Gibraltar on June 21, he found the long-awaited letter from Uncle Ned suggesting they meet in Geneva. Lowell immediately sailed to Genoa, bought a Sardinian pony, and set off with great enthusiasm to cross the Alps on horseback. The trip was not a success. The flies were terrible, pestering the horse and forcing Lowell to sleep by day and travel by night. While the drama and romance of the landscape increased in the moonlight, as long as it held, the beauty was more than a little eerie, even lugubrious. Lowell crossed the Alps at Mont Cenis and followed the river valley below the Massif de la Vanoise to Chambéry. Thence he went up through the middle of the Savoy, passing along the Lac de Bourget and through Annecy. He had named his horse Jip, after the family's Scottish terrier, but he began to call it Gyp, having just read Matthew Arnold's new poem, "The Scholar-Gipsy." In the poem an Oxford scholar is forced by poverty and by fatigue at "knocking at preferment's door" to wander with Gypsies, who initiate him into the mysteries of "gypsy-lore." His old friends occasionally glimpse him, wild-eyed, oddly dressed, possessed, but eventually he disappears into the oblivion of nomadic life. The poem depicts the ways in which youthful ardor and enthusiasms "are sapped by life in the world." Arnold's tone is elegiac and melancholic, expressing a bittersweet incomprehension of wasted talent. The poem resonated strongly in Lowell, encapsulating the irony between his heartfelt 1854 evocation of godlike youth burning with ideals and his present predicament: ill, useless, of uncertain future, wandering in foreign lands.[3]

Once in Geneva Ned Jackson, an experienced traveler and quintessential bourgeois gentleman, came to his aid. Unlike his striving nephew, Ned, five years his senior, had never shown any special talent: no one in or out of the family ever suggested that the qualities of Patrick Tracy Jackson were manifest in him. He intuitively gravitated toward ease, was wedded to the comforts of an unambitious life, and may even have felt that, as the much younger son in a family of capable, self-sacrificing women who had been willing to do nearly everything for him, he was the lucky one.

The two men spent August doing very little. Ned fed Charlie regular meals, returned him to the modest exercise of walking in the hills above Lake Geneva, and reintroduced him to polite society in the form of other Bostonians, some indeed family. Lowell's health began to stabilize. Some color came back into his cheeks. When Ned left Geneva in early September he handed Charlie on to the Frank Lowells, who were living up the lake from Geneva, between Lausanne and Montreux, at Vevey, where a substantial American community could be found. A Monsieur Sillig ran a boarding school for boys, which was filled with Americans whose families were touring Europe or escaping Italy's summer heat in the pleasant hotels that overlooked the lake. Ned believed that the influence of his cousin Frank (the only surviving son of old Francis Cabot Lowell) would continue in the same style. Conservative in politics and in approach to life, Frank had married his second cousin and was living a sober, patrician, and uneventful life.

Charlie continued to take long walks to Lausanne or in the hills, going to his cousins' for evenings of conversation and whist with the gentlemen, or for tea with the ladies. Georgina Lowell, known as Nina, was Charlie's age and suffered from some unspecified nervous condition, but she was a bright, eager girl who had been a student at Anna Lowell's school and was devoted to literature. Georgina was infatuated with Henry Higginson, or "Wild Harry," as she called him. She and Charlie discussed literature and their mutual friends. Charlie expounded on Shakespeare and asked for her opinions about Pauline and Ida Agassiz. They talked about Cervantes. Nina asked about Stephen Perkins and John Bancroft. Lowell told her that save Shakespeare there was no book he enjoyed as much as *Don Quixote*. They debated the comparative merits of men and women. Nina defended her own sex but found herself won over by Charlie's arguments. After a week of such conversations, Nina, with some surprise, realized that Charlie and his friends talked about young ladies as much as she and her friends discussed young men. She found him fascinating and confided to her diary, "I think C[harles] L[owell] an improving person to be with."[4]

Charlie's classmate Horace Furness appeared in Vevey for a few days, on his way south to Italy. After two years in Europe, Furness was part of what Henry Adams called the "deputation" of Harvard graduates sent abroad "to polish off in the elegant cities of Europe, and obtain that knowledge of the modern languages so necessary to the present age." Furness had just come from an expedition with another classmate and mutual friend from Hasty Pudding productions, William S. Haseltine, who had been studying painting at the Düsseldorf Academy. Furness, Haseltine, and some of his American friends from the academy, including Albert Bierstadt, had spent the summer traveling down the Rhine Valley and then up the Ahr and Nahe Rivers, sketching as they went. They had stayed in inns, explored the countryside for scenic spots, absorbed the beauty of isolated and romantic landscapes, dined well, and enjoyed the region's sweet white wines. Furness could not recommend it too highly to Lowell, as the two friends lolled on the banks of Lake Geneva, Furness puffing on his pipe, Lowell eating plums, reminiscing over old times and laying in plans for the future. Furness encouraged Charlie to come with him to Italy, where he intended to rejoin his artist friends. Charlie readily agreed, but then his cough returned—perhaps because of Furness's pipe smoke, though Lowell insisted this was good for him—and Furness departed without his friend.[5]

Lowell's two months in Switzerland did him immeasurable good, but beneath the surface he was troubled. It had been easier to sell his pony than to shake off his identification with Arnold's Scholar-Gipsy. Although the comforts offered by his conservative relatives improved his health, they exacerbated his mental unease. He began to "smoke" in the way he so disliked. He had made arrangements to join his aunt Mary Lowell Putnam in Florence and had even-written to the American consul in Constantinople with the idea of wintering in Turkey, but he was secretly scheming to abandon his European tour. His homesickness was acute, but it was not "home" that he missed so much as the feeling of being part of things.

Civil war, or some low-grade version of it, appeared to have erupted in Kansas. The newspapers were full of sensational reports of Missourians known as Border Ruffians raiding the northern settlements, many of which were sponsored by the Emigrant Aid Societies, which had been established throughout the northern states to ensure that Kansas had a majority of set- tlers who opposed slavery and would thus become a free state. Not only was there fighting in Kansas, but after Massachusetts senator Charles Sumner denounced the most egregious violence in a speech, "The Crime Against Kansas," he had been brutally attacked and seriously injured while at his desk in the Senate Chamber by a South Carolina congressman.

The furor that followed was perhaps even more provocative: "Bleeding Kansas" was matched by "Bleeding Sumner." His attacker, Congressman Preston Brooks, previously considered of little consequence, was now claimed by the South as a hero defending its honor. Sumner, previously considered extreme and egotistical, was taken up by the North as a martyr to the intolerance and excessive demands of the Slave Power. The southern press not only defended Brooks but drove home the social slight implied in the attack: gentlemen duel, but only social inferiors are beaten; dueling would have been too good for "vulgar Abolitionists," who were "getting above themselves" by being "impudent to gentlemen." Such ranting helped to unify northern indignation, and even moderate newspapers queried: "Are we to be chastised as they chastise their slaves? Are we too, slaves for life, a target for their brutal blows, when we do not comport ourselves to please them?"[6]

Lowell wanted to go to Kansas and do something useful. While he had been sailing the Atlantic and recuperating in the backcountry of Spain, both his family and friends at home had been involved in varying degrees: some gave money, some prepared supplies for settlers, some were active in the New England Emigrant Aid Society, and some even went to Kansas. Lowell was especially galvanized by a letter from Frank Sanborn, written just after his return in August from Kansas, where he had gone as an agent of the Em- igrant Aid Society. Sanborn reported an inflammatory situation there: north- erners outnumbered southerners by a large majority (thanks to the Emigrant Aid Societies' efforts), but the territorial administration was under southern control and maintained itself by rigged elections and phony ballots. This corrupt government had drawn up a constitution that, in northern eyes, mocked true justice. In an attempt to contest such connivance, northern settlers had established their own provisional government, and now both governments—one legal but corrupt, the other illegal but representative— wanted to be recognized by Congress. Meanwhile chaos reigned.

In Kansas, Sanborn believed, he had found the "most practical form in which the struggle for freedom has ever presented itself." Filled with fervor, he was fed up with the usual talk, tired of the quick fading away of interest after a flurry of indignation. It infuriated him that people seemed to think that decrying the sorry state of affairs was all that was required of them: "I see in almost every person traces of indecision which is fatal to any good settlement . . . we are all . . . held back . . . for some personal reason." Sanborn was "determined . . . to cut through all these meshes and do thoroughly what I have been so long talking about."[7]

Sanborn spent most of his time in Iowa establishing a safe route for supplies sent to settlers, especially guns (including a shipment from the Ames Company). Although the ostensible purpose of the Emigrant Aid Society was to subsidize settlers from the North moving to Kansas, once violence broke out it was decided that supplying settlers with arms was a defensive necessity.

Sanborn's few days in Kansas had been enough to extinguish any thoughts he might have had of settling there. Personally terrified of violence, he scrupulously removed himself from any place at the first hint of it, and he persuaded himself that he could best contribute to the cause by "executive power," not "armed settlement." Safe in his Boston office, his high ideals were reserved for the exhortation of others to do what he himself would not. Thus he became secretary of the Emigrant Aid Society in Boston with the purpose of radicalizing it. (Charlie's family was strongly represented in this organization. Uncle Patrick Jackson was its treasurer, Uncle Sam Cabot was on its board, and Aunt Hannah marshaled the forces of the women in the family to prepare and make clothing for the settlers.) Sanborn wanted to broaden its base in Massachusetts and to use its funds and connections to organize and systematize the struggle. His letter had an alarming effect on Lowell, who hurriedly wrote on September 10 to both Higginson and Bancroft warning them not to sail for Europe until they heard from him again. He explained that he might go to Kansas himself, and he proposed that Higginson ought to go as well. Exactly what Charlie thought he would do in Kansas was vague, but he cautioned Higginson not to "breath[e] a word of this to any one."[8]

By September 16 Charlie had abandoned the plan, fearing that his health would not stand the strain. He wrote again to Higginson and Bancroft, urging them to come to Europe after all, making clear that he would be in Florence by October 20 and that he intended to stay in Italy through the winter. To salve their honor over Kansas, Higginson, who had just inherited some money from a grandparent, donated sufficient funds to pay for a family to move there. He told Lowell of this and, as he sailed for Liverpool, wrote to his skeptical father, "I'll do my best for C[harlie] in pecuniary ways. I've got plenty for both. Now don't shake your head . . . what is money good for if not to spend for one's friends and to help them?"[9]

Lowell left Vevey and arrived in Milan on September 28, joining up with Furness and friends and finding a cache of letters from home awaiting him. Since leaving Boston in March, his letters home had given almost no clues as to his health. His bantering offhand manner, invariably cheerful, nevertheless often struck a mordant or morbid note. Discouraging his mother from worrying about him, he wrote that he was "in an agony of enjoyment all the time." He shook off maternal concern by saying that "my only fear now is that which drove the tyrant of Samos to throw his ring into the sea,— I am frightened and oppressed by the terrible good fortune which always has attended me, by the kindnesses which I have done nothing to earn and which I can never repay."

This was an illusion to the story of Polycrates, in Herodotus's *Histories*, a ruler so lucky that he aroused suspicion and feared that the gods would punish him. To counter this premonition, Polycrates threw a valuable ring into the sea; yet a fisherman caught the fish that swallowed the ring, and it was returned to him. Such extraordinary luck caused his main benefactor, the Pharaoh, to withdraw his support, and Polycrates was crucified. The parable was intended to prove that even the luckiest of men will be the cause of their own destruction.

Lowell also insisted on his good spirits by quoting Emerson, "I sail with God the seas." And while this sounded like the spirit of adventure, his mother knew the full quotation: "Never strike sail to any. Come into port greatly or sail with God the seas." She understood that Charlie preferred to put a brave face on things. His independence and self-reliance, even his cheerfulness, had an undertow: he concealed more than he told. This was worrying, considering how foolishly he had ignored early warning signs of illness and how reluctantly he had embraced the need to live as an invalid in order to get well. He wrote infrequently and claimed that his hair was still too short to have a photograph taken. His mother assumed he was hiding his condition from her. Harriet wrote to tell him of the anxiety he caused their mother and that she, his grandmother, and his aunts all insisted he write regularly.[10]

And so at the end of September, safely in Milan, having wrestled with his Kansas question, Lowell finally gave his mother an account of himself. "You say I have failed—true," he began; "but on my long voyage this seemed to me a mark of the gods' peculiar favour,—to those whom they love they send early warnings. Better to fail now, when the choice of my career is my own, than two years hence when my ties would have been more binding . . . I have failed at the right moment."

His decision to go into the iron business, he insisted, had not been made on account of his sisters and certainly not his mother. He explained, "You were successful and that is its own reward. I certainly would not have worked ten or fifteen years to give you the largest fortune in Boston." Exonerating both his sisters and his mother from any responsibility for his destroyed health, he continued, "But with dear Father, it was quite a different case,—to him my success would have been an immense gratification." This explanation of his motives implies that Charlie's identification with his father was more intimate and deeper than previously acknowledged. (Perhaps with his own "failure" he found a circumstantial commonality.) Charlie explained that if his father liked his new position at the Athenaeum, "then I too have done with commerce." It also reveals a new perspective on his mother's self-sacrifice, as if he had risen above "the mist" of guilt and blame to recognize his mother as a success and his father as the failure or victim.

Charlie then analyzed his own mistakes. He had hoped to lead a double life, he conceded, making a fortune by day and studying by night. He admitted that it had been an attempt to be all things, scholar for himself, businessman for his family, and that that was his mistake. His initial desolation, he confessed, had come from the realization that this double life would have to stop. His first reaction had been to swear off books and continue with business, putting his duty before his pleasure. He had considered it crucial to his pride and maturation that he make the transition from being cared for to caring for others. He had even resisted invalidism because it jeopardized and delayed that step. Then had come his father's twenty-first-birthday letter, received during the early months of his illness, with its healing effects. Charlie had changed his plans, accepted the invalid life, and committed himself to getting better. His health still demanded that he pass the winter in Italy "spending grandmother's money," he admitted, and he did so with the residue of shame.[11]*

By January 1857 Charlie had joined Aunt Mary Lowell Putnam and her family in Florence. Safe in the care of his aunt, well fed and well tended, he explored the city, touring the Uffizi and the galleries of the Pitti Palace. He read voraciously from the libraries of his new acquaintances and soon had mastered conversational Italian. He delighted in the social life of Florence, with its curious mix of the high-minded, the pleasure-seeking, and the artistic. A number of families from the old Winter Street enclave were there: the Charles Paines, the Elliot Cabots, and the Thomas Carys. Other Bostonians included Lowell's distant cousin Mrs. Sophia Amory Eckley and Miss Isabella Blagden, both devotees of Elizabeth Barrett Browning, who with her husband, Robert, was the center of Florence's émigré community. Elfin, deeply unfashionable, and inordinately shy, Elizabeth Browning had found her power as a poet in Florence, living as she wished, her eccentricities blossoming. She and her following practiced spiritualism—the power of moving tables and communing with the dead. Émigrés suspicious of objects whizzing about a room and enigmatic messages received from long-departed parents or babies preferred the company of Robert Browning, revered not only for his poetry but for his steady good sense and amiable temperament.

Another Florence celebrity was the American sculptor Hiram Powers. His *Greek Slave*, exhibited at the Crystal Palace in 1851, had a reputation in America and Europe as the most significant piece of modern sculpture. Despite having lived in Florence since 1837, Powers remained a Vermont Yankee farmer's son, pragmatic, plainspoken, plain living, and hospitable. The grand old man of expatriate Florence was Seymour Kirkup, an English

---

*Anna's reply, written in her inimitably forthright manner, was courageous: "Be easy, and be happy; enjoy what time and place bring, and cultivate patience—this for your own sake. What matter is it how those little things go. While we expected to do some great things we could not be provoked to have little things thwart us, but we need not live long to find our greatest are quite unimportant to the world, and that the lesson we have to learn is quite a different one. Perhaps those who seem to do a great deal feel more keenly than others what is denied them. I cannot remember the childish year in which I did not feel in my inmost depths my inability in all directions to which my tastes and desires tended. Well dear fellow, if we are ever together again we shall sympathize as we never did before. It is long till that time comes."

painter who had buried Keats, had been at Viareggio when Shelley drowned, and who owned Shelley's sofa, on which he often lay, hoping that the poet's ghost would appear to him. But it was Dante with whom Kirkup communed daily. As a Dante scholar and expert, he owned Dante manuscripts and had discovered Giotto's portrait of him. His clothes threadbare, his hair long and unkempt, he lived simply in two rooms where all lovers of Dante sought him out.

Florence was also the home of the English novelist and travel writer Fanny Trollope, who lived with her son Thomas and his beautiful, popular wife, Theodosia. Fanny Trollope was ubiquitous but not always welcome. Indefatigable, opinionated, and relentlessly middle class, she was notorious for her good-humored callousness, her superficial industry, and her immense popular success. Her book on America, *Domestic Manners of the Americans*, had a huge readership but was far from flattering. Villino Trollope was a social calling spot for private theatricals and "Saturday evenings."

In February, when Higginson and Perkins got to Florence, they found Lowell free of his cough but nervous and excited. The three friends then set off for Rome, which was full of Americans, and where they could board with Boston families. At the center of the American community was one of James Russell Lowell's earliest friends, William Wetmore Story, the rebellious son of the late Supreme Court justice Joseph Story. Like James Russell Lowell, William Story had made his bow to the conventional life and gone to law school. But with the death of his father in 1845 he broke free, moved to Rome, and became a sculptor. He was a companionable man with a sociable wife. Their home in the Casa Cabrale became a gathering place for American and British artists, historians, classicists, collectors, and writers. Lowell joined up with his classmate William Haseltine and through him met the younger American artists living on the cheap in the American quarter near the Spanish Steps. At Monaldini's Library one could receive letters and read the English papers. The Americans banked at Hooker & Plowden's, met their friends at Nazzarri's or Spillman's tearooms or, for the more serious-minded, the Lepre Restaurant in the Via Condotti, and took coffee across the road at the Caffè Greco.

At the Storys' Casa Cabrale, Charlie Lowell encountered such varied figures as Aunt Mary's close friend the historian John L. Motley, the art critic Anna Jameson, the painter Sir Frederick Leighton, and the English novelist Elizabeth Gaskell; even Franz Liszt joined the company. The conversation had tremendous breadth. Two British converts to Catholicism, Henry Edward Manning (later archdeacon) and his colleague Aubrey de Vere, were nearly always there. As is often the case with new converts, they found it difficult to resist discussing their new faith, which was not to everyone's taste. One Bostonian listened as long as he could, then declared, "I don't care one jot about your Apostolic succession, I don't know anything about such matters, but what I do know is that your Popes are not much like the Apostles."

Controversy was stirred up when the Storys had as their house guest Harriet Beecher Stowe. The popularity of *Uncle Tom's Cabin* (1852) was so enormous, her fame so complete, that even Mrs. Browning in Florence had been apprehensive about meeting her. But Stowe's simplicity and humility charmed many, and her profoundly religious outlook was widely respected. With Stowe, however, came talk of slavery. Inevitably she told many of the true tales on which her novel had been based. Particularly upsetting to southerners and their sympathizers were the powerful stories of the person from whom Milly was drawn: Sojourner Truth. As one listener put it, "The American Eagle was ruffled." Among those ruffled were the Ticknors, dyed-in-the-wool Whigs; the Paines and the Frank Lowells, rich from cotton mills; and William Preston, a much-respected art collector whose son had been one of Charlie's southern classmates at Harvard. They all stayed away from the Story residence while Stowe was there. They found "Roman skies less blue for sheltering her" and regretted "that a woman who had so discredited her country should not remain at home."

An American in Rome who was often at the Storys' and who strongly influenced Lowell's art historical education was Charles Eliot Norton, whom Charlie had known at Harvard. In age midway between Charlie and his uncle James, Norton had been a frequent visitor to the Quincy Street house, one of the Cambridge circle who made it so attractive to students. In the summer of 1855 Norton and James Russell Lowell had become fast friends, taking a mule trip through Sardinia together. They were to remain friends for life. Both were the adored and adoring sons of clergymen of the old school. But where Reverend Lowell had been gentle and liberal, Reverend Andrews Norton had been fiery and conservative.

Norton's capacity for friendship was remarkable, but in the winter of 1856–57 he had only begun his life of vast acquaintances. Like Charlie, Norton had found his business career interrupted by poor health, consumption touching his lungs as well. Many other Americans went to Rome for their health, but Norton may have been the most instructive to Charlie, given their common interests and background. Having come to Italy for his health, Norton was rapidly developing an interest in art history that would become the consuming passion of his life. He knew and admired John Ruskin; everyone agreed that Norton had a calming effect on that temperamental and unstable genius.[12]

After a highly social breakfast at the Casa Cabrale, Charlie often joined an expedition of these various men and women to visit the Pantheon, St. Peter's, the Vatican galleries, a palazzo, or the Colosseum. He repeatedly visited the art galleries and, under the care of greater enthusiasts, tried to absorb the education offered him; he confessed that he had "a most superb ignorance of the history of Art and Artists." Encouraged to admire Giotto and Fra Angelico, he found himself staring at the frescoes and paintings "with curiosity but without sympathy." Repeated visits did not change this sense of distance. Nor did Lowell's taste conform to the more conventional aesthetic that rated Raphael supreme. Although most of his companions felt uplifted and morally improved by Raphael's and Perugino's beautiful Madonnas, Lowell did not. These, he emphatically insisted, *I do not enjoy at all.* Indeed, he did not warm to Christian subjects generally, although he took great pleasure in cathedrals.

Lowell suspected that his taste shocked his learned tutors: "Art is by no means my province." His attraction to a painting was less to its plastic and painterly qualities than to its literary and evocative capacities, and to its personal associations. Titian's painting *Faith* (portraying Doge Antonio Grimati kneeling before Faith) looked like his cousin Lucy Russel, he declared, "but Lucy as she ought to be—a radiant face and a face that 'knows no shadow of turning.' " Lucy in fact was humpbacked, having Pott's disease, a form of the consumption that had killed her mother. She had grown up in their grandmother's house, her father having remarried and started a new family, requiring Lucy only when her stepmother was ill or in childbirth.[13]

A particular face by Giorgione spurred Charlie to tell his mother that he "had made a new friend . . . the most deep-eyed of the earth." Of another Giorgione (at the Accademia) he remarked that it was one of which Byron had said "one might go mad because it cannot walk out of its frame": this was an old woman holding a scroll on which was the inscription "COL TEMPO." A Venus and Bacchus by Tintoretto (most likely *Bacchus and Ariadne*, now in the Doge's Palace in Venice) struck him as something he might take as "my aim, my ideal in life—and certainly it did give me a push, a swing, which I think I shall never entirely lose."[14]

The Americans were struck by the sharp contrasts between beggars hanging about the entrances to fabulous palaces, the beauty of gallery rooms compared with the filthy streets, a humdrum fish-seller's stall set up beside an ancient column or a collapsed arch. Pickpockets were prayerful. The bourgeoisie talked in church. And everywhere beggars demanded coins. The Americans would also go off to the many ateliers where their fellow countrymen worked. Visits to one artist's studio inevitably led to others, to a meal, to yet more studio visits, then perhaps to the Caffè Greco for coffee. In the evenings there were theatricals, plays, concerts, and conversation.

In a letter to Johnny Bancroft, urging him to come to Europe, Lowell best revealed how this kind of life was benefiting him: "Come out here, not with the intention of devoting yourself to any art, or to all of them, but simply that you may become acquainted with yourself,—come out to 'sfogare' yourself—it is astounding how the smoke clears away when one is here looking at the whole concern from afar,—come for your own sake and for us who love you."[15]

Rome was a long way from Boston. Not only were social mores relaxed, but American and British émigrés largely lived without any overt plan or compelling ambition. They stayed in Rome until their health improved or until they were invited to join a party going somewhere else. They were waiting for money. They were escaping or avoiding some other fate. Artists were waiting for the luck of meeting a collector, of selling a picture, waiting for the next turn of the wheel. In such an environment Lowell found it easier to let go of his worries about his future duties and responsibilities. "Science" remained his goal, but he began to recognize that "usefulness" as defined in Boston was a narrow term. Exploring the Roman countryside, he began to judge places by whether they were "another lovely spot to loafe" and declared that the pleasantest day he had spent in Rome was one in which he had lolled atop the Caracalla baths watching the landscape change as the sun crossed the sky—a vast improvement over filing iron.

At the end of May, Higginson, Perkins, and Lowell set off for Dresden intending to take most of the summer for the trip. They bought two horses and a cart. Stephen or Henry or both rode in the cart with the luggage, while Charlie went on horseback, unless he was tired, in which case he stretched out on a bed of luggage in the cart. While Henry's horse and cart were sturdy fare, bought from a hauler and used to the humdrum life, Charlie's horse, from the *campagna*, had never worn shoes and was quite spirited. Horses and cart had not come cheap, and Henry paid for Charlie's share, writing to his father from Venice that "it is a pretty considerable expense but it ought to do C. much good—indeed, he is already rather better than in Rome."[16]

Traveling through the Italian countryside on horseback with good companions proved excellent for Lowell's health. He was able to build up his strength without overtaxing himself. As he regained his stamina, his confidence increased. "Our present mode of traveling suits me beyond my expectation," Charlie reported. Following what was said to be Hannibal's route to Etruria, they traveled early and spent the heat of the day in long siestas, setting off again in the late afternoon. Lowell's horse, despite its former semi-wild life in the *campagna*, settled into the routine: "That cavallino works as well, eats as fast, sleeps as sound as his more staid companion, and life is to him tenfold less bitter; our midday siesta is a season of ever new delights to him, he rejoices in the songs of the birds, in the rustling of leaves, in the wind that shakes his mane."[17]

Their trip took them through ancient chestnut forests, or more properly plantations, where the trees lined up in rows as perfect as one would find in a cornfield. From Modena to Bologna they traveled across equally scrupulously cultivated terrain. Lowell was not overly charmed by the "monotonous regularity," although the "festoons of vines" and "the waving surface of the wheatfields" was beautiful. After a few days in Venice, where Lowell became feverish, they struck northward through Treviso to the Tyrolese Alps. He was riding on horseback the whole time now, some thirty to thirty-five miles a day through a superb landscape of steep valleys, fast-rushing streams, strong light and cool shadows, rich pastures, and rocky peaks. When they reached high altitudes he had to walk his horse. One day they spent seven hours traversing a glacier and felt "a wonderful exhilaration." Their excitement went beyond an enthusiasm for the landscape. After crossing one steep mountain pass, they felt an "intense overwhelming passion" to cross many more.[18]

During their long siestas and over their evening meals, the three companions discussed many things—religion, free will, and lesser subjects—but most particularly news from America. The Supreme Court in early March 1857 had decided the *Dred Scott* case, in which a slave sued for freedom on the basis of longtime residence in a free state. The opinion by the proslavery Chief Justice Roger Taney held that black men, free or slave, were denied the right to sue in a federal court. The founders, Taney argued, never intended free blacks to be U.S. citizens, and they were not part of Jefferson's "we" as in "We, the people." Furthermore, he wrote, the only protection the

Constitution offered the slave was the Fifth Amendment, which guaranteed that without due process of law a man could not lose life, liberty, or property. An amendment intended to guarantee life and liberty reinforced instead the slaves' subjugation as property. Taney's argument threatened to supersede state laws banning slavery, just as the Fugitive Slave Law had overridden other state statutes. The *Dred Scott* decision horrified all three friends. Deeply pessimistic, Perkins believed that there was no reward in human life and that "the best people are the unhappiest." He claimed that he wanted to "annihilate his soul." Higginson, more timidly, supposed that now and then rewards did come on earth.[19]

From Salzburg they followed the Danube through Linz to Vienna. There they went to operas and concerts, which Henry enjoyed immensely, but Charlie's health deteriorated, and once again they set off, this time to the spa at Bad Ishl, then up through Bohemia to Prague and, finally, Dresden. After three months on the road, they sold their horses, all agreeing they were "glad to put off our dusty riding garments and settle down into civilization."[20]

Johnny Bancroft joined them in Dresden. He took up Charlie's care and Henry returned to Vienna to devote himself to music. For a month and a half Lowell and Bancroft lived with the German family of a professor Muller, who taught history at the cadet school. Johnny was studying painting, Charlie German. But he was now convinced that fresh air and outdoor exercise were his best cure. Daily he rode two hours, rowed for one hour, and did "a good deal of walking"; still he missed the outdoor life. Among the curiosities Lowell found in Dresden were the military maneuvers on the outskirts of the city, where some thirty thousand Saxon troops reenacted the Battle of Dresden, fought in 1813 on the very same ground. Over the course of a week Lowell watched as soldiers dramatized Napoleon's last major victory on German soil. Then, as the weather turned cold in October, he headed south. He planned to spend the winter in North Africa, contacts in Dresden having supplied him with the names of French military officers in Algiers.[21]

Before he left Rome in May, Charlie had written to his mother, "I have entirely decided to stay abroad another winter,—not that I am not well enough now, but, because I can be better, the doctor says. You, I see, are much more afraid of my growing selfish than of my becoming unfitted for business. It is a selfish enough life I am leading, I know."[22]

This was exactly Anna's fear. Assured that her son was no longer at death's door, she was anxious to have him home again. It had disturbed her that Charlie's early letters had told her little and dwelt excessively on his debts and duties. Now she was upset that he hardly mentioned them, that he wrote of "loafing" days away, that he joked ironically about his obligations. She feared he was growing too comfortable with a life from which he had excluded all work—perhaps he was finding it "gracious as roses." She begged him to return to America with his mind "as far as possible made up" regarding his future. While she was much more broad-minded than her parents' generation, she nevertheless was ambivalent about the effects of too much time spent in Europe (where she herself had never been). Europe was all very well; it was necessary for reasons of health; it gave polish to Americans and exposed them to the finer aspects of culture; but it did have its dangers. At its worst, Europe might make an American decadent, effete, languid, and self-indulgent.

In this concern Anna found a soulmate in Henry's father, her old friend George Higginson. He did not understand his son's devotion to music and was distressed that his son's small inheritance (from his own father) was now being squandered on quixotic dreams and self-indulgent pleasures. Moreover he had three other sons to worry about, and like the Lowells had lost his money in the Panic of 1837. Neither Anna Lowell nor George Higginson was pleased to have a son keeping company with the likes of Stephen Perkins and Johnny Bancroft. Perkins had a reputation for laziness that even his friends acknowledged. Though laziness was all very well for him since he would inherit a fortune, it would not do for Lowell or Higginson. Bancroft had always been a bit of a wild card—he had lost $17,000 in less than a year and could not settle on a profession. His brother was even worse: Anna had watched him waste his Harvard years with drink and partying, only to go to Europe and in less than six months marry a French girl (at least so they were told), get her pregnant, and live in France entirely dependent on handouts from his father.

Needless to say, in his letters home Charlie did not mention anything that even suggested what he might be "getting up to." Certainly he had acquired a taste for wine. He and Henry knew enough of beers and breweries to contemplate running such a business in Vienna. Rome had been full of attractive young women, but Charlie was unlikely to have strayed. His health did not suit a life of excessive hedonism, his personality even less. Although he was high-spirited and fond of fun, loving banter and humor, he had a serious, almost frightening earnestness at his core.

Boston culture demanded that young men play their part in the family unit. Lowell's search for his inner self, his interest in "self-culture," and his Transcendentalist individualism showed his chafing at this dictum. Europe afforded him freedom simply by distancing him from his family. It released him from his omnipresent sense of obligation. Still, his plan to make a fortune had not been abandoned. Another winter, he explained, "will make me almost as good a worker as I ever was . . . Whether it be a railway, a rolling-mill, a machine shop, or a cotton-factory, depends not so much on me as on circumstances,—but I am quite convinced that for ten or fifteen years my true field is in manufactures."

Charlie posted this letter and headed south to Algiers, stopping in Vienna to see Henry Higginson, in Florence to visit Aunt Mary, and then in Marseilles, where he took a boat, arriving in Algiers in the first days of November 1857. He boarded with a Republican exile recommended by Aunt Mary, a Madame Girault—a "motherly French lady," he told his mother, adding, "you see there is no chance of my ever becoming a man; I find some one to take your place wherever I go."[23]

Algiers was a polyglot city. French officers, in elegant uniforms, paraded the streets while fierce Zoaves in turbans and flowing trousers massed in the squares. Lowell found jaunty Parisian tourists who looked vaguely uncomfortable, "starch-collared" Englishmen with guidebook in hand, and exiles from Hungary, Poland, and Spain. Arab nomads proudly girdled in camel skins, turbaned Moors, Africans, Bisberi water-carriers, Maltese, and Jews all crowded into the narrow streets of this port. The public squares were filled with people smoking cigars and playing hazard and vagabonds lounging on benches. Tourists were plagued by Arab boys carrying boxes and brushes, determined to shine their shoes.

For the first month the weather was surprisingly benign. Lowell found he could sit writing by an open window and declared he was enjoying his "surroundings as Adam and Eve enjoyed Paradise, according to Mr. Carlyle." He slept late, rode in the morning, breakfasted at a café, walked in the main square, dined with his French teacher, rode again in the afternoon, and ate again at six with an Englishman, "a very pleasant fellow, who sketches in water colors." The two then went to a club to play billiards or chess and cards. Lowell went shooting in the Medeah with many French Republican exiles, who had been shipped in huge numbers to Algiers after the military coup d'état of 1851–52 that had made Louis Napoleon emperor. His French teacher was one such exile, and Aunt Mary put him in touch

with a Frenchwoman of Republican sympathies whose son was also consumptive.

By December, however, it was clear to Lowell that he was still ill. To Higginson he confessed in the New Year that "I have spent more money and got
less benefit than from any three months since I left home." In early February
he headed back to Rome via Tunis, where he explored the ruins of
Carthage, and Malta. When not aboard ship, he was traveling again on
horseback, convinced that only when riding was his health assuredly good.
He booked passage to Naples and from there rode to Rome.[24]

But Italy was suffering an unusually harsh winter, and Rome was not
pleasant. He had trouble shaking off his cough. The large, dank, unheated
Roman apartments were not suited to the freezing cold; nor did he find the
companionship he had so enjoyed the year before. To his mother he wrote,
"Roman society, so far as I have seen it, is trivial beyond belief,—perhaps the
artists keep all their deep and serious life for their marble and their canvas,
but, except Hawthorne, I doubt if there is an earnest, thinking American at
Rome."[25]

Lowell had been befriended by the author Nathaniel Hawthorne (a
friend of Uncle James) and his wife, Sophia, whose older sister, Elizabeth
Peabody, had championed Charlie's mother in the 1840s, when they were
among the few women included in the Transcendentalist Conversations
held at Elizabeth's bookstore. Once again Lowell toured the galleries. This
time he avoided the forgiving and loving Madonnas and turned his attention
to the work of Michelangelo. At the Pitti Palace he was riveted by a painting
called *Three Fates*. (Attributed to Michelangelo at the time, it is now
thought to be by Francesco Salviati. The painting had also fascinated Emerson, who had it copied and wrote of it in *The Conduct of Life*.) The Moerae,
or Fates, are the three daughters of Erebus who control the individual and
inescapable destiny of each mortal being: Clotho spins the thread of life;
Lachesis embodies Chance, or Luck, and with her rod measures the length
of the thread of each human life; and Atropos is inescapable fate who with
her shears cuts the thread. Most Americans tried to convince themselves
that something forgiving and pitying showed in their faces. Hawthorne went
again and again to study the painting, looking for some sign of mercy, but he
could find only "a slight compunction" in Lachesis. Just beginning what
would become *The Marble Faun*, he was fascinated and horrified by the
Fates' "terrible, stern, passionless severity, neither loving nor hating us . . . If
they were angry, or had the least spite against human kind, it would render

them tolerable. They are a great work, containing and representing the very idea that makes a belief in fate such a cold torture to the human soul. God give me the sure belief in His Providence." Lowell, however, found the picture cathartic. "The old crone in the background holding the distaff and sending forth to eternity one monotonous, unheeding shriek, is crushing,— she is better than a Greek tragedy." The painting was "the most instructive I have met."[26]

But his favorite was one of Fortuna, or "the lady with the wheel," as Lowell familiarly called her. There are, in fact, two goddesses of fortune. Tyche offers riches, luck, and plenty from her cornucopia. She is an irresponsible figure whose actions are governed by impulse and chance, and she is often depicted juggling. Nemesis carries the wheel—originally representing the solar year, another image of time—and wreaks vengeance on those who too arrogantly enjoy the riches heaped on them by capricious Tyche. As the year turns from the plenty of summer to the barrenness of winter, so the wheel turns, and so human life progresses from good to bad, from blessings to privation.

Lowell's letters home are full of classical allusions. Almost every one of his letters referred to his "luck" and "good fortune." He told his mother, "I shall trust as usual to the Gods." In a later letter he explained that "the Gods will hold me responsible and I am too superstitious to provoke the avenging Goddess." His classical studies, his love of Plato, his fondness for epithets that alluded to that philosopher, and the prominence of Greek myth in his Commencement Day oration indicate an allegiance to the ancient world. But what might have simply been an affectation in a student became a more deeply held devotion during his months in Europe. He wrote of trusting to the gods, of how the gods "send you such chances," of "the gifts of Gods," of having "a great deal to thank the Gods for," of how "the wheel must turn sometime," of thanking "Fortune for playing me an ill turn now and then," of being "frightened when my spoke points too long at the zenith."[27]

In establishing his curious relationship with "the Gods" and Fortuna particularly, Lowell found a way to understand the events of his life. The image of Fortune's turning wheel may have best described his plunge into dependence at just the moment he believed he might begin to be independent; into needing care at a time he intended to care for others; into finding the price of illness to be the privilege of travel; into discovering that while great things had been demanded of him when he was healthy, his family indulged him now that he was ill. The classical imagery may have helped him retain his dignity in the face of his illness. If illness was an "early warning," if he was a favorite of the gods, if they were watching his movements, gauging the height of his spokes, then he was engaged in a heroic struggle. In this sense his catharsis at the indifference of the Fates was offset by his belief that the gods did play favorites.

Lowell's return to Rome brought home to him the effects of the financial crisis that was engulfing much of the American and even the European economies. The Panic of 1857 had started when French, Russian, and Balkan wheat returned to the European marketplace after the end of the Crimean War in 1856; this greatly reduced the demand for American wheat, and the price of flour and wheat collapsed. At first it seemed that the crisis would affect only the financial markets and speculators, but it intensified when American farmers refused to sell their crops at the new low prices. In reaction, the stock market dropped, railroad shares plunged, and banks began to hoard specie and to call in loans. By late September the entire economy was affected. John Murray Forbes wrote Lowell tell him he was on his way to London to secure a loan from Baring to rescue the Michigan Central Railroad, which had stopped paying its floating debt. Forbes also reported that J. K. Mills, for whom Lowell's uncle Patrick worked, had failed, leaving Patrick on the edge of bankruptcy. As money became increasingly tight, many of the Americans in Rome went home. Lowell noticed a large pile of mail awaiting his cousin Frank Lowell and wondered whether he had already left for Boston. The entire American community in Florence went into a tailspin as stock values plummeted.

Back in Boston, Anna Lowell's finances were also affected, and she was considering leaving Massachusetts for a more clement environment, perhaps the West, perhaps to Virginia. Hypothetically the idea of Virginia appealed to Charlie, who imagined "it would be far better than the West—we should continue to live in the last half of the 19th century and not fall back a generation as most Western men do." It even matched a scheme he and Henry Higginson had concocted in their travels, by which they and Jim Savage and Johnny Bancroft would all move to Virginia "to cultivate the vine and olive, to think none but high thoughts, to speak none but weighty words, and to become, in short, the worthies of our age."[28]

But when he realized that his mother was seriously considering the move and had in fact made an exploratory visit in the spring of 1857, Charlie's attitude quickly sobered. Now he opposed migration generally and most particularly to Virginia. "As long as the question of slavery there is undecided," he explained, "free settlers, however cultivated, will be under a taboo,— may even be in danger from personal attack from the vagabond whites. As visitors, you are courteously received; as settlers, you would find things changed. Nothing would induce me to expose the girls to it." He thought the emancipation of Virginia slaves might take a century, but even if it took only ten years, he understood that Virginia's debts would be high, its infrastructure poor.

In any case Anna reckoned she would be unable to abide such close proximity to what she considered the supreme evil. She now turned to the idea of moving west. This suggestion also alarmed Charlie: "Have you decided to emigrate *en masse*? . . . I wish you would give me some idea of your plan . . . How much land you intend to buy,—how you intend to cultivate it, &c? . . . You speak of Quincy [Illinois] as a promising place." Lowell imagined that Quincy might one day become a "great grain-centre" and that "some one will make fortunes: but successful speculation requires a talent by itself, of which I have never seen in myself the slightest proof."[29]

Nor did Lowell like the prospect of spending the rest of his days on a farm. He wanted to know if there was "likely to be any chance for manufacturing, rather than farming . . . In anything connected with manufactures, or even with the lower branches of railroad management, ability will answer, and that I once had." He could not understand his mother's rush to leave Massachusetts. "Why talk of emigration? . . . if it is on my account, I hope at the end of another year to find all climates alike . . . if it proves better for [Harriet] to go West, I go there as gayly as a horse to battle." But he did not see the need for such worrying now. Nor did he think it made sense for them to be making such huge plans by letter, without waiting for his return. "You must not make up your mind at all before seeing me. I certainly should be utterly unwilling to drag either Father or the girls away from Cambridge."[30]

Lowell's second winter in Europe had not been much of a success. He had clung stubbornly to his plans, hoping that his health would further improve, but it did not. Keeping his disappointment from his family, in April 1858 he confessed to Higginson:

> My strongest feeling at the moment (burnt into me by the events of the last six months) is to make no promises which I am not sure to be able to keep. But in my present state of health of what can I be sure? That damned Algiers showed me clearly that for the next six or seven years I must have no engagements which would involve either much

excitement or much confinement. . . . I shall have to fight shy of temptations to very great activity until I am thirty. Every little over-exertion I feel much more markedly than quite a sudden change of weather.

It left him at loose ends as to what he might do with his life once he re-turned home, and he explained, "I have lost all confidence in myself. It is rather a shameful confession, but it is the fact."[31]

It had taken two years and much spending of "grandmother's money," but Lowell, now ready to accept Great-uncle Jackson's prescription for the moderated cautious life of an invalid, prepared to leave Europe. From Rome he went to Paris to visit the famous pathologist Pierre Louis, who had trained Boston's most eminent doctors and was highly respected as an au-thority. Louis examined Lowell and declared that his tuberculosis was in re-mission. His right lung was damaged, the breath shallow and feeble, but the left lung appeared unscarred. Lowell took this as good news. His spirits rose. He told his mother not to make plans until she had seen him. His two years in Europe had restored him. He knew he could not attempt his former dou-ble life. Rather than reenter the world of business and money, he preferred to live quietly, studying mathematics under the mentorship of his Harvard professor and Cambridge neighbor, Benjamin Peirce. However, if the family finances required it, he would pursue Forbes's proposal of April 1856 that af-ter his European trip he spend a few years in the West working on one of Forbes's railroads.

During his last days in Europe, he reveled in Parisian theater and the Louvre. By July 2 he was at Liverpool ready to board a steamer for home. Af-ter dining on "beastly roast beef, and still more beastly stout," Lowell wrote Higginson a stout-influenced farewell: "Henry, Apple of my eye—I write to thee not because the mood is upon me, not because there is news to tell thee, nor yet because I labour under a pressure of private opinion, and must let out to some one or burst my *dura mater*. No, I write to say *Farewell*. God speed thee, for in ten days the great waters will stretch between thee and me, in ten days I shall be kissing my mother's forehead. I kiss thee adieu on ei-ther cheek, sweet friend."[32]

SEVEN

LIFE IN THE WEST

1858–60

When Lowell returned to Cambridge at the end of July, he found his mother "good, better, best." The satisfaction of seeing her favorite son safely returned—if not in perfect health, then immeasurably healthier than when he had left—brought a glow to Anna. But Charlie's return home was bittersweet, his happiness infused with the curious knowledge that the lives of his friends and family had gone on quite fully without him. A reunion of his college class helped to drive the point home: many of his classmates were now settled in careers and marrying. They had joined the Suffolk County bar, become partners in family companies, were managing mills. Enmeshed in their work and their romances, preoccupied with recent gossip and local news, they seemed distant to Charlie, who was sadly aware of the contrast between their solid, predictable Boston world and his own as yet uncertain fate.

His younger brother James, always the baby of the family, had matured from a schoolboy to a scholar, graduating, as his brother had, first in his class and giving the valedictory address at Harvard commencement. He was now a handsome, well-built man. His gentle nature had developed into an easygoing manner, and he joined Boston's social scene more fully than Charlie ever had. If he did not glow as brightly as his elder brother, win so many accolades, or make such an impression, neither did he intimidate. He had established a good income tutoring other boys; the money he intended to use for law school. Charlie wrote that he considered Jim "more of a man than myself."

The greatest surprise for Charlie was his adoring sister Harriet, who had grieved so when he left the family home. For three years her letters had saddened him as she wrote of her isolation and the gap that the loss of his companionship created in her life. Within a few days of his return George Putnam, his old college classmate, came to see him. George and Harriet had deepened their acquaintance over the previous winter, when ice-skating on Fresh Pond had been in vogue, and Putnam had taught her to skate. Harriet had told Charlie of her adventures on the ice, but nothing in her letters had singled Putnam out from among the many young men who called at Quincy Street or conveyed her feelings toward him. George wanted to marry Harriet, and he asked Charlie for his approval; having received it, he approached Harriet's parents. The engagement pleased everyone, but in passing on the news to Henry Higginson, Charlie could not hide his shock: "The [sister] who was going to migrate with me is engaged, and of course lost to *me*. I'm a different man to what I was, Henry—worse I fear—less hopeful, I know."[1]

In many ways Lowell's return reawakened old instincts within him. These had started with the financial crisis and its siren call of "necessity." His mother's letters presuming his continued invalidism had reignited old childhood humiliations, and her plans for emigrating had driven "necessity" to the highest pitch. Ironically, his friend George Putnam, treating him as the paterfamilias, showed him his own immaturity. As he gave his blessing to George and Harriet, he had to concede to himself that he was far from being the head of the family. He was still a young man without a profession, with much to prove and little to show for himself. After a scant week in Cambridge, he and his mother went down to Naushon Island, at the mouth of Buzzard's Bay on the south coast of Massachusetts, as John Murray Forbes's guests, whence Lowell wrote to Johnny Bancroft in August 1858:

> I am now down at Naushon,—getting up muscle and coaching young Forbes through Algebra and History. It is the finest island on the whole Atlantic coast,—horses *ad libitum*,—guns enough for a regiment,—and a squadron of sailboats. The house is filled with a constantly changing crowd of visitors,—who are always the best people in the country, each in his department. The woods are part of the primeval forest, and you canter out of them on to a stretch of downs, unsurpassed on this side of the water. Am I not a lucky dog to tumble into such a jollitude, and be paid for it too?[2]

Few visitors left without being smitten by Naushon's beauties and the Forbeses' hospitality. It was on Naushon that Forbes indulged in, and indulged, his greatest love: his family, embracing young and old, distant cousins, near relations, and the few people who, by virtue of devotion and familiarity, had become familial. A revolving roster of these visitors filled the clapboard Mansion House that stood like a sentinel on a hilltop above the island's harbor, meadows, and rolling hills. Broad piazzas took the breeze from these expanses; within, the house was spacious and rambling—it had grown over the years to accommodate the many guests. The Mansion House was so called only in comparison to the farm buildings nearby; it had few pretensions to grandeur. Unadorned, comfortable, it conformed to the spirit of the rugged island landscape.

Among the guests were relics of New England's past, sea captains from New Bedford and venerable partners of old China trade firms. These acerbic old men, their time nearly run, sat in ample armchairs on the broad porches, old age having mellowed them somewhat. Grateful for a game of chess, they now turned a more indulgent eye toward a younger generation they barely understood. Near and distant relations, friends and acquaintances, arrived by sailboat—Naushon being but a stop on a cruise—or stayed all summer, like the impoverished family of Mrs. Sarah Forbes's twin sister, Mary Watson.

When Lowell arrived in August, the Ralph Waldo Emerson family was there. Friendships between the Forbes and Emerson children, all about the same ages, were strong. Yet in almost every way Emerson and Forbes were dissimilar: Forbes was a dynamic entrepreneur, a pragmatist, schooled by the world; Emerson was a scholar, ill equipped for practical matters. Certainly their mutual attraction was that of opposites, but both shared a natural caution and a propensity for the long view. And if Forbes admired Emerson's articulate wisdom, Emerson was deeply impressed by Forbes: "How little this man suspects, with his sympathy for men and his respect for lettered and scientific people, that he is not likely ever to meet a man who is superior to himself."[3]

The young dominated the island. Of Forbes's six children, the eldest, at twenty, were the twins, Ellen and Alice; William was eighteen and at Harvard, Mary was fourteen, Malcolm eleven, Sarah only six. Their companions that summer were their Watson cousins, the Emerson and Shaw children, several Russells and Perkinses, and Alexander Agassiz. Among the older girls was Ellen Emerson, nineteen, and her sister Edith, seventeen. Sue Shaw was nineteen, and Anna Russell eighteen. Effie Shaw was fifteen, only a year older than Mary Forbes, and Nellie Shaw at thirteen was a year younger. Matching this gaggle of girls was a mixture of friends, classmates, and cousins of William Forbes. Two of his closest friends were the cousins Henry

Sturgis Russell and Robert Gould Shaw, both members of the Harvard Class of 1860 (and second cousins of young Forbes). Another second cousin was Charles Eliot Perkins, eighteen, present with his cousin Stephen Perkins, Lowell's traveling companion.

Days were spent out of doors. There was always a group eager to swim, to sail, to fish for perch, to explore the island on foot or on horseback, and to picnic under a great oak at West End Pond, where the boys rowed the girls about in a flat-bottomed boat. Evenings were devoted to dancing and singing, to card playing and billiards, or to games of charades. Rainy days were passed with chess, reading, the composition of poetic epistles to a particularly old and irascible pony, Johnny Crapeau, or to the two monstrous beech trees, Apollo and Briarius.[4]

Forbes's older son, William, to whom Lowell was now ostensibly a tutor, was a strapping, good-hearted, high-spirited, and well-liked young man. He was neither as bright nor as hardworking as his father would have liked. Benefiting from his father's wealth and affection, he had a security of place and an over-trusting faith in his own good luck that his father regarded with a wary eye. Forbes adored his eldest son and knew that his happy-go-lucky temperament was in many ways the consequence of his affection, but he feared that Will lacked the drive and ambition to make something of himself. It had been Forbes's experience that the sons of wealthy fathers were often spoiled for a profession. Perhaps he hoped that Lowell's more restless or questing qualities would rub off on his son.

Although few of these young people had met Lowell before, they had almost all been visitors to his mother's house, were friendly with his siblings, and knew of him by reputation. Quite a few of the older girls had attended Anna Lowell's school, and the others had absorbed their exalted veneration of her. The boys knew Anna's house well, too; she had continued her hospitality toward Harvard students. Her Quincy Street home remained a gathering spot for students, lecturers, tutors, and young ladies. Since their Cuba trip, young Malcolm Forbes had idolized Lowell, singing his praises with the enthusiasm of an eleven-year-old. The Shaw children had learned of Lowell from Frank Barlow, who, through the efforts of Anna and Emerson, had spent a year living with them while he prepared young Rob Shaw for Harvard. Both Emerson girls greatly admired the entire Lowell family: Ellen's crush on Anna was complete, and Edith, a very young seventeen, was to board at her home that autumn while she attended the new Agassiz School at the end of Quincy Street. Both girls understood their father's interest in and respect for Anna and her son.

Charlie quickly gained the trust and esteem of this company. He took the girls out riding or rowing, and his easy charm and attentive manners flattered them. The young men were impressed by his ease with horses, for they, like most New England boys, had more enthusiasm for than expertise in riding. Knowing he was consumptive, they admired how lightly he wore his years of illness. His tales of European adventure, particularly his time in Algiers, and his expeditions on horseback gave him an air of romance and originality. His confidence, talents, and magnetism made him attractive, and the young people found it quite easy to fall in with his enthusiasms. Like his cousin Nina, these young people found him "an improving sort of person." As in his Harvard days, he quite naturally assumed the role of leader. And as a leader, he was of them but not like them, more mature, confident, and experienced. Charlie seemed to move so effortlessly from the games of the young to the more serious conversation of the older men, that the young looked to him with awe.

Forbes had brought Lowell to Naushon not simply to entertain and improve his son. He wanted to observe Charlie, to assess for himself just how well the young man really was. He needed to decide where in his western railroad network Lowell might be of greatest use and to prepare him for his new employment. Forbes had become involved in western rail work in the mid-1840s, when the state of Michigan had decided to sell three railroad lines that it had over-optimistically begun to build. With other wealthy ex–China traders from Boston and New York known as the Forbes Group, Forbes had bought the Michigan Central Railroad and begun to complete that line, racing against the new owners of the Michigan Southern, which connected Pittsburgh, Philadelphia, and Baltimore and might potentially eclipse New England manufactures and Boston shipping if it got to Chicago first. But the race did not end there.

When the owners of the Southern realized the Central would open sooner, they raised the stakes, buying a franchise for a rail line beyond Chicago running due west to the Mississippi. The Forbes-led Central cast its eye farther west as well. In a complicated series of maneuvers, the group also bought up a number of lines running southwest from Chicago to two termini on the Mississippi. Barely had work begun on these new lines when the possibility of building a transcontinental railroad again increased the financial gamble. Forbes bought into two more franchises, both intended to connect the Missouri and Mississippi Rivers, one crossing the state of Missouri, the other crossing Iowa and terminating where the Platte joins the Missouri. Thus by 1857 Forbes was building railroads stretching from Boston to the Missouri River.

Forbes was not alone in taking the plunge into railroads. Like the "iron fever" of the 1830s, railroading in the 1840s and 1850s aroused enormous interest. It too was characterized by overspeculation and less-than-adequate sober reflection. But the marvels of railroad technology were such that only a curmudgeon would not yield to wild optimism and ambition. To men used to the horse, the ox, and the mule, rail speed seemed to defy nature, turning what had once been a three-week journey into a three-day trip. Even more significant was the railroad's independence from basic geography.

Earlier settlements in the West had been located close to the only practical means of transportation, the river systems; settlers, like salmon, had traveled upriver from the sea. But the great river system was that of the Missouri and Mississippi Rivers, leading down to New Orleans and the Gulf of Mexico, an inconvenient terminus to New England manufacturers and shipowners. A direct route from the Midwest to the Atlantic ports would be of far greater benefit to them, and only the railroad, because it could traverse watersheds, could accomplish this, connecting the previously unconnected. It was an excellent example of Lowell's idea that the world advances by "impossibilities achieved," for the railroad made the impossible a scheduled stop on its route. The "impossibility" that Forbes was intent on achieving, along with the other northeastern investors, was a transportation network that rendered the Mississippi River obsolete.

Building a railroad involved enormous sums of money, far exceeding the cost of building even the largest mill or the financial resources of a partnership of the wealthiest men in America. Thus, while a railroad's financiers served as its directors, they were required to subscribe huge numbers of other stockholders to whom the directors were responsible and who expected the corporation to pay dividends. Thus began the modern stock market.

No one had previously attempted to administer and manage such a complex business organization. Apart from the tremendous capital sums a railroad required, nobody anticipated the expense that daily operation would entail. The innovations introduced by the textile mills of New England had brought some sophistication into American corporate organization and structure, but a modest railroad cost seven times as much to run as the largest industrial mill and employed two or three times as many men. Unlike a canal, which, whatever its length, was nothing more than a water-filled ditch, a railroad was not mere track: its constantly employed assets, all requiring maintenance and repair, including engines, cars, terminals, stations, warehouses, bridges, and telegraph lines. Beyond that came the headaches of operation: scheduling passengers and freight and establishing reliable timetables. Above all, one grim financial truth: a railroad's operating costs remained constant, whether it transported three passengers or three thousand, three pounds of freight or three tons.

Many railroads were insufficiently funded. Quite a few worsened their situation by paying out dividends from early profits without anticipating maintenance expenses. Some failed to pay off their huge construction loans. Not until the Panic of 1857 did the fiscal shortsightedness become obvious. When the price of western crops dropped and farmers refused to send them to market, the railroads lost freight income. When banks reacted to the crisis by tightening their loan policies, railroads could not borrow working capital. The stock market as a source of funds failed, shares dropping to less than half their previous value. As the panic spread to the manufacturing Northeast, factories shut down, thus accelerating loss of freight and compounding the squeeze.

Two months into the crisis, Michigan Central, Forbes's most mature and profitable railroad, found itself on the edge of collapse. With a fortune sunk in expensive, unrealizable, and (for the time being) worthless assets, the railroad neither had funds nor could raise any. If it failed, Forbes would sustain a huge loss, which would jeopardize his other railroad investments as well. The value lay in their totality, not in the separate parts. To meet this crisis, Forbes, resorting to the methods of his youth, went personally to England in 1857 to Baring Brothers, the bankers with whom he had both commercial and personal links dating back to his youth in the China trade. The Barings provided him with a $3 million loan, an indication of their faith in his credibility, integrity, and ability, but the help came at a cost. Guaranteed personally by Forbes, the loan deepened his commitment to Michigan Central. Fortunately for Forbes, the loan saw the railroad through the banking crisis, while countless other reputable firms and railroads went under.

Keenly aware of the various weaknesses in railroading's financial and administrative underpinnings, Forbes now regarded his railroad ventures with a new wariness. Modern financial instruments like stocks and bonds were all very well, but they were "fair weather" friends, not to be relied on in troubled times. Equally, a corporate structure that separated the management of the railroad from its shareholders made it extremely difficult for the board of directors or even the president (which Forbes was) to keep a close eye on the company's financial health. As president, Forbes readily recognized that although a financier could not run a railroad, an engineer could do nothing but run it.

To operate his railroads, Forbes wanted men whom he knew personally and could trust. He wanted them to feel the personal obligation that he had had when as a young man he had traded for his uncles in Canton. Just as he had propped up the railroad with personal bonds procured the old-fashioned way, he wanted to infuse into the new corporate system a judicious sprinkling of individuals who understood the old system of personal obligation, mutual interest, and fealty that had been at the core of the New England merchants' sea-trading ventures and far-flung operations. Charlie Lowell was such a man. Forbes was convinced of his integrity and sense of obligation. Thus, when Forbes went to Europe to obtain the loan in October 1857, he told Lowell the railroad position he wanted him to fill. Two years earlier Lowell had considered himself "engaged" to Forbes. Now Forbes needed Lowell. During the Naushon visit he reinforced the ties that secured Lowell's fealty.

Lowell's month on Naushon demonstrated certain basic New England values: a clannish love of family, a devotion to the beauties and freedoms of the natural world, an unpretentious and bookish love of literary and philosophical thought and discussion. Emerson and Anna Lowell initiated the sort of animated conversation typical of Lowell family gatherings and of which Lowell had always been so fond. Questions of the day, literary musings, and philosophical ruminations were debated partly to entertain, partly to exercise the mind, and partly from genuine interest. Gathered together in a setting removed from Boston's social demands and distinctions, enjoying a return to the perhaps innocent and childlike pleasures of the natural world, the various generations mingled, old and young, politically conservative and socially experimental, very rich and much less so, all on a common footing.

It was a world well familiar to Charlie for "Aunt-Hill," the Jackson place in Beverly, had operated on the same principles. He found an easy comfort in playing chess with the old governor, engaging Emerson in serious conversation, amusing the girls by rowing them about the Deerwood Lake, and shooting with the boys.

Before he left Europe, Charlie had advised Henry Higginson, "I think you can squeeze more pleasure out of old Boston, squeezed as it is." Certainly his month on Naushon offered him that opportunity. "How could a returned European better pass his first month?" he wrote Higginson. "I am galloping through one month of life more distracting than Paris, more attracting than Naples; and what have I to say to thee, thou whey-drinking, backward-looking old hydropath? Get thou behind me, man, thou work'st i' the earth." Still, Lowell recognized that he had lost the selfish freedom he had enjoyed in Europe and was daunted by what awaited him. "By the time this hits thee in the pit of the stomach, I shall probably be in the far West. Cheerful, is it not? More than a week ahead I have ceased to look, but the West stares me in the face whenever I open my eyes. A railway probably; salary small, but a chance ahead if found smart—cheerful again—you know I hate smartness." But there was nothing he could do to avoid this fate, and so, he explained to Higginson, "I live in the moment—I breathe an atmosphere of rifles and fishing tackle and saddle horses—and I snap my fingers at ideas, at thoughts, at sentiments—how could a departing Westerner better pass his last month?"

Yet even in this carefree mood, Lowell had a serious point to make. Explaining the challenge before him, he wrote Higginson: "It is easy enough to live alone in Cambridge, in Boston, in Europe, and never know that you are nobody. In Missouri or Iowa this will be harder,—the shaking up comes oftener . . . It's no use being a feller out there, unless you're a hell of a feller. But then it's scarcely worth while to be a feller at all, I admit."[5]

By mid-September 1858 Lowell had started work as assistant treasurer and land agent for the Burlington & Missouri River Railroad Company at Burlington, in southeastern Iowa. Unlike Detroit or Chicago or other midwestern towns, Burlington was not too muddy. It sat on high ground, two bluffs overlooking Hawkeye Creek, where it met the Mississippi River, and many of its buildings were built of locally quarried stone, which gave them a more substantial appearance than the clapboard storefronts typical of so many western towns. Nevertheless Burlington had, as Lowell wrote his mother, "a half-fledged look, the pin-feathers being still very apparent,—but the savage sullenness of the Mississippi tones it down in a measure, and seems to *justify* a semi-demi-civilization."[6]

The manner in which Iowa had been settled was very different from what coastal New England had experienced some two hundred years before. The speed of new settlements, the centrality of their commercial interests, and a heterodox population were distinguishing features. Burlington was only three years older than Lowell himself: the land on which it was built had been Indian territory until 1832, when the Sac Indians were defeated in what became known as the Black Hawk War but was more accurately a slaughter of Indians that culminated a series of treaty violations between the Sac, protesting against the encroachment of white settlers, and those white settlers eager to encroach. The new treaty, by which the Sac ceded a fifty-mile-wide band of land on the western bank of the Mississippi, was considered a triumph of Andrew Jackson's presidency largely because it distracted Americans from more contentious economic issues (the closing of the Second Bank of the United States especially). Barely was the ink dry on the document when settlers poured across the Mississippi to settle the Iowa prairie.

These first settlers were farmers from Missouri, southern Illinois, Indiana, and Kentucky. Like most southerners, they shunned towns and cared little for government or civic life. They were sympathetic to slavery and suspicious of big business, banks, and industry. Fiercely individualistic populist Democrats, they dominated Iowa's early political development and established the tone of Burlington, where, as Lowell explained, "every man is a law unto himself, and such a law." Their leader was Augustus C. Dodge, who had fought in the Black Hawk War and as territorial governor had brought Iowa to statehood in 1846, with a state constitution that banned banks and blacks—free or slave. Becoming one of Iowa's first senators, Dodge staunchly defended southern interests and in 1854 introduced the fateful Kansas-Nebraska Bill.[7]

Burlington's position as a port on the Mississippi naturally did much to determine its character. The Mississippi was a highway for barges, and its steamboats, then at their peak of popularity, brought in a constant flow of people, goods, and entertainment. Down along its swampy edge on a section known as Willow Patch, the river people lived—a transient and seasonal community of raftsmen, fishermen, bargers, and ferrymen. Marvels like the *Floating Palace* came by, "a gorgeous spectacle, made partly of glass, and equipped with both chimes and calliope." Rounding the bend in the river and coming into view from Burlington's bluffs, its calliope would strike up a familiar tune like "The Girl I Left Behind Me." The music attracted crowds along the banks that cheered as the steamer docked.

Because of the steamers, plenty of people in Burlington were "just passing through"—card sharks, tricksters, confidence men, preachers without Bibles, doctors with the latest patent medicine, lawyers good at drawing up wills, and foreign gentlemen deprived of their vast wealth and titled estates by some cruel tyranny, evil uncle, or scheming cousin. Everyone had a story to tell, few of them true; the art of the confidence game found many practitioners. The steamboats also brought execrable vaudeville acts entertaining those who could bear to watch them. For brief spells the heady atmosphere of New Orleans would fill the "Porkopolis of Iowa."

The town received this title because of two large pork-packing plants in Burlington run by German immigrants (who made up roughly one-third of its population). These Lutheran liberals, industrious and culturally distinct, also ran breweries and gave musical concerts that, Lowell claimed, gave Burlington "a certain cosmopolitan character." Logging mills along the Black Hawk Creek had attracted Swedish migrants, while the railroad had brought the Irish, who lived in the Hibernia section of town; for several years Hungarian Kossuthites plotted the building of a socialist society called New Buda just outside town (after a few Iowa winters, the Hungarians moved to Texas); and Mormons settled briefly in Iowa before trekking on to Utah. Other Iowa communities included Quakers, as well as a small following of the French utopian Charles Fourier, who mixed elements of free love and socialist principles to establish a harmonious "phalanstery," or ideal community, and of course, Yankees.[8]

At first these had been a distinct minority, but by the late 1850s they made up the majority of the Iowa population. Coming from New Hampshire, Vermont, western New York, Ohio, and Michigan, they were townsmen interested in shops, commerce, schools, and churches. It was, in the main, these men who "improved" Burlington, erecting its stone buildings and trying to give it substance, a look of success and permanence. They encouraged commerce and business and the exploitation or development of Burlington as the market town for the surrounding farms.

Burlington's Yankee citizens recognized that the town's future development lay with rail. They understood intrinsically the looming inevitability of a transcontinental railroad, and they wanted to be part of it. One Iowan described how the state was "as central in location in the United States as the 'bull's eye' to a shooting target . . . therefore, *the line of inland communication* between the people residing on the Atlantic coast and those on the Pacific coast — other things being equal — must cross this delta — and although there will, no doubt, in time, be many routes of Rail Road across the Continent — some one will be the *great thoroughfare*."[9] The advantages of being part of a great thoroughfare were obvious for commerce even more than for migration. As a central point for railroad transport to the east, Chicago's markets, both national and international, were huge and its prices higher. But the cost of building a railroad far exceeded the means of Burlington or of the state of Iowa, with its antibank constitution. To find capital, Burlington's ex–New Englanders looked to the Northeast, in particular to New Englanders with an interest in railroads. This is how the Burlington & Missouri River Railroad had come to Forbes's attention and became the westernmost line owned by the Forbes Group.

In his position as assistant treasurer, Charlie Lowell handled funds and served as chief clerk and accountant. He paid all the bills, collected revenue, and reported to the treasurer in Boston, J. N. Denison. His closest colleague was the railroad's vice president and superintendent, John G. Read, whose principal task was to engineer and build the line. Both Read and Lowell reported directly to Boston, and while their status was roughly equal, their duties were entirely different. Still, since the B&MR was a very small concern, it was natural that they shared their tasks. A strong friendship and mutual trust quickly developed, and the two men worked together well. The only other company officer was the ticket agent, a Bohemian named Leo Carper. Under these officers were the Irish laborers engaged in building the railroad and a number of German technicians. Nearby, in neighboring Fairfield, was the general agent, Bernhardt Henn, who had served as the main liaison between Burlington's first citizens and the railroad's eastern financiers. Henn had also spent several years in Washington as the railroad liaison with the General Land Office. He had retired from active duty but remained a strong ally of the B&MR.

The creation of the Burlington & Missouri River Railroad coincided with the rise of the Republican Party in Iowa and its neighboring states. In 1854 James Grimes, a New Hampshire man and Burlington's leading Republican, became Iowa's governor. In 1855, the year the B&MR was incorporated, Republican-Whigs gained control of Iowa's lower house. The abolitionist James Harlan became Iowa's junior senator in Washington, filling the seat vacated by Senator Dodge when he was appointed minister to Spain. By 1857 Iowa had a new constitution with reforms that permitted banks and corporate enterprise—all favorable to railroads—and a spurt of building resulted.

For his first six months Lowell lived at a public house, an establishment that combined the rooms of a boardinghouse with the downstairs parlors of a saloon. He had little privacy and little peace. Quickly developing a reputation as the resident intellectual, he often found his evenings interrupted by some fellow in search of edification. After a long day, the challenge of giving a twenty-minute explanation of Swedenborg, Lowell complained, "rather melts the brain,"[10] the more so when he wanted to guard his time jealously to read or write. Nor was he free of the noise and violence that a public house invariably sustained. But he was well placed to watch electoral politics, specifically the 1858 senatorial campaign of Governor Grimes, who wished to fill the seat vacated by George W. Jones, a staunch Democrat and ardent friend of slavery who had just accepted an appointment as minister to New Grenada. In Illinois the Republican Abraham Lincoln, a little-known lawyer, was opposing the region's leading political figure, Stephen Douglas. Both men put in appearances in Iowa. In October Lincoln spoke in Burlington to a packed audience. Shortly thereafter Douglas attended the opening of the first thirty-five miles of the B&MR. In both Senate races, Iowa and Illinois, Republicans sought to replace powerful Democrats, but here the similarities ended. Grimes was far better established than Lincoln and had minimal opposition.

Charlie Lowell voted for the first time in this election, supporting a solid Republican ticket. When the votes were counted, Iowa had gone Republican, with two Republican senators and a Republican governor. Through the campaigning Lowell had become acquainted with most of the leading citizens of southern Iowa, and with key Republicans such as Grimes, Harlan, and the new governor, Samuel P. Lowe. The Republican Party in Iowa had drawn heavily on the support of immigrants, especially Germans, to develop a broad Free Soil base. Midwestern farmers opposed slavery not on moral or religious grounds but for the practical reason that they did not want to compete with slave labor, either directly in their own state or indirectly in neighboring states. Antislavery pamphlets were freely circulated everywhere: Iowans had played and continued to play a part in the Underground Railroad and in the free settlement of Kansas Territory, which lay to the west and southwest. Grimes supported the work of the New England Emigrant Aid Society. While governor, he had made possible the appropriation of fifteen hundred guns from the Iowa arsenal by Kansas militia fighters. In 1856, when Frank Sanborn made his trip to Kansas, he had stayed with Grimes. The two men, both from New Hampshire, shared many acquaintances. Sanborn had negotiated the safe conduct of men, goods, and guns through Iowa, procuring the use of the contacts, "way-stations," and apparatus of the Iowa underground for the Kansas struggle.

By 1858, however, the Kansas crisis had largely abated. A new territorial governor had quelled most of the fighting by initiating a credible process toward statehood. Northerners now outnumbered southerners, ensuring that Kansas would become a free state. The local Emigrant Aid workers in Kansas had divorced themselves from free-state militia fighters and joined the process of peaceful resolution. Republicans had been elected to all state offices. Kansas would soon be admitted as a free state—and a Republican one at that. Thus when Lowell wrote Henry Higginson claiming there was no longer any "border spice left"[11] in Burlington, he meant that violence, raids, and free-state militias were a thing of the past. The fighting in Kansas had largely ended. Indeed Kansas would soon join the midwestern states as they rapidly became hardcore Republican, despite the reelection of the Democrat from Illinois, Stephen Douglas.

However, in late December 1857 a vicious attack on Fort Scott in Kansas followed by a raid into Missouri in January 1858 had threatened to reignite the violence. A gang of Kansas free-settlers had invaded Missouri and attacked a number of farms, murdering and butchering the men, robbing the houses, and stealing the slaves. The leader was a fanatical abolitionist named John Brown. In Kansas and surrounding states many people had for years thought Brown insane; now virtually all were convinced of it. The raid was universally condemned. Kansas already offered a bounty of $350 for Brown's capture. Missouri now put out a reward of $3,000 and the President of the United States offered $250.

Taking the freed slaves with him, Brown had fled east to Tabor, Iowa. This religious community, situated just south of the final terminus of the B&MR, had served as an armory, a refuge, and a hospital for Free-Soilers in the Kansas struggle since 1854. But even in Tabor Brown found that his violence had lost him sympathy. Using safe houses established in 1856 by Frank Sanborn, Brown crossed Iowa, taking with him the guns and ammunition that had been stored in Tabor and gathering along the way four local recruits. In mid-March 1859 he was headed farther east to provoke the "final contest": encouraging slaves across the South to rise up and rebel.

Since January 1857 Brown's primary supporter and confidant had been Frank Sanborn. Throughout the year Sanborn, who found Brown a heroic figure, promoted his interests among radical abolitionists—men like Dr. Samuel G. Howe and Luther Stearns—as well as members of liberal Boston society (including Anna Lowell, John Murray Forbes, and Ralph Waldo Emerson) and more moderate men like Charlie's uncle Pat Jackson, treasurer of the Emigrant Aid Society, and his uncle Dr. Samuel Cabot, a generous donor to John Brown and the cause of free settlement in Kansas. In July 1858 just before Charlie headed out to Iowa, both he and Sanborn attended reunion dinners at Harvard. Did they discuss Kansas, John Brown, or any aspect of the Emigrant Aid Society's activities? Did Sanborn put Lowell in touch with another Harvard classmate, Benjamin Lyman, whom Sanborn had successfully recruited to work as the Emigrant Aid Society's agent in Lawrence, Kansas, and as such knew something of Brown's movements? Did Sanborn provide Brown with an introduction to Lowell in Iowa? He certainly did this for another Kansas militia fighter, Captain Charles Stewart, an Englishman who later volunteered for the Union army. But we cannot establish whether Charlie Lowell was even aware of John Brown's existence at this point. Nor is there any mention of the Missouri raid in Lowell's letters to his mother.

Instead, we learn that after six months of paying high prices (Lowell complained that he paid at least thirty-five dollars a month for room and board), he persuaded the B&MR's ticket agent, Leo Carper, to go in with him on renting a small house half a mile out of town with two acres, a milk cow, a dog called Punch, and a pup by the name of Grouse. The cottage was homey, with sweetbriar growing on it, a quaint blue and brown carpet, and a good fireplace. Lowell hung the walls with photographs of Italian art: a Masaccio over the fireplace, to its left Raphael's *Hours*, and, on the right, his favorite, Michelangelo's *Fortune*.[12] His mother had sent him several boxes of books: Spenser, Chaucer, *Pilgrim's Progress*, Pascal's *Provincial Letters*, his old textbook on curves and functions, a German grammar, Spanish, English, and Greek dictionaries, Emerson's *Latest Poems*, *The Philosophy of Immanuel Kant*, and recently published works by Charles Darwin and Henry Thomas Buckle. For his health Lowell rode two hours a day, whatever the weather, and often worked late into the night rather than miss an afternoon's ride.

The thought of Charlie's efforts at housekeeping caused much mirth at home. His sisters wrote teasing letters, to which he replied with mock indignation. But his description of his homemade pea soup, "with which the spoon is loath to part," did not tempt. He claimed that "if architecture is frozen music, cooking is melody boiled and roast," and undoubtedly his food was as mangled as a melody would be if subjected to such treatment. But he wanted to display his boiled mutton, at least "one of our successful efforts in that line."

While Charlie made the best of life in Burlington, he made no bones about its limitations. "Do not fancy that I shall hold on here from any fear of the future," he wrote home. "That is a thraldom I am entirely free from." When Anna wondered whether six months in Iowa might not be good for Harriet, Charlie wrote back, "Do not think of bringing Hatty out here,—it is no place for women; they can't stand the climate or the mode of life, and the society is cliquish to an extent unknown in the East."[13]

One of the saddest things of his life in Burlington became "the absence of new interests, and the gradual scaling off of the old ones." Although he had told Higginson that the West would make "a feller" of him, he now qualified that idea. "The West may make a man strong, massy, rock-like,— never large and generous and manly. There are no new roots tempted out,—but the old ones, if they are left, may tap deeper." He wrote Higginson, "I am getting over vague Charleynesses about inner life. I am drying, my lad, drying,—if I ever do burn, you will see less smoke."[14]

In June 1859 Charlie Perkins, then only eighteen, whom Lowell had met on Naushon, joined Lowell as chief clerk, taking on most of the accounting and payroll jobs and helping Lowell to manage the B&MR's land mortgage. It was this aspect of the B&MR that came in for attack in August 1859, when Augustus Dodge ran for governor. He had never liked "damned Yankees," and, freshly returned from Spain, he mounted a vicious campaign in an effort to regain control of the state. Falling back on the populism of the region, Dodge attempted to tar Iowa Republicans with the brush of big business, using the railroad to do so. In 1858 Forbes had moved the treasurer's office east to Boston, and the ex-treasurer, a local citizen, was persuaded to spread allegations that the eastern owners were buying up land along the railroad for their own benefit, and a faction of citizens called for the resignation of the superintendent, John Read.

Although no evidence has surfaced suggesting that these allegations were true, it was not surprising that they were made. The eastern stockholders and directors who had initially been the railroad's saviors were now regarded as shadowy, unknown figures, perhaps taking control. Railroad finance was complicated. To explain it properly was to introduce the controversial subjects of banks, mortgages, stocks, and bonds, which midwestern populists found deeply suspect and feverishly complicated, especially after the Panic of 1857. Grounds for the ex-treasurer's suspicions may have been created by the curious circumstances surrounding the B&MR's third mortgage. The federal government had passed laws that created a railroad land-grant scheme: railroads were given the land adjacent to their tracks to sell to underwrite construction costs. The land was not available, however, until a railroad had completed twenty-five miles of road by a certain date, and even then it would come only in parcels with each twenty-five miles of track completed thereafter.

It was a generous scheme, but the B&MR had no funds with which to meet the grant's requirements of construction, for it was already twice mortgaged and still underbuilt. By October 1858 Forbes successfully persuaded a few colleagues to guarantee personally a million-dollar mortgage, which served as a kind of bridge loan until the land grant came through, at which time the new assets would underwrite the loan. These personal guarantors created a trust into which the proceeds of the sales of the promised land grant would go, earmarked to repay this million-dollar loan. As further security, they made themselves trustees.*

For people generally suspicious of banking, this financial arrangement perhaps too closely resembled fancy footwork. The long, involved explanations needed to make the situation clear may have sounded to Burlington people like a confidence game. Nevertheless in September another twenty-five miles of track were completed. The B&MR now reached the Des Moines River, roughly halfway across the state, and posters announced that this was "25 miles further west than any other railroad in Iowa." On September 1, a day of festivities celebrated the feat. Railroad cars brought more than 2,500 people to Ottumwa, the westernmost terminus, for speeches, a parade, dancing, and a picnic on the depot grounds. The partying went on all night with dancing, and champagne flowed freely. Antirailroad suspicions vanished. The land grant went through. In November Dodge was defeated, which sealed the fate of Iowa's Democrats. But Lowell also had his own ambivalence. To Higginson he explained:

> Railroading, I fancy, is as honourable as other kinds of business, — you
> know I put them all below honest mechanic handiwork. What makes
> railroading dangerous is the fact that the roads here are built too early.
> Build a cheap road two thirds through a new country, mortgage this
> to build the other one third; then find that the business of the country

---

*Forbes had originally promised this $1 million in March 1857. Then the Panic of 1857 hit, and the crisis with the Michigan Central. Eventually he arranged bonds at 8 percent due in 1883, and raised $833,000. This third mortgage became known as the land mortgage.

is too light to keep the road in thorough running order, to pay interest
on bonds, and to give dividends to needy stockholders,—this is the
history of most Western roads, and this complicates things. In the adjustment of this conflict of interests, the ideal, the good road, perfect
in all its parts, is apt to be lost sight of, and a man simply does the
day's work that lies nearest him, better or worse according to his honesty and talent. This is not cheering, is it, old boy?[15]

Indeed it was not, but Lowell was only beginning to understand the complexities. As land agent, he was in charge of procuring and administering the
railroad land grant received in September 1859 after the track to Ottumwa
was completed. Lowell first had to survey the land, establish clear title to it,
and then organize a program by which the railroad might sell it off. Simple
enough on the surface, in fact it was a morass of red tape, fraud, and contradictory statutes. Although the land-grant legislation gave the B&MR rights
to some 300,000 acres, fully one quarter of this land was contested or compromised by two prior congressional acts—the Preemption Act of 1841 and
the Swamp Act of 1850—both intended, like the railroad's land grant, to promote western settlement. While this was achieved, speculators had abused
the situation; in the land-rich West nothing aroused jealousy and dirty dealings quite so much as land. Speculation had been briefly checked during
the 1857 Panic, but as Lowell discovered, by 1859 it had vigorously resumed.
    Establishing clear title under these circumstances was far from easy. The
surveyors had to establish fair selling prices and investigate numerous claims
against the railroad lands—some of them legitimate, of course, but experiences in Missouri and Michigan suggested that a high proportion would
prove fraudulent. Lowell rejected several surveyors whose methods struck
him as too casual and finally hired two men: Hans Thielsen, a Swede who
had done the original railroad survey, and Harvard classmate John W. Ames,
who had landed penniless in Mendota. His instructions to them were precise and detailed, and he included far more extensive work than a simple
survey. The two men were to gather information on any rock or mineral deposits; to chart wells, springs, ponds, rivers, and creeks; to determine the fer-
tility of the soil and the type of vegetation; to record any buildings; and to
establish the access to the nearest road, village, and town. He equipped the
men with odometers and with questionnaires for local people to fill out. He
wanted them to work quickly, but he counseled them to be careful—particularly as the original survey submitted in 1857 on short notice had been slop-

pily done—to "make your examinations as thorough & your reports as full as if on each 40 acres you were writing to your ladylove & describing the Paradise where you hoped to pass with her a blissful middleage!" Lowell underlined the idea that the "final object of the examination is to get data for the correct *valuation of each 40.*"[16]

With well over 200,000 acres to sell, a difference of a few cents per acre would signify a considerable sum of money. The value of the land had the potential to vary from $1.25 an acre (charged to preemptioners) to as much as $10.50 an acre (which the Hannibal & St. Joseph Railroad was receiving for some of its land).

The original survey had supposedly marked out the railroad's forty-acre allotments, but Lowell's surveyors had terrible trouble finding the markers, many of which were stakes vaguely dropped somewhere near the location. Cold winter weather and horrendous living conditions added to the difficulties. Farmhouses were scarce. At the end of the day the men had to ride as much as four or five miles to find shelter—often only a crude construction that already housed stage drivers, movers, and workmen. Thielsen wrote that he had passed the night in "a constant rotary motion [before a fire] thawing & warming one side while we cooled & froze the other." Some reports sent back to Lowell were written in barely legible pencil because their ink had frozen. Others arrived buckled and smeared from the wet; still others were unreadable, having been written without candlelight. As spring came, the alternating rain and snow made a foot-thick slush on the ground that exhausted horses and made walking almost impossible. So Thielsen and Ames took longer and the work cost more than scheduled, but Lowell assured them not to worry about expense: "I will try to save it elsewhere. The aggregate is trifling compared with the advantage we may reap from knowing exactly what we are selling."[17]

One way in which Lowell proposed to make up lost time and expense was in investigating the many claims against the railroad. To Ames and Thielsen he wrote, "Keep it constantly before the farmers that we are a *railroad* company & not a *land* company—that settlers are more important to us than a high price for our land—& that no claims will be used as an engine of injustice; it would be a miserable policy."[18]

That some claims were fraudulent is beyond doubt; in some cases the fraud was flagrant. But Lowell chose to distinguish among the levels of fraud. He regarded it as petty quibbling to challenge minor infractions or corner-cutting in which a bona fide settler might have indulged. Reports from the surveyors made clear that a good portion of the claims made under the Preemption Act of 1841 were fraudulent only by inadvertence, coming from farmers settled on the wrong land, from naïve farmers who had been "done wrong" by corrupt state officials, or from those who made only slightly improper claims out of poverty, ignorance, and fear. As far as Lowell was concerned, if the net result was to put settlers on the land, he would not argue technicalities. "Pat the children on the head, swear they are the image of their father, and leave all in a good humor. However valid our claim, and however valuable the land, I fancy it will always be our policy to charge bona fide residents only our minimum rates. Therefore by all means save time and avoid offense."[19]

Claims invoking the 1850 Swamp Act he regarded in a different light. Intended to provide states with an incentive to improve poor-quality or useless lands, the act required that the state drain, dike, and levee swamplands and then sell them to subsidize further improvement. But the law was easily abused. In Iowa the state legislature devolved the responsibility for the Swamp Act onto the various counties, then permitted the proceeds from the sale of swamplands to be spent on new town buildings and town amenities. But in many parts of sparsely settled Iowa a county might have only one or two families or even no residents whatsoever. Speculators quickly jumped on the scheme, filing fraudulent or grossly exaggerated claims and tying up land for years, waiting for its value to rise but contributing nothing. Lowell was ruthless in uncovering this fraud. In a letter to a state official Lowell noted, "We are beginning to find that he who buildeth a railroad west of the Mississippi must also find a population and build up business."[20]

On October 17, 1859, John Brown and his gang of eighteen men stormed and occupied the United States Arsenal at Harpers Ferry, Virginia. Their purpose was to foment a slave rebellion that would spread down the Allegheny Mountains into the South in the form of guerrilla bands of runaway or liberated slaves leading hit-and-run attacks on plantations. Brown's raid failed utterly in its purpose. Not one slave joined the rebellion. Having taken control of the arsenal, the raiders almost immediately found themselves trapped in the building. They did more damage to themselves than to anyone else; the first man killed in the incident was black. They were captured largely because of their own incompetence; nevertheless the incident was enough to incite panic. Rumors of slave rebellions coursed through the

South, exciting fear, outrage, and frenzied mob hysteria. In the North the raid was recognized as "misguided, wild, and apparently insane," as the abolitionist William Lloyd Garrison put it.*

Brown accepted his capture, his trial for treason, and his fate of hanging on December 2 with the equanimity of a man who had long been looking for martyrdom. His composure and his effective use of the trial as a national pulpit contributed to that martyrdom. Northerners were impressed by his iron resolve and the manly way in which he faced death. As a result northern public opinion differentiated between the treasonous act and the man's personal nobility. Emerson felt he had made "the gallows as glorious as the cross." Brown gained international prominence: Victor Hugo championed him as "a hero and martyr."[21]

During his trial Brown maintained that he had been working alone. But his papers contained letters making clear the source of his funds—the Kansas Aid Committee, a radical branch of the New England Emigrant Aid Society—and implicating some of its members in the raid. The possibility of a terrorist conspiracy against the South, funded and plotted by New England abolitionists, was political dynamite, deeply embarrassing to the newly successful Republican Party and shaming for the North generally, as it fed the worst suspicions of the South. A Senate committee held investigative hearings for six months to determine whether there had been a larger conspiracy. Of the six men implicated and dubbed the "Secret Six," most were well known to Charlie Lowell. Reverend Theodore Parker, his mother's cousin by marriage, was one of them; he was now abroad dying of tuberculosis. The abolitionist minister Thomas Wentworth Higginson, who had received a saber slash eight years earlier while freeing Thomas Sims, was a friend. His wife was an invalid, and boarded with Anna Lowell at Quincy Street. Higginson openly advocated violent resistance to slavery, and after Frank Sanborn, he was Brown's closest supporter and conspirator in the East. Sanborn was of course Charlie's college friend and a constant presence in the Lowell house. He was a particular favorite of Anna Lowell (who had helped him start his school in Concord). It is scarcely possible

---

*In August 1859 the secretary of war received two anonymous letters from Iowa warning of a planned attack on Harpers Ferry but ignored them as the work of a crank. This leaves open to speculation as to who and how many in Iowa's antislavery community knew of the intended raid. It is hard to believe that Brown's movements through Iowa were not broadly known among the Iowa antislavery men with whom Lowell was friendly, but knowledge of Brown's planned attack, its location, and its timing would have been more closely guarded.

that in their correspondence, mother and son would not have discussed John Brown, the Harpers Ferry raid, the conspiracy, and the work of Sanborn and Higginson. Sanborn had solicited Aunt Hannah's husband, Dr. Cabot, to join the Secret Six. The doctor learned enough of the plan to know he did not want to be part of it.

Like many abolitionists, Anna was also a pacifist. Her fundamental respect for the law prevented her from approving of any effort to break it. But even she knew enough of Sanborn's militant activities to have quarreled with him. As late as January 1860, three months after the raid, Sanborn was still trying to convince Anna that John Brown "was right." Although no traces of her letters to Charlie survive, we know from his replies that she wrote him detailed reports. At the end of January, responding to news that Sanborn had fled to Canada rather than testify before Congress, Lowell asked, "I am sorry that Sanborn is not going to Washington—what is the trouble—is he afraid of implicating others?" Anna's reply must have been scornful, for it elicited this forgiving comment: "Do not be too hard on Sanborn—if he is melodramatic, he is honestly and earnestly so; there is nothing dilletanti about him—he is free from that folly at least."[22]

After his work on the railroad, Charlie no longer believed that, as Sanborn had written in 1856, Kansas presented "the most practical form in which the struggle for freedom had presented itself." His experiences in Iowa confirmed his loathing of slavery and his desire to see it eradicated, but he had come to regard Brown and the Kansas struggle as most westerners did. What in Boston appeared the glory of a freedom fight, in Kansas looked like the murder and mayhem of yet another land grab by common desperadoes and cattle thieves.

Lowell's correspondence dwelt more fully on the Iowa visit of a George Ashburner, of Russell & Co. in Hong Kong, whom Lowell entertained in his farmhouse; three days later Ashburner offered Lowell a job in his Calcutta office, an offer that amounted to the management of the company's opium trade between Turkey, where the poppies were procured, and Canton, where the opium was delivered to runners who smuggled it into China. The offer appeared "on one of our most Arctic days—mercury at zero with a wind," so the idea of a tropical climate alone was enough to tempt him. He recognized that the position in Calcutta was excellent and the offer a compliment, but he refused it nonetheless. Scruples about the propriety of smuggling drugs had "little or no weight" in his refusal. Nor did his mother express qualms. She went so far as to propose her brother Ned for the job instead.[23]

Charlie feared that India's humidity and heat would ultimately grind him down. Although a healthy man is a free agent, he explained that his own situation was different: "a fellow who has been ill feels that his kindred have a new claim on him." Specifically Lowell meant his mother. Her "hold upon me has increased tenfold within four years . . . I cannot disappoint her . . . the long separation would be very hard upon her." He apparently had accepted and assumed with grace his obligation to live a prudent life. His intention was to get well and, once recovered, to pursue some of his old ambitions. Meanwhile he needed a dry climate where he could exercise daily. Writing to Forbes, Lowell noted that although he had been sorely tempted, "the Jacksons belong so distinctly to the useful, and not the ornamental half of mankind—that supposing an independence secured, I am *sure* I shall be happier with hand and head in good working order than with unlimited means of enjoyment." He told his mother that the offer had been "a chance to steal a march on Fortune,—and I believe Fortune will be none the less kind to me, that I have let the chance pass."[24]

What Charlie did not mention was that Anna had also developed "a cough." With her own health in question, she intended to spend part of every year with her son in Iowa. His letters to her were now marked by ease and affection. "You must remember," he wrote, "when you are well I am well; you are the very root of my life now and will be perhaps forever." They recommended books to each other, and she sent large parcels of them to Iowa, which he read imagining her reactions and the conversations they might have. In this pleasure he found something he called selfishness: "I am selfish in every way. It is my nature: but this is a selfishness which your own yearning should make you in part excuse: I am selfish by very dint of having you too much in my heart, and not by forgetting you."[25]

The old ribbing is gone. The guarded acknowledgment of her toughness has vanished. His letters read almost like love letters, though he did not write often and reserved his tenderest expressions for explaining how homesicknesses prevented his writing: "I know how poets ease their hearts by writing out their sorrow, but I am no poet, and the heaviness on my heart is a sweet heaviness which I do not wish to shake off, I wish to gust it fully." Lowell still suffered from a lack of intellectual companionship, which he understood as his need for "human sympathy." But he insisted that he nurtured a greater sense of intimacy and connection by *not* writing. To write would make "object what I now enjoy as subject."[26]

As Harriet's wedding plans moved forward, Anna wrote her son expressing her general relief and pleasure with his life, remarking, "All we want is a wife." The comment raised his hackles: "What does this mean about marrying? No such disloyal sentiment was ever breathed by *me*. A wife—I should as soon think of applying the indefinite article to *a* mother. At present I am not against marriage, but certainly not for it—if ever I meet *the* wife, the matter may have some interest for me." Writing to Henry Higginson, Charlie asked whether he could find him a "true-hearted, violet-eyed woman" like the Giorgione that had so captured his imagination in Italy. Yet his search for the ideal woman did not mean his idea of marriage had improved. In April he wrote his mother, complaining, "As to the groomsman business . . . I am sorry to disappoint Hatty but I cannot really give my countenance so far to the institution of marriage. Cannot George persuade [Jim] Savage?" In June 1860, when Charlie went east for Harriet's wedding, he told Henry, "I have come twelve hundred miles, as you will know, to see the matrimonial noose adjusted around the first of our family."[27]

Charlie did not seem to believe any longer in the sort of plotted, schemed life that had preoccupied him at Harvard. "Don't bother with plans," he told Henry, "but be governed by circumstance. Damn it, a man who has got himself up as much as you ought to be happy enough anywhere. Even I manage that, since I was abroad, and as for use,—mind your own business, and you cannot help being useful." As he discouraged Henry from excessive earnestness, he reminded him of where he, too, would return. His letters to Henry, still in Europe, employed the adjective *puritan* with new frequency. From the "Puritan Isle" of Naushon, he had called his oldest friend a "whey-drinking, backward-looking old hydropath." From the "Puritan city" of Boston, the "levity" of Henry's letter from Düsseldorf "was more grating to my serious mind than it might have been in the city of Burlington." To the suggestion that he join Henry and Johnny in Europe for the summer, Charlie replied that "ten years from now" he would live "in a little Italian villa, and . . . enjoy the sunshine and the gray olives and the people, cattle, and the fullness of Italy." But were these ten years the same as the "five or ten years among men and things" that would "educate" him, as he had declared to Stephen, or the same ten years that he had told his mother would "complete his character," or perhaps the same "ten years to make the largest fortune in Boston" or the same ten years which his great-uncle had demanded he devote to "climate, living where the air was dry, and where the weather invited to exercise"?[28]

Whenever Lowell mentioned "ten years," the implication was a decade of apprenticeship—to make money, to educate himself, to regain his health —after which he would achieve a certain freedom. In every instance, he assumes a period of duty, obligation, a sort of indenture for self-tempering or refinement. In his earliest references he meant freedom to pursue some philanthropic reform. When he first had a job, he sought the freedom to return to books, theories, and the life of the mind. After his European odyssey the goal was freedom to return to Italy. As Lowell became more "useful," his future dreams involved the selfish "happiness" he had experienced in Europe. Reconciling himself to his Iowa sojourn, he had told his mother: "Gold digging till I am 35, then—big nugget or empty pockets, I shall vote myself free." To George Ashburner he explained, "My first duty is to earn an independence, enough to support myself and one or both of my sisters, if necessary. We are all brought up to economy and shall not require more than I can reasonably hope to lay by in 10 or 15 years in the West."[29]

In the autumn of 1860 Lowell received a position as ironmaster of the Mount Savage Iron Works near Cumberland, Maryland. He accepted with alacrity. This return to his old love of ironwork and his earlier pursuit of a career in manufacturing perhaps signaled that he was once again well enough to "toil terribly." In his resignation letter to Denison, treasurer of the B&MR, Lowell wrote:

> I know I may assume without vanity that you will be sorry to hear I have resigned my place on B.&M.—I know it because I am sorry myself to tell you so, though I am changing to a business which has always had the strongest attractions for me. I have never got over the "iron-fever," and when a place was offered me at Mt. Savage, though the pecuniary prospect was no better than at Burlington, the chance to become an iron-master was too good to be refused.[30]

Two years in Iowa had vastly improved Lowell's health and spirits. His work on the B&MR had been difficult and demanding, and he had carried it out with sense, good spirit, and integrity. Although he had spent barely a year and a half on the land grant, he had established its policies, set its tone, and trained young Charles Eliot Perkins to take his place. Lowell's respect for Perkins was strong; his letters to Denison and to Forbes assured them: "Perkins is an exceedingly smart man . . . I would suggest that he would command respect in almost any position, for his judgment is excellent . . .

No endorsement [of Perkins] is needed from me, but I offer my guaranty that both personally and B.M.ically you will be glad you have got him."[31]

The new plan pleased Forbes, since he owned the Mount Savage Iron Works and was simply transferring Lowell to another element of his interests. The object at Mount Savage would be much the same as it had been at Burlington: putting a somewhat troublesome investment on a stable footing.

Lowell felt profound satisfaction in taking this new position. The cautious years of half measures, of scrupulous attention to his health, of delaying and deferring his ambitions and interests, appeared to have paid off. With a greater sense of well-being, self-knowledge, and conviction, Lowell left Burlington and moved to Maryland.

EIGHT

THE BORDER STATE OF MARYLAND

1860–61

The peculiar geography of Maryland, quintessentially a border state looking both north and south, emphasized its diversity. The central, eastern portion much resembled Virginia, to the southwest, and 54 percent of its population was slave. Large tobacco plantations with magnificent houses were home to many of Maryland's oldest families. One in nine whites owned slaves. Measured by all the standards a northerner like Charlie Lowell would apply, the area was backward: there were few towns, schools, churches, or hospitals, and the roads were of very poor quality.

On the far side of the Chesapeake Bay was Maryland's Eastern Shore, an isolated peninsula, home mostly to "watermen" living off the bay and its estuaries. Only one in twenty whites there owned slaves, and half the black population was free. The Eastern Shore's sandy soil, too poor for tobacco, was rich in orchards and small farms. Here was one of the few places where slavery was disappearing for entirely pragmatic reasons.

Western Maryland, shaped like a long finger pointing west across the Alleghenies, took on a northern orientation largely because of its railroads, coalfields, and industry. Only one in fifty-eight of its white population owned slaves, usually only one. Through the Cumberland Gap, where the Potomac River cuts through the Allegheny Mountains across a rugged landscape, early pioneers moved west: through old mountains, their peaks worn down to windswept knobs, with steep sides, narrow valleys, and hollows, at the bottom of which ran rocky, fast-moving creeks.

Seven miles west of Cumberland, in one of those clefts, stood Mount Savage, amid one of the southernmost iron and coal deposits in the eastern Alleghenies, a counterpart to Lycoming in the North. The Cumberland & Pennsylvania Railroad connected the area to Pittsburgh, while the Baltimore & Ohio Railroad gave access both east and west.

The history of the Mount Savage Iron Works illustrates the vagaries of the iron business. Opened in the ill-fated year of 1837, the company joined the race to build a hot-blast furnace and won it, producing the first heavy iron railroad rails in America by 1844. These two achievements earned it "the highest honors in connection with the American iron trade." By 1845 the company was turning out two hundred tons of iron a week. Despite this successful early history, within a decade the original company was bankrupt. Shortly thereafter John Murray Forbes bought it; in 1853 Mount Savage resumed operations, the business growing and the town's population doubling every two years. A highly aggressive firm, Mount Savage gave Lowell's old employer Abram Hewitt his principal competition in rail manufacture.[1]

The move to Mount Savage coincided with the election of 1860. Charlie had been an early Lincoln supporter. "Deliberately I prefer Lincoln to Seward," he had written from Iowa in May, at the time of the Republican convention in Chicago. Most New England Republicans had supported the New York senator William H. Seward, who had coined the terms "a higher law" and "irrepressible conflict." But he was rejected nevertheless, partly because of his connection to the corrupt New York boss Thurlow Weed and also because he had tempered his earlier unequivocal statements against slavery. Lowell explained, "Lincoln is emphatic on the irrepressible conflict, without *if* or *but*." More important, Lincoln was a midwesterner with a regional reputation, and he could split if not steal midwestern voters from Douglas. Lowell explained that if an easterner had been picked, Iowa "would have gone for Douglas." Forbes was a delegate to the Chicago convention and had voted for Lincoln, believing him the party's best chance of winning the election, but he cautioned a friend, "There is some danger that we shall be disgusted with a repetition of the log-cabin and hard-cider style of campaigning which was so successful in the Harrison election." The election would hang on how the Midwest voted.[2]

The Republicans' task was to continue the assault on Douglas that Lincoln had begun in 1858. They needed to show Douglas to be a man heavily compromised by the Slave Power, the aristocratic plantation owners whose oligarchic despotism had for decades been the main impediment to American economic development. Obstructing the development of new states and expansion into new territories, they had held up railroad charters, land grants, and other federal legislation that benefited western settlers. (This did not mean that the South was anti-expansionist: through the 1850s it had pressed for an invasion of Cuba and Nicaragua as fertile fields to expand the slave culture.)

But the election was further complicated when both parties split along regional lines, thus creating four parties with four candidates. In April at the Democratic convention southern delegates had walked out rather than support Stephen Douglas. Shock at the Harpers Ferry raid, fear of further violence, suspicions of conspiracy, and the North's having made a martyr of John Brown created among southerners an intense distrust of all Yankees. A second meeting did not heal the rift. The southern Democrats supported Kentucky senator John C. Breckenridge, and the northern delegates stuck with Douglas, who campaigned as a national candidate claiming that only he could save the Union. Meanwhile the last gasp of the old Whig Party, in the form of the Constitutional Union Party, fielded John Bell of Tennessee for president, with Edward Everett from Massachusetts as vice president.

This fracturing of the vote favored the little-known Republican candidate, and Lincoln's election in November 1860 provoked an immediate and frenzied furor in the South. Lowell found his five months as ironmaster in Maryland overshadowed by the political tensions increasing everywhere in the country. At a northern-owned ironworks in a border state sharply divided between its agricultural slave-owning eastern half and its mountainous, industrial western half, he was in a position to observe many facets of the slavery issue and to feel acutely the implications of the political dilemma concerning it. "Living in a border state," he wrote his mother, "politics are personally too interesting for me to enjoy the papers. It is hard to see clearly."[3]

In the southern press peaceful submission to a Lincoln administration was presented as the equivalent of suicide; agitation for secession began immediately. Lincoln was seen as a radical and revolutionary leader at the head of a central government that wished to usurp the authority of the individual states in order to impose an oppressive and penurious regime. In what has been called a "pre-emptive counter-revolution," the states of the Deep South, led by South Carolina, began to secede, justifying their actions by rhetorically linking them to "the Spirit of 1776."[4]*

The spring of 1860 saw a general exodus of northerners—tutors, adminis-

---

*Most southerners, slave owners or not, believed that American democracy required slave labor. Slavery put all white men above "the menial class" and united them in a "true aristocracy." Even if they could not afford to own slaves themselves, they believed the liberty to do so was the basis of democracy and that without slave labor, the equality of white men would inevitably be destroyed.

trators, businessmen, and agents—from the South. Ties to the South were so weak that most northerners, ignorant of southern opinion, lacked personal experience with the South or its people. Thus when Lowell found himself in New Orleans on iron business for most of December 1860, he was one of a very few northerners who witnessed firsthand a rally supporting South Carolina's secession. "It was an instructive spectacle," Charlie wrote home. "I wonder whether the signers of our Declaration of Independence looked as silly as those fellows." Lowell could not take the southern passion for secession seriously despite the heated atmosphere. "The *vote* of New Orleans city will show a large majority for Union," he declared.[5]

At the same time in Boston Anna had attended a rally at Faneuil Hall to commemorate the anniversary of John Brown's hanging, a meeting intended to build support for Massachusetts's new Republican governor, John Albion Andrew, the abolitionist lawyer who had defended Brown and his conspirators. Instead, a band of thugs broke up the gathering, beat some free blacks, and threatened Wendell Phillips's life. Anna wrote to Charlie of her alarm, shock, and shame at what she described as the suppression of free speech. His reply makes clear that he recognized the provincialism of Massachusetts's radicals.

> I have no sympathy with those John-Brownists, nor do I believe they will make much out of the "Free-Speech" cry. It was a piece of rowdyism to break up their meeting, but at the same time a proof the more how free speech is in Massachusetts. Fancy a parcel of Union-savers breaking up a fanatical Southern-rights meeting in New Orleans, and you have an exact parallel. But in New Orleans a Union-lover dare not speak under his breath. Beyond "co-operation" no man's courage hath yet ventured. This to be sure means "time" and "time" means "submission"; but even co-operation finds few and feeble advocates.[6]

Lowell was referring to moderate southerners who, seeking to calm the agitation by arguing to wait and see what the Republican president would do before seceding, were mocked for their caution.

Little more than a month later Louisiana seceded. Lowell, like almost all northerners, realized he had miscalculated. Although well aware that political discussion was suppressed in the South, he had been sure it would not act against its own self-interest, and the economic arguments against secession were compelling. The South had weathered the Panic of 1857 because of its near monopoly on the supply of cotton for British and French mills. In 1858 the South Carolinian James Hammond had crowed, "The slaveholding South is now the controlling power of the world . . . No power on earth dares . . . to make war on cotton. Cotton is king."[7] But this hubris rested on simplistic economic analysis. By late 1859 and 1860 most railroading men had become convinced that the Cotton Kingdom would not last. The Panic of 1857 had also revealed how the economies of the North and West were, thanks to the railroads, integrated with European markets. The price of grain in Burlington, Iowa, was linked to political events in the Crimea, as Lowell already knew from his experience in the winter of 1855 buying western wheat for France. This was the beginning of an international economy, with interrelated vulnerabilities, whose real measure of economic health was the ability to rebound from temporary setbacks. The South's failure to diversify its economy and its feeble infrastructure confirmed its shortsightedness, a point evident to New Englanders with business there. And without Yankee banking instruments, the South would have trouble raising the funds to begin to repair its neglect.

In December 1860 Henry Varnum Poor, a railroad analyst who for years had been following closely the effect of the railroads on patterns of trade, declared in a *New York Times* editorial, "The peaceable effect of Secession may be to close [the Mississippi's] mouth, in which event the entire trade of the Valley could be easily, and in the end to the convenience of all, sent over the Northern and Eastern [railroad] routes."[8] Lowell, like most responsible railroad men, respected Poor's analysis and opinion.

To Henry Higginson, who had just returned from Europe and now had to begin serious work, Charlie wrote in late December that he took Poor's analysis of the American economy seriously, and placed little trust in what he had seen in New Orleans, but he could not predict events: "If you have any respectable mode of getting through your days, and do not feel yourself in danger of becoming a demned disreputable, dissatisfied loafer, I should advise you to be in no hurry to plunge into trade. Cotton is unthroned, but Corn is not yet king, and meanwhile Chance rules. The South is just now a mere mob, and *no man* can tell whither a mob may rush."[9]

On January 20, 1861, after years of declining health and repeated strokes, Reverend Lowell died. He had served as pastor of the West Church for fifty-five years—a remarkably long tenure, especially considering the doctrinal controversies of the period. Perhaps for this reason, Lowell had stubbornly refused to enter into any of the controversies and took no denomination, declaring that "Christian" would suffice. Ministry and good works, not theology, were his emphasis, and this won him the love and loyalty of his huge congregation, all of whom he had known personally. The reverend's death marked the passing of an era. Born before the Revolution, Charles Lowell had been the youngest of the Lowell-Jackson children raised in that "system of seclusion" begun on the High Street of Newburyport and perpetuated within the houses and alleyways of Winter Street and Temple Court.

Perhaps distracted by his grandfather's death, Charlie did not grasp the severity of the political crisis. As late as the end of January 1861, after the secession of five states, he continued to take a strongly economic view of events. Writing to his mother, "One thing is *clear*," he declared, "that the South have struck a blow at their Cotton King which he will never get well over. The mischief is already done. Cotton must and will be raised elsewhere, too. Whether or no the agitators succeed in their political game of brag, it is certain they will repent hereafter the damage to their material interests in the Union or out of it."[10]

But compromise efforts to save the Union failed whether in the Senate, in the House, or at a Virginia Peace Convention, which met in February at Washington. There, leading citizens from the northern states hoped to restore past regional civility. Massachusetts had at first refused to participate, but Charles Francis Adams finally persuaded Governor Andrew to show a willingness to participate. However, the Massachusetts legislature so hampered its state delegation that the exercise was futile. Nevertheless Lowell wrote a letter of support to John Murray Forbes, one of the delegates, saying, "If Massachusetts stands where Charles Francis Adams has put her, it seems to me she will be right, and will look right in history. I did not know till now that Webster was so nearly correct in his 7th of March speech. I have always supposed he stretched the facts to suit his purposes." This approval of Adams and reappraisal of Webster represented a remarkable moderation of his previous views—an influence, no doubt, of his experiences in railroading.

As the peace convention was foundering, the seven seceded states were convening in Mobile to establish a confederacy. Lowell referred to them as "Benjamin & Co.," after Louisiana's Senator Judah P. Benjamin. Thus while northern states searched for a compromise, debating whether too much would be given away, or whether the bullying of the South was all brag, or whether Lincoln's inauguration would quell talk of secession, the seceded states were creating their own constitution, establishing a cabinet, and appointing a president. Compromise never really had a chance.

Meanwhile even more states seceded, until the entire Deep South had removed itself from the Union. Still Lowell was not too worried, though he doubted "if any compromise which did not virtually acknowledge the right of secession would be acceptable here [in Maryland]." Early in February he attended a Union meeting near Mount Savage, in Maryland. He described it as "more anti-slavery than Faneuil Hall dares to be" but acknowledged that Maryland still generally supported the South. Lowell was not thinking that secession would inevitably mean civil war. He considered it just as likely that the South, with its "fighting mania," would set off on an empire-building scheme. For decades southerners had been interested in U.S. expansion southward as a means of increasing slaveholding territories and ensuring its political power (viz., the Mexican War). An attack on Cuba or Nicaragua (both long coveted by southerners) would provoke Britain or Spain to defend its interests in the Western Hemisphere. This, Lowell thought, would drive the Confederacy to seek Union military support, thus "enabling us to re-cement the Union on *our* terms."[11]

By late March, however, Lowell was baffled. Lincoln's long-awaited inauguration made little difference to the simmering crisis. He remained an enigmatic, equivocating figure. Meanwhile the Confederacy had united under a constitution, installed a president and a cabinet, and was demanding international recognition. As each state seceded, it had taken control of federal property within its borders: mints, arsenals, customs houses, forts, and federal buildings. South Carolina was the exception. In Charleston harbor Fort Sumter remained under the command of Colonel Robert Anderson, who, despite the continued demands of South Carolina's new government, had refused to vacate it. As the months passed and his supplies ran low, Anderson's position became increasingly awkward.

South Carolina's secessionist representatives were forcing the issue with characteristic pugnacity, demanding the fort and challenging the federal government's right to maintain it. If South Carolina could force the government to abandon Sumter, it could use that act to legitimize secession, claiming that the federal government had recognized the new Confederacy and was allowing the peaceful dismemberment of the Union. Lincoln had sworn at his inauguration to uphold, protect, and defend the Union as it stood. Now his first presidential act threatened to be recognition of the Confederate states; tacit admission of dissolution. Lincoln stalled, refusing either to meet the South Carolina delegation or to receive their letters.

Lowell was not convinced by Lincoln's game of "possum." "Lincoln must *act* soon," he wrote his mother. He thought that Lincoln's inaction would irretrievably damage his authority and saw two possible courses: Lincoln might force the crisis by asserting federal power, such as collecting taxes in the southern states; alternatively, if Lincoln wanted to avert war, then he could recognize the "Cotton Confederacy" and simultaneously recommend a constitutional amendment to prevent any future secession. "It is absurd to talk of *national* deliberation with seven States in open revolution; but if attempted, not Slavery but Secession should be forever laid. Let the States that claim it as a right make a Confederacy, and the States that do not claim it a Union."

This attitude closely tracked that of his uncle, James Russell Lowell, who in the February issue of *The Atlantic Monthly* had contributed an article, "E Pluribus Unum," which argued that the United States was "a unitary and indivisible nation, with a national life to protect, a national power to maintain, and national rights to defend." To the question of what to do if more states seceded, James humorously suggested that "we shall need something like a Fugitive Law for runaway republics."[12]

Pandering to the border states did not strike Charlie as wise: "I sincerely hope that Lincoln will not consult too nicely what is *acceptable* even to the Border States." He wanted Lincoln "to take his stand on the principles which the framers of the Constitution stood upon, and if there comes a collision, [to] call upon the Border States *alone* to aid him—I believe they would at once rally to sustain him, even in a course which they would now pronounce totally *un*acceptable." But Lincoln in fact wisely took the extreme opposite tack. The ensuing events would almost certainly not have followed Lowell's scenario.

On April 12, the confrontation at Fort Sumter came. While supply ships attempted to land, South Carolina guns reduced the fort to rubble. On April 14 Lincoln called on the states to produce 75,000 troops. Lowell fired off a note to his mother: "this war news is so startling that I do not quite know where I am." Yet his reaction was entirely practical: "I fear our Government will be hard pushed for the next six months—it can raise 75,000 men easily enough, but can it use them?"[13]

Lowell went to Baltimore on business and stayed on through the weekend of April 17 because a secessionist convention had convened there. With the outbreak of hostilities, the pro-Southern forces in Maryland had shifted into high gear. Recruiters for the Confederacy were active in the city; South Carolina's Palmetto flag was a frequent sight. Gangs milled about. Attempting to appease the border states, Lincoln had maneuvered to make it appear that the South was the aggressor and that troops were needed for the defense of the Union, or at least of federal property. Most Marylanders, however strong their pro-Union inclinations, were emotionally tied to the South. They would not participate in the use of force or coercion against it. News that Virginia's state convention had passed an ordinance of secession that same weekend further heated the situation.

On the evening of April 18, Baltimore's "Southern Rights Convention" endorsed a number of resolutions supporting secession. It was obvious to everyone that if Maryland seceded, the United States would find its capital, legislature, executive, and government apparatus well inside Confederate territory.

In Boston Lincoln's call to arms of April 14 met an immediate response. Decades of popular ambivalence appeared to end in an instant. Emerson described it as "an affair of instincts . . . we did not know we had them; . . . —and now a sentiment mightier than logic, wide as light, strong as gravity, reaches into the college, the bank, the farm-house, and the church. It is the day of the populace; they are wiser than their teachers . . . I will never again speak lightly of a crowd." Charles Eliot Norton, more conservative, more deliberate, reflecting the traditional New England patrician fear of mobs and the irrational, tried to cast the new war spirit in the light of sober judgment, as an expression of a naturally conservative people. It was not a "contagion of a short-lived popular excitement" but a result of the people's "conservative love of order, government, and law." The Russian ambassador had a more pragmatic interpretation of events: "The stagnation of business and industry threw thousands of persons onto the streets who found relief only in the army."[14]

This last observation was sadly true. Over the preceding months, the loss of southern markets had hit Massachusetts factories badly. Even more to the point, under the astute and courageous leadership of Governor Andrew, the state had been preparing for war even while Lowell was doubting war would ever come. Thanks to this advance preparation, Massachusetts almost immediately shipped four regiments south under General Benjamin F. Butler, the former Democratic legislator and state senator, now a brigadier general. Three more followed by train. Within two days of Lincoln's call for troops, the Sixth Massachusetts Regiment had headed south.

Northern troops intended for the defense of Washington had to change trains in Baltimore, marching across the city to the southern depot. Were

Baltimore to block their passage, Washington would be completely defenseless. Even before the war began, the Confederacy would control the capital. That very day, April 18, two companies of artillery passing through Baltimore had been subjected to random verbal harassment, but nothing more. Now, with the excitement of the convention, Baltimoreans were urged to arm themselves and prevent more northern troops from heading south. Both the governor of Maryland and the mayor of Baltimore believed they could no longer control the mobs. They telegraphed to Boston that no more troops should be sent through Baltimore. Andrew ignored the warning.

Chaos was now nearly complete. Distrust in the reliability of the Baltimore authorities encouraged Massachusetts to provide no information about its troops' arrival. As rumors swirled that more regiments were on their way, the mood of the gangs grew more and more restive. City officials were unable to take preparatory steps. Definitive word came only when the railroad signaled the imminent arrival of the train shortly before eleven a.m. on April 19. The soldiers were the Sixth Massachusetts and a regiment of Pennsylvania uniformed militia, seventeen hundred men all together. As word spread through the Baltimore mobs that troops had arrived, the recognition of the Massachusetts uniforms as "abolitionist" added fuel to the mobs' fury.

The plan had been to move the troops in small groups (on the mistaken assumption that they would be less obtrusive). They were duly dispatched from the depot company by company, taking horse-drawn trolleys along the mile-and-a-half route through the busiest commercial area of downtown Baltimore. As word spread of what was afoot, mobs massed along the streets, obstructing the track with bricks, sand, and other objects. Rocks and paving stones struck the trolleys. Although the first companies arrived unharmed at the southern depot, each successive trolley took longer and arrived more battered. Eventually no more came. Two hundred men were missing.

The Baltimore police and the mayor had for some unexplained reason stationed themselves at the southern depot. Of course they could offer no help to the troops that had not yet arrived. When it became clear that the missing two hundred men were stranded, the mayor dashed toward the northern station, encountering a violent mob surrounding the last companies of Massachusetts men as they marched double-time down the main thoroughfare. Bricks, cobblestones, and an occasional bullet flew. The mayor tried to restore order by marching at the head of the troops, slowing their pace, and uttering a clear verbal defense. But within a few minutes stones once again began to fly. Rioters assaulted soldiers and seized their muskets. One soldier panicked and fired; then the whole line began shooting. The horrified mayor waved his umbrella wildly and rushed about, screaming, "For God's sake, don't shoot!" But it was not until a large police detachment arrived and placed itself between the troops and the mob, with orders to fire on the Baltimore mob if necessary, that the rioters retreated.

The last of the Massachusetts troops left Baltimore at one p.m. Two hours in the city had left four soldiers dead and three dozen wounded, twelve citizens dead and an unknown number wounded. The Pennsylvania militia, which had never left the first station, returned by the next train to Philadelphia. Baltimore remained in an explosive state. The mayor and governor tried, with small success, to calm the crowd that evening at a mass meeting. The governor in particular was deeply shaken by events, and his speech reflected his exhaustion and distress. "I love my State and I love the Union, but I will suffer my right arm to be torn from my body before I will raise it to strike a sister State." The mayor was helpless. With an unappeasable mob, a distraught governor, and no clear support from either Washington or other states, the civic leaders could not prevent further violence. Deciding in a late-night meeting to destroy the railroad bridges connecting Baltimore to the North, the next day they sent out the home guard and the Baltimore police to burn them. By the evening of April 20 Baltimore had cut itself off from the North. One official explained, "Baltimore was veritably crazy."[15]

The city was filled with armed men, some of them newly deputized policemen. Of these a number were eager for another confrontation with federal troops. Militia from other counties, along with private citizens, poured into Baltimore, all eager for a fight. Maryland's moderation and neutrality evaporated. It was ready to secede, despite the pro-Union sympathies of its leading politicians.

Charlie Lowell assumed Maryland would secede. He recognized that he had been entirely wrong in his earlier assessments. Living in the more modernized western part of Maryland, he had failed to consider the southern sentiments on the Eastern Shore. Over the course of that night and the next day, he managed to get to Washington. With rail lines torn up and the borders closed, Lowell arrived after "several detentions." He was traveling with the English captain Charles Stewart, an abolitionist and guerrilla from Kansas days. Stewart had spent the last several years in the West, where he had helped runaway slaves escape from Missouri and Kansas into Iowa; he had also become involved with Kansas Free State militias. In this capacity he had come to know Frank Sanborn, whom he had visited in Concord. Sanborn believed that Stewart had been "besieged, shot at, cut with a bowie knife, &c., passing thro' the ordinary Kansas experiences" and intended to fund his further enterprises. How and when Sanborn introduced Stewart to Lowell is unknown—whether in Iowa or more recently—but he was a remarkably fortunate traveling companion with whom to cross closed borders and evade authority at the outbreak of a civil war.[16]

From a letter Lowell wrote his mother that same evening, it is clear that the catalyst to Lowell's abandoning Mount Savage to join the Union cause was not the attack on Fort Sumter but the shooting of Massachusetts men in Baltimore: "I want to see the Baltimore traitors put on trial at once, and armed rebellion everywhere crushed out." Lowell's newfound patriotism was closely interlinked with a new pride in, and loyalty to, his state. "Henceforth I will always hail from Massachusetts," he wrote on the envelope of this letter home.[17]

PART II

THE MINOTAUR

Action, then, is the Minotaur which claims and devours our youths: Athens bewailed the seven who yearly left her shore; with us scarce seven remain, and we urge the victims to their fate.

—Charles Russell Lowell, Commencement Day oration, 1854

The Gentlemen's War

NINE

A REGULAR COMMISSION

1861–62

On April 21, when Charlie Lowell arrived in Washington, the capital was largely deserted. Hotels had emptied, shops were boarded up, houses vacant, offices closed. A skeleton staff ran the government. The city lay suspended in stillness. What news reached it was bad: rail lines were ripped up, roads were closed, the telegraph was down, mail had stopped. The Norfolk Navy Yard was lost, the arsenal at Harpers Ferry destroyed, the bridges across the Potomac burned. Rumors of attack and sabotage were rife.

Lowell arranged to stay with Count Adam Gurowski, a one-eyed Polish revolutionary who, exiled in America, worked as a translator for the State Department and had become friends with liberal Americans such as Mary Lowell Putnam, James Russell Lowell, and the abolitionist Wendell Phillips. Gurowski was an abolitionist himself, but his main appeal to Lowell was precisely that he was a foreigner, a safer haven at a time when the sympathies of most Washingtonians were unclear and invasion from Virginia was a feared prospect.

Gurowski was a member of Clay's Guards, one of two informal companies created over the previous week to defend the capital. Led by the Republican senator Cassius Clay, it patrolled the streets and guarded Willard's Hotel, the grandest and largest hotel-cum-boardinghouse in the city, which was used by senators, diplomats, and other important visitors. The other company, the Frontier Guards, under the former Kansas fighter, now senator, James Lane, was quartered in the Executive Mansion to guard the president. These two companies were commanded by Major David Hunter, an abolitionist and a personal friend of Lincoln's. They were essentially vigilantes: untrained and unreliable but unquestioningly loyal.

The real defense of Washington rested on a handful of regular companies under Major Irvin McDowell at the Capitol and Captain William Franklin at the Treasury, and on the reconstituted district militia commanded by Colonel Charles P. Stone, who was quickly promoted to general. In the defensive strategy devised by Stone and the army commander General Winfield Scott, the Treasury was to be the final citadel of defense against a Confederate attack. Both men knew that their plan was more symbolic than potentially effective. The capital—entirely within the borders of slaveholding states, its citizenry largely composed of southerners sympathetic to the Confederacy, and unlikely to get significant reinforcements to the inadequate federal garrison—was a ripe plum to be picked almost at will.

Lowell immediately set about finding a position in the Union army. Unimpressed with the vigilante companies and influenced by Captain Stewart, who quickly became an aide on Stone's staff, Lowell tried for a place in the regular army, not one of the state volunteer regiments. "While the *volunteers* will furnish fully their share of military talent, and more than their share of food for powder, it will fall mainly on the *Regular* organization to keep the armies in the field and to keep them moving."[1] As a civilian with no military experience, it was clear that he would need help. He wrote to Massachusetts senator Charles Sumner, whom he had never met, presenting his qualifications. He mentioned that he could "speak and write English, French, and Italian, and read German and Spanish," and that he had once known "enough of Mathematics to put me at the head of my class in Harvard"; he claimed to be "a tolerable proficient with the small sword and singlestick" (from his exercises in Algiers) and to be able to "ride a horse as far and bring him in as fresh as any other man." (He probably knew more about horses than most northerners.) Finally, he wrote, "I am twenty-six years of age, and believe I possess more or less of that moral courage about taking responsibility which seems at present to be found only in Southern officers."

Lowell named his uncle, James Russell Lowell, and his mentor, John Murray Forbes, as two men who could "put you in the way of hearing more about my qualifications." Neither belonged to Senator Sumner's inner circle, but James Lowell, as editor of *The Atlantic Monthly*, was a respected Republican spokesman and politically astute, while Forbes was a highly active and philanthropic Massachusetts Republican. Lowell explained his presence in Washington despite the closed border and suggested that by corresponding through Gurowski (whom Sumner knew and who had access to the diplomatic bag), they could circumvent the disruption of mail and telegraph communication between Washington and the North. He concluded,

"I should prefer the artillery. I believe, with a week or two of preparation, I could pass the examinations."[2]

The letter was forthright both in its request and in Lowell's estimation of himself. This quality perhaps distinguishes it from the countless others that Sumner and every other politician received in the following months. Lowell made no attempt to flatter either Sumner or himself. He was not falsely modest; nor did he try to conform to the ideal profile of an artillery officer. But he did communicate the urgency of the moment most forcefully. The letter reads as if it had been written before its author had even unpacked the modest contents of his carpetbag: two flannel shirts and six collars.

A similar urgency informs Lowell's hurried note to Uncle Ned asking, and assuming, that Ned Jackson would make arrangements for credit (pledged against his pay due from Mount Savage), as he had come away with no money. "I have come down here anticipating that Lincoln's 'masterly inactivity' would soon force a crisis," he added.

Masterly inactivity is exactly what Lincoln's game had been. But despite its political success, playing possum had done nothing to prepare the North, much less Washington, for war. Lowell was not dismayed: "I was fortunate to be in Baltimore last Sunday and to be here [Washington] at present: how Jim and Henry will envy me." He meant Jim Savage and Henry Higginson, but he might have meant any number of others: most young men shared this urge to be present and to take part. It was described at the time as "the fire fed by love of adventure, contagion of example, fear of losing the chance of participating in the great events of the time, desire for personal distinction." In short, war fever.

Unlike most young men, Lowell imagined neither that the task ahead would be simple and easy nor that the war would be over quickly. He did not see his contribution as a temporary interruption to civilian life. He wrote to Sumner, "Whether the Union stands or falls . . . the profession of arms will henceforth be more desirable and more respected . . . the army will again become a profession . . . I want to be in a position to take the best advantage of it." For Lowell this meant a post in the regular army.[3]

During the first week of war, Lowell succeeded in obtaining an interview with the secretary of war. Simon Cameron must have looked at him skeptically: a slight, rather shabby young man with boyish looks—curling locks, a somewhat pretty face, barely enough facial hair to shave. What did this jaded and corrupt former Democratic senator from Pennsylvania make of

Lowell's earnest, enthusiastic, forthright manner? "You, young man," Cameron boomed, "what do you know of a horse?"

Lowell repeated what he had written to Sumner: "Enough to take a hard day's work out of him and to bring him back fresh at night." After the interview Lowell wrote home that Secretary Cameron had promised him a second lieutenancy in the flying artillery.[4]

It was a stroke of luck that Lowell had been able to meet Cameron so early, for within a week the sleepy little southern town with its unfinished Capitol and its muddy streets was overwhelmed by twenty thousand volunteer troops. The first to arrive, on April 25, was the Seventh New York Regiment. All of beleaguered Washington turned out to cheer as, with bands playing, flags flying, and uniforms ablaze with shiny buttons and gold braid, they marched to salute the president. The fact that they were militiamen, signed on for only thirty days, and that those thirty days would represent, in many cases, their entire service in the Union cause, was beside the point. They were greeted with enthusiasm for what they symbolized: the fighting North.

Other regiments quickly followed. By May 1 Washington was swarming with young men and their paraphernalia. The first to arrive camped in federal buildings; the others swarmed over the Mall and any other available open ground. Also descending on the capital were scores, even hundreds, of patriotic or self-serving men, all eager to grasp the opportunity presented by war. Willard's Hotel, to which Lowell moved once he had obtained credit, was jammed with "crowds of long-limbed, nervous, eagerlooking men, in loose black garments, undulating shirt collars, vast conceptions in hatting and booting, angular with documents and pregnant with demand." To anyone who would listen, these do-gooders, busybodies, and instant experts expounded their urgent theories and requests. They blocked corridors, filled lobbies, and ignored signs asking them "to move on from in front of the cigarstand."[5]

In the Seventh New York Regiment were Frank Barlow and Rob Shaw, friends ever since Barlow had lived with the Shaw family in 1856 as a tutor preparing Rob for Harvard. Lowell and Shaw had last seen each other on Naushon Island. Because the Seventh was a thirty-day militia, both Barlow and Shaw were eager to obtain a more permanent appointment in a volunteer regiment. Barlow, since leaving Harvard and tutoring young Shaw, had become a lawyer and moved to New York City; after an engagement of over three years, he had married the day before he left New York. He now sought a place for himself in a New York volunteer regiment.

Also in Washington were other friends and acquaintances of Lowell's, seeking positions for themselves on the staff of senior officers and making other special requests. One of the first Lowell ran into was Wilder Dwight, from the class ahead of him at Harvard and a cousin of his close friend Johnny Bancroft. Dwight was in Washington to get permission to form the Second Massachusetts Volunteer Infantry. He intended it to be a crack regiment; he had secured regular officers as its colonel and lieutenant colonel, taking only the majority himself. Among his captains were many of Lowell's friends, James Savage and Henry Higginson among them. Dwight offered both Lowell and Shaw a captaincy. Lowell chose to wait for his commission in the regular army. Shaw joined Dwight and the Second Massachusetts Infantry despite being envious of Lowell's imagination and guts in writing to Sumner for help in securing a regular commission. He was ready to resign his commission in the Second Massachusetts if he too could find a cavalry commission. He wrote his mother, "I think he [Lowell] is the cleverest young man I know & will do well in any position," and Mrs. Shaw wrote Lowell's uncle James, "Rob has lost his heart to your nephew Charles Lowell at Washington."[6]

By late May there were between 200,000 and 250,000 men, largely untrained, in Washington. As Lowell had predicted, the Union could "raise 75,000 men easily enough" but was at a loss to know what to do with them. The weeks passed, and "not the first step [was] made to organize them into an army, to form brigades, not to say divisions." Citizen enthusiasm turned to petulance and dismay as the noise of drilling, bugling, drumming, and weapons firing frightened women and children. The problems of hygiene were never properly addressed because everybody thought the war would be over in a few weeks.[7]

The regular army itself was faced with a massive and disorienting reorganization: roughly a third of its officers had resigned to join the Confederacy. Its commander, General Winfield Scott, was seventy-four years old and suffered from gout, so standing on his own two feet was excruciating for him. The militia defending the District of Columbia was a motley crew, and the rest of the army—on paper 18,093 men; in fact 16,367—was stationed at outposts in the West. However much northerners were now eager for war, the overwhelming truth was that the Union was unprepared. One visitor's apposite comment was that "Washington was not only unprepared for its *defense*, it was also unprepared for its defenders."[8]

Aware that it could not possibly handle the enormous influx of green troops, the federal government in late April declared that all volunteer regiments raised in the various states were the responsibility of their state governments until they actually joined an army on a campaign. This shifted the responsibility for housing and provisioning the volunteers from the federal to the state level, which meant that the troops in Washington had to rely for their well-being on the generosity and industriousness of families, hometowns, and local voluntary organizations that were hundreds of miles away.

In the case of Massachusetts, Governor Andrew sent a delegation to Washington to assess the condition of the state's regiments and to advise on how best to serve them. Among the worthies were Dr. Samuel G. Howe, one of Sanborn's Secret Six and a former hero of the Greek Revolution, and Judge E. R. Hoar, a man with a strong Republican record and the Concord resident who had issued the writ of habeas corpus that prevented Sanborn's extradition. But John Murray Forbes stepped in with both the means and the method of supplying troops, making available two of his transport steamers, the *Spaulding* and the *State of Maine*. Using his vast commercial network, he became an unofficial commissary or quartermaster, organizing the provision of everything from potatoes to ice to blankets.

By May 7 Judge Hoar was sufficiently impressed by Lowell to write to Forbes that he was "sensible, efficient and a trump into the bargain." He recommended him to Governor Andrew as the man to fill Massachusetts's pressing need for a general agent in the capital. On May 10, unaware of Hoar's suggestion, Lowell himself had independently spotted this need, writing to Forbes, "An agent ought to be sent here permanently to manage Massachusetts' interests. A vast deal of official and unofficial time and patience is wasted by new men going over and over old ground. Where so much is to be done it ought to be done by the best man and with the best tact. Otherwise it will be undone and done wrong. Any service I can render meanwhile will be a real gratification . . . Will you yourself request whoever comes as agent to call on me for what work I can do?"[9] His observation was purely practical—he had not been looking for this post. Instead he entertained the idea of raising a regiment of Maryland volunteers from Allegheny County. Together with Captain Stewart he crossed over the Potomac into Virginia and scouted around there, making a second reconnaissance later in the week. For a brief twenty-four hours he thought he would be made the censor of telegraphic communications at Baltimore under General Nathaniel P. Banks, an early Republican leader in Massachusetts and former Speaker of the House, but this came to nothing.

His was a waiting game while his letter to Sumner made the rounds of Boston gathering endorsements. His mother's cousin Henry Lee, an aide to Governor Andrew, procured a recommendation from the governor, but in the meantime Andrew appointed Lowell as Massachusetts's general agent, with duties to include the care of the transport ships and the responsibility for receiving, storing, and disposing of all goods shipped for troops. Lowell's daily communications by telegram with Governor Andrew ranged across a variety of subjects: whether he could sell the federal government potatoes at under two dollars a barrel, or the recovery of a load of hay that had been rained on, or Andrew's dismay at a U.S. officer's rudeness regarding the comfort of his men. All requests made by the various Massachusetts regiments had to go through Lowell. He had to retrieve all mislaid or appropriated property or at least to secure compensation for it. When the troops needed soap but instead received "hundreds of chests of oolong teas, tons of white crushed sugar, and then a whole cargo of ice!" he had to sell the ice immediately, from a ship moored off Annapolis. Thus it was that he served as a sort of supercargo for Governor Andrew.[10]

As the month wore on, in Washington's endemic atmosphere of flattery and aggressive self-promotion, exacerbated by "war fever," Lowell felt the noose of being Massachusetts's general agent tightening around his neck. Although urged by various sources to take the post as a permanent appointment, he resisted, for it would have jeopardized his chances in the regular army. Fielding telegrams about the price of potatoes, he felt he was "the only one of our family who is not doing or giving something." Letters from home only irritated this sentiment since they described how "about 1100 young men including all the Cabots and all of our male relations had been since January drilling daily under a French ex-Colonel of Zouaves." Many of his friends were in uniform and accustoming themselves to military life by doing a month's garrison duty at Fort Independence, in Boston Harbor. His younger brother, Jim, having raised a company, was now assured of his commission as first lieutenant in the Twentieth Massachusetts Infantry, and Charlie wrote home that he was sure that Jim "has a far better experience of military realities" than he had. His sister Anna had organized—and then put their mother and her cousin Amelia Jackson (Mrs. Oliver Wendell) Holmes in charge of—the Union Hall Association, which arranged relief work for the wives of volunteers by taking government contracts for uniforms, bandages, et cetera and offering out the sewing to these wives. Anna was now training to qualify as a nurse, under the draconian system instituted for army nurses by the formidable Dorothea Dix, who had a reputation for championing institutional reform of prisons and insane asylums and was now the superintendent of nurses for the Union army. Only Harriet was not involved, as she was in the early stages of pregnancy.[11]

"I feel quite ashamed at wasting so much time about a personal matter [his commission]," Charlie wrote home. "Military science I have absolutely none,—military talent I am too ignorant yet to recognize,—but my education and experience in business and in the working of men may, if wanted, be made available at once in the Regular Army: the Acting Commissary for this whole military district is only a Lieutenant of Artillery." Immediately his father wrote back, "You stand well with the authorities, especially with Cameron," reminding him that the scope of his present position was wide. It gave him a chance to understand the military system, to prove himself, and to reinforce the good impression he had made on Secretary Cameron. "It is looked as a favor on your part to give your services to the State, and not as a favor conferred by the State on you. You could not stand better. This will give you a claim for something better than a Second Lieutenant." Charles Lowell clearly desired his son to do well in the army. Before his fall from grace, he himself had been colonel of the Independent Corps of Cadets, a largely ceremonial role but one of the few prestigious military positions in Massachusetts. He had friends within the state's military structure and now made every effort to use these connections to promote Charlie. They were not very useful, however. Of greater value was Forbes's approbation, but Forbes wanted to keep him in his present administrative post.

Charlie was intent on receiving a commission. Both to Judge Hoar and to one of Governor Andrew's private advisers, he wrote that he would serve as general agent only until the right man could be sent out permanently: "He should be a man of age and weight, should be able to put the screws on Cameron occasionally." To Forbes, Charlie explained: "I do not change my purpose . . . am only sorry that there has been a misunderstanding." That confusion persisted was testament to Forbes's stubbornness in wanting Lowell for his own purposes. Forbes's endorsement of Lowell to Sumner was masterfully double-edged: "Lowell is a trump, full of brains and quick-witted. I want him in various places, so he is a valuable man for everybody." Not only conveying Lowell's abilities but laying claim to them, Forbes implied that unless Lowell was offered a position of sufficient consequence, Forbes had plenty of uses for him. It also had been a warning that this young man was not to be used as so much "food for powder."[12]

As May drew to a close, Lowell's optimism began to flag. Despite Cameron's promises, he had received no commission, and his options were narrowing. Cameron, assuming that cavalry would play no significant role in a short war that would be largely reliant on volunteer troops, admonished, "Accept no cavalry." Cavalry regiments were expensive to equip and maintain, with a training period much longer than that of the infantry. Nevertheless, one new cavalry regiment was commissioned, and Lowell was the only civilian to receive a commission in it. He exulted. "The thing is as sure as anything of that sort can be made in Washington."[13]

The U.S. Cavalry at this point consisted of five regiments used for duty at western forts and along borders. They collected Indian bounty, escorted western settlers, and occasionally skirmished with Indians; it was a career dull beyond dreaming. A veteran cavalry officer wrote,

> Take a boy of sixteen from his mother's apron strings, shut him up under constant surveillance for four years at West Point, send him out to a two-company post upon the frontier where he does little but play seven-up and drink whiskey at the sutler's, and by the time he is forty-five . . . he will furnish the most complete illustration of suppressed mental development of which nature is capable.[14]

If cavalry morale was never in prime condition, it certainly was not improved by the departure in 1861 of many of its best officers—Robert E. Lee, Albert Sidney Johnston, Joseph E. Johnston, J.E.B. Stuart, J. B. Hood, and Fitzhugh Lee—the finest officers in the Confederate army. The Union cavalry did not come into its own until later in the war, when a new generation of officers emerged, young men like Wesley Merritt, George Custer, and Philip Sheridan, unknown and untried at the beginning of the war.

But Lowell understood only dimly the organization he was about to join. For the moment he was content to have obtained a commission. He resigned as general agent and went home for a quick visit, arriving in Cambridge in time for the flag presentation on June 26 of Wilder Dwight's Second Massachusetts Regiment, which had been training for almost two months at the former Brook Farm, now called Camp Andrew. At this ceremony the regiment was presented with the flags it would carry into battle. Fine speeches were made; a review of sorts was put on. The regiment in its splendid uniforms marched and formed lines of battle and paraded, proving its adeptness at precision drill.

Many of Lowell's old classmates from the Boston Latin School were also in the Second Massachusetts: Henry Lee Higginson, Jim Savage, Richard Cary, Greeley Curtis, Richard Goodwin, and William Sedgwick. Most were single men who had not yet settled into permanent domestic or business relationships, although Cary and Sedgwick were married with small children. Stephen Perkins had been slow to sign up. After doing garrison duty in May at Fort Independence, he knew that he would loathe military life. He wasn't sure whether war would decide anything at all, whether the fight would gain the prize. But eventually he succumbed and took up a commission as second lieutenant under Savage. To those who asked why, he said only that the army was "an ancient and honorable profession."[15]

Among the spectators were college friends who had not enlisted. Some were married, with small children or widowed mothers to look after. Others, like Lowell's brother-in-law George Putnam, were compromised by physical failings—poor eyesight, bad legs, weak constitutions. Some, like Frank Sanborn, simply knew they were not up to the task, and a few others like Charles Adams were still undecided. Adams had joined the Fourth Battalion of the state militia and done garrison duty at Fort Independence but had not volunteered. Adams's indecision hinged on a keen sense of divided loyalties. His father, the newly appointed minister to Great Britain, had just sailed for England, leaving Charles in charge of the family's financial and real property, and Adams felt he must honor his father's wishes. He bitterly regretted that he had not joined up immediately in April during the first wave of patriotism, before he had been saddled with this family responsibility, but he had not quite marshaled the courage directly to disobey his father.

Many young men were commissioned as officers in other regiments. Lowell's brother Jim and his cousin Willy Putnam were in the Twentieth Regiment, known as the Harvard Regiment since so many of its officers were graduates of the college. Jim and Willy had paired up as first and second lieutenants under Captain George Schmidt, the German instructor at Harvard. The regiment's colonel was William Lee, a civil engineer and West Point graduate; Lieutenant-Colonel Francis Palfrey was also an acquaintance of Lowell's. Hoping to join the Twentieth was Wendell Holmes, a second cousin, and there were many other recent graduates—Caspar Crowninshield, Henry Howard Sturgis, William F. Bartlett, and Henry Abbott among them. The regiment's major was Paul Revere, Lowell's old Latin School classmate and a member of the Winter Street gang.

These young men were motivated by what Emerson had called "an affair of instincts"; they could not explain what had taken hold of them. Years later Higginson described his conversation with Jim Savage after Lincoln's call for troops. Savage, like many radical abolitionists, had claimed to be content, even eager, to see the South leave the Union. But when the time came, the two friends simply told each other, "I'm going." As Henry explained, "Of course we were." And they had, Jim as captain and Henry as his lieutenant, mirroring their childhood days of playing and fighting on the Common.[16]

All talk among these old friends was practical and immediate: about the minutiae of military life, its uniforms, its language, its protocol. They were as united in their enthusiasm for action as in their ignorance of what this might mean. When Henry Higginson (in training and unable to do it himself) sent a note to his father asking, "Will you get Charlie a pistol from me?"[17] he did not consider the pistol an instrument of death; instead it symbolized their shared status as officers.

Nor was Charlie Lowell "in the least bloodthirsty," but he did admit, "Like every young soldier, I am anxious for one battle as an experience." The desire to experience a battle was largely a matter of bearing witness, and of being involved in a key event of one's times. There was also the more abstract spiritual quest—to be tested, to know oneself, to discover what kind of man one was. Lowell claimed to be "too apathetic to get up such a feeling against the worst traitor among them as to desire to personally slay him." The reality that one might be killed or might have to kill dawned only slowly and incrementally. Only after Lowell had sworn his oath of allegiance, donned his cavalry uniform, and had his hair cut did he say, "You would not like to see me in uniform—I look like a butcher."[18]

Many young men volunteered because they considered the American experiment in self-government an example for the world; now that it was imperiled, so were the principles of democratic self-rule. Would American democracy end in fratricidal slaughter, as the French Revolution had? Lowell and most if not all of his friends had a direct personal or familial connection to the American Revolution. His friend Paul Revere was the grandson and namesake of the silversmith and Revolutionary War hero whose memory had been given new life in April, when *The Atlantic Monthly* published a new poem by Henry Wadsworth Longfellow, "Paul Revere's Ride," beginning with the now famous lines that almost every schoolchild knows: "Listen my children and you shall hear / Of the midnight ride of Paul Revere." The poem was an instant success. It appealed immediately to northerners' sense of urgency, to the call for action. It spoke of the effect that courageous men might have in the history of their times. It would have been hard for the grandson of such a hero not to join and fight, which all the Revere boys did. And when Charles Adams finally gathered his courage to defy his father and enlist, he explained that "it would have been an actual disgrace had his family, of all possible families American, been wholly unrepresented in the field."[19] Each generation of Adamses had played a vital part in American life. His great-grandfather had been the second president, his grandfather the sixth; his own father had served long years in the House of Representatives and assisted in the birth of the Free Soil and Republican Parties. He did not want his own generation to be the one to fail.

Revere and Adams were exceptional only inasmuch as their names are still remembered today as connected to the American Revolution. But they were typical of Lowell's friends in this respect. Charlie himself knew that his great-grandfather John Lowell had roomed with James Madison when they met in Philadelphia at the Continental Congresses and had been instrumental in writing the Massachusetts state constitution; another great-grandfather, Jonathan Jackson, had been among the first to contribute ships to the fledgling U.S. Navy. Virtually all Lowell's friends could claim at least one ancestor who had been a Founding Father in some degree, participated in a continental or state congress, or actually fought in the Revolutionary War. In their homes were ancient weapons that had killed Redcoats, and copies of state and federal constitutions. So the desire of these young men to preserve the Union, to defend its Constitution and its principles, was not an abstract or philosophical attitude but one imbued with almost hereditary, even proprietary feelings, perhaps even some of the irrational protectiveness one has for family—sentiments that these men might never have known they possessed had the war not come. It was an aspect of their patriotism that was expressed only obliquely.

Lowell's motives were even more complex. He wrote to Charlie Perkins that he would not have thought of taking up a soldier's life "were it not for a muddled and twisted idea that somehow or other this fight was going to be one in which decent men ought to engage for the sake of *humanity*." By humanity Lowell meant something akin to the general cause of human rights. He was speaking of abolition: "It seems to me that within a year the slavery question will again take a prominent place, and that many cases will arise in which we may get fearfully in the wrong if we put our cause wholly in the hands of fighting men and foreign legions." Writing to his mother, Lowell had described two potential outcomes. The first was a "short war and a separation": the northern states, caring little about slavery and having no taste for war or fratricidal slaughter, would content themselves with a dissolved Union and the knowledge that slavery was now confined within the boundaries of another country. Alternatively, if the Union decided to destroy slavery, Lowell believed it would be a long war in which "we subdue them," for the South would not willingly abandon slavery as an economic system. Although the difficulties involved in "subduing" the Confederacy were beyond imagining at this early stage, Lowell was implying that gentlemen, or "decent men," with their sense of personal honor and of duty, would ensure that the fighting did not disintegrate into bestial combat.[20]

On July 1 Lowell had taken the oath of allegiance: he was now "fairly in the U.S. Army" as a captain in the Sixth U.S. Cavalry, and he reported for recruiting duty in Pittsburgh. Riding some twenty-five miles a day to draw in men from a largely Democratic and thus less prowar area of western Pennsylvania, Lowell found the pickings slim. A few weeks later he was transferred to Ohio's Western Reserve, a Republican stronghold, but even there recruiting was very slow. Most able young men had already joined state volunteer regiments, and Lowell found the work "dreadfully tedious." He set up a recruiting office on the main street of Warren, Ohio, the principal town, and became known as the agent of "that Cavalry Company." The office became a favorite place for idle clerks and daguerreotypists. A large poster of a mounted soldier hung on the street to entice young men, but few enlisted.[21]

One who did described how Lowell, who had been standing in a nearby doorway, sauntered over as soon as he paused before the recruiting poster and began a conversation: "Young man, don't you wish to enlist?" The nineteen-year-old explained that he intended to join the Twenty-third Ohio Volunteers, but Lowell pointed out the advantages of the cavalry service and the regular army—and was so persuasive that within fifteen minutes the young man decided "to accept his opinion of what was best for me to do." As the days stretched by, Lowell described himself as "a mounted officer without a horse, a Captain without a Lieutenant or a command, a recruiting officer without a Sergeant and with but one enlisted man."[22]

News of the humiliating Union defeat on July 21 at Bull Run further discouraged Lowell. The battle had been undertaken in response to political pressure, not military wisdom. General Scott, a Virginian, had devised the least aggressive and least destructive war plan possible. He imposed a blockade on the South, denying southerners the profits of their exports and the imports on which they depended. Dubbed the Anaconda Plan because it was a matter of slow strangulation, it had several virtues. It avoided outright civil war and thus offered greater hope for a reunification of the nation; it also avoided overtaxing an army of untrained men and inexperienced officers. Unfortunately the northern public, under the illusion that with the first battle the Confederate rank and file would abandon its aristocratic and undemocratic leaders, was impatient for success. Political pressure was such that a battle became unavoidable. Bull Run was the result. Hence with the Union defeat there, popular morale in the North plummeted.

Yet Lowell, with his unconventional view that the war would be a long one, was ready to accept a certain degree of initial failure. The defeat did not trouble him as much as the behavior of Union officers afterward. He heard stories of them "skulking about Washington . . . letting their names go home in the lists of killed . . . entirely ignoring the commands of their superiors, and the moral and physical needs of their men." He thought their conduct proved they had "no sense of the situation and no sentiment for their cause. Fancy Jim or Willy behaving so!" he exclaimed to his mother. And he was especially piqued because such behavior confirmed all the worst southern prejudices about the character of northerners. In his letter to Sumner, he had said he believed he possessed "more or less of that moral courage about taking responsibility which seems at present to be found only in Southern officers," and on April 29 he had told his brother Jim that "if Southern gentlemen enlist, Northern gentlemen must also." Again Lowell was reminded of his Harvard classmates from the South: "I know that my Southern classmates in the Rebel ranks would never have treated their companies of poor white trash so contemptuously: they respect them too much as means for a great end."[23]

The southern officers' sense of superiority had been a leitmotif in North-South tensions for at least ten years—the most egregious expression being Congressman Brooks's beating of Senator Sumner (in itself a snub, since if Brooks had regarded Sumner as a gentleman, he would have challenged him to a duel). But as Lowell's allusion to "poor white trash" suggests, class was also an issue in the North. Lowell and his friends were, after all, descendants of the "Lobster princes," and the condescension of southern gentlemen rankled. That northerners appeared less arrogant in their demeanor was attributable to their less stable social order and to differences of style. A mercantile and industrial culture had as many distinctions and divisions of class as an agrarian plantation society. But in the close-knit world of Boston, one seldom felt the need for any kind of self-promotion, and well-born Yankees regarded boastful behavior as unforgivably uncouth. At Harvard, when southerners scorned polishing their own boots, northerners had insisted that to fail to do so was worse. But Lowell was not in Boston. In the Sixth U.S. Cavalry the field officers were southerners (even after the defections of so many of them to the Confederacy), and the Union army continued to embody the values and snobberies that southern culture associated with military leadership.

Lieutenant-Colonel William H. Emory was a Marylander whose wife was a granddaughter of Benjamin Franklin and the best friend of Mrs. Jefferson Davis. Their son had joined the Confederate navy, and in the brief period in early May when it appeared that Maryland would secede, Emory had resigned from the cavalry—or rather, his commission had been resigned for him by his Maryland brothers, and despite his wife's personal entreaties with President Lincoln, it could not be got back. Instead, Emory was offered a new commission in the Sixth U.S. Cavalry and served the Union loyally throughout the war. Second in command was Major Lawrence Williams, another southerner and a cousin of Mrs. Robert E. Lee (herself a descendant of Martha Custis Washington). Charlie Lowell, the only officer from civilian life and with no prior record of service, had a difficult time. The discomfort of his predicament added vehemence to his denunciation of irresponsible officers.

The day after Bull Run, President Lincoln put the Army of the Potomac into the hands of General George Brinton McClellan, a stocky, handsome man who seemed destined for great things. He presented himself as a man of action. In a report submitted in early August, he made clear that only military success would end the South's rebellion. In this respect McClellan was a more aggressive leader than Scott, but only by a few degrees, for his war policy was deeply conciliatory. Nevertheless McClellan encouraged the press and the public to imagine that he would be an American "Napoleon." Unusually, he lived in Washington with his new wife, away from his troops, and cut a fine figure in the capital's society. He had a penchant for foreign staff officers, most notably the Duke of Chartres and the Count of Paris of the French legitimist royal family, and he was partial to veterans of the Crimean War. Clever, conscientious, and hardworking, he tackled administrative and organizational challenges that had been heretofore ignored. He procured proper equipment and set up supply procedures, all with the purpose of molding the mass of men assembled in Washington into an army. He entertained lavishly. As part of his efforts to improve morale and to gain publicity, he frequently staged grand reviews, and the army was often paraded through Washington.[24]

One of General McClellan's first steps was to establish a training program for officers, teaching them tactical drills, army regulations, the posting of sentinels, field marches, and the like. Establishing a board of inquiry to review officers' conduct, he made a not-so-subtle attempt to weed out inefficient political appointees and generally improve military professionalism. Almost immediately 170 officers resigned rather than be forced to defend their credentials.

A regular cavalry regiment had twelve companies, and as a captain Lowell was in charge of one of them. Under his command were two commissioned line officers, a first lieutenant and a second lieutenant; fifteen noncommissioned officers—a first sergeant, a quartermaster, a commissary sergeant, four sergeants, and eight corporals; and between 56 and 72 men, including two musicians, two farriers, a saddler, and a wagoner. At the end of August Lowell and his company were sent to the Camp of Instruction. East of the city, it was not a pleasant place, squeezed between a poorhouse and a graveyard. With 650 men in the camp, 44 horses, and no arms, Captain Lowell and the Sixth U.S. Cavalry were trained by the veteran General Silas Casey, a strict drillmaster.

Whatever romantic illusions Lowell and the new recruits held about belonging to a cavalry regiment were quickly shed. The primary task of an officer was to accustom his men to obeying orders, to working precisely and in unison. This was a challenge to both officers and men, since it is debatable which was the more tedious, drilling or being drilled. Column into line, line into column. Squad drill, company drill, battalion drill, regimental drill, dress parade at sundown. Endless marching.

Officers neglected their duty for much the same reason that enlisted men did: weariness, boredom, perversity, the need for privacy or release. Whatever the rank, drink was a problem both within and without the camp. More important, many officers disliked giving orders and, even more, seeing that they were carried out. They did not want to be unpopular, did not like the isolation of their position, and did not want to hold themselves apart from the camaraderie of the men.

Officers had to enforce basic principles of personal hygiene, which the men often disregarded. They had to combat dirty clothes, missing buttons, a mix-and-match approach to uniforms, filthy unkempt hair, and a tremendous reluctance to bathe. Given the disregard of basic sanitary procedures, illness was a constant danger; the tedious and unpleasant task of keeping water pure was of great importance. Officers had to make sure that the men and their quarters, their cooking gear, their arms, and their accoutrements were clean, and they had to oversee the care of the horses.

Many of the enlisted men had never previously ridden horses, and if they had, their mounts had usually been old plowhorses or ponies accustomed to being hitched to traps. So the cavalry recruits were united in their fear and ignorance of horses. The ignorance could be remedied; the fear was harder to combat. Nor did northern boys know much about firearms. They might handle a telescope with expertise, but as one officer explained, an armed raw recruit was "more likely to shoot off his horse's ears or kill his next comrade."[25] It was, then, a blessing that horses, being expensive, were slow to arrive. Lowell was a more than competent equestrian, having had at least one horse almost continuously in his care since 1856. When the horses did arrive in mid-September, he had to teach the men to ride. Needless to say, problems multiplied when the men and their mounts were pushed too quickly. A neophyte cavalryman might just manage to control his horse if given space and calm, but the attempts of an entire company of poor riders on skittish or bad horses were not only comic but often dangerous. Bruises, sprains, and broken bones resulted.

Teaching a man how to care for his horse was not the same as ensuring that he did so. The beast's needs came first: the soldier had to rise early to water and feed the horse, groom and saddle it up, before having his own breakfast, and at day's end he had to picket, water, feed, and groom his horse before taking his own meal or rest. As summer gave way to autumn and heavy rain, the cavalry camp, on a clay bank just above the eastern branch of the Potomac, was no place to find oneself. After three hours' drill the horses, begrimed with the splatters and spray of wet clay, presented a daunting sight to a raw recruit with curry brush in hand. "It opens his eyes to some of the advantages of infantry,"[26] Lowell wrote home in masterly understatement.

To meet his new responsibilities, Lowell had to commit himself to a prodigious study of manuals both theoretical and practical. It required acute observation of his fellow officers and an ability to stay one step ahead of his men. Twice a week the officers assembled to be instructed in "tactics" and the theory behind them. A variety of texts were used: McClellan's *Regulations and Instructions*, Hardee's *Tactics*, and the *Revised United States Army Regulations of 1861*. The standard text on cavalry had been *Poinsett Tactics*, essentially a translation of the French cavalry manual. McClellan's rigor was paying off in better-trained troops and greater morale, which was not lost on Lowell, but it was still a tedious time that tested his convictions, while battles were fought and his friends took the field without him.

At its mouth the Potomac River was wide and deep, making a direct attack on Washington impracticable from the south, but upriver from the capital were numerous sites where Confederate troops might easily ford the river and swoop down upon the capital. One such position was at Ball's Bluff, overhanging the Potomac near Leesburg, Virginia, which was then occupied by the Confederates. In October General McClellan found himself in much the same position as Scott had in July: with the Confederates in so advantageous a position, the political pressure to take some kind of action was overwhelming. McClellan ordered "a slight demonstration," hoping this show of force would persuade the Confederates to back off and thereby satisfy his critics. General Charles Stone sent in Union troops under the command of Colonel Edward Baker, a former Oregon senator, a close friend of Lincoln's, and a man with no military experience. Among these troops was the as-yet-untested Twentieth Massachusetts Regiment. Baker, overeager for a fight, committed multiple errors: poor planning, terrible communication, and inexperience characterized the Union action.

News of the battle on October 21 spread quickly to Washington. Within twenty-four hours a casualty list was published. From this Lowell learned that his cousin had been killed and his brother and many friends wounded. Immediately he rode over to the regimental hospital to find Jim, do what he could, and get details of the battle. Wounded in the fleshy part of the thigh, Jim had been treated and was now waiting to be shipped back to Boston on sick leave. As Jim gave an account of events, Charlie could see that he had found his first battle deeply shocking.

Laboriously Jim described all the stages by which the Twentieth had reached the battlefield. He recalled Willy's debate over bringing his overcoat and field glasses, and he detailed the anxious wait at the base of the hundred-foot bluff, including the slice of ham and bread each cousin had eaten just before orders came. When Jim's Company E had finally been ordered up over the bluff, it did not know that the rest of the Union forces were in retreat. As it came over the bluff, it encountered the rebels, sheltered by woods, lying in wait. Opening on the men, the rebels fired low and accurately into the regiment, which was now trapped on the narrow piece of open ground—"one of the most complete slaughter pens ever devised," explained one of Jim's fellow captains, Henry L. Abbott. Another captain, William F. Bartlett, described how the men began to panic as "bullets flew like hail." Orders came for the men to lie down. But Jim and his officers continued to walk among them. In pointed contrast to Bull Run, they meant to set an example for their men, and it worked. Once on the ground, the men calmed and followed orders: they were to stand only to fire and then lie down again to reload. Following orders of their own, Jim and Willy started forward with their captain. The Twentieth's adjutant, Charles Peirson, was hit. Willy went to help him and was shot in the bowels. Jim went to help him and was hit in the thigh. Captain Schmidt was shot in the head. Jim's cousin, Wendell Holmes of Company A, waved his sword and shouted, "Will no one follow me?" He was hit in the chest. In Company C the captain was shot four or five times. After barely an hour of fighting the Twentieth was forced to retreat.[27]

Willy, in excruciating pain and recognizing that his bowel wound was fatal, refused to be moved. Jim, with only one good leg, could do nothing for him and had to leave him, which he hardly found easy to recount. After this his narrative lost much of its coherence. Dragging his wounded leg, Jim made his way to the edge of the bluff, trampling over the wounded and dead underfoot. The "ground was smoking and covered with blood," while the sound of artillery fire was deafening, punctuated by the screams of horses and men dying in agony. Thirteen of the regiment's twenty-two officers were wounded or dead. Jim could find no support in organizing the men, who began to panic as they scrambled down the steep cliff.

Fortunately Norwood "Pen" Hallowell, a fellow lieutenant, found him at the clifftop. Hallowell was soaking wet, having swum across the river to find wood to make a raft and then poled back. As he helped Jim down the cliff, they witnessed a Dantesque scene: the rebels were shooting and sinking the boats and makeshift rafts filled with men and wounded who were trying to retreat. The river was full of bodies—some swimming, some clinging to logs, others dead or in the throes of drowning. Their screams filled the air. Worst of all, in the struggle to survive, "man clutched at man, and the strong who might have escaped were dragged down by the weaker."[28]

Hallowell managed to get both Jim and Wendell to an island in the river, where a field hospital was set up. There Jim found Willy again. Henry Sturgis, a lieutenant who heretofore had shown little promise, had refused to abandon him despite his protests, had scooped him up in his arms, and had carried him down the cliff and into one of the few boats making the cross-ing. At the field hospital Willy refused all treatment, "saying he knew the wound was mortal and it would only be more pain for nothing."[29] He was given morphine. Jim's leg was quickly treated, the bullet easily extracted, and then Jim too was left. All around them the doctors worked: mangled, crushed, and splintered limbs were amputated and thrown on a growing pile; simple wounds were bandaged; the worst cases were given morphine. In the predawn hours, when firing had begun again, the island was evacu-ated. The wounded were carried in blankets down to boats and ferried to the Maryland shore, where they were loaded into a canal boat headed for Ed-ward's Ferry. Many were further wounded when part of the canal boat col-lapsed, sending a shower of debris down on those in the hold. It was at this point that Jim's narrative lost all coherence.

His own wound meant little to Jim, and he had never thought it was seri-ous, but he seemed utterly bewildered by his own helplessness. Despite all logic it weighed on his conscience that he had left Willy on the field. After the horrifying scenes of unnecessary and vicious death in the river, his mind shut down, and he could tell his brother little more. But Charlie needed to know more. From what Jim said, all the officers had behaved well, but the entire affair made so little sense. Their orders had been too vague, and then, it would seem, they had been abandoned. Fortunately the Second Massa-chusetts Infantry had marched all night through pouring rain, arriving at the river's edge on the Maryland shore opposite Ball's Bluff in the early dawn of October 22, when the wounded men were being loaded for transport. These men were also at the hospital, and Charlie turned to his friends in that regi-ment to find out more.

On the morning of October 22, many of the Second's officers were see-ing, if not their own younger brothers and cousins, then the younger broth-ers of their friends, whom they had last seen at the Harvard autumn ritual of interclass football games. They were impressed by the man in charge of the Twentieth, eighteen-year-old Caspar Crowninshield. None of the Twenti-eth's field officers had made it across the river: Colonel William Lee could not swim, Lieutenant-Colonel Frank Palfrey had been slightly wounded, and Major Paul Revere's scruples had not allowed him to abandon them: they had all been taken prisoner. With more than half the captains killed, Crowninshield, as captain of Company D, was the regiment's senior officer. He was dressed in only a borrowed overcoat and his drawers, his uniform having been lost in the river crossing; a former hero of the first boat of the

Harvard crew, he had had no trouble swimming. Crowninshield gave a very good account, explaining the lack of organization, the inadequate supply of boats, and the poor communication. His composure impressed them all. Dwight remarked that "only once, when he spoke of the terrible scene in the river . . . did he seem to think of the horrors."[30]

Henry Higginson told Charlie that almost as soon as they arrived at Ball's Bluff, a runner had found him and said that Willy wanted to see him. Although Henry told Rob Shaw that Willy "talked as calmly about the fight as if he were in perfect health," he now told Charlie that Willy "could hardly speak." Last messages were passed on, and Henry believed his presence had calmed Willy. Wilder Dwight also went to see him and described him as "bright, but evidently sinking." His composure was probably due to the heavy dose of morphine that dulled his pain as he prepared for the ambulance journey to the regimental hospital. He and Wendell Holmes were loaded into a two-wheeled horse-drawn wagon. The jolting and bumping were so horrendous that Wendell, lying next to Willy, passed out. He woke hearing someone say, "It is a beautiful face," and he knew that Willy was dead.[31]

Such a sad and miserable death was beyond words.* Charlie's reaction to the death of his cousin and the wounding of his brother was to fall into silence like that which had gripped him when he first became ill in 1856. His parents once again became anxious. By December he still had not written, and his father made him a visit, bringing with him a photograph of Willy, which Charlie was pleased to have, and a rather clever writing case that impressed his fellow officers and that carried the not-so-subtle hint for him to write more often. But when he did, on Christmas Day, it was only to say: "What is the use of writing just now? . . . Every day is exactly like every other day and like every day for every man in the army. Jim can tell you exactly what I do from day break to bedtime."[32]

While there was truth to this, it was perhaps even truer that Lowell was depressed. The most he could manage to explain to his mother was that the "life is totally different from any thing I have tried heretofore, and I have not yet got wonted to it, I am still in a semi-bewildered state." To Charlie Perkins, his old colleague on the B&MR and housemate, he wrote, "I wish I could see you for an hour or two. I hardly know myself in this new style of

---

*Aunt Mary was told that Willy had died "in sleep quietly and gradually" lying next to his cousin Jim.

life, and though I fancy it much, I still see everything 'through a glass darkly.' I feel as though I were in a dream, and positively yearn for some old fact, like yourself, occasionally." It was inevitable that after only a few months as a cavalry captain he would only "know in part," but his frustrations were not with his life as an officer.[33]

Lowell's allusion to the oft-quoted passage from First Corinthians attested to his grief: "For now we see through a glass, darkly; but then face to face: now I know in part; but then shall I know even as also I am known." This text was, as it is today, a regular feature of many funeral services, consoling those who are struggling to understand the cruelty of death. Charlie had grown up with Willy Putnam, although he had been more naturally Jim's playmate, while Willy's older brother Alfred had been Charlie's exact contemporary. But Alfred had died in 1856 during Charlie's own period of illness, and when he was traveling and living with the Putnams he became especially close to Willy. Now Willy, too, was dead.

He was at a loss to know what to say to Aunt Mary. When Alfred had died, it had been easier somehow: he had stepped in as the surrogate child whom she could pamper and fuss over and mother in lieu of her own. Now, with the stale artifice of a letter, what was there to say? Uncle James had written that "there is something very painful to me in the hoarse hollowness of her voice." In fact her grief was extreme. His mother reported to Charlie that Mary Putnam had gone to collect Willy's body at the railyard stables in Boston. (Her husband was incapacitated by a stroke, which the family had kept secret from Willy.) He was in a rough wooden box, and nothing had been done to clean him up. His hair was matted with sweat and blood, but his long dark eyelashes made his cheeks look that much fairer, and his lips were smiling, which seemed to confirm his innocence, his youth, and his wretched death. On seeing her beloved and last son, Anna continued, Aunt Mary had found that "a strange peace stole into her heart & the words came 'Peace I leave unto you — my peace I give unto you.'" These were the words that Christ used when comforting his disciples after the Last Supper and after he washed their feet. Among the more religious women in the family, Aunt Mary's experience was given the significance of a visitation.[34]

Even if you did not accept the "visitation," as Charlie most definitely did not, Willy was a hero and had already begun to be transformed into a martyr. When Governor Andrew came to call on the Putnams to express condolences, he was much affected by Willy's sister, Georgina, who answered his ring, saying, as tears streamed down her face, "Governor Andrew, we thanked you when we got Willy's commission and we thank you now." His funeral service reinforced the martyr image; one text was from the passage in the Gospels in which Christ prepares his disciples for his death: "He that loseth his life for my sake shall find it . . . For what is a man profited, if he shall gain the whole world, and lose his own soul?" In his homily the minister said, "And he did lose it for Christ's sake, for he lost it in the spirit of a noble self sacrifice for country & freedom & not for country alone, but for humanity—in this way his [Willy's] youthful eye saw a way opened for the deliverance of the captive."[35]

Mary Putnam had already begun to circulate her son's last letter, written the week before his death, in which Willy had agreed with the maxim "A century of civil war is better than a day of slavery . . . Human being never drew sword in a better cause than ours." While many northerners did eventually come to embrace emancipation as one of the aims of the war, very few embraced it so early, so ardently, and so purely as did Willy Putnam. President Lincoln had earlier tried to play down the slavery issue and had struck down orders by General John C. Frémont emancipating slaves under his jurisdiction as military governor of Missouri. To Radical Republicans in the North, this action had demonstrated confusion and a lack of leadership. But while Lincoln could risk alienating the radicals, he could not afford to alienate the moderate Unionists of Kentucky or Maryland. "I think to lose Kentucky is nearly the same as to lose the whole game," Lincoln explained. "Kentucky gone we cannot hold Missouri, nor, as I think, Maryland." But these were cautions regarding the war's start. The conclusion of the war would hinge on the slavery question.[36]

Willy had written: "God grant that every river in this land of ours may run with blood, and every city be laid in ashes rather than this war should come to an end without the utter destruction of every vestige of this curse so monstrous."[37] In this conviction he was very much his mother's son: they had shared a passionate abolitionism informed by religious conviction, and with his death it now became imperative for his mother that the war become one against slavery.

To this end she arranged a formal ceremony in Boston on Christmas Day in which the Twentieth Massachusetts was presented with a silk memorial ensign made by Georgina Putnam and her cousins Anna and Harriet Lowell. On one side was a pine tree, symbol of Massachusetts, the words "Ball's Bluff," and the inscription "Stand in the Evil Day." On the other were the state motto and an arm whose hand grasped a sword (adapted from the Lowell coat of arms). In the presentation speech the soldiers were promised that Massachusetts "will never forget your hard, faithful, glorious though defeated services on that day."[38]

Charlie was unable to obtain leave to return to Boston for Willy's funeral or for the birth of his nephew, one month to the day after Ball's Bluff. His sister Harriet, breaking with the tradition of naming the eldest son after his father or grandfather, called him William Lowell Putnam after her cousin. The arrival of the Beautiful Bunch, or just Bunch, as the baby quickly came to be known, coincided with the return to Boston of Jim Lowell and the other wounded officers of the Twentieth.

And so amid the grief over Willy Putnam's death and the potent message of his martyrdom began a Boston winter of parties and visits, making much of Jim and Wendell and the other officers who were not so badly wounded as to be removed from all society. Cousin Lucy wrote, "The wounded hero is so well that he can be feted and made much of without any risk of tiring him, and it is a real pleasure to look at him." Her brother Cabot wrote, "Jim got back and looks as well as can be . . . They serenaded him the evening he arrived." Edward Emerson, who was living at the Lowells' for his first year at Harvard, asked his sister, "Don't you envy them? Wounded for their country! They can feel it has cost them something." They had had their taste of battle and survived. They had been wounded nobly. Jim and even Wendell had been transformed into men. They had "put away childish things": they had had their baptism by fire.[39]

Charlie Lowell as yet had not. Six months earlier he had told his mother that he suspected the volunteer troops would supply "more than their share of food for powder." It had not yet dawned on him that his own flesh and blood would be that food. Nor could he have imagined his own reaction. The incompetence of the military action at Ball's Bluff, its stupidity and mismanagement, infuriated him because it confirmed in his mind the offensive feeling that Willy's death had been a waste. And while he agreed with Uncle James that Willy's death was "noble," this did not rid him of the feeling of needless waste. But he could not share this sentiment with those at home. The more Willy was ennobled in death, the more impossible it was for Charlie to express his own feelings. He wrote to Charlie Perkins saying that "decent men" ought to join up "for the sake of humanity . . . within a year the Slavery question will again take a prominent place," but he did not tie that opinion to Willy's death and saw it rather as the inevitable conclusion of political minds.[40]

The political logic notwithstanding, Charlie was experiencing feelings that he could hardly put words to—unease at the thought of battle, yet deep chagrin that he had not yet fought in one; profound rage at Willy's innocence, as well as a sense that it was inexpressibly precious; and a complete bafflement about larger questions. The gods had not protected Willy, and Charlie's own special relationship with them was also in question. Was his safety a sign of their neglect? His fall from favor? Or did Charlie now recognize the brutal indifference Hawthorne had identified as the chilling truth expressed in Michangelo's *Three Fates*?

TEN

THE PENINSULA CAMPAIGN

1862

Charlie Lowell's cavalry camp was only a short ride from Washington. Despite the demands of his commission, he managed to get to Washington frequently enough to send home reports via friends that he saw "a great many people."[1]

And indeed, he had friends sprinkled about on the staffs of various generals, as well as many acquaintances in the War Department and the administration of the regular army made during his time as Massachusetts general agent. Also, he had access to privileged political figures through Massachusetts congressman Samuel Hooper, whose wife was a close friend of his mother's and whose children had been part of the Winter Place set. Hooper was a radical and a Republican, like both Massachusetts senators. The senators occupied powerful positions (Sumner as chairman of the Senate Foreign Relations Committee, and Henry Wilson as chairman of the Senate Military Affairs Committee). Lowell used his friendship with the Hoopers to become acquainted with both these men.

Well placed to pick up rumors, gossip, and genuine news, Lowell heard criticism of the government from every point of the political spectrum. Lincoln's "masterly inactivity" may have successfully constructed a unifying alliance for defense of the Union at a time when even that was a precarious notion, but as he continued to play possum in the hopes of retaining the border states, he was failing to provide any clear direction to the war effort. Many Americans believed that the country desperately needed strong leadership and that lack of it permitted chaos to reign, confusion to abound, and incompetence to be the order of the day.

Senator Wilson, in alliance with other Radical Republicans, notably Iowa's senator and Lowell's friend James Grimes, succeeded in forming a Committee on the Conduct of the War, ostensibly a Senate oversight committee with the power both to investigate corruption within the War Department and to apportion and assign blame for military failures. Although intended constructively, the committee was often petty and partisan and was seldom without controversy. It had a political agenda: to check and control Lincoln's moderating tendencies and to keep the prosecution of the war from foundering on the shoals of appeasement.

General McClellan wanted to create a mammoth army that would force any sane opponent to sue for peace. He believed that the Union's vastly superior force, acting simultaneously in the East and the West, on land and sea, could "crush the rebellion at one blow [and] terminate the war in one campaign."[2] This monolithic military force, he insisted, must scrupulously avoid any interference with civilian life. The fighting would remain between armies, which would help to preserve Confederate civilians' goodwill for the Union, a critical component in any future reconciliation. His goal was still the voluntary return of the Confederate states to the Union, and he presumed a predilection toward peace in the South that probably didn't exist. (Northerners consistently assumed a greater Union sympathy within the southern states than was the case.)

McClellan's plan, dismissed by historians as quixotic and symptomatic of an inability to act in conditions short of perfection, at the time won almost instant support from President Lincoln, the public, and the army, for the relatively conservative mood of the nation demanded reunification and was deeply ambivalent about and distrustful of the slavery question. For precisely this reason, McClellan did not gain the support of the Radical Republicans in Congress, and Senator Wilson, in his powerful position as chairman of the Committee on the Conduct of the War, was determined to oppose the plan.

Understanding this unappeasable opposition, McClellan became increasingly secretive, revealing nothing to the cabinet or even the president. His plan, he explained, demanded patience. But patience, however useful or even necessary from a military point of view, was in short supply, and in February 1862 McClellan, after stubborn procrastination, finally revealed his plan for a coordinated naval and land campaign that would move his entire force to the lower Chesapeake Bay, by which route he would attack Richmond. At the same time armies to the west would drive into the Confederacy. The plan had two principal drawbacks: the Union army would no longer stand between the Confederate army camped at Manassas (the town closest to the battle site along the Bull Run) and its goal, Washington, thus putting the defense of the capital once again in question; and the logistics were staggering. The bulk of the army would have to be transported south by steamer to Fortress Monroe, at the mouth of the James River, where it would march up the peninsula between the James and York Rivers, some sixty miles, to assault Richmond. If done speedily, the element of surprise might allow Union troops to get close to Richmond before the Confederates could mount a stout defense. But transporting 100,000 men, their animals, and their provisions was not easily done, and retaining the element of surprise would be almost impossible.

While the administration and McClellan debated, the Confederates outmaneuvered them. On March 9 General Joseph E. Johnston, commanding the Confederate troops, abandoned Manassas and headed south to form a line closer to Richmond. The following day the Union cavalry, including the Sixth U.S. Cavalry and Lowell, made a reconnaissance of the area. Most of Manassas had been burned, but at Centerville the guns that McClellan had so feared turned out to be logs carved to resemble cannon—"Quaker guns," as the newspapers dubbed them. It was also obvious that the number of Confederate troops had been grossly exaggerated. Galled and humiliated, McClellan began to move.

Most of the Union army was already at Fortress Monroe when the Sixth U.S. Cavalry arrived on the evening of March 30, 1862. On each vessel lanterns swung in the wind and bobbed as the boats rocked in the surf, making a "most brilliant and beautiful illumination."[3] Lowell anticipated that with vast numbers of troops congregating on this spot, he would have a chance to hunt up some of his friends. That very evening he had seen the boat carrying the Twentieth Massachusetts dock, and had had just enough time to rush over and greet his brother Jim, freshly returned to his regiment. But the next morning the situation was too chaotic and the officers were too busy, himself included.

Transporting an entire army and all it needed to survive was an administrative feat of huge proportions—a testament to what McClellan did best— and Lowell was busy unloading troops and provisions and making sure that everyone and everything under his command reached its correct destination. Adding to the complexity was the almost immediate acknowledgment that delay had allowed Johnston to reinforce the fort at Yorktown. McClellan assumed it was now too heavily defended to attack. (This was not in fact true, but McClellan once again fell for a Confederate deception, as he had for "Quaker guns.") And so the Sixth U.S. Cavalry led the army, in heavy rain, as it took up its position outside Yorktown. Over the next month, Mc-

Clellan's army laid siege but despite carefully placed heavy artillery batteries, no shelling occurred.

In early May, just before McClellan was finally ready to order a massive bombardment, the rebels evacuated Yorktown. The Union army followed, again with the cavalry in the lead. At Williamsburg, where the peninsula narrows and the Confederates had a fort, the Sixth U.S. Cavalry had their first engagement, fighting in the early hours of May 5. Lowell, commanding a squadron (Companies K and E), led the charge on Fort MacGruder. In their advance position and after long delays, the anticipation of battle was quickly transformed into the most intense anxiety. Lowell's men were green: they knew nothing of battle, and the siege of Yorktown had taught them nothing. During the evacuation they had occupied only what the Confederates had abandoned. Far from suffering from false bravado, the men mostly were very frightened. Even before the fighting began, one of his men reported his sergeant drunk. On investigating, Lowell learned that the sergeant, who was indeed suffering from "Dutch courage," was riding about, waving his pistol, and insisting that if any one of his six men did not charge and kill twenty rebels, he would be put in the guardhouse. Lowell had him arrested and took charge of the men himself. Lowell's main task was to get the men to advance at all. Barely had they begun to move when he came upon a lieutenant cowering behind a tree stump.

"Captain! Say, Captain!" the lieutenant cried. "Have you seen my horse?"[4]

Lowell's only recourse was to order the lieutenant up behind him and to ride to the rear to get him off the field. Returning to the front, Lowell could see that without their commanding officers his men had lost formation. They were fighting in pockets, and the companies had become scattered. Lowell joined those who were putting up the best resistance and rallied them to make another charge. They started off, and the rebels charged as well. At the point of "shock," when the two opposing forces should have met and fought, enough men had dropped out so that there was plenty of room for the horses to make room for one another, and the two lines rode past each other. The odd shot was fired, there was some yelling and waving of sabers, but by and large the effect was not unlike boats in a busy harbor viewed from a distance—balletic, graceful, and inconsequential. It was hardly combat.

This situation did not last. As Lowell turned to re-form his men, he saw riderless horses running amok and men on foot seeking shelter. Some of his men, still mounted but having lost control of their horses, rode on past him into enemy lines. There was nothing he could do for them, and with only a handful of his original command, he started back. The rebels, too, were returning to their own lines.

Taking advantage of this situation, Lowell rode up alongside a retreating rebel soldier and ordered the man to surrender. The rebel, instead of following battlefield protocol, raised his shotgun and at point-blank range aimed it directly at Lowell. "Drop that!" Lowell barked. The order was sufficient for the rebel to lower the gun as he fired, and the shot blew to pieces Lowell's coat, strapped behind him. Coolly Lowell took the gun and the man prisoner.[5]

There was a lull in the fighting. Lowell's squadron was ordered out to recover lost horses and saddles, a maneuver that exposed them to fire. As Lowell worked among the men he noticed they ducked as bullets whistled past. Urging them to keep moving, he explained that there was no point in ducking *after* hearing the bullets' whistle; by then it was too late. Instead, he explained, they should be sure to always keep moving. It was the best way to lengthen the odds of being hit.

The skirmish was over before Lowell knew it. Between the enormous tasks of educating his men and keeping them alive, he had been too busy to register that he had been himself under fire, except during the episode with the recalcitrant prisoner and his shotgun. Lowell's barked command had come from an instinct that was as surprising to him as the gun itself had been. Not until that evening, when his orderly held up the ruined coat as if it were a trophy, did the reality of the moment hit him. His orderly saw the bullet-ridden coat as proof that Lowell was lucky, but Lowell demanded that the coat be jettisoned. Above the orderly's protests he gave it to a camp follower, insisting it was "unlucky."

After this skirmish Lowell's squadron was rarely under heavy fire. As part of the Cavalry Reserve under the command of the Mexican war veteran General Philip Cooke, most of the Sixth U.S. Cavalry's work was in reconnaissance—patrolling the outskirts of the Union lines, serving as guards, and performing sabotage. The rebels continued their retreat up the peninsula toward Richmond. The Sixth pursued, skirmishing every day with the rear of the Confederate army for reconnaissance. Swinging up to the north, they destroyed the railroad bridges over the Pamunkey and the South and North Anna Rivers. They fired artillery into the engine of an oncoming rebel train. They tore up the railroad track, built a fire, heated the railroad bars, and bent them. But they made no attempt at classic cavalry action. The terrain was considered unsuitable: the roads were narrow, the woods tangled thickets, the ground low and swampy.

The Sixth U.S. Cavalry did their work well, working fast and riding off with equal haste at the rare times when enemy fire was directed at them. While on patrol, Lowell insisted that his men keep their horses saddled. He did not permit them large campfires or tents. The men grumbled, but they soon had occasion to be grateful. On June 13, when they stopped for their midday meal, a large force of rebel cavalry charged their camp, killing and capturing virtually all the men in the other squadron who had unsaddled their horses or set up camp. Lowell's men, with no camp to impede them and with their horses ready, were able to mount and flee. Chased across the Pamunkey, Lowell sent one company ahead with instructions to build fires to represent campfires; the other gained their colleagues time by firing on rebels as they tried to cross the Pamunkey, forcing them back to search for a safer way across. Lowell's men then hightailed it for the pseudo-campfires, where they lined up. When the rebels approached, they assumed the entire cavalry was out to defend its camp, and withdrew.

Lowell's men then reported that Confederate cavalry were headed behind federal lines. Bad orders and poor strategy from General Cooke unfortunately meant that despite their swift escape, the Sixth U.S. Cavalry was slow to pursue the rebels, who turned out to be J.E.B. Stuart and his cavalry, on their famous ride around the Army of the Potomac.

Stuart's ride was of great psychological value: it fed Confederate confidence, perpetuated the image of Union incompetence, and reconfirmed all the old prejudices about southern finesse and Yankee bumpkins. More important, McClellan came to doubt his ability to keep his supply lines open. The Sixth U.S. Cavalry was ordered to retire down the peninsula to Fortress Monroe, burning excess supplies and bridges as it went. McClellan had decided to shift his base of operations from Fortress Monroe to Harrison's Landing, more than halfway upriver to Richmond.

This was the end of Lowell's Peninsula campaign. He had demonstrated to himself and to his superiors his reliability on reconnaissance, his powers of command, his coolness under fire, and his quick thinking. He had established a good reputation among his men and beyond. Many officers boasted of their command over their own men, but few had ventured to give orders to an enemy soldier. The anecdote of Lowell and the rebel soldier captured the general consensus about Lowell: he had a natural "capacity of ruling men, which was the most remarkable of his gifts." The story was repeated throughout the army and got into the newspapers, earning him a reputation for bravery. But Lowell never acknowledged the incident except to say, "You can usually make a man obey you if you speak quickly enough and with authority."[6]

Nevertheless it was not a campaign of any significance for the cavalry. Union generals did not use their cavalry well; nor did the cavalry itself have a very good idea of its proper use. Stuart's ride around the Union army had made clear to even the dimmest cavalryman that there was something "radically wrong with the way they were used and led." Whatever the cavalry's reputation might have been at the start of the war, soldiers now began to ask, "Who ever saw a dead cavalryman?"[7]

As soon as he arrived at Harrison's Landing on July 8, Lowell went to the headquarters of the Twentieth, wanting news of his brother. During the initial months of the campaign he had seen Jim frequently enough to know that the infantry was doing the real fighting in the peninsula and bearing the worst of the summer climate. The swampy low ground was given to insects, oppressive heat, and a suffocating humidity; an unusually rainy season exacerbated the humidity and the insects. During the month-long siege of Yorktown, infantry soldiers had lived off biscuits bought from the ubiquitous contrabands, or ex-slaves, and crabs caught in the estuary. They had also caught a variety of infectious diseases: measles, mumps, smallpox, and consumption. Curiously, the big burly men from rural areas fared the worst, while the scraggly city volunteers were relatively immune. All the troops succumbed to dysentery and malaria; many suffered badly from diarrhea, the Twentieth Massachusetts among them and Jim Lowell in particular. The remedy was thought to be quinine and whiskey.

In addition to illness, Jim had been suffering a crisis of confidence as he headed back into battle this second time with greater awareness of what to expect. As the rebels retreated and the federals advanced, both armies, fully equipped, jockeyed about trying to find a place to stand and fight, skirmishing, snipers picking off the pickets. As the days of skirmishing became weeks, Jim felt confused. He did not understand what was going on; nor did any other line officer. He did not consider this "a real fight" and did not want to be shot in such circumstances.

For encouragement he turned to his brother, as well as to letters from home. His mother wrote with advice to bear up, to make the best of it, to be cheerful and assume the best in others. But once again it was his father who offered the needed tonic:

> Every real brave man must have doubt of his courage, till it has been put to actual proof under fire. This is the statement of all the greatest generals. Some never went into battle without positive fear. I never doubted your courage . . . I have never . . . had a moment's anxiety about your principles, your conduct, or your doing your duty on all occasions, and under all circumstances . . . My darling boy, from the time you entered the world till now you have been nothing but a source of unmingled pleasure and joy to your mother and me.[8]

This was Charles Lowell at his very best, offering his gentle younger son the unconditional love that calmed his troubled soul. But even receiving this most loving letter was not enough to stave off a morbid unease. Jim was, as he told a classmate, "almost certain of being killed before it was over." In March at the beginning of the campaign, Jim had sent in a short piece for his Harvard class album: "As we may have a great fight some of these fine days, I send you my life, since other wise I might lose it, for your battles are dangerous things and it won't do to risk too much in them." The same day he had written his mother: "If I die I wish to leave all my small property to Anna." At the end of June, when the army began to move again, Jim matter-of-factly explained to a friend, "I don't want to be shot in a skirmish or on picket but in a real fight." By that time Charlie knew only that Jim was in the thickest of the fighting.[9]

When he arrived at the camp of the Twentieth on July 8, Charlie had no idea of Jim's fate. Fellow officers—friends from childhood—told him the story. They described the initial relief when in mid-June the regimental bands, which had been banned from playing for more than a month, had been ordered to strike up, and the march toward Richmond began. Soon came the discomfort of mud, rain, and sweltering heat. The ranks, already depleted by typhoid, were suffering from scurvy. Marching in extreme heat was dangerous. Even the healthy could become fatally dehydrated if they were not accustomed to the weather. The rebels were retreating so quickly that they had no time to bury their dead. Union soldiers constantly came across bits of soldiers—a skull, a rib cage, some clothing still adhering. The climate ensured that bodies rapidly decomposed, and the sights were dreadful.

And so on June 25 the Twentieth Massachusetts began what became known as the Seven Days, a series of battles on the outskirts of Richmond in which casualties for both sides were very high. Each day a hard-won skirmish advanced or held the Union line; then in the evening would come an order from McClellan to withdraw, whereupon the Twentieth's commanding general, John Sedgwick, would pull back and reestablish the line. The next day another nasty battle would result in Sedgwick's holding the line, after which would come another order to retreat. The weather continued excruciatingly hot. The men, overcome with thirst, were dropping from exhaustion and dehydration. So it went for Oak Grove, Mechanicsville, Gaines's Mill, and Savage's Station.

Leaving Savage's Station on June 29, the Twentieth Massachusetts burned what they could not take with them and marched all night, arriving near White Oak Swamp. After a brief rest the men were marched double-quick up to Nelson's farm, Glendale, where there was no water. When the fighting started, part of another division receiving the main Confederate assault cracked and fled, streaming through Sedgwick's men to the rear. Despite this panic around them, Sedgwick's men held the line, partly thanks to their commander's own passionate actions: joining the line and spurring his men on, Sedgwick was not deterred by the wounding of his horse, its death, his own leg wound, or the killing of his second horse. As the advance began, Wendell Holmes described looking down the line and catching Jim's eye. The two cousins saluted each other and then went forward to plug the gap. Courage did not prevent the Twentieth from being flanked and nearly surrounded. Confusion broke out, and stragglers from other regiments added to the chaos. The guns became so hot that they could not be fired. Some men braced ramrods against trees to force the charges into the barrels. "When next I looked," Wendell explained, "he was gone."[10]

Jim had not at first thought he was wounded. Only when he found he was too weak to stand did he realize he had been shot in the lower stomach, like Willy. His men came to his aid, but Jim waved them on. Henry Patten, an old school friend who had replaced Willy as Jim's second lieutenant, wanted to stay with him, but Jim ordered him to take command. An orderly carried Jim back to the farmhouse serving as a field hospital, where the doctors, unable to do anything else, gave him morphine and ether. Shortly, Patten was carried in with a leg wound. Jim had Patten put next to him and took his friend's hand. Patten reported that Jim asked if the wound was mortal, and the doctor replied, "You better look upon it so."[11]

As darkness fell, McClellan's orders to retreat came down the line. The officers of the regiment gathered around Jim. His wound was too severe to move him, and in any event, they believed he would die before dawn. Patten wanted to stay with him, but Jim, as his superior officer, refused permission. Patten asked him if he had any words for home, and Jim said, "Tell them how it was Pat." Then he amended this, saying he wanted his father to know he was "dressing his line when he fell."[12] He had already written home: all that there was to say had been said. He shook hands with his friends. He gave his sword to Palfrey, his lieutenant-colonel, for safekeeping. The doctors gave Jim more morphine. The Twentieth once again abandoned their hard-won position and left Jim to be overrun by the rebels. Tears streamed down Palfrey's face as he recalled these events for Charlie.

They marched through the night of June 30 to Malvern Hill. From this brilliant strategic position they fought the next day, winning an unqualified Union victory, but again McClellan ordered a retreat. In a raging downpour, again through the night, the men of the Twentieth Massachusetts marched back to Harrison's Landing, where they collapsed: exhausted, hungry, filthy, weary, in shock. They were met by, among other people, young Anna Lowell, serving as a nurse aboard the *Daniel Webster*, one of the hospital transport ships evacuating the wounded up to hospitals in Washington and New York. Charlie had had considerable anxiety about his sister going so near the battlefield. Jim had written, "I would not have Anna leave the boat, where there is some civilization and humanizing influence." Her mother had written to her, "I am quite glad you cannot get about more. The middle of the river is the safest place for you . . . I am glad you are there at so important a time. You will remember it with pleasure all your life . . . I believe you have courage to go through with all that can be demanded of you." When Anna learned of Jim's wound, she immediately set about trying to reach him, only eight miles away. Sadly she was not allowed through the lines, and she had returned to her work on the *Daniel Webster*, caring for the vast numbers of wounded being loaded aboard ship. Palfrey gave her Jim's sword and belt, and soon the ship and Anna, carrying Jim's few possessions, sailed north. Charlie had missed his sister by only a few hours.[13]

Jim's fate after he fell into enemy hands was unknown. George Putnam, who was also working at Harrison's Landing on the hospital transports, used his free time to investigate, finding out the names and regiments of the doctors left in charge of the wounded before he, too, had to sail north. He was keen that the elder Anna Lowell be discouraged from believing that Jim might have survived. In letters to Harriet, George urged her not to encourage her mother in false hopes. If Jim had lived, he explained, he would have been "a most wretched invalid all his life instead of closing so beautifully and fittingly a life so happy and nobly as his has been." Wendell wrote his mother, Amelia Jackson Holmes (Anna Lowell's friend and cousin), that he himself "suffered the most intense anxiety and everything possible—you can't conceive the wear and tear—Lowell is probably dead bowels cut." The next day he wrote again, repeating, "Poor [Jim] Lowell was hit just as Willy Putnam was & had to be left behind—beyond doubt dead." The younger Anna, from her experience aboard the transport, knew enough of wounds to appreciate not only the inevitability of Jim's death but the pain he had suffered before it came. And yet, without confirmation of his death, their mother refused to give up hope.[14]

Also on July 8, as Charlie learned of his brother's fate, President Lincoln had visited McClellan at Harrison's Landing to discuss the conduct of the war, but nothing was resolved. The two men talked at cross-purposes. Lincoln tried to make clear that goals, rationales, and laudable strategies would be vindicated only by a victory. McClellan, unaware that his own conduct was in question, was high-handed with the president and insisted on his old demands of extravagant preparedness before starting a siege of Richmond. He demanded more troops, time to regroup, and renewed commitment from Lincoln: once he had these, and once he had restored the military machine to his liking, he was sure that the Union army would prevail. None of his requests were granted.

McClellan also gave Lincoln a letter detailing his criticisms of the president's political policies and war aims. As commander of the Army of the Potomac, he was well within his rights to offer confidential advice, particularly on military matters. His advice contained a great deal of politics confirming how closely political and military goals were intertwined. Behind the debate over whether to continue on to Richmond was a larger political power struggle about control of the Union war effort. McClellan, a conservative Democrat, urged Lincoln not to bow to Radical Republican pressures for the emancipation of slaves. Peace, he believed, could be achieved only by a voluntary restoration of the Union, which would be impossible if slavery became an issue. The army would not fight for abolition or emancipation, only for Union, he insisted.

Two days later, on July 10, Captain Charles Lowell was appointed to General McClellan's staff. He could not have failed to grasp the poor communication between the general's headquarters and Washington: confusion, rumor, and an ill-defined paralysis reigned at Harrison's Landing. Although the professional soldiers maintained their sanguine attitude, they recognized that McClellan had been hesitant and overcautious. Even his own brigade generals were upset: an opportunity had been missed, and in his caution McClellan had squandered lives.

Many of his European staff officers had left or were leaving. Although McClellan had weeded out the great mass of political appointees in the army, his own staff contained many gentlemen civilians who were only now being moved on: John Jacob Astor, Lowell's friend Powell Mason, and the Philadelphian William Biddle. McClellan had discovered them to be nearly useless. What he wanted now, he explained to his wife, was efficient military men to do the "really serious work, especially under fire."[15] In fact Lowell had been recommended to him in January by George Bancroft (Johnny's father), a prominent Democrat who supported McClellan, believing him to be a "deep thinker." To fill staff positions, McClellan recruited solely from the cavalry: Captains George Custer, Arthur McClellan (a nephew), Charles Lowell, and William S. Abert. It was flattering for Lowell to find himself in such company and estimated by such criteria, but for the time being he had precious little work under fire.

Because of the skills he had developed as Massachusetts general agent, Lowell was assigned to superintend the inspection of the army's First Corps. Performing essentially administrative tasks, he gained firsthand experience of McClellan's best qualities: his organizational skills and his ability to make efficient and rational the task of supplying a vast army. But it was just this sort of work that Lowell had found so dissatisfying as general agent.

Charlie used his extra time to hunt down the doctors who had treated Jim and to find his burial site. The uncertainty surrounding his brother's last days agitated him. He had no illusion that Jim might have survived, but the thought of his pain, loneliness, and possible maltreatment in enemy hands was upsetting. After several weeks Charlie found the doctors who could tell him of Jim's last hours. Jim had lived until July 4 and was buried beneath a tree on the battlefield where he had received his mortal wound, Glendale. He wrote his mother, "It is painful to think that you were still in suspense about dear Jim . . . I am glad the little fellow was not moved to Richmond, merely to die and to be buried where we never could find him."[16] As with most soldiers, it mattered deeply to Charlie that Jim's body could be retrieved and was not fated to become like the anonymous bones he was now seeing littered across former battle sites.

He also told his mother that one of the doctors, deeply impressed by Jim, recalled that Jim had talked at length about the war and why he had fought. The doctor had told the Confederate officers to talk to him if they wished to see how a "true and brave Northern soldier thought and felt."[17] Charlie had qualms about the reliability of this report, because none of the officers of the Twentieth believed that Jim had been in any condition to speak articulately about anything. Still, he kept his doubts to himself and reported what he had learned. It was possible that with enough morphine, Jim might have lost contact with his physical condition. Perhaps in his dying hours he had achieved a clarity of vision and articulation that was part of the onset of death.

On the basis of what the doctors told him, Charlie gained a new respect for his younger brother, yet he could not banish thoughts of the potential torment of Jim's last days. He took some relief in knowing that Jim's geniality and idealism persisted to the end. But this too was painful. Charlie felt unbearable chagrin and anguish that so dearly loved and so good a person had become yet more "food for powder." A certain unspecified rage set in. This was not uncommon among the soldiers. Palfrey was deeply bitter, complaining that he regarded McClellan as a failure. Frank Barlow, now a colonel commanding two New York regiments and whom Charlie had made a point of seeking out during the campaign, was characteristically blunt in his frustration: "I am thoroughly disgusted . . . You have no idea of the imbecility of management . . . It is considered generally that McClellan has been completely outwitted."[18] Despite Jim's manifest courage, high principles, and fine values, Charlie couldn't help feeling his brother's life had been wasted.

These were suspicions that Charlie could not share generally—certainly not with those at home—and his colleagues in the regular army would have considered them unprofessional. The closer Lowell moved to the West Point graduates who formed the inner circle of the Union army's command, the more pervasive he found an aristocratic southern tone. Many of the officers regarded Confederate officers as comrades and valued them as former colleagues and old friends. Major Lawrence Williams of the Sixth U.S. Cavalry, a cousin of Mrs. Robert E. Lee's, had tried to visit her and her daughter, in residence near Hanover Court House, on May 15. When he reached the regiment's pickets, a lieutenant warned him back within the lines, and later that night he was arrested by his own men outside Union lines for "alleged communication with the enemy."* General Philip Cooke, commanding the Union cavalry, was the father-in-law of J.E.B. Stuart, who had so effortlessly humiliated it. McClellan and Joe Johnston, opposing generals during the initial phase of the campaign, were close personal friends. George Custer, Lowell's fellow aide-de-camp, used the lull in the fighting to attend the wedding of an old West Point classmate—John W. Lea of Mississippi, now a Confederate officer. He participated fully in the week of festivities with no unease.

This behavior confirmed what Lowell had recognized the year before: the regular army officers fought with an eye toward their own honor, not with the zeal of political passion. Most had an apolitical view of the war: almost universally they resented civilian interference in military matters. Lowell admired this professionalism and acquired many aspects of it, but his admiration was qualified as he reacted to the experience of war and to its losses. He could not maintain his colleagues' apolitical distance.

And yet his attitude also differed from his family's compelling need to believe that first Willy's and now Jim's death had some meaning. Aunt Hannah declared, "I believe that not one drop of blood is shed in vain! That these pure & holy sacrifices will purchase the redemption of our country from the guilt of injustice and oppression." All the helplessness Charlie had felt at Willy's death was now magnified. Aunt Mary's grief then was nothing compared to what he now felt for his mother, who poured out her heart to him, while he could only reply: "Your last two letters bring me very near to him and also to you and Father—nearer than I might ever have been. Do, dear Mother, write to me a little oftener and try and help me to be a little more

---

*Williams maintained that he had wanted to make a purely social call on his cousin, and on May 17 he was released and resumed command of the regiment. A few weeks later, when Lee took command of the Confederate troops, Major Williams was relieved of his command and spent the rest of the war guarding New York Harbor.

That he came under suspicion may have been partly due to his brother, William Orton Williams, who had also been in the cavalry but had resigned in June 1861 following a scandalous incident in which he shot a man for not saluting him. When examined, Orton Williams had declared, "For his ignorance, I pitied him; for his insolence, I forgave him; for his insubordination, I slew him." Resignation seemed the best thing under the circumstances. He then joined the Confederates but found that even rebel soldiers refused to fight under him, and his career as an officer was over. Eventually he and yet another cousin were caught in a Union camp wearing disguises. The two men were executed as spies. (William H. Carter, *From Yorktown to Santiago with the Sixth U.S. Cavalry* [Baltimore: Friedenwald, 1900], p. 33.)

like what you saw me as a little child. Your really loving son." The gentle tenderness of this note was uncharacteristic, as if he were instinctively attempting to assume some of his younger brother's qualities.[19]

Without a body there was no funeral, but Reverend Bartol, a little less than a year after he had commemorated the life of William Lowell Putnam, now gave a sermon for James Jackson Lowell. For the extended family, he raised this thought: "How strange that those two cousins, so pure, lofty, and peerlessly lovely in their character, should alone, of all we have known, be killed."[20] John Lothrop Motley, a family friend, attended the service for Jim. Afterward he wrote:

> There is something most touching in the fact that those two youths, Putnam and Lowell, both scions of our most honoured families, and both distinguished among their equals for talent, character, accomplishment, and virtue, for all that make youth VENERABLE, should have been among the earliest victims of this infernal conspiracy of slaveholders. I know not if such a thought is likely to comfort the mourners, but it is nevertheless most certain that when such SEED is SOWN the harvest to be reaped by the country will be almost priceless.[21]

Henry Higginson wrote his own brother, Jim, after the death of Jim Lowell: "You will feel very sorry if you have no hand in the struggle—whether we sink or swim. We are fighting against slavery, present or future, and we are struggling for the right of mankind to be educated and to think; come and do your part." Soon not only Jim Higginson but the youngest Higginson brother, Frank, had enlisted. But Charlie Lowell had no one in particular to recruit; his remaining cousins had already rushed to enlist. When the Peninsula campaign began, his cousin Cabot Jackson Russel, who was then not yet sixteen, had told his father, "If anything has happened to either of them [Jim or Charlie], Father, I shall want to enlist as soon as I get back." His father sent him on an expedition to the West, hoping to distract him from the cause, but when Cabot read of Jim's death, he telegraphed from a western train depot, "Now I shall have to fight." By September he was sworn in as a sergeant in the Forty-fourth Massachusetts Infantry along with another cousin, Pat Jackson, and their schoolmates Wilkie and Bob James.[22]

Lowell's sensitivity about the volunteer regiments being "food for powder" may have been strong, but he did not express vengeful or even vaguely

bloodthirsty thoughts. Aware of the cavalry's poor performance and basic ir-
relevance in the Peninsula campaign, he was an easy mark for guilty feelings
about his relative comfort, ease, and security. His staff appointment, which
took him even farther from danger, had come at a time when he might have
been glad to distract his mind from a sense of inadequacy, but it was characteristic of him to internalize his emotional turbulence. Rather than exhort-
ing others to do their bit for the cause, he oriented himself to his own
possibilities for action.

On July 23, ten days after becoming an aide to McClellan, Lowell wrote
to his mother's cousin Henry Lee, now an aide to Governor Andrew, requesting to command a volunteer Massachusetts regiment. Reviewing his
qualifications, he pointed out that he had been trained "in a 'crack' regiment" and had been privileged to command a squadron. He offered Generals William Emory (his former colonel) and George Stoneman (brigade
commander) as references. Then he said, "Perhaps you think me too
young—it is eight years to-day since I graduated—I have to apologize to myself for being so old." He mentioned Frank Barlow as an example of a young
man from civilian life who had quickly risen in the army.[23]

Other regular officers were taking commands of volunteer regiments to
help raise their quality, but Lowell's desire to associate himself more closely
with his home state also had less practical, more personal motives. The letter to Lee, written within days of his brother's death, was undoubtedly a reaction to that news. The depth of feeling among Jim's regimental colleagues
impressed Lowell. Listening to Patten and Holmes, seeing Palfrey in tears,
Lowell had recognized their bond of loyalty, forged by years of intimacy in
infancy, during school days, and now further deepened by fighting together.
The loyalty of comrades has been said to be perhaps the most powerful force
animating a soldier's motive for fighting and for finding within himself the
capacity for self-sacrifice that on a battlefield becomes heroics. More subtly,
it is essential in helping a soldier face death.

Lowell's wish to command a regiment also suggests his discontent with
his position as aide-de-camp to McClellan. McClellan's conservative military policy reflected his politics, and he was cultivated as a presidential candidate by powerful Democratic friends who were now stroking his ego by
suggesting he take over the government. Meant only as flattery and wishful
thinking, such comments helped to delude McClellan further.

When the third-rate general John Pope was brought east in late June to
command the Army of Virginia, McClellan fumed that the secretary of war,

Edwin Stanton, an old friend, was an "unmitigated scoundrel" whose capacity for betrayal was worse than "Judas Iscariot." McClellan was equally enraged by Lincoln's appointment of Henry Halleck, whom McClellan felt was showing his "cloven hoof," as "Commander-in-Chief" of Union forces. Compounding his anger was Halleck's order to McClellan at the end of July to return to Alexandria and coordinate with Pope in the Second Bull Run campaign. McClellan was so offended that he failed to acknowledge the order; instead he waited two weeks and only then returned and, after docking, leisurely marched the Army of the Potomac toward Alexandria. He was teasing the boundaries of insubordination. He vented his anger by jokingly entertaining the idea of marching on Washington with his "large military family" to persuade the government that it should treat him "more politely."[24]

Pope's campaign was not going well. McClellan dropped hints that if he were given command of both armies, he could save the day. When these hints were ignored, he found yet more excuses to move slowly. Although he did arrive in Alexandria by August 28, he refused to give assistance to Pope, who was fighting the culminating battle of the campaign, Second Bull Run. Other generals loyal to McClellan also refused to aid Pope: Fitz-John Porter, McClellan's closest colleague, was subsequently court-martialed.

As a military man, Lowell had some sympathy for the contempt with which McClellan's faction regarded Pope. Although clever politically and the darling of the Radical Republicans, Pope had always had low credibility among his military superiors, his fellow generals, and the men fighting under him. Compounding the problem, he had needlessly and ineptly alienated a huge segment of the army that was still loyal to McClellan with pointless snide references to his failings. Lowell was shocked by this infighting among the generals, particularly when he came to feel the price paid in the lives of his friends. Warren Dutton Russell, another Lowell cousin, of the Eighteenth Massachusetts, was killed at Second Bull Run. Warren had been "standing close by the colors of his regiment, waving his sword and cheering on his men in a charge, [when] grape-shot struck him in the neck and killed him instantly."[25] In the same battle Lowell's companion on the Burlington & Missouri River Railroad, John Read, was also killed.

Worst of all was the fate of the Second Massachusetts Infantry, which had been fighting all summer in the Shenandoah Valley campaign under the command of the Massachusetts politician-turned-general Nathaniel Banks. On August 9, eager to prove his military worth and believing that reinforcements were on the way, Banks rashly attacked General Thomas "Stonewall" Jackson's division at Cedar Mountain. At first, although outnumbered two to one, the Union men succeeded in driving back Jackson's forces, but then Jackson rode to the front, rallied his troops, and as another Confederate division came to his aid, counterattacked: the Union troops were driven back with severe losses. Banks lost 30 percent of his army; of the Second Massachusetts's twenty-three officers, sixteen were killed or wounded, with many of Lowell's oldest friends on the casualty list.

It wasn't until the end of August, when McClellan's army finally reached Alexandria, that Lowell was able to hear firsthand of the fighting at Cedar Mountain. The joy of finding old friends among the Union armies massed on the hills of Alexandria was sobered by the news of so many deaths. Higginson and Adams, both formerly of the Second, were now in the First Massachusetts Cavalry and thus safe. So was Rob Shaw, who as a staff officer to General Porter had not been in the fight. This troubled Shaw's conscience, particularly as it had fallen to him to find and identify his dead comrades, to arrange transport of their bodies home, and to write letters of condolence. Now he once again told the story, this time to Lowell, Higginson, and Adams.

Richard Goodwin, their old Latin School classmate and a member of Lowell's Harvard class of 1854, had been so ill he could not keep up with his regiment and needed his servant to help him walk. He fell behind as the men marched uphill to battle. Hardly had he reached the front when both he and his servant were killed, neither having actually fought. Richard Cary, a frail young man who had been in the gang from the Temple Court days, had also been ill. When he fell, a rebel soldier left a dipper of water for him and then, after he died, came back to rob him. At the urging of Cary's sergeant, who lay wounded beside him, the Confederate gave back a locket with a picture of Cary's wife. When Shaw found Cary's body he could hardly believe he was dead, he seemed so peaceful. Jim Savage, recently promoted to major, and Henry Russell were prisoners. Savage's horse had been shot from under him. His first wound had broken the upper bone of his right arm, the second had shattered the lower bone of his right leg, and a spent ball had damaged his left hip. Russell was tying a tourniquet on his friend's leg when the two were taken prisoner.

Higginson and Savage had ruled the Winter Street gang, led the games on the Common, and fought off the other gangs. Savage had always been physically robust, a great athlete and outdoorsman, so his friends had had great confidence in his physical abilities and strength; not realizing how bad his wounds were, Lowell and Higginson did not fear for him. Instead they took comfort in the fact that Russell was with him, for they knew that Savage needed companionship to keep up his spirits: left to his own devices, he would turn inward and descend into melancholy, as had happened with the death of his mother and two sisters. While at Harvard, he had become a devout Christian and in his earnest, quiet way impressed people with his moral purity, creating an atmosphere in which there was no place for coarse or vulgar talk. He was an ardent abolitionist, described by Cary as "one of those who came out to whip the rebels [and] free all the niggers."[26] But his depression made him inflexible and curiously inept. They all felt that the presence of Russell would help Savage survive imprisonment.

Hardest of all to accept was the death of Stephen Perkins. He too had been ill and refused to stay out of the fight at Cedar Mountain. While the regiment waited for the rebel counterattack, his enlisted men lay on the ground as Perkins, like the other officers, stayed on his feet, exposed to enemy fire. (As at Ball's Bluff, this needless exposure was in marked and self-conscious contrast to Union officers at Bull Run the year before.) Perkins was struck in the hand as the fighting started but wrapped a handkerchief around the wound and continued. Only when the regiment retreated under heavy fire was he killed. When Shaw found his body, it had been badly disfigured; he had been shot three times in the head.

Perkins, like Savage, had been a magnificent physical specimen, tall and powerfully built, with a kind of Grecian beauty. And like Savage, he had been deeply reserved. To a cousin who indifferently remarked that the war was unlikely to have much effect on her life, Perkins had replied: "I don't know that it will make any difference in your life, but it is likely to make a very great difference to mine." And he had been greatly liked. Charles Adams called him "the choicest mind I ever knew" and described him as "mature and self-respecting; one who thought much, and looked quite through the acts of men." Adams recalled, "He always impressed me with a sense of my own inferiority, and his friendship was a compliment." Perkins's death cut him to the quick.[27]

As they sat among the dog tents covering the hillsides of Alexandria, Henry Higginson and Charlie Lowell recalled their European journey on horseback with Stephen Perkins. Out of time and place, with whole nights to huddle around a campfire and blistering hot days to sit out in the shade, they had talked, "not content with the affairs of this world, being what one now would call real reformers or radicals, and measuring everything by their own foot rule." Perkins had spoken in a quiet, reflective, and observant way, Lowell with greater flamboyance — sarcastic, ironic, exploratory. Their conversations had ranged across the spectrum, from slavery (all three had considered going to Kansas) to the soul. Perkins, it will be recalled, had been the pessimist, confessing that there were times when he "would like to annihilate his soul" because he did not believe that "the good person receives his reward on this earth," that in fact "the best people are the unhappiest." Not surprisingly, it was Perkins who had posed the question, "I wonder whether we shall go on constantly expecting life to unfold itself, and the great possibilities to appear in us and outside of us, until we are surprised that death has come for us, when we hardly seem to ourselves to have lived." Now death had come for Stephen Perkins. He was twenty-six.[28]

Lowell knew that Perkins had been almost sublimely unsuited to military life. Cary and Goodwin had been equally improbable soldiers. Their disregard of their own inadequacies had a certain nobility, and Lowell would have been the last person to disrespect them for it, but he felt heartsick when contrasting the sangfroid he admired in his colleagues in the regular army with the qualities of his fallen friends. He also recognized that he shared his friends' rage. Rob Shaw wrote, "I long for the day when we shall attack the Rebels with an overwhelming force and annihilate them. May I live long enough to see them running before us hacked to little pieces." Shaw was not troubled by his rage or by his desire for revenge, which he thought was righteous. He was disturbed more by the callousness he discovered within himself on the battlefield of Cedar Mountain — "to step about among heaps of dead bodies, many of them . . . friends and acquaintances, without — any particular emotion." But to Lowell such control was admirable; he had long struggled with his own strong feelings, and admired friends like Potter who were contained and whose fires did not "smoke." His own explosive rage could not be expressed either in vengeful talk or in exhortations to enlist but lay coiled within him.[29]

In addition to responding to the many deaths and injuries of their colleagues and old friends, Lowell, Higginson, Adams, and Shaw were confounded by the general state of affairs. The campaigning of the summer of 1862 had ended with the disastrous battle of Second Bull Run. It had reduced the Union army to a mob, its officers to mutinous thoughts and outright insubordination. Pope's army had returned to Washington in a shambles, its morale exceedingly low. Once again rumors circulated of a potential coup. Charles Adams was shocked by what he encountered in Washington: "Our rulers seem to me to be crazy. The air of this city seems thick with treachery; our army seems in danger of utter demoralization . . . Everything is ripe for a terrible panic, the end of which I cannot see or even imagine."[30]

It is interesting to note the distance Lowell had come in less than three years. In the winter of 1859–60 he had been on the outer edge of an abolitionist circle, at the core of which was the radical and treasonous conspiracy to raid Harpers Ferry. By September 1862 he had served two months on the staff of a conservative general whose friends and officers grumbled and joked about the need for a coup d'état. During both these periods Lowell's correspondence is thin, leading one to speculate that at some stage outright suppression of material may have occurred. But the lack of information in his letters may also represent the sort of self-censorship or internal suppression that he exhibited during his illness. Perhaps for his mother's benefit, perhaps for his own, perhaps both, Lowell did not use his letters home to unburden himself emotionally. As he had written in 1858, he did not find it comforting to do so. In fact, Lowell's letters seem more like means of preparing arguments on which to act than as cathartic effusions.

It is also possible that Lowell did not take either the radicals or the conservatives seriously. Judging by the scorn with which he referred to "John Brownists" in late 1860, and by the speed with which he began his campaign to leave McClellan's staff, we can safely infer that his own radicalism and patriotism embraced neither self-destruction nor treason. Neither was "useful." Within the government McClellan's behavior had driven Secretary of War Stanton and Secretary of the Treasury Salmon P. Chase (the former senator from Pennsylvania) to draft a document demanding that McClellan be cashiered. Both men understood and feared McClellan's political ambitions. Lincoln, however, stepped in. Local and state elections were not far off, and the president desperately needed a break in the bad luck and mismanagement of the Union army. It could not be allowed to dissolve, as was now threatened. And so Pope's failure was McClellan's salvation. Lincoln was forced to acknowledge that McClellan was the best commanding general the Union had to offer. Despite the active protest of his most powerful cabinet secretaries, as well as his own frustrations and distrust, Lincoln ordered McClellan to take command of all the troops that had fallen back from the Bull Run battlefield to Washington.

Lowell and his companions could not have known the details of this crisis, but they certainly understood its general dimensions. Higginson and

Adams wanted to know what Shaw, on Porter's staff, and Lowell, on McClellan's, thought of the general. Lowell described McClellan as a great strategist and a brilliant administrator. Comparing him to the Duke of Wellington, the man who had defeated Napoleon, Lowell described him as a master of command—controlling everything, thinking of everything, bullying, supremely in charge. But Lowell also offered a warning: when it was time to act he had observed McClellan's curious vacillation and irresolution. "Unlike the Duke of Wellington, when he [McClellan] does come to strike, he doesn't . . . do the best thing—strike hard."[31]

ELEVEN

ANTIETAM

September 17, 1862

As soon as all the corps of the Army of the Potomac and the Army of Virginia (Pope's) were put under General McClellan's command, Charlie Lowell, as a member of the general's staff, was thrown into the organizational challenge of reprovisioning and equipping the army. This task was made more difficult because General Robert E. Lee, aware of the crisis in the Union command, acted boldly. By September 7 he had brought the Confederate army into Maryland. His invasion of Union territory appeared to threaten perhaps Baltimore, perhaps Washington, and perhaps Pennsylvania. His men were confident, cocky, and contemptuous. McClellan followed Lee, but cautiously, still focused on refitting the army and restoring its morale. Even a fortuitous discovery of Lee's orders, revealing the position of his divided troops and their extreme vulnerability, failed to arouse an instinct for bold and decisive action. McClellan had a perfect opportunity to seize the gaps at South Mountain, the northern tip of the Blue Ridge, thereby preventing Lee's army from reunifying, but he waited twenty-four hours before he acted. When on September 14 he did order an attack, Lee's troops had occupied the passes, and all the Union action did was alert Lee to the danger he was in. And so he ordered his scattered divisions to gather around Sharpsburg, Maryland, a town along Antietam Creek, overlooking the Potomac River. When Lee issued this order, it was his intention to retreat back into Virginia and the Shenandoah Valley. But the next day the Confederate position was strengthened when forces under Stonewall Jackson took the Union garrison at Harpers Ferry, which McClellan had failed to reinforce. This success emboldened Lee, who decided to make a stand at Sharpsburg.

With McClellan again in command, morale improved. The men felt they were taken care of—supplied, fed, trained. The officers felt the army had a firm leader again. This renewed confidence helped to turn the discouragement of the summer's campaigning into a sort of bitter anger. Fear of yet another defeat, so soon after the catastrophe at Bull Run, added a certain mettle to the soldiers; it was stronger than their actual fear of battle or their sense of being ill used by their generals. These factors fed into a particularly strange atmosphere as the armies approached each other. One historian has claimed that the old cliché of "seeing red" seemed to apply collectively: a kind of battle-madness or fury gripped the Union army, and "the very landscape . . . turned red."[1]

On the evening of September 15 both armies were at Sharpsburg. McClellan had the numerical advantage and claimed he would strike the next day, but he did not. Instead he hesitated. From his headquarters on the high ground on the east side of Antietam Creek, he could see the central portion of the battleground but could not make out the north flank, where he planned the attack to start the following morning. Nor did he have any sense of the wooded areas. He did not use the cavalry for reconnaissance, and curiously, none of the Union generals felt the need to scout out the ground. Thus they had no knowledge of how the Confederate forces were positioned or what the battleground was like; nor were they aware that Lee's army had been reinforced by the arrival of Stonewall Jackson's men.

Instead McClellan remained focused on his chain of command, making unconventional changes among his generals. Porter, his most loyal and trusted general, whose Fifth Corps was one of the strongest, was put in the reserve, as was the entire Union cavalry under Alfred E. Pleasonton. Ambrose Burnside, an old and trusted friend to whom McClellan felt tremendous loyalty and personal affection, had annoyed the general by his lack of initiative at South Mountain. Instead of confronting him, McClellan sent Burnside's First Corps under Joseph Hooker to the opposite side of the battlefield with orders to initiate the attack the next morning. This promotion of Hooker had the effect of punishing Burnside, who was now in the humiliating position of simply relaying orders from McClellan's headquarters to his remaining corps commander, General Jacob Cox. On the eve of battle McClellan had inexplicably wounded Burnside's pride, and yet he continued to rely on this friend whose judgment he mistrusted and whose pride he had hurt. Compounding this error, McClellan ordered cavalry veteran General Edwin Sumner, now an infantry corps commander, to support Hooker's attack as ordered. This required Sumner to report to a subordinate officer, something no officer found palatable. McClellan was frustrated with Sumner, thinking him old, slow, and stupid, but he gave no explanation and again continued to rely on a general he had offended. In Lowell's estimate, these were half-measures; McClellan should have relieved Sumner entirely.

Throughout the battle of Antietam, Lowell was deployed carrying messages and relaying information between McClellan and his generals. He was in a very good position from which to gain insight into the overall action. The battle began just after dawn, around 6 a.m., on September 17, when Hooker's First Corps attacked in the northernmost sector of the field, just out of view of headquarters, where everyone relied on the sounds of battle to learn what was going on—the boom of artillery cannon, the pacing of infantry volleys and their return. After an hour and a half McClellan sent an aide north with orders that Hooker be reinforced, and he sent Lowell to General Burnside, at the southernmost end of the field, with an order to move. As Lowell returned to headquarters, he believed that this next phase of the battle would see a two-pronged attack. Hooker, once reinforced, would renew fighting in the north while Burnside would cross Antietam Creek and engage the Confederates from the south. Once these flanking movements were under way, the center would attack, and then with one big push the Union troops would drive the Confederates back to the banks of the Potomac River, which at this point were steep and impossible to ford.[2]

What actually happened was very different. There was a pause in the fighting: something was wrong with the northern flanking action. Lowell was dispatched to investigate. As he rode off, he lost sight of the battlefield, but the ominous silence confirmed that Burnside had not started fighting. Arriving on the northern outskirts of the battlefield, he learned that General Sumner's Second Corps had failed to act in concert with General Joseph Mansfield's Twelfth Corps. Although ordered to support Hooker at 7:20 a.m., Sumner's men had been slowed down, first as they forded Antietam Creek, waist deep and fast-moving, then on the steep creek bank. Even the mile-long trek over undulating farmland had complications, for their way was obstructed by fences, patches of woods, and barnyards, which all had to be navigated while staying in formation. As a result, Mansfield's men were on the field first. These veteran troops, the Second Massachusetts among them, drove the Confederates back amid terrible slaughter. Mansfield himself was mortally wounded. Hooker was wounded in the foot and despite his protests was taken from the field when he grew faint from loss of blood; once in the rear, he lost consciousness. It was now about 9 a.m., and Sumner's men were on the field. Sumner had been impatient to attack since first light, and now he behaved rashly: he forged ahead without a briefing. He had received no intelligence, made no reconnaissance, and spurned advice. As Lowell followed them through a cornfield, its stalks now trodden underfoot and littered with men, the division became hopelessly tangled. Making matters worse, as Sumner plunged his corps into the fight, he closed up the three lines of General John Sedgwick's lead division and marched at the front, not noticing the gap he had opened in the Union line. This the Confederates exploited; as Sedgwick's men pushed into the West Woods, they attacked. Just as Lowell rode up to Sumner, "a holocaust engulfed Sedgwick's command."[3] Shell, spherical case, shrapnel, grape, canister, and even railroad iron and nails were relentlessly fired at them: whole sections of a line went down, as the men fell like dominoes. Explosions of artillery shook the ground. The deafening rumble was punctuated by high-pitched screaming, the snap and crack of trees hit, another shattering explosion. A sulfurous smell filled the air. Clouds of smoke obscured vision.

With the three lines bunched together, the second and third lines couldn't shoot without firing on their own men. Among the regiments caught in this maelstrom of shells and utter confusion was the Twentieth Massachusetts. Lowell thought he recognized the flag as he rode up, but the woods were now so filled with smoke that very little could be made out. Sumner, hatless, ran about waving his arms violently. He was signaling to retreat, but amid the smoke and confusion he and his signals meant nothing, and nothing could be done from a distance.

Lowell spotted the brigade flag, and as he rode up, he found Sedgwick frantically riding among his men. Almost immediately Sedgwick was shot through the leg, and a bullet broke his wrist; his horse was shot and collapsed. Against advice, Sedgwick refused to leave the field. He remounted, though his broken wrist made it impossible for him to control his horse; he was shot in the shoulder, fainted, and was carried off the field.

As Lowell rode on into the West Woods, shells bursting around him, whole clumps of men dropped together, lines crumbled and broke. Three-quarter-inch iron balls could disembowel a man or blow arms and legs right off. Limbs were hanging in the trees. The shock of such viciousness stopped men cold, and even the unwounded were profoundly disoriented when splattered with their messmates' insides. Every instinct told the men to escape the hailstorm of artillery fire raining down on them. Here on the front line Lowell found the Twentieth, their chain of command fractured because so many field officers were wounded. Their line and field officers could not grasp that they were being attacked from three sides, and once the men, who understood this, saw that they knew more than their officers, all authority was lost. Fear overtook them, and they began to flee.

A mass panic acquires an energy of its own—not from fear, but from the step beyond: terror. Men in a panic shut down completely: beyond reason, they are so possessed that no words or actions can reach them. In this instance, as they fled their overly cramped lines, they immediately incurred new problems. Some ran toward the enemy, but even those who didn't were in terrible danger. Randomly fleeing with their backs to enemy fire, they could offer no resistance and could only be potential victims.

Although cavalry action on the peninsula had not taught Lowell much, he had learned that only the coolest sangfroid had the power to check the force of panic, and only a sense of relative safety would afford men time to gather their wits. He rode out among the men and put his horse between them and the enemy, partly to shelter them, partly to shame them. But once in the line of fire, he became, of course, a target himself. His saber scabbard was struck and torn to pieces, but he himself was uninjured. The close call only animated him the more. One general described how "his eyes glistened and his face literally shone with . . . spirit and intelligence."[4] He seemed to be everywhere at once, riding among the men, whacking some with his saber, shouting to others, essentially herding them into retreat.

When the men reached the cornfield and its comparative safety, they were able to form a defensive line and hold. Meanwhile Mansfield's men renewed their attack, which helped draw Confederate fire away from Sumner's men. The panic was over. With the situation stabilized, Lowell withdrew. He had been diverted from his task barely twenty minutes, and now he hurried to report on the setbacks in the northern sector. Only as he attempted the steep climb up to headquarters did he notice that his horse, Berold, a large chestnut, was visibly flagging. Several times Berold stumbled and recovered slowly, and then before the summit he gave out.

Lowell dismounted and went to find his orderly, Frank Robbins. He told him to switch his saddle to Bob, another horse (given him by John Murray Forbes), and went to drink some water. When Robbins took the saddle off Berold, he found "two great lumps on each side of him as big as a hen's egg,"[5] where bullets had lodged under the saddle. He called to his captain, and Lowell examined Berold's wounds while Robbins switched the saddle. As he did so, he detached Lowell's overcoat, which had been rolled on the back of the saddle like a blanket. Shaking it out, he saw it was riddled with bullet holes. Lowell did not pause, however, and rode off on Bob, leaving Robbins to count the holes in yet another ruined overcoat.

By the time Lowell reached McClellan, the battle had moved on. Union troops were attacking in midfield around Sunken Road, in full view of head-quarters. This Confederate stronghold had seemed impregnable, with the rebels well hidden from view and in a position to mow down any assault made on them. This they did effectively, as McClellan and his staff watched from their porch, tension pulsating among them. All they could see of the battle was the stalemate and slaughter in the center. From the sound of the gunfire, they knew the northern attack was growing increasingly desultory. And still there was silence from the south. Repeatedly aides had been sent to Burnside with orders to attack, and each had returned with assurances that the attack was imminent, but still it did not come. McClellan remained alarmingly passive and unperturbed, which exacerbated the tension. Occa-sionally one or another group of officers heatedly discussed something, but mostly the men communicated with the most minimal of gestures. Binocu-lars passed from one to another, a word or two was mumbled, and the briefest of words were exchanged. McClellan and Porter held themselves aloof. An aide would bustle off to his horse, or another would return. A re-port would be made, and the information would move among the groups.

The contrast between the lack of action at headquarters and the frenzy of the fighting around Sunken Road heightened the tension, particularly because neither extreme brought results. Finally Frank Barlow, serving in General John C. Caldwell's brigade, led an assault that at great cost suc-ceeded in breaking the weakest and most exposed section of the road. The Confederates then found themselves too closely massed to defend them-selves, and they were mowed down in turn: Sunken Road became Bloody Lane. This breakthrough lanced the Union tension at headquarters and brought action.

Burnside's maddening and inexplicable failure to advance finally be-came intolerable. McClellan sent Colonel Keyes, one of his most trusted aides, with the authority to relieve Burnside if he refused to move. As Keyes rode off, some of the staff despaired. Lieutenant James Wilson confessed to Lowell that earlier in the morning he had been distressed enough to have persuaded George Smalley, a reporter for the New York Times, to ride to Hooker and propose that he take over the army. Since he did this without any authorization and without the support of any higher officer, Wilson, an aide-de-camp, was essentially proposing a coup. By the time Smalley reached Hooker's headquarters, that general, wounded in the foot, was no longer capable of command—fortunately. Astounded by his audacity, Lowell sympathized with Wilson's anguish. As Lowell saw it, "If McClellan had been a little ugly, he would have dropped Burnside right out, at nine o'clock, and somebody would have made the attack at once." Lowell knew Burnside and considered him patriotic and loyal but "of very ordinary intelligence and still less ability (for a general officer I mean of course)," as well as having a rather weak character.[6] Essentially he thought that personal niceties had interfered with McClellan's judgment: the general could not muster the ruthlessness necessary for effective command.

Fortunately, Colonel Keyes successfully motivated Burnside, who finally gave the order to start across the bridge over the Antietam. But by now the Confederates had reinforced their southern position. Cox's corps crossed the bridge slowly, at great cost, and then began to attack the Confederates from the southeast, while Sumner's Second and Third Divisions reentered the fight from the northeast. Briefly, and only in the midafternoon, the Union army appeared to be fulfilling its ambition of a double flanking movement. But the momentum was soon lost, although the fighting went on till dusk. The lack of coordination among the Union generals had permitted Lee to concentrate his troops on each assault individually instead of being forced to fight on all fronts.

As darkness fell, the roar of battle was replaced by the moans of the wounded and dying. Both armies slept where they had fought. Union officers assumed that the battle would be renewed the next morning when, many of them believed, they stood a good chance of destroying Lee's army. Even the troops, exhausted and devastated and dreading the thought, were ready to fight. Everyone remembered that Porter's corps had sat out the entire battle: fresh troops for the renewed fight.

The next day the troops awoke early and waited for orders to renew the battle: the Confederates with considerable dread, the Union almost eagerly. But the orders never came. McClellan let the opportunity pass largely because he did not realize it existed. To some degree, that is perhaps understandable: his men had suffered the worst day of battle ever experienced, with 12,500 men—one-quarter of those who went into action—killed, wounded, or missing. Combined losses of the Union and Confederate armies were almost 23,000 men for twelve hours of battle. All through the night reports had come to headquarters detailing the devastation, information that was almost indigestible in its enormity.[7]

By midday a truce was agreed on, and both sides began to tend to their dead and dying. Charlie Lowell's first concern was the fate of the Twentieth Massachusetts, which he knew had endured some of the worst fighting. Their losses were the highest of any division. Responsibility for the tragedy lay entirely with Sumner: his blind fidelity to inadequate orders, his rashness, and his indefensible decision to mass the men. As Lowell rode to their camp, he crossed a battlefield littered with corpses, in some places so thickly that there was no space for Lowell's horse to pick a way among them. Some bodies were mangled and torn to pieces, stripped of clothing, shoes, weapons—sometimes because of looting, but often because the simple force of the firepower had blown off the clothing. Hundreds of mangled horses were littered about, along with the detritus of war: guns, carriages, wagons, equipment of every kind. Crops were trampled, barns knocked to pieces, buildings scarred and burned. The landscape bore no resemblance to what it had been the day before. Lowell wandered through this wasteland trying to distinguish the wounded from the dead, to find friends who might be helped or at least dignified. Some men slept as if dead, using corpses as pillows. Others wandered in a delirium. They were filthy, their faces blackened by gunpowder and streaked with sweat.

Death and injury were everywhere. At the field hospitals Lowell passed mounds of amputated limbs piled like cordwood outside the entrances. Bodies shook in death throes or simply from shock. The ill, the dead, and the injured were so filthy, they were hardly recognizable as men. Then there were men bragging manically, adrenaline and shock animating their actions; they too had a ghoulish inhumanity, the whites of their eyes shockingly large in their dirt-streaked faces. Lowell had seen nothing like this on the peninsula. Cavalry skirmishing, while nasty enough, had had nothing of this overwhelming abundance of destruction.

Lowell found the Twentieth at their campfires, sleeping or eating in a daze, reacting to their trauma with profound hunger or profound fatigue. Frank Palfrey, his tall, thin frame collapsed, was badly wounded. Paul Revere, only slightly wounded, was in command. As he told Lowell of the condition of the regiment, he leaned against his horse and fell asleep in midsentence. His older brother, the Twentieth's able regimental surgeon Edward Revere, had been killed at noon as he tended a wounded man.

Frank Barlow had taken refuge in a nearby house, where his wife, a nurse, was tending him. Barlow had been badly wounded in the groin in the assault that had broken Confederate control of Sunken Road. Now he slept, his devoted wife at his side. In the same house were Wendell Holmes and Pen Hallowell, both wounded. Holmes had been shot through the base of his neck without the ball's having hit anything vital, spine or artery, and his adrenaline was still high. Hallowell's arm had been broken and badly smashed, and he was terrified that it would be amputated if he went to a field hospital; Holmes devised a splint for it. Ned Hallowell, having found his older brother after searching with mounting fear, had collapsed in a corner of the room, delirious with fever.

Riding on to the Second Massachusetts's camp, Lowell discovered Wilder Dwight mortally wounded, his pelvis shattered. Loss of blood had brought on the symptoms of shock. He had been given extra doses of morphine and could not possibly live long. Nursing him was one of his men, Private Rupert Sadler, whom Dwight had recruited. Dwight had been ill before the battle but nevertheless joined the fight when the regiment was first sent in to support Hooker. When he felt morale failing, he had tried to rally his men by taking a captured rebel flag and walking up to their front line. As he was waving the flag, he was shot in the left wrist and then in the left hip, the shot shattering the joint. Almost immediately the regiment had to retreat, leaving him lying in a field open to enemy fire. Knowing that his hip wound was fatal, Dwight took out some paper and tried to write to his mother. Sadler explained to Lowell that he owed Dwight, a lawyer who had successfully defended him in a manslaughter case, his life, so it had seemed only natural to creep out to him, give him water, take the letter, and also insist on carrying him carefully to a safer spot. Later in the day, when the regiment was again forced to retreat, the loyal friend again crept out and carried Dwight to the rear. Now he would stay with Dwight until death released him.

Lowell looked at the shivering man, his body twitching in pain, his mind largely insensible to the world around him. One year and six months almost to the day, the two had met outside Willard's Hotel in the first days of the war, when Dwight came to Washington to speed through approval for the formation of the Second Massachusetts Infantry. He had struck Lowell as someone who was sure to last the war and go on to greater things.

Also sedated was Bill Sedgwick, Dwight's cousin. Shot in the spine while rallying his men, Sedgwick had been knocked from his horse. The spine wound had paralyzed one leg. He too pulled out paper to write. With shocking composure, despite "very great pain" and shells bursting all around him, he wrote that he prayed to God to forgive his sins, "to bless and comfort my darling wife and children, my dearest mother and sisters."[8] Two things he wanted his friends to know: he fell doing his duty, and he had not yet uttered a groan. For eight hours he remained trapped by fire before he was moved to safety. Lowell had never liked Bill Sedgwick much, finding him fastidious and dull. Now he lay dying, filthy and sweat-streaked, in fitful drug-induced sleep.

Rob Shaw was fine. Early on he had been hit by a spent ball, as the Second had started into the fight; he had been knocked senseless for a brief time and bruised. But he had been lucky: there were many wounded, many killed. Among those who survived, each story combined ill luck and good luck; they told of the random cruelty of war and of equally random courageous acts.

Late in the afternoon Lowell rode away from the unreal scene and stopped at the camp of the First Massachusetts Cavalry, which had not been in the fight and was untouched. Charles Adams confessed he had slept through the middle of the day; Henry Higginson did not understand why his regiment had remained in reserve and why the fighting had not been renewed. Night fell, and the enemy fires began to glow in the distance. The officers of the First were hoping they would be called into action, but Lowell was of two minds. From the comfortable perspective of the camps of the reserve troops, logic seemed to argue that now was the time to strike in order to destroy Lee's army, but for the ravaged men of the Twentieth and the Second, logic argued that exhausted troops could not so quickly take up the fight again.

Before he slept that night Charlie Lowell composed for his mother a brief account of the battle and the fate of family friends. "This is not a pleasant letter," he ended. He told nothing of his own exposure under fire, his shattered scabbard, his wounded horse or ruined coat. He did not mention a nasty bruise on the thigh and around the hip from the impact of the smashed scabbard, which was nothing in comparison to the suffering around him. In a letter to John Murray Forbes he managed to say more: "I have had my usual good luck, but shall have to buy a new saber and shall have one horse the less to ride for a month or two." Fortunately "Bob Logic," the horse given him by Forbes, although in the fight, "was untouched." Lowell was able to assure Forbes that his son Will Forbes and all the First Massachusetts Cavalry were safe. Then Lowell sat in the dark, waiting for sleep.[9]

Although Lowell acknowledged "my usual good luck," things were more complicated than that. When Lowell's orderly, Frank Robbins, had marveled at Lowell's luck and wanted to keep his bullet-riddled overcoat as proof, Lowell had once again snatched it back and given it to a camp follower, saying it was "unlucky" to keep such things. (Robbins did keep the shivered scabbard but only by hiding it.)

The next morning, as the mist cleared, it became evident that Lee's army had vanished. It had withdrawn across the Potomac under cover of night. The battle was over. McClellan became euphoric. He telegraphed Halleck: "Our victory was complete. The enemy is driven back into Virginia. Maryland and Pennsylvania are now safe." He wrote his wife: "I fought the battle splendidly . . . it was a masterpiece of art . . . I feel some little pride in having, with a beaten & demoralized army, defeated Lee so utterly."[10]

Lowell was significantly less fulsome. He wrote both his mother and John Murray Forbes that he believed the Antietam victory to be "a complete one," but he was more tentative about its implications, telling Forbes that it was only "decisive in so far as it clears Maryland," and his mother that the battle was not so decisive "as could have been wished." McClellan's failure to renew the fight on the second day troubled Lowell, and he was not alone. A number of staff officers believed that another opportunity to destroy Lee's army had been lost. (It has been convincingly argued that McClellan had six "highly favorable opportunities" to do precisely this.) McClellan had violated some of the most "established principles of the military art."[11]

The private misgivings of some of McClellan's staff were nothing compared to the reaction of Lincoln's administration. And yet so confident was McClellan that he was God's "instrument for saving the nation" that he demanded that his "Judas,"[12] Secretary of War Stanton, be removed and that he himself be made commander-in-chief, eclipsing Halleck. Lincoln brushed aside these grandiose demands and seized the victory of Antietam for his own purposes. On September 22 he presented the nation with the Emancipation Proclamation, a dry legalistic document of questionable constitutionality that pleased no one. Calling on the rebelling states to rejoin the Union, Lincoln announced that if they did not do so by January 1, 1863, their slaves would be considered free. The proclamation's symbolic value was enormous, however, and its repercussions profound; in the North, a conservative war policy in favor of the restoration of the Union with slavery intact was no longer possible. The Union army had become a liberating force.

Lowell was initially nonplussed by the Emancipation Proclamation. As a stand on principle, it lacked moral force since it had been made so late in the day. Nor was its political value immediately apparent, other than as a means of dividing public opinion within the Union. It appeared to be a war measure but a dubious one. Its immediate effect was to force a crisis at the highest echelons of the regular army, particularly among officers close to McClellan. General Porter, for example, complained it was the "absurd proclamation of a political coward" that would only "prolong the war by rousing the bitter feelings of the South." One reporter for a Democratic paper wrote his editor that he had observed among officers "a large promise of a fearful revolution . . . that will startle the Country and give us a military Dictator."[13]

As discontent among the officers came to Lincoln's attention, he acted boldly, making an example of Major John J. Key, an unfortunate officer on Halleck's staff who had mistakenly tried to answer the question that was on everyone's lips: why hadn't McClellan destroyed Lee's army? Key replied, "That is not the game. The object is that neither army shall get much advantage of the other; that both shall be kept in the field till they are exhausted, when we will make a compromise and save slavery."[14] Quite whom Major Key imagined he was speaking for is unclear, but he was crudely expressing a view far worse than the policy of conciliation that General Scott had initially put forward, that McClellan had then modified, and that conservative circles still supported. Key suggested that the army was running its own show and that the loyalty of Union officers to their Confederate confreres outweighed their loyalty to the Union. For once Lincoln was unequivocal: on September 27, after interviewing Key, Lincoln summarily cashiered the major.

That very afternoon Lowell was in Washington, at the War Department, delivering to the secretary of war the thirty-nine enemy flags captured at Antietam, the first victory of the Union's eastern campaign. This was a great honor, and Lowell was justifiably proud to have been chosen for it. At the War Department Stanton greeted him brusquely: "What do you want, young man?"

Lowell explained.

"Fetch them in and stand them up in the corner," Stanton said.

After doing so, Lowell awaited further instruction, a commendation, or a message of congratulations to return to McClellan. Usually a small ceremony marked such an event: the favored officer, representing the army in the field, was feted by the government and had a chance to make a good impression on the key executive dignitaries.

After a long pause, Stanton turned around in his chair. "Have you any other business with me, young man?" he asked.

"No," Lowell replied.

"Good-day, sir," was Stanton's response. Thus ended the interview.

Nothing could have more clearly conveyed the depth of chill in relations between McClellan and the government. When Lowell returned to headquarters, he described his interview with Stanton in tones that were "amused, aggravated and insulted."[15]

While in Washington delivering the battle flags, Lowell had been surprised to learn of Jim Savage's death. He had thought Jim was getting along well despite his many wounds. Savage's brother-in-law had family in Virginia and they made sure Jim was treated considerately by his captors, but his shattered leg had refused to mend and was eventually amputated; the stump had bled profusely; it had to be reopened and the arteries retied, by which time Savage was in very poor condition. He had lingered on and died of exhaustion and infections on September 22, the day of the Emancipation Proclamation.

This coincidence aroused bitter feelings in Lowell. Savage's abolitionism had been profoundly Christian. His faith and his abolitionism were one. Like Charlie's grandfather Lowell, Savage had never spoken of wrath, retribution, or evil but instead had prayed for deliverance, redemption, and forgiveness. It was a faith that Lowell esteemed, though he did not have the temperament for it himself. Now he reckoned he had always attributed to Savage the power of invulnerability. His death seemed even worse and more inconceivable than that of Stephen Perkins.

On October 1 Lincoln visited General McClellan at Antietam and was taken over the battlefield. His purpose was to urge McClellan to pursue Lee, but still the army failed to do so. Throughout October Lincoln and Halleck tried without success to get McClellan to move on Richmond, but he claimed that neither his men nor his horses were ready for battle. On October 25 Lincoln asked, "Will you pardon me for asking what the horses of your army have done since the battle of Antietam that fatigues anything?" This did succeed in getting McClellan to make a start south, crossing the Potomac in an effort to get between Richmond and Lee's army, regrouping in the Shenandoah Valley. But the start was too late, and McClellan's progress too slow. Lincoln complained he had "tried long enough to bore with an auger too dull to take hold."[16] The only reason for Lincoln to retain McClellan was to prevent any last-minute controversy that might affect the midterm election. It was clear to the Republicans that McClellan was not only a military failure but a political threat, since he was a strong supporter of the Peace Democrats and their most likely candidate for president in 1864. McClellan, still imagining himself the nation's savior, grew increasingly adept at blaming others for his own mistakes and at making outrageous demands.

Lowell was baffled. Lincoln's passivity was incongruous with true leadership. Sometimes under the domination of Seward or McClellan, at other times a pawn of the Radical Republicans in Congress, Lincoln seemed too easily led himself. Lowell also recognized McClellan's failings and the pointless and petty jealousies among the generals. Lowell continued to do his duty for leaders he felt did not deserve and had not earned his loyalty. He continued to believe in the subordination of the military to civil governance, and had no patience either for many officers' contempt for civilian authority or for their conservative politics. And yet he hoped that his request of July 23 to Henry Lee to command a volunteer regiment of Massachusetts men would soon bear fruit, but he had heard nothing.

Then, on October 25, Charlie Lowell received a letter, not from Governor Andrew but from Amos Adams Lawrence, proposing that he, with the rank of major, command a cavalry "battalion of gentlemen" for "home use i.e. in the militia."[17] Lowell had little idea what to make of this proposal, for it seemed beside the point: the U.S. Army did not recognize a battalion as an independent military unit, so permission would never be granted by the War Department; moreover, a militia was composed of men signed on for nine months—far too short a time to train cavalry.

Lowell considered Amos Lawrence the embodiment of the Cotton Whig heritage: he had a cotton textile fortune, a stepmother from South Carolina, and an uncle who was the last Boston Whig of national significance. He had helped to foment the riots that had broken up antislavery meetings in Boston since 1835 and that had culminated in a riot in December 1860, when Lawrence himself ran for governor in a futile bid to revive the traditional Whig compromise position under the guise of the Constitutional Union Party. Lowell thought he was out of touch, cocooned in the comfort and self-congratulation of Beacon Hill, unable to assess the requirements of the times.

Proper Bostonians had the idea that a regiment's moral and social tone was important. Good "breeding" would help a man withstand the bestiality of war, it was thought. Aunt Mary had made a strenuous effort to get Willy Putnam into the regiment commanded by William Greene because under his patrician eye her son's moral character, she believed, would survive intact the rigors of war. Lowell had seemed to endorse this view in 1860, when he wrote about "decent men" and the southerner's sense of moral responsibility. But his perspective had changed. The experience of battle convinced him that entirely different standards applied. Not only had he seen many "gentlemen" fail under fire, but even when the codes of gentlemanly conduct were adhered to, the result was often still incompetence and death. He believed the requisite battlefield qualities were decisiveness and ruthlessness. It helped to be able to transform that peculiar mix of fear, rage, and courage which possesses a man under fire into action—in the case of an officer, considered action.

"What do you mean by gentlemen?" Lowell, weary in all ways, replied. "Drivers of gigs?"[18]

Lowell then contacted John Murray Forbes, recognizing that he needed an advocate who would shepherd Lawrence's proposal toward a realistic plan. After all, Forbes, a key adviser to the governor, from the war's start had established himself as practical, resourceful, and efficient. Lowell explained to Forbes why it was necessary to decline Lawrence's offer, but he also made clear to what he would agree: "I should like very much to take command of a Second Massachusetts Cavalry." He explained that the War Department, although eager to release regular officers to train and command volunteer regiments so as to improve their quality, would never grant him permission to command an unrecognized independent military unit like a battalion. Lowell warned that such a request would be granted only "through improper influence and in defiance of General Orders . . . I do not care to attempt it."

Lowell's adherence to military protocol confirmed his apparent commitment to a military career. Underlining this point, he brought up a point of honor. As captain in the Sixth U.S. Cavalry, he commanded a battalion; he was in essence an "acting" major. To accept Lawrence's offer would have given him only the "rank and pay of Major" and, he explained to Forbes, "I want to keep my record clearer than that." The terms of advancement mattered to him. He also questioned the inherent integrity of the idea. Lawrence wanted to have the principal voice in naming the battalion's officers, but Lowell wanted the right to weed them out later. He asked whether

Lawrence would be able to keep officers in place should they prove "incompetent." Lowell's question reflected his willingness to bend to political reality but not to be dominated by purely political considerations.[19]

Fortunately Lawrence was a better man than Lowell had estimated. Uncle Patrick Jackson smoothed over Lowell's sarcastic letter to Lawrence, whom he knew well, by explaining Charlie's grief over the death of his brother on the peninsula. To his credit, Lawrence not only put aside the affront but saw merit in Lowell's objections and quickly came around. He agreed to bankroll not just a battalion but an entire regiment of cavalry with Lowell as colonel. By the last week of October, Lowell was already absorbed in this new task, recruiting officers from the regiments of his old friends. He wanted officers with experience of cavalry if possible, of war at least.

On November 2 Lowell and his friends in the First Massachusetts Cavalry tried to get a nearby farmer to give them supper. At first the farmer's wife insisted that she had nothing to spare for them. But after Lowell chatted her up, she gave them "a very good supper" and promised them breakfast. After the meal Lowell explained his mission to his friends. Higginson and Adams were high-ranking captains and vital to the morale of the regiment. Neither thought they could leave it to join him, but their advice was valuable. Both recommended Caspar Crowninshield, who at Ball's Bluff had assumed command of the Twentieth during its retreat. A tall, well-built man, Crowninshield was in fact too tall for the ideal cavalryman, but after Ball's Bluff he had joined the First Massachusetts Cavalry and had since gained considerable experience in it. Though something of a snob, having grown up under the wing of his extremely wealthy grandfather, David Sears, he came well recommended by Rob Shaw, his former roommate, and by Charles Adams, his brother-in-law. Crowninshield was certainly not a radical. He had volunteered "to show to the world that we have a government, and that a Republic is not a vain idea," and to show the South that "we are not to be bullied."[20] He loathed Lincoln and hated blacks.

Will Forbes was Lowell's choice for first captain. Commissioned as a second lieutenant in the First Massachusetts Cavalry, he so far had had little chance to distinguish himself, but he had good sense and was entirely trustworthy and universally liked. Lowell believed he could help to establish the regiment's tone and morale. In addition, he was the son of John Murray Forbes.

Francis Washburn, a young man whom Lowell did not know, came highly recommended. An abolitionist from Worcester who had studied engineering in Europe and at the Lawrence Sheffield Scientific School, he was admired and respected among his fellow officers in the First Massachusetts Cavalry. Louis Cabot, whom Lowell had known since infancy, was adept at accounting and had a good knowledge of horses, but he wasn't much of a soldier. Adams probably insisted that if Lowell were to take one of their best officers, Washburn, he would also have to take one or two they would not miss. That evening Lowell shared Will Forbes's tent, and Will reported to his mother that Lowell "coughed once or twice during the night and was restless as usual."[21] This would suggest that Lowell's lung problems were not entirely cleared up.

A few days later Lowell visited the Second, where he particularly wanted to recruit Rob Shaw and Henry Russell. Russell, paroled at the end of October, had stopped in Boston long enough to become engaged to Mary Forbes (second daughter of John Murray Forbes) before rejoining his regiment, which he did not want to leave. Shaw was tempted by Lowell's offer largely because he relished the prospect of working with Lowell, Crowninshield, and Forbes, but in the end loyalty to the Second Infantry and all it had suffered at Cedar Mountain and Antietam prevailed. That not much was left of the original regiment made it all the harder to leave it. Also, although in June 1861 Shaw had envied Lowell for joining the cavalry, he now had a prejudice against it, claiming that "most of them are so bad that we don't think much of them, excepting for the advantage they have in running away." He looked upon a cavalry commission as a "safe place" and did not want one. The door was left open, however, for Shaw and Russell to change their minds.[22]

Lowell proceeded to fill other commissions and was once again in daily telegraphic communication with Governor Andrew, wiring names back and forth until November 9, when he was officially relieved of duty on Mc-Clellan's staff and from the Sixth U.S. Cavalry and ordered to report to Governor Andrew. This was Election Day, and the same day as McClellan's carefully engineered dismissal, which began within hours of the polls closing. A senior military figure in the War Department delivered a letter to Mc-Clellan relieving him of command. He was to be replaced, ironically, by Ambrose Burnside, whom few believed up to the job, including himself. (He had already twice refused on the grounds that he was not qualified.)

Within McClellan's circle, the general's removal was received with outrage. As the shocking news swirled through army headquarters, Lowell quietly went about putting his things together and left for Boston immediately. He missed the army's great show of support for McClellan on November 10, the drunken ranting of fellow staff members that evening, and McClellan's tearful farewell on November 11. McClellan's war was over, and Charlie Lowell was headed toward his own regiment.

The Second Massachusetts Cavalry

TWELVE

RAISING A REGIMENT

1862–63

When Charlie Lowell came home on leave in early November 1862, life at his mother's house in Cambridge was entirely recognizable to him. As in the past, an inexhaustible supply of young people—boys from Harvard College across the street and girls from the Agassiz school down the road—used the Lowell house as a gathering place. Georgina Lowell Putnam, Willy's sister, was often there. Emerson's daughters Edith and Ellen, idolizing Anna Lowell as they did, visited as often as they could. Their brother, Edward, was an undergraduate and a regular. And Anna still took in lodgers, at the moment a Lowell cousin preparing to enter Harvard. The Agassiz and Felton girls, being neighbors, were daily in the house: coming to tea, to find a walking companion, to issue an invitation, or to organize a reading of Shakespeare or a German play. In addition to all these young people, James Russell Lowell and his daughter Mabel were frequent visitors. There was also a regular swirl of junior professors, extended family, and bright young men who thrived on Anna's conversation.

But Charlie noticed changes, too. Since Jim's death Harriet and her infant son, William Lowell Putnam, now stayed for long stretches in the house (to the frustration of her husband, George Putnam). The baby, called the Beautiful Bunch, was a joyful distraction for his mourning grandparents. For hours Charlie's father would sing "Yankee Doodle" to Bunch, who loved the attention and always got it. Often the indulgent grandfather Charles was not told that Bunch was in the house, because once in his arms, Charles seldom gave him up to others. Anna too delighted in the baby, though he could "never fill [Jim's] place."[1] She talked frequently of her son, tried to write a short piece on his life, and like many grieving parents proudly relived his triumphs with whoever would listen.

The house on Quincy Street had also become a center for war news, and once Charlie returned home, there was further reason for this. Almost every one of the cousinly families—the Holmeses, Storrows, Paines, Russels, Jacksons, and Higginsons, as well as the extended Forbes clan—had sons in the army. The women in these households volunteered at the Sanitary Commission preparing and packing boxes of supplies for soldiers and hospitals. Almost all of them knit endless supplies of hats, mittens, and socks and devoted inordinate amounts of time to preparing boxes to send to their sons, husbands, and brothers. Officers sent home long request lists asking for books, cigars, and specific items of food or clothing, as well as sheet music for the regimental band, books for the regimental library, and supplies for the regimental hospital. These requests were zealously fulfilled, the women competing to outdo one another. No mother wanted to be in the position of learning that her son was mooching off a friend's crate from home. Secrets of special finds, methods of procurement, and even tricks of shipping were jealously guarded and only selectively shared.

A similar competition concerned news from both the front and the statehouse. When young ladies gathered, they achieved status by having news to tell. The exalted ones were the actual recipients of letters; a second tier included those with whom the letters were shared, an inner circle of family and closest friends; a third tier was an unstable gray zone of intimacy, where portions of a letter could and might be read aloud.

The circle of young women at the Lowell house on Quincy Street gained a sense of vicarious experience from Anna Lowell and her cousin Amelia Holmes, both of whom went daily to the Union Hall in Boston, where they ran a relief center for the wives of enlisted men. Procuring commissions for sewn garments, mostly army uniforms, Anna and Amelia arranged contract sewing for the wives of soldiers that gave them supplemental income. Anna used her connections to numerous officers to intercede on the behalf of distressed wives or mothers wanting news, details, or special attention. Sometimes it was a matter of an enlisted man who had lost touch with his family or been wounded and was unable to communicate. Other times it was more serious: a name appearing on a casualty list without confirmation from a regimental officer. In still other cases it was the tricky business of trying to compel an enlisted man to provide for his family from his pay, or simply to write. Friends worried that Anna was working herself to the point of exhaustion. Emerson believed it was grief that drove the "devotion of herself & all her family to the public service,"[2] and there was some truth to this.

Very few women, young or old, even attempted what the younger Anna had accomplished by becoming a nurse, and those who did often broke down under the strain. Louisa May Alcott, only two years older than Anna, lasted only three months, but Anna lasted out the war. She was now at the Armory Hospital in Washington, which, being nearest the docks where the transports brought the wounded, received the worst cases.

When Anna Lowell wrote to her daughter, "For his [Jim's] sake I could nurse many soldiers," Anna chafed. "That is not my feeling exactly and never was. I have some pleasure in it now for little Jim's sake, but why I wanted to come—was because I knew it was my 'one talent' and did not want to be an unprofitable servant."[3] She had begun her nursing before Jim had even been wounded. It was a genuine contribution to the war, and she wanted it recognized in its own right. Her grief was private and inconsolable, but however intensely felt, her loss was not special or singular. To aggrandize it would be a delusion. Anna had seen too much suffering to imagine that Jim's death was unique or that she, in her pain, had any special claims. Unlike her aunt Mary, she was not the recipient of a visitation: Jim had died along with thousands of others, luckier than some, not as lucky as others. And she, like thousands of sisters, had lost forever and irredeemably her favorite brother. It was a hard but unavoidable truth.

Years before, Charlie Lowell had commented that it was easy to live in Cambridge and "never know that you are nobody." Years of traveling and living away from home had confirmed the truth of this remark even before the war broke out. Young Anna, like many of the young officers for whom war was their first experience away from home, learned the lesson under the most painful circumstances. A powerful example was Frank Palfrey, lieutenant-colonel of the Twentieth. Ball's Bluff, the Seven Days, and then the West Woods of Antietam, where he was wounded, were rough experiences for a cosseted young man of whom, before the war, the senior partner in his law firm, George S. Hillard, had said, "He is such a favorite in society that he has to go out more than he ought. It distracts him, but among the young ladies he is so liked that the temptation is too much." Shipped home after Antietam, his brother John went to fetch him from the depot and found him but "a bundle of dirty, bloody rags on the floor of a baggage car, after a continuous jostle of a hundred and forty miles."[4]

Palfrey blamed McClellan, he blamed the government, and he blamed the entire military and administrative mismanagement of the war. And he never did return to his regiment. The fatigue of nearly constant marching and fighting, with no chance to recoup strength or relieve the anxiety and strain of inglorious and desultory campaigning, had worn him down. "If I could have known a year ago, how things were to be managed," he said, "I never would have taken up arms." Once home he became angry at how people there continued to shroud the dead in mantles of nobility, instead of recognizing the reality of death's commonplace misery. "When parents tire of having their children die by thousands in camps and field," Palfrey wrote, "then the war will be so conducted as to bring victory."[5]

Slowly during the autumn of 1862 the price of war was finally coming home. In 1861 the death of Willy Putnam had seemed exceptional and the Boston community had reacted by emphasizing his unique qualities. As late as July 1862 people had reacted to the death of Jim Lowell by pondering the significance of the deaths of those two boys in particular. But by the end of the year there were too many grieving families to single out any one as exceptional. In awakening people to the full reality of the war, martyrs or heroes were less effective than deaths too numerous to count, pain too deep to feel.

Palfrey, like Anna, was also expressing the great divide between what the soldier in the field or the nurse in the hospital knew and what those at home whose experience was only vicarious could grasp. In many families this gap was unbridgeable. And in this sense Charlie Lowell was lucky, for his mother, through her work at Union Hall, had a deeper, more complex understanding of the experience of the Union soldier and the war's social costs than most women. Yet even her sympathy had limits.

Shortly after his return home Charlie had argued to his mother that it was impossible to defeat the Confederacy, and precisely because it was impossible, it would have to be done. His mother thought this seeming contradiction was yet another "Charleyism," another sophistical flourish, and reported it to her daughter as an example of his terrierlike argumentative style. But this easy dismissal missed the point: Charlie was saying that the political unity of the Confederacy and its superior military talent had, in two years of war, forged a fighting power that the Union had not mastered or equaled, nor had the Union yet found the resolve to win, and yet it would have to win.

Lowell had first claimed the success of an impossibility in 1854 in his Commencement Day oration, when he said, "The world always advances by impossibilities achieved." In explaining the virtues of youth, he had observed that an insurmountable obstacle in an earlier generation is often overcome in the next. The spur to such a thought had been his experience of witnessing the return of Anthony Burns to slavery. Lowell and Higginson, traipsing over the bridge to Cambridge that evening, had recognized that their parents' generation had failed: they could not see beyond the slave's status as property to recognize his humanity. In 1854 Lowell had insisted that a moral revolution was possible: the task of abolishing slavery would fall to his generation. Now that possibility was closer to becoming a reality, yet it seemed as elusive as ever. A year and a half of war had achieved very little beyond the hideous death toll best demonstrated at Antietam and Shiloh. The Union remained fractious while the Confederates appeared impervious to failure.

Wendell Holmes also had parents whose experience might have made them more understanding. His mother worked with Anna Lowell at Union Hall, and his father, a doctor, might have been presumed to have a capacity for understanding trauma and the effects of mass suffering. Not so. After Antietam, when Holmes had written his parents, "I've pretty much made up my mind that the South have achieved their independence & I am almost ready to hope spring will see an end . . . believe me, we never shall lick 'em," Dr. Holmes had reacted harshly, accusing his son of loss of faith in the cause. Wendell replied angrily, telling his father he was "ignorant . . . I never I believe have shown, as you seemed to hint, any wavering in my belief in the right of our cause . . . I am to be sure heartily tired and half worn out body and mind by this life, but I believe I am as ready as ever to do my duty." His frustration was with the "terrible experience & still more the mismanagement."[6]

It was the experience of the war and its bungled prosecution, not the reasons for the war or even its success or failure, that was wearing down young men like Wendell Holmes and angering Frank Barlow and Rob Shaw. Barlow believed that only a radical change in the Union's leadership would prevent a Confederate victory. The experience of war itself—the fighting, the dying, the surviving—was changing them, and changing how they thought, in ways that were all but impossible for others to understand. Experience stripped away the veneer of genteel life, cultural ritual, civilized expectations, and their own self-conceits. In extreme conditions they had experienced something intensely real and true, truer perhaps than anything else in their lives. Stephen Perkins's midnight speculation among the glaciers of the Alps had been hauntingly apt: life before the war had been about unfolding and about possibilities, about things that now seemed to them hardly to qualify as "life." Now that they knew death and had made irrevocable choices, the very shape of life had changed. As they struggled to express their new knowledge, most of their initial attempts made even less sense than their proposed remedies.

An extreme example is provided in a letter written by Wendell Holmes describing his days in the camp hospital because of dysentery while the battle of Fredericksburg was being fought: "It's odd how indifferent one gets to the sight of death—perhaps, because one gets aristocratic and don't value a common life—Then they are apt to be so dirty it seems natural—'Dust to Dust'—I would do anything that lay in my power but it doesn't much affect my feelings."[7] The power of this incoherent confession lies in its indifference to the niceties of political correctness, polite society, or precise articulation. And read out of context, it would indict Holmes as a terrible snob: an officer who could not appreciate his men or was so overwhelmed by his failure to protect them that he reacted with chilling inhumanity. But Holmes's uncomfortable comment was a frank acceptance of the desanctification of human life that is so evident in war. The great division between the dead and the living was a primal hierarchy: the living were the aristocrats. One might sacrifice one's own life to save another life, but once that life was spent, it had to be abandoned. The dead were irretrievably dead; sentiment was irrelevant; it was necessary to be utterly realistic and turn one's attention to the living. Wendell Holmes's ability to cling to this hierarchy gave him a longer life in the Twentieth Massachusetts Regiment than Palfrey.

The families of these young men heard their exhaustion, sensed their despair, and understood it as defeatism, so they checked their sons or offered palliatives to keep up morale. But what sounded defeatist at home was realistic to those in the field, and "palliatives" or even "morale" missed the point. The challenge for each soldier was to find the will to face battle again, and there was precious little to grasp hold of that wouldn't come away in his hand. This new knowledge first dawned as a negative: they would never beat the South; their leaders were no good. Then came the insistence on a contradiction: it could not be won but would have to be won; indifference to the dead was an embrace of life; worn out and exhausted, believing in nothing, they would still do their duty, as Holmes put it.

Henry Higginson agreed with Holmes that the Confederates were a superior fighting force, and yet like Lowell, he was convinced that the war could have only one outcome:

> I cannot for the life of me, see any other possible way for us than to whip them: we have no ground on which to make peace—and can-

not have any, until we or they have given in—beaten. Peace cannot
last if made now . . . Besides, this is all we can do for mankind . . .
fighting for freedom for man, for the right and the good, for God. My
whole religion (that is my whole belief and hope in everything, in
life, in man, in woman, in music, in good, in the beautiful, in the real
truth) rests on the questions now really before us.[8]

Henry was insisting that peace would have to resolve the issue of slavery.
The North had to win because he could not envisage a world in which it
lost. This was his declaration of faith and, more subtly, sheer will. When
Holmes so many decades later tried to describe "the soldier's faith," he too
reduced the soldier's motivation to what at first seems frighteningly thin. A
soldier fought for a "cause he little understands," following a plan about
which he knows nothing, employing a "blindly accepted duty." And while
this recipe sounds deeply cynical, Holmes further explained that "to fight
out a war, you must believe something and want something with all your
might." Only from that small kernel of absolute belief could a soldier find
the "internal resources" to accept his fate and to "do his duty."[9]

Surprisingly, Charlie Lowell in short order found one civilian who
seemed to understand these subtle paradoxes. Within the last year William
James had become a regular caller at Quincy Street. He had not volunteered for military service: he had a bad back, and his father, a committed
pacifist, had discouraged him from enlisting. Now this small and contained
young man with a slender face appeared in the Quincy Street front parlor.
James "looked at C[harlie] with great curiosity," Anna noted. Here was the
colonel James had heard the women talking about, and yet off duty Charlie
Lowell was a slight man, still boyish despite his attempt at a mustache, without the slightest air of pretension, and quite shabbily dressed. Once James
locked eyes with Lowell, however, he recognized authority and single-
mindedness, and Lowell, for his part, "pricked up his ears as if he smelt a familiar." The two men immediately began talking "loud all the time
contradicting and questioning all each other said. The difficulty was to keep
in the opposition all the time." Anna was surprised that "there was a quality
in their talk so strikingly the same."

Their subject was the sorry state of public affairs. "J[ames] rejoiced in the
fatal apathy wh[ich] made us contented with every thing second rate. He
was curious to see where it could leave us. C[harlie] traced it to our
common schools. We began with liking second rate books and ended by

choosing second rate men,—the nation which lived on a second rate hash has become second rate—(this was aimed at our breakfast)." Describing this encounter to her daughter, Anna concluded, "When J[ames] had gone C[harlie] stretched himself like one who has been roused, and never made a disparaging remark."[10]

Behind this jousting between James and Lowell lay the old debate, reawakened by the war, about "great men" or heroes. Several months previously Wendell Phillips had given a speech in which he described Lincoln as a "first-rate *second-rate* man."[11] Although abolitionist criticism of Lincoln had abated with the Emancipation Proclamation, Phillips's phrase survived because it captured a more generalized prevailing opinion: at a time of such dire national crisis, there were no "great men" to lead.

It had long been assumed that men like Washington and Jefferson and Adams had achieved greatness because the times had given them the scope. Americans understood their Founding Fathers in these terms: the gentleman farmer or local silversmith, who in time of revolution rose to greatness as the occasion demanded, became a Founding Father and then, with peace, returned to the farm or workshop. James Russell Lowell, in *The Atlantic Monthly*, wrote, "It is only first-rate events that call for and mould first-rate characters." Hawthorne at about the same time commented, "A hero cannot be a hero, unless in a heroic world."[12] And yet the nation now again faced severe crisis, and the times cried out for heroes, but they were not forthcoming.

Thus the ironic twist in "rejoicing" at the second rate: the first rate was an impossibility; third-rate men like Pope and Burnside were a disaster. A second-rate president like Lincoln and a second-rate general like McClellan were the best to be hoped for. Rob Shaw had defended McClellan with the argument, "If he is not a very great general, he is the best we have." Behind the bitter ironic humor of Charlie Lowell and Will James was the admission that the need for heroes would not necessarily be filled, that events would not necessarily "mold" first-rate characters. Frank Barlow wrote his brothers on July 12 that "unless there is a radical change in the leaders, the enemy will whip us again and again." The betrayal soldiers had suffered at the hands of poor leaders was beginning to drive sane men mad; Frank Palfrey was but one example.[13]

Charlie was not sure that a change in leaders would solve the problem. Instead, he believed Americans were being challenged to transform their basic understanding of their relationship to their leaders. The court-martialing of Fitz-John Porter for his failure to support General Pope at Second Bull Run was instructive. Emphasizing this point in a letter to Henry Higginson, Charlie described Porter's insubordination as "un-officer-like and dangerous." Porter had "heard Pope say the enemy was here, or there, or in the bag, and always found it quite to the contrary, and unconsciously he said, 'This is not war, this is chance, I cannot do anything here,' and he rather let things slide. He was no worse than twenty thousand others. This sort of feeling was growing in the army, and . . . it must be stopped." Despite or because of people becoming reconciled to poor leadership, they were recognizing that "there is something for every man to do."[14] The war was becoming a popular effort, and popular resolve would prove more effective than strong leadership.

It is an interesting opinion, considering that Lowell had begun the war believing that the greatest influence would come from the regular army. By July 1862, despite recognizing that the volunteer troops were, as he had predicted, "food for powder," he had reversed himself and wanted to command state volunteer troops. And now he was proposing that "good people" were needed on the home front more than on the battlefield. He expanded on this idea in a letter to Higginson, noting that many of the men he had most admired before the war and naturally looked to for leadership had faded from the public scene, but pleased that "others shine out, whom we had overlooked." Governor Andrew was such a man. In 1861, at the onset of the national crisis, John Albion Andrew had taken office assured of the antipathy of those key leaders in business and philanthropy whose cooperation success in Massachusetts politics still required. A populist evangelical from Maine, he was a lawyer and an abolitionist who belonged to the radical wing of the Republican Party and had distinguished himself by providing legal services to John Brown, the Secret Six, and John Brown's family. At best patrician Bostonians considered him an impractical idealist, at worst a fanatic. The danger to Massachusetts at the start of the war was that if the economic power of the state turned against Governor Andrew, the state risked paralysis. But unlike the grudge-holding, bitter Senator Sumner, Andrew proved an expansive man with the ability to forge effective and unifying alliances, permitting those of more conservative and tentative politics to be coaxed to adjust to his more radical perspective. Lowell's admiration for him grew daily. He told one friend that it had been worth coming home "if only to get acquainted with him." As the two men worked on the formation of the Second Massachusetts Cavalry, Andrew was quickly coming to appreciate Lowell. Soon he ended a directive, "What I have failed fully or clearly to express you will understand by your inspiration." Lowell wrote Higginson, "I find myself judging men entirely now by their standard of public spirit."[15]

Amos Lawrence was one of those he judged. On November 18, ten days after arriving in Boston, Lowell was initiated into the inner workings of Governor Andrew's war cabinet at a dinner party given by Lawrence. Since Lawrence had agreed to fund the Second Massachusetts Cavalry, Lowell had decided he deserved closer examination. In the mid-1850s Lawrence had been one of the major sources of funds for the New England Emigrant Aid Society—hence the naming of Lawrence, Kansas—and had wholeheartedly supported the northern settlers in Kansas, helping to supply them with guns. He had even given money to John Brown for his activities there (without fully understanding their violent nature), though he had never supported or even considered the more radical turn taken by the Secret Six and had been horrified by John Brown's raid on Harpers Ferry. Better understanding the southern reaction to Brown's insurrection than most New Englanders, and desirous to mitigate the political damage the raid had caused, Lawrence had been one of the initiators of the Constitutional Union Party and its candidate for governor of Massachusetts. But once the South shelled Fort Sumter and war was declared, Lawrence threw his support behind his former rival, Governor Andrew.

John Murray Forbes's presence in Andrew's war cabinet was an essential element in Lawrence's willingness and ability to work with the governor. The two men shared a business sense, an intense practicality, a personal friendship (although their families were not close), and a deep patriotism. Their partnership guaranteed a broad base of support throughout the state: it began with the fairly conservative, self-interested concern to continue getting a supply of cotton to the Massachusetts mills, but it pushed Lawrence into leadership on increasingly liberal causes and became the cornerstone of Massachusetts's war effort.

Henry Lee had been the ideal person to propose Lowell's colonelcy to Governor Andrew. He was one of three men, "all representing different wings of the Boston elite," whom the governor had appointed to his personal staff. Charming, funny, with a quiet wisdom and patience that easily went unnoticed, Lee's work for the governor was a strong link in the chain that established a working accommodation between the governor's political power and the men whose wealth and connections actually ran Boston.

Since Andrew, being a populist governor, saw everyone who requested an audience with him and answered every letter, he and his assistants were always overworked. And political pressure on him was especially intense because of the military contracts to be filled. In this hectic circumstance, Lee's frank pronouncements on the many petitioners often clarified murky waters for him. (Once he stated, "That man is a damned thief, and you have no business to put him in charge of Uncle Sam's property.") Lowell's petition had arrived at a time when Andrew was very reluctant to give McClellan more Massachusetts men to be butchered for no clear purpose. He belonged to that group of Radical Republicans who saw McClellan's conservative politics at the root of his military lackluster. Andrew further believed that between Seward, Stanton, and McClellan, Lincoln was being deflected from his true course, which must lead to the righteous and principled emancipation of the slaves and the unequivocal suppression of the southern oligarchy. By the summer of 1862 Andrew felt urgently the need to "save the President from the infamy of ruining his country." Even Lincoln's Emancipation Proclamation disappointed him. He recognized the "mighty act," even called it "great" and "sublime," but he complained that it was "slow, somewhat halting, and wrong in delay."[16]

Since the beginning of the war, whenever the federal government dragged its heels, Andrew had initiated public-private partnerships in Massachusetts that advanced his radical yet practical agenda. One of the first was the Boston Education Commission, of which he was honorary president and which was run by many of the men who had backed the New England Emigrant Aid Society. Two of Lowell's uncles, Patrick Jackson and Samuel Cabot, as well as John Murray Forbes and Amos Lawrence, were members. Using Port Royal Island and other sea islands off the South Carolina coast, where plantations had been abandoned after federal troops gained control in January 1862, the commission established a community of contrabands, or ex-slaves, with two objectives: the continued production of cotton for northern mills, and preparation of the ex-slaves for freedom. So successful was the project that it secured federal funds, despite the fact that within the last year Lincoln had twice chastised generals for emancipating slaves under their military authority, most especially in May 1862, when General David Hunter, commanding the Department of the South, in which Port Royal lay, "issued a sweeping declaration of martial law abolishing slavery." The commission wisely made no mention of actual status, but rather emphasized the purely practical requirements of freedom by sending down a contingent of young Bostonians to teach the three R's and the fundamentals of citizenship: an emancipation curriculum.[17]

Andrew's success had taken advantage of two practical considerations: the need of Massachusetts mills for a steady supply of cotton, and the huge number of ex-slaves massing within Union lines. Solving those immediate problems, he had pushed the government unwittingly closer to recognizing the human rights of the ex-slave. He had also established a modus operandi for other projects that were funded by industrialists and manned by idealists, practical solutions paving the way for liberalization. He had done this by mending the rancorous political split of the 1840s and 1850s: Conscience and Cotton were once again united.

In the late spring of 1862 Andrew had appointed John Murray Forbes chairman of the Committee of a Hundred, a partnership of business leaders concerned with sustaining an industrial workforce while delivering the required quota of men to the Union army. Forbes visited the plantations of the Boston Education Commission and liked what he saw there. Morality and justice aside, common sense endorsed emancipation as a war measure: the South would be robbed of its slave labor, and the newly freed workers could be used to fuel the northern industrial machine. The Committee of a Hundred began to pave the way for a pragmatic solution to the military manpower question: the use of ex-slaves as soldiers.

In the summer of 1862 Andrew began to explore the possibility of creating other such communities while contributing to the naval blockade of the Confederacy. Union troops had taken New Orleans in April 1862 but didn't control the Mississippi. Blockade runners could supply the Confederacy via an overland route from Mexico through Texas and Louisiana, then slip across the Mississippi at any number of points. The Union army had a strong interest in closing this source of supply, and there was some serious discussion of mounting an expedition to win back Texas (in addition to the campaign to gain control of the Mississippi). Andrew recognized that a Union-controlled Texas might be an ideal place to pioneer emancipation while obtaining yet more cotton for northern mills. He began to promote a military expedition to liberate Texas and establish such a community. At its head, he hoped, would be General Nathaniel P. Banks, former governor of Massachusetts, now in charge of the Defenses of Washington. The plan received authorization, if not much support, in Washington.

Then on September 15 Andrew received a request from Massachusetts natives in California who wanted to contribute to the Union cause.[18] California's governor, Leland Stanford, was sympathetic to the Confederacy, and California, as a state, supplied no troops to the war. But Captain J. Sewall Reed, formerly of Dorchester, Massachusetts, proposed raising a cavalry company for the Union; if Massachusetts would pay their passage east, these California men would fight under her flag. Immediately negotiations began. On October 22 Lawrence had agreed to underwrite the venture, and Andrew telegraphed Reed in California to proceed with recruitment. Meanwhile Lowell was approached by both Forbes and Lawrence. Unlike many governors, Governor Andrew was particularly rigorous in selecting candidates for colonelcies. He recognized and supported the need for military integrity and resisted the pressure to fill positions out of political expediency. In choosing Lowell as colonel, he knew he had a cavalry officer who would ensure the professionalism of the Massachusetts regiment and whose political support he could count on. In this larger context, Lawrence's proposal for a cavalry battalion was not half as crazy as Lowell had first supposed, but it was still highly irregular. His reservations about accepting this command appear to have been the first "reality check" on a project that was well outside the permit of any governor of any state. Fortunately Lawrence signed on to underwrite an entire regiment, and the Second Massachusetts Cavalry was begun.

Forbes imagined that the Texas expedition would involve minimal fighting. He intended the Second Massachusetts Cavalry to be a safe place and was loading the regiment with his own people. To be extra safe, he also procured the surgeon of the First Massachusetts Cavalry. Lowell was sympathetic to Forbes's intention; he too wanted his friends out of harm's way. His reservations concerned whether he should be one of those for whom a "safe" place was procured. He would never have resigned his regular commission for a safe place. His ambition was to create a superior cavalry regiment, as evidenced by the fierceness with which he protected his right to weed out politically appointed officers. Between Lowell and Governor Andrew a daily correspondence, in addition to frequent consultations, grew up almost entirely devoted to the myriad petitions before them for commissions. And Lowell was quick to discover that the political dimension to raising a regiment was not confined to the commissioning of officers.

In the winter of 1862–63 officers were easier to find than men to fill the ranks. Patriotism and romance were still motives for volunteering, but the enthusiasm and peer pressure that had overwhelmed Massachusetts men in 1861 had pretty well run its course. Right after the Peninsula campaign and Antietam had come another, smaller wave of grimmer volunteers, but those men were now in regiments. Towns across the state sponsored fairs to whip up enthusiasm, but men barely trickled in. Not only had the realities of war taken the edge off the romance, but the war economy was booming. With more than 100,000 men already under arms, Massachusetts was suffering a shortage of skilled labor. Pay was good, and business leaders were unwilling to sacrifice their labor force.

The Second Massachusetts Cavalry hoped to draw recruits from the ranks of unskilled labor. Posters served as the main advertisement and enticement. One that was prepared for Captain Forbes survives. In huge type it declared MAJ. GEN. BANKS' GRAND EXPEDITION, referring to the Texas experiment.* Appealing to the romance associated with cavalry, it prominently displayed a picture of a mounted cavalry officer on a galloping black horse, holding his sword aloft as if leading a charge and looking back over his shoulder as if to ask who was following behind him. Below, in large type, were the names of Colonel Lowell, Major Crowninshield, and Captain Forbes, along with Amos A. Lawrence as "Special Recruiting Officer." At the very bottom was announced "a preference given for Light Weights."[19] The ideal cavalryman was considered to be about 130 pounds, no older than twenty-two, and of small stature. This preference for small men was based on the same criterion used for jockeys: a small man would not tire a horse as quickly. In reality the need for recruits was such that no one was turned away, whatever their size or age.

On January 4, 1863, Captain J. Sewall Reed's California company, calling itself the California Hundred, arrived in Boston and immediately boosted morale. In forming his company Reed had selected men carefully, and Lowell was instantly delighted. The men knew horses, knew fighting, and had lived a rougher, more independent life than their eastern compatriots. Newspapers speculated on "how many Indians they are in the habit of killing before breakfast." They were reported as each having "a thousand scalps" to their name, and some were said to have "brought lassoes with them." One man, the only native-born Californian among them, was the best *vaquero* in the state. Most of them were New Englanders who had

---

*The Second Massachusetts Infantry had been under Banks's command at Cedar Mountain. Henry Lee, who believed that Banks should have resigned after Cedar Mountain, spoke of its dead officers as having been murdered by Banks. Recruiting, however, was a political, not a military, exercise. As he was a former Speaker of the House and a former Know-Nothing-turned-Republican governor, Banks's name pulled in recruits.

emigrated west during the Gold Rush years. Lowell was so pleased with the Californians that Reed became the first ranking captain; the California Hundred became Company A.[20]

Because so many men had applied to the California Hundred, a second proposal was made to Governor Andrew offering an entire battalion (four more companies) of four hundred men under the command of Major De Witt Clinton Thompson, the former sheriff of San Francisco. These men would be known as the California Battalion, to distinguish them from the California Hundred. Andrew immediately accepted, assuming the men could be mustered immediately, and requested that they take the steamer on February 11, less than a month away. Unfortunately the California Battalion ran into intense political controversy from California's secessionist element under Copperhead governor Leland Stanford, and it was delayed. But this impediment was not known in Boston. Optimistic that more Californians were on the way, Lowell became more exacting about the quality of his Massachusetts recruits and officers. Governor Andrew also changed his estimates, though for more complex reasons.

For some time, Andrew and his Committee of a Hundred had been working to secure the use of freed slaves as soldiers. Lawrence, who had originally opposed the plan, now argued, "Let us take what we can get. Negroes where well commanded make useful soldiers." Their use would preserve the workforce and, if successful in averting a draft, would prevent civil unrest within the state. Many supporters of this idea envisaged essentially a formalization of the present use of ex-slaves, who were flooding the army in newly liberated areas as well as in the District of Columbia and the border states; they were being used primarily for hard labor and as cooks, laundresses, and other servants. "Colored troops" would be not armed soldiers but labor brigades.[21]

Governor Andrew had something else in mind, however. He wanted to organize a model regiment of black soldiers and insisted on two things: the Negro regiment must be counted as a regular volunteer regiment from Massachusetts, taking its natural place in the sequencing as the Fifty-fourth Massachusetts Infantry (not the First Colored Massachusetts Troops); and second, white field officers would command it—"young men of military experience, of firm anti-slavery principles, ambitious, superior to a vulgar contempt for color, and having faith in the capacity of colored men for military service."[22] The two officers he wished as colonel and lieutenant-colonel of the new regiment were Lowell's friend Robert G. Shaw and Pen Hallowell, the man who had rescued Jim Lowell at Ball's Bluff and been wounded with Holmes at Antietam. (Philadelphia Quakers, all three Hallowell boys had been educated at Harvard, and their home served as a halfway house and hospital for Massachusetts officers. Their father belonged to the abolitionists' inner circle: he was the man who had brought John Brown's body north after the hanging.)

Hallowell did not hesitate, but Shaw at first refused the offer, as he had refused the captaincy with Lowell's regiment. The same considerations of loyalty to his regiment weighed heavily on him. Also, Shaw had just proposed to a young woman and was anxiously awaiting her response. He was aware that his three years would be up in June 1864, and he was reluctant to sign on for another three-year commitment. He was, in this sense, gauging his "safest" move, but safety was only part of the issue—he had rejected Lowell's offer because it was *too* safe. Essentially Shaw, like many other young men, wanted to do his duty honorably, but he didn't want to do more than his duty. After a sleepless night, however, he changed his mind and accepted.

"You will be very glad to hear that Bob Shaw is to be Colonel and Norwood Hallowell Lt. Colonel of the Governor's Negro regiment," Lowell wrote to his mother. "It is very important that it should be started soberly, and not spoilt by too much fanaticism. Bob Shaw is not a fanatic." Governor Andrew had been absolutely on target in his desire for high-caliber officers. By the end of the week, Lowell was promoting the regiment to his friends. He told one friend that having Shaw as colonel and Forbes as a backer meant that the regiment "is likely to be a success."[23]

With Lowell committed to the project, the governor decided to put the Fifty-fourth into the training camp at Readville, nine miles southwest of Boston, on a portion of the old Brook Farm, with the Second Massachusetts Cavalry. Those who applied to join the Second Massachusetts Cavalry whom Lowell knew to be committed abolitionists he deflected into the Fifty-fourth: Frank Higginson, the youngest of the Higginson boys; Wilkie and Bob James, the youngest of the four James brothers; and his own young cousin Cabot Russel. These young men had all been students at the model school about which Sanborn and Lowell had theorized during their college days and which Sanborn, with the encouragement of Emerson and Anna Lowell, had set up at Concord. It had many innovative features, among them coeducation and an open learning plan. But far and away the most radical element was Sanborn's politics. In the months following the hanging of John Brown, his role as the agent provocateur of the Secret Six was perfectly grasped by his students, and they were all fired with the zeal of activist abolitionism and the excitement of subversion. Young, politically radical and militarily inexperienced, they received commissions of higher rank in the Fifty-fourth than they would have procured in a white regiment, but it would be a mistake to imagine that they joined out of ambition for higher rank. No officer was so ambitious of rank that he would lead men in battle who he thought would not fight.

Andrew's aggressive promotion of black troops was not universally supported in Massachusetts, nor within the army. The distinctions among those who did not support emancipation as a war goal, those who did not condone the use of black troops, and those whose support was clouded by prejudice and bigotry are perhaps too fine to draw. But young white men were not flocking to officer black troops. The men who did believed black troops would fight.

Ironically and certainly not coincidentally, the official announcement of the formation of the Fifty-fourth Regiment was simultaneous with a much-celebrated visit to Boston by General McClellan. He was not a guest of the state but had been invited by conservative patrician Bostonians with the ostensible motive of paying tribute to his military leadership. But as the *Springfield Republican* reported, "No stranger ever goes to Boston unless he wants something and no one is invited unless the city wants something of him."[24] In fact, the visit was an attempt to test the waters for McClellan's bid for the Democratic presidential nomination and to rally support for an anti-administration platform. McClellan was a guest of the Copperheads, those northerners whose avowed desire was peace at any price. (McClellan actually was something of a moderate, being a War Democrat rather than a Copperhead—meaning that he wanted to win the war to restore the Union, though not to emancipate the slaves.)

The national mood was complex and confused. Throughout the North a strong Democratic vote at the 1862 midterm election had expressed the populace's displeasure with Lincoln, with the Emancipation Proclamation, and with the Union army's inconclusive performance. It was intended as a check on the growing influence of the Radical Republicans. And in Massachusetts, which had seen the rise of Democratic opposition in the form of the Massachusetts People's Party but where conservatives had been unable to unseat Andrew, Boston was abuzz with talk of peace. While some Copperheads opposed emancipation, many others were simply overwhelmed by the horror of civil war. They turned away from war with disgust and lost their enthusiasm for the cause, believing that nothing was worth the violence, injury, and death. Peace on almost any terms was better than fratricidal slaughter.

Lowell did not meet with McClellan while he was in Boston. He did not attend any of the soirées and receptions, the formal dance, or any other event that would have put him in McClellan's path. His loyalty was now to Governor Andrew and to a more radical prosecution of the war. Still, he respected McClellan as a general who for a time had provided critical leadership and contributed vitally to the Union cause. He spoke up privately on many occasions, discussing his experience of McClellan and his estimation of him as a military commander. His measured criticism, careful analysis, and detailed explanation of the disaster with Burnside at Antietam helped his listeners find the delicate balance of praising the general without supporting his political ambitions.

Lowell joined with a constellation of businessmen to found the Union Club shortly after the departure of "the Hero of one hundred ungained victories," as they referred to McClellan. Its aim was to bring together men of either party for "the encouragement and dissemination of patriotic sentiment and opinion." It set up quarters in Abbott Lawrence's old house on Park Street. The club welcomed anyone who continued to support the government despite its poor leadership and desultory military efforts. Edward Everett was the first president, but he was a figurehead. The club especially embraced men who supported the Emancipation Proclamation and the Negro Army Bill and was run by Samuel G. Ward of Baring Brothers, John Murray Forbes, Amos Lawrence, and younger men like Lowell and his uncle's great friend Charles Eliot Norton, who had become editor at the New England Loyal Publication Society, a complementary organization whose purpose was to produce pamphlets and broadsides supporting the Union cause, rallying patriotic feeling, and arguing against the Copperheads. Lowell also became involved in a petition to get Frank Barlow appointed brigadier-general of an all-black brigade. Because his regiment trained alongside the Fifty-fourth, Lowell spoke from experience and used concrete anecdotes when he rallied support for the black regiment at every forum, public and private.[25]

On February 15 Lowell wrote to Higginson that the founding of the Union Club was evidence that "public opinion here is getting stouter." By April some two hundred members had signed on to the Union Club. Most of them were ex–Somerset Club members who disliked the way that club had gravitated "very strongly towards the Sesech sympathies." Forbes, voicing his characteristic prejudices, complained that at the Somerset Club men lived "by wine, cards, tobacco, and billiards for their cheap stimulants and timekillers." They thought themselves "aristocratic and gentleman-like and they look up to the idle slave-owners with respect, as being more permanently idle than themselves." Confirming Forbes's prejudices, Somerset Club members referred to the new club as the Sambo Club.[26]

THIRTEEN

ROMANCE AND MUTINY

Spring 1863

Inevitably the raising of two new regiments brought many officers home to recruit. Others returned on leave once the army had moved into winter quarters. The wounded also returned. The presence of so many men in uniform caused considerable excitement in Boston. Both young ladies and young men filled diaries and letters with rumors and advance news of who had received which commission, and with anecdotes attesting to the courage, idealism, and worthiness of various officers. The atmosphere was one of excitement and optimism. Parties were given. Everyone wanted to be seen with the brave young men in uniform.

The Forbeses in particular entertained often, and Lowell eagerly took up a return to society. However interesting Iowa, Maryland, Washington, and the army may have been, his companionship had been largely confined to men and professional associations. Just twenty-eight, he now placed high on his agenda the company of young ladies. There was, in Boston at this time, a surfeit of young women ready to admire the courageous young colonel. Many of them were pretty, charming, and well bred. Several caught Charlie's eye. There was a Miss Ashburner, mention of whose name caused Lowell to exhibit a "burning blush."[1] Anna Lowell believed him to be much taken with Ida Agassiz, who had been the object of many questions he had put to his cousin Georgina Lowell some five years before. Then, at a party at the Forbeses' in early January, Effie Shaw stood out.

The beguiling younger sister of his much-admired and -admiring friend Rob Shaw wore an exquisitely fitted dress, trimmed and ornamented with flair. She was small and delicate, with a careful daintiness. What distinguished her immediately from all the other pretty, charming, cultivated young women was her voice, which was low, vibrant, and enormously compelling. At eighteen, she had not forgotten her earlier encounter with Charlie Lowell: they had met on Naushon Island when Effie was only fifteen.

One friend described her then as "always reading American History and wishing her ancestors had had more to do with things."[2]

Her war diary's first entry, dated July 23, 1861, noted the men of her acquaintance in the army, chief among them "Capt. Lowell of the U.S.A." She had heard and read her brother's admiring and envious reports about him. Rob believed Lowell to be the most "brilliant" man in the army. The clarity of ambition and the forthright actions that had so impressed Rob also thrilled Effie. She came frequently from New York to Boston, staying with cousins, the Forbeses particularly, who gave her entrée into the circle of young women who admired Anna Lowell, and Effie was steeped in admiration for the Lowell family. Compared to her own home on Staten Island, the Quincy Street house was an important social hub, and compared with her own retiring mother, afflicted with a variety of nonspecific maladies, Anna was dynamism personified. The previous winter she had danced with the wounded Jim Lowell. She recorded his death in her diary, writing, "Poor mother! I won't say poor son, for he died for the country and such Martyrs are not to be pitied."[3]

Effie had, from the first, been interested in the formation of the Second Massachusetts Cavalry. Her letters to Rob in November 1862 made it clear that she wanted him to accept the offered captain's commission in it, and when he refused, she kept him informed on the regiment's progress anyway, perhaps thinking he might change his mind. Now she was spending the winter at the Forbeses' and thus followed every step in its development. Of course when Rob took on the colonelcy of the Fifty-fourth Regiment, Effie was proud beyond measure. If his war career was to be hers vicariously, this new position was all she could have dreamed.

In the meantime Effie watched and waited for her opportunities with Colonel Lowell. At the Forbes party she was in her element. The way she took her brother's arm, whispered in his ear, and looked up into his face to catch his response—all these excited Charlie, who had had a special closeness to his own younger sister. As he drew Effie into conversation, he was pleased that she remembered him, knew so much about his regiment, and wished Rob would join it. He was delighted that she seemed to fit so seamlessly into Boston society and yet had lived most of her life elsewhere.

Charlie had not previously had any deep attachment to a member of the opposite sex. In 1857, during the horse-packing trip with Higginson and Perkins in Europe, he had conceived the fantasy of marrying a Russian. His years in Iowa had not encouraged him to relinquish his fantasies. He told his mother that western society was "cliquish to an extent unknown in the East." And instead of engaging in it, he had corresponded with two young women—one his cousin Nina Lowell, a purely platonic friend, and an unknown young lady in Cambridge. In October 1859 he inquired of Higginson whether he knew of any "true-hearted, violet-eyed woman," but given the profound sadness of his family circumstances—a mad grandmother, an addle-headed aunt, and his parents' compromised marriage—it is not surprising that he was, in 1860, at the time of Harriet's wedding, still ambivalent about the rewards of marriage. For a young man so unresolved about his life goals, the entanglements of marriage would, as he had written Henry Higginson, easily appear a "noose."[4]

He was in much the same position as his grandfather Jackson and many other young New Englanders had been, forced to make his fortune in foreign parts, and unable financially or practically to marry until he could live a more certain life. But his emotional development was also a factor: for all his intellectual precosity, he had not shown much emotional sophistication. As a toddler he had had great charm and been a favorite at his dame school, but as a boy he had been surly and angry. As a college student, he had been excessively intellectual, living at home and forging few profound relationships beyond his family. Once a young man, he had lived almost exclusively in remote places. But the family problems had now eased, Harriet was married, young Anna was showing remarkable independence, and he had matured. His last year and a half in the army had put matters of life and death in a stark perspective.

The most potent factor was his relationship with his mother. Twenty years before, she had admitted that he was her favorite. The years had not changed that, and their special alliance is clear in their letters. He was, more than a son, her partner in the family fortunes. This was a bond that would be difficult to supersede. When he scolded her for encouraging him to find "a" wife, he had insisted that to surmount the obstacles to marriage he would need not "a" wife but "the" wife. Anna's unique aspects as "the" mother had set the standard. Charlie never described them, but we can safely assume that he recognized in his mother a woman of formidable strength, immense intellectual vitality, and despite her toughness a profound loyalty.

Now he found himself beguiled by a very young woman who shared many of these characteristics. Effie, like Anna, had a charm, style, and wit that outshone her physical beauty. Both women were idolized and envied by their contemporaries. Both excelled in the traditional feminine skills but combined them with unusual intellectuality and originality of thought. Finally both women had enormous strength of will: deep reserves of independence and self-confidence that most women, even of their social station, lacked. Effie also had youth and fortune, an artistic sensibility, and the strong influence of her father and Rob.

At the Forbeses', the two renewed their acquaintance, and in the swirl of parties that followed a mutual attraction was cemented. A party celebrating Henry Russell's precipitate engagement to Mary Forbes, John Murray Forbes's eldest daughter, set the tone for a rash of new alliances in 1863. Rob Shaw became engaged to Annie Haggerty, a friend of his sister Susie's. Henry Russell's sister married Alexander Agassiz. There were many parties: Aunt Mary had a dinner for the officers of the Fifty-fourth, and Dr. Hooper had another. There was a party at Papanti's, the dance hall of Boston. Henry Lee gave a party. Charlie went out every night and told his mother, "I am almost afraid to write how gay I am getting."[5] By Valentine's Day Effie and Charlie were passing messages back and forth via Rob, whom both saw daily. Then on March 7 the news became official: they were engaged. The speed of the courtship alone invited speculation. Rumor had it that they had seen each other only nine times. This rumor certainly captured the whirlwind nature of the courtship of barely two months. Gossip quickly attended to the fittingness of the match, the qualities of the two lovers, and among the older generation, the dynastic significance of a Shaw-Lowell alliance.

Charlie wrote to Aunt Ellen, "You can tell Ned and any body else, not to take the trouble to contradict the report that I am engaged to Miss Effie Shaw, if he hears it—indeed he may mention it when he chooses. If you wish to write to the young lady and condole with her, I shall not be jealous; she admits that every one with whom she has talked about me ends by saying 'but he has no heart;' so you need not feel delicate about showing your sympathy with her in her misfortune."[6]

Charlie had never escaped his stereotyping from boyhood. He was still, in some circles, considered the bluff, rough boy of his Latin School days, and to some degree this was true. In twenty-eight years he had not given his heart to any except his mother and his sister. He had no childhood sweethearts, no heady romance in college, no long line of adoring young women. Nor had he ever made a fool of himself. He had never been disappointed in love. At once inexperienced and vulnerable, as well as potentially cruel in his naïveté, his combination of blindness and thoughtlessness deterred anyone from approaching too closely. He was, emotionally, still a virgin.

Effie also had a heartless streak. Her callousness toward another young man had once occasioned censure from her brother. "Your treatment of James Jackson struck me as being very brutal," Rob wrote. "I can imagine the poor devil's feelings, while a lot of girls were laughing at him." John Palfrey, an accomplished engineer and West Point graduate, wrote his brother Frank,

> As to the engagements, I bear Col. Chas. Lowell's with great equanimity. He is a good fellow, and worthy of a better fate. If the young woman's manner is as forbidding to him as it was to me when I had the honor . . . he must be even a braver officer than he has the credit of being. I should think she might be economical and useful by the way she knit on a huge gray stocking, and tugged with her little finger at the ball which had got away from her under some chairs. Perhaps however she did not care to waste her smiles on one who was neither a negro nor a volunteer.[7]

Effie and Charlie were both new to the game of romance. Hers was a strong personality used to a liberal home environment in which women were allowed their point of view. Nevertheless her devotion to her brother and her father was entire, and she took their disagreements or chastisements meekly and trustingly. There was something of the bluestocking about her—slightly too earnest, somewhat too daunting for Palfrey. But by many lights, not only her own, that was not necessarily a defect. She was seen to have "character," and this was appreciated.

James Russell Lowell, carried away with "this good luck of Charlie's," wrote Mrs. Shaw that Effie's "force of character & good sense" would "assure both to herself & Charlie a happy life." This is an interesting comment, given the family history, and suggests some of the qualities that made Effie "the" wife. The two had an instinctive sympathy about ideas and also mannerisms. They were both lovers of grand ideas but also precise, almost finicky, perfectionists. They both had ideal expectations and took no comfort in approximations.[8]

Rob Shaw was immensely pleased that the sister closest to him should marry a man of whom he was so fond. He wrote a friend, "It is a very satisfactory affair for us all and especially for me—as I like him very much, and she and I have always been together, more than any other two of the family." Her parents initially wanted to postpone the engagement, arguing that Effie, barely eighteen, was too young. On March 10, however, Charlie escorted Effie to Staten Island, and after this meeting the Shaws gave way to the insistence of the happy couple. A very relieved Charlie wrote his mother in a fairly giddy mood, "Nothing particular to tell you—not engaged *again*, don't be alarmed." He then arranged for his mother and sister Anna to visit the Shaws on their return from Washington to Boston.[9]

Mrs. Shaw wrote to James Russell Lowell that "this new son . . . suits us exactly!" James was Effie's godfather, in fact, and he wrote a very long letter trying to claim as much responsibility for the affair as he could. To Charlie he explained, "You could not have done anything better for yourself or your friends, & as for me, the name of her & hers is associated with my dearest recollections, the happiest & most hopeful days of my life." Anna Lowell wrote to her daughter Anna, "Patrick and Sue rejoice greatly for me—so does every body. I cannot walk in the street without continual stoppings and congratulations." Hattie wrote to Anna, "Is it not delightful for Charley and indeed all of us—Effie is charming I wish you could be here."[10]

Parties were given for the engaged pair: tea parties, dinner parties. Uncle Pat Jackson had a dinner. Uncle James had a dinner. Ella and Arthur Lyman had a dinner. The Lees and the Higginsons had parties. Henry Higginson wrote expansively to Effie:

> I am sure no man was ever luckier or happier than he—The boy always did have the greatest luck in everything & deserved it too, but he has crowned all his successes by this last greatest piece of good-fortune . . . how very near & dear Charley has been to me for nearly twenty years, how he has helped & guided & comforted & sympathized with me in everything—Always & invariably the same true, staunch friend . . . One might almost have foreseen that Charley for liking Bob so much would inevitably fall in love with his sister, who so resembled him—One thing you have already accomplished for Charley—You have softened him for the world, tho' he was always soft enough to me . . . By a letter from my sister I see that all the girls in Boston are wild about your engagement! Charley's regiment ought to fill up on the strength of it.[11]

But the regiment did not fill up, and recruitment was so slow that in mid-February the regiment was broken up. The First Battalion, or first four companies, including the California Hundred, were sent to the front under the command of Major Caspar Crowninshield. Remaining at Readville, the training camp, were the company officers awaiting a new crop of recruits to be trained.

The initial days or weeks of training were unpleasant but crucial. Establishing authority and respect for that authority was the first task for an officer, and it was difficult to get men to settle into the routine and discipline of military life. Grumbling and complaining were endemic, as men used to liberty submitted to regimentation. For the early volunteers, it had been a privilege to fight, and they had jostled for the opportunity. In contrast men who joined the Union army later, many for the bounty, often had no idealistic or patriotic attachment to the war. Their commitment to the cause was minimal, and having joined in gangs, their loyalty was to their gang leaders rather than to the army's chain of command. Many were "roughs" or "scalawags" with a history of brawling, heavy drinking, and hard labor; some of them were criminals or petty criminals whose prison sentences had been commuted in exchange for their volunteering.

Physical restraint was frequently needed to control a man who was on the rampage from rage or drink. Lowell tried to respect his men, to be fair but strict, and never to be needlessly cruel. The sergeants themselves were often the strictest disciplinarians, their authority being paramount but fragile, since they were usually from the same social class as the privates. Lowell knew that in countless instances that never reached him, sergeants got the upper hand. The enlisted men breathed the air of grievance: they were convinced the system was stacked against them. They complained of being clamped in irons and put in cells for minor infractions or for no reason at all. Usually the offense was one form or another of insubordination—defying orders, refusing to recognize a superior, sometimes simply asserting autonomy or pride. Behavior that, before volunteering, any man would have considered well within his rights was now punishable.

Many privates complained that they didn't want to follow orders, didn't like wearing a uniform, and didn't like the food. Lowell wanted them to recognize that they had joined a system and that it would do them no good to question it generally. On January 25, 1863, he issued a general order establishing a method for lodging complaints that would reinforce the command structure. First, he insisted that the complaint be specific: if a uniform didn't fit, if the meat was bad, if a specific disciplinary incident was inappropriate, then he could remedy the problem. Second, he insisted that an order first be obeyed and only then objected to. Although in training camp the men were not exposed to situations in which following orders would save their lives, it was there that they had to acquire the reflexes that would see them through the dangers of battle: the most important was an immediate response to orders. However idiotic endless drills might seem, it was essential preparation. If they were to accept a system that robbed them of their freedom, they had to have faith that it was just, and Lowell admonished his officers to listen carefully to the men's objections when made at the appropriate time and place.

Although Lowell repeated in his general order that quarrels between privates were to be settled by sergeants (only the sergeants were in a position to take the measure of the men and to understand the history behind the flare-ups and feuds that erupted as they lived in cramped quarters), the sergeants quickly learned that when a complaint did reach him, Lowell would always hear what the private had to say, and "if there was a doubt Lowell always gave the private the benefit of it rather than the officer."[12] Early flare-ups had to be handled properly, but many of the sergeants, too, were new at their job and needed training. Line officers were young and lacked the confidence befitting their authority. They often had less physical presence than the mature enlisted men under their command, who might have spent years in physical labor on farms, docks, and factories. Since a failure to exert authority might set an unalterable pattern, the young, uncertain, and inexperienced officers sometimes resorted to extreme measures.

Will Forbes proved himself invaluable during these early days. In one instance a "big lout" began acting out during drill. He was ordered to the guardhouse, resisted, knocked down his sergeant, and started a scuffle. Voices were raised. Hearing the noise, Will rushed out of his tent, "seized the fellow by the throat and pinned him against the guard house wall while the sergeant put him in irons." The man was kept pinned to the shed until his fury passed. Forbes's prompt action, reinforced with physical strength, had restored order and won him respect from the men. He had shown he was not averse to using his strength but had not abused his rank. He had established his authority.[13]

Some cases of unduly severe punishment required investigation. In February two men complained of improper treatment, saying they had been locked in a cell for two days and received no bounty. In reporting on this case, Lowell explained that the men, drunk at the time, had told their lieutenant that "unless they got into a company that suited them, they should not stay long."[14] Obviously the regiment could not function if enlisted men could pick and choose which company they joined. They were locked up until they sobered to prevent them from acting on such a foolish impulse and as an example to others. Lowell's threat to deny their bounty was intended similarly: he had assumed that in their present mood the minute they had it they would, like so many others, desert, but once they sobered up better judgment would prevail.

Lowell, indeed all the officers, would have been happy without these recruits of minimal commitment and resistant attitude. Unfortunately, they needed them, and experienced officers knew that initial resistance to the system was not necessarily a harbinger of poor performance as a soldier. A period of adjustment was necessary for everyone. Only after a recruit settled could one get a clearer idea of his potential. Each batch of new recruits required the same unpleasant "breaking in," and some proceeded more smoothly than others.

On April 9 Lowell arrived at his recruiting office at 2 City Hall Avenue and School Street, in downtown Boston, to find a mutiny in progress.[15] His recruiting officer, George Quincy, briefed him. It was muster-in day for Company G, which Lieutenant Archibald McKendry, one of the original members of the California Hundred, had raised with great effort. Promised a promotion to captain, McKendry had remained in Boston after his original company had sailed for Virginia in February. It is not clear why Lowell picked him out for promotion, but he ultimately became colonel of the regiment, was never wounded, and was one of the few officers who was invariably present and ready for duty.

At about eight-thirty in the morning, in the drilling room in the basement of the recruiting office, one of the company sergeants, Ansom Burlingham, had tried to put irons on a drunken recruit. Another recruit, William Lynch, accosted him, struck him in the face, and said, "You shan't do that to any man in this place." An eighteen-year-old private called Frank Drew, an Englishman, then shouted, "Kill the son of a bitch of a sergeant." William Johnson, a twenty-one-year-old farmer, yelled, "Kill the sergeant, damn him, kill him." The men attacked Burlingham, punching him in the face and head, but he fled up the stairs to the main office, leaving the angry men trapped below.

Burlingham explained the situation to Lieutenant McKendry and Quincy. The two officers then went down to the basement, where the men were still upset. McKendry ordered the sergeant to put Lynch in irons. Lynch replied, "No man in the room can iron me." When McKendry repeated the order, the men drew their swords. McKendry tried to deflect the confrontation: he "ordered the men into line and commenced the morning drill." At first it seemed to be the right tack: the men all fell in, and the incident might have ended there, although the power struggle would have required an eventual resolution. But Quincy had meanwhile run up the street for the police, and returned with four officers, all of whom went down to the basement.

Enough time had elapsed that the fury of the earlier moment had subsided, although not completely. Most of the men were drilling and following orders but also doing a lot of cursing. Once the men saw the police and their clubs, the cursing got much worse and the men grew tense. As the police started to move, the men insulted them, then rushed them with drawn sabers. The police quickly retreated upstairs.

It was at this point that Lowell arrived. Going down to the basement, he ordered the men to halt and to face forward. He ordered Lynch to step forward, then ordered him ironed. The men, obedient till this point, broke ranks and "with fearful oaths swore the irons should not be put on." Lowell asked for a weapon, and Quincy gave him a Colt revolver. He warned the men that they were in a state of mutiny and liable to be court-martialed; they could be sentenced to death for these infractions. He reminded them of his general order about complaints: "The order must be obeyed. After it is obeyed, I will hear what you have to say, and will decide the case on its merits, but it must be obeyed first." He continued talking, using "every possible persuasion to have them come to order." He finished by saying, "God knows, I don't want to kill any of you; but I shall shoot the first man who resists."

His speech had no effect. He was appealing to their reason, but the men were too inflamed to respond. Perhaps they were too drunk, or perhaps he was simply too late: rebellion erupted, and the men slashed about with their sabers; a corporal was cut on the head, and Quincy was slashed on the wrist. The men rushed the policemen, who again promptly fled—a success that gave the men courage. One young recruit lunged at a lieutenant, who escaped the hit. Somehow, in this melee, Lynch was successfully ironed, which further angered the men. Another young recruit, William Pendergast, in a lightning-quick move, lunged for McKendry's breast. Lowell stepped almost between them and fired. Pendergast staggered and fell to the floor. The men immediately gathered around him. He did not writhe or speak. In less than four minutes he was dead. A twenty-two-year-old English sailor named

Daniel Riley shook his fist in Lowell's face and shouted, "Damn you, shoot me, shoot me if you dare." Lynch called on the men to mutiny. James Thompson, an Irish laborer, shouted, "The boys were right, . . . Col. Lowell [is] a son of a bitch, and a coward for shooting Pendergast." Others swore they would never obey orders again. They taunted Lowell, shouting that he had killed one man and had "got to kill some more or he wouldn't go out of there alive." Lynch in his irons "stepped up to Lowell and raising his hands said, 'Comrades, he has shot that man, and I'm bound to revenge his blood.'"

Lowell ordered Sergeant Burlingham to take Lynch to the Tombs, the colloquial term for the city jails used for detaining prisoners awaiting trial. As the sergeant went up to him, Lynch struck him with his ironed wrists and was dragged away, yelling that he would kill him. The departure of Lynch seemed to quell the mutiny. The men fell into line and gave up their rebellion. McKendry resumed command.

Lowell left the recruiting office and went directly to the statehouse, where he reported to Colonel Day, provost-marshal general of Massachusetts, who refused to arrest him. Lowell then reported to Governor Andrew, whose outer office was open to the public; one could walk in without an audience. Saluting the governor, Lowell said, "I have to report to you, sir, that in the discharge of my duty, I have shot a man." He saluted again and left. The governor told the men gathered around him, "I need nothing more. Colonel Lowell is as humane as he is brave."[16]

By now the news had spread about town, and a huge crowd had gathered outside the statehouse. Among them were several men who knew Lowell and came to his support. One said, "I could not take my eyes off of him. I glory in him. He's as stringy as a wild partridge,—he can't keep still a minute. He is all muscle—such a man will never have any flesh." Another explained, "I was with Lowell at the [English] High School, and if he did it, it is right." A "civic dignitary" declared Lowell was "just the man we want for Mayor." William Bowditch, who did not know Lowell personally, stopped and thanked him; in his diary that evening Bowditch noted, "All the community, save Copperheads, agree with me."[17]

At the inquest the next day, the jury found that Lowell "shot the deceased in the discharge of his duty, and in defense of the life of one of his officers, the company being at the time in a state of revolt." The court determined that William Lynch, who had claimed to be a New York laborer, was in fact a Londoner named Jack King and a "fighting man." He had served in the regular army and "could not plead ignorance." Five other men, considered co-conspirators, were confined in the Tombs and court-martialed. One was acquitted, Lynch was executed in June, and the four others were sentenced to hard labor. The dead man, William Pendergast, was twenty-three. Born in Ireland, he was said to have a wife in New York, but she was never located.* At the time of Lynch's execution Lowell wrote to Effie, "Lynch was a very bold fellow and a natural leader of men . . . I took quite a fancy to him for the force of character he showed during the confusion—but he was a bad man."[18]

The affair and the inquest were fully reported in the Boston papers. The *Boston Journal*, the newspaper of record, printed most of the inquest testimony in an attempt to exonerate Lowell. The *Boston Courier*, an anti-Republican, anti-administration, and antiwar paper, took a more critical position. Complaining that officers had grown more officious, that they showed increasing contempt for enlisted men, and that they received their commissions only through influence, the *Courier* claimed that the killing of Pendergast was an expression of class prejudice. Certainly both sides of the class divide attempted to make political capital out of the incident.

Two years of war had done nothing to improve the prejudice that most Bostonians felt about the Irish. Even enlightened northerners had little sympathy for the Irish (an irony in itself, given the outpouring of compassion for the Irish in 1848). Familiarity had bred contempt. Liberals vastly preferred the emancipated slave. W. T. Strong, considering the future, claimed, "It is impossible to name any standard of requisites for the full rights of citizenship which will give a vote to the Celt and exclude the Negro."[19]†

It has been said, "Of all the ethnic antagonisms that have arisen in the turbulence of American social development few have such a distinctly rancorous history as that between the Irish and the Black."[20] Indeed, the intense racism of the Irish, who already formed the bulk of the Democratic vote in

---

*After the war Effie Lowell tried to find the wife but failed and came to believe she did not exist.

†Deepening the irony, when Frederick Douglass visited Ireland in the 1840s, he was stunned by the sight of an Irish farmer; describing his "open, uneducated mouth—the long, gaunt arm—. . . the shuffling gait—the retreating forehead and vacant expression." These terms might be dismissed as pure prejudice if they had not come from a man who clearly was experiencing the shock of recognition, for he was reminded of "my own cruelly abused people." He knew that generations of profound poverty, heavy manual labor, and unrelenting oppression had an undeniable effect on any population, white or black.

Boston, made them particularly hostile to the Emancipation Proclamation. Once the war turned into a war for freedom, Irish patriotism flagged. They took an antiwar, peace-at-any-price position, becoming the bedrock of Copperhead support. Prejudice against the black soldiers of the Fifty-fourth was intense—there had been several incidents of violence—but the situation grew worse in March, when a national conscription law was passed. If selected to serve the Union, a wealthy draftee could hire a substitute or pay $300 to purchase an exemption. In other words, the draft applied only to the poor. In Boston this meant the Irish. Their resentment and anger at this law not only reflected their lack of support for the Union cause but also confirmed their feeling that a healthy dose of hypocrisy lay behind Boston's high ideals.

In this climate most of Boston reacted prejudicially when word went around that drunken recruits had rebelled and that Lowell had shot a mutineering Irishman. The Irish were confirmed in believing that Protestant liberalism's high ideals were a mask for base hypocrisy, while Brahmin Boston admired the firm hand that one of their own had taken with a people they regarded as ignorant, drunken, and treasonous. Lowell's reputation was hugely enhanced. Acclaimed as a man of swift decisive action, a man unafraid of bearing responsibilities, he was inundated with visitors, cards, and public support. But his impatience with bounty-jumpers and his annoyance with "scalawag" recruits was not the prejudice of a Brahmin against the Irish but the frustration of an officer wanting good men. He would take them whatever and however they came, and he knew from experience that the Irish made great fighters.

The death of Pendergast had been a shock for Lowell. As he described his dilemma to Uncle James, he explained that he had risked shooting his own lieutenant unless he shot high, in which case he risked killing Pendergast; and if he did not shoot, he risked letting his lieutenant be fatally wounded. He considered it his responsibility to restore order and believed he was compelled to shoot. Another officer, George Quincy, had already been wounded in the arm taking a blow intended for Lowell.

Thus after two years of war Lowell had killed his first man, an Irishman not yet mustered into his own regiment in downtown Boston. It was a strange anomaly. He had wished to experience a battle, he had been ambitious to rise to positions of greater military responsibility, and yet he had thought he did not need to have a direct hand in killing. Lowell had thought his responsibilities as an officer were to train his men for battle and, once in battle, to interpret the orders of generals and see that they were carried out; to rally them, lead them, keep them at their task. His family had been surprised, even skeptical, to learn that he had never killed anyone. Lowell became quite intense on the point. He insisted that an officer was not "called upon to kill." He believed the most he needed to do was to scatter and demoralize the enemy, and he told his mother he had not yet "seen any occasion to" do more. Lowell was not alone in holding to this view—most of his friends agreed with him. Anna marveled that Frank Barlow, recovering from his Antietam wound, shared Lowell's belief, confessing that he did not even know how to shoot and rarely actually loaded his revolver.

As early as 1861, Orestes Brownson had written, "We must not only have the courage to be killed, but we must have . . . the harder courage to kill," advice that had fallen on deaf ears. Even after suffering the losses of the peninsula, many young men like Lowell retained lofty ideas of moral purity and were troubled by their desire for revenge and by the general "hardening" of their moral compasses. The battle of Antietam had been a breaking point, however, and thereafter the idea of a gentlemanly war was gradually abandoned. Lowell's abhorrence of personal acts of violence in part reflected the pacifism that had accompanied his liberal abolitionist upbringing. But it also expressed the aristocratic, Romantic standard he had set for himself and wished to project to others. He had a reputation for coolness under fire, and such courage was nurtured by stoicism and self-control, by a surmounting of fear. He was believed to have an "absolute indifference" to danger. His self-image relied on this indifference. He could ride among killers and amid killing and be untouched. Much as he had persuaded his Harvard classmates that he did not need to study to excel at schoolwork, now he cultivated an image of perfect courage, of utter fearlessness. To engage in combat, to enter the fray, would have altered that self-image.[21]

Such thinking conformed to the values behind the Romantic revival of the chivalric tradition. Sir Walter Scott's novels *Waverley* and *Ivanhoe* had been the bread and butter that fed the imagination of Lowell's generation. Victory in war was the reward of moral courage over cowardice, of virtue over meanness. This was a distinction between the heroes of the ancient world, Hercules or Achilles, and those of the Romantic ideal, Ivanhoe, Richard the Lionheart, and Robin Hood. The chivalric tradition as reinterpreted by the Romantics was one of moral purity: a knight must be without fear, yes, but also beyond reproach.

In evaluating his own conduct on April 9, Lowell believed he had acted to protect his officers, restore order, and establish authority. The shock of killing, the rage of the men—these things deeply appalled him. He had turned himself in to the provost-marshal because he thought he had been at fault as an officer, although he could not see what he might have done differently. What he could not know was that this nasty yet not-exceptional incident was an augur of the future. The war was about to take a new turn.

On the following Sunday the entire family went to church, where Reverend Bartol preached in support of Lowell's action, endorsing it as an expression of divinely guided rightness for the godly cause of abolition. Bartol heaped glory on Lowell as a man of action, of a kind sorely lacking in the Union cause. Lowell's private opinion was wholehearted regret, and his response, when he discussed the sermon later with his family, was sardonic laughter about this contorted support. Afterward Anna Lowell reported that he "has shut up again" and whistled "whenever he is alone."[22]

This self-protective retreat was abetted by the fortuitous arrival of the belated California Battalion on April 15, two months behind schedule. Under the command of Major De Witt Clinton Thompson, these three companies of strong, eager Californians, like the original California Hundred, were received as a blessing. (The fourth company was delayed yet another month.) Immediately they were bustled out to the training camp at Readville, where trouble quickly arose. The Californians were appalled by the high prices of the war economy in New England, and there was a serious misunderstanding about the payment of their bounty. From the first, these officers and men alike prickled and fussed over their position within the regiment. Many were uneasy about fighting under the Massachusetts flag. They were suspicious of this abolitionist governor with his punky recruits, his Copperhead community, and a staff that, they thought, cheated them of money every which way. They also disapproved of the Fifty-fourth Regiment, calling its enlisted men "blackbirds" who had "flocked" to Uncle Sam for food and clothing and would leave when they felt like it. At the April 30 review, the Californians took offense when Governor Andrew and Secretary of the Treasury Salmon Chase visited the Fifty-fourth first and spent more time inspecting them. The Fifty-fourth's dress parade was "a ludicrous sight," they claimed. What galled particularly was to be "put on a footing of equality." This and the financial angle were the kernel of their festering resentment about serving under the Massachusetts flag. One Californian complained, "Massachusetts has treated us in a scandalous and shabby manner. We are under *no* obligations to her."[23]

Carrying out a plan made in mid-March, Anna Lowell now moved into a boardinghouse at Readville, where Effie and Annie Haggerty, Rob Shaw's fiancée, could also come for extended visits. This made for extremely pleasant living arrangements, and neither Lowell nor Shaw, focused almost exclusively on training their men, had to travel to see his sweetheart, so the engaged pairs had more time together.

It is interesting that the mutiny did not dim Charlie's romance with Effie. His natural aloofness and the fact of his having killed a man made him somewhat intimidating, and he had always been daunting. So new and potentially fragile a relationship as his romance might well have foundered under the strain of responding to the crisis, but this did not happen. Few young women had Effie's sophistication and passion. Of all the Shaw children, she had inherited her parents' political and social zeal. Her mother, described as a woman of "unbending strength," was particularly committed to the cause of abolition. Her closest friend was Lydia Maria Child, who, after Harriet Beecher Stowe, was the woman author who had done the most to awaken in American society a moral outrage against slavery. Effie's father was a philanthropist and a literary man who was described as always exercising "a wise and sound discretion." Both of the elder Shaws were committed to social reform, and in their younger days they had been Transcendentalists who financially supported Brook Farm.[24]

From an early age Effie had been encouraged to make small charitable gestures, and she was now working for the Sanitary Commission, a civilian organization of volunteers who provided medical supplies, nurses, doctors, boat and ambulance transport, and many other humanitarian services. Not only knitting socks and mittens for soldiers, she was also packing boxes for shipment. Like her mother, she was a passionate and religious abolitionist, but unlike the older pacifist generation, she did not shrink from violence; in her diary she repeatedly expressed her anxiety over her limited role (and that of all women) in the war effort.

After Antietam Effie wrote, "All our young men who take their lives in their hands and go out and battle for the right grow noble and grand in the act, and when they come back (perhaps only half of those who went) I hope they will find that the women have grown with them in the long hours of agony." She understood that the fighting men were being transformed by war and that their experiences were foreign to the young women of her generation. How would they understand each other? Her comment is particularly poignant because she had always been so close to her older brother

Rob. Effie comforted herself by considering, "We can work though we can't enlist, and we do."

Effie would have liked to be a soldier. She adored Rob and through his enlistment vicariously imagined her own. "I'm not an atom afraid of death and the enthusiasm of the moment would be sublime . . . I would give anything to be one of them. I cannot express what a sense of admiration and delight fills my soul when I think of the noble fellows advancing, retreating, charging and dying."

In her zeal for action she romanticized the sacrifices made by others.

> All the accounts of brave deeds, bayonet charges, calmly receiving the fire of the enemy and withholding their own, and all the stirring accounts of courageous men, make one so long to be with them . . . I think one loses sight of the wounds and suffering, both of the enemy and one's own force, in thinking of the sublime whole, the grand forward movement of thousands of men marching "into the jaws of death," calmly and coolly . . . I should think a man would be afraid to be a coward in front of his men, all looking to him for example. I should think he'd go and shoot himself.

Her mother hated to hear her talk thus, and her father gave her stern reminders of the price paid for glory and the losses involved. Both her father and Rob did much to educate her about a soldier's life. After one of Rob's visits Effie confided to her diary, "[Rob] said tonight, poor boy, that he wished we were done with this fighting, and expected to be 'slaughtered before it was over.' I suppose they must all feel so, seeing so many of their friends and companions dying around them."[25]

Nevertheless she did not lose her zeal. Her diary entries remind one of Anna Lowell's writings as she watched the Panic of 1837 affect friends and neighbors without having any notion of the impact it would have on her own life. Effie's innate sense of her own courage appears to be naïve overconfidence, but her writing also reflects how she channeled her envy of the officers into empathy, infusing it with a thirst for glory and a taste for war equal to that felt by the men who enlisted in 1861. Perhaps it is not surprising that the mutiny Lowell faced in Boston brought the couple closer together, for he responded to the crisis in just the way Effie hoped and imagined she would have. His horror at having killed a man only made the act more romantic and Lowell yet more deserving of her empathy. Effie genuinely sup-

John Lowell (1743–1802), Lowell's great-grandfather, a maritime lawyer and member of the Constitutional Conventions, in a portrait by Edward Savage.

Jonathan Jackson (1743–1810), Lowell's great-grandfather, an "opulent merchant" before the Revolution and a conservative revolutionary. Photogravure of a painting by John Singleton Copley.

Patrick Tracy (1711–89). Born in Ireland, he rose from common sailor to become the preeminent merchant of pre-Revolutionary Newburyport. Photogravure of a painting by John Trumbull.

Patrick Tracy Jackson (1780–1847), Lowell's maternal grandfather, at the peak of his powers in 1835.

James Russell Lowell in 1866. (Courtesy of Harvard University Archives)

Reverend Charles Lowell (1782–1861), Lowell's paternal grandfather and a beloved minister, one of the few in Boston to speak out against slavery.

Elmwood, Reverend Charles Lowell's house in Cambridge, described as an "abode of angels," where Lowell spent the first five years of his life. (Courtesy of Harvard University Archives)

Lowell's mother, Anna C. J. Lowell, at the end of the war.

Lowell with his father, Charles Russell Lowell, Sr. (1807–70), around 1843, when the elder Lowell was running a dry-goods shop, Lowell & Hinckley, in south Boston.

Lowell as a Harvard undergraduate. (Courtesy of Harvard University Archives)

Frank Sanborn was one of Lowell's intellectual comrades. An abolitionist, he was the most intimately connected to John Brown of all the "Secret Six." (Courtesy of Harvard University Archives)

John C. Bancroft, son of the famous historian and diplomat, grew up at Brook Farm. (Courtesy of Harvard University Archives)

George Putnam, Lowell's future brother-in-law, was one of the few who could keep up with him in mathematics.

Benjamin Peirce, Lowell's favorite professor, was a mystical mathematician who pioneered in probability theory and statistics. (Courtesy of Harvard University Archives)

Ralph Waldo Emerson in 1854. He considered Lowell one of his protégé "mystics." (Courtesy of Library of Congress, Prints and Photographs Division, Civil War Photographs)

John Murray Forbes, China trader and railroad pioneer, who became Lowell's friend and mentor in the mid-1850s. (Courtesy of Forbes family)

Nathaniel Hawthorne, with whom Lowell wandered the art galleries of Rome. (Courtesy of Peabody-Essex Museum)

First Lieutenant James Jackson Lowell of the Twentieth Massachusetts Infantry, Lowell's younger brother.

Lowell's cousin Warren Dutton Russell, killed at Second Bull Run. (Courtesy of Harvard University Archives)

Richard Cary, a friend from Temple Court days, killed at Cedar Mountain. (Mass.-MOLLUS)

Stephen Perkins, with whom Lowell crossed the Alps, also killed at Cedar Mountain. (Courtesy of Harvard University Archives)

James Savage, leader of the Beacon Street Cowards, Lowell's childhood gang. (USAMHI)

Lowell's classmate Richard Goodwin, killed at Cedar Mountain. (Mass.-MOLLUS)

Wilkie James when he was recuperating from wounds received at Fort Wagner, leaning on a crutch and wearing the black arm-band of mourning. He never recovered from the horror of that battle. (USAMHI)

Lowell's cousin Cabot Jackson Russel, mortally wounded on the parapet at Fort Wagner. His body, which was never found, was probably swept into the mass grave along with those of the enlisted men. (Courtesy of Harvard University Archives)

William Lowell Putnam, another of Lowell's cousins, killed at Ball's Bluff. (Dayton VA Archive)

Lowell's close friend Robert Gould Shaw, killed at Fort Wagner.

MAJ. GEN. BANKS'
GRAND EXPEDITION.

2nd MASS. CAVALRY
FIRST BATTALION, 1
Col. C. R. LOWELL, Major CASPAR CROWNINSHIELD

CAPT. W. H. FORBES

Wants Recruits for his Company, in the above Regiment. A preference given to Light Weights.

$100 — UNITED STATES BOUNTY
$50 — CITY BOUNTY, CASH IN HAND
$13 — ADVANCE PAY, and STATE AID TO FAMILIES

PAY PER MONTH:

TO A SERGEANT MAJOR. QUARTERMASTER SERGEANT, PRINCIPAL MUSICIAN and CHIEF BUGLER EACH		$21
TO THE FIRST SERGEANT OF A COMPANY	20 — BUGLERS	13
ORDNANCE SERGEANT and HOSPITAL STEWARDS	22 — MUSICIANS	12
ALL OTHER SERGEANTS, EACH	17 — FARRIERS, BLACKSMITHS and ARTIFICERS	15
CORPORALS	14 — PRIVATES	13

Horses, Arms, Accoutrements, Uniforms, Clothing, Rations, and Medical Attendance, all furnished by Government.

 HEADQUARTERS, 113 WASHINGTON STREET, BOSTON.
AMOS A. LAWRENCE, Special Recruiting Officer.

F. A. SEARLE, STEAM PRINTER, JOURNAL BUILDING. 118 WASHINGTON STREET, BOSTON.

Recruiting poster for Lowell's regiment. (Courtesy of Forbes family)

Captain William Hathaway Forbes, Lowell's most trusted officer. (Courtesy of Forbes family)

First Major Caspar Crowninshield was strong and well liked, and war eventually made him a good officer. (USAMHI)

Will Forbes, Louis Cabot, Henry Russell, and Rob Shaw, with Ida Agassiz, Edith and Ellen Emerson, Alice and Mary Forbes, and Annie Russell at Readville in March 1863. (Courtesy of Forbes family)

Effie Shaw with Lowell in March 1863, after their engagement was announced.

Governor John A. Andrew, Massachusetts's war governor. (Mass.-MOLLUS)

Major De Witt C. Thompson of the California Battalion, who never reconciled himself to serving under the Massachusetts flag and resigned in August 1864, just as the regiment joined Sheridan in the Shenandoah Valley campaign. (Sutter's Fort State Historical Park)

Captain Charles Eigenbrodt of Company E, California Battalion, a first-rate officer who was killed on August 25, 1864. (Sutter's Fort State Historical Park)

The Second Massachusetts Cavalry camp at Vienna, Virginia, showing the denuded landscape, the wooden stockade, the dog tents, the stables, and the officers' Sibley tents. (USAMHI)

Captain J. Sewall Reed of Company A (the California Hundred), a much-admired officer killed in an ambush on February 22, 1864. (USAMHI)

Private Samuel Corbett of the California Hundred was one of the men involved in the Front Royal affair. (USAMHI)

George Towle of the California Hundred was Lowell's orderly; he believed that Lowell's luck worked for him, too. (Courtesy of Wayne Sherman)

Samuel L. Backus, Company L, was one of the "duty men" forming the core of the regiment. (USAMHI)

Frederick Quant of the California Hundred, another duty man, was troubled by the burning of the Shenandoah Valley. (Vallejo Naval and Historical Museum)

Herman Melville visited Lowell's camp in April 1864. (Berkshire Athenaeum, Pittsfield, Massachusetts)

Lieutenant Henry E. Alvord, an abolitionist from western Massachusetts, wrote that with Lowell he had found a "second home." (USAMHI)

John Singleton Mosby with his Partisan Rangers. (Courtesy of Maryland Historical Society)

Henry Lee Higginson, Lowell's oldest and closest friend. The photograph was taken in Vienna, where he attended the opera, during 1857. (Courtesy of Harvard University Archives)

Lowell's cousin Oliver Wendell Holmes, wounded at Ball's Bluff and again at Antietam. (USAMHI)

Frank Barlow with General Winfield Scott Hancock. Left for dead at Gettysburg, Barlow recovered and rose to the rank of major-general. He had hoped to lead a Colored Division, but the death of his wife, to whom he had twice owed his life, undid him, and he left the war. (USAMHI)

Philip Sheridan and his generals—James H. Wilson, Wesley Merritt, Thomas C. Devin, and George Armstrong Custer. (Courtesy of Library of Congress, Prints and Photographs Division, Civil War Photographs)

Rufus Smith, originally in Company F, assumed command of Company A after Captain Reed's death and was mortally wounded in the early fighting at Cedar Creek. (USAMHI)

Lieutenant William Henry Harrison Hussey of Company A, wounded at Cedar Creek. (Courtesy of Mike Fitzpatrick)

A portrait of Lowell made in the Shenandoah Valley. (USAMHI)

Effie Shaw Lowell in 1869, as she emerged from her depression and began to become "a useful citizen."

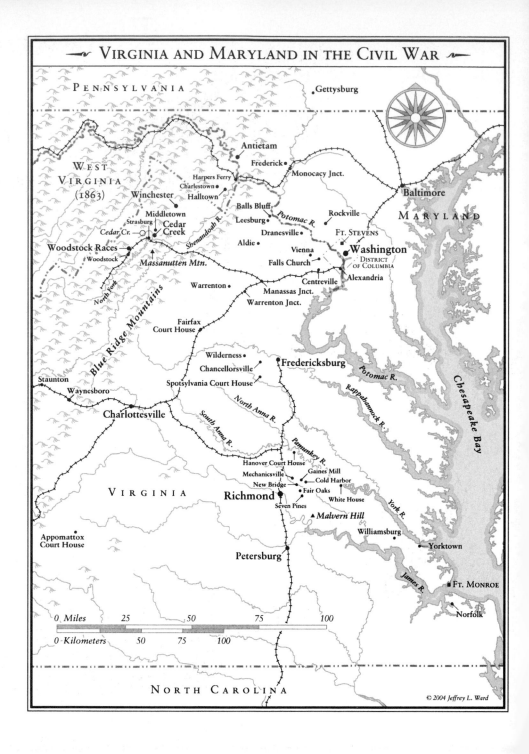

VIRGINIA AND MARYLAND IN THE CIVIL WAR

PENNSYLVANIA

Gettysburg

WEST
VIRGINIA
(1863)

Antietam

Frederick •

Harpers Ferry
Charlestown •
Halltown

Monocacy Jnct.

Baltimore

MARYLAND

Winchester

Middletown

Strasburg   Cedar
Cedar Cr. ○— Creek

Woodstock Races •
• Woodstock

Massanutten Mtn.

Shenandoah R.

North Fork

Balls Bluff •
Leesburg •
Dranesville •
Aldie •

Rockville •

FT. STEVENS

Washington
DISTRICT
OF COLUMBIA

Potomac R.

Vienna •

Falls Church •

Alexandria

Centreville •
Warrenton •   Manassas Jnct.
Warrenton Jnct.

Fairfax
Court House •

Blue Ridge Mountains

Wilderness •
Chancellorsville •
Spotsylvania Court House •

Fredericksburg

Potomac R.

Staunton •
Waynesboro •

Charlottesville

South Anna R.

North Anna R.

Rappahannock R.

Chesapeake Bay

VIRGINIA

Richmond

Hanover Court House •
Mechanicsville •   Gaines Mill
New Bridge •   • Cold Harbor
• Fair Oaks   White House
Seven Pines •

Pamunkey R.

York R.

▲ Malvern Hill

Williamsburg •

Appomattox
Court House •

Petersburg

Yorktown •

James R.

■ FT. MONROE

Norfolk •

0 Miles   25   50   75   100

0 Kilometers   50   75   100

NORTH CAROLINA

© 2004 Jeffrey L. Ward

ported him both in his decisiveness and in his anguish over its consequences.

The fact that Effie Shaw was living at Readville created a huge buzz
among the young ladies of Boston. Her independence and her access to the
hard, gritty truths of the male province of army life enhanced her status. She
appeared to have everything: social prestige, her own beauty, and the reflected glory of her brother and her fiancé. To the young women of Boston,
this was glamour. Lizzie Putnam, Charlie Lowell's cousin and the admirer
of James Savage, first met Effie on April 30 when the Ladies Committee
went to Readville to see the Fifty-fourth Regiment.

Effie was "sitting on a packing box, at the camp in Readville, the afternoon sun striking across the pheasant's feather in her hat, and lighting up
her delicate complexion, her fair hair and fine brow." Lizzie mused that
Effie's face "seemed like an alabaster vase with the light shining through." At
the same review Charlie's aunt Ellen Jackson and cousin Lucy Russel (sister
to Cabot Russel in the Fifty-fourth Regiment) were most impressed by Effie
dressed in a riding habit and pantaloons. She had wound Lowell's colonel's
sash around her body so that it resembled a short blouse. She looked beautiful, somewhat exotic, and slightly intimidating. Anna commented tersely
that such a get-up "would never have appeared in mother's family." Lucy
conceded she had great aplomb.[26]

At the marriage of Henry Russell and Mary Forbes in early May, Ellen
Emerson noted that Charlie Lowell wore his colonel's uniform for the first
time. He had shaved off his scraggly beard and was particularly handsome,
while Effie was beautiful in white, "with the ribbons of the Country." Edith
Emerson had thought that Charlie would pair up with Ida Agassiz and was
delighted that her friend Effie had been chosen. Edith thought Effie was "as
beautiful and fresh as a water lily, wearing a white dress and for a breast pin
she wore a silver eagle like a colonel's only it was of the purest and most delicate silver." The effect was both stylish and distinctive. "Effie, in everything
she says, does, or looks is sweeter and more beautiful than anybody else."[27]

On April 30, at a review of the Second Massachusetts Cavalry, Charlie
and Effie further impressed those who knew them. When the couple rode
up on horseback to greet the Lowell family, they "towered above the crowd
on foot," and Bunch (the baby), who showed no interest in the troops, insisted on climbing up and joining Charlie. Some thirty years later William
James recalled the moment vividly. They rode up near him with the sun behind them, and their looming shapes outlined against the bright sunlight

seemed to exaggerate their godliness. He thought they "looked so like a king and queen that he did not venture to speak to them."[28]

They were a gilded couple expressing the patriotism of the times. For young men like William James, Lowell was the epitome of the correct response to the demands of the moment—a cavalry colonel with his prancing black stallion, his reputation, his beautiful fiancée. For Lizzie Putnam, something so ordinary as sitting on packing crates became iconic of Effie's exalted uniqueness, her brother the colonel of the first black regiment, her fiancé a cavalry colonel.

Anna Lowell described Charlie and Effie stopping by the Quincy Street house on their way out to Readville in early May, when Governor Andrew and Secretary of the Treasury Chase were to review the Fifty-fourth Regiment. Effie was riding Berold, the chestnut whom Charlie had ridden into the West Woods at Antietam and whose wounds had left him no longer fit for battle; Charlie had given him to Effie. To match her horse, Effie wore a black habit and veil. Charlie was riding Ruksh, a large black stallion. Anna had never seen him ride before and was awed. He rode, she thought, with great dignity, and he and Effie "turned back to kiss Bunch, for of course the whole population of the house was out—and then rode round the corner."[29] Her favorite son, whom she had always cherished and adored while indulging his immaturities, was now a man who took her breath away.

FOURTEEN

DEFENDING THE CAPITAL

Summer 1863

I date this May 15, 1863,—ought it to be 1864?—it seems to me a month since this morning and at least a year since Tuesday noon.

—Charles Russell Lowell to Effie Shaw

On May 12 the Second Massachusetts Cavalry left New England for the front. The order had come five days before, on May 7, as the nation absorbed news of the Union defeat at Chancellorsville, Virginia, just south of the Rappahannock River. The campaign that spring had begun with the intention of catching General Lee's army in a pincer movement that would crush it and drive it back on Richmond. But General "Fighting Joe" Hooker, who now commanded the Department and Army of the Potomac, had failed to seize the moment. After four days of fighting in the dense second-growth forest known as the Wilderness, some nine miles west of Fredericksburg, he had been outgeneraled, and 15 percent of the Army of the Potomac had been killed or wounded. The hospitals around Washington were overflowing, and the call had gone out for fresh troops.

From Readville the Second Massachusetts Cavalry marched to Boston, where it was loaded onto a steamer and chuffed off, arriving at Jersey City in the early morning of May 13. It took all day to unload the regiment, water the horses, march to the train depot, and reload onto a train that took the troops to Camden in the middle of the night. They unloaded, crossed the Delaware River by ferry, had breakfast in Philadelphia, and were on the 6 a.m. train to Baltimore, where yet another day was spent changing trains. The regiment left Baltimore at 5 p.m., arriving in Washington at two in the morning of May 15. Lowell proudly told Effie that the regiment had suffered only eleven deserters and one dead horse, and it had picked up six new horses. He had a "very strong guard detailed and kept it on duty for the trip."[1]

Lowell was returning to army life after six months at home—not to army headquarters but to a small camp east of the capital at the Camp of Instruction, which was on the edge of an orchard not far from where he had started with the Sixth U.S. Cavalry. Lowell and Will Forbes shared a tent on a hilltop that looked down on the company tents neatly laid out along the hillside and on the horses grazing under the trees. It was a "pretty scene," Lowell assured Effie that first day, but he confessed that the campfires "have contrived to get up a jolly blue smoke."[2] Writing the next day to his lieutenant-colonel, however, Lowell was all business.

As in 1861, a new cavalry regiment in 1863 offered plenty of incidents of incompetence. The Second Massachusetts Cavalry lacked cartridges, ordnance, and equipment for farrier work. More important, horses had been supplied only two or three days before they left their home state. When Lowell reported for duty in Virginia, he requested ten days to fit out his horses and train up his men. He was given four, and on May 20 General Silas B. Casey, who had been commanding the Camp of Instruction since August 1861, reviewed the regiment.

A review gave a regiment the opportunity to show off its accomplishments: how beautifully it maintained its line, how instantaneous was its discipline. But at the Second's review, quite the reverse occurred. When General Casey asked that the regiment go around at a gallop, "I smiled," Lowell reported to Effie, "for I thought of Casey's probable fate—one Major-General less, dead of a review, ridden over by wild horses." Dutifully the companies formed a straightish line. Lowell ordered, "Draw sabers," whereupon with a great clatter and rattle the men's sabers were pulled from their scabbards and waved over their horses' heads. The untrained horses shied, bolted, and plunged. "When I made the last turn," Lowell recalled, "I glanced backward, the column was half a mile wide where I could last see it and seemed to stretch *ad infinitum*." Despite the chaos, "straight in front in the old place was troublesome Casey, smiling and satisfied as ever." Lowell re-formed the line, including half a dozen riderless horses, and presented the regiment. "Don't blush for us," he told Effie. "We are entirely satisfied with our own appearances."[3] All experienced cavalrymen knew that four days was not long enough to learn to ride.

The point of the review had been not to demonstrate perfection but to assess progress: Casey was looking for assurance that Lowell had his regiment in hand. By this criterion the men and Lowell passed with flying colors.

They were eager for action. Lowell made the rounds of army headquarters, looking up old contacts. The mood was depressingly familiar. Like General McClellan, General Hooker had good administrative skills and fine fighting talk, but he failed to act decisively. This failure, and his dodging of blame, irreparably undermined the trust of his officers (and eventually the administration). "The officers whom I see from the Army of the Potomac give such discouraging accounts of its discipline and *morale*, of the bickerings and jealousies among the general officers, and of the general wrongness of things, that I hesitate about taking steps to get ordered there," Lowell wrote his lieutenant-colonel on May 23. But he had inured himself to disappointment in leaders. More important, he recognized there was work to do: "You may rely upon it, Harry, *Lee* will not remain idle if *we* do; he will send a column into Maryland again when the crops are ready."[4] To threaten Washington, the Confederate army under General Lee was again using the Shenandoah Valley as its route north, where he would ford the Potomac to the north and then swing down on the city through Maryland.

If Lowell was to participate in the campaign to come, he needed to get his regiment reunited (Major Crowninshield and the First Battalion, on detached service since February, were now stationed at Gloucester Point, at the mouth of the York River directly opposite Yorktown where the Peninsula campaign had started). Then he needed his regiment assigned to the command of a general who would use it well. He hoped to join the newly organized cavalry corps of the Army of the Potomac. Its Third Division was commanded by General David McM. Gregg, an old Sixth U.S. Cavalry colleague, and initially Lowell had good reason to be optimistic that the cavalry chief, General George Stoneman, under whom Lowell had served on the peninsula, would assign him to Gregg.* But on May 22 Stoneman became the scapegoat for Hooker's failure at Chancellorsville. He was replaced by General Alfred E. Pleasonton. Nine days later, on May 31, General Casey attached the regiment to the Defenses North of the Potomac, under the

---

*The corps had just completed a raid that, from the cavalry point of view, was the first time in the war that it was properly used. Instead of being tied down to infantry the cavalry freely ranged through Confederate territory, destroying bridges, wrecking rail and telegraph lines, and doing whatever other damage was possible "without violating any of the recognized rules of civilized warfare." Such success promised future cavalry raids.

command of General Samuel P. Heintzelman, and ordered it to Camp Brightwood, eight miles northwest of Washington. From there it was to guard outposts north of Washington and to scout in front of the forts defending the capital.

Thus by June 1 Lowell's troops had technically taken the field, but theirs was an ultradefensive position, some forty miles from the enemy. Lowell complained, "I feel as if I were playing soldier here, and that I always disliked in peace, and disliked still more in war." Adding to the sham was Heintzelman's order to conduct night alarms; these drills meant leaping out of bed, saddling up, and riding out, only to learn that nothing was there. After a week of false alarms and sleepless nights for no purpose, Lowell's men were tired, jaded, and cynical. Even Will Forbes lost his patience, complaining that the alarms were "somewhat played out." Exercises like these did as much damage as good, Lowell felt. Whatever they taught the men about "readiness," they encouraged them equally to think that officers gave orders just to make work for them. And this, he thought, was a greater evil, undermining the delicate trust between officers and men.[5]

Lowell kept the new recruits on a short leash, subjecting them to constant drilling. The bugle first blew at 5:30 a.m., when the men rose, dressed, and answered to roll call. After their horses were watered, fed, cleaned, and inspected, a second bugle call summoned them to breakfast. Dress parade at eight was followed by individual and company drill. By ten-thirty men and horses alike needed a rest; then both were fed. From two until four in the afternoon, they alternated between squadron and regimental drill, after which horses and men were fed again. Retreat was sounded. The men had two hours of leisure until the bugle went for roll call and, at nine, taps.

In addition to imposing this strict schedule, Lowell issued various regulations and special orders. In his letters to Effie, Lowell complained that new officers were too chummy with the men and didn't enforce their authority. He had to reprimand one officer for sloppy bookkeeping. He insisted that the men wear proper uniforms, carry passes, refrain from drinking, never gallop in camp, and water their horses in an orderly manner. It was hard to keep the camp clean, and he complained that "it is so hard to make men understand that the only way to keep tolerably clean is to keep perfectly clean."[6] It was a matter of sanitation and health, of course. Carelessness in camp was not solely the province of the men, however. At one point a runaway horse and buggy nearly mowed down Lowell's tent, but luckily it hit a tree first, destroying the buggy, whose proprietors turned out to be two fellow officers. Only when the men had performed well did he lighten the guard, which permitted them greater freedom in camp, but he was ready to lower the boom if they abused his comparative leniency.

When the men were given three-day passes, they went to Washington, drank themselves blind, and failed to return to camp. Officers had to hunt them down in jails or hospitals, a job made more difficult when the men were so crazed with alcohol that they were unrecognizable or incapable of identifying themselves. Even more pitiable, the men fought when drunk and in several cases cut one another up badly. The California Hundred had all taken a pledge of abstinence in San Francisco, but they too succumbed to the temptations of the bottle.

In the long history of army life, it has never been possible to make soldiers enjoy many aspects of their work. Lowell's strict drill regimen did not even aspire to enjoyment. Hence his soldiers, like all soldiers, complained, and his officers, like all officers, bore the brunt of these complaints. Lowell believed this grumbling among the men would disappear not with reforms or rationalizations, but rather with the knowledge, respect, and trust established under fire. Failure there could not be compensated for by any amount of bonhomie in camp or by any enlightened camp policies. To be effective on a field of battle, a soldier had to respond to orders even if panicked, to resist the natural instinct to avoid fire, and to fight instead of flee. Until his men were battle-tested, neither Lowell nor his men would know how effective their training had been. The best one could hope for was their grudging acceptance of the necessity of performing onerous tasks. He was therefore eager for the real thing—to get his men into action quickly.

Unfortunately, the real thing was not what was in store for the Second Massachusetts Cavalry, assigned to the Defenses of Washington at Camp Brightwood. Picket duty was not about fighting, and it bore almost no resemblance to a young man's notion of soldiering. Intended solely to alert the main army to an approaching enemy, pickets set the outer perimeter of the army's defensive circle, with mounted vedettes standing guard for two-hour stretches. A mile or so to their rear was the picket reserve, about fifteen men ready to ride out at a moment's notice. Citizens or soldiers attempting to pass through the pickets were stopped. If they had passes or knew the password, they were let through. The enemy might probe the picket—a shot or two might be fired—and thus the two armies would jockey for position or signs of vulnerability. In good weather picket duty was boring; in bad it was miserable. Scouting was somewhat better. Usually a lieutenant and forty men broken into squadrons rode over an assigned area looking for signs of the Confederate army. They might also find stragglers, reclaim lost horses, or gather intelligence. The men enjoyed the comparative liberty of being on a scouting party, particularly when the weather was fine.

Lowell wrote to Effie every day as a complement to the pedestrian affairs of regimental life. He wanted letters from her to be a tonic, to remind both of them of "the hope of . . . pleasanter circumstances." They made plans to travel together in Europe, to Italy and the Alps. Lowell liked the idea of going down the Nile and considered these future plans good for his soul. But he also wrote to Effie as a confidant, reporting frankly on his military life, offering more detail and opinion than he had ever given his mother, and confessing his ambitions and frustrations to her. He was sometimes asking a lot of his fiancée, though she was considerably better informed than most girls. Her family constantly discussed the major issues of the day, Rob had always written openly and informatively to her, and she exhibited a maturity that far exceeded her age. But her understanding was vicarious: she was only nineteen, and sometimes Lowell got too far ahead of her and frightened her.[7]

One such case was his report of his interview with Secretary of War Stanton, who summoned Lowell on May 22. Since the previous September, when he had snubbed Lowell, the secretary had radically altered his opinion of the young officer. Now, Lowell told Effie, Stanton felicitously offered to do "anything and everything I wanted to make [the Second Massachusetts Cavalry] an 'Ironside' regiment." (The term referred to the USS *Constitution*, called "Old Ironsides" because it was made of Georgia oak as dense as iron. In the War of 1812 British cannonballs had bounced off it.) Quite how that would be done Lowell had no idea, but he promised to make it "a good regiment." And Stanton congratulated Lowell on his handling of the mutiny at School Street, explaining that had he not been away when it occurred, he would have written "a personal letter of thanks."[8] Somewhat flummoxed by this praise, Lowell changed the subject, requesting that his first battalion, serving on the Yorktown peninsula since February, now rejoin the regiment. Stanton agreed, and Lowell accepted his promise graciously, keeping his skepticism to himself, for he did not trust Stanton: having been snubbed when delivering the captured flags from a much-needed victory, he was now being treated as an admired protégé because he had killed one of his own soldiers.

Effie was spooked not only by Lowell's report of the discussion of the School Street affair but by the implications of an "Ironside" regiment. By return mail she wrote that she wished he might get "out of harness" because of a "breakdown," and then they could begin their travels in Europe. She meant that a relapse of consumption, or even a threatened relapse, was an honorable reason for him to resign his commission, but to Lowell this was a flirtation with even greater danger. Her suggestion made him "a little superstitious," and on May 29, with an eye on "Fortuna," Lowell set parameters, defining the line between the fantasies that helped him meet his responsibilities and those that didn't. He used a cavalryman's image to explain: "We do not own ourselves and have no right to even wish ourselves out of harness. Collars are our proper 'wear,' I am afraid, and we ought to enjoy going well up to them."[9] He did not want to have the sort of doubts and longings that might turn him into a skittish, shying horse that wouldn't take the bit. He did not want to lose his nerve.

Their letters also explored philosophies and attitudes that would inform their future life together. On May 24 Lowell sent Effie a motto inscribed around the portrait, hanging in Elmwood, of his grandfather's grandfather, Reverend John Lowell of Newburyport: "*In necessitas unitas; in nonnecessariis libertas; in omnibus caritas*," which he translated as "In essentials, unity; in non-essentials, freedom; in all things, love." He saw it as a sort of guiding "principle," he told her, that offered latitude for individuality, at least until freedom threatened unity. One can easily imagine the Sunday dinners at Elmwood with Reverend Lowell at the head of the table listening to his children debate and argue and, as things grew heated, his calling their attention to the portrait of his grandfather and quoting the motto as a gentle reminder, a plea for tolerance, moderation, and a sense of proportion.

Applied to a marriage, his grandfather's motto had a lot going for it. Lowell thought the motto would smooth away many differences if written over "every young fireside,"[10] particularly if the mediation of differences were guided by *caritas*. He may also have meant it as a hint to Effie that however much he loved her and would stand by her, he did not always agree with her and did not share all her passionate convictions and harsh judgments. What they were both to learn was that he had some of his own. Lowell believed that "no two persons ought to believe exactly alike . . . the truth must be seen from different sides by different people . . . each person much cling to the one which is most real, most internal, most near to him."[11] (This very modern notion of self and selfhood, keenly sensitive to the Romantic emphasis on the individual, is interestingly applied here to the context of marriage.)

Effie wanted their future children to have household duties so that they would develop a sense of responsibility and cooperation. Lowell responded jokingly: "Excellent—no family should be without them,—let us order a small lot at once."[12] Humor may have been the only way he could mask the immense distance that he felt separated him from Effie. He was living a life consumed with duties—he was, as he had just written, "in harness," and it was all but impossible to imagine a world of *concocted* duties, there being so many real ones. Ironic humor was his bridge.

His own growing up had in any case involved real responsibilities, out of necessity, not theory. He did not mention this, however, and instead ruminated that "in a world where it would seem so easy to enjoy,—this conscience should so often come in to make us 'move on.'" Carlyle, among others, he told Effie, believed that "conscience is the sign of man's fall"; it was the fruit of knowledge, the reason for man's banishment from paradise.[13] Lowell's linkage of childhood duties, man's fall, conscience, and paradise was typically Romantic. On one level he was implying that in his relationship with Effie he had found what felt like paradise, and it was his conscience that forced his return to army life.

But he was also exhibiting a more complex understanding than he had shown when, as a student, he had first examined the subject of work and paradise. As a young man he had been a reformer and had resisted man's fated labor. After he left Harvard, he had struggled with his mother over the nature of work itself, castigating her for adhering to the old New England belief in duty and work as a kind of faith. Work, he had insisted, need not be all drudgery, and he had struggled to find its glory. In those days there had been no mention of paradise, only heroic labor. "It is Heroes that we must try to be," he had told his mother.[14] Now, with new eyes and new experience, he revisited the old theme. Recognizing the grandiosity behind his youthful vision of heroes, he was far more reconciled to what he now regarded as the human condition. Having found a personal happiness, Charlie could now speculate to Effie that the compensation for man's fate of conscience and labor might be spontaneous joy, and that these moments of joy might be a state more divine than what even the most elevated conscience (or heroic labor) could achieve.

Lowell was finally taking steps to approve a regimental chaplain, a post that heretofore he had shown no interest in filling. To Johnny Bancroft, he confessed that he "should like to be at home, even to go to church"[15] and described the part he would play in the regimental services: reading a chapter or two from the New Testament. But this desire for the comfort and habit of faith did not mean that he had reconciled himself to conventional religion. Lowell believed "Heaven is here, everywhere, if we could only see God." The Unitarians and Transcendentalists of Lowell's childhood, from his grandfather to Emerson, placed great emphasis on Christ as God incarnate: "Would you see God, see me." They understood it as an exhortation to "firsthand" faith. They wanted to reinvigorate Christianity, and to transport religious experience beyond the church walls, and so they had emphasized the miraculous in life, the sublime in nature, and the divinity of man. But Lowell did not explain how he thought we might "see God." Indeed the implication was that we cannot. Nor did he put much faith in the idea of an afterlife. "It is not to be much dwelt upon," he suggested, "only enough to make one content with death as a change not infinitely different from sleep."[16]

The most conventional of Lowell's religious attitudes concerned prayer. For him, prayer was "not an asking, but a thanking mood." The world was created "for the glory of God," and man was intended to glorify God; Lowell felt this was best done by being thankful. "Just how we are to show our thankfulness is a more searching question," he wrote Effie; "I think not by depreciating this world to exalt another, perhaps by 'bene vivere,' by loving well both man and bird and beast." By "bene vivere" Lowell did not mean "the good life" or "good living" but using one's life well, living a fully realized life.[17]

Obviously this was not organized religion, and in some respects it hardly qualified as religion. One suspects that for the benefit of his bride-to-be he was recasting as a very liberal Christianity his old ideas about the relationship between conscience and duty, and the importance of work in a man's life—all related to his interpretations of Wordsworth, Carlyle, and Emerson. Perhaps he was establishing the common ground on which they might meet. Like her mother and his own, Effie had a strong and conventional Christian faith. She attended church regularly and took the sermons to heart. Her faith was activist: she believed in good works. But this difference between them was not unusual. The women in many New England families believed deeply, even fervently, while the men doubted, speculated, theorized, or simply lapsed. In Lowell's case, his comments to Effie hark back to the ideas he had put forward a decade earlier, when he wrote to his friends Sanborn and Potter about his ideal club aimed at the full realization of each individual's expressive powers and his request that his clubmates make an "integer" of him.

Shortly after getting to Washington, Lowell had received accounts from both his mother and Effie of the flag presentation of the Fifty-fourth Regiment. Reading these moved Lowell to reflect on the previous six months. On May 23 he wrote Shaw a congratulatory letter: "I feel like telling you now, old fellow (as an officer and outsider, and not as your friend and brother), how very manly I thought it of you then to undertake the experiment." His letter included advice on preventive measures against malaria. Sounding oddly like his mother, Lowell went into considerable detail about the need to take quinine with whiskey in liberal doses. His regimental doctor, he explained, who had served briefly on the Carolina coast, believed that this treatment drastically reduced the odds of succumbing to the disease.

"Your regiment has proved such an entire success—has given such good promise of taking a very high place . . . that it is easy to forget the circumstances under which you took hold of it," he wrote. (But Shaw had not forgotten. A week later he wrote Annie, "Just remember our own doubts and fears, and other people's sneering and pitying remarks, when we began last winter, and then look at the perfect triumph of last Thursday . . . Everyone I saw from the Governor's staff [who had always given us rather the cold shoulder] down, had nothing but words of praise.") A few days later Lowell wrote Effie an amusing account of having his hair cut at the barbershop at Willard's, Washington's swank hotel, where he received royal treatment from the black attendants who recognized him as a Massachusetts colonel; the barber told him they favored all things from Massachusetts because, unlike everywhere else, the Fifty-fourth had been allowed to join the white troops, taking its regimental number in the regular sequence. Lowell enjoyed answering their questions about the Fifty-fourth and gave them as much information as he could, although he did not mention his own association with it. "Had I said the word, I believe they would have pressed all the offices of their trade upon me, willy-nilly, and instead of my short bristles, I should have left with a curled wig perfumed and oiled."[18]

As both Shaw and Lowell knew, the Fifty-fourth Regiment, having taken the field, would now be tested in an entirely new way. Rob's challenge was to prove that his men could fight. The practical obstacles were now largely military ones. The plan was for the Fifty-fourth to form the core of a new "colored" brigade, including the few black regiments that had been organized, recruited, and trained in parts of the South where many ex-slaves had congregated around Union troops holding bits of Confederate territory—in the islands off Georgia, in New Orleans, and in places along the Mississippi River.

The danger was that these troops would be made to function as work gangs, which is how the army had used, and was using, the ex-slaves who flooded its camps, from among whom most of the black soldiers were being recruited. There was considerable doubt or uncertainty, even among those sympathetic to the cause, about whether the ex-slaves could withstand the rigors of battle. The fear was that slavery's harsh conditions and abuse might have broken their spirit. But the officers who had intimate exposure to the Fifty-fourth—officers of the regiment itself and of the Second Massachusetts Cavalry—knew that the odds in favor of success were high. Furthermore, Lowell believed that once blacks had fought, then "the question of slavery and the disposition of the slaves becomes comparatively easy of solution"— they would have earned their citizenship.[19]

Believing it was imperative that the regiment serve under a sympathetic brigade commander, Lowell had taken the initiative of writing to Senator Sumner recommending Frank Barlow for the job. But Barlow, wounded at Gettysburg, had been passed over. After some confusion, Governor Andrew succeeded in getting the Fifty-fourth sent to General David Hunter at Hilton Head, South Carolina, where, he and Shaw believed, they would "be appreciated and allowed a place in . . . active war."[20] The fate of the Fifty-fourth now rested in the hands of the military establishment, and the careful behind-the-scenes manipulations of powerful and sympathetic friends would no longer have much influence.

The regiment was near the colonies of the Boston Education Commission at Port Royal and Hilton Head, where Thomas Higginson and James Montgomery were brigaded under General Hunter. Both these men had credentials that Governor Andrew respected. Higginson had been one of the Secret Six, and Montgomery had been part of the Kansas fighting. Hunter was an abolitionist, had seen fighting in Kansas, and had been an early convert to the use of black troops. Lowell had last personally encountered Hunter in the early days of the war, when he commanded Clay's Battalion, the vigilante organization to which Count Gurowski belonged. He knew he was not very professional and lacked credibility in the military establishment.

Then came news that on June 9 Darien, a small coastal town in Georgia (which Lowell had visited in 1856), had been pillaged and burned by troops under Colonel Montgomery, the Fifty-fourth Massachusetts among them. The purpose of this destruction was obscure. The town was deserted except for women, the old, and some slaves. No resistance was offered when federal troops entered the town, and federal gunboats had habitually passed it without event. Shaw had had to participate in the Darien raid, although he had held his men back from the greater excesses of pillage. Troubled by the event, he wrote to Lowell, "Don't you think . . . the destruction of a defense-less town, containing only a few non-combatants, is unjustifiable, and contrary to all rules of warfare?"[21]

Shaw told Lowell that when questioned on his reasons for burning the town, Montgomery had replied, "Southerners must be made to feel that this was a real war, and that they were to be swept away by the hand of God, like the Jews of old." Shaw accused Montgomery of having a "hatred of every-thing Southern," but he claimed that "he only hated them as being enemies of liberty & he had good reason to hate every enemy of liberty," arguing that brutal tactics were justified because the South had declared that it would return any captured black soldier into slavery and kill any white officer of black troops. Shaw was silenced by this reply, yet he thought that burning houses lived in solely by women and children was "most barbarous—more so than the hanging of every man we take in arms." He hadn't been able to stand up to Montgomery, but he afterward wrote, "In theory it may seem all right to some, but when it comes to being made the instrument of the Lord's vengeance, I myself don't like it."[22]

Lowell couldn't have agreed more. And the misadventure confirmed his suspicions about Hunter: he and Montgomery were both renegades. Guerrilla fighting in Kansas had made acceptable to them a number of tactics that should never become military policy, or so Lowell was convinced, but he did not have much more practical experience than Shaw. He had only just completed his first scout on Confederate soil.

North of the Potomac, on June 10, the day after Darien, Lowell had been ordered out to chase guerrillas who attacked and burned the camp of the Sixth Michigan Cavalry. Following their trail to Poolesville, Maryland, the Second Massachusetts Cavalry crossed the Potomac at White's Ford (White was one of several local guerrilla leaders) and rode onto Confederate soil for the first time. Lowell sent out flankers and skirmishers, standard procedure for a scouting party in enemy territory. The trail led to Leesburg, Virginia, the town nearest to Ball's Bluff, and Lowell's men charged the town, which was shut up tight with only the odd old man scuttling for cover.

Although his men insisted that the rebels they were pursuing had taken shelter in civilian houses, Lowell forbade them to touch anything or search any homes as they marched through town. The guerrillas' trail led southwest down the Little River Turnpike to Aldie, and then six miles west to Middleburg. Just as Lowell was preparing to enter that town, where he supposed he would find the guerrillas, a party of four hundred federal cavalrymen rode in from there with the news that the guerrillas had disbanded, then vanished back to their farms and regular life. There was nothing to do but turn around and head home. Despite their 150-mile scout with only hardtack to eat, Lowell did not allow his men to forage. Although the Californians admitted that forage was stealing by another name, they deeply resented Lowell's fastidiousness. They believed that "if we hope for success in putting down this hellish rebellion we must get over our nice points of etiquette." One Californian sarcastically complained that to "satisfy our hunger would not be pursuing a 'conciliatory policy.' "[23]

From the start of the war, Lowell had been preoccupied with the problem of controlling the bestial instincts that emerge in warfare. When Shaw had been picked as colonel of the Fifty-fourth, his optimism had increased, for "Shaw is not a fanatic,"[24] as he explained to his mother. Colonel James Montgomery was precisely the sort of fanatic Lowell feared would do more harm than good. Wanting to help his friend, Lowell thought of writing to Secretary Stanton, but his position as an army officer made it difficult, and he did not want to be accused of insubordination. It would do no good to antagonize the secretary of war. Lowell settled on writing a letter dated June 26 to William Whiting, the man in the War Department in charge of reviewing policy on black troops. Lowell did not mention any personal association with the Fifty-fourth but confined his comments to newspaper accounts of the Darien incident and represented himself as a disinterested officer concerned with war policy. His point was simple: "It is not war, it is piracy — expeditions in which pillaging is attempted by order will infallibly degenerate into raids in which *indiscriminate* pillaging will be the rule."[25] Lowell, an emancipationist, did not subscribe to conciliation, nor was he fearful of antagonizing the South (as McClellan had been). His concern was the potential destruction of the good reputation of the black troops and of turning an army into a violent mob.

Lowell followed up this letter by meeting with Senator Sumner. The two men talked about the future of black troops. Sumner suggested that by the end of the summer Stanton's hope of having some 200,000 black troops might be realized. Lowell thought this was "rather wild." (It was: by war's end the U.S. Colored Troops totaled only 187,000.) But optimistic minds were already racing to the fruits of success. Lowell was deeply stimulated by Sumner's speculations on the duration, outcome, and result of the war. Now that emancipation was a reality and African Americans were bearing arms in the Union army, Sumner, like Lowell, believed that the war would be a long one. "[Sumner] does not find in history any record of such great changes as we expect to see, having been brought about except with long wars and great suffering." Lowell happily confessed to Effie that he thought his ideas about the war "excellent because they agree with mine."[26]

But Lowell did not agree with Sumner's ideas about a peace. The enormous task of reorganizing the South and its institutions was one that few people agreed on in theory and hardly anyone had discussed in practice. To Lowell, Sumner seemed too vindictive, too punitive, too ready to strip the southern states of their power. Considering the demands of peace made Lowell feel the limitations of being a professional soldier, and he wasn't sure that he was prepared to meet the challenges of the future. "After the war, how much there will be to do," he had already written Effie, "and how little opportunity a fellow in the field has to prepare himself for the sort of doing that will be required: it makes me quite sad sometimes." He thought the work could not "be done until a new generation, better educated in such things than the present, takes hold of it. How many years it took to form our present Constitution."[27]

Thoughts of peace and the future led Lowell to consider how war had changed him. As a young man, he had found appealing the Transcendentalist idea that through self-culture one might apprehend the real in a philosophical or religious sense, might "see God," as he said to Effie. But Lowell no longer believed this could be done in a retreat from the world. His strongest moments and his fullest use of himself, he had learned, came not in isolation and the perfect articulation of inner thought but in action. His experience of the battlefield had brought vividly into perspective Emerson's maxim "Action is man thinking." Lowell now understood that his powers of leadership could not be exercised in isolation. "I wonder whether my theories about self-culture, &c., would ever have been modified so much, whether I should ever have seen what a necessary failure they lead to, had it not been for this war." The force of his personality, his confidence among his peers, the willingness of men to follow him had come together on the battlefield and he had tasted that very real power within himself. He had no doubts about what it meant. "I wish I could feel as sure of doing my duty elsewhere as I am of doing it on the field of battle—that is so little a part of an officer's and patriot's duty now." His ease in battle was real, and it had taught him "the great secret of doing, is in seeing what is to be done."[28]

Almost as soon as Lowell had finished this letter, he received news that on June 17 the First Massachusetts Cavalry had been badly mauled in a skirmish at Aldie, about thirty miles west of Washington, losing half its men. Immediately Lowell went to Alexandria, where the wounded were being brought in, and searched through the stretchers. He found Henry Higginson with a great saber slash across his face, an arm and a leg broken, bad bruises, and, most worryingly, a pistol bullet lodged near the base of his spine. He had been hit in much the same place as had William Sedgwick at Antietam; Sedgwick had been paralyzed from the waist down and died within two weeks. Remembering this, Lowell telegraphed Henry's father to come immediately, then arranged to have his friend moved to the Armory Hospital in Washington, where his sister Anna could look after him. She got Henry the best treatment possible and the attention of its one excellent surgeon, Dr. D. Willard Bliss. But even Dr. Bliss recommended that the bullet be extracted in Boston. It was near enough to the spine that mismanagement of its removal might result in paralysis.

Henry's version of what had happened at Aldie was very unclear. Leading two squadrons, he had been ordered to make a feint by charging the enemy but not actually engaging. (He was substantially outnumbered.) One of his squadrons had overrun the mark. Higginson had gone after it and had succeeded in extracting his men without exciting the accomplished Virginian, Colonel Thomas Rosser, and his superior forces into pursuing them. Then, in a move that defies explanation, one of Higginson's captains (the brother of the regiment's colonel) decided to taunt the Confederates. At this the rebels turned in full force and mercilessly chased down Higginson's men. The taunting captain was mortally wounded, Jim Higginson was captured, and Henry too—then shot and left for dead. He escaped recapture by crawling away through the woods for some distance until he collapsed.

Once Henry's father arrived, he was slung in a hammock and shipped back to Boston, now essentially out of the war. From Charles Adams, Lowell learned that the Fourth New York Cavalry had failed to support the First Massachusetts, but Adams conceded that the blame lay with the stupidity of the First Massachusetts's own captain in taunting the enemy. To the officers of his own regiment, who had once belonged to the First, Lowell repeated only that the Fourth New York Cavalry had "left our men unprotected."[29]

This nasty wounding of his oldest and closest friend through the stupidity of his own officers and the neglect of other troops disheartened Charlie. Worse, Higginson had been shot when he was down, wounded, and already a prisoner. Charlie did not mention this to anyone, but Jim Higginson, who had been there, wrote from prison that he had noted it "for future reference." The whole experience had altogether changed Jim. He no longer believed that an officer's function was only to direct others; he was ready to engage in combat himself. "My scruples have vanished," he declared to his younger brother Frank.[30]

Lowell had little time to consider his scruples. While in Washington, he was given new orders. The fracas at Aldie had been a small part of General Lee's overall movement north. State militias in Maryland and Pennsylvania were called out, impromptu fortifications thrown up. The Second Massachusetts Cavalry, still attached to the Defenses North of the Potomac, was ordered to move to Poolesville and to picket the Potomac River between the mouth of the Monocacy and Great Falls, but Lowell was not content with this assignment. Nor were any of his men.

Major Thompson, the Californian, appealed directly to the general-in-chief. (Before the war he and Hooker had had a real estate partnership in northern California.) His battalion was assigned as Hooker's escort. At 10 p.m. on June 26, as a result of a separate interview with General Hooker, Lowell got orders to march for Knoxville, Maryland, to join General Henry Slocum of the Twelfth Corps. On June 27 at 8:30 a.m. he started his men off marching twenty-five miles west and then bivouacked. Meanwhile urgent telegrams recalling him chased after him, and when Lowell finally received them, the new orders were contradictory, coming from different sources. Hooker, in the field, ordered him to report to General William H. French, while General Heintzelman, in Washington, countermanded this order. In the predawn hours of June 28, Lowell obeyed Heintzelman because "he was backed by Halleck" and, against all his desires, returned to the mouth of the Monocacy. There Lowell learned that J.E.B. Stuart and his Confederate cavalry had already crossed "at the very ford I was especially to watch; that there had been no picket there at all, and no notice had gone either to Washington or to Hooker till nearly twelve hours after the crossing."[31] Hoping to mitigate the damage, Lowell set off immediately in pursuit of Stuart and caught up, urging his advance guard to tail Stuart with less than a mile between them. They rode through Rockville and Brookville, taking their first prisoners.

The Second Massachusetts Cavalry then returned to Poolesville and were immediately ordered to a new camp, where they spent the three days of the battle of Gettysburg patrolling the Potomac and arresting citizens thought to be guerrillas in the Rockville area of Maryland. The camp of the Second Massachusetts Cavalry was on Seneca Creek as it curved around an oak grove at the base of a hill. In the hot weather they bathed, read, and felt bored, idle, and wasted. Will Forbes reported to his family, "The Colonel made one attempt to get into the Army of the Potomac and was ordered back, and now we must lie here quietly till something turns up." As reports of a big battle came in, the men had plenty of time to think and talk. It galled them to be so idle during such a huge confrontation. Lowell wrote Effie, "Don't you wish that your Colonel was one who belonged to the Army of the Potomac? . . . I have done all I dare to get away . . . I suppose there will come a time when the regiment will have a chance." Nor was his mood improved by his conviction that once the dust settled, he would be cashiered and "disgraced forever." He did not feel he deserved the blame for Stuart's breakthrough but knew that it would be easy for Hooker to pin it on him. Fortunately for Lowell, he had been merely a pawn in a larger game. On June 27, the day of Lowell's march, Halleck had forced Hooker to resign his command of the Union army. The unpicketed ford and the conflicting telegrams Lowell received had been the result of confusion during the power struggle between Hooker and Halleck.[32]

Interestingly and perhaps justifiably, Lowell was never reprimanded or even blamed for the disastrous twenty-four hours during which his portion of the Potomac had not been picketed. Stuart's successful crossing of the river had allowed him to commence another raid around the Union army as it moved north after General Lee. By the time the battle of Gettysburg was over, it was clear that Stuart's famous ride, which had separated him from Lee's army for a week, depriving it of vital intelligence, had significantly contributed to the Union victory. In other words, the absence of Lowell's pickets on the Potomac had given the Union army an instrumental advantage at Gettysburg, since it permitted Stuart to engage in a folly that, if he had been challenged, he might easily have abandoned and returned to serve a more useful purpose for Lee's army.*

Lowell's satisfaction in the Union victory at Gettysburg included his relief that Hooker had been relieved. "A victory under Hooker," Lowell explained, "might have been almost as bad as a defeat." He considered Hooker "an adventurer and his popularity would have been very dangerous I think

---

*The two times Stuart's cavalry circled the Union army—in June 1862 and June 1863— Lowell's regiment was the only one in its immediate path.

to the republic." General George Meade was "a good man and a modest man," but Lowell credited the Gettysburg victory to "Fortune" and to "the Army itself."[33] It confirmed his conviction that soldiers and officers were finding out how to fight despite bad or indifferent leaders.

Among those killed at Gettysburg were yet more friends of Lowell's from the Twentieth. Sumner Paine, Lowell's second cousin, had joined in May as soon as he turned eighteen. Wounded in the face on the battle's second day, he fought on the third day, resisting Pickett's charge. He was hit by a ball that broke his leg. Continuing to command on one knee, Paine was urging his men on, waving his sword, when he was struck by a shell and instantly killed. Henry Ropes was hit by shell fragments and lived long enough to say, "I am killed." (He had described the feeling of being shot at Antietam as being like "fishes nibbling.") And in the same charge that killed Paine and Ropes, Paul Revere was mortally wounded by a bullet from a canister shot. He had been taken prisoner at Ball's Bluff, threatened with being hanged in retaliation for Union policy on Confederate privateers, badly afflicted by malaria during the Seven Days, wounded at Antietam, and killed at Gettysburg. It was honorable service. Revere had not had much talent for leading officers or men, being too rigid and interfering, but as a man he was much admired, courageous, reliable—in the word of the day, "manly."[34]

The most upsetting news for Lowell personally was that Frank Barlow had been wounded and left for dead. Serving under General Winfield Scott Hancock, he had been shot on the first day in the terrible fighting after General John Reynolds's men relieved General John Buford and his Reserve Brigade. The bullet had exited at the spine, and Barlow was paralyzed in his arms and legs. His life was saved by an aide to the Confederate general Jubal Early, who had had Barlow transported to the rear, where word was passed through the lines to Barlow's wife, a nurse. She immediately went to him. The bullet had passed through his body but had hit nothing vital, and although his spine was traumatized, it was undamaged. Slowly he regained the use of his limbs. Barlow was very lucky, both in the nature of his wound and in the assiduous devotion and competence of his wife.

Simultaneous with the Union victory at Gettysburg was the Confederate surrender of Vicksburg after six weeks of siege. Control of the Mississippi River was now in Union hands. Isolated from its western states and no longer capable of receiving supplies from them, the Confederacy was seriously, perhaps fatally, compromised. This was the most significant Union victory to date. But victory made Lowell anxious: it was "going to be more difficult to use victories than to bear defeats." He had expressed this idea to his mother shortly after leaving Boston, and now it was truer than ever. "We have had few victories, but have been on the whole successful. We are now going to gain victories and find them comparatively useless."[35] This kind of comment was guaranteed to provoke her, but Lowell had a serious point.

Throughout 1861–63 the Union's humiliations and defeats had steeled people's nerve, focused their determination. Northern preachers had used the defeats as moral lessons, finding in the results of battle the angry God of the Old Testament meting out justice and retribution for the sins of slavery. Both his mother and Effie had largely accepted this way of viewing the war. But Lowell disagreed with Effie's "Jewish faith," as he called it, meaning the tendency among New Englanders to see themselves as the chosen people, as God's elect. Lowell was not convinced that "God's plan" was knowable. He admitted that "when a nation, or a man, has to learn a thing it is clutched by the throat and held down till it does learn it," but to believe that human suffering should be read as a specific divine message he considered "arrogating too much for ourselves." By way of example, he teasingly asked her, "How do you adapt this victory to your theory—do you give up the theory, or do you expound the victory as an indication that we have been sufficiently humiliated, have mended our ways and are now all right?"[36]

Whatever the divine plan might be, the individual was at best merely a pawn, perhaps only a bystander: "Not all nations, and not all men, do have to learn things . . . most fall untaught. Why may not we? Why may not we fall by victory? May it not be the South that is being taught?" Charlie no longer believed that there was any message or meaning in either suffering or success, as he had when he thought tuberculosis was an early warning from the gods and a sign of being especially favored. "Many nations fail, that one may become great; ours will fail, unless we gird up our loins and do an honest and humble day's work, without trying to do the thing by the job or to get a great nation made by any patent process. It is not safe to say that we shall not have victories till we are ready for them; we shall have victories, and whether or not we are ready for them depends upon ourselves."[37]

Effie still had a lustful enthusiasm for the glory of war. Unlike her father and Rob, who chastised and remonstrated with her callous enthusiasms, Lowell took a different tack. Urging patience, he wrote, "I believe more in 'keeping gunpowder dry' than you do, but am quite convinced that we are likely to suffer a great deal before the end of this." In the same letter he wrote, "Wars are bad, but there are many things far worse,"[38] and a bad peace was one of these. There were critical realities and issues still unsolved that would have to be part of any ultimate resolution (most obviously the status of ex-slaves), and Lowell, mindful of his conversation with Senator Sumner, hoped that victory would not be snatched at hastily. With his eyes on a radical and transformative peace, Charlie knew that the war would go on, and this meant sustaining a willingness to fight. Effie's ambition and infatuation with glory were stimulants to him.

On July 11 Lowell's regiment was finally given a chance. As General Lee's army retreated south from Gettysburg, General Meade needed to know where its advance was. Lowell was ordered to scout northern Virginia east of the Blue Ridge Mountains. At Paris, Virginia, he found a small number of Confederates and chased them up to Ashby's Gap, one of the passes into the Shenandoah Valley. Defending the pass were mounted and dismounted Confederates, who fired on them. Lowell personally led the charge to dislodge dismounted men behind a stone wall. Two men alongside him were killed, while another was taken prisoner. James Hawkins, a Californian in Company L, was shot in the head; his horse was then shot and fell on him, breaking his left arm and two ribs. (When he returned to camp, there was no end of surprise that his head wound had not been fatal.) Although this frontal assault failed, Lowell used two companies to flank the rebels and, it being too hazy to see much from the gap, then followed them into the Shenandoah Valley, until he hit a picket some miles south on the west side of the river. He had taken twelve prisoners, and most of his own wounded were from Company E, Eigenbrodt's, which had made the failed frontal assault. The next day on the return journey, Lowell charged into Leesburg and this time permitted a search of the houses but turned up only one officer and two privates. That evening when the men camped for the night at a milk house, Lowell did not post a guard there until his men had helped themselves to milk and butter. He and his regiment were rightly proud of this maiden skirmish of the Second Massachusetts Cavalry, a short, nasty one. Lowell won the praise of Heintzelman via his immediate superior, Colonel Joseph H. Taylor, and the promise that "if an opportunity arises, you shall have it."[39]

For the next two days, July 16 and 17, "we lay by the roadside, booted and saddled,—waiting for orders," Lowell wrote Effie. Unfortunately the orders, when they came, were desultory. He was told to report to General Rufus King at Centreville, cavalry headquarters for the Department of Washington on the edge of the old Bull Run battlefield. The detritus of war was everywhere—broken carriages, caissons, and ordnance of all kinds. Solid shots and shells littered the ground, some exploded but most still charged. Knapsacks, muskets, and other accoutrements lay about. In the chaos of collapsing shelters, broken-down fireplaces, rifle pits, and the remains of earthworks could be found small personal touches: carved on a large tree were the initials of the Seventh South Carolina Regiment and the names of several of its members—a reminder of "how near the rebel troops had been to Washington."[40]

More to the point were the skeletons lying uncovered and exposed to view, "not one or two, but hundreds." Even bodies that had been buried were emerging from their shallow graves as rain and weather settled and eroded the earth thrown over them. This devastated landscape, these signs of the neglect and disrespect for soldiers' mortal remains, drove home to all the men of the regiment the horror of death in battle. Both battles at Bull Run had ended with a Union retreat, which had not allowed time to collect and bury the Union dead. But even if it had, only some of the horror would have been eliminated: the inadequacies of hasty burial were a matter of degree. Lowell still had haunting thoughts about Jim's body, which he had not been able to retrieve. Knowing the spot and knowing that Jim had been buried, he had imagined he was safe. But now it was not so certain. Only a few days before Lowell had been extolling the Gettysburg victory, which came on the anniversary of Jim's death, and had told Effie, "The little fellow was very happy,—he thought the war would soon be over, that everything was going right, and that everybody was as high-minded and courageous as himself."[41]

Hearing of the deaths of so many of his college friends, Charlie naturally became nostalgic about the innocent prewar era. "People used to tell me, when I was at Cambridge that those were to be the happiest years of my life," Charlie wrote Effie, but "people were wrong." Uncle James had exhorted him to believe that "Experience is a dumb, dead thing; / The victory is in believing." And although he could now understand his uncle's pain, Charlie thought not: "Dissatisfied as I have always been with myself, I have yet found that, as I grew older, I enjoyed more and more."

Lowell did not mention to Effie the grisly sights at Bull Run or his own dark thoughts about the death of friends, but he did tell her that he had stopped to pick a morning glory to send her and then, on second thought, had crushed it and thrown it away. "The association was not pleasant; and yet it was pleasant to see that morning-glories could bloom on, right in the

midst of our worries and disgraces." Although Wordsworth remained his favorite poet, it was Emerson he urged her to read, in particular "Each and
All," in which the poet takes up the Romantic question of the relationship of
Beauty and Truth to Experience and Innocence. He wanted Effie to recognize that Emerson was putting the truth of idealistic young hope in a context: life could not be understood piecemeal. Attempts to pluck beauty and
reject the rest were an "unripe and childish . . . desire to appropriate" and
were futile. As Charlie put it, "everything is ours to enjoy, nothing is ours to
encage; open, we are as wide as Nature; closed, we are too narrow to enjoy a
sea-shell's beauty."[42]

Under General King, Lowell's orders were to protect Washington and to deter or prevent any guerrilla action near it. Guerrilla operations in northern
Virginia had increased dramatically during 1863, and both Union and Confederate newspapers found that the ease with which guerrillas were effectively humiliating and embarrassing the Union army made good copy.
During the Gettysburg campaign, rebel guerrillas had successfully harassed
the Union army's rear. The army, if it were to follow up on the Gettysburg
victory, would clearly have to hold at least a portion of northern Virginia. Essentially the Second Massachusetts Cavalry had two objectives: a defensive
one, to protect the fords on the Potomac and prevent Lee from going north
again either to threaten the capital or to carry the war onto northern soil;
and an offensive one, to extend the Union army's lines of supply, railroads
and main roads, permitting it to make aggressive incursions into the Confederacy unhampered by attacks on its rear.

On the face of it the orders were clear. But Lowell had in fact entered
one of the grayest zones of warfare. Classic military texts did not discuss irregular maneuvers, and most military experts did not even recognize them.
Only in *The Art of War* by Baron Jomini, a volume well thumbed by volunteer officers at the war's start, did the subject of an inflamed citizenry
come up in detail. Referring to the guerrilla fighting in Spain during the
Napoleonic War, Jomini described a "people's war" as "the most formidable
of all" and to be avoided.[43]

In May 1861 an American book, *International Law; or Rules of Regulat-
ing the Intercourse of States in Peace and War*, reiterated the traditional idea
that modern warfare was waged between armies in the field, with civilians
wholly outside the conflict. Occupying armies had to be careful not to cre-

ate a "bitter and implacable" hatred among an abused citizenry. Forage, because it tended to degenerate into pillage, was "impolitic and unjust" and moreover antiquated: it was "coming into general disuse among the most civilized nations." The book's author was Henry Halleck, who by the summer of 1862 was commander-in-chief of the Union army. By then General Halleck had seen enough of war to replace General McClellan's conciliatory civilian policy with a series of general orders that formed the basis of a more pragmatic one. Halleck understood that the people of the Confederacy were not neutral and that many of them aided and abetted guerrilla bands. Under Halleck's system, guerrilla attacks on the Union army would earn punitive actions against the local civilians among whom the guerrillas were to be found. He wanted it clear that communities that harbored guerrillas would be held responsible for them. The theory was that guerrillas could not operate without local support, and harsh sanctions would turn the locals against them. His goal was to subdue civilian activity and return the war to a conventional struggle between armies.

In April 1863 Halleck issued General Order No. 100, which became known as Lieber's Code, after Francis Lieber, the staunch Prussian antislavery activist who had drafted it; ten years earlier he had written *Civil Liberty and Self-Government*. Lieber did not countenance any hostile act "which makes the return to peace unnecessarily difficult," and he thought soldiers committing prohibited "wanton" acts should be shot on the spot. He distinguished between bushwhackers, whom he regarded as common criminals, and guerrillas, whom he defined as sanctioned by the Confederate army and therefore subject to soldiers' protocol, but Lieber did not discuss how the distinction between the two could be made. He was equally fuzzy on treatment of civilians. His code failed to set clear limits and allowed for a frighteningly broad range of confiscation and destruction in the name of military necessity or measures "indispensable for securing the ends of the war." Actual implementation of the code relied on the judgment of commanding officers. (Colonel Montgomery had actually used Lieber's Code to justify his pillage of Darien.)[44]

Some Confederate guerrillas were outlaws, rank opportunists, horse thieves, or smugglers who were using the excuses of war to glorify their criminality. Some were bands of bushwhackers or vigilantes who openly supported the Confederacy yet operated outside its army. They burned Unionists' barns or attacked small, vulnerable targets. Will Forbes explained to his father, "They watch us without letting us know of their presence, and hang on our rear with a small party to see if we have any stragglers. If one of them should fire he would be run down at once unless he had a clear road and fast horse." Lieber's Code dictated that when apprehended, these bush-whackers should be treated as common criminals and subjected to civil law. Regularly Lowell's men were sent out to arrest those suspected of abetting the Confederates or belonging to bushwhacking bands. It was miserable work. To Effie, Lowell said, "It brings me in contact with too many citi-zens,—and sometimes with mothers and children."[45]

This section of northern Virginia had paid dearly for its secession. Fences had been dismantled and used for firewood. Without fences, farmers had abandoned their livestock, and fields that should have been dotted with cows were empty and unkempt. Most of Centreville's private houses had been burned or torn down. The devastation of town and country had left the citizens in "awful straits," and the Union soldiers could not help feeling compassion for them, even the once-wealthy landowners who were now de-void of land, slaves, and income. One soldier described, "I have seen ladies who, before the war broke out, considered themselves . . . altogether too good to work, but who are now to be seen peddling pies, cakes, and such things, to Union soldiers—not because they have any sympathy for our cause, but because they are driven to it by straits of necessity, with starvation staring them in the face." And yet compassion for their plight did not pre-vent Lowell's men from feeling that it was deserved. This was the price of war, and the Confederates had wanted war. But the men of the Second Massachusetts Cavalry failed to appreciate what it would actually mean for them to live among this population.

Almost every soldier and officer of the regiment had at least one story il-luminating the difficulty of his position. One Californian sergeant, trying to reconcile himself to his work, wrote that to be a good cavalry soldier one "is required to have a heart as hard as adamant, and a determination which nothing can change." He told of being sent out to capture horses, and at one farm, where he prepared to lead off a horse, he was confronted by an old lady and her daughters, one of whom threw "herself on her knees and, with uplifted eyes" begged him to spare "poor old Tobe." Sensing she had won his sympathy, she began to recite the horse's life story, while another daugh-ter threw her arms around the old horse's neck, kissing it and sobbing loudly. The soldier recalled, "I felt like saying: 'Young ladies, keep your poor old horse, and if that does not satisfy you, take mine, too.' "[46]

Lieutenant Henry Alvord, a young Massachusetts officer, had "uncondi-tional" orders to arrest a man who was the sole source of support for his mother, "an old helpless lady of eighty-five." Alvord told himself, "Such is civil war," and made the arrest. Later that night on the return journey he and the arrested man went to check on the old mother. She was "crouched over a few warm ashes with not one stick of wood." Alvord hesitated "between humanity and obedience," then shaved the orders by letting the man stay another night, on the promise that he bring himself in the next day. "I was surprised at finding him true to his word," Alvord wrote: he had been prepared to face Lowell with his failure to carry out orders. The man took "the oath," meaning he swore allegiance to the Union, and was permitted to return home. That story ended well, but Alvord conceded that many did not.[47]

Lowell himself described to Effie how he was moved by an old mother's forbearance at the loss of her only son. She was a "Quakerlike looking old lady, very neat and quiet." Lowell found her failure to beg more affecting than if she had. In another case, as he questioned a sixteen-year-old bushwhacker who told him everything he wanted to hear, Lowell felt that it was almost unfair to question him, "he was such a babe."[48]

As the experiences mounted, Lieutenant Alvord wondered "if a man is kept long enough in this part of Virginia at such a time he will forget what it is to feel at all." Yet long before the men's hearts could be hardened by the harshness of federal policy, they learned how utterly ineffective it was. Arresting citizens and jailing or expelling them sounded meet and proper until one was faced with the actual task of doing so. With the administration of loyalty oaths, at least on paper Halleck had what he wanted: "A broad line of distinction must be drawn between friends and enemies, between the loyal and the disloyal." But this was not how it seemed to the soldiers of the Second Massachusetts Cavalry on the front line, where an oath was not an oath and prison was not prison. Most civilians happily swore their loyalty oaths and then returned equally happily to their former Confederate work. Any one of Lowell's men might have written, "You may see them in the day time at the farm-houses, protesting their loyalty, and with a long, sober face, ready to swear that they are 'union men.' As soon as night comes, then they arm themselves, assemble at some rendezvous, and from there sail out to rob and plunder on the highway."[49]

Only truly pigheaded Virginians refused to swear the Union oath; they were sent into Washington as prisoners. But Lowell discovered that they were sent back "almost as fast as I sent them there," which made arresting them hardly worth the exercise. Halleck's "broad line of distinction" was rapidly blurring. And so when a private approached his sergeant saying, "I have caught a copperhead, a real snake this time; what shall I do with him?" the sergeant's immediate reply was, "I suppose the only thing you can do is to swear him and let him go."[50]

There were other ironies as well. When on July 25 Lowell captured a lieutenant-colonel who had been drafting men for the Confederate army, he told Effie drily, "You see I'm 'opposed to the draft' as unconstitutional." He was alluding ironically to the Copperhead position on the controversial drafts in the North. Like so many veteran soldiers, he resented those who stayed clear of the war while those he loved were fighting and being killed. He would have liked a draft with no substitutions: "Why should not all go who are chosen?"[51] Yet as an officer he believed that drafted men were worse than useless because their morale was so poor and they dragged down the other enlisted men. He did not want them in his regiment. Lowell was also writing in full knowledge of the antidraft riots that were taking place in many northern cities, the result of the Union's first attempt, on July 11, to impose the draft. In New York City, a riot started in the draft office and spread across the city; for four days a mob largely comprising Irishmen attacked black men, women, and children, killing many and hanging some from lampposts. They looted businesses and set fires. By July 17, when the fury of the mob subsided, more than a thousand people were dead or wounded. Lowell did not yet know that on Staten Island a mob had surrounded the Shaws' house and threatened it with fire. As one of the state's most prominent abolitionist families, they were an obvious target.

Lowell used ironic humor to express his feelings about a world turned upside down, signaling to Effie the moral ambiguity with which he would, over the next year and a half, become all too familiar. Within the states still in the Union, Lowell supported the government and scorned the Copperhead opposition. As a federal officer policing occupied territory of the Confederacy, he protected draft dodgers and arrested recruiting officers. He put aside his sense of decency and common humanity and treated harshly, even on occasion brutally, civilians who a few years before had been his fellow citizens, people who, but for luck, might have been neighbors: he had not forgotten the fantasy his mother had entertained in 1858 of moving the family to Virginia.

On July 26, almost ten days after the fact, Lowell received reports of an assault on Fort Wagner, an engineering marvel of moats, pits, and walls with which the Confederates were defending the mouth of Charleston Bay. Two Union brigades had been involved, but what mattered to Lowell was that the Fifty-fourth had led the charge and been devastated on the fort's slopes. Lowell's first response was to hope that the news was wrong, but he was already writing of Rob Shaw in the past tense. He asked his mother to send him everything she learned, telling her that Shaw "was to me one of the most attractive men I ever knew." Asking for news coming through official channels and not in the papers, he also wrote to Henry Russell, still in Boston with the last of the Second Massachusetts Cavalry: "If he is dead, they've killed one of the dearest fellows that ever was."[52]

On July 18 Fort Wagner had been heavily shelled all day before the Fifty-fourth Regiment began a bayonet charge across a spit of sand narrowed by high tide. Shaw was on the left, in the lead near the flag. As they approached, the Confederates began to drop hand grenades and lighted shells on the men. Once Shaw reached the top of the parapet, he turned, sword held high, to wave his men on. He was hit by a bullet in the chest and fell into the fort. The Union flag was briefly planted on the parapet, and the men of the Fifty-fourth kept on coming over the parapet and into the fort, where hand-to-hand combat began. But their ranks were depleted, and the supporting columns were slow in following up. Within an hour they had to retreat. Two-thirds of the Fifty-fourth's officers and nearly half its men were dead, missing, or wounded. The beach for some three-quarters of a mile was strewn with the bodies of black and white soldiers.

Due to the magnitude of the regiment's losses, suspicions arose almost immediately about the misuse of the Fifty-fourth Regiment. One Union general was reported to have said, "Put those d——d niggers from Massachusetts in the advance; we may as well get rid of them one time as another."[53] Certainly prejudice against and suspicion about black troops were rife; the assault was guaranteed to involve enormous casualties; and commanders who had no sympathy for the abolitionist cause were looking for ways to get around what they foresaw as the difficulty of getting white troops to fight alongside black ones. Was the allegation that black troops had been used on a suicidal mission warranted?

The Union's commanding general in Charleston, Quincy Adams Gillmore, an artillery specialist whose reputation had been made in forcing the 1862 surrender of Fort Pulaski (which had defended the harbor at Savannah, Georgia), had not been deterred when one of his generals argued that a frontal assault on Fort Wagner was bound to fail. Shaw, like others, assumed that Gillmore would lay siege in the same way that he had taken Fort Pulaski, with overwhelming artillery power, which would have incurred fewer casualties. But Gillmore had not wanted to do so. Perhaps he was using his men without a true appreciation for the limitations of infantry, and perhaps he was simply inadequate. What is certain is that he made the decision for a frontal assault *before* the Fifty-fourth was asked to lead it. In fact, the very first assault, the day before, used white troops; it had failed, with heavy casualties. Neither this failed first attempt nor the advice of his generals deflected Gillmore; nor did the failure of the Fifty-fourth. Third and fourth assaults were made. General George C. Strong, the Massachusetts officer who had offered Shaw the privilege of leading the charge on July 16, was mortally wounded in the third attempt, and Colonel Haldimand S. Putnam, who had tried to get the plan altered, was also killed. In the end Fort Wagner was taken, but it was an expensive exercise. Ill use of troops at the hands of bad generals was hardly new; a veteran soldier would have considered it naïve, perhaps even insulting, to imagine that the incompetence occurred only in order to squander black troops.

In the first reports Shaw's body had been listed as missing, and some hope remained that he was still alive. But even in the unlikely case that he had survived, his fate would have been very uncertain. In December 1862, to discourage Union recruitment of black troops, the Confederate Congress had declared that captured white officers commanding black troops would be put to death and captured black soldiers sold into slavery. But when the Confederate commander of Fort Wagner confirmed Shaw's death, he announced that Shaw's body had been stripped of its uniform and tossed into the ditch that had been dug as the Massachusetts grave for black soldiers. The Confederates intended this announcement as a humiliation—the ultimate in disrespect.

It had the opposite effect. Lowell wrote Effie, "I am thankful they buried him 'with his niggers'; they were brave men and they were his men." Shaw's father wrote to that same effect both to the press and to the regimental surgeon. He gave explicit instructions to General Gillmore that once Fort Wagner was taken, he was to "forbid the desecration of my son's grave," a request that raised the symbolic stakes of the entire game. The father was violating the habitual protocol of death in war: that the fallen soldiers should be recovered and brought home. Soldiers felt strongly about this; everyone did. By leaving Rob's body in the mass grave, his father turned a Confederate act of contempt into a symbol of martyrdom. He had, at least metaphorically, reclaimed his son's body and consecrated the ground where he was buried. The mass grave immediately became a symbol of the abolitionist cause: black and white, privileged and abused, brave men treated as beasts, were buried there as one.[54]

The confusion over the fate of soldiers at Fort Wagner was not limited to the case of Rob Shaw. Lowell's younger cousin Cabot Russel was also missing. Frank Higginson reported that Cabot had been near the top of the parapet when he was wounded. Captain William H. Simpkins had called a sergeant, and together they had tried to save Cabot, but as they were picking him up, Simpkins was hit and fell on top of Cabot, dying instantly. The sergeant reported that Cabot then asked him twice to move farther away as he was drawing fire. He believed that Cabot had been hit in the leg and perhaps the breast.

Cabot's father immediately left New York City, where he lived, for Charleston. There he wandered the hospitals, hunted up chaplains, scrounged and knocked on doors, but to no avail. He did find Cabot's closest friend, Wilkie James, younger brother of William and Henry James, in a hospital. Wilkie had been badly wounded on his right side and in his left foot. Like Russel, he had been with Shaw on the parapet. The senior Russel arranged to bring him north by boat, and they arrived together at Newport, Rhode Island, where the Jameses were then living. Like a figure out of Homeric legend, Russel led the stretcher-bearers to the Jameses' house and had them set the wounded boy-soldier down just inside the door. Henry James in his old age recalled the scene as "some object presented in high relief against the evening sky of the west," with himself sitting beside the stretcher and Russel "erect and dry-eyed at the guarded feast of our relief."[55] (Wilkie's recovery was slow, complicated by mental anguish as well as physical pain.)

The effect on northern public opinion of the Fifty-fourth's failed assault on Fort Wagner was tremendous. While it was not the first instance of black troops under fire, it was the first example of a serious battle in which black troops had played so dramatic and heroic a part. It confirmed beyond a doubt their abilities and their bravery. However much the common Union soldier disliked the black man, he knew enough of war to recognize courage when he saw it. However much the general public was indifferent to the cause of black freedom—accepting emancipation as a war measure, the use of black troops as a pragmatic solution to a shortage of manpower, and the freedom of all slaves as an extremely conditional eventuality—Fort Wagner punctured the rationalizations and struck at the collective imagination. The assault on Fort Wagner confirmed for all but the stubbornest Copperheads that the war would end with the liberation of African Americans. In this cause Shaw became a martyr both in his self-sacrifice and in his unconsecrated burial.*

For some twenty-five years the abolitionist movement had strengthened itself by cultivating images of martyrdom drawing on the Christian model. In 1835, the year of Lowell's birth, the beating of William Lloyd Garrison had garnered new supporters in Massachusetts; in 1837 Elijah Lovejoy's death at Alton, Illinois, defending his presses had linked abolition with freedom of the press and further expanded its membership; *Uncle Tom's Cabin*, published in 1852, had popularized the movement; in the 1850s the fugitive slaves who were returned to slavery as martyrs to unjust laws had aroused still more adherents; and even the hanging of John Brown in 1859 was understood as the martyrdom of a visionary. After Governor Andrew's election, public events in Massachusetts regularly featured William Lloyd Garrison holding a bust of John Brown, a kind of double-header in the martyrdom game.

At the flag presentation of the Fifty-fourth in May 1863, Governor Andrew had made it clear that Shaw had inherited the abolitionist mantle. Carriages and extra trains had brought about a thousand people, black and white, to Readville. A flag presentation (at which the regiment became the official representative of the state on the field of battle) was always an emotional event, but in this case it was supercharged. The governor presented the American flag, a gift from the young ladies of Boston; then the flag of Massachusetts, a gift from the Relief Society, a committee of "colored ladies of Boston"; an emblematic banner from the city of Boston representing the Goddess of Liberty; and finally, a white silk banner bearing an inscription and a golden cross on a golden star, which Andrew called "the sacred, holy

---

*W.E.B. DuBois, writing in the 1930s, remarked ironically that Fort Wagner proved that the black man could kill as well as any white man, and only then was he recognized as a man. Actually, they had scant opportunity for killing. Only for a brief time on the ramparts did the Fifty-fourth engage in actual combat. What the Fifty-fourth Regiment proved on the slopes of Fort Wagner was that white officers and black men had the moral courage to walk, then run into the jaws of death as nobly as the ancient heroes of the western European tradition. It was this that, in the eyes of a prejudiced nation, made them men. (It is ironic that such evidence came hot on the heels of the New York draft riots, which left many blacks dead, some hung from lampposts, the worst example of rioting the United States has ever witnessed.)

cross, representing passion, the highest heroism . . . It is the emblem of Christianity." It was the first and perhaps only overtly Christian banner of the Civil War. (The inscription would have been recognizable to everyone present, even though it was in Latin. It referred to the vision of Constantine: a flaming cross inscribed IN HOC SIGNO VINCES, "By this sign thou shalt conquer.") Governor Andrew explained, "We are fighting now a battle not merely for country, not merely for humanity, not only for civilization, but for the religion of our Lord itself. When this cause shall ultimately fail, if ever failure at the last shall be possible, it will only fail when the last patriot, the last philanthropist, and the last Christian shall have tasted death, and left no descendants behind them upon the soil of Massachusetts."

This was the voice of Andrew the abolitionist, the man who had passionately attempted to defend John Brown, who had counseled Luther Stearns and Dr. Samuel G. Howe. The flag had been given, he went on, by the mother, sister, friends, and relatives of "one of the dearest and noblest soldier-boys of Massachusetts," by which Andrew meant Willy Putnam. Aunt Mary had galvanized the entire Lowell and Putnam families to offer this banner to the Fifty-fourth, including her high Cotton Whig cousins the John Amory Lowells. Andrew said that Putnam, one of Boston's first martyred officers, had "tasted death for an immortal cause." He urged the regiment to "follow the splendid example, the sweet devotion mingled with manly, heroic character, of which the life, character, and death of Lieutenant Putnam was one example!" In the eyes of his abolitionist audience, Shaw had already started down the road to martyrdom.[56]

Five days later Shaw's youngest sister, Nellie, watched the regiment marching through Boston to board ship and recalled that her brother, "riding at its head, looked up and kissed his sword, his face was as the face of an angel and I felt perfectly sure he would never come back." John Greenleaf Whittier, who was also there, recalled a similar reaction: "he seemed to me beautiful and awful, as an angel of God come down to lead the host of freedom to victory." Henry James was so moved by the event that he described it twice in his memoirs, even though he was not there. In this context Shaw was rapidly transformed from a competent officer and attractive young man into a hero, and ultimately, as Lydia Maria Child wrote, Shaw had "gone to join the glorious army of martyrs."[57]

Most abolitionists thought of martyrdom as a regenerative force with moral power. Lost lives were dropped "into the fruitful soil of humanity" to become "seed of a new national and human life."[58] This cult of the martyr gave meaning to suffering, turning loss into sacrifice and connecting personal anguish to a larger altruistic goal. Perhaps most important, it restored the concept of a moral universe with a moral purpose. The mourners did not then have to consider the possibility that their own pain might have been avoided, that it was unnecessary or meaningless.

After Shaw's death Charlie Lowell, too, began to adopt elements of this martyr mentality. Lowell had celebrated the victory at Gettysburg especially because it came on the anniversary of Jim's death, tacitly acknowledging that it helped to compensate for his loss. But he was clear that Jim had been mistaken when he imagined that "the war would soon be over, that everything was going right, and that everybody was as high-minded and courageous as himself." Yet after Fort Wagner Lowell changed. In a letter to Henry Russell, his own lieutenant-colonel and Shaw's closest friend, he acknowledged, "I felt thankful that you and he were out of the Second at Gettysburg,—I thought of you both as surely safe, I had always felt of Rob too, that he was not going to be killed." Instead, as Lowell had described those whom God believed needed to learn, he was "clutched by the throat." In daily letters to Effie, trying to come to grips with his own feelings and to comfort his fiancée, he was frustrated by the inadequacy of words, the inviolability of her grief and his own. "How I wish I could see you now to comfort you," he wrote her. "I wish I could *write* you some word of love and comfort."[59]

To his mother, he tried to mitigate the pain of his loss. "It cannot be so hard for such a man to die—it is not so hard for his friends to lose him," he wrote. Charlie wanted to believe that a man who is more at peace with himself, and in his relationships with others, leaves behind less regret, less that is undone and unsaid. For Charlie this spiritual integrity became an achievement. He tried to express his sense of "Rob's usefulness . . . how the beauty of his character had been becoming a power, widely felt, how his life had become something more than a promise." This was the same tack he had taken after the death of his brother Jim, reinforcing the idea of a good man's completeness of character. "Will [Forbes] and I have been talking over the good fellows who have gone before in this war,—fellows whom Rob loved so much, many of them: there is none who has been so widely and so dearly loved as he." Good men are already resolved beings, and so their lives, however short, have a wholeness that is often lacking in less happy people.[60]

He dwelt on what he saw as Shaw's justice to others. He told his mother that he "had such a single and loyal and kindly heart: I don't believe he ever did an unkind or thoughtless act without trying to make up for it afterwards . . . in that, he was like Jimmy."[61] Charlie, like his mother, recognized that he himself lacked the "softer virtues." He thought of himself, as his fiancée had been warned, as heartless. That hardness, his clarity of thought, his pragmatic harshness, and his capacity to deny or compartmentalize his emotions helped him to survive.

But he was aware of regrets: "I am very sorry that I did not more than half bid Rob good-bye that Tuesday. It is a little thing, but I wish it had been otherwise." Charlie had never properly responded to Shaw's letter of June 20, in which he had written, "I have often thought since I left, of our meetings at Harper's Ferry, and how little I supposed then that we should be so intimately connected. I hope this war will not finish one or both of us and that we shall live to know each other well . . . I remember, at Susie's just after you were engaged you said to me: 'Am not I a lucky fellow?' and I must say, I think you are. There are not many girls like Effie."[62]

On July 28, two days after learning the news, Charlie wrote, "Effie I am under very sacred bonds to be good and gentle and noble—to my Aunt Mary, I must be Willy [Putnam]—to my mother and father, Jim—and now to your Mother, as far as I can, Rob." Part of a martyr's power lies in his moral superiority. He is made out to have been of purer, finer stuff and thus "too good" for this world. As Charlie learned more and more about Shaw's actions at Fort Wagner, he increasingly spoke of his friend's death as ideal and necessary. "Everything that comes about Rob," he told Effie, "shows his death to have been more and more completely that which every soldier and every man would long to die, but it is given to very few, for very few do their duty as Rob had."[63]

Charlie learned that in preparing for the assault on Fort Wagner, Shaw had given his valuables and letters to a journalist and told Pen Hallowell of his premonition that he would not live. He needed time alone, he brooded, and he found it difficult to follow conversation. But by the time he was ready to lead his men, he was in good cheer. He gave instructions to his officers. Hallowell said, "I am sure he felt ready to meet his fate."

In the preattack pep talk, the commanding general asked, "Who will carry the flag if this man falls?" There was a silence among the men, and then Shaw spoke up: "I will." The men cheered. The officers shook hands. Shaw reminded his men that the whole nation looked to them and would follow their actions. "I want you to prove yourselves,"[64] he said. As he spoke, the corners of his mouth twitched in his effort at self-control. Then the march began. As the fire from the fort became unbearable, the regiment broke into a headlong charge in which Shaw did not stop until, as he crested the parapet, he was killed.

Shaw knew his fate, accepted it, and met it with courage. The fact that he felt the eyes of the nation watching him helped steel his nerve. His friend Theodore Lyman wrote about him: "In peace times he would have lived and died a quiet, manly, happy-tempered fellow; but the peril forced his true spirit into action, and now his name stands as that of one who gave up his life spotless of low ambition, of cowardice, of immorality."[65] Undoubtedly this is true. Shaw's behavior was an example of what Lowell had meant two years before when he wrote that because of the slavery question, the war had to be fought by "decent men" and not fighting men.

"That is the time to die," Charlie wrote Effie, "when one is happiest, or rather I mean that is the time when we wish those we love to die: Rob was very happy too at the head of his regiment where he died . . . it is a very great comfort to know that his life had such a perfect ending." He acknowledged, "I see now that the best Colonel of the best black regiment had to die, it was a sacrifice we owed,—and how could it have been paid more gloriously?"[66]

PART III

THE DYER'S HAND

—◈—

While mankind is constantly rising to higher ideals, there is always danger that the individual may sink to lower ones . . . Apart from the fact that in changing wishes to wills and wills to deeds much is always lost that is never missed, . . . gratified vanity may become a syren to lure man to destruction. The ideal power may stoop to form pictures of worldly success. Or he may flatter himself that he is still true to his ideal, when to every one else it is clear that his nature is subdued to that it works in, like the dyer's hand.
                    —Charles Russell Lowell, Commencement Day oration, 1854

Mosby and Inglorious War

FIFTEEN

INGLORIOUS WARFARE

August–September 1863

In the last days of July 1863, Major Caspar Crowninshield and the First Battalion, which had been on detached service since February, arrived in Centreville. The Second Massachusetts Cavalry was united for the first time. Lowell now faced the challenge of creating a coherent, unified, and effective regiment from its various constituent parts. Lowell's initial liking for Captain J. Sewall Reed, who commanded the California Hundred, or Company A, had been confirmed by the past six months on detached service, when, despite the differences in their life experiences, Reed had forged effective relationships with Major Crowninshield and the other Boston officers. His company had become the core of the First Battalion.

Reed, ten years older than his fellow captains, had no money and little book education. Originally from Dorchester, Massachusetts, he had left home in 1849 at seventeen with one of his younger brothers to pan for gold in the Sierras. After two years in Nevada City without luck, they had returned to San Francisco, where Reed served on the Vigilance Committee of that city. In 1856 he set off for Central and South America once again in search of gold but failed quickly. In 1858 he went north into British Columbia, but that too ended without result. None of his ventures had paid off financially, but he had learned a lot about men, good and bad. He went home to Boston long enough to marry and then returned to San Francisco. The advent of war led him to join the Dragoons, but when it became clear that these California troops would not be sent east to join the war, he contracted with his home state to raise a company of the best men he could find, and he had done well.[1] The California Hundred was an impressive company. In fact the Californians were without question the better fighting men. Their knowledge of horses, their familiarity with weaponry, and their morale, patriotism, and resourcefulness were qualities unmatched by the Bay Staters.

In addition to the California Hundred there was the California Battalion, perhaps equally talented, raised in the first quarter of 1863 by Major De Witt Clinton Thompson, who was originally from a locally prominent military family in western Massachusetts. Thompson had made a comfortable fortune in real estate and become a leading citizen in San Francisco. He owned property in Sonoma County with General Hooker. In 1861 he had been appointed to General Halleck's staff, and after Halleck went east, Thompson became the sheriff of San Francisco. Yet for all his accomplishments, connections, and maturity (at thirty-seven he was the oldest man in the regiment), he had an awkward presence: an overly thick black beard hid most of his gaunt face; he had a scrawny physique; and his pale eyes gave him an unsettling intensity.

Of the California captains belonging to the California Battalion, Charles Eigenbrodt, commanding Company E, came from a successful farming family on Long Island and had become a serious rancher in Alameda County, from which he had recruited most of his men. Eigenbrodt was thirty-six at the time of enlistment and had a benevolently patrician mien. Tall, well built, with a thick blond mustache and beard and a level gaze, he was utterly reliable.

David A. DeMerritt, formerly of the Sacramento Rangers, commanding Company F, made an excellent first impression on Lowell but broke his leg in his first week. The thirty-three-year-old with a gaunt, slightly haunted look was plagued by mishap and never fulfilled the promise he had first shown.

Commanding Company L was Zabdiel Boylston Adams (named for the Boston doctor who first promoted the smallpox vaccine), twenty-nine, an impatient, hard-driving officer who had already been reprimanded for sloppy bookkeeping and court-martialed for swearing at his men. Although he was exonerated by his fellow officers, the incident left a bad taste among his men. Nevertheless, Company L was one of the regiment's best, rivaled only by Company E.

Only slightly less impressive was George A. Manning, of Company M, twenty-seven, handsome, well liked, and earnest, a first-rate officer. Archibald McKendry, originally of the California Hundred and the ranking first lieutenant, had already been promoted and had raised his own company in Boston. Many other California lieutenants were officers of quality and by the end of the war would hold most of the regiment's major commissions. But among the California officers were quite a few older men who were not pleased to be serving under the boyish Lowell and his other young officers.

These were all problems that Lowell assumed would work themselves out as everyone got acquainted.

The Massachusetts officers, for their part, were a mixed bag. Lieutenant-Colonel Henry Russell had stayed in Boston to recruit more men and represent regimental interests at the statehouse. This task was usually given to a lesser or noncommissioned officer, but Russell was John Murray Forbes's son-in-law, and it seems clear that he was in Boston to be kept "safe," as Lowell had written him in July. Lowell was happy enough with this arrangement—Russell, despite being taken prisoner at Cedar Mountain in August 1862, had not distinguished himself in the field. Instead, Crowninshield, the ranking major, had been commanding the First Battalion since February. Now Lowell made him acting regimental commander, filling the role that should have gone to Russell. This did not sit well with the California major, Thompson, who despite lacking any experience in the field believed he was the more qualified officer. He was ten years older, had far greater administrative experience, had been a successful entrepreneur in San Francisco, and had excellent connections to both Generals Hooker (now useless) and Halleck. But Thompson lacked seniority (his battalion was the last to be mustered), he had no experience in the field, and unlike Reed, he had failed to forge an alliance with any of the Massachusetts officers.

Crowninshield was twenty and, save the war, knew little of the world beyond Boston, where his maternal grandfather, David Sears, was the wealthy patriarch of an influential family. In almost every respect he was the epitome of a Boston fop, except for one thing: he was a powerfully built man—tall and strong—and a superb athlete, having been the star oarsman on the first Harvard crew, and at Ball's Bluff he had shown a potential for courage and leadership. Francis Washburn, captain of Company D, was also twenty-five. From central Massachusetts, Washburn was an abolitionist, had studied engineering, and had proven himself an excellent officer in the First Massachusetts Cavalry. Reliant on his own talents, Washburn had none of the arrogance of Crowninshield but a good deal more earnestness. William Forbes, only twenty-two, had Lowell's entire trust. He had good instincts but lacked experience. Charles Rice and George Holman, captains of Companies I and K, respectively, were, by Lowell's admission, too inexperienced, as were many of the lieutenants—Louis Cabot, Lewis Dabney, Goodwin Stone, and seventeen-year-old Henry Alvord, who had attended Norwich Military Academy and thus was more useful than the other lieutenants.

These young men were directed to staff appointments and the multitude of administrative tasks—provost-marshal, quartermaster, or adjutant—that reflected the corporate nature of the regiment and brigade, and for which the Californians had little interest.

Lowell wanted to spread his reliable soldiers throughout the regiment, to be sure that however he configured the scouts, patrols, or pickets, he was guaranteed a core of good officers and good fighting men. Thus when he divided the regiment into three battalions under the command of the three senior officers—Major Crowninshield, Captain Reed, and Major Thompson—he departed from convention by not assigning companies to battalions in ranking order. Instead, he filled each battalion with half California companies, half Massachusetts. In this fashion he attempted to balance his regiment.

The disparities within his command were compounded on August 1, when Lowell was given two undermanned, half-formed regiments: the Thirteenth and Sixteenth New York Cavalries. Called the Independent Cavalry Brigade, this was all the cavalry in the Department of Washington, and Lowell was now, at least technically, a brigade commander. Despite having West Pointers for its two senior officers, the Sixteenth was hardly an exemplary unit, and it had been further discredited by a scandal involving its lieutenant-colonel, George H. Hollister. Accused of groping southern women, Hollister evidently swung both ways and, it was discovered, had crept into the beds of various less-than-willing junior officers and sergeants.[2]

The Thirteenth New York Cavalry was an amalgamation of several partially raised regiments, under the command of Henry S. Gansevoort, a patrician of Dutch extraction from Albany, and it had a reputation for unreliability. A brave man endowed with a boundless sense of his own entitlement, Gansevoort was absent from command for extended periods: he suffered from chronic malaria and venereal disease. One of the regiment's majors, Douglas Frazar, was determined to unseat him and take the colonelcy himself, so he worked assiduously to sow disharmony among the officers. Frazar was fond of drink and on at least one occasion was sufficiently inebriated while on duty that Lowell included this fact in a report. The New Yorkers had poor morale and gave no fight at all when bushwhacked. The men of the Second Massachusetts Cavalry resented the New Yorkers' incompetence because it increased their own workload. The Californians in particular were contemptuous, calling them "Dutch" men, not because many of them were of German extraction but because they relied on "Dutch courage."[*]

Lowell's main adversary was John Singleton Mosby and his Partisan Rangers, a detached cavalry unit that functioned with a high degree of autonomy and yet was sanctioned by the Confederate army. A protégé of the great cavalryman J.E.B. Stuart, Mosby had served as a scout in the Peninsula campaign, and it was his reconnaissance that had led to Stuart's ride around McClellan's army, the success of which gave him a taste for further irregular action. By December 1862 Stuart had agreed to Mosby's proposal that a detached unit of Partisan Rangers be raised in Virginia with the intention of menacing the Union army's rear.

In March 1863, using a deserter from the Fifth New York Cavalry as a guide and with only a handful of men, Mosby kidnapped a drunken General Edwin H. Stoughton from his own headquarters at a small town in Virginia called Fairfax Court House and marched him through Union lines. It was an exploit of minimal military value, but the publicity was phenomenal and Mosby's ranks swelled thereafter. Confederate papers gloried in his audacity and published Stuart's report that spoke of Mosby's "brilliant exploit." In Union papers, outrage was the order of the day. The army was humiliated. Lincoln, when informed of the event, remarked that he regretted the lost horses more than the general: generals were easier to replace.

Mosby was two years older than Lowell and came from central Virginia. His college education had been interrupted by a short term in prison for unlawful shooting: he had shot, fortunately not killing, a fellow student with a reputation as a bully. This brush with the law was evidently an inspiration: by 1855 Mosby was licensed as a lawyer with a practice in Charlottesville. In 1857 he married a woman whose family was prominent in Kentucky politics.

Lowell and Mosby shared certain qualities. Physically they both had the small and wiry physique that was ideal for a cavalryman. Neither was singu-

---

[*]On one occasion a California scout named Sergeant Gustavus C. Doane was so busy raiding a sutler's pantry of "a very large loaf of bread and a crock of butter" that he failed to respond to the alarm that Mosby's Rangers were about to attack. As a result he was captured—on the face of it a case of insubordination and pillage in which the unwise Doane had proved his folly. But later that day Doane came strolling into camp whistling happily and with a story to tell. He had put on a German accent when Mosby's men questioned him, pretending he was part of the Thirteenth New York Cavalry. Mosby had taken his horse and equipment and set him free, telling him to "go to camp and get more."

lar in appearance, their eyes being the feature best expressing their force of will and character. Both were recognized as brave, and subordinates were reluctant to disappoint them. Asking much of themselves and of others, both were reckoned as frighteningly tough. Neither man had much brag in him, preferring to stick to results and taking a certain satisfaction in being a realist, or at least being thought a realist. The combination of these qualities could make them appear cold, heartless, and devoid of feeling. Closer to the truth was that both men controlled their inner selves with iron discipline.

Perhaps the greatest distinction between the two men was that Mosby "had no magnetism." One of Mosby's own men recalled that he was "cold as an iceberg, and to shake hands with him was like having the fire itching symptoms of a congestive chill . . . cold, indifferent, and utterly selfish." They were both readers. Mosby had with him a small library—Shakespeare, Plutarch, Irving and Hazlitt's *Life of Napoleon*. Lowell's included John Stuart Mill on political economy, Adolphe Thiers's *History of the Consulate and the Empire*, and standard texts on military law and tactics.[3]

Mosby's Confederacy, as the ground of his operations was called, consisted of a triangular wedge in the heart of northern Virginia: the area west from Alexandria to the Blue Ridge Mountains and the gaps into the Shenandoah Valley, with the Warrenton Turnpike the southern boundary and the Leesburg Pike the northern one. In the northernmost tip of this triangle were found Quaker communities and German settlements that were neutral or supported the Union, but by and large the farmers of northern Virginia supported the Confederacy. Rolling countryside, ideal for horse travel, was interrupted by wooded areas where ambushes were easy. The roads were sunk below the fields, shaded by trees that prevented a clear view. The towns—sometimes no more than a crossroad with a church, a mill, a post office, and a few modest homes—tended to be located in hollows near fast water, which ran the ubiquitous mills. Farther west the beautiful countryside opened up, with large estates forming a sharp contrast to the sad little towns. It is hard to imagine that Union soldiers patrolling here, or picketing a lazy crossroads, wouldn't have fallen into a reverie of summer lassitude, relaxing their guard, sucking on grass, snoozing in the shade of a tree with the loud hum of insect life convincing them that all was right with the world and the war a distant dream—a perfect moment for Mosby to strike.

And strike he did. Using the element of surprise and acting with speed, the Rangers would attack and then disappear into the woods, confounding the federal soldiers who had become accustomed to days of numbing routine. Virtually every citizen was a friend to Mosby and fed him a constant stream of intelligence about federal movements, which allowed for subtle last-minute shifts of plan and gave tremendous agility to Ranger actions. Many new recruits were local boys who knew the countryside inside out. Pouncing on stray Union cavalrymen was amusing, and a good source for horses and guns, but swooping down on the provision-laden wagons of the private merchants or sutlers was even better. Technically sutlers were not permitted military protection and often traveled without escort of any kind, leaving them exceedingly vulnerable to attack by guerrillas. All too often Lowell found himself repeating a pattern: a telegram would arrive reporting that the Rangers had attacked a wagon train and ordering him to pursue. His men would gallop off, recover what property they could, tend the wounded, and then set out on Mosby's trail. But the alarm would have come too late to catch him, the trail would be cold, and the Rangers would have disappeared.

After a number of fruitless pursuits of Mosby's cold trail, Lowell changed his approach. He decided to intercept Mosby's escape by picketing various crossroads that he calculated Mosby would have to use. This more aggressive tactic gave his men a chance to skirmish, but it was an unsatisfactory opportunity: the minute the fight became "hot," the Rangers would abandon their booty and skedaddle; the Second Massachusetts Cavalry would pursue, but the Rangers would outrun them, scatter, and again disappear into the local population; Lowell's men would gather up the abandoned wagons, mules, jettisoned food or clothing, and occasional prisoners and head back to their camp at cavalry headquarters in Centreville. It became typical that Lowell would recover most of whatever the Rangers had raided in a matter of hours. But his men were wounded, even killed, in these petty fracases over supplies. And they were still cheated of a "fair fight."

Neither Lowell nor any man in his regiment liked "to have men killed in such an 'inglorious warfare,'" as he wrote to Effie, and he repeated the phrase to John Murray Forbes. Newspaper accounts made out that Mosby was a master of terror, but as Lowell explained to Forbes, "You must not exaggerate the danger. Mosby is more keen to plunder than to murder; he always runs if he can." Lowell's men considered the Rangers' hit-and-run technique cowardly, too much like robbery. One private, Sam Hanscom, writing home, explained, "They don't want to fight but rob trains is their game." In pursuing him, they felt more like policemen than soldiers. Lowell described Mosby as "an old rat" with "a great many holes."[4]*

On August 12 Lowell presented two proposals to his superiors in King's division of the Second Corps that, he hoped, would rationalize the system, making the roads safer and also permitting a more successful and systematic pursuit of Mosby. His first reform was aimed at reducing vulnerability: wanting to put sutlers' wagons on the same footing as government supply trains, he proposed establishing an escort of thirty to fifty men that would travel once daily between Alexandria and cavalry headquarters at Centreville, at irregular times. Technically sutlers were not allowed to sell liquor to the troops, but most kept a supply on hand for officers, and this traffic was permitted as long as it was handled discreetly. To bolster his proposal, Lowell implied that sutlers were acquiring unofficial escorts by making their whiskey supplies "very easily obtainable" and "it is not uncommon to see both officers and men drunk."[5]

Lowell further explained that a larger problem was the looting of sutlers' wagons by the Union's own "stray cavalrymen." After the Rangers commandeered, looted, and abandoned the wagons, Lowell's men would recover them and regularly pocket what they could: canned peaches, turkey breast, and other comestibles, or as one Californian wrote home, "everything good."[6] Lowell suggested that "good officers" were needed to command detachments that escorted trains carrying cattle to the troops: Fresh beef was second to alcohol in popularity with the enlisted men. Since the army was beginning to fear that it would be liable for huge claims against lost property, Lowell's comments added real force to his recommendation.

Lowell's second proposal was aimed at establishing a stronger footing for the Union troops in the Virginia countryside. With so many of the local people sympathetic to the Confederacy, it was hard to find information at all, and harder still to trust the tidbits and rumors that did come forward. One lieutenant complained that "every rebel on a horse or mule is 'mosby.' " Fol-

---

*Forbes was worried about officers, easily identified by their uniform, being picked off by hidden Rangers. Lowell was irritated by this concern. "As to insignia of rank, I never encourage my officers to wear any conspicuously," he told Forbes. More to the point, he explained, most were not "distinguishable at 100 yds." Lowell added that he personally felt that if he were "to be shot from behind a fence [he] would still rather be in uniform than out of it," but he assured Forbes he did not say this to the officers. Then he got to the point: "I will take as good care of Will as I can. I really do not think you need feel anxious." But the men as well as the officers were anxious.

lowing bad tips Lowell's men went everywhere, riding constantly for twelve hours at a stretch, "over horrid roads and down and up terribly steep ravines," deep into the hills running north from Bull Run. Only once, in a predawn raid, did they come upon a large group of men, but Mosby had been warned and the Rangers fled through the pass into the mists of the Shenandoah Valley. Although some of Lowell's men believed they had found "the long-sought-for place,"[7] Lowell himself decided it was only a temporary camp and not an established hideout.

Lowell wanted a system for rewarding citizens who brought in reliable information on Mosby's whereabouts or plans. He did not imagine that people loyal to the Union would come by useful information easily. The few Union sympathizers in Virginia were at best isolated from the larger community and more likely to need protection than to offer assistance. One William Tyson, of Tyson's Corner in eastern Virginia, fifteen miles from Washington, had paid dearly for his vote against secession and loyalty to the Union. He had been a wealthy landowner with a large family before the war; Mosby had put out word to capture him, and he was now in fairly desperate circumstances, with most of his estate destroyed, his house and barn burned. Tyson rarely slept at home but instead moved about randomly, trying to stay one step ahead of the Rangers.[8]

Lowell thought that problems within the guerrilla ranks might possibly produce an outcast or malcontent, and that the prospect of a reward for betrayal, or of security in becoming a paid informant, might create a turncoat. The offer of protection and recompense might successfully attract a man like "Big Yankee" Ames, a deserter from the Union at the time of the Emancipation Proclamation, who had become invaluable serving Mosby as a guide to the Union camps. By return messenger, Lowell's reforms were accepted and implemented. Immediately the number of attacks on sutlers' wagons dropped.

On August 22 Governor Andrew's office forwarded to Lowell, for his endorsement, a request that Major Thompson had written on August 20 to Colonel Lafayette Baker (commanding the District of Columbia Rangers), requesting his help getting the California companies transferred to his command and back to California. Thompson's letter contained a number of inaccuracies: he implied that he himself had raised all five California companies, and he wrote as if the California Hundred (raised by Captain Reed in December 1862) were part of his battalion (raised in March 1863), ignoring the existence of Captain Reed and the fact that the California Hundred had only just met their fellow Californians. Then he alleged that the California Battalion had been destroyed "by a small clique of young Boston Aristocracy, who to advance their own personal interests have already broken the agreement, pledges, good faith and honorable obligations" that the California Battalion would not be broken up and would remain under Thompson's command. He claimed that Lowell's motive for reorganizing the regiment was to provide this clique of aristocrats with a decent command (implying that the Massachusetts recruits were worthless).

But the reorganization of the regiment had been motivated by a desire to improve its quality. Neither Lowell, Andrew, nor anyone else representing Massachusetts had given Thompson "pledges, good faith and honorable obligations"[9] promising exclusive command of any men beyond the rights inherent in a major's commission. But even if they had, no responsible colonel would have honored them: this was precisely the sort of political interference made under the pressure of recruitment against which Lowell, in his negotiations with Lawrence, had been careful to protect himself. It would have shown poor military judgment to honor any promise that worked against the best interests of the regiment as a whole.

The officers of the Second Massachusetts Cavalry did appear as a small clique of young Boston aristocrats. Cliquishness was a fact of life in all volunteer regiments, a by-product of the political process by which recruitment worked. The Second and the Twentieth Massachusetts Infantry and the First Massachusetts Cavalry (from which many Second Massachusetts Cavalry officers came) were heavily officered by Harvard graduates and sons of the Boston aristocracy. But within the Second Massachusetts Cavalry, the officers represented a broader constituency: officers came not only from Boston but from western Massachusetts and from Essex County. There was a world of difference between Caspar Crowninshield and Francis Washburn and still more Goodwin Stone, a Transcendentalist scholar from Newburyport. And Thompson himself, who came from a long line of military men from western Massachusetts, knew that the Second Massachusetts Cavalry was one of the state's most broadly constituted regiments. Nevertheless Lowell was vulnerable on one point: the desire to load the regiment with officers who were also friends and relations had been an open and avowed goal (even if not very successful, since the formation of the Fifty-fourth had taken precedence); Forbes implicitly relied on Lowell to protect these young men, and Lowell recognized the obligation.

In his endorsement of Thompson's request, Lowell made no mention of the erroneous statements and did not defend himself against Thompson's accusations, for he knew that the request would ultimately arrive at the desk of General Halleck, on whose staff Thompson had served in 1861 before Halleck was summoned east. Lowell was not entirely sure what their relationship was worth. Thompson's claim to exclusive command of the California Battalion rested on assurances Halleck had made in February as part of the complex maneuvering to work around California's governor, Leland Stanford, who had attempted to stir up political controversy and prevent the battalion from leaving the state. Thompson now claimed that these assurances gave him authority to operate without subordination to any higher authority save Halleck. But Lowell knew that no such privilege had been granted. It would have been highly irregular—not even intimate personal connection to General Halleck was sufficient cause, without a compelling objective and overwhelming justification.

So Lowell simply disregarded most of Thompson's letter. Insisting that the entire matter was a "misapprehension as to Major Thompson's wishes," he explained that Thompson really wanted to raise a whole new regiment in California, some of the officers of course coming from the present regiment. This was a scheme that appealed to many "distinguished Californians" (senators and others) in Washington. Thompson had met with them, and they had agreed "to raise the money to pay back Massachusetts." Lowell recognized that Thompson was a "restless fellow and pretty persistent," but even so Lowell was not worried. He explained that "Thompson is not fit to command a platoon and his officers know it."[10] Nevertheless Lowell did his best to stymie Thompson's plan. His endorsement explained that Thompson had two special requests: he wanted his officers approved by the War Department and not the governor of the state, by which means he believed he could "avoid all *political* appointments"; and he wanted the regiment to be accepted and its transportation paid by the federal government, not a state. (Not in a million years would either of these requests be granted. Halleck and Lowell both knew this.) Lowell was reminding Halleck that Thompson, not he, was the political appointee, owing his rank to Halleck, and furthermore, with Leland Stanford, a Copperhead, as governor, California would send no troops to the Union army. This was all that needed saying to remind Halleck how and why California men were fighting under the Massachusetts flag.

Lowell then made three points, the most important of which concerned "*the men.*" He praised them, saying they were of the quality of "our first Eastern regiments—all young, vigorous and zealous—all hating a rebel—*too good* for hunting horse thieves . . . worth three of the ordinary recruits now picked up in our Eastern Cities. This is my deliberate opinion, *after experience.*"[11] Lowell was signaling that while he was willing to lose Thompson and the usual number of junior officers typically taken to form the core of a new regiment, he would not give up his men; nor, he inferred, should Halleck. And in his reference to horse thieves, Lowell acknowledged the source of the trouble: no one in the regiment wanted to be fighting Mosby; they had been raised and trained for a better fate.

Artfully, Lowell had frustrated Thompson's plan without providing Halleck or Thompson with any ammunition against him. As he sent off his endorsement, he hoped that Thompson would soon be on his way back to California and that the regiment could then settle down. Shortly thereafter he also wrote to Brigadier-General L. Thomas, the adjutant general (in a letter that began, "In Justice to the Captains of the California Battalion"). He proposed hair-splitting distinctions that would adjust the muster dates, alter the ranking, and allow him to promote deserving officers to command squadrons "to which I am unable on the present roster consistently to assign them."[12] Army protocol required that promotion follow rank, which was determined not by skill but by the date companies had been mustered into the regiment. With a little creative rearrangement of dates, Lowell was able to improve the seniority of the California captains, giving them precedence over the Massachusetts captains who had not panned out. He believed that with his regiment evenly balanced, and with his reforms for escort duty, he had rationalized the system, thereby reducing the damage Mosby could do.

But on August 24 a detachment of twenty-six men from Lowell's brigade, under the command of Lieutenant Hollis C. Pinkham, went to the cavalry depot at Washington to turn in the regiment's overworked horses and bring back a hundred remounts; on their return journey that evening Mosby ambushed the detachment. The story, as it emerged, was a sad tale of missteps leading to disaster. Lieutenant Pinkham had put a Sergeant Varnum in charge, and under normal circumstances Varnum could easily have held off the raiders. But the regular escort that left Arlington for Centreville failed to operate that day. Rather than wait for another, Varnum had set off unescorted. The hundred remount horses were untrained and all but unmanageable. To keep them under control, each of his twenty-six men was riding one horse and leading three remounts on as short a line as possible, and even that didn't work easily; progress was slow.

As the detachment reached a small clearing near Coyle's Tavern, the site of an ambush two weeks before, it too was ambushed. Mosby had been following them, waiting for this clearing to pounce. At the sound of gunfire the horses panicked and began to stampede down the road. Controlling one panicking horse is difficult, but each man had four. The unlucky men were thrown and trampled; the lucky ones were those who could dismount and jump clear. Then a second lot of Rangers attacked from the direction of the stampede. At this new sign of alarm in their path, the panicked horses doubled back into the melee, further trampling the injured and unwary, while the Union men who had successfully dismounted—about half of them— took shelter behind a fence from which they could return fire. But, unprepared, they quickly ran out of ammunition. The fight became one of hand-to-hand combat. Varnum held "a rebel by the throat" and beat "him over the head with an empty pistol" until a Ranger put a gun to his head. He was killed instantly. Most of the horses were captured. Of the twenty-six men, two were killed, one mortally wounded, seven captured. In the skirmish William F. Short of Company A and Carlos M. Jenkins of Company E had both shot and wounded Mosby in the chest and groin. The odds were good, they thought, that he could not ride to flee, and a few men dashed to Centreville to bring help.[13]

Within two hours of the attack Lowell sent out two squadrons: one to recover the dead and wounded and to collect the lost horses, the other to search for Mosby. It hardly need be said what capturing Mosby would have done for the reputation of the Second Massachusetts Cavalry and its colonel, but the effort failed due to the disappearance of the squadron leader, Captain David A. DeMerritt. He had become deluded and believed that his own regiment intended to hang him. Twice he rode off at a gallop and was twice chased down. He disappeared for good on the third attempt after dark. Mosby and a few of his men were safely hidden in the woods while the Second Massachusetts Cavalry thundered up and down the roads searching for their crazed captain. When DeMerritt returned to camp the next day, the regimental surgeon assessed his condition as "entirely harmless." His breakdown was caused by exhaustion and the pain from refracturing his broken leg. DeMerritt was "one of my best fellows," Lowell wrote to Effie. He had given him the "most important post" and been let down.[14]

Although the regiment had the satisfaction of knowing it had shot and wounded Mosby, the harder truth was that the wounded Mosby had slipped through their fingers. Emotions ran high among the men of the Second

Massachusetts Cavalry. Humiliated by the ambush, frustrated with themselves for letting Mosby get by, angry that popular men had died, and bewildered by the insanity of an admired captain, the men were looking to lay blame. "I sincerely hope that whoever it may be [responsible], will be made to suffer the greatest punishment allowed," wrote Private Thomas Barnstead of the California Hundred. A sergeant of Company L wrote home to California that "it was a gross piece of negligence to send over one hundred horses with only men enough to lead them, without an escort of any kind, over a road infested by guerrillas, just waiting for opportunities to rob and plunder." A good portion of the regiment was happy to blame their colonel.

While Lowell commanded the brigade, Crowninshield was the commanding officer of the regiment, the one who had made the arrangements and issued the orders to Lieutenant Pinkham. Writing the day after the ambush, Crowninshield put the blame on Pinkham, who had "contrary to orders started without the Regular Guard which comes out every day." Because Pinkham was an officer of the Thirteenth New York Cavalry, Secretary Stanton and General Heintzelman assumed the troops involved were from that regiment, but Lowell quickly cleared up the confusion and took responsibility. Heintzelman demanded from Lowell a thorough and immediate report, while Stanton ordered a court of inquiry and named George Stoneman to head it. Lowell was upset at potentially falling out with Stoneman, who had hinted he would assign him command of one of the three cavalry depots projected for the Cavalry Bureau: a cushy post for a man about to marry. Lowell ruefully wrote Effie that it "would have been very pleasant winter-quarters." And yet he accepted the blame, telling her that "a commanding officer is to blame for everything that goes wrong under him."[15]

The humiliation was so severe that Lowell's men had trouble appreciating that Mosby had wounded himself on a trivial errand. His attack on Sergeant Varnum's detail had been serendipitous, his real purpose on the morning of August 24 having been an attack on the Orange & Alexandria rail line that ran between Alexandria and points southwest, a valuable line of supply for the Army of the Potomac camped along the Rappahannock and Rapidan Rivers, as it had been most of the summer and would be again if Richmond were ever to be taken. Generals Lee and Stuart had repeatedly requested that Mosby attack railroad lines, but he had done so only three times. His failure to do so again caused exasperation in the Confederate command.

However much the generals wanted train crashes and bent rails, Mosby, or at least his Rangers, preferred attacking sutler wagons and stealing horses. Mosby allowed his men to keep the spoils of war. They profited from their raids, selling goods on the black market or simply keeping friends and family supplied with food and themselves in drink. This was a key factor in Ranger recruitment and a real limit on Mosby's control of his men. When well supplied with booze, the Rangers failed to turn out for Mosby, whatever the nature of the intended raid. Thus on August 24 they passed up a chance to do lasting damage in favor of capturing horses. The Rangers had taken advantage of the Second Massachusetts Cavalry refitting itself with new horses to do the same for themselves. (An epidemic of hoof-and-mouth disease affected a huge number of horses both within the army and at the cavalry depot, as well as the equine population of Virginia generally.) Although this sort of exploit became the stuff of legend, it in fact served only the narrowest of mercenary interests.

On August 29 Cabot Russel's father met directly with President Lincoln. Since his failure to find his son in the hospitals of Charleston, he had gone to Washington, where he pursued his connections until he procured a private interview. In May the Confederate Congress had resolved that captured white officers commanding black troops would be hanged. After Fort Wagner the Confederates had refused a flag of truce, provided no information on prisoners taken, and only reluctantly declared that, save Shaw's body, they held no officers. Rumors of executions had been rife. When the Confederates announced the civil trial of prisoners from the Fifty-fourth accused of being escaped slaves committing insurrection, Lincoln had countered with a new policy: for every Union soldier executed, a Confederate prisoner would be; for every soldier returned to slavery, a Confederate prisoner would serve hard labor. In response, on August 10 the trial was aborted and the men fell into limbo, neither civilians nor soldiers.

Russel now urged the president "to refuse to exchange at all until he had brought by his refusal, the rebels to acknowledge the right of the black troops and their officers as equal to those of any other troops and any other officers." The president was reluctant to take this stand, feeling that the country did not support "their having equal rights" and that it was not fair to the other Union prisoners. That evening Russel reported that Lincoln had acted "like a man who had been badgered about negroes and negro regiments and their officers till he had lost his patience. He certainly talked very unreasonably and I am sure could not on reflection maintain to his conscience the ground he took." Lowell had long been displeased with Lincoln's stand: he would have preferred execution instead of hard labor as retaliation for soldiers sold into slavery. Conferring with Russel after the meeting, Lowell reported that their only hope now was "to write to everyone . . . and thus create such a storm of letters that Cabot shall in course of time hear of some of them."[16]

The family began to marshal their forces. Lowell told Forbes that he would no longer recommend and recruit officers, "if the Government is going to rate them so much cheaper than officers of white troops. In the case of the Fifty-Fourth it seems to me that Massachusetts is involved, — that she ought to demand that her officers be treated all alike; but it is discreditable that the Government should make it necessary." Since Shaw's death Lowell had renewed his commitment to black troops, maintaining a dialogue with Senator Sumner on the subject. With Forbes, who was making plans for more black regiments, he discussed whom to recruit as a brigade commander. If black cavalry were to be established, Lowell wanted to be involved. So did Will Forbes. Lowell planted the idea with his other officers. He believed that "the black business" would not end with the war but would become a "career."[17]

After the Coyle's Tavern fiasco, General Heintzelman ordered Lowell to "clear out the whole country inside of Manassas Junction." He meant to force all civilians sympathetic to the Confederacy between Manassas or Centreville and Alexandria to migrate. Southern Unionists, loyal to the United States, were to be accorded full protection. Neutrals, helping neither side and confining themselves to their daily tasks, were offered protection in exchange for their "passivity." But secessionists who aided and abetted the enemy were not spared. Their property could be seized and confiscated. Foraging, billeting, and requisitions of any kind were to start with them. And they could be expelled from their communities. In fact, Halleck recommended this as a means of saving effort and aggravation, although he left such decisions to the discretion of the local commander. Colonel J. H. Taylor, chief of staff to the command general, Samuel P. Heintzelman, had already issued general orders: "No mercy need be shown to bushwhackers. These guerrillas must be destroyed."

But Lowell did not act: after a humiliating incident, generals typically vented their frustration by sending out orders like these full of spleen but vague in detail. And while many in the Union army, frustrated by the failed attempt to capture the countless guerrillas, came to believe in a "policy of extermination," Lowell was not one of them. In September he received specific orders "to burn the houses of all persons actively assisting Mosby." He knew that if he complied literally with these orders, hardly a house would be left standing. Instead he reserved the torch for two mills and a house that was a known rendezvous. The mills were used to supply the Confederate army with grain and, as such, were a fair target in the Union policy of destroying matériel that was of potential or assured use to the enemy. The house, he explained to Effie, belonged to a man who engaged in sustained secessionist activities: he had shot a Union soldier in cold blood, then shot the "Negro who informed on him." The family were given notice to move their furniture and valuables, and Lowell detailed his men to help in moving the heavy furniture — clearly not a wanton act.[18]

In fact, so deliberate was Lowell that he even sent Mosby a letter explaining his policy. He assured Mosby that a house would not be burned simply because it was the home of a Ranger. Only houses used as "rendezvous" would suffer the torch. Lowell reckoned he would do more burning, but, he told Effie, it "will be done with all possible consideration." He wanted to discuss this policy with her: "I hope you will always write about such things: it will make me more considerate, and in such cases one cannot be too considerate."[19] Consideration is an interesting requirement for dealing with an enemy as crafty as Mosby. What did Lowell have in mind? Burning all the homes of those who abetted Mosby would have denuded the countryside and made the secessionists even more militant, potentially inflaming the situation. Burning "rendezvous" sites, however, gave people a choice, creating what Lowell hoped would become a means of accomplishing Halleck's goal of separating the guerrilla band from the community that supported it. It was a clever strategy, compromised only by Lowell's lack of solid intelligence.

Lowell wanted to believe that he and his men were fighting an "honorable foe," and that if treated as such, Mosby would behave honorably. This was a matter of pride and morale and his own sense of honor. The men were asked to burn houses, to requisition horses, to arrest citizens, and most worrying of all, to "deny" to the enemy crops or whatever might be of material benefit. At every level of the regimental hierarchy, Lowell included, the moral ambiguity of the work affected morale. The result was that almost everyone in the regiment, not just Major Thompson, wanted to escape their assignment.

Since Gettysburg, Lowell had known of three possible escapes for his unit from the tedium of chasing Mosby. On August 28 General Nathaniel P.

Banks made the last of repeated requests to the secretary of war for the Second Massachusetts Cavalry to serve under his command. Complaining that the regiment had been "raised expressly for my command," he asked, at least, for Lowell, who, he claimed, was "nearly as important to us as his regiment" and was needed to "infuse the necessary vigour" into his cavalry. These requests only encouraged General Heintzelman, who had a reputation of being "greedy" for troops, to hang on to Lowell and the Second Massachusetts. On September 8 General Halleck dismissed General Banks's request, explaining, "I need simply to mention the fact that it [Lowell's regiment] is the only one we have for scouts and pickets in front of Washington."[20] He also refused General William S. Rosencrans's request that the Second Massachusetts join the Army of the Cumberland. This left only Lowell's most desired chance for seeing action: since June 1863 General David Gregg, a former colleague in the Sixth U.S. Cavalry and now a division commander in the Cavalry Corps, had repeatedly asked for Lowell's transfer to his division in the Army of the Potomac, where he intended Lowell to command a real five-regiment brigade. These requests had gone unanswered, sustaining the hope that they might eventually be honored, particularly in early September, when General Meade was preparing the Army of the Potomac to march south.

But on September 13 Lowell received orders to establish a series of pickets along the fordable sections of the Potomac River, with a permanent station on the Maryland side at the mouth of Muddy Branch, some twenty miles north of Washington along the Chesapeake & Ohio Canal. He was to maintain and expand the defensive postings while the Army of the Potomac headed south to confront Lee's army on the Rappahannock. Lowell returned to camp to find brigades of cavalry, infantry, and baggage trains, all belonging to the Army of the Potomac, passing by Centreville while "we stay here forever," as Will Forbes put it in a letter to his sister. The trains looked "like long serpents winding down our hillside across the brook and up behind the earthworks."[21] As regiment after regiment went through, the regimental band played on, stopping only when the last troops crested the far hill and disappeared from view.

Writing to Henry Higginson that evening, Lowell could not refrain from making the complaint he had successfully kept out of his letters to Effie and Forbes. Telling Henry that the Fifty-fourth Regiment was historic, he mocked his own as "mythic." A regiment he had started to recruit in November 1862 was still not up to full strength and had not been united in the field until August. Intended for the conquest of the Mississippi, the Second Massachusetts Cavalry was still in the East, assigned to the defense of Washington; the Mississippi, thanks to the victory at Vicksburg, was now under Union control. The Army of the Potomac was headed south to take Richmond, while his men were chasing horse thieves and were so disunited as to fail to acknowledge they came from the same regiment. As other troops passed by, they asked the inevitable question, "What regiment." The answer varied: the Massachusetts men said, "Second Massachusetts Cavalry," while the Californians replied, "California Hundred" or "California Battalion."[22]

Lowell, perhaps recalling promises of an "Ironside" regiment, blamed Secretary Stanton and adopted a sarcastic tone as he told Higginson, "We are an independent, fancy department . . . and we take no interest in wars or rumors of war . . . Stanton is *very fond* of us, and keeps us where it is safe — the 'front' nearest Washington, whereby I am debarred from the rightful command of a brigade of five regiments in Gregg's division."[23]

Only reluctantly, with this sarcastic and facetious complaint, did Lowell finally walk into his "collar" and resign himself to make the best of his "inglorious warfare." As he considered the order for a station at Muddy Branch, he reckoned it was a perfect opportunity to give Major Thompson the independence he craved and, with a bit of luck, salve his offended ego. Lowell's relationship with Thompson was "anything but pleasant." Lowell had to take no official notice of Thompson's scheming, and Thompson, suspecting that Lowell did know, "wears a very hang dog look whenever I meet him."[24] It was a tiresome charade, and Lowell was glad to put an end to it. But Thompson failed to see his opportunity and regarded the assignment as "banishment." Lowell did use the Muddy Branch station as a kind of R&R spot for his brigade, rotating his overworked men in and out. This was something the men needed, especially as the cold and rainy season began, but it was a slight to Thompson. Despite his threats and the humiliation to which Lowell subjected him, Thompson did not resign. Instead, he nursed his festering resentments, and the boil was yet to be lanced.

What Lowell did not know was that John Murray Forbes was doing all he could to put the brakes on Lowell's rise in the army. George Putnam had gone to see Forbes in Boston about plans for the "Colored Troops" and learned that he feared Lowell was "in great danger of being made a brigadier." George cautioned his wife not to repeat this fact to anyone as "Mr. F[orbes] wouldn't wish to be understood as reluctant that C[harlie] should be promoted." Instead, Lowell and Forbes continued their correspondence about black troops. Lowell admitted that he wanted to "help make it clear that the black troops are *the* instrument which alone can end the rebellion; [Shaw] died to prove the fact that blacks will fight . . . I do not want to see his proof drop useless for want of strong men and good officers to act upon it. I did what little I could to help the Fifty-fourth for his sake and for its own sake before, but since July 18th, I think I can do more."[25]

On September 15 Governor Andrew went to see Lincoln and Lowell went to see Secretary Stanton, who offered him the position of provost-marshal general of the District of Columbia. Stanton believed Lowell had "the right nerve and the right character" for the job. But after a short talk during which Lowell explained his ambitions, Stanton agreed that it was not the right job. It was, as Lowell explained to Effie, "not strictly *military*." Lowell then lobbied Stanton to stop all prisoner exchanges until the Confederacy recognized officers of black troops on the same footing as white. Lowell came away feeling moderately optimistic. Writing to Forbes, he described how Governor Andrew had found Lincoln much more sympathetic than Russel had. Stanton had assured Lowell that an officer had been sent to Charleston to reiterate the demands that had been made to General P.G.T. Beauregard, the commanding Confederate general, and, if he failed again to respond, then Stanton was willing to refuse all exchanges and to persuade Lincoln that this was the right action. "I have good hopes that Stanton and Andrew together may keep the President from disgracing himself and us."[26]

This pressure did elicit from General Beauregard's staff the statement that the Confederates held no officers of the Fifty-fourth. They claimed that they had found none except Shaw. The Lowell-Jackson family were convinced that Beauregard was lying. Anna Lowell spoke for all of them on September 20 when she mused, "It is very singular that they have never mentioned the Lieut. Col. and Maj. whom they at first said they had captured, nor reported them as dead. Neither were Cabot and Simpkins mentioned with Shaw."[27] To this day it remains a mystery what did happen to Cabot Russel. Most likely he was buried at Fort Wagner along with Simpkins, but when and how they died and whether they joined Shaw in the mass grave or were buried separately, together, or with other enlisted men is unknown. The last account of Cabot described his cries through the night for water heard by other wounded soldiers.

Supporters of the Fifty-fourth like George William Curtis, married to Effie's older sister and a journalist of considerable reputation, felt that the Confederates had irreparably broken the protocols of war and that Union war policy should become equally ruthless. Lowell disagreed, and he was frustrated by the failure of the Lincoln administration to take a clear position. "I do not think I am 'discouraged,' Effie," Lowell wrote. "I have the greatest confidence in Stanton, in his heart at any rate and therefore sufficiently in his head. I have *no* confidence in Lincoln or Seward or Blair— *none* in General Halleck, whom I consider a miserable shuffler, hiding his ignorance and his failures with a lawyer's speciousness."[28] Although Lowell favored a draconian retaliatory response to Confederate abuse of prisoners, he did not support a more generalized retaliatory action against the Confederates.

Despite his feelings of "inglorious war," of hating to have men killed on ambush, his contempt for "police work," and his belief that Mosby was "an old rat" with "a great many holes," Lowell now insisted to Effie that "Mosby is an honourable foe, and should be treated as such." He acknowledged, and deeply disliked, the "falsehoods of Beauregard," but he insisted that "we have acknowledged them as belligerents, and we must treat them accordingly.[29]

The Californians did not believe Mosby was an honorable foe, and they did not much care for the rules of war or for Mosby's "belligerent" status. The men hated the work and came to hate the officers who made them do it. The injustices of the army rankled because they were the same injustices and capricious privileges of a class system. At the top of the hierarchy was their colonel, Charles Russell Lowell, the man who engineered their misery and whom the Californians still resented for breaking them up. A *Daily Alta California* letter made their animus clear: "All the knowledge that he possesses of fighting Indians or guerrillas has been acquired by reading Sylvanus Cobb's stories in the *New York Ledger*, while burning the 'midnight oil' at Harvard." This bilious jibe made light of the fact that combating guerrillas was a controversial problem without any clear answer, to put it mildly. Nevertheless the letter insisted that if the War Department would let Major Thompson "have absolute command of his California battalion and of the California Hundred" and "let us fight the guerrillas our own way, either as we hunt Indians or at their own game of bushwhacking [we] will soon make short work of the guerrillas."[30]

The last week of September the Californians were given their chance when Captain Reed sent out a small detail of Company A on foot—the regiment was still short of horses. They returned with four prisoners, of whom James Wilson was supposedly one of the "worst rebel captains." He had been arrested and paroled twice before and was an early member of Mosby's band but not a captain. The Californians told lurid stories of how Wilson had killed federal soldiers by slitting their throats and then ritually mutilated their corpses. But the Massachusetts men did not believe these "tall tales."[31]

On September 27 Mosby, fully recuperated from his wounds, decided to announce his return by kidnapping the Union governor of Virginia (that slice of it under Union control). Mosby and his men successfully sneaked into Alexandria, only to discover that Governor Francis H. Pierpont was not home. Discouraged, the Rangers decided to go after one of the governor's aides, Daniel H. Dulaney, who lived at Rose Hill, not far south of Alexandria. They chose him because his son, another Daniel, was riding with Mosby and took great delight in taking his father captive. Like the kidnapping of General Stoughton the previous March, this publicity stunt was hard to live down but was of no material consequence. Mosby, in fact, was under serious attack from generals in the Confederate army. General Jubal Early scorned the Rangers: "They are a nuisance and an evil . . . a band of thieves, stealing, pillaging, plundering, and doing every manner of mischief and crime. They are a terror to the citizens and an injury to the cause . . . They never fight; can't be made to fight. Their leaders are generally brave, but few of the men are good soldiers and have engaged in this business for the sake of gain."

General Thomas Rosser complained that his companies from Loudoun, Fauquier, and Fairfax Counties were increasingly disgruntled with regular army life as they learned, heard, and saw more of the carefree life of Mosby's Rangers. They too wanted to stay at home, keep what they captured, and be free of the duties of camp life. Even J.E.B. Stuart, Mosby's stout defender, was forced to concede that the Rangers operated at only one-quarter their nominal strength. Although General Lee appreciated Mosby's potential, he was exasperated because he could only partially control him, and he suspected that Mosby could only partially control his men. Lee wanted to see them do more strategic damage to Union railroads, telegraphs, and other lines of supply and communication. Mosby defended his Rangers by claiming that his success was not quantifiable in that way. Instead, he described himself as a fly on the rump of a horse—persistently annoying and requiring greater and greater resources to be got rid of. He argued that he and his men tied down federal troops in defensive and rearguard actions. (In fact, it was just Lowell's brigade and one other battalion assigned to antiguerrilla work.) But for the time being, such an argument, and General Stuart's support, persuaded Lee to encourage rather than censor Mosby and his Rangers, particularly as they could be immediately useful.

General Meade had once again failed to seize his moment on Confederate soil, and once again Lee responded aggressively to Union hesitation. By the first days of October he was pushing the Army of the Potomac north. Both armies were headed toward Centreville as if to fight yet a third battle of Bull Run, although if the actions of the early summer were any indication, Lee might well swing north into Maryland and Pennsylvania again, or attack Washington from the north.

Lowell put forward a plan to establish an outer ring of the defenses around Washington using the cavalry camps at Fairfax Court House, Centreville, and Muddy Branch. He proposed a new cavalry camp to be his own headquarters, at Vienna, Virginia, which in a few days' time would be the new terminus of the Loudoun & Hampshire Railroad, only now reopening. (Originally the line had extended to Leesburg, but in 1861 the Confederate army destroyed the track at Reston. By October 1863 it had been repaired to Vienna, but no further: Leesburg was of insufficient strategic value.) Vienna sat on the northern road between Alexandria and Leesburg. Lowell believed that by making it headquarters for his Independent Cavalry Brigade, he would kill two birds with one stone: reduce Washington's vulnerability to the north, and secure an essential supply depot.

He also proposed a set of pickets at Germantown, Lewinsville, and Annandale. Patrols would pass by daily and relieve the men on picket duty on a rotating basis. Patrols every two or four hours between these posts and the other cavalry camps would keep the roads invariably full of soldiers, and vedettes at night would guard the main roads. Lowell proposed blocking the smaller roads with felled trees. He wanted the patrols also to serve as escorts for sutler and other supply wagons. By careful planning, Lowell organized the most effective use of his men to protect the greatest area.

These plans were immediately accepted, and by the second week in October the Second Massachusetts Cavalry had moved to Vienna and were constructing their winter quarters on a south-facing slope, with a stream at the bottom of the valley. The surrounding countryside was largely secessionist, although the town of Vienna itself had a high percentage of Union families. The local hotel was requisitioned for a hospital, the schoolhouse for a mess hall, and the schoolmarm, "a smart Yankee kind of girl," as the cook. A large house on the hill became brigade headquarters, and senior officers occupied smaller houses. The line officers had rectangular tents on the upper slope of the hill. Building materials were appropriated to make wooden floors and wooden boarding for walls up to the height of a low dado railing, three and a half feet. To heat their tents, officers either built brick chimneys for open fires or procured wood-burning stoves. Desks, tables, chairs, and bedsteads added to their comfort, many of them built by the camp carpenter, Valorus Dearborn, a member of the California Hundred whose time in California had not softened the sharp edges of his Maine childhood; he was taciturn even in his diary. Will Forbes was Dearborn's largest client, and once Dearborn had built a mantelpiece for his fireplace, he felt "as comfortable as possible."[32]

Several dogs were attached to the command: Jack, a bulldog, and two terriers called Nip and Chicken, as well as some nameless pointers. Lowell had a partiality to terriers, as his family had always had them, and these terriers would set up a howling contest with the dogs of the town so that the nights were filled with "growling, inciting, threatening and whining in tribulation."[33]

Lowell's reforms had rationalized the Union response to Mosby and other guerrillas, and Union forces had carved out a reasonable area of control over Loudoun and Fauquier Counties, Mosby's Confederacy. His escorts had reduced the incidence of raids on sutler wagons, and the Vienna depot now protected Union supply lines. But whatever was saved in manpower by this efficiency was more than lost by the punishing schedule of pickets, patrols, and escorts required to keep the main thoroughfares free of guerrillas. Patrol and escort duty created a constant gnawing anxiety that at any moment Mosby might strike, although most of the time he didn't. What had been a pleasant enough duty during the summer became profoundly unpleasant in the autumn, with its rain and cold nights. While on duty it was next to impossible to sleep, and the men spent only one in four nights in bed in camp. Although the Vienna camp had few occurrences of the diseases associated with poor sanitation (cholera, chronic bowel issues) and the infectious diseases, and although it was spared the despair of having three men die of such diseases for every man killed in battle, the hospital was filling with men suffering from diseases of exposure and exhaustion, from rheumatism, diarrhea, and fevers. One private complained that picket duty was "just killing men and accomplishing nothing for Rebels are so scarce about here as $20,000 gold pieces."[34]

Although it seemed to a private that picket and patrol duty was work done to no good purpose, he was wrong. Mosby and his informants were watching the Union actions carefully. The Rangers had no desire to encounter Lowell's men unless it was in an ambush of their own planning. Lowell's constant patrols drove the Rangers off certain roads and forced them to take alternate routes, change their objectives, search out less-well-guarded areas and more obscure venues, or simply hide in the woods. Roads that Mosby's Rangers had once ridden with impunity no longer offered safe passage. Lowell's vigilance contributed to keeping Mosby deeper in Virginia and diminished his area of operation. Lowell regularly reported to headquarters, "everything quiet in this vicinity," or as a popular wartime song put it, "All Quiet Along the Potomac Tonight." The seeming scarcity of rebels was a sign of success, though this fact was not readily appreciated by the men.

Scouting, unpredictable and risky, was preferred over anything else, even the boredom of remaining in camp. One might always hope to find Mosby's headquarters and flush out his men. Scouts ranged far afield for days at a time, and in good weather the work was arduous but pleasant. As autumn turned to winter, the scouting parties set out and rode all day in pouring rain, often had to swim across flooded fords, and set up camp in still more rain. Cooking anything but coffee was nigh impossible, for the rain soaked their knapsacks and ruined the hardtack. Sleeping out when soaking wet, with only a thin marching blanket for warmth, was harsh. Eating bad food, getting little sleep, sitting in the saddle for "ten hours at a stretch without dismounting,"[35] on a horse also poorly fed and just as wet, was fun as long as the men could hope that soon they would find and surprise Mosby.

This never happened. The wet, tired, and hungry men of the Second Massachusetts Cavalry could only watch as the rebels disappeared through various gaps into the Shenandoah Valley. Their tired horses were no match for the Rangers' fresh ones. The only outcome was the long ride back to camp and the inevitable rotation to Muddy Branch to recoup their strength in lighter duty where, bitter and exhausted, they cursed their lot. On October 29 their misery came to a head: a constellation of disgruntled Californians cooling their heels at Muddy Branch signed a petition to the secretary of war asking to be put on active service with the Rangers of the District of Columbia, commanded by the same Colonel Lafayette Baker to whom Major Thompson had appealed in August.

The day before, Lowell had gone on a ten-day leave. His request, made only a week earlier, had mentioned "private reasons of great importance."[36] His purpose was to marry. It had not been easy for him to obtain a leave: he had hoped for twenty days but had been given only half that and on only two days' notice. Once his telegram with this news reached Effie in Boston, she left a note at the Sanitary Commission, where she had been working, saying she would not be in the next week for personal reasons and apologizing for the inconvenience. His parents and sister rushed down to New York barely in time for the service.

Originally Effie's parents had felt that because of her youth a long engagement was wise, but with Rob Shaw's death things had changed, and the Shaws had dropped their objections to an early wedding. As news of their impending marriage spread, practical questions arose. Henry Higginson wrote Charlie asking how he planned to marry "without 'daily bread.' " He replied, "Daily bread sinks into insignificance by the side of the other more important things which the war has made uncertain, and I know now that it would be unwise to allow a possible want of 'daily bread' in the future to prevent the certainty of even a month's happiness in the present. In peace times this would not be so clear." In this one respect, Charlie conceded, "This war is perhaps a personal Godsend."

In peacetime he would not have had much chance of marrying Effie. Her family was many times wealthier than his, and while the Shaws were open-minded idealists for whom worldly wealth was by no means the only measure of a man, and while their wealth was such that Effie could choose a husband without having to consider his financial position too closely, nevertheless she would have been marrying "beneath her." Charlie's pride would not have permitted such a scenario. But with the glamour of a colonel's eagles resting on his shoulders and with his reputation for courage established, he was deemed a catch. He took his opportunity, and as he told Henry, "I am going to marry upon nothing; I am going to make my wife as happy upon nothing as if I could give her a fortune." His officer's pay was enough for the simple life they would have to live during wartime. After the war, he supposed, "there will [not] be more men than there are places for them to fill."[37]

Higginson, emboldened by Charlie's attitude, took his chances and once again asked Ida Agassiz to marry him. The previous winter she had turned him down, but this time, laid out on a divan with his spine wound and with a glamorous crescent saber scar across his cheek, she could not resist. Charlie was quick to congratulate him. "You've been a great deal of trouble to me for the last 25 years, Henry, a great deal of trouble," he teased. "I should have been very willing to continue to take care of you . . . Still, old fellow, I am very, very glad to turn you over to so much better hands." Charlie was fond of Ida, and she and Effie had become fast friends. He was confident that his deepest friendship from childhood would survive both their marriages. Charlie had been slow to warm to the entanglements of love and marriage, but having found Effie, he was no longer ambivalent. "Henry, don't tell me about your being happy, wait three months; then, as you begin to see how happiness grows, you may begin to talk about it."[38]

On October 31, in a very simple and small ceremony on Staten Island, Charlie and Effie were married. His family stayed on for a few days so the two families could get further acquainted. Anna felt quite easy with Effie, having seen much of her in Boston and Cambridge and having lived with her at the boardinghouse in Readville, but she was not and had never been an intimate of Mrs. Shaw, although their social circles had once overlapped. In her letter describing the visit to her daughter Anna, one can detect a note of envy. Effie and her younger sister, Nellie, sewed in the evenings, neighbors came to call, the house was "perfectly charming and their style of life easy and luxurious." The Shaws' was a happiness "unmarred by misfortune," she remarked. Yet the Shaws had lost their son Rob only three months before. And Anna also had lost a son. By "misfortune," she has to have been thinking of her own—her husband's failure and the financial burdens she had shouldered. It was a small but telling comment.[39]

Charlie and Effie went off on their honeymoon—a few nights in Hartford—before returning together to Washington, where they stopped to see his sister Anna, whom Effie had not yet met. The next day Charlie brought Effie to the Vienna camp. It was quite unusual for a wife to accompany an officer into the field, and it would have been impossible while on campaign, but at a permanent camp near a town only a short distance from the capital, Lowell hoped it would be acceptable to both his fellow officers and his new bride. Nevertheless, most of the officers did not approve. Major Crowninshield told his mother that "camp is hardly the place for a young girl just married." Major Will Forbes and Dr. Oscar DeWolf were not so disapproving but had doubted that Effie's parents would let her come. When Forbes finally had word that Effie was indeed on her way, he was dismayed to find Lowell had left the house he shared with Dr. DeWolf in a state of rampant bachelor chaos: "coats, hats boots trunks, books, etc. etc. in disarray about the rooms." It was "a nice little white cottage under some tall trees, almost in the camp, a pretty place," but it needed work. The old woman who owned the place was persuaded to clean it up, and Forbes, eager for the house "to have an appearance of comfort" to greet the young bride, went to great lengths to procure some andirons and fire tools, some tables, and a tablecloth. Dr. DeWolf offered a picture.[40]

Despite Forbes's best efforts, Effie initially felt out of her depth. She was the only wife at the camp, she was only nineteen, and her privileged upbringing had given her maturity but not the practical experience of running a household. Anna, with her contacts in Washington hospitals, arranged for a woman to work as housekeeper, a welcome addition, but the good woman did not last long. On November 19 Charlie told his mother that Effie was "very much afraid of imposing on my 'relatives' (meaning mother and sisters) and of being regarded by them as a bore and an incapable, — so if I ask for anything hereafter, you must know it is done secretly. Is not this a very sad state of things already?" His mother sent recipes, which were less welcome. Charlie accidentally threw them in the fire and told his mother not to bother to recopy them. Effie and he were growing "exceedingly corpulent"[41] on dry toast cooked on the open fire, he insisted.

Rather than fussing about the house and getting frustrated by the inconveniences of housekeeping, for which she had little training and no interest, Effie turned her efforts to other things. Of an evening they occasionally entertained other officers, but more often Effie read aloud to him, starting with passages from *The Faerie Queen*. Lowell took enormous pleasure as he lay before the fire and listened to Effie's beautiful low voice, enjoying the text "to the full." Like his men, he was taxed to his limits of endurance, and a good deal of his free time was spent sleeping. Effie had to tiptoe about the house and find things to do. She organized a writing class for the camp contrabands, and she quickly made a place for herself as an assistant to the regimental chaplain, Charles Humphreys, visiting and nursing the wounded men. From the years she had lived in Europe as a child, she spoke French, Italian, and German and thus could converse with many soldiers in their native languages. She wrote letters to their relatives, an important job that earned her a valued place. More generally she brought warmth and empathy to the regiment, whether in hospitality for officers at headquarters, or in the tenderness to the ill or dying men in the hospital. "If it wasn't for the hospital I don't know what I should do," Effie confessed to her mother-in-law.[42]

Effie became a familiar presence about the camp, trudging through the ubiquitous mud in gumboots—hardly elegant but nevertheless very feminine. For the rest of her life she received letters from these men recalling the value of her care and concern for their comfort. Her family at home in New

York, reading newspaper reports of how the guerrillas were getting increasingly bold, feared that Effie was confined to camp. This was not so. Daily she went for a ride on Berold, the horse Lowell had ridden at Antietam. "It will be encouraging to you to know that Berold has not deteriorated in her hands," Charlie wrote his mother, but "has rather improved,—so there are hopes that I may be returned to you as good as ever."[43]

This curious statement withheld all the genuine feeling Charlie expressed that very same day to Higginson: "I wish you and Ida could make as pleasant arrangements for winter-quarters as E. and I have made." But he remained guarded with his mother, unwilling to share with her his new happiness. In 1858 he had written that his mother was "the very root of my life now and will be perhaps forever." Now Effie was. He may not have been entirely sure that his mother was content with this transfer of affection, particularly now that Jim was dead. Her expression of envy for the Shaws' lifestyle had perhaps tipped her hand. Whether from guilt or loyalty, Charlie did not share his new happiness with his mother.[44]

He had promised Effie he would give up leading scouting expeditions, which he acknowledged were the greatest avoidable danger. He did not give them up entirely. Still, he did his best to spend as few nights away as possible. He did not have to tell the men he was eager to spend the night with his bride or that the company of his wife was preferable to a thin blanket and his horse's hot breath. The men without wives of their own could only sigh indulgently at their colonel's ardor and at the inequities of an army system that permitted his pleasure but not their own. Such a state of affairs hardly eased their resentments.

SIXTEEN

ALL QUIET ALONG THE POTOMAC
Winter 1863–64

Lowell had returned from his honeymoon to find that affairs had been somewhat mismanaged during his absence. Awaiting his attention was news that a deserter from Mosby's Rangers had presented himself at Vienna offering to turn informant, and that Major Crowninshield had sent this man into Washington as if he were just another prisoner. Certainly he was right to be suspicious of anyone who purported to be a turncoat, but Lowell was nonetheless annoyed that Crowninshield had taken the safe route and sent the man on to let someone else make the judgment about his reliability. Once out of their hands, they might never get him back. Lowell immediately requested that the man be returned to him.

More problematic was a petition that the disgruntled Californians had submitted to the War Department, now waiting for Lowell's endorsement. Their request was to transfer to the First District of Columbia Cavalry under Colonel Baker, to whom Major Thompson had appealed back in August, immediately arousing the suspicion that Thompson was behind the request. Upset that the affair had been allowed to get as far as it did without his knowledge, Lowell ordered Thompson to Vienna and sent Will Forbes and George Holman to inspect his camp for infractions. They found a broad range of lapses in discipline and good order, which Thompson was ordered to correct; more important, Holman learned that Thompson had been sowing discontent: a string of letters had been published in the California newspapers complaining about and criticizing Lowell's command.

Lowell had known of these letters for months but had deliberately not read them, telling Effie on August 4, "You must never allow anything you see in the papers to disturb you . . . one man who has been roughed and feels aggrieved can easily profess to express the feelings of a company."[1] But when presented with the full record, Lowell was stunned. Not because he believed the letters themselves would have any real effect—he understood that they were published months out of date and for the consumption of a California audience that had no power to affect things one way or the other. Indeed, as such, they were, in isolation, perhaps the safest means possible of venting frustration.

But what the letters proved more effectively than Lowell could have conceived was that Thompson had been actively, even brazenly, promoting dissension, spreading lies, feeding discontent, and nursing grudges. The letters were signed T.H.M. and it took only a quick search of the roster to establish that Thompson had been using as his mouthpiece Thomas H. Merry, originally of Company L under the command of Captain Zabdiel Boylston Adams, but promoted to sergeant of Company M and then detached to serve under Major Thompson. Originally from New York, Merry had immigrated to California in 1850 and had been living in San Francisco when the war started, twenty-three years old and a college graduate. His letters described Major Thompson and "friends of the battalion in Washington" as working to sever its connection to the Second Massachusetts Cavalry. He claimed that if Hooker had remained in command, the California Battalion would already be "out of this detested regiment."

Merry's letters to the *Daily Alta California* alleged that from the moment the battalion crossed Panama in March 1863, it was consistently subjected to malice and injustice, the culprits being Governor Andrew and Massachusetts's governing officials, who had treated them "in a most niggardly and contemptible manner." After Lowell reorganized the regiment in August, the letters shifted to criticizing Colonel Lowell, who "has done all in his power to spite us, both officers and men."[2]

When Lowell finally confronted Thompson about the petition, Thompson at first claimed he had not heard of it until a month later, on November 27. Then he described earlier conversations with regimental officers in which the fact of the petition had been discussed, the earliest on November 2, three days after it was written. He explained, "I gave them [the reports he had heard] little thought as I was constantly engaged with my military duties and supposed they had been sent to the Secretary of War he would either approve or reject them and that would end the matter."[3] This was disingenuous. The chain of command required Thompson to report what he learned of the petition to Crowninshield, the acting commanding officer. The fact was, as Lowell learned from other sources, Thompson had been the force behind the petition, which had been circulated with sufficient secrecy that Crowninshield had had no hint of what was up. Caspar was now so mad that he wanted to personally punch Thompson. Charlie confessed to Henry Russell, his lieutenant-colonel in Boston, "I rather like the excitement."[4]

Crowninshield would ultimately prove to be consistently what he had shown himself to be at Ball's Bluff: a reliable and good officer. But his natural qualities of leadership, his impressive athleticism, and his easygoing disposition were marred by emotional immaturity, an overblown sense of entitlement, and intense ambition. He had left the Twentieth because he felt that his service at Ball's Bluff had not earned him the recognition he thought he deserved, and this sense of aggrievement had made him enemies. Now in the Second Massachusetts Cavalry he once again found potential threats to his advancement. The possibility that Henry Russell, the lieutenant-colonel, would join the regiment and thus rob him of his de facto command gnawed at Crowninshield, and his suspicion and distrust were excited by Major Thompson's oppositional and uncooperative behavior. (Crowninshield claimed in a letter of early August to his mother that officers older than he bore him no grudge. He was probably comparing the camaraderie of Captain Reed with the chilly reserve of Major Thompson.) Both Thompson and Crowninshield were ambitious for advancement and never bridged their rivalry.

Many of Merry's diatribes against Lowell applied more aptly to Crowninshield, pampered child of the Boston aristocracy, and this may explain why Crowninshield moved swiftly, insisting that Merry be separated from Thompson and returned to Vienna. Merry "has availed himself of opportunities to disturb the good order of the Regt," Crowninshield explained. "His continuance on Det[ached] Ser[vice] is undesirable."[5] Despite Thompson's protests, Lowell backed Crowninshield's demand: Merry was returned to his own company. But this was the strongest action taken. Lowell could not take either Thompson or Merry seriously.

Instead he focused on what he saw as the heart of the men's complaints. In mid-November he had made reforms, adding reserves to the pickets, enlarging the picket parties, and giving his less reliable troops, the Thirteenth New York Cavalry, more escort duty within the protected areas where no raids had occurred for some time. But he could lighten the men's work only so much without jeopardizing his effectiveness. Beyond this it was a matter of morale: he wanted more of the men to understand what Private Samuel Backus, a member of Company L like Merry, understood instinctively. Writing home at virtually the same time that the others were signing the petition,

Backus confirmed that the company suffered hardships both on scout and on picket duty, but he seemed immune to the grumbling. He took in stride the privations of weather and poor food. He ate what he could and slept when he could, even if that meant lying in cold mud and keeping hold of his horse's bridle. What the grumblers described as deliberate maneuvers against them, Backus took to be impersonal facts. More important, he believed there was a purpose behind Lowell's strict orders: "We have to do all this to keep from being taken by surprise by the rebs, who are always ready to take advantage of any chance that presents itself to pounce on us." What to the grumblers was gratuitous torment Backus believed was sensible caution. His respect for the Ranger menace did not preclude a healthy estimate of the regiment's success: "we have crippled the gang of Mosby more than any other troops ever did before."[6] Blessed with sturdy health and a balanced mind, instinctively grasping the essential nature of the business, Backus was the sort of trooper a colonel prayed for. Lowell knew such men were rare. But what did the most for regimental morale was the return from Washington of Mosby's deserter.

Charlie Binns was a resident of Falls Church (where the Union cavalry had its headquarters) and with his stepson had joined the Rangers in July 1863. While inebriated in November, he had committed "an act of rascality"[7] that was severe enough for Mosby, who usually offered his men considerable latitude, to order his arrest. Rather than face Mosby's punishment, Binns turned himself in at Vienna with an offer to serve as a guide in lieu of a prison term. Under close questioning, Binns revealed that the Rangers had no base camp, no headquarters. This explained why Lowell had failed to find it. Instead, they were scattered in a large number of safe houses around Aldie and west to the Blue Ridge, where they lived as sporadic boarders or spur-of-the-moment guests until the signal went out to gather for a raid.

Merry had written, "Let us fight the guerrillas our own way, either as we hunt Indians or at their own game of bushwhacking." Up until now Lowell had not seen how to make use of the Californians' experience with "Indian hunting" while avoiding a breakdown of discipline. Now he thought he did. If Charlie Binns's intelligence was dependable, the idea of sneaking up on the Rangers became a realistic possibility. Suspicion of Binns was strong, however, and one of Lowell's men was ordered to watch him at all times, with orders to shoot if it became clear Binns was leading them into an ambush.

With some apprehension, on November 18 Lowell sent out a scouting party of about one hundred men from the Second Massachusetts Cavalry under the command of Captain William M. Rumery, a Californian. Only twenty-five were mounted. Cavalrymen did not like being used as infantry, and the expedition set off with much grumbling. Moreover, they set out in "the very worst rain that ever brought into requisition India rubber overcoats and boots." A Massachusetts officer said it was "as cold as Christmas."[8]

The first night out Rumery plied Binns with whiskey, figuring that the influence of alcohol would encourage him to divulge information. But Rumery got drunk faster than Binns, and once their captain had passed out, two of the privates were able to smash the whiskey bottle. Thereafter the raiding of Rangers' homes went better. With Binns as their guide, they moved with stealth, sneaking up on and surrounding houses undetected. Rangers were captured in their sleep. "The application to their heads of a loaded revolver caused them to deliver up their firearms and themselves without making any disturbance,"[9] one trooper explained.

On the third day out the group met up with another hundred men under Lowell, well within the heart of Mosby's Confederacy, between Middleburg and Rector's Cross Road (Atoka). Rumery delivered his twenty-three prisoners and reported no casualties. On the strength of the intelligence gathered, Lowell divided his men into four parties to make another foray with orders to gather that evening at Mount Zion Church, near Aldie. Eighteen more Rangers were captured, one was killed, and one escaped. Also taken were seven smugglers and horse thieves; thirty horses were added to the command, about half with equipment—all this without loss or injury, save that one private guarding the prisoners accidentally shot himself when he slipped while leaning on his carbine. Despite this misfortune Lowell was pleased. More Rangers had been captured in this foray than in all the summer months combined, and most were from the original core of Rangers. In his report he praised Captain Rumery for his "great judgment" and recommended that Binns be kept as a government scout and paid accordingly.[10]

A few days later another scout using Binns started off with eighty Californians under the command of Captain Adams. They swept out beyond the Bull Run Mountains, then headed back down the Little River Turnpike to Aldie. There they turned north and followed the line of the mountains to Leesburg, returning south via the Leesburg Pike and Dranesville. In the first several houses raided they found no rebels. Finally one David Hixon, "one of the worst Desperadoes of Moseby's guerrillas," as one Californian wrote home, was found at his father's house in his large feather bed. (Hixon had been arrested several times and paroled from the Old Capitol Prison just as frequently.) The family burst into tears, the four daughters creating a Greek chorus of woe. But when the "plantation Negroes" learned of the capture, they "began clapping their hands and jumping for very joy, and begged us 'to take old masa too.' "[11] And so the Californians took the father of the family as well.

Binns next led them to a tannery. No rebels were found, but the Californians did find a Confederate warehouse and ate well. They then went to a house near Leesburg, where they captured two Rangers who were indignant at being surprised. The next house was the home of a Union man called Ellsworth, whose family was nonetheless "intensely Sesech." The house was searched with no success. Then a slave accepted the bribe of a "calico dress" and assured them that "Bill" was at home. Searching again, Binns took the lead. He crept up into the attic and found "Bill" wedged between the attic ceiling and the rafters. Once again the women of the family set up a barrage of tears and screams. The youngest and most beautiful ground her teeth and looked as "savage as a meat-axe" and kept saying, "Oh! If hate could kill!" The pro-Union father of this household bade his son adieu, saying, "I told you to keep out of the rebel service, but you would not mind me; now you are going to prison, and I don't want you to return till the war is over."

The Californians by now heartily approved of Binns. His information permitted them to travel at night, "so as to keep our approach from being known to the rebels and their sympathizers," and rest during the day. Binns led the Californians to believe that many of the men they found were lieutenants, or captains, or notorious Ranger officers. And yet they weren't. In some cases they weren't Rangers at all. The closest thing to a complete roster of the Rangers does not include any mention of a man named Ellsworth or of a number of other men captured. It is possible that this Bill Ellsworth abetted the Rangers in some ad hoc capacity, or was engaged in some other clandestine activity. Perhaps Binns deceived the Californians. He needed to keep his position as a valued guide, and the Rangers weren't being found in the numbers he had promised. (By unfortunate coincidence, Mosby and fifty of his men were south of Warrenton at the time.)[12]

There is no doubt that if the Californians had successfully captured Mosby and his five main captains in their beds, the Rangers would have been finished and the Second Massachusetts Cavalry famous forever. For a short time both officers and men believed that Binns had given them the wherewithal to finish off Mosby. One claimed that their successful captures left "Mosby but about twenty of his old men, and it will be impossible for him to get recruits enough to make up another effective gang."[13] But this was far from the case. Mosby had plenty of men left and no trouble recruiting more. But the success of the raids was not entirely a matter of captured Rangers. Binns identified the Rangers' safe houses even if they found no Rangers on their first attempts. And return they did. Regularly Lowell sent out scouts to disrupt the Rangers' sleep, and Mosby was forced to establish patrols within his Confederacy who were on the lookout for federal raiders. Late-night raids continued to catch more Rangers and sent many more shinnying down drainpipes and scurrying, half dressed, into haylofts. The "safe houses" were no longer safe.

The Union officers had known all along that Virginians were abetting the guerrillas and even riding with them on raids; now Binns put names and faces to these mysterious figures. With this greater familiarity came greater license. Over the next month they took horses, much needed by the regiment, almost without compunction. Pretty daughters still made appeals that horses be spared, and Captain Adams's "gallantry got the best of him" still, but the men were hardening their hearts. Firearms were confiscated, as well as cattle, chickens, turkeys, and sundry other items to aid the "comfort of our boy's 'inner man.' " The troopers wrote home about discovering storehouses of provisions intended for the rebel army. Happily the men loaded themselves with corncakes, butter, and apples. They described how, finding "no rebels . . . We did, however, find the pantry." One Californian absconded with "a handsome bed quilt with the United States coat of arms in each corner." Now, when they saw a good rail fence, they halted to use it to make their fires. On several occasions when Lowell accompanied a scout, he put strict limits on such foraging, posting guards around corncribs and such. These limits were not popular, and the men were not deterred—they tried to dig under, abandoning the effort only because it was too difficult.[14]

Given the nature of their work, broken into small details and requiring interaction with locals, the men had innumerable other temptations—some petty, some grave—for avoiding duty and getting into trouble. To disguise forbidden activity—drinking, whoring, gambling, illegally trading in guns and horses—any number of excuses could be given: a delayed patrol, a few lost hours on scout, or a detour required to meet an escort. But equally often the motive for avoiding work was innocent: to enjoy a home-cooked meal, to savor the ambiance of home life, to escape momentarily the routine of camp life and all-male conversation. One trooper, a trumpeter, took a shine to a local lady who was musical; they sang duets together, and he was delighted to attend her wedding.

For such reasons the men preferred active duty to camp, with its repetitive and boring routine. The worst challenges to morale came at payday. With money in their pockets the men gambled till their pockets were empty. As long as they could pay for it, whiskey was irresistible and could be obtained from sutlers despite regulations to the contrary.

Charles A. Humphreys, the young regimental chaplain, tried to contain the damage of payday: he arranged to have regular sums sent home, partly for the benefit of families and partly so that the money ran out sooner. But the chaplain, in a revealing admission, insisted that the officers needed to take the lead. He reported at least two instances of officers "intoxicated when on duty."[15] Humphreys was also troubled by the prevalence of swearing and the degree to which the men had perfected that art. Under especially arduous circumstances, an enlisted man could incorporate five or six allusions to one or another version of the Almighty in a single sentence. Horses were the usual object of these fulminations on the injustices of life as lived by the troopers of the Second Massachusetts Cavalry. And after a trooper had exhausted his imagination, cursing his way out of a bad mood or a problem, the opportunity presented itself to start all over again as a form of humor or jesting, with other troopers an all-too-willing audience for such performances.

Humphreys rather tartly pointed out to Lowell that in this matter the officers were no better than the men. Officers cursed not only horses but men, especially their servants. Lowell conceded as much. Swearing was a pervasive problem, and he was not blameless himself. No longer was his favorite expostulation, "By Plato!" And breaking himself of the habit was harder than he had anticipated. He did not throw his full weight behind this effort: the eradication of profanity did not take pride of place.

The troops did, of course, have legitimate pastimes. Humphreys ran a large and wide-ranging camp library. There were no end of card and board games to play. Inevitably horses dominated the men's leisure as well as their work. The drudgery of horse maintenance was cursed, the responsibility resented, and yet the power and speed of a fine horse, the prowess or skill at subduing and training one, provoked universal interest, and discussions of horses and their management went on ad infinitum. Officers and men devoted most of their free time to horse races, with at least one or two a day. Company competed against company, and Company A, the California Hundred, almost always won.

Officers also competed, but not against the men. Lowell was the hands-down winner. He had the ideal cavalryman's build and could make the most of any horse, even the sorry nags that passed for government horses. Will Forbes explained, "He is so light that no one can fairly run against him." Men like Eigenbrodt and Manning and Reed were mature, thickly muscled men, too large and heavy for horse racing, and all the California captains had the disadvantage of having only government horses, since they lacked the connections to acquire admirable steeds privately. Forbes took considerable trouble to get good horses, and Lowell was covetous of them. Forbes had a handsome thoroughbred, flighty and strong willed, that jumped well but needed training. It proved too difficult for Forbes to handle, and Lowell successfully traded for it. The truth was that Forbes was too big for any horse — he would never get the best out of one. Crowninshield, too, was too big to win races, though this did not prevent him from horse mania. He had a large, strong sorrel stallion, Jim, that could carry him. Jim had once knocked him "almost senseless," had "nearly killed" his orderly, and on another occasion had broken a sergeant's leg. Lowell liked difficult horses and believed that unless they initially resisted, showing a healthy dose of high-spiritedness, he could have no faith in them.[16]

John Murray Forbes came for a long visit over Thanksgiving. He stayed in his son's tent, taking the bed while Will slept on the floor. Quite a few of the officers enjoyed quail shooting, and some of the captains took Forbes hunting with a "couple of armed orderlies and a couple of pointers." Because they rarely hunted beyond "neutral ground," little was ever shot. More successful were riding expeditions. One trip to Fairfax Court House included Lowell, Effie, Will Forbes and his father, along with the ubiquitous orderlies. They rode cross-country, "jumping brooks, wading swamps, galloping and scurrying," Forbes reported to his wife. The countryside was beautiful, with open fields and cleared woods. Effie, on Berold, was full of spirit. They got home in time for tea at sundown. Forbes thought Lowell's headquarters was a modest place with "one good parlor, made cheery with red curtains."[17]

Most officers smoked, believing it was a preventive for malaria, and it probably did keep mosquitoes away. Major Crowninshield and Captain Louis Cabot were fond of an evening cigar. They worried about their investments in the war economy, and several, with the aid of family hampers filled with books, set their own course of reading. Forbes, Reed, Humphreys, and Crowninshield formed an officers' quartet to which they devoted a huge portion of their free time. Will had his sister Alice send sheet music. Reed was already friendly with Crowninshield and the circle of Boston officers who had served on detachment with him. Now he got to know Forbes, who, thanks to his natural amiability, forged ties with Californians like George Manning, William Rumery, Rufus Smith, John W. Sim, and others who, of an evening, gathered around a huge blazing log to sing old songs and learn new ones. The German, French, and Irish soldiers sang their own songs and the Americans joined in. The eastern boys learned songs from the mines, songs from Alta California, and songs from the long overland journey, while many of the songs picked up from sailors were known by all.

Singing often dissolved into storytelling, with the Californians taking the lead. Tales of following the Overland Trail and gold mining became favorites. Reed told of his time among the Indians of the Pacific Northwest. Some of these stories were true, but the Californians were great braggarts, and many of the Boston men found it hard to believe some of the tales, however much they enjoyed the telling. Still, the Californians had seen the world, and their life experiences opened up new vistas to the young easterners.

Not only tales of adventure but differences in demeanor intrigued the Massachusetts men. They were impressed by the Californian "habit of saying just what they mean and pretty much what they please." California flamboyance extended to dress. Although on parade the Californians wore their uniforms with dignity, the rest of the time their eccentricities were given full rein, with "Scotch caps, some dress caps; some dressed in ragged overalls, some in stable frocks—once white—and some in jackets."[18] But the most distinguishing feature was the black felt slouch hat, which they preferred to the more military forage cap. The Bostonian officers either wore government-issue uniforms, as Lowell did, or uniforms made by their private tailors, as Crowninshield did.

Thanksgiving was a festive occasion. The chaplain brought the text of Edward Everett's address at Gettysburg the week before; this, rather than Lincoln's shorter speech, was being widely read and considered. But the perfect late autumn day—bright, clear, and sunny—was not a serious one. The morning involved horse races, and then the Massachusetts officers dined by invitation with the California officers, who told or retold stories of western exploits for the elder Forbes's benefit. In the afternoon yet more racing took place. Company A, the California Hundred, won.

Unfortunately not even holidays and music did enough to strengthen the overall cohesion of the regiment. In regular soldiering, for men engaged in skirmishes and battles with a clear enemy, regimental solidarity gave some solace. A regiment's status in the larger army structure gave its men an identity and a context in which to set their difficult work. But Lowell's brigade had neither of these luxuries. Frustrated by an enemy who could not be found, or engaged, and was glimpsed only as peaceable citizenry until, with an ambush, he struck with deadly force and without a clear identity, Lowell's discontented men believed they had the worst post in the entire Union army.

As Lowell persisted in sending his scouting parties to Ranger safe houses, Mosby took his revenge, starting in December, by targeting the regiment's vedettes and picket stations. On the night of December 9 some twenty-five Rangers approached the Tyson's Corner crossroads picket post. When the guards ordered them to halt and give the password, they claimed to know it—and by this ruse got close enough to charge. But the trick was on them. The men in the vedette, showing their "Yankee ingenuity," had strung telegraph wire across the road at a height that would knock a man off his horse. When the Rangers charged, they hit the wire and were thrown from their horses: they suffered casualties and, worse, a deep wound to their pride.

The next day, December 10, Major Thompson notified Lowell that four men stationed at Muddy Branch had robbed a home and deserted on December 3. The goods were recovered from their hiding place in a haystack, but the men were not. They had told locals they intended to join Mosby. Major Thompson warned, "They are very smart men and dangerous men if they get with Mosbys gang they will—if they are disposed—be very troublesome."[19] Embittered members of the regiment deserting to Mosby posed a huge danger to the success and the safety of the Union forces. Lowell had been after Mosby long enough to have learned how important deserters and informants were to his success.

We have no evidence that any of the four men reached Mosby. This is significant, because if Mosby had wanted them to reach him, he would have arranged it. Four Union deserters, without arms or funds in territory hostile to them, telling locals of their desire to join him (no doubt in an attempt to avoid whatever summary justice awaited them), could have been picked up by Mosby in a matter of hours.

That evening, December 10, about thirty guerrillas attacked the Lewinsville picket station, which was manned by six troops. Misled by a pro-

Union local, the Rangers did not realize that there was a reserve of an additional fifteen Union men in the woods. Since the complaints of late October, Lowell had made improvements in the picket detail, doubling the number of men and providing a reserve of fifteen men camped in the woods. Thus the Rangers attacking the picket post were unprepared when the reserve picket emerged from the woods and began to fight. Once the Rangers began to take casualties, they fled. In the fracas, however, the officer in charge of the reserve was thrown from his horse, and without his direction his men failed to pursue.

On December 13 the Germantown picket post was caught by surprise when about twenty Rangers crawled up and, without warning, opened fire at close quarters. Two men were killed, four horses taken. Pickets, at least with regular armies in conventional fighting, functioned as territorial markers, not as targets. It was considered murderous and cowardly to treat them as the latter, and at least one enlisted man wanted to see any rebel carrying arms caught near a picket station "hung to the nearest tree. Woe be to the one that should be caught by us!"[20] Despite Lowell's reforms the men still could have no fires, and after the long cold nights dawn came as a welcome relief. The men could move back to the road, light a fire, thaw out, and get some sleep. It did not help that Virginia was experiencing one of its coldest winters.

Another rash of picket attacks took place on December 20, notably one against a post at Hunter's Mill, manned by members of Company E. They stood their ground for some time despite being badly outnumbered, but eventually they were forced to retreat, leaving behind two men wounded (one was thought dead, having been shot in the head). As the Rangers gathered their booty and seized their prisoner, the picket reserve turned out, and this time they did pursue. Seeing this larger force, the rebels fled. Instead of simply abandoning the prisoner, Oscar Burnap from Company E, a Ranger shot him in the chest at close range. The bullet missed his heart by an inch; he lived to tell what had happened to him, and through the regiment passed a wave of indignation and revulsion. One Californian observed, "The step from a traitor to a murderer seems to be easily taken."[21]* Two more men de-

---

*By the end of 1863 General Lee had concurred with the Confederate secretary of war's intention to disband all guerrilla units or incorporate them into the army. When Mosby learned of Lee's recommendation, he went to Richmond to plead his case. The result was that while all other partisan groups were mustered into the Confederate army, a tentative exemption was made for Mosby. He had survived, but only just.

serted in December, one from Company I, the other from Forbes's Company B.

On Christmas Eve two more picket posts were attacked, but Lowell had dismounted the advance pickets, and there were no horses to steal. On Christmas Day, after shooting matches, games, and the typical Christmas dinner, Lowell sent out a small scout with Binns to Leesburg. They returned December 27 with eight prisoners, and the next day Lowell led a scout divided into three separate parties. They returned December 31, having netted thirty-odd prisoners and ten citizens. General Halleck spent the New Year with Lowell's brigade at Vienna and was there to witness the return of these successful scouts.

On January 7, 1864, a Springfield man in Company K, John Parks, deserted. On January 11 John Jones, a Californian of Company E stationed at Muddy Branch, deserted. Then on January 14 the Vienna camp was raided by Rangers and seventeen horses were taken. The manner of the raid indicated that the Rangers had had a guide. Fortunately all they wanted was horses, but the seed for potential disaster had been planted. With an insider's knowledge of the Union camp, Mosby would have the capacity to inflict significant casualties. He had recently used information supplied by an escaped prisoner to raid the headquarters near Harpers Ferry of Major Henry Cole, whose battalion was the only other unit assigned to counter Mosby. Lowell respected Cole's loyal local men highly. Luckily the attempt had been foiled by an especially alert sentry, but it indicated Mosby's ambitions and audacity. It was curious that Mosby used his guide to Lowell's camp only to steal horses: why didn't he attempt more? Perhaps the Vienna camp was too large, the defeat against Cole too fresh. Still, Vienna was vulnerable. Cole ran a sleek operation, but Lowell's three brigades were hardly sleek.

On January 15 William Harris of Melrose, another member of Forbes's company, deserted. It was getting colder and colder. And on January 24 Private William E. Ormsby of Company E of the California Battalion, assigned to picket duty at Lewinsville, made one round and disappeared, absconding with two of the regiment's best horses, their accoutrements, and two Colt revolvers. Search parties failed to find him. His desertion was duly recorded. Things were quiet for two weeks until on February 4 John Hayes, a Boston recruit to the California Hundred freshly arrived, also deserted.

The next day a scouting party under the command of Captain Reed returned to camp very early in the morning with Private Ormsby, his arms tied behind his back, his feet tied to the saddle girth. He was dressed in "full rebel uniform." Reed's small advance party had been passing Aldie Mill when it was ambushed. As the main body of Reed's men rode up, the Rangers realized they were outmanned, and all fled but one, who lingered long enough to shoot at Sergeant Benjamin F. Partridge. As the man rode off, however, his horse stumbled while leaping a ditch. He climbed free and ran off on foot, but Sergeant Partridge ran him down and confirmed what he had suspected: the "Ranger" was William Ormsby. By this time both men had already emptied their pistols, but Partridge held his empty pistol in Ormsby's face, threatening him for some time, until Reed and others intervened.

As the news of Ormsby's recapture flew around the Vienna camp, the men stopped what they were doing and gathered in groups to discuss it. The mood became volatile. Attempts to impose order were ignored. Lowell immediately ordered a drumhead court-martial. Convened whenever a commander deemed it necessary, this procedure was intended to deal with extreme or unusual circumstances and emergencies in the field but was a dubious form of justice, compromising legal niceties in the interest of speed. Stripping down the regular court-martial panel to the minimum three officers needed to proceed, Lowell detailed Major Frazar of the Thirteenth New York Cavalry and Captain Adams of Company L, with Major Forbes presiding. Lieutenant Lewis Dabney was appointed judge advocate. Ormsby requested that the chaplain defend him. The charges included desertion, delivering himself and his arms and horses to the enemy, and, most important, treason: he had been captured "dressed in Rebel uniform and armed and in the act of using his arms against the United States." Within two hours of Ormsby's return to camp, the court convened. For three hours, while the court-martial panel heard testimony and deliberated in private, the regiment awaited the verdict in a state of suspended shock. Lowell made sure a complete transcript was made of his order for the court-martial and for its proceedings—the only such record for the entire war.[22]

Who was William Ormsby? What led to this event? Born somewhere between 1843 and 1848 in Massachusetts, he was in Colesburg, Iowa, in 1861, where he joined a mule train to California. In April 1863, only marginally underage, he enlisted in Company E of the California Battalion. After the battalion was moved to Vienna, Ormsby volunteered to be the mail carrier, making the round-trip journey between Alexandria and Vienna every other day, the regiment's very own Pony Express. In this independent position he had ample opportunity to rub shoulders with locals and occasionally be chased by Mosby's men. "Pony" Ormsby stood only five foot three and was, even among the Californians, recognized as an accomplished horseman; hence his nickname.

Ormsby's migratory and highly independent life from a youthful age had not severed all family connections. He had been trying to see his brother when, in early November, he received a three-day pass to Arlington. His troubles began when he returned to camp with a bad horse, and his commanding officer, Captain Eigenbrodt, at the urging of Sergeant Partridge, brought charges against Ormsby for horse-trading. He was arrested and confined in the guardhouse to await trial on November 16. For a variety of bureaucratic reasons that earlier court-martial panel failed to convene until December 16. At his trial Ormsby did not deny that he had made a trade or that his new horse was of poor quality, but he insisted that he had made the trade because his own horse had had an injured foot and a cold—which was plausible, given the shabby state of most government horses and the poor care they received. He claimed that he had had only two hours left on his pass, and knowing his horse could not carry him home in that time, he had traded with a "nigger" who gave him a bad horse but one that would make the journey. It was therefore his desire to comply with orders and to return to camp on time, Ormsby explained, that had forced him to trade his horse at a disadvantage.[23]

Horse-trading was ubiquitous. When the circumstances were beneficial to the U.S. government, it was overlooked, though usually soldiers traded their horses and their guns for inferior horses, making up the difference in cash. Many cavalry regimental order books contained threats that men caught trading horses "and receiving return money" would be immediately transferred to the infantry. Ormsby's trade had included fifteen dollars.

His punishment—being docked three months' pay and assigned to one month of extra duty—was harsh, especially considering that he had already spent a month in the guardhouse. But the horse shortage that the entire Union cavalry was suffering that winter—hoof-and-mouth disease was rampant—helps to explain the anger of the officers. Punishments generally were severe, particularly those meted out by sergeants. One private was hung by the thumbs, another was tied hand and feet to a post, yet another confined to a slave pen—all for what the men considered the crime of disobeying petty orders, such as a refusal to muck out the stables or to perform other unpleasant but necessary camp duties. Usually what lay behind such incidents was a power struggle—either a sergeant wishing to force acknowledgment of his authority or privates unwilling to do so. We can best understand Lowell's willingness to "give the private the benefit of the doubt" in the context of these conflicts. In any event, Ormsby had suffered through the month of extra duty. Then he deserted, not impulsively but in a well-planned escape in the wee hours of January 24.

As the men waited on the court, there was considerable sympathy for Ormsby, given the harsh sentence he had been given in December. They considered the injustice, like their more general complaints, as part of the social combat between enlisted men and officers. The fantasy of shooting one's sergeant is perhaps a sine qua non of soldiering. Equally believable was the less amusing possibility that if caught after attempting to do so, one's sergeant would indeed blow one's head off. A mixture of envy and sympathy for Ormsby was palpable. Ormsby had appeared pretty drunk when he was brought into camp. He had, in his own defense, claimed to be "so drunk I couldn't see nothing at all" and "could scarcely stand up." Another rumor had it that a woman was involved—the chaplain made allusions to "the blandishments of the Southern Beauty." Had he deserted to protest his harsh treatment, or to go after a girl? Had he sold out his company in revenge, or because he was too drunk to think clearly? Had Mosby captured him, or had he sought him out? Was there malice in his behavior, or had Ormsby stumbled into his treason? So the men debated among themselves.[24]

Company E was a hard-driving, no-nonsense unit that fought hard, was widely respected, and had good morale; it had the lowest rate of desertion in the regiment. Yet there had been trouble in Company E, and Captain Eigenbrodt had long been frustrated by the elusive Mosby. Vulnerable to Thompson's cabals of discontent, members of that company were among those who had signed the petition of October 29 requesting to be transferred from the regiment. But when their petition failed, with Thompson and Merry at least momentarily cowed and with Lowell's modifications in the schedule, most of the men of Company E accepted their lot and settled down. Still, even those who continued to resent their work and their colonel believed a huge gulf divided their discontent from treason, particularly helping Mosby, a man they had learned to hate as a coward, a thief, a scoundrel, and a murderer. Even less palatable was the idea of betraying one's own company. Although Partridge was a tough sergeant, many of the men wished there had been a bullet in his empty pistol.

Before the court the facts of the case were not disputed, but the facts played differently among the officers. Speaking in his own defense, Ormsby explained, "I had no idea of leaving this place to join any rebel command at all." His intention had been to go home and see his parents, more specifically to meet his mother in New York. He admitted to taking the horses so as to sell them to raise the money to get north. He claimed that before this plan was put into effect, three of Mosby's men found him at Aldie, took his horses and his guns, and left him "with a widow lady" at Middleburg. Then they reappeared and took him to somewhere near Aldie. But Ormsby also mentioned that he "was acquainted down there with some ladies. I was going down to see them." On the way he was distracted by an invitation to get some liquor. He and another young man went off and got drunk. He claimed that it was while returning from this binge that he had accidentally run into Mosby's men, just as Reed showed up. It was no ambush at all, only an astounding coincidence. He had been firing at the rebels, not at his sergeant, and his flight, first on horseback and then on foot, was made in the confusion of drink. The horse and weapons he had when captured had been given him by his drinking buddy.

Ormsby was hoping the court would conclude that it was all a big mistake. He presented himself as a decent man wanting to see his mother, waylaid by Mosby, corrupted by drink, subject to bad luck. The few unintentional shots fired off happened, by pure coincidence, to be in the direction of his former sergeant. This tale was almost credible, particularly for those officers who could not bear to confront the motives behind treason. But unfortunately Ormsby did not end his testimony there. He admitted to having seen Mosby twice. He acknowledged that Mosby had promised him either a pass into Texas or safe passage across the Potomac at Point of Rocks. In a rush of contrition he confessed, "I know I done wrong and I'm sorry for it and I think I was always counted a sober man when I was here and always done my duty very well."[25]

Which of Ormsby's various motives and versions of events was to be believed? Why, the officers wondered, would Mosby have made such promises? He and his Rangers were used to robbing federal soldiers without a backward glance. Ormsby must have offered more. Ormsby claimed that it was only accidentally that the Rangers ran into Lowell's men, which was probably true, since Ormsby could not have known Reed's route, but the officers concluded that Mosby had intended to use Ormsby to get into the Vienna camp or possibly one of the picket posts.

No one on the court-martial panel doubted that Ormsby had deliberately shot at his own sergeant and company, contrary to his claim of its being accidental. And although no one mentioned that only an empty pistol saved Ormsby's life, the officers were well aware of the fact. But they sympathized with Partridge: simply by enforcing army regulations, each of them had given more than one enlisted man a reason for wishing them dead. Nothing brought the point home quite so clearly. At 8 a.m. the court returned a unanimous verdict of guilty.

By the book, the next step was to forward the court's verdict to Washington by telegraph, with the prisoner following under armed escort. There the appropriate punishment would be determined and carried out. Desertion and treason merited death unless, of course, Ormsby was pardoned. President Lincoln had a reputation for generous pardons, particularly of deserters and particularly for crimes committed under the influence of alcohol. Lowell ordered the court to reconvene at seven-thirty the next morning. The postponement of the sentence for a day may have been a tactic to ensure Ormsby's safety until he left for Washington, but Lowell was also buying himself some time to consider his course of action.

Neither desertion nor summary execution was rare: each corps in the Army of the Potomac had its own gallows, and by the winter of 1863–64 desertion rates were high enough that an execution took place almost every Friday. Not every deserter was executed, but the punishment was meted out to teach the men a lesson or to put on a brake when the steady trickle of desertion increased to rates the commanding officers found intolerable. And desertion rates among the Second Massachusetts Cavalry were at their highest.[26]

According to army regulations, a summary execution was justified only when it was impossible to carry out the usual protocol. But what could be justified in the Army of the Tennessee could not in the Defenses of Washington, since only a scant seventeen-mile ride would bring the court-martial findings from the latter to army headquarters. Lowell knew that he would be violating military law if he carried out the execution in Vienna and that he could himself be court-martialed. His experience in Boston had shown him that there was a broad consensus among the powerful to support decisive if brutal action against insubordinate soldiers, and he may have believed that he was not taking a great risk. He probably felt he had an ironclad case: Ormsby was a traitor. For troops engaged in counterguerrilla warfare, such behavior was beyond the pale, and Lowell believed he could defend himself on that point.

Nevertheless Lowell was putting his career on the line. Why was he willing to risk so much to carry out a summary execution? In his working life he had shown a "common touch" that had won him the respect and admiration of the men who worked under him. Time and again he had shown a tolerance for the "learning curve." In his troubles with Thompson and Merry, he had remained remarkably sanguine. He was generally recognized to be harsh but fair. Yet Lowell—so rational in most situations, so generous with the enemy—was hotheaded when his authority was challenged from within. Something about insubordination drove him to a particular fury. The year before, he had tried a man for desertion, hoping to discourage bounty-jumpers. Then he had killed a man while trying to quell a mutiny. And now he was on the verge of taking unequivocal action again. In each of these situations Lowell acted against someone who, he believed, had failed to meet the demands of his situation, had failed to achieve the necessary sublimation of the self to society's larger demands—which for Lowell was second nature.

Lowell's large New England family had fostered strength of character, powers of leadership, great independence of judgment, and an identity that was essentially corporate. When faced with Ormsby and his heedless, reckless, unthinking endangerment of the brigade, Lowell suffered a failure of sympathy. (One is reminded of Patrick Tracy Jackson's reaction to Lowell's father's foolhardiness at the Lycoming Coal Company: the more he tried to understand, the further he traveled from empathy.) Ormsby's behavior was beyond his comprehension. Did he see an aspect of his own rebellious self in this young man? Was it horror at rediscovering his old rage, only now with the roles reversed, himself now the authority figure? Lowell's own childhood dreams of mutiny expressed feelings so powerful and dangerous that he had had no means of recognizing them.

Certainly what Lowell told himself, or Effie, or anyone who cared to ask, was that he wished to use Ormsby as an example for the brigade. The rash of winter desertions carried with it a host of new rumors of betrayal. Proof was not positive, but Mosby's successful raid on the Vienna horse line could have succeeded only with insider knowledge. The attack on Major Cole's headquarters had certainly been based on detailed knowledge of the camp. Whether out of venality or stupidity Ormsby put the safety of the brigade at risk, and Lowell would not tolerate that. He believed that no one was more important than the greater good. If Willy, and Jim, and Stephen Perkins, and Jim Savage, and Rob Shaw had all been sacrificed, then William

"Pony" Ormsby would have to be sacrificed, too. Lowell recognized the vast distinction between self-sacrifice and sacrifice, but he believed that an officer's duty was to take responsibility for the sacrifice of men.

What Lowell could not have anticipated was Ormsby's willingness to cooperate in making precisely the point Lowell wanted to impress upon the brigade. At seven-thirty the next morning, a Sunday, the court reconvened to hear the sentence. Lowell ordered Ormsby "shot to death with musketry," with the entire brigade witnessing the event. Humphreys, the regimental chaplain who had served as defense counsel, delivered the news to Ormsby, whose first reaction was relief that he was to escape hanging. All morning the chaplain and the condemned man remained in conference. As he recalled it forty years later, Humphreys considered it "the hardest duty that ever fell to my lot." Ormsby was a callow youth, he thought, who had led a thoughtless life devoid of good judgment, sound principles, or even a sense of propriety, and now he was having to face the consequences of his actions in the harshest way possible.[27]

By midday the entire brigade was assembled in a large field forming three sides of a hollow square. Into this square marched the regimental band playing a funeral dirge, and a cart bearing the coffin, the condemned man, and the chaplain. Ormsby and the chaplain got down from the cart and walked the last short distance. Some in the regiment thought Ormsby was moving with "firm and steady step," but Humphreys recalled that Ormsby leaned heavily on his arm and "leaned still more closely on my faith." At the center of the square the wagon halted, and Ormsby helped to unload his coffin.[28]

The band ceased playing. The charge, the conviction, and the sentence were read out. Ormsby was given a chance to say some last words. He stepped forward. Turning to Captain Eigenbrodt, he asked his former captain to forgive him. "I am guilty and my punishment is just." Twisting to face the whole regiment, he told them to take warning from him. "I want you to know that I did not desert because I didn't believe in our cause. I know it is right. And it is right that I should die for deserting it."[29]

Then he spoke of his sure sense that the Union would win. He believed that soon the Stars and Stripes would once again float over the entire nation. With that he said good-bye.

The silence in the field was palpable. Humphreys said a prayer, commended the condemned man to the mercy of God, bound his eyes with a handkerchief, shook his hand, and said, "Now, die like a man."[30]

Ormsby sat down on his coffin, placed his hand upon his heart, and, patting the target pinned over it, said, "Boys, I hope you fire well."[31]

Six men, Californians all, aimed Sharps carbines at him, of which only five were loaded. The sergeant gave the order, and at half past twelve in the afternoon he was shot twice in the left breast. Ormsby was dead. The field was silent. The courage and patriotism of the condemned man had transformed the moment into something both terrible and beautiful. The entire brigade was stunned.

Slowly the burial detail came forward and began to dig Ormsby's grave. Slowly the brigade, man by man, marched past the stricken body and dispersed back to their tents. Ormsby was buried on the site of his execution in an unmarked grave, as befitted a traitor and a deserter. Yet it was universally agreed that his last words were completely unanticipated and transformed the event: contempt for the feckless youth became something like awe. A fellow member of Company E approached the chaplain, wondering what he had said to convince Ormsby to speak as he had. Humphreys rejected any credit, saying that it was the "awful presence of death" that had brought forth Ormsby's eloquence and bravery. "Whole years of thoughtless wandering and heedless sin" were sloughed off in Ormsby's last hours, in which he achieved "marvelous insight." The regiment recognized what they believed to be redemption. The young man had seized the moment almost as assuredly as Shaw had. He had embraced his own death, turning execution into self-sacrifice, and in the eeriest way possible, he had died for the cause he was being executed for having betrayed.

Will Forbes had served on the panel of both courts-martial, had heard all the testimony, and bore no little responsibility both for the delays in Ormsby's first trial and for the harshness of the sentence. During the second trial he heard Ormsby's affecting confession. For the rest of his life he referred to Ormsby's execution as "the most sickening experience of [my] army life" (five months of which were later spent in open stockade prison camps similar to Andersonville but farther south). Among enlisted men the event was noted in diaries, and Ormsby's bravery at the last was remarked on. Otherwise remarkably little was said. Valorus Dearborn, the Californian born in Maine, spoke for all, with a mastery of understatement typical of his native state: "Sad, sad, indeed."[32]

SEVENTEEN

FIGHTING THE GRAY GHOST

Spring 1864

The reaction in Washington was almost exactly as Lowell had imagined. Not only was there no severe reprimand, but the Ormsby matter was completely ignored. However momentous an event it had been for the members of the Second Massachusetts Cavalry, it was of no consequence to the War Department. When Lowell did receive departmental word two days later, it was orders to report to the Cavalry Bureau on temporary duty. Here were the cushy winter quarters he had coveted for Effie and himself in September, a comfort he had feared, even presumed, he might lose.

During Lowell's last weekend at Vienna in late February, he sent out Captain Reed, commanding the First Battalion, including Company A, and accompanied by Charlie Binns, with a "roving commission" to travel wherever he wanted in search of guerrillas. Meanwhile the rest of the camp participated in field sports in celebration of Washington's birthday: sack races and horse races. Come evening, with the games over, Lowell left for Giesboro and Forbes took Effie for a short ride, returning to camp at sundown. Almost immediately two men rode up "looking pale as death" and gave news of an ambush just outside the town of Dranesville on the Leesburg Pike, saying the men had been "cut to pieces" and "scattered in every direction."[1]

Forbes gathered some men and immediately rode up to Dranesville. He had with him Chaplain Humphreys, Dr. DeWolf, and a wagon for the wounded. On their way they encountered Reed's men, who had fled the ambush and taken to the woods, singly or in small groups. Each man who turned up gave new details of the disaster. All agreed that Reed was certainly dead.

Taking with him one of the survivors, Will Forbes led the party on to Dranesville. The cold weather had broken and the night was warm, the moon was large, the sky clear, so the road was illuminated almost as brightly as in daytime. They arrived at the spot, two miles beyond Dranesville, where

Mosby and the Rangers had ambushed the men, deserted now except for the dead and dying. They found Captain Reed and eight men dead. Reed had been stripped of his uniform; his horse, accoutrements, and one of his revolvers were gone. He wore only his long underwear. He had been shot in the arm and, at close range, in the eye. His face was largely destroyed. As the silver-white moonlight shone down on his stripped body, surrounded by the curious and nonsensical debris of a skirmish, Forbes recalled the sound of Reed's tenor voice singing his part in their quartet.

The cries of the wounded did not permit him to linger over this morbid memory. He ordered the dead to be loaded onto the open wagon while the doctor tended to the eight wounded men. Forbes sent a man around to the nearest farm to appropriate some kind of cart or wagon for them. Most of the wounded had been thrown from their horses, and their legs were badly broken. Even loading them into the cart was difficult, and they "screamed with agony."[2] Two dying men were left on the field, the doctor believing it would be inhumane to submit them to the journey.

Forbes walked the skirmish ground with George Buhrer of Company C, who had been in the advance party and had escaped. He questioned him closely. Buhrer admitted that Reed had had no thought "of danger." They "had too much confidence in the absence of Rebels and were marching along in route style, without special caution." The men in the rear were straggling badly, so Captain Manning rode to the rear to urge Lieutenant Dabney "to keep the men closed up." He paused to light a cigar and glance at his watch, then rode up to the head of the column and barely had reached his place when the advance party was attacked.[3]

While Manning had been in the rear, the sixteen-man advance party, with Reed and Binns in command, had spotted three Rangers up ahead and had ridden on some forty yards to capture them when a larger group of Rangers, their decoy successful, attacked and surrounded the advance guard. Binns was a marked man and only death awaited him if captured. There was nothing to do but charge right through the guerrillas, which a few, including Binns and Reed and Buhrer, managed to do. Buhrer was thrown from his horse but without injury, and he ran for cover in the woods.

Captain Manning with the main body, meanwhile, came under attack from the right and prepared to receive a charge. But none came. Instead, the Rangers, well hidden in the woods and never showing themselves, poured a murderous fire on Manning's men. They received four volleys of fire "standing in line. Not a man had broken from the ranks."[4] Manning's horse was hit and collapsed, got up, and then rolled into the ditch on the side of the road, with Manning pinned under it. Manning lost consciousness and did not come to until the fight was over and he was a prisoner.

Reed tried to rally his unnerved men, but the detail of the Sixteenth New York broke and scattered, exacerbating the confusion by firing randomly in all directions. Dabney's straggling men in the rear fled en masse. (The Rangers laughed at them, thinking the soldiers were so frightened that they had jumped into the river and drowned, but Dabney's men in fact swam the Potomac and arrived without loss at Muddy Branch.) Reed and a small party of men continued to fight.

Then, as if the day hadn't had enough surprises, Reed was charged by what could only be described as a renegade Saracen. Mounted on a heavy gray stallion, dressed in a gray suit with a massive slouch hat plumed with feathers, a dark, swarthy man careened toward him, whirling swords in each hand, screaming German curses. In the face of this extraordinary apparition, Reed, who was wounded in the arm, made a gesture that appeared to be signaling surrender and perhaps was. The renegade Saracen in any case took it as surrender and signaled Reed to go to the rear, then continued on into the fight. As he turned his back, Reed shot him. Another guerrilla then shot Reed in the eye, and he died instantly. This final encounter had been with Baron von Massow, son of the chamberlain to the King of Prussia, who survived his wounding to become a future chief of cavalry in the Imperial German Army.[5]

With Manning trapped under his horse, Reed killed, and most of the men having fled, Buhrer decided it was time he fled, too, and took off through the woods, emerging only when he saw Forbes riding toward Dranesville. Forbes did not learn how the skirmish ended, but he could well imagine. Without officers, the men could have continued to fight for only a short time, and most likely anyone who hadn't fled by then was taken prisoner and was now well on his way to a Confederate prison. All that was left were dead horses, some destroyed fencing, blood-soaked grass, and the odd buckle, button, or remnant of clothing. As they made their way back to camp along roads rutted and pitted from the cold winter, the wagons were jolted and "the cries of the wounded were excruciating."[6] One soldier died before camp was reached at midmorning.

The next day Captain Adams headed back to Dranesville hoping to learn more, to discover the fate of the two men left behind, to find stragglers and other wounded men, and to recover horses. On his way he picked up reports that the rebels, some "three hundred strong . . . were waiting to give us a warm reception." Having only a small detail with him, Adams did not consider it safe to continue and he returned to camp, where the story of the ambush was pieced together. Of some 125 men sent out on the scout, only 40 returned to Vienna. With 9 killed and 8 wounded, the rest were presumed captured. Captain George Manning and his brother, Lieutenant William Manning, both respected Californians, were beyond doubt prisoners; some 68 enlisted men were missing and assumed to be prisoners. The *Washington Star*, in an account of the disaster two days after the event, reported that 50 to 75 prisoners had been taken. Adding a last-minute news flash, the papers reported Dabney's escape and the safe arrival, after swimming the river, of 42 men at Muddy Branch. Adjusting the figures, they claimed that "not more than twenty prisoners" remained in rebel hands. The real number was 26.

Humiliated, a member of Company A admitted, "We have been licked like the devil." Dranesville had been a disaster for the entire regiment. The remaining Californians discovered that the grief and depression of the Massachusetts soldiers were equal to their own. The chaplain noted that in three days and nights of "exhausting labors" he had lost ten pounds and was sapped of his "vitality."[7] Reed had been much admired. Lowell's endorsement we know. Humphreys, Forbes, and Crowninshield abandoned their quartet for a month, not having the heart to sing without Reed or to replace him. (Eventually Lieutenant Josiah A. Baldwin, one of Reed's best friends, asked to take his place, and the quartet was revived.) One of the Californians, a sergeant from Company F, wrote that Reed "was worth more to us than nearly all the other Officers."[8] That his horse had been stolen was no great surprise; nor was the loss of his revolver. But the fact that his body had been stripped of clothing made a deep impression on everyone. Undoubtedly the presence of Captain Reed's wife in camp added to the gloom. She had come down for a visit and was there to receive her husband's body when the wagon returned on the morning of February 23.

Reed had died devoid of property. His former company collected funds to pay for his embalming. His wife was given his last effects: his remaining pistol and the bullet that killed him. She and Chaplain Humphreys took Reed's body back to Dorchester. Awaiting her was their only child, a boy, who was incapacitated from birth by nephritis or Bright's disease. Reed had been so well liked that it was especially painful to realize how meager his estate was, how paltry his circumstances. Crowninshield was beside himself and asked his mother to give money to Reed's widow. He explained, "I miss poor Capt. Reed very much . . . he was honest & brave & a great friend of mine." And he was quick to defend Reed, declaring that the ambush "was not owing to any carelessness on his part," for Reed "was marching his men as we always march." Crowninshield ordered out a larger party looking for a fight with Mosby. For two days they scoured Loudoun County but had no luck. After this Crowninshield calmed down, admitted that Reed should have sent out flankers, and became exceedingly cautious himself. He did not scout far beyond Vienna, leaving Mosby free run of the area around Leesburg. For the next month Mosby complained that he had few opportunities because the federals "exert great vigilance."[9]

For the next several weekends Lowell returned to Vienna. He believed that Mosby had planned the ambush "very cleverly" and had made "a great effort to get together men and to get them where he wanted them." Lowell predicted that after such an effort "there is likely to be quite a quiet time." But his brief, as he told John Murray Forbes in a letter, was "to straighten out the Cavalry Depot . . . There has been no head here, and there was a sad want of system." One might think this assignment was the army's, or at least Stanton or Halleck's, response to Lowell's summary justice, but there is no evidence to support this assumption. The Cavalry Bureau had been, since its inception in July 1863, the source of much angst and acrimony within the cavalry. Both General Halleck and Secretary Stanton found its problems mystifyingly insoluble. The number of horses shipped from Giesboro to regiments in the field was well over twice the number these regiments claimed to have received. Those that did arrive were considered worn out and inferior, while the Cavalry Bureau claimed that certain cavalry commanders were "horse-killers"—Pleasonton, Kilpatrick, Custer. More troubling was the six-month report revealing that every man in the Cavalry Corps had been remounted three times in the previous six months. If this became the pattern, then 435,000 horses would be required for 1864 alone. It was highly doubtful that so many would be available and quite clear that the government would not be able to afford them. The Cavalry Bureau was perpetuating the problems it had been created to resolve.[10]

Stanton wanted a man with administrative talent and the willingness to take responsibility to institute reforms. James H. Wilson came recommended by Charles Dana, Stanton's undersecretary. During the battle of Antietam Wilson had been so distraught at the lost opportunities that he sent an emissary, the newspaperman George Smalley, to Hooker asking him to take over the Union army and finish the fight. But Hooker was wounded too severely to act on the audacious proposal. Since then Wilson had raised a volunteer regiment, served in varying capacities in the West, and ended up on Grant's staff. Two years younger than Lowell, belonging to the West Point Class of 1860, Wilson was a rising star in the army. It was a compliment that Wilson wanted Lowell to help in the job of reforming the Cavalry Bureau. Once again his administrative skills were being rewarded, but Lowell did not want to leave his brigade at such a delicate moment. He put his case to Secretary Stanton, General Christopher Augur (who had replaced General Rufus King as commander of the Defenses North of the Potomac), and General Wilson himself. All three assured him that he would be at the Cavalry Bureau only "two or three months."[11] Wilson had been promised that his own appointment would be for sixty days, long enough to whip the bureau into shape, before joining the summer campaigns. Wilson made the same promises to Lowell.

Their first task was to stop the corruption. Purchasing depots were required to have inspection boards with the right to reject horses and brand them. By this method the quality of horseflesh entering the cavalry could be monitored. Next came the necessity of controlling the suppliers. Adequate regulations existed, but they were not enforced. It had become commonplace for horse suppliers to subcontract to others in order to fulfill a contract. When this practice continued despite warnings, Lowell and Wilson arrested and court-martialed the offenders. This disruption of the status quo was contested, but when the secretary of war supported the Cavalry Bureau, the suppliers were forced to settle down to a more honest supply of horses and their "quality greatly improved."[12]

Other questions before the Cavalry Bureau included methods of instruction, standardization, organization, reconditioning tired horses, and finding a function for "unserviceable horses." But most important was the question of ordnance. A wide variety of carbines was in use. Many were not good and not liked by the men. The most effective was the Sharps. But a new innovation was the Spencer carbine, an early version of the repeating rifle: seven shots could be fired without having to reload. Heavier than a regular carbine, the Spencer also required retraining men to learn how to fire and load. But it was obviously a superior weapon. Under Wilson the Cavalry Bureau made arrangements to procure these weapons for the cavalry. Lowell could see that, like so much involving government contracts, there would be uncertainty and delay in the delivery of those new weapons, and that a lowly brigade such as his might never receive a consignment. He contacted John Murray Forbes and promoted the Spencer carbine, explaining, "If our men had had them [at Dranesville] perhaps they would have given a better account of themselves."[13] Forbes was persuaded to arrange an independent supply of Spencer carbines for the Second Massachusetts Cavalry.

Lowell was also finalizing the lists of officers of the Second Massachusetts Cavalry who would be transferred to form the core of the Fourth and Fifth Massachusetts Cavalry, two new black regiments. Twenty-five men transferred, including Captains Washburn, Cabot, and Adams, a handful of lieutenants and noncommissioned officers, and eleven more men. In the regimental reshuffle, the biggest change came when Henry Russell, the absent lieutenant-colonel, resigned to become colonel of the Fifth Massachusetts Cavalry—an eventuality for which Crowninshield had been praying. His pleasure at now being promoted to lieutenant-colonel was tinged with relief and the knowledge that he well deserved it. He had been effectively doing the work of a lieutenant-colonel for six months.

Almost as soon as he was promoted, and in the absence of Lowell's less confrontational style, Crowninshield once again fought with Thompson over control of the regiment. Thompson, taking advantage of Lowell's absence, persuaded General Augur to have the First Battalion ordered to Muddy Branch. Since August 1863 it had been commanded by Frank Washburn, but, in the first days of March, he left the regiment to become lieutenant-colonel of the Fourth Massachusetts Cavalry, one of Forbes's black regiments. And since August it had contained three of the five California companies, making it the best of the regiment's three battalions. Immediately suspicious of Thompson's motives, Crowninshield substituted Massachusetts for California companies before sending the battalion. Thompson, on receiving this newly configured battalion, retaliated by refusing to send the Third Battalion back to Vienna, the post with the larger duty. All through March the two officers fought over the makeup and placement of the First Battalion. Crowninshield complained that he did not have enough men (and he did not); Thompson complained about the First Battalion having been rejiggered.

When called to account, Crowninshield stood his ground, insisting he had the authority to designate which companies made up a battalion. But he also took Thompson to task for insubordination: "It is well known here that Major Thompson has openly stated his intention of getting certain companies away from the Regiment," he wrote to headquarters in Washington, and was "continually endeavoring to create dissatisfaction among the enlisted men of the Regiment." Thompson's intrigues, he said, "would greatly impair the efficiency of a Regt. and the Authority of the Commanding Officer." For good measure he added that Thompson was "totally lax in matters of discipline and drill and entirely ignorant of nearly all the other duties of a Cavalry Officer." He suggested that Colonel Lowell would confirm his opinion and that Captain DeMerritt, of the California Battalion, who had recently inspected Thompson's command at Lowell's request, could also be consulted. Thompson received orders from General Augur to return the battalion in question. Explaining the situation to John Murray Forbes, Lowell wrote, "He is a miserable fellow I *know*; we *all* know it, his own officers all know it, but it is hard to make it apparent. There is so much meanness round Washington that we naturally shall get credit for treating him meanly. The sure cure for the whole trouble is to get the regiment ordered into the field . . . Thompson will resign the moment the regiment is ordered to the field."[14]

Incidental to Crowninshield's success with Thompson was that he also neutralized Thompson's lackey, Sergeant Merry. Since November, when Merry and Thompson had been separated, Merry's letters to the California newspapers had lost some of their vitriol, and now they changed altogether. Merry's next letter, written March 25, announced that Major Crowninshield was "a fine officer" and "one of the very few Massachusetts officers who have treated the Californians as men and patriots should be treated." Because of his decency Crowninshield had "won a strong hold on their [the Californians'] affection."[15]

While Crowninshield was solidifying his position as lieutenant-colonel and acting commander of the Second Massachusetts Cavalry, the Union army as a whole was undergoing a transformation. On March 10 Ulysses S. Grant was elevated to lieutenant-general and given the title of general-in-chief of the Union army; Halleck was made chief of staff. Grant had been instrumental in recapturing the Mississippi and lands west. With hindsight it is clear that after the victory at Vicksburg, the momentum had shifted, and a Union triumph in the war was virtually inevitable. But that was not apparent in late 1863 and early 1864, and the mood in the North was anything but confident. Copperheadism was strong. Many feared that Lincoln would be ousted and a peace platform would prevail in the next election, especially if the war dragged on with high casualties and little to show for them. Nevertheless the appointment of Grant set a new tone, and there was excitement in the air when Grant came east. Lincoln famously said of Grant, "He fights." The simplicity of the statement should not underrate its force. Grant fought stubbornly. He was willing to keep fighting when many more talented men pulled back. He was willing to carry the burden of ordering men to their death. He did not, as he explained, "count the dead." It would be a mistake to believe that he was insensitive to numbers or that he lacked a moral dimension that permitted him to slaughter men. This has, in some quarters, been the characterization of Sherman and Grant and the Union war effort in its final phase generally, but it is neither accurate nor fair. The point to make here is that Grant and the leadership he issued into command had no qualms about destroying the Confederate army, recognizing this to be as important, if not more so, than capturing Richmond.

In the cavalry, sharp changes were made. Pleasonton was sent west, while Grant brought east Philip Henry Sheridan. When Wilson's sixty days were up, he was given a division and told to join the Cavalry Corps under Sheridan. Lowell, after his sixty days at the Cavalry Bureau, returned to his brigade at Vienna on April 3 with his hope of joining the Cavalry Corps for the summer campaigns momentarily dashed. As soon as General Augur learned that General Wilson intended to keep Lowell with him, he applied to get Lowell back at Vienna under his control. That evening the regimental band serenaded him and Effie. Lowell told the men that he was happy to be back and wasted no time retaking charge of his brigade.

The day after his return, Lowell resumed the heavy schedule of constant scouts and patrols. One member of the first scout, Valorus Dearborn, the carpenter, noted that "it was tough—dark, cold and wet—the worst night I have experienced for a long time. No fires to sit by and no chance to sleep."[16] In particular Lowell wanted to investigate what Mosby was doing to the north of them, where no scouts had been since late February.

By April 7 the scout returned with the news that all along the Potomac the winter melt had made fords impassable, which prevented Virginia farmers from selling their grain across the river in Maryland; given this delay, Mosby was doing the smart thing and appropriating it for Confederate use. Word was coming from local citizens that Mosby was raiding the barns of Quakers and Union sympathizers across Loudoun County, subjecting them to the traditional tithe of 10 percent and taking grain and animals without compensation.

Lowell ordered a second scout to the northeastern section of Virginia. As the brigade made preparations, three men turned up looking for Lieutenant-Colonel Henry S. Gansevoort of the Thirteenth New York Cavalry. Gansevoort was not in camp, but Lieutenant Edwin Lansing, serving on Lowell's brigade staff, was a cousin and immediately recognized these men as family. They were two of Gansevoort's cousins, Herman Melville and his brother Alan. The third man was a former law partner of Gansevoort's, George Brewster, newly commissioned as a captain in the Thirteenth New York Cavalry. The Melville brothers had decided to accompany Brewster as he joined his new regiment. While Brewster went off to assume his new command, Lansing brought the Melvilles to brigade headquarters.

Melville's reputation within New England was on a par with that of Richard Henry Dana: the two men had been responsible for bringing the life of the common seaman before the world. The camp library included Melville's two most successful travel novels, *Typee* and *Omoo*. Since 1851, when *Moby-Dick* was published, Melville's reputation had declined. That novel and *Pierre*, published shortly thereafter, had not pleased the reading public. Hit hard by these failures, Melville was only now attempting to resurrect his writing career. He had in mind a book about war. During the winter his cousin Henry Gansevoort had often been in New York recuperating from various fevers. He had given Melville some sense of Lowell, the Vienna camp, and their "inglorious warfare" against Mosby. Now he wished to see it for himself. Lansing, who admired Lowell enormously, made introductions, and the Melville brothers took tea at brigade headquarters, served to them by Effie Shaw Lowell. (Melville was married to Effie's distant cousin, and Effie's father, Francis G. Shaw, had been Melville's publisher for a time.)

As he watched the demure young woman before him pouring tea, Melville might well have thought about the romance of her brother's death and her new marriage. For five months Effie had been living in camp, visiting soldiers, tending the wounded, generally making herself useful. In these early days of April the countryside was still bleak, the ground a mire of mud. Nevertheless Effie was riding on horseback daily outside the safety of the Vienna camp. She was, with her excellent manners, her intelligence, and her grit, entirely original. Melville recognized that Lowell was not, as the Californians believed, just another effete easterner. Lowell, like Melville, knew the shame of a failed father, of relying on a mother's connections and wits, of being "the poor relation." Both men came from distinguished patrician families but held insecure, uncertain places in that world of privilege. Neither could afford the self-assurance of Henry Gansevoort or Caspar Crown-inshield or Will Forbes.

Both men had lived double lives: their mental world of rarefied thought, difficult to share with others; their physical world rougher and more practical than their upbringing had prepared them for. Both men knew and admired Hawthorne, Melville obsessively and problematically. Hawthorne's failing health (he was to die in May 1864) was a point of reference for them. Lowell and Hawthorne had spent hours in Rome transfixed by the *Three Fates*, attributed to Michelangelo: the chilly detachment of the old crones drove Hawthorne to a deeper embrace of a forgiving God, while Lowell reveled in the cathartic power of such supreme indifference. Melville, too, had been in Rome and admired the *Three Fates*, but earlier, in 1857, and he was one of the few people who might have appreciated both Hawthorne's and Lowell's responses.

Melville was eager to learn what he could of the war. Lowell had little sympathy for journalists and a very low regard for the accuracy of their reports, but he recognized Melville as something entirely different. Melville's desire to make art out of war interested him, and he invited the novelist along on a scout—an opportunity he quickly accepted, despite the potential risks and his own unpreparedness. Alan Melville returned to Washington, while Herman stayed on.

The next morning, April 18, Melville rode out with the scouting party. He was in the lead with Lowell and Major Frazar of the Thirteenth New York Cavalry, who was serving as Lowell's second in command, and their guide, "Yankee" Davis, a Virginian who like Binns had deserted Mosby and was working as a Union scout. Behind them was a column of 250 cavalry-men traveling four abreast—an impressive sight.

The day before Melville had been struck by how casually Lowell dressed, in a simple cavalry coat and the regulation forage cap of the common soldier, with its long front brim to shade his eyes. Now Lowell wore his full uniform. His single-breasted jacket had a simple narrow lapel and plain flat buttons—austere compared with the double-breasted jacket and specially chosen brass buttons most officers preferred. Nor did Lowell wear a shoulder strap to designate his rank. His light blue cavalry trousers were trimmed with dark blue piping. Melville noticed that Lowell's modest style was copied by Forbes and some of the other Massachusetts soldiers. Despite the lack of ostentation, Lowell cut an impressive figure. He sat well in the saddle and wore the red sash of an officer, with its long tassle over which his scabbard was buckled, and on horseback his excellent posture and commanding manner had extra effect.

Within a short distance of the camp, the bugles were put away and the noncombatants fell to the rear: the regimental doctor with his green sash, the chaplain in black, the hospital steward, the ambulance, and Melville. Flankers were thrown out, and the column established a defensive order. An advance guard traveled some forty paces in the lead to give warning of ambush, and a rear guard served the same purpose in the back. They traveled at a fast pace, in silence, without straggling. Soon they left the pike and traveled cross-country for further concealment.

They stopped at various farms, where Lowell learned that Mosby's quartermaster, Major Hibbs, had requisitioned most of the grain around Leesburg without paying for it and stored it in remote barns. A few wagonloads of corn were left behind, perhaps in lieu of payment, but the farmers were coming to resent Mosby's failure to reimburse them. The possibility of receiving payment from federal quartermasters helped to divide loyalties within Loudoun County.

Outside Leesburg, the advance guard reported sighting rebels, and a ripple of tension ran through the scouting party. Lowell gave the order to charge. As the men responded, the noise became deafening. But the men knew their parts without having to hear orders. Once the horses began to gallop, the contagion of example worked on man and horse alike. Humphreys described that "one is borne along in the rush and tumult of the onset and can hardly think of fear."[17] But in fact the chase came to nothing: the Rangers vanished into the countryside.

When evening closed in, Lowell camped just outside Leesburg, resting his horses and men in anticipation of the next day's raid. They were now deep into Mosby's Confederacy, no fires were lit, and the horses remained saddled. It was too cold to sleep, and the men sat or lay on the ground and talked. They told Melville the story of Coyle's Tavern, of the cold-blooded murder of Oscar Burnap, of the summary execution of "Pony" Ormsby, of the ambush of Captain Reed and the California Hundred. As the men talked, it was clear that the fight against Mosby had become intimate and personal: they knew each other, their strengths and weaknesses. Just the tone of their voices conveyed all the contradictory passions of the regiment's relationship with Mosby, its suspicion of civilians, and its betrayal by their own. The vision of war offered him by the Second Massachusetts Cavalry had little glory.

The next morning the scouting party set out to visit more farms and gather more intelligence. An unexpected run-in with some of Mosby's men yielded prisoners, who were brought to Lowell for questioning and then guarded. One tried to break for the woods, but a guard tackled him, and as the prisoner went down, his head smashed against a tree. After some confusion his injuries were recognized as mortal and he was left behind. It was, for all the witnesses, one of those moments—rare in civil life, in war too frequent—when the unexpected reveals the omnipotence of death. The snip of Atropos's scissors could almost be heard.

Lowell planned to use the cover of night to send detachments throughout the Aldie area, sweeping as far west and south as Rectortown and Upperville, to catch Rangers in their sleep once again. But a reconnaissance to Aldie revealed that Mosby knew of Lowell's presence and had left a message sending his regards. Was it a gesture of contempt or a gentlemanly salute? Either way, Lowell changed his plans, deciding to call on a wedding party that very evening in Leesburg, but he did not move quickly enough and his men arrived after the party had broken up. Mosby's men had been "ready to fight," or perhaps not: in the evening skirmish in the streets of Leesburg, Lowell's report says that "the captain in charge believes his own party firing without orders in the rear, did at least half the mischief."[18] Three men were wounded, one killed most likely by their own men.

The second night out there was no more anticipation. The scout was over. The men slept soundly and the next morning returned to camp. Several days later Melville returned to Washington. He took with him a desultory experience and a wealth of anecdotes. Over the next two years Melville wrote poems about the war, publishing them in 1866 as *Battle-Pieces and Aspects of the War.* His longest, "The Scout Toward Aldie," was based on the three days he spent with Lowell; "On the Grave of a Young Cavalry Officer Killed in the Valley of Virginia" was written about Lowell after his death. The novella *Billy Budd*, written over a decade later and published only posthumously, finds in the tale of William Ormsby and Lowell's summary execution the eternal tension between the individual and the demands of the social order. Ormsby's statement before he was shot served as the inspiration for Billy Budd's "God bless Captain Vere." The effect of Ormsby's words was not unlike that of Budd's, as Melville describes how, "watched by the wedged mass of upturned faces, Billy ascended; and ascending took the full rose of the dawn."[19]

By the end of April Lowell had several informants and showed considerable discretion in his interpretation of information, whether from citizens or men in his own brigade. Based on what he learned, he made a third scout to the Blue Ridge, passing through towns like Upperville and Paris, in the heart of Mosby's Confederacy. He gave clear instructions to Lieutenant Alvord about which houses and which cupboards to search in the hopes of finding Mosby's private hiding place. Fortunately Alvord searched with a remarkable tenacity, explaining, "I knew there must be a hole for the fox somewhere, and I stuck to it till I found it." Eventually, he discovered a loose threshold in the kitchen on the ground floor of a house mentioned by his informant. This, taken up, revealed that the floor of the cupboard was in fact a trap door. Once he climbed down, Alvord found himself in an underground apartment. Hanging on the wall was a satchel filled with Mosby's private papers, including his two commissions as captain and major of the Partisan Rangers. There were both Confederate and Union uniforms, sabers, carbines, and other weaponry. They found and pocketed "trinkets in the shape of rings, and ornaments carved from bone." Alvord and his men supposed the bones were human, but "DeWolf thinks the one I showed him is not." Crowninshield nevertheless sent his mother a ring, telling her it was "made out of a Yankee bone."[20] After ten months Mosby's hideout had been found.

Alvord brought in twenty-three prisoners and as many horses. They also found huge quantities of wool and tobacco, some $25,000 worth of blockade-run goods, which they confiscated, and three blockade runners, whom they took prisoner. Lowell's success at finding Mosby's hideout was the apex of a successful and aggressive campaign that received praise from his superiors. On April 26 General Robert O. Tyler wrote to General Augur, "With Colonel Lowell in command of the cavalry, I have no fear of trouble." Five days later Tyler again praised Lowell to Augur: "I have the honor to commend to the favorable attention of the commanding general the activity and excellent conduct of Colonel Lowell." General Augur was moved to write, "I desire to commend in strong terms the zeal and ability displayed by Colonel Lowell in these various expeditions."[21]

Lowell's reports now grew increasingly frank. He acknowledged that he had not pursued Mosby once because he had "fourteen miles and at least six hours start" and "the roads are so dusty that a pursuing party would be seen for miles and miles, and time given to hide or escape." A number of his reports relayed information that he asterisked with the comment, "I consider this doubtful," showing that he did not fully trust the officers of the Thirteenth New York Cavalry, just as his men did not trust the enlisted men of that regiment. He reported "friendly fire" when he suspected it. He confessed that his picket offered "no resistance." Of one raid, Lowell wrote only, "Do not know that we did any damage at all."[22]

At the end of the last scout Captain DeMerritt shot himself in the foot as he was returning his pistol to its holster. DeMerritt had broken a leg, rebroken it, gone insane, recovered, and now shot himself; his bad luck had a pathological edge to it. But whatever lay behind this repeated incapacitation was quickly forgotten by Lowell when, as he approached camp, Effie came running to greet him and tell him her news: she was pregnant. Once this news was communicated to the family, Anna came to visit. She thought Effie looked "wonderfully well" and was astounded that she made virtually no concessions to her condition. Effie still went riding and led her mother-in-law into the woods surrounding the camp to collect pansies and violets, which Anna took home to Cambridge. Anna learned a great many stories about Mosby and Lowell's men. One story had Lowell and an orderly separated from the rest of the party as they pursued Mosby on tired, jaded horses. Mosby had not recognized Lowell and later claimed that if he had, he "would have had him." Anna could scarcely believe this tale, but her son conceded it was true and asked her not to repeat it. From all she learned, Anna was led to believe that Charlie would remain at Vienna "for a long time, because his regt. know the country perfectly." They had settled into a routine, and felt that they were finally gaining the edge on their wily opponent. The regimental band was learning the music to *Lucrezia Borgia*. Forbes was reading the poetry of Robert Burns. Cabot was reading *Don Quixote* in the original Spanish. One of the Californians, C. Mason Kinne, married a local girl.[23]

Then on May 24 Lowell was ordered to abandon Vienna and move his brigade to Fairfax Court House, as part of the preparations for Grant's intended summer campaign. As soon as the federals left Vienna, Mosby came in to punish Unionists who had worked with them, carrying off two Union citizens. Lowell's response was to order his men to "bring in about a dozen of the most prominent secesh citizens about the country as a gentle reminder that we can take about 10 to 1 if they commence that game." It was not a pleasant job. Arresting an elderly man named Rogers at his lovely place near Aldie upset Will Forbes: Rogers was friendly with many of the officers, including Lowell, and therefore "felt no apprehension at our approach." This "most respectable, wealthy old chap" had six sons in the Confederate army, one of whom had been killed. And when Forbes explained that he had come to arrest him, Rogers thought it was a joke, but once he understood the situation, he "made the best of it." Forbes commented, "This is miserable work, stealing round in the night and taking citizens and soldiers out of their beds." Ten months before, Alvord had worried that the work in Virginia would harden their hearts. But they were still capable of self-disgust, and of loathing their work. Even the generally upbeat Forbes found his morale slumping. He had been leading scouts regularly throughout the spring and by early June complained of having to "ride through that hateful country of which we are so tired . . . If we've got to be soldiers, Heaven send us soldiers' work to do, and policemen for the business we are now doing."[24]

This sense of their own uselessness was doubtless exacerbated by knowing that the summer campaign had started without them. In the first weeks of June change did come, but it was not especially welcome. Mosby's Rangers attacked a train of Union ambulances that were bringing wounded men back from the Wilderness. Stealing what they could and taking the horses, the Rangers abandoned the wounded men. This kind of action earned Mosby a notoriety that humiliated even his Confederate commanders. However much he purported to be a legitimate warrior, and however much Lowell wanted to believe that he was "an honorable foe," the pretense was sometimes hard to maintain.

Lowell was ordered to provide escort for another rescue attempt. On June 8 seven hundred men set out. Early the next morning fifty ambulances joined them and the convoy continued south. They were headed for a field hospital at Locust Grove, in the Wilderness—second-growth forest that was a thicket of impenetrable scrubby vegetation growing on marshy ground. The ambulances traveled on a plank road carved out of the terrain. As the men passed along, they were shocked by evidence of fighting such as they had never seen. The side of the road was "strewn with decayed bodies." In some places the dead lay in their lines of battle. The trees were "torn and shivered by the sleet of bullets that stormed through these woods." In some spots spontaneous fires had laid waste whole areas, and charred remains were evidence of the wounded who had been burned alive. The dead, "their blackened skulls grinning horribly," were too numerous to count. Captain Goodwin Stone, a Harvard graduate, wrote: "Imagine the two or three hundred men that used to gather for our football games lying dead about the Delta." He was alluding to the annual autumn football game between freshmen and sophomores. Such an allusion was not so far-fetched. Many of the decaying corpses had bits of paper pinned to their sleeves, identifications done as the last acts of dying men. Quite a few were members of the Twentieth Massachusetts Infantry.[25]

As the ambulance escort rode along, the men came upon three or four teams of Virginians with wagons "loaded with stuff they had picked up on the battlefield . . . They were in good business with buzzards robbing the dead," sardonically commented one Californian. Crows and turkey buzzards followed the armies and, after battle, feasted on the remains left on the fields. The ambulances stopped first at the hospital at Parker's Store, where the wounded who were no longer strong enough to withstand transport had to be left. Next, at Locust Grove, they found about forty dead and forty wounded, mostly amputees, who were overjoyed to see them. The rebel doctors in charge of these hospitals "were drunk when we got there and had quite a lot of rifled whiskey on hand still." There wasn't enough room in the ambulances for forty passengers, but somehow they made room; several of Lowell's men carried wounded men on their backs rather than leave them behind. One overloaded ambulance tipped over while crossing a ford on the way back, and one wounded man died and was buried on the road.[26]

Soon after their return to Falls Church the weather turned extremely hot. Almost everything and everyone ground to a halt. Boredom and heat took their toll. Having witnessed enough of the Wilderness to understand how nasty and dogged the fighting was as Grant pressed on toward Richmond, their own work seemed inconsequential. Even Will Forbes, who possessed the greatest equanimity of all Lowell's officers, wrote to his sister, "I'm restless here, Alice, and want more work. Life is a lazy thing here and I've got work enough in me, but it spoils a man to spend all his days doing nothing."[27] Forbes had finished reading Burns and a biography of Theodore Parker. He had taken up the cornet and was getting the runs from eating too many ripe cherries. Indeed, a detachment of New Yorkers had been caught in the cherry trees by Mosby's men and Lowell reported their capture. After an Independence Day festivity of horse racing and jumping, Forbes set out with 150 men on another scout of the area between Aldie and Leesburg, watching for any rebel troops coming through the gaps in the Blue Ridge Mountains.

Three days later troopers from Forbes's party returned to camp around 3 a.m. with a terrible story: the scout had been attacked. Mosby had had an artillery piece. Things had gone unaccountably wrong. Forbes was thought to be wounded or worse. Leaving about 4 a.m. with a party of 250 men and four ambulances, Lowell reached the site about eleven-thirty that morn-ing—a series of fields between a farmhouse on a hilltop, where the fighting had started, and a church on lower ground, which was being used as a hos-pital. The fields were strewn with "guns, pistols, blankets and equipment of all kinds . . . horses, wounded and maddened with pain and fright, dashed wildly over the battleground." Twelve horses and four soldiers had been left for dead. They buried the soldiers. In the church they found about forty wounded men, many of them mortally injured. These were loaded into the ambulances and sent back to Falls Church.

Lowell went over the entire skirmish ground with the utmost care, recon-structing what had happened. On the evening of July 6 Forbes and his men had just finished dining when forward pickets started firing. The pickets' warning shots were heeded: the men mounted, and at least the first two squadrons formed in "an excellent position" at the top of a sloping field. The third was forming when Forbes ordered the first platoon to fire their car-bines. "Here was the first mistake," Lowell surmised. On May 23 the regi-ment had been supplied with Spencer repeating carbines. The men had only just started accustoming themselves to the new weapon, which was much heavier than a regular carbine. To fire it, a trooper needed two hands. This meant that the men had to let go of the reins of their jittery horses. "Had the order been given to draw sabers and charge," Lowell suggested, "the rebels would never have got their gun off." Lowell's analysis suggests how he thought the situation might have been handled: he believed there had been an opportunity to charge, which would have gathered momentum and built morale. That alone would have steadied horses and men alike. Also, the Union forces would then have taken the advantage and deter-mined the action.

Instead, Mosby fired his artillery gun, a Napoleon, a twelve-pound how-itzer drawn by six horses. The shot went high and wide over the heads of the Union men, but neither horses nor men were prepared for its explosion. Even though the shell "burst entirely too high," pandemonium ensued. Forbes had reported the week before that Mosby had an artillery piece, Low-ell remembered, and he had included the information in his report and dis-cussed it with his captains; their supposition had been that Mosby intended to renew his attacks on the railroad. Given his hit-and-run technique, it had not occurred to them that he might lug it about the countryside to attack scouting parties. Mosby used the federal confusion to take down a fence, which allowed his men the chance to charge on open ground.

As Lowell assessed the action, Will Forbes had responded to the problem of the panicking horses by ordering his men to dismount and one squadron to move position. In essence, he was reacting to events and correcting errors already committed rather than responding aggressively: this was a mistake. "The rebels saw their chance, gave a yell, and our men, in the confusion of the moment, broke." Lowell confessed, "I have only to report a perfect rout and a chase for five to seven miles." The only officer not killed, captured, or wounded was Lieutenant Henry Kuhls.[28]

As Lowell wrote to Will Forbes's father that evening, "Will did not leave the field till every man had passed out: emptied his revolver, cut one man with his sabre, and lunged through Mosby's coat." In the skirmish Forbes had lunged at Mosby a second time; this thrust was kept from striking home only by a Ranger throwing himself between Forbes's saber and Mosby. It was, Mosby conceded years later, the closest he came to death. Mosby then fired at Forbes, whose horse thrust his head up at just that moment and took the bullet. The shot brought the stallion down and pinned Forbes underneath. Only then did he surrender. Will, once taken, was sent to the nearby house of Mrs. Davis, the mother of the scout "Yankee" Davis. He left a message there "to tell Col. Lowell that he did not surrender till he was pinned to the ground by his horse and two fellows were over him with sabers."[29]

Lowell spent three hours on the field, then searched the woods, went to the Davis house, then to Centreville, and was disappointed to pick up only six stragglers: the Confederates had captured fifty-seven prisoners. The *Washington Evening Star* reported, "This is Moseby's bravest and largest capture and there is something about it almost unaccountable, when we know how efficient this cavalry force [Lowell's command] had been heretofore, the numerous times they have fought Moseby the past year, and the number of captures we have made."[30] The point was well taken. All year the Second Massachusetts Cavalry had claimed that Mosby did not fight fairly, that he would not stand and fight. But here was an instance of a fair fight of equal forces.

Two factors may have contributed to the "unaccountable." Forbes's units included a fair number of green men and officers. A third of them were New Yorkers (from the Thirteenth this time, not the Sixteenth), but the hard core of the Second Massachusetts Cavalry knew them to be prone to panic and always the first to break. Devoid of discipline, these troops promoted chaos. There was also a fresh influx of recruits from Boston under the newly commissioned Captain Charles W. Amory, a young man with no experience. A cousin of Major Crowninshield and nephew of the Charles Amory on Governor Andrew's staff, his was a political appointment if ever there was one. Young Captain Amory knew nothing of war or commanding men, and ever since arriving in Virginia with the regiment, he had been unwell. He hardly qualified as an officer, let alone one to handle men in a crisis. Although Amory did try to assist Forbes, he was thrown from his horse as it jumped a fence and taken prisoner.*

Forbes's other captain and second in command was Goodwin Stone, the brilliant scholar and Transcendentalist abolitionist from Newburyport. Stone was a gentle but resolute man, tall and slenderly built but strong, with an earnest, attentive face. At the beginning of his service Stone wrote home, "I think myself fortunate in being connected in this regiment with so many officers who have been in service with Regular Army officers and acquired their discipline and habit of command." By September 1863, after three months of guerrilla fighting, it was clear that Stone did not have much stomach for the assignment, and he was ready to leave the army: "there are men enough with more taste for bushwhacking to officer a national police-gang."[31] But Stone, a conscientious officer, stayed with the regiment and was given command of Adams's Company L when Adams transferred to the Fifth Cavalry. Stone was extremely proud of his company and served them with great assiduousness. But at Aldie he had only eight men from his company with him; the rest of his squadron were New Yorkers.

After Forbes's capture Stone had tried to take command, but the situation was beyond his control. Clotted around Forbes was a tangled thicket of "horses madly leaping in the pangs of death, riders crushed beneath their ruthless feet; then the panic-stricken crowd galloping over their fallen companions, and closely followed by the insolent foe." When his New Yorkers took off, Stone tried to halt their headlong flight, briefly making "a stand in the road," but he was shot through the spine and lost control of his legs. After that there was no one left to even attempt to rally the men. Recalling the experience years later, Humphreys explained, "Panic knows no law either in its origin or growth, and sometimes seizes men before they are aware, and spreads from one to another like wild-fire." Stone had just enough strength to cling to his horse as it fled along with all the others some fourteen miles. He was convinced that "if he had only had his own company, he might have

---

*Amory became ill from bad water while in prison, and although he was released in October, his health was ruined.

driven Mosby after all, and that it might just as well have been the other way." He died of his wound ten days later. Lowell concluded his report, "I think the chance was an excellent one to whip Mosby and take his gun. I have no doubt Forbes thought so too."[32]

In his letter to John Murray Forbes, Lowell went to great lengths to convince himself and Will's father that the disaster had been a hazard of chance. He needed to believe that Will could not have behaved foolishly and that he, Lowell, had not behaved irresponsibly. He had done his best to keep Will safe, but since April that had been hard. Throughout the winter Forbes had been president of the court-martial board, which had kept him from going on scout. But with so many officers captured or dead, it was hard not to use him. Lowell wrote Forbes, "I believe Will expected, and intended, to have the gun. He missed it by one of those turns of fortune that must be expected in Cavalry."

Stone, Forbes, and Lowell had all believed the skirmish could have gone either way. Lowell told Will's father, "That he missed doing exactly the right thing at exactly the right time at Aldie, we can see now—he will never make that mistake again! It only makes *me* feel that I should probably slip up myself some day just where I thought myself strongest."[33] But another argument, made mostly well after the war, was that by going over the same ground too frequently on his three-day scout, Forbes had given the locals and Mosby too good a chance to draw a bead on the scouting party, track it, pick the ground, and calculate the odds. There is some truth to this argument, but the larger truth was that only a force capable of eternal vigilance could have bested Mosby. And eternal vigilance is a chimera. The Union men were being worn down. Long before they had learned from experience, many of them died or were captured.

Mosby gave assurances that Will would not be taken farther south than the relatively decent prisoner-of-war camps in Virginia. Lowell wrote Forbes that Will "will be well-treated by Mosby I know. I should not be surprised if yet he escaped and came into camp." Will Forbes did escape but was recaptured and sent to the horrendous open stockade prisons of Columbia, South Carolina, and Macon, Georgia. He was then moved to the jail in downtown Charleston, to serve as a living shield against the bombardment of that city by the federals. Paroled in time to be at Appomattox, Forbes knew that Mosby had refused to surrender, disbanding his men instead. In later years Forbes explained his capture thus: "That acts of violence quite unwarranted were repeatedly committed by the men of [Mosby's] band is true, but my observation was that he tried to keep his men as before said, within the bounds of legitimate warfare."[34] Forbes went to great lengths to renew his connection with Mosby and to find him a sinecure. Mosby responded to this gesture. He became a Republican and accepted posts of various kinds from several Republican presidents. While this was undoubtedly the safest and wisest postwar policy, it does nothing to relieve the sustained quandary as to the true nature of their fight. Had Mosby been an honorable foe or an old rat? Had the Second Massachusetts Cavalry almost outsmarted Mosby, or had they simply played the straight man for his pranks?

The Shenandoah Valley Campaign

EIGHTEEN

REAL CAVALRY FIGHTING

"Follow the enemy to the death. Wherever he goes let our troops go also."
— Ulysses S. Grant to Philip H. Sheridan, August 1, 1864

On July 5, the day Will Forbes's scout set out for Aldie, Lieutenant Henry E. Alvord, serving as the provost-marshal of the brigade, brought to Colonel Lowell's attention a letter that one of his spies had intercepted. Written on June 23 by a South Carolina cavalry colonel to his sweetheart, the letter gave details about an impending attack on Washington by some fifty thousand Confederates and described the route as via Harpers Ferry. Alvord regularly intercepted letters between this lady and her Confederate beau, and he was sure this one was genuine and an intelligence coup. Lowell forwarded the letter with Alvord's explanation of its authenticity to General Christopher Augur, commanding the Defenses of Washington. There the intelligence appeared to die the quiet death of neglect.[1]

The Confederate cavalry usually moved north in late June and early July. Streams and fords were at their lowest in the dry season, giving them many opportunities to cross the Potomac and pursue a classic Confederate strategy: create a diversion by sending an army onto Union soil. Grant, at great cost to his own troops, had for two months been keeping the pressure on Lee. After the grueling bloody draw in early May at the Wilderness west of Fredericksburg, he had moved farther south to Spotsylvania, for a sustained week of yet more stubborn fighting. Then on to Cold Harbor, where the fighting continued through early June. His goal was Richmond, capital of the Confederacy. At present he was laying siege to Petersburg, a town roughly fifteen miles southeast of Richmond, pressing Lee's army relentlessly. Additionally, General David Hunter, last seen in South Carolina commanding colored troops, was now commanding the Army of West Virginia and ravaging the Shenandoah Valley. He had burned the Virginia Military Institute and was moving north, burning towns and plantations. The effect of this destruction was terrible for morale within the Confederacy. Lee, needing to ease the pressure on his troops, sent General Jubal Early to deter Hunter. This Early did, and to his own surprise, Hunter moved west, leaving the valley free of Union troops. Early seized his moment and, without waiting for orders, moved down the valley to Harpers Ferry. When he reached the bottom of the valley on July 3, General Halleck telegraphed Grant with the concern that Early would cross into Maryland.

Grant, who had not wanted to repeat the cautious mistakes of his predecessors, had not made adequate provision for the defense of Washington. Compounding this error and despite Halleck's telegram, he trusted intelligence that wrongly insisted that Early had never left Petersburg. On July 4 Early forded the Potomac. Again Halleck telegraphed Grant, who now awakened to the crisis and dispatched from his own troops one division and the dismounted cavalry of the Sixth Corps, but they would be days arriving.

By July 6 Early had extorted $20,000 from the village of Hagerstown, Maryland. The next day he found shoes for his men. On July 8 and 9 he took the town of Frederick, extorting $200,000 there. Meanwhile federal troops under General Lew Wallace arrived from Baltimore. Two companies under Major Thompson—Eigenbrodt's Company E and Manning's Company M (under Partridge who, since his encounter with Ormsby, had been promoted to lieutenant)—which had been picketing fords on the Monocacy River and the Frederick Pike, now fell back to their camp at Muddy Branch.

On July 9 at the battle of Monocacy the Confederates drove back General Wallace's hastily assembled force, and shortly thereafter Major Thompson withdrew his battalion from Muddy Branch. As the Confederates advanced, Thompson began to retreat along with the rest of the Union army back onto the Defenses of Washington, most critically to Fort Stevens at Tenalytown, where his men manned the rifle pits. In response to this news, Grant dispatched the rest of the Sixth Corps, but for the time being Early's troops had only a ragtag assembly of troops standing between them and Washington.

Meanwhile Lowell and the main body of his brigade remained at Falls Church, their camp in Virginia. It looked as though, once again, Lowell's men would be held back as the reserve of the reserve, but on July 10 orders came: Lowell was to send one regiment to join General Augur at Fort Stevens, while two regiments continued at Falls Church lest yet more Confederate troops arrive from the south. Recognizing that this was perhaps his last chance to prove himself and join in the season's campaigning, Lowell sent an orderly to General Augur requesting that he be allowed to join the detached regiment. Augur agreed. Lowell turned over command of the two New York regiments to Colonel Lazelle and led the Second Massachusetts Cavalry to join Augur at Fort Stevens. He told the men that this was their chance, perhaps their only chance, to earn a place within the fighting armies: to escape the Defenses of Washington and their hated assignment to thwart Mosby.

At Fort Stevens on the evening of July 10 Lowell was immediately able to appreciate the situation. Simply put, General Augur did not have enough men. Troops were being called in from whatever source, arriving in detached units, as Lowell's had. Many had been assembled from the detachments at the remount camp. Lowell was told to command whatever assortment of detached cavalry was available the next morning. Thus on July 11 he had under him between 750 and 800 men, and his first assignment was to provide Augur with reconnaissance. He was to obtain intelligence on where the Confederate army was, in what force, and where it appeared to be headed. He had the added job of delaying the Confederate advance in whatever way possible, buying time until the Sixth Corps arrived.

The weather was fearsomely hot. For two weeks a sustained heat wave had hung over the area, and a drought of forty-one days had dried up creek beds and limited available well water. Tempers frayed. Early's men, worn down by weeks of marching, were fainting from heat and collapsing from dehydration. A cavalry camp in high summer is a loathsome place; the flies alone are enough to drive strong men mad. Cavalry on the move in drought-like conditions made dust clouds that choked the riders and could be seen for miles. Yet ironically, the heat created a haze that rose in layers or waves off the overheated earth and obscured even such obvious signs as the dust cloud of an army on the move. Visibility was good only in the early morning and the late evening.

Even so, Lowell's difficulty was not so much locating where Early's army was as determining its numbers, and whether the huge dust trails represented the main body or a diversionary force. This sort of information could be established only by getting close and skirmishing. Having sent out squadrons along a number of roads, he himself led a party of men on the Rockville Pike, the obvious route. Near Rockville he quickly recognized this was the route of Early's main army. His men began to skirmish with enemy forces, falling back slowly toward Fort Stevens. In this position of advance skirmish line, they were subjected to constant daylong shelling from Confederate cannons.

Few things are more destructive to the nerves than artillery fire. The cannons were beyond range, and so Lowell's men could do nothing to halt the incessant drone as gun after gun fired and the attendant explosions shook the earth. "The light that followed the monster shells on their semi-circular four mile flight through the heavens was beautiful indeed," recalled one of Lowell's troopers, "and the noise of their explosion shocked earth and air."[2] The screaming of a shell was rivaled only by the cacophony of its bursting. A wagon could be blown to smithereens, sent flying for yards. Even small objects blown with such force became deadly and even when not, earth or men or parts thereof, while unlikely to inflict wounds, had a shocking effect when hitting men at high speed. The smoke and the noise obscured the obvious, a sense of time evaporated, and the destruction of people and things created a living hell.

Earlier that week Mosby's use of one artillery piece firing just once had been enough to destabilize Will Forbes's battalion. Mindful of Forbes's crisis, Lowell had directed the officers to prepare their men for artillery fire. Now, in front of Fort Stevens, under Lowell's command neither the men nor the horses of the Second Massachusetts Cavalry were fazed. They remained steady and stayed at their work, disregarding the heavy fire around them.

The next day Lowell's men once again ventured down the Rockville Pike. Lowell split his force to give the appearance of more men, and then he attacked, himself leading on the right and Crowninshield on the left. The Confederates were driven back about a mile, retreating in haste. Lowell then took over their old position and held it until day's end, when again he withdrew slowly back to Fort Stevens.

Meanwhile the First and Second Divisions of the Sixth Corps, some ten thousand men, arrived. Washington was safe and the crisis to the Union averted. That evening Union commanders went to bed assuming that General Early would attack the next morning, and they may even have relished the thought. The Confederate army was dangerously exposed, weary from heat and lack of water and living off the land. Here was a chance, now that the Union troops were appropriately reinforced, for them to cripple, if not destroy, their opponent.

Dawn broke on July 13 with no enemy in sight. Lowell's cavalry was sent out to find it. Once again they rode up the Rockville Pike, and just outside

Rockville Lowell captured badly demoralized Confederate stragglers. As he questioned them, he realized he was on the flank of a fast-retreating Confederate army. (Early had learned that Union reinforcements had arrived. His objective in any case had been not to take Washington but to divert Union troops from Petersburg.) With mounting frustration, Lowell followed the dust cloud of Confederates getting farther and farther away. When he reached Rockville, Lowell sent two squadrons under Crowninshield to keep watch on the Confederates, while the remainder of his men rested their horses and found water, and he sent a report. Like all the reports he sent over these days, this one was extremely thorough, precise, and concise. Balancing facts with analysis, Lowell provided information and drew conclusions from that intelligence. An opportunity, he believed, was fast being missed. As Lowell wrote, on the porch of a house along the main street, he became increasingly disturbed by firing from Crowninshield's direction: it seemed too heavy. Lowell sent his orderly, Frank Robbins, to Crowninshield with the reminder "not to urge a fight," but it was too late.[3]

Unbeknownst to them, Lowell had so effectively harassed the Confederate retreat that Early had ordered General Bradley Johnson and his famed "Maryland Line" to drive the federals away. Johnson's men took cover in a plantation of dense pines near a small stream, where the federals were likely to stop, and many of Crowninshield's men did stop. As they began to remount and ride away, the Confederate cavalry charged, catching them by surprise. Things quickly became chaotic. The dust was so bad that it was all but impossible to distinguish between friend or enemy; many Union men were taken prisoner. Soldiers who remounted and fled did so under cover and went back down the Rockville Pike and straight into town.

By the time Robbins came dashing back with news of the ambush, Lowell had already formed his men into platoons. He was ordering them out of Rockville when the retreating elements of Crowninshield's squadron, in many cases riderless horses, came careening into town and smacked straight into them. Among them was the odd Confederate cavalryman, but it was impossible to distinguish them with all the dust, frightened horses, and thrown riders. In the chaos and panicked disorder, Lowell's horse was hit, and he was thrown to the ground. Stunned, he lay there unmoving, long enough to frighten his staff. But then he was up, and remounted, and once again in command. There was no time for delay. As the disorderly mass of men and horses attempted to flee, Lowell gauged the distance to the open field beyond town. His men were alert to his command. The enemy was bearing down hard and would be in Rockville momentarily. To do nothing would result in the entire regiment's being overwhelmed and captured. At any moment the men would recognize the hopelessness of their situation and panic. Grabbing the men's attention by waving his hat, Lowell leaped from his horse and shouted, "Dismount! And let your horses go!"[4]

About thirty-five or forty men from Companies E and F did so. (In later years a few claimed that Lowell had not ordered but asked, "Boys will you dismount?" Others claimed that everyone obeyed instantaneously.) Lowell formed a hasty line across the road and ordered his men to hold their fire as the Confederate cavalry bore down upon them. Only when the enemy was close enough that the dust did not obscure the situation (one private claimed the rebels were within twenty feet) did Lowell order the first volley. Some horses went down, while others shied and pulled up or veered off. But the rebels kept on. Lowell ordered a second volley. This time the rebels reined in. Sparing the stunned Confederates no time, Lowell ran forward, waving his men on. They followed, firing freely. A private from Company F described how "the pitiful sight of a wounded foeman clutching for dear life to the neck of his horse" made such an impression that he forgot for a moment the battle around him.[5]

The Confederates turned back, some fleeing, others taking refuge in back alleys, but Lowell and the men of Companies E and F held them in check. Behind them their own troops gathered the abandoned horses and remounted; most made an orderly withdrawal. By then the rebels were successfully flanking Lowell and the men fighting with him. They were surrounded and cut off from the main body of Union troops, but they still had their horses, so they remounted and charged, hoping to break through the Confederate line. As Lowell was remounting, a rebel rode up, brought a musket level with him, and told him to surrender. Instead Lowell lowered his pistol and fired into the man's face, simultaneously spurred his horse, and dashed to federal lines. He was the last of his men to reach safety. They had all come through.

This small skirmish cost the regiment dearly. Thirty-two men had been taken prisoner, and close to the same number were wounded and killed. In his report, Lowell did not gloss over the crisis. He explained that the men had been "mostly enveloped by the enemy and were very severely whipped."[6] At headquarters his account caused a flurry of telegrams among the various forts: the loss of his troops represented a significant setback and raised the question of whether Early was on the advance again.

Typically, commanding officers were reluctant to report bad news and habitually understated their failures or losses. Assuming this to be the case with Lowell, General Heintzelman dispatched an aide to investigate the extent of his losses and the nature of the action. In his aide's report, two factors stand in marked contrast to Lowell's acknowledgment of failure. The first is numerical. Lowell's regiment was fighting off two brigades: that he succeeded at all was extraordinary. Union troops were used to fighting with a large numerical advantage (usually even more than they realized, as they invariably overestimated the size of Confederate troops). Since Grant had taken command, the Army of the Potomac had been taking more aggressive action, as had been the case in the West, but this aggression was based on the assumption that federal troops had the numerical advantage and could take casualties. Lowell had shown that he could fight beyond this, as the Confederates had been fighting all along, with wits outweighing manpower.

The second factor is that Lowell had executed a brilliant maneuver that came to have a huge part in the making of the federal cavalry: he had dismounted his men. Even within the regular cavalry, dismounted action was only slowly catching on. Historically speaking, the Union army thought of cavalry action as almost exclusively reconnaissance or as a shock tactic, the effect of the charge. Dismounted action was first used selectively by the hard core of the regular cavalry, General Buford's Reserve Brigade, and then by the Cavalry Corps.* But Lowell's men had been conducting dismounted actions since November 1863. Their problems procuring horses (thanks to hoof-and-mouth disease and Coyle's Tavern), had forced them to innovate in ways that other cavalry, particularly volunteer, had not. To the Californians, it was part of hunting Mosby "Indian fashion," which was how Buford had also learned to fight dismounted. The entire regiment reckoned it was the only way to preserve the element of surprise against Mosby.

Another factor, not mentioned in the report but undoubtedly noted throughout the hierarchy, was that Lowell's men had Spencer carbines, the most advanced weapon of the war (with which Forbes had supplied them in May). Lowell and General Wilson were responsible for ordering them for the cavalry, but they were in short supply, and Wilson's own troops would not be armed with Spencers until later in the month. If doubts lingered about these new weapons, they vanished with this skirmish: watching the

---

*At Gettysburg, General Buford initiated the battle by a dismounted action that took and held the "high ground" of ridges outside the town.

Confederate cavalry reel back, even the dimmest wits in the company understood that carrying Spencers was better than doubling their numbers. Lowell's vastly outnumbered and not very experienced men had survived a cavalry charge made by veterans, because they were armed with advanced weaponry. As Lieutenant Edward Thompson of Company E exulted, "One little routed Brigade held their ground against the 'Maryland Brigade' and Stonewall Jackson's old brigade."[7]

Thus it was that almost a year to the day after Ashby's Gap, the Second Massachusetts Cavalry finally came into its own in its first genuine engagement against a conventional foe, their first chance at the "real" fighting they had all wanted for more than a year. Their esprit de corps was first rate. Artillery fire had not fazed them, and they had worked well with troops they did not know. They had responded well in a crisis, showing openness to innovation and all the manifestations of well-trained troops. Any doubts about the men's confidence in their officers were gone.

Lowell had proven himself as a commander as well. He had displayed quick thinking, determination, control of his men, and sheer courage. To Private Samuel Backus, the Rockville skirmish was "a marked instance of [Lowell's] genius for command." To tell cavalrymen to let their horses go was to fly in the face of their training, and yet his men had obeyed him instantly. This sort of trust could not be bought or induced, only earned. However harsh Lowell's discipline, however much the men had blamed him for their troubles, they paid him the ultimate compliment: they trusted him with their lives. And he had done the same: a private explained that if they hadn't followed his orders, Lowell would have been taken prisoner for sure. Returning that evening to Fort Stevens, the small regiment went past other troops, and the inevitable question came: what regiment did they belong to? A year ago, the answer had varied with the company. Now to a man they answered, "Second Massachusetts Cavalry."[8]

Lowell had also won the respect of his superiors. General Benjamin Hardin in particular recognized that he had pretty well saved the day. Endorsing Lieutenant Warner's report that unequivocally stated, "I am greatly indebted to Colonel C. R. Lowell" for his reconnaissance and effective action, Hardin explained that Lowell's information was "always reliable." General Augur now understood what his subordinate, General Tyler, had meant when he praised the "activity and excellent conduct of Colonel Lowell" and explained that "with Colonel Lowell in command of the cavalry, I have no fear of trouble." Augur commended "in strong terms the zeal and ability displayed by Colonel Lowell." The high command could finally appreciate the manner in which Lowell's reports needed to be read. His was not the voice of the anxious volunteer eager to make a good impression and just as eager to minimize error. There was nothing a superior officer wanted more from a subordinate than to know that he understood orders, could take charge of unexpected contingencies, and would carry through on orders whatever the outcome. These things Lowell proved at Rockville.[9]

His reward was that he retained the men under him, doubling the size of his previous command. This included the detachments he had acquired in the crisis—a squadron of the Eighth Illinois Cavalry that had been cut off from its regiment; a battalion of the Seventh Michigan Cavalry under Major Darling; part of the Sixth Pennsylvania Cavalry under Captain Leiper that had been gathered from the remount camp; the entire Sixteenth Pennsylvania Cavalry under Major Fry; the Seventeenth Pennsylvania Cavalry under Major Durland; and a battery of artillery. Officially now the Provisional Brigade, it numbered between 1,900 and 2,500 men. Their experience at Rockville had been a good baptism, but Lowell still had to work hard in these early weeks to unite these various troops. Fortunately the men were busy and he kept them at their work, forging new bonds without giving them time for complaints.

He was told to report to General Horatio G. Wright, commanding the Sixth Corps. The rest of July was given over to considerable marching and much confusion, as Generals William W. Averell and Wright failed to make a decisive and coordinated effort to destroy Early's army, which at first fled back into the Shenandoah Valley. But when the opportunity presented itself on July 29, Early came back over the Potomac for the second time, heading north to Chambersburg. On July 30 he held the town at ransom, attempting to extort $500,000 and then, failing to receive the cash, he burned it to the ground. This was General Early's revenge for General Hunter's destruction in the Shenandoah Valley. He explained, "It was time to open the eyes of the North to the enormity, by an example in the way of retaliation."[10]

Lieutenant Alvord wrote home, "The rebels fight better every day, and our men just the opposite." Major Crowninshield was also demoralized. He had no patience for General Early or General Hunter and told his mother, "I am tired and disgusted with the war and it would take precious little now to induce me to resign my commission." Lowell drily commented to Effie, "Lincoln's popularity must daily diminish when such imbecility flourishes under his very eyes." Two Confederate invasions of Union soil in one month were also too much for General Grant. The time had come for the Union army to take control of the Shenandoah Valley. He reorganized the command structure of the Eastern Army.[11]

Grant had brought together the Departments of West Virginia and Washington and created the Middle Military Division. Over the objections of General Halleck, Secretary Stanton, and even President Lincoln, he gave the command to Major-General Philip H. Sheridan and told him to "follow the enemy to the death. Wherever he goes let our troops go also."[12] On August 8 Lowell was ordered to join the Cavalry Corps of Sheridan's command, his Provisional Brigade to become the Third Brigade of its First Division. For more than a year, Lowell had been trying to find an assignment within this Cavalry Corps, and now he had it. He and the Second Massachusetts Cavalry were to leave Mosby behind.

That very day Major Thompson resigned. Since the incident at Rockville, he had had an awkward time. Ordered to cooperate with another major who outranked him, he'd repeated many of the errors he had made with Crowninshield, and in short order a remarkably similar complaint was again made to Generals Augur and Taylor at headquarters. Only five months before, the two generals had been drawn into the petty power squabbles between Thompson and Crowninshield, and neither wanted to repeat that tedious performance. Whatever patience or sympathy Thompson might have originally garnered had been exhausted, especially since Lowell, whom he had undermined and insulted as a political appointee, had in the present crisis proven himself. General Augur, in particular, was now a wholehearted supporter of Colonel Lowell.

To Thompson, the significance of the order for Lowell to gather his men and join Sheridan in the field was that it put the onus on him to submit to the chain of command and the hated Bostonians. He chose instead to resign, giving as his reason the broken promise of an independent command. In his endorsement of Thompson's resignation letter, Lowell stated plainly that this action would be "for the good of the regiment."[13]

In contrast to the loss of Major Thompson, Major Henry Cole's First Maryland Cavalry was assigned to the Third Brigade. By experience and reputation, Cole might have legitimately resented his situation, for he had raised the battalion in western Maryland (the area whence Lowell had imagined raising his own regiment three years earlier), had always functioned semiautonomously, and had fought doggedly and expertly in northwestern Virginia against Mosby and other guerrillas with far greater success and independence than had Lowell's men at Vienna. But Cole was not a man to stand on ceremony. His men fell into line within the Third Brigade without hesitation, quickly earning a valued place.

Since Lowell had left Falls Church, Effie had moved into Washington and Lowell had seen her when he could. But now that he had officially joined a campaign and she was finishing her sixth month of pregnancy, she went home to have their baby. For nine months she had shared his life in the field, coming as close to war as any woman she knew, and laying the foundation of her marriage. This special intimacy was now at an end. They had known this moment of parting would come, and they had both prayed for his advancement and an escape from "inglorious warfare," but the parting was difficult with unforeseen ambivalences. And yet it was over before they knew it.

It had been two years since Lowell was part of an army campaign. Then he had been an aide; now he was an acting brigadier-general. Other changes were equally marked. The Union cavalry had sat out the Antietam campaign, or served solely as messengers and reconnaissance. The joke had been, "Have you ever seen a dead cavalryman?" Rob Shaw had not been the only one who subsequently refused to join the cavalry because its reputation was so poor. Now there was an independent Cavalry Corps with three divisions. Starting on August 8 Lowell's Third Brigade formed the advance as the Union forces moved up the Shenandoah Valley and Early's forces slowly retreated. Daily the two forces performed an almost ritualized duet: Early's men formed a line of battle and skirmished with Lowell's cavalry, then retired before the Union infantry reached them. As Lowell explained to Effie, "It is not by any means certain that either general intends to fight."[14] Thus Early bought time for his infantry to retreat up the valley, and thus Lowell's men, followed by the rest of Sheridan's army, hurried them on their way.

This duet continued until they reached Strasburg, a small town on the Shenandoah River where the Manassas Gap Railroad turned south toward the centers for grain and other foodstuffs—towns like New Market, Harrisonburg, and Staunton. At Strasburg the Confederates made a stand. There was a railroad to protect, but more important, the Shenandoah River divided here, with a north and south fork separated into two valleys by the Massanutten Mountains. Early had wanted to travel via the South Fork, through Front Royal, where he had several options: to slip across the Blue Ridge east into Virginia, or receive reinforcements via the same route. Sheridan forced Early to take the Strasburg route, which offered neither option.

But even so Sheridan's intelligence revealed that two divisions of Confederate infantry with twenty pieces of artillery had entered the Shenandoah Valley via Front Royal on their way to join Early, and he began to appreciate the difficulty of controlling this split section of the valley south of Strasburg. A reinforcing Confederate division might slip in behind him and cut his army off from its lines of supply and retreat, then attack him on two fronts. Barring that disaster, it was also clear that this section of the Shenandoah Valley, being much narrower, was less than ideal for battle, particularly for cavalry. Both Stanton and Halleck in private conferences with Sheridan had cautioned against a defeat. He recalled in his memoirs, "The fact that the Presidential election was impending made me doubly [cautious], the authorities at Washington having impressed upon me that the defeat of my army might be followed by the overthrow of the party in power."[15]

Rather than risk such an outcome, Sheridan decided to retreat, drawing Early after him toward Harpers Ferry, where his chances of controlling the terms of engagement were better. On August 16 Lowell was summoned to Sheridan's headquarters and issued special instructions: having formed the advance up the valley, his brigade now formed the rear guard of the federal retreat from Strasburg. Once again they took the brunt of the skirmishing. But they had additional orders to burn all the barns holding grain and forage and to drive in every horse, mule, ox, and cow between Strasburg and Winchester. The order came directly from General Grant and therefore had to be carried out.[16]

Although Grant had famously said that crows flying over the valley would need to pack their own provisions, his final qualification is seldom remembered: that the army was to be scrupulous in "giving regular vouchers for such as will be taken from loyal citizens in the country through which you march." Even as it destroyed, the federal army was to maintain Lieber's distinctions among civilians. Sheridan used Lowell's men to initiate the destruction because of their experience in Loudoun County, explaining in his order of August 16 that it was a "delicate, but necessary, duty." No private houses were to be burned, and enough food for private consumption was to be left. Frank Robbins recalled that one farmer asked if he might keep his cow: "The colonel said he could have it, but he thought the rebels would take it." It was, Lowell wrote Effie, "a miserable duty."[17]

At night the men were not allowed fires, and they slept poorly, anticipating rebel retaliation. Their job was to buy time for the army as it got away; their risk was being overwhelmed themselves. Since the beginning of the war, Lowell had been advocating greater self-reliance—whether in disregarding the relatively petty complaint that the troops were overprovided for with an excess of tea and ice or in advancing the philosophic belief that defeat taught much-needed lessons. He wanted to see greater commitment among the Union troops, his own men in particular. His regiment's experience with Mosby had reinforced the point: rescue would never come in time (a truth learned from bitter experience), and so acceptance of the hardships of their duty and a belief in themselves were the only real safeguards the men had against a wily foe. It is perhaps not surprising that an ex-disciple of Emerson should believe in a soldier's self-reliance; now his belief was to be tested.

In one engagement he had his men mount a piece of wood on wheels. With this improvised apparatus, he ordered a squadron of his men to pretend they were light artillery and make a stand on a hill. They went through the motions of setting up and loading their "cannon." Immediately the Confederates shifted their fire to the fake cannon, allowing Lowell to move the rest of his cavalry out of range. This ruse, borrowed from the Confederates at Manassas, worked well enough to get the brigade safely off, but all too quickly the Confederates charged the hill, took it, discovered the trick, and were ready to charge down the hill after them. The slow-moving ammunition wagons were in jeopardy. To protect them, Lowell had to charge the hill that the Confederates now dominated. He used a technique that would become his signature: he dismounted some portion of his men behind stone walls as skirmishers to provide cover while his mounted men charged. Splitting his men like this appeared risky but actually improved their odds, since the Confederates had to divide their firepower between two targets. His orderly described Lowell on his horse behind the stone wall that protected his skirmishers when an artillery shell hit the wall: "for a good while I could not see him for the dust and stones that flew over and around him."[18] But the wagons were able to move off, and the ammunition was safe.

On another occasion, the men awoke to discover that their new camp at Summit Point had been almost completely surrounded by rebels. Recognizing that they could be overrun, Lowell ordered the band's fife and drum to strike up marching tunes. The rebels, assuming that the cavalry was reinforced by infantry, left the brigade alone. The next morning, in the wee hours, Lowell's men fought their way out. His orderly recalled only that "we whipped them." In fact, Lowell and the Second Massachusetts Cavalry drove the Confederates back three miles, killing a captain, a lieutenant, and a number of privates and taking prisoners. These men were completely baffled at being taken prisoner by cavalry. "Where is your infantry?"[19] they asked. Lowell's trick with the drums had worked perfectly. This ingenuity also earned him large reserves of credit with his men. They liked his quick thinking. After a year of playing the straight man to Mosby's prankster, they welcomed the change. The men had accused Mosby of not fighting fair; they meant that Mosby surprised them. Now they recognized that they could use surprise to their own advantage.

Throughout the war, out of necessity, the Confederate army fought against the odds. Relying on superior skill and fighting spirit and better generalship, the Confederates had quickly recognized that numerical superiority was not as important as a general like McClellan believed. Federal morale had been badly damaged by early failures, bad generals, and divisiveness among Union leaders, so this lesson was less obvious and harder to learn. While fighting Mosby, the excuse the men had given for all their failures was that they were outnumbered. On many occasions they had accused Lowell of foolhardiness in his willingness to fight against odds. But since the Rockville fight this accusation was no longer made, even in private letters or diaries. And now, as the Union infantry retreated all the way back to Halltown and Harpers Ferry, it was forgotten.

Sheridan had hoped that by drawing General Early down into the lower section of the Shenandoah Valley, he would find favorable and advantageous conditions under which to attack him. He had even imagined that the Confederates might once again cross the Potomac into Maryland, where they could be attacked with greater assurance of victory. But this possibility was frustrated by two factors. Early's army had accidentally encountered federal cavalry at Winchester in a brief skirmish that had been enough to halt his northern movement. Then the dry, droughtlike weather broke, and for several days torrential rain flooded fords along the Potomac, foreclosing any opportunity for Early to cross into Maryland.

Throughout this period Sheridan had a mania for intelligence, wanting reports and updates with the intensity of a man anxious for his "perfect" moment and place. Both armies were jockeying for position, trying to find the ground on which to fight, hesitating, probing. Lowell was frequently summoned to the general's tent for special instructions. Sheridan used Lowell's men, separated from the rest of the cavalry, for reconnaissance. Riding cross-country and sticking to ridgetops, Lowell wrote reports and almost immediately received requests for yet more information. And in this capacity both

his men and Cole's proved themselves invaluable as scouts. Their knowledge of this art had been honed by fighting guerrillas in Loudoun County.
They thought nothing of lying in a hog pen all night to observe Confederate
movements.

But such subterfuge was only one aspect of their work. Lowell had to
skirmish daily, even when he was not protecting Sheridan's retreat. Parties of
men were sent out to probe the Confederate position, to tweak the skirmish
line, and by the Confederates' response to determine their strength. Sometimes they had to initiate enough of a skirmish to take prisoners and from
them learn intelligence. This was usually done by swift swoops upon the
skirmish line.

On August 25 a squadron under Captain Eigenbrodt was sent to probe an
aspect of the Confederate position behind a stone wall just outside of Hall
town. As Eigenbrodt led the charge against this strongly held position, he
was shot through the heart, as well as in other places, and died instantly. Although several of his men were with him when he fell, his body was left on
the field. At the cost of Eigenbrodt's death and unrecovered body, prisoners
were taken and valuable intelligence was gained.

The regiment reacted intensely to the death of Charles Eigenbrodt. Born
in 1825, ten years before Lowell, he belonged to a patrician Dutch family of
old New York that owned farms in western Long Island (now Queens and
Brooklyn). At twenty Eigenbrodt had gone west exploring and leading a
daredevil life before he settled down and became a successful businessman
in Stockton and San Francisco. Eventually he moved to Alameda County,
across the bay from San Francisco, where he owned a prosperous ranch and
became a pillar of the community. His company of the California Battalion
had been raised almost exclusively in Alameda County, and its desertion
rate was by far the lowest in the regiment, William Ormsby notwithstanding.
A large reason for their high morale was that the men formed a united and
coherent unit: they were friends, with loyalties to Eigenbrodt and to each
other. But sorrow over Eigenbrodt's death extended beyond his own company. He was the last of the original California captains. Reed had been
killed; Manning was a prisoner of war; Adams, never popular, had transferred to the Fifth Massachusetts Cavalry; DeMerritt had been unfit for service since he shot himself in the foot in April; and Thompson, their only
major, had resigned.

From Lowell's point of view Eigenbrodt had been the best of them and
was irreplaceable. Eigenbrodt had never been close to the Bostonians, being

substantially older, and had kept to himself. Though he had had strong criticisms of Lowell's command at first, he had sobered up when Lowell reasserted his control in November 1863. It was Eigenbrodt (and Reed) who had shown Lowell how to use the regiment's lack of horses to attack Mosby dismounted in "Indian style." His steadiness had persuaded Lowell of the effectiveness of this approach. They had forged an alliance based not on friendship but on mutual respect. "Captain Eigenbrodt was truly one of the bravest of the brave,"[20] one of his men wrote in his diary. His death put the men in a fighting mood.

Here in the Shenandoah Valley, the challenges of their work had changed. To satisfy Sheridan's mania for intelligence, they needed to make lightning-quick charges against entrenched infantry positions. The courage to do so was different from the self-reliance the men knew well from escaping desperate situations like Rockville. The death of a loved and highly professional captain appeared to confirm that such charges were suicidal. Independent-minded Americans did not offer their officers the blind obedience that Europeans schooled by a rigid class system expected: they needed to believe in their orders. From experience Lowell knew this to be particularly true of the Californians.

The next afternoon, August 26, another reconnaissance was ordered, probing the same forward enemy position. This time Lowell took charge. He led Eigenbrodt's battalion through some woods, following the Confederate skirmish line, until they could see, some three to four hundred yards beyond the trees, its extreme right edge. With hardly a pause, Lowell plunged into a hollow. The men followed, riding to within two hundred yards of the position. Then, ordering them to attack "as foragers," meaning in open order, Lowell rose out of the hollow, formed the men in line, and led his four companies out onto the open field. Years later one veteran recalled that the action was so swiftly undertaken that the men were upon the Confederates before they could reload.

Of course it was not quite that clean. The Confederates had piled up fence rails to create a barricade or breastwork that could not be jumped and had to be dismantled. A handful of men, including Lowell, provided the fighting distraction while this was done. Private Samuel Backus described Lowell riding along the barricade as his men tore it down, "whacking their [Confederate] leveled muskets with his saber." The regimental doctor, Oscar DeWolf, from western Massachusetts and Lowell's tentmate for the campaign, explained, "Such a noble scorn of death and danger they never saw before, and it inspired them with a courage that quailed at nothing." Two of the men were clubbed to death as they worked; others suffered shattered limbs or had their skulls fractured.[21]

It was the second charge that went swiftly as Lowell led them, leaping over the remains of the rails, in among the Confederates. General Sheridan, who happened to be watching, commented to his orderly, "Lowell is a brave man."[22] Hand-to-hand combat followed. The brutal fighting was brief. The assault had been so swift and so unrelenting that Lowell's men carried off seventy-four prisoners, including a lieutenant-colonel and three captains.

Lowell's willingness to fight and take risks became a new model for Eigenbrodt's men. But this was only part of it. On August 27 Lowell again went out with the Second Massachusetts to probe the Confederate line, testing their new position near Charlestown. All day they skirmished, charging various points along the line and being driven back. By day's end, in addition to their official assignment, they had what they had been looking for: the bodies of Captain Eigenbrodt and of the two men from the California Hundred who had been clubbed to death at the rail fence. Eigenbrodt's body was to be embalmed and sent to his family in Long Island; the two Californians were buried with military honors.

Riding the old Manassas battlefield, arriving at the scene of their own ambushed men, and, most of all, collecting the wounded from the Wilderness had burned into the consciousness of the entire regiment the importance of this last tribute. Lowell had responded to the death of Eigenbrodt by instinctively getting what the men needed to remain loyal to him: he had made sure that the bodies of their dead were recovered. More important, on August 26 and 27, the men learned not only that Lowell was brave but that he would not send them where "he would not go himself."[23] By taking Eigenbrodt's place, Lowell was proving to the men that what they feared might be suicidal could be done and survived. He had reestablished the integrity of his orders—an essential, perhaps *the* essential, factor in an officer's ability to lead his men successfully.

Since Rockville, when the company had responded instantly to his orders, Lowell had played favorites and made his reasons clear to the entire brigade: Companies E and F were willing to fight the Confederates even when the odds were against them. This favoritism did not sow discord or create resentments. The men had changed their attitude. Old prejudices, whether against Irish scum or pampered Boston officers, were now abandoned as the men were tested under fire. Prejudice gave way to fact. They knew one another. The threshing machine of battle had separated the wheat from the chaff, and there was no longer confusion about who the fighters were. Many of the men had "shell fever" and ceased to function when subjected to artillery fire. Others lost their nerve in a charge. They were said to have "slow horses." There were men who were spooked, ruled by fear, and unable to control their fear. Their instinct was flight, and no amount of military discipline or drill could affect that. Modern studies reveal that statistically only 25 percent of soldiers in an army are actually capable of using their weapons in battle. The rest are subject to "the slows" or "shell fever" or whatever name one gives to the paralysis that is a natural response to fear.

Instinctively the men understood that this capacity or incapacity to function under fire was beyond anyone's control. Although some men scorned the shirkers, even resented them, most accepted them as a fact of life and did their best to ignore them. By and large the response was purely practical: no one wanted to fight surrounded by shirkers; far better to cut them out at the start and go into battle surrounded by men whom one could rely upon. Samuel Backus explained that only forty out of the hundred men in his company could be relied upon in battle. Nevertheless he considered his company (Company A) to be "a fighting lot." The men who could fight were worked to the bone. They knew they were "duty men," and took a gritty pride in the fact that they could, and would, do their duty.

These men believed that almost every effort to improve their effectiveness also protected them. They knew that those who panicked and fled, turned their backs on the enemy and ran, were hit much faster. Flight was an effective strategy only when employed with strategic care, well before the battle began. Standing still was the next worst thing to do, since it offered the enemy an easy target.

An example came on September 13, when the regiment was given the task of clearing several fords on the Opequon Creek that were well defended by the Confederates. Company A was broken into parties to try various fords. As they waited for the return of one party, the company was drawn up together on the riverbank within range of the sharpshooters defending the ford. Nearly every shot the Confederates fired hit a man or horse—eleven men were killed or wounded. Yet the company never fired a shot. They simply sat on their horses "like bumps on logs, and serve[d] as targets for the Confederate sharpshooters."

Most regretted was the death of the regimental carpenter, Valorus Dearborn, who was shot clean through the temple. Dearborn had been a "duty man." Belonging to Company A, he was part of the hard core of the regiment, entirely reliable, given to few words, slow yet firm in his judgments. Lowell's orderly George W. Towle was one of his comrades and explained, "Dearborn was in every sense of the word a fine man and a good soldier." His death, particularly its needlessness, angered the men. They had sat exposed on the bank for no more than five minutes. It might have been half that, and yet it had been an expensive error, the result of the "crass stupidity" of their line officers.[24]

The duty men knew there was great protection in keeping moving. Lowell taught them that when they no longer had any props to aid them, their only ally was speed itself. Moving was good, but moving fast was best of all, even if it meant heading straight toward enemy fire. However reckless it seemed to the untutored eye, experienced troopers quickly recognized that Lowell's instructions were based on a sound principle. He showed them how far they could ride in the time it took the enemy to reload. A charge like the one he made following Eigenbrodt's death looked like guts and was called a "moral victory," but it was actually calculated. The trick was to force the enemy to fire and then charge immediately. The men would then have to withstand only one volley before they got close enough to use their sabers.

The greatest and most damaging failing in a line officer was hesitation. It opened the door to doubt and confusion among the men or, worse, to ambivalence and, most disastrous of all, to panic. (Forbes's hesitation at Aldie was a tragic example.) At precisely those moments of potential hesitation, Lowell had shown an ability to use landscape, surprise, inventiveness, and sheer daring to take or keep control of the situation. The men trusted this capacity. Starting a charge is one example. Lowell's men responded instantly to his orders—but not without calculation on his part. Regularly he rode from the rear, up alongside the men, gave them his order, and immediately spurred his horse forward; he got his officers to do the same. He knew the men's horses would instinctively follow the lead of any spirited stallion. Forcing the pace in this fashion pushed the men through whatever internal indecision might be affecting them, and they would find themselves obeying him before they even knew it, swept along in the momentum created by their horses.

Hesitation might also be reckoned a failure to anticipate. Of necessity an officer had to respond to circumstances: he must anticipate and take charge of actions, and try to turn the course of events to advantage. This was a quality Lowell's men remarked on. George Towle recalled that when he would report on events on the battlefield, Lowell often replied, "I know it, I have given the necessary orders." One of the men explained, "The colonel's quick perception always foiled them." Another recalled, "The movements of his thoughts were like flashes of lightning." Sheridan also appreciated Lowell's ability to anticipate events, recalling after the war, "I never had to tell him what to do. He had always seen and done it."[25]

Thus it was that the Second Massachusetts Cavalry developed methods and techniques that improved their odds. They began to grasp the nature of those elusive qualities that make a great fighting force: confidence, esprit de corps, imagination, audacity, courage and bravery (of course), clear thinking under pressure, a profound realism, and calculation. This training would prove invaluable, and it had come at a price: the regiment had lost seventy-five men in heavy skirmishing and almost daily brutal encounters. Camped on the hills overlooking the main army at the appropriately named Summit Point, east of Opequon Creek, on the ridge road from Winchester to Harpers Ferry, Lowell was waking regularly at 3:30 a.m. and rarely sleeping even half the night without interruption. In the forward exposed position of his brigade, sleep for all the men and officers was a chancy thing: two-hour naps snatched at any moment, day or night. The night of September 4 was not atypical. Lowell was interrupted five times before 1 a.m., when he received an order to be ready at 3 a.m. He asked his sentry to wake him at two-thirty, but in fact it was he who woke the sentry. The knowledge that this would be the case had made him restless enough to awake several times during that hour-and-a-half interval. With so little sleep, he wrote Effie, he was not "fresh." Crowninshield wrote home that week with the complaint that he was "very dirty and covered with fleas" and had "not felt very smart for the last week." But Lowell found time to shave, wash, and brush himself. The lack of sleep would not show. Dr. DeWolf thought Lowell looked his healthiest during these months of campaigning. He noted that Lowell never appeared tired or worn, after a sixty-mile ride seeming as fresh "as when he set out," while the men about him were weary and ready to drop.[26]

A not-so-subtle shift in mentality was under way. Confederate prisoners were saying they had never seen "such cavalry fighting before." Within the Cavalry Corps, Lowell and his men were beginning to earn a place. He had begun the campaign as a relative unknown. After a month in the Cavalry Corps, both Lowell and the Second Massachusetts Cavalry had developed "a very good reputation in the army."[27] The trend in the army was now so strongly toward boy generals that his youthful looks no longer counted against him. Lowell's division commander was Wesley Merritt, and he too looked like a boy. Only six months older than Lowell, Merritt had graduated from West Point in 1860. He had started the war serving as an aide to General Philip Cooke in the Department of Washington under General Heintzelman, then served as aide-de-camp to General Stoneman, and finally under General John Buford. On Buford's death in 1863, Merritt had assumed command of the Reserve Brigade. His boyish looks, slender build, and intellectual air were deceiving: he was tough as nails with a driving ambition. Recognized as preserving "an absolute coolness" in battle, off the battlefield Merritt's coolness was less attractive. He was not easily approachable.[28]

Decked out in velvet jacket, lace trim, golden curls, and a "pouting" face, General George Armstrong Custer commanded the First Brigade. Lowell had known Custer on McClellan's staff, but they had never been close. Custer was brave and clever and knew how to get the best from his men but Lowell found him too much of a dandy, too self-regarding, too fond of publicity. Wilson, Merritt, and Lowell all loathed Custer. No one questioned his abilities, but it was insufferable to be around him.

General Thomas C. Devin, commanding the Second Brigade, was not a West Pointer. An Irishman from New York City, he had risen by his own intelligence under the approving eye of General Buford. (Buford's mentorship was a stamp of approval that was, in many ways, better than being a West Point graduate: one became an insider and yet remained unknown, immune to the gossip and petty jealousies that dogged West Point connections.) William Averell, an older man and the ranking cavalry general, was prickly and disliked by both Merritt and Custer.

Commanding the Cavalry Corps was General Alfred A. Torbert, an infantryman like Sheridan. He never distinguished himself for his skill but was very well liked and a peacemaker among many brilliant but egotistical cavalry commanders. Torbert was two years older than Lowell and sported huge, thick side whiskers.

General Philip Sheridan, commanding all these young men at the age of thirty-three, was a wiry, pugnacious Irishman whose parents had immigrated first to Albany and later to Ohio. He graduated from West Point in 1853 in the bottom third of the class and served for eight years on the frontier. At the war's start he commanded the Second Michigan Cavalry, in the western theater where, after a series of bold and successful actions, Grant promoted him. At Missionary Ridge in November 1863, his decisiveness made him a favorite, and Grant brought him east in April 1864 to command the newly formed Cavalry Corps of the Army of the Potomac. Although his experience was entirely with infantry, Sheridan had the physique of a cavalryman. He stood not over five foot three. More important, his natural aggression turned the cavalry to best advantage. The result had been a series of dramatic raids in the early summer of 1864. Now Sheridan commanded an entire army.

Lowell liked him, calling him "the first General I have seen who puts as much heart and time and thought into his work as if he were doing it for his own exclusive profit. He works like a mill-owner or an iron-master." It is an interesting comment. Lowell had admired General McClellan for his administrative efficiency, for his capacities of organization and structural expediency, and for his ability to supply the army and keep it supplied. McClellan had been an engineer by training who before the war had left the army and worked for the Illinois Central Railroad. Sheridan, on the other hand, had spent his career in those western forts notorious for their destruction of initiative—too much whiskey, too many card games, too little to do—and yet it was Sheridan whom Lowell considered the entrepreneur.[29]

In a letter to John Murray Forbes, Lowell explained, "I have great confidence in Sheridan. He works at this business as if he were working for himself, watches everything himself . . . And keeps his officers pretty well up to their work. If the campaign does not succeed, it will not be for want of interest and energy on his part." Lowell said that Sheridan had no vainglory: "never sleeps, never worries, is never cross but isn't afraid to come down on a man who deserves it." This had been McClellan's great fault in Lowell's eyes: his half-measures with Burnside and Sumner had jeopardized the success of the Antietam battle. But Sheridan took responsibility, and in his dealings with his subordinates he made them do so as well. When Lowell said that Sheridan worked as if "for his own exclusive profit," he meant that Sheridan wanted not to be *seen* to be a good general but to *be* one, by winning battles. This was not the usual "might makes right" logic, for Lowell went on to say that he admired Sheridan "whether he succeeds or fails."[30]*

And Sheridan admired Lowell: confirmation of this fact came on September 9 with Lowell's promotion to command of the Reserve Brigade. When Lowell had applied for a regular commission in the army, he had predicted that the volunteer army would supply talent "and more than their

---

*Lowell was proposing that a ruthless concern with results was the proper attitude for conducting a war, as opposed to the more moderate and scrupulous considerations of someone like McClellan.

share of food for powder." He had said it would be the responsibility of the regular army to "keep the armies in the field and to keep them moving." Now he would command just such regular troops: the First, Second, Fifth, and Sixth U.S. Cavalries, this last being his old regiment. Lowell was also given Battery D of the Second U.S. Artillery. These troops were the backbone of the Union effort, and command of the Reserve Brigade was a distinct privilege—it was the legendary General John Buford's old command. A slouching man with a round face and drooping mustache, who dressed shabbily and whose pockets bulged with his pipe and tobacco pouch, Buford defied the stereotype of a cavalry officer as an elegant aristocratic figure. From his prewar experience Buford understood the potential of dismounted tactics and was instrumental in introducing to the Union cavalry the flexibility that combined the finesse of dismounted action (for the actual impact, or "shock") with the power of the classical charge (for pursuit), a technique that assured cavalry would prevail over infantry. Despite his brilliance, Buford's rise within the army had been slow. He lacked political connections, had an intense dislike of reporters, was personally modest, and failed to draw either publicity or mentors. But his subordinates adored him, and "the praise of John Buford was more highly esteemed by the officers under his command than a brevet commission."[31] Because Buford died in December 1863 of typhoid and exhaustion, his influence must be recognized by the example he set and the men he mentored who carried on his ideas after his untimely death. Assuming command of the Reserve Brigade, Lowell inherited the mantle of a cavalry legend.

Lowell responded to his advancement rather coolly. He told John Murray Forbes that he had had no hint that he would be made a brigadier. He confessed his new command was a sign that Sheridan was "entirely satisfied with what we have done," but he refused to supply Forbes with specific news, saying that he had only once seen his name in the papers since leaving Falls Church in June: "So I really don't know what I have done or where I have been." He did confess to Effie that "today has quite changed the face of things," but he also wrote to her, "Much more is expected . . . than from [an officer] commanding a little patched-up affair like my last command." He found that it was a difficult brigade to command, for "there are many prides and prejudices." These veterans did not want a volunteer colonel commanding them and were even prejudiced against a non–West Point graduate, despite Lowell's experience with the Sixth.[32] "I don't think I now care at all about being a Brigadier-General . . . I am perfectly satisfied to be

a Colonel, if I can always have a brigade to command." It is a curious attitude, since Lowell had never before shown a want of ambition, but he was
undoubtedly influenced by a letter he had just received from Governor Andrew's secretary, Albert G. Browne, who had attended the Latin School with
him. Browne's reason for writing was to solicit Lowell's opinion on the mood
among Massachusetts soldiers, a preliminary testing of the waters to see how,
if allowed, they would vote.[33]

On September 7 George McClellan accepted the Democratic Party's
nomination in a speech that laid out his conditions for peace. Although
McClellan had refused to join the Copperheads in declaring the war a failure, his notion of peace was one that would never last. He envisioned a reunion of the country in which each returning state would be readmitted
with "all its constitutional rights." This was entirely unacceptable to Lowell,
who considered it "contemptible." Whatever shred of loyalty he still felt for
the general was now severed. "Honestly," he wrote Effie, "I believe that if by
chance McClellan is elected, the North will split before his four years are
passed and we shall be left in the condition of the South American republics, or worse." The nation would become either "one despotism" or
many small warring republics. Three days later Lowell unequivocally stated
to his mother that "four years under McClellan would destroy what is left of
the Republic." To almost everyone, he repeated his confidence that Lincoln
would be reelected: "If success to our arms will further Lincoln's chances, I
feel as if each one of us, both in the army and at home, [has] a tenfold motive for exertion now." The Republican platform insisted on unconditional
surrender and the emancipation of all slaves. After so much fighting and so
many killed, Lowell believed that the only durable peace was one that irrev-
ocably expunged the greatest stain on, and the greatest threat to, the experiment in democracy that was the United States: slavery and the slave power.
To his friends who had left the army, he wrote, "Labour for recruits and for
Linkum [the standard way of conveying the president's name in black di-
alect], and you will do more than by sabring six Confederates."[34]

The critical nub of Browne's letter was his report on the other Massachusetts troops and the fate of their mutual friends. The Twentieth had been
mustered out in July, its numbers so small that there was no question of
reenlistment. A look back at its extraordinary history was a daunting thing.
Begun in naïveté, the Twentieth had been, in many respects, a nightmare
fantasy of college boys who had no business in war. But the regiment had
matured and done good service at the price of the lives of its men and offi-

cers. Among Lowell's connections in it, only his cousin Wendell Holmes, a rail-thin shell of a twenty-one-year-old, was still alive. Lowell had seen him in Washington just as he was mustered out of the war, profoundly grateful to have done "his duty." By June 1864 the war had so ground him down that he had been ready to resign even without his parents' approbation.

The Second Massachusetts Infantry now had only three of its original officers. The First Massachusetts Cavalry was so riven by poor commanding officers that none of Lowell's friends remained with it. Greeley Curtis and Charles Adams both had taken an extended leave of absence due to ill health. Curtis was "much damaged by war," as Charles Adams explained, but Adams too was mentally and physically exhausted. Tired of the "carnival of death,"[35] Adams had malaria and other intestinal complications. Despite the light work of escort duty at the headquarters of the Army of the Potomac, and a subsequent appointment as lieutenant-colonel of Henry Russell's Fifth Cavalry, Adams was repeatedly shipped home to regain strength.

More alarming to Lowell, and the real point of Browne's letter, was the news that Frank Barlow had broken down completely. On July 27 he had learned of the unexpected death of his wife from yellow fever. Theirs had been an intense romance, and they had married the day after war was declared. The next day Barlow had left for Washington and begun his meteoric rise within the volunteer army. As a lieutenant-colonel in the Sixty-first New York Infantry, he had served on the Peninsula, been wounded at Antietam, and recovered to fight at Fredericksburg and at Gettysburg, where he was left for dead. His wife, who all this time had been serving as a nurse in field hospitals, found him, and under her care he recovered to lead a division at Spotsylvania and receive his brevet as major-general under General Hancock. One of the boy generals, Barlow was fond of a checked shirt and a string tie. His lanky elegant frame was well captured by Winslow Homer in his painting *Prisoners from the Front*.

Barlow was a hard man. He judged harshly, finding most things and people inadequate. He spoke what he knew to be the truth, regardless of people's feelings, and he was as far from a sentimentalist as was possible. Most of his friends believed that he would have improved as a friend if he had had more tact; consideration was too much to ask. Yet Barlow's laconic manner, his bluntness, and his relentless, almost merciless, realism had made him an excellent warrior. Lowell had admired and envied him his success: of their circle Barlow had risen well beyond the rest. Lowell had used him as a yardstick and always found himself wanting.

The nature of Barlow's collapse was unnerving. On learning of his wife's death he requested leave to go to her but was refused. That evening grief overcame him, and by morning he had fragmented in ways that were beyond his ability to articulate. Granted a fifteen-day leave, he returned to his mother's house in Concord.

Lowell now wrote him a long letter, though he knew well that words were useless to affect Barlow in this early stage of grief and exhaustion. A decade before, the two of them had been disciples of Emerson and had followed the effects of the Compromise of 1850 in all its detail. They had stayed up late honing their passion for Justice and Right, following the events involving fugitive slaves in Boston, and railing against the insanity and moral cowardice of society. Lowell knew enough not to dismiss their shared passion. For Barlow it went back even farther: having grown up at Brook Farm, like Johnny Bancroft, he was literally a child of Transcendentalism. His passion for reform was fed by the shame of his father's pecuniary disappointment and inability to meet his marital obligations. When natural authority is such a disappointment, the soul of a reformer is born.

"Take care of yourself, old fellow," Lowell wrote. "Just get your mother to take you to some quiet place and make much of you—don't think too much of campaigns and of elections." Recognizing in his friend the same remorseless spirit that he himself possessed, Lowell strove to assuage any worries about Lincoln or the army or the desire for peace. These could all wait and would be attended to by others, like Lowell, who were still in the game. "What you want is rest and care," Lowell insisted. "Don't be foolish . . . and neglect them." The tables had turned on their fates. Six months before, Lowell had been desperate to leave Vienna and get himself into the real fighting, and he had written Barlow offering to dismount his men if they could serve under him. Now Frank was out of the game entirely, and his own star was rising. For Barlow's sake, Lowell wanted to undo or discount their old conversations. "I remember we said to each other six months ago, that the man who wasn't in the coming campaign might as well count out. Bah! It hasn't proved. There are as many campaigns for a fellow as there are half years to his life." And he offered Barlow a revised sense of mission: "Unless you give yourself some time now, you will never half complete your career . . . There are better things to be done in the Country, Barlow, than fighting, and you must save yourself for them too." It was the wisest and most apt comment of the letter, and this was precisely what Barlow did.[36]

Lowell also wrote to Henry Higginson, who on July 22, having secured a staff position with Barlow, had returned to the front. But he quickly found that his spine wound still gave him trouble—not the kind that would kill him or make him crazy, but he was no longer fit for days in the saddle. Barlow's collapse five days later speeded the inevitable. Higginson respectfully and respectably resigned and escorted the ailing Barlow, who could not bear to be left alone, back to Concord.

But Higginson was crushed neither physically nor emotionally. He had spent the better part of the past year recuperating in Boston and had snagged the girl of his dreams, Ida Agassiz. He was returning to her and the prospect of marrying her in December. Lowell wrote to him jovially and lightheartedly: Henry was now the man to envy. He teased him by boasting of all the unpleasant aspects of army life: "I drink no sugar in my coffee, butter and eggs are unobtainable . . . army beef is still only 13 cents." How else, he wanted to know, could an officer live on his pay? Lowell saw Higginson as leading the way back into civilian life and wanted to know how it was done. He mockingly admonished him to "live like a plain Republican, mindful of the beauty and the duty of simplicity. Nothing fancy now, Sir, if you please." He explained that it was disreputable to spend money "when there are so many poor officers," meaning, of course, himself.

But then he grew serious and told Henry, "Don't grow rich; if you once begin, you will find it much more difficult to be a useful citizen. That's what I preach to you and Wendell Holmes and Johnny and all other young people of our persuasion . . . The useful citizen is a mighty unpretending hero. But we are not going to have any Country very long unless such heroism is developed. Being a soldier, it *does* seem to me that I should like nothing else so well as being a useful citizen . . . Well, trying to be one, I mean."[37]

Lowell acknowledged that he would stay in the army until war's end or injury. To Henry he swore that he had lost all ambition. Claiming to have given up any thought of an intellectual career, he wrote, "All I now care about is to be a useful citizen with money enough to buy bread and firewood, and to teach my children how to ride on horseback and look strangers in the face, especially Southern strangers."[38] These are feelings that suit a man who is retiring from battle far better than one who is in the midst of a grueling campaign and has just been elevated to an honored command. How much did he express his true views, and how much were these words of comfort?

In trying to console Barlow, Lowell had suggested that he would now do the fighting while Barlow preserved himself for the future. He assumed that their common goal would be achieved by teamwork: a sort of baton passing. And to Higginson, Lowell gave the task of leading their mutual return to civilian life. Voicing his deep longing for that life, he confessed that he very much looked forward to a "pleasanter career" as a useful citizen, "one in which E. can be even a more better half."[39] His reference to how he and Effie might build a life together after the war suggests that his "integer" theory of relationship—that he needed his friends to make him whole—was still very much alive, however much he disliked theories. In this corporate idea, we are completed by others, and we find our wholeness in our friendships.

Whatever a psychiatrist might say about its implications for the full development of an individuated self, the theory suggests a great aptitude for friendship and collective action. Never in Lowell's letters did he speak of his ambitions outside the context of some corporate structure: his family, his circle of friends, his regiment, his marriage. This supposes that he could only conceive of his ambitions within the context of what he could contribute to the greater whole.

By the middle of September Lowell had given the Reserve Brigade new colors—the old flag had worn out. Made of red, white, and blue silk, with crossed sabers in a white triangle, Lowell described it as "the prettiest color in the army." Teasingly he told Effie, "You'll wonder at me, being willing to carry anything so 'gaudy,' but my well-known modesty enabled me to do it." This was typical Lowell: happy to wear a government-issue uniform and even to ride a government horse, and yet fussing over the silk guidon that his brigade would carry into battle.[40]

He did not want wealth because he loved money or wanted leisure. He did not want success because he needed to show off or be admired. His motives were interior—to live up to the family name, to compensate for his father's failure, to recoup the family fortune—and these were not so much ambitions as duties he owed to those he loved. He had brought their complexities to his experience of the war. His successes and opportunities in the army left him dissatisfied and, worse, feeling inadequate. The early deaths of friends and family exacerbated these feelings. His administrative work in Washington had seemed as "nothing." The regular cavalry had not taken the brunt of battle on the Peninsula. His elevation to McClellan's staff had been too safe. At Antietam he had demonstrated his valor, his integrity, and his moral ability in battle. But still Lowell was not satisfied.

Although he had acquitted himself on the Peninsula and at Antietam, he was horrified by battle, confessing to his aunt after Antietam that he never wanted to be in another one. He had never been bloodthirsty, wanting battle only as "an experience," and his first reaction to wearing a uniform was that he "looked like a butcher." Yet battle had given him a sense of himself, indeed had transformed his sense of self. None of his old theories—"What I have wasted through crude and stupid theories!" he wrote—added up to anything compared to those critical moments of action in which the great challenge was to see what needed to be done and to do it. In July 1863 he had written Effie these thoughts, ruefully commenting, "I wish I could feel as sure of doing my duty elsewhere as I am of doing it on the field of battle—that is so little a part of an officer's and patriot's duty now." So however much he hated battle, he had the capacity to fight, and he knew it. This self-knowledge was what he had always craved: he had found what Carlyle would have called his work.

He did not care whether he was made a brigadier or not; he asked only for the *duty* of a brigadier. He was now "where he could do good," where he could be useful. In his letter to Effie telling her of his promotion, he explained, "I am now where, if there is anything to be done for Mr. Linkum in the way of fighting, I may have a chance to do it." His reference to "Linkum" indicates what it was about Lincoln that garnered Lowell's support. He wanted to end the war, he wanted to end slavery, and he believed that Lincoln's reelection was the best hope of achieving those ends.[41]

NINETEEN

WINCHESTER

September 19, 1864

Since early August Generals Sheridan and Early had jockeyed for position, and by the second week of September both Confederate and Union commanders had begun to wonder about Sheridan's determination. Early was convinced he was facing yet another Union general afraid to fight. The mood in the Union army was bafflement about its frequent returns to Harpers Ferry, whence the campaign had begun. When troops once again began to push up the valley, a joke ran through the camps about "Harper's Weekly," a play on the title of the popular magazine of that name. Less amusingly, northern newspapers were criticizing Sheridan and doubting his capacities.

Grant was rightly concerned. "I had reason to believe," Sheridan wrote in his memoirs, "that the administration was a little afraid to have a decisive battle fought at this time, for fear it might go against us and have a bad effect on the November elections."[1] He decided to circumvent General Halleck's moderating influence (his orders to Sheridan were relayed through Halleck) and meet Sheridan in the Shenandoah Valley, at Charlestown, on September 17. There he learned that Sheridan's caution did indeed result from Halleck's and Secretary Stanton's admonitions about the political perils of a Union defeat. The two generals reestablished their mutual resolve for bold action, whatever the warnings from the War Department, and Sheridan was ready to take the offensive. He wanted to attack Early at Winchester, a prosperous town on the west bank of the Opequon, some miles west of the Shenandoah River, in the flat land between these two rivers. He proposed a two-pronged action—the cavalry attacking from the northeast, the infantry from the east. Grant gave him the green light, and Sheridan immediately put his plan into effect.

Following orders from his division commander, General Merritt, Lowell roused his brigade on September 19 at 1 a.m. from their camp at Ripon, just east of Summit Point, and was on the move by two. In the predawn light, Lowell's first task was to cross the Opequon at Seiver's Ford. Custer's men and General Thomas Devin's were using other fords, but in each case the river ran well below the height of the fields and had steep banks caused by erosion. Despite heavy fire from the enemy across the river, Lowell posted skirmishers, and Captain Theophilus Rodenbough, of the Second U.S. Cavalry, led his troops down the bank, across the stream, and on up the opposite incline, right into the rebel position. It was a repeat of his now well-tried technique, combining the speed of the horse with the deadly fire of dismounted men armed with Spencer carbines. Hardly firing a shot, Rodenbough's men overwhelmed the Virginians and took prisoners. Merritt reported that the action was "done in fine style."[2]

But once across the Opequon, Lowell's men encountered Confederate infantry entrenched behind earthworks, stone walls, and rail breastworks along the crest of a long, gently sloped wooded hill. The fighting to dislodge them was slow and nasty. The Confederates were so sure of their excellent position that they placed their battle flag prominently at their front as a challenge or taunt, as if to say to Lowell's men: If you damn Yankees want the flag, come and get it. After a morning of hard fighting, Lowell's men were incensed. They charged up the slope to "the very muzzles of the enemy's guns." Private Backus recalled, "It seemed rash, yes! Foolhardy to charge a line of infantry so well posted, but we did, Colonel Lowell leading the charge with the Second U.S. Cavalry." Though they failed to get the flag or hold the position, the men were strangely invigorated by the effort. Backus explained that "the moral effect of the charge was equal to a victory."[3]

Finally the Confederates' left flank crumbled and they began to retreat. Union forces followed, pressing them hard. By now Lowell's and Custer's brigades had linked up and were headed south down the Valley Pike, and for about an hour the two cavalry divisions pushed back the Confederate cavalry until it found shelter in a wood. Dislodging them was difficult, but by early afternoon Merritt ordered a total of five brigades of cavalry forward. First skirmishers advanced in small groups, sprinting for cover and firing. Behind them, across a front half a mile wide and three mounted men deep, some seven thousand horsemen went forward at a walk. The bands played national airs. Sabers glistened, while the flags and guidons added a picturesque element, as the Union cavalry began a slow trot.

With few options, the Confederates took the initiative and charged Custer's men in the middle of the federal line. At this action Merritt gave the order, and the entire line, yelling like maniacs, drew sabers and charged. Beneath the spectacle and the yelling, the thunderous noise of seven thousand horses' hooves pounding forward rumbled up from the earth. The horses, catching the excitement, were barely under control. The distinction between a stampede and a charge was hardly possible to make, until the Union cavalry began to wheel, flanking Early's left. It was a sight the Confederates had not seen before: raw power on a scale that was until then unimaginable. Early's men simply gave way.

Few Union cavalrymen attempted to describe this experience, for it defied words. After the war a number of them tried, but by then the conventional images invoked by observers and newspapermen were dominant. Most made it sound like a parade, mentioning the flags, the shine of the sabers, the unity of action. Sheridan wrote of the cavalry as "the thunderbolt of battle." Another officer used similar weather imagery: "It was like a thunder-clap out of a clear sky, and the bolt struck home." One described a charge as bursting "like a storm of case-shot." Many insisted it was "the grandest sight I saw during my army life."[4]

But it was not a parade, and very quickly the objectivity with which one can view a spectacle was discarded. One cavalryman attempted to go deeper:

> The sense of power and audacity that possesses the cavalier, the unity with his steed, both are perfect. The horse is as wild as the man: with glaring eye-balls and red nostrils he rushes frantically forward at the very top of his speed, with huge bounds, as different from the rhythmic precision of the gallop as the sweep of the hurricane is from the rustle of the breeze. Horse and rider are drunk with excitement, feeling and seeing nothing but the cloud of dust, the scattered flying figures, conscious of only one mad desire, to reach them, to smite, smite, smite![5]

This drunken contagion of power drove the Union cavalry forward.

A cavalry charge rarely if ever results in "shock," that is to say, in headlong contact. Either the numbers of charging horsemen are so reduced that only a few make contact, or else the line being charged gives way. Anyone who has tried to take a horse over even a low jump knows that horses are unwilling to run full tilt at something they do not want to jump: they will veer off or stop entirely. Whether because of the horse or the rider, cavalrymen know that a certain number of them will drop out before reaching the enemy. (It is a classic moment for "the slows.") Nor will an enemy horse stand still to receive the impact of a headlong charge. Thus it was not unusual for cavalry engagements to resemble a form of Scottish dancing: enough charging horses dropped out to permit the opposing horses to move aside to avoid impact, and the two forces would gallop past each other only to turn and repeat the exercise. This was hardly battle that an infantryman would recognize.

But when a cavalry charge had the power that the Union forces achieved at Winchester, the opposition simply crumbled, as Early's men did. The Confederate cavalry fell back on its infantry, and both fled through woods and emerged onto open fields, the Union cavalry hot on their heels. A Confederate artillery piece positioned in another copse on the outskirts of Winchester began to pummel the edge of the wood, preventing the federal cavalry from continuing their pursuit. This checked the charge, kept the whole line of Union cavalry pinned in the woods, and threatened to halt the advance. The Reserve Brigade was nearest to the artillery. "Charge and get the guns," Lowell yelled, and took off. The bugle sounded, and the Second U.S. Cavalry followed him. The Confederate battery fired musketry straight at them, and for a moment the leading squadron was checked. "Forward! Forward!" Lowell shouted, echoed by Captain Rodenbough.

The men gave a maniacal scream and resumed their gallop. Without breaking front, they leaped across a blind ditch, and then, as Rodenbough recalled, "we were face to face with the enemy." The attacking federals confronted a stunned opponent. The boldness of the charge, the refusal to be repulsed, and the sheer heroism of the Union forces had caught the rebels off guard. Many of them broke and fled as Lowell's regulars sabered them. But the rebels manning the cannons kept their heads and fired. In the explosion several horses were killed, including Lowell's, and Captain Rodenbough, who was next to Lowell, had his arm torn off. When the air cleared, Lowell, having mounted a stray horse, was still there and had taken possession of the artillery piece.[6]

The Confederates no longer offered any substantial resistance. Since early that morning, when Lowell charged their entrenched position, the Confederate infantry had been resisting the Union cavalry, and by now they were desperate. Their general, John C. Breckenridge, a former Kentucky senator and in 1860 a candidate for president, formed them into a hollow square.

As the Union cavalry approached this square, Lowell must have been struck by the sight. This had been Wellington's successful tactic to withstand Napoleon's cavalry at Waterloo. All West Point graduates and most officers would have recognized this strongest of defensive positions. Officers could control men in a square with greater ease than on the line, and the men felt much safer: the wounded could retreat into the square, protected by their comrades; the sense of group solidarity among men formed in a square was very strong.

But the square had no moral effect on the Union cavalry whatsoever. Their charge overran and destroyed it. The men broke and ran in all directions, and the rebel army became a mob mobilized by fear. Whatever connection had existed between officers and men was broken. One Yankee recalled this part of the battle as "a carnival of death."[7] Across the landscape a primal scene was being enacted. Men on horseback were slaughtering men on the ground. Artillery was now useless, and the sounds of battle were no longer deafening but a kind of articulated chaos. Even the gunfire was not so heavy. Instead the screams of dying men and horses competed with the maniacal hollering of the conquerors. Horsemen gored, hacked, slashed, and stabbed whatever came within their reach. The Confederate army was driven back into Winchester and through the town. In the chaos and smoke, with fighting on all sides, the difficulty was to stay with one's unit, to not become engulfed and overwhelmed by the manifest carnival of killing—at which point one became victim rather than killer.

That evening in the Union cavalry camps, the men exulted around campfires. Exhaustion and euphoria kept adrenaline pumping through them. The light of the fires exaggerated their smoke- and sweat-streaked faces, filthy from battle, the whites of their eyes, their glistening teeth, and the hollows of their cheeks. Some were grieving over their own dead, sacrificed in this orgy of killing, but there had been few Union casualties, and these had occurred mostly in the early fighting, before the glorious charge. The men knew they had participated in something unique, and they had tasted power on a heretofore unimaginable scale. After years of fearing the Confederates, and of hearing long-winded editorializing about Confederate aristocratic superiority and the southerners' inherent martial virtue, as contrasted with the hopelessly middle-class, spineless, shopkeeper northern mentality, of all that humble pie that had had to be eaten, now finally they had tasted not only victory but the collapse of the enemy. The men exulted at the omnipotence of their destruction. Victory and destruction were analogous. This fact worked like a powerful drug: for some it was a stimulant, for others a narcotic. A year earlier Lowell had wondered how the Union troops would handle victory. Writing Effie, he had argued that victories would come "whether or no we are ready for them."[8] Now he witnessed one at first hand.

Within the cavalry, victory excited jealousies. Between Merritt and Custer there had always been an intense rivalry that impelled both commanders to do their best. A few days before the battle Custer had been given a division to command, which had intensified this rivalry. Now Custer believed he had outperformed Merritt, and he did not hesitate to revel in this conviction. As the officers celebrated, Custer teased Lowell, asking why he had no battle flags to show.

"Oh, flags do not hurt anybody," Lowell replied. "Why don't you capture some artillery?"[9] It was a good riposte, and everyone who heard it laughed, but Lowell had not really been joking.

Military historians agree that the Union cavalry in this battle had finally been used "right." The power unleashed had no equal on earth, but the next evening, writing to Effie, Lowell sounded anything but victorious. He did not communicate any triumph. He gave few details, describing nothing of what he had seen, or felt, or done, except to say that Billy, Will Forbes's horse, which he had been riding at Winchester, had been "shot in three places and is dead."[10]

Lowell also wrote to Alice Forbes, Will's closest sibling, only two years older than he. To her he did not justify having used Billy—he simply explained the situation. The charge that killed Billy had failed, "but not through any fault of men or horses." If before the charge, he had had an orderly nearby, he would have swapped horses, but that had not been possible. He spoke of his resolve to get Will a new horse, "but of course he can never replace Billy." It was a most respectful and considerate letter, especially when one remembers how much else was demanding Lowell's immediate attention. One senses that Lowell needed to write to Alice: he may have needed to create for himself a psychic island of civility. Writing to a thoughtful young Boston girl was a way of so doing.[11]

Horses mattered to cavalrymen—not just in the abstract, but in the particular. A horse was a huge investment in man-hours, training it to the battlefield and to the demands of cavalry. An excellent mount was a testament to its owner's horsemanship and required constant attention—feeding, watering, cleaning, saddling, unsaddling, and shoeing—tasks that however boring and repetitive made a huge difference in the life and quality of a horse. But these various forms of investment had a distinct payoff: a good mount could make the difference between life and death. Horse and rider had to be "one."

Many horses had ordinary names: Crowninshield called his favorite horse Jim. Will Forbes's two horses were Billy and Dick. Lowell had Nig, "the gray," and innumerable nameless government horses. But he also had three whose names resonated: Berold, Atalanta, and Ruksh. Berold, now Effie's horse, was always mentioned in their letters as grazing happily, with a spectacular valley view, or wearing a red blanket.* Atalanta, of whom we have no physical description, had been a gift from John Murray Forbes. Lowell had had high hopes for her and had invested many hours in her training, but at the end of August she was stolen from the line.

That left Ruksh, the horse that had been wounded at Rockville. Ruksh was named for the horse ridden by the warrior Rustum in Matthew Arnold's adaptation of the Persian epic *Sohrab and Rustum*. The poem depicts a single combat between two warriors. Sohrab, a young man of mysterious birth who has fantasies about the father he never knew, fights with the Tartars; Rustum, the greatest of the Persian warriors, is haunted by his failure to have any progeny. The two men battle, and only after Rustum mortally wounds Sohrab do they discover that they are father and son. When Sohrab dies in his father's arms, Ruksh, Rustum's black stallion, as formidable as his owner, gives out an anguished scream that speaks for his master's agony of guilt and regret. The week before Winchester, Lowell took Ruksh out, and he was wounded for the third and last time. Shot in the foreleg, he was ruined for life. Perhaps it was just as well that a horse freighted with so resonant a name should have amounted to so little.

Lowell had hoped to train up "the gray." On August 24 he had written Effie that he was going to use the gray "habitually," but shortly thereafter she

---

*Berold, a chestnut, was named after the horse in Browning's *The Flight of the Duchess*. This long poem is told in the voice of the servant of an Italian duke who lives under the sway of his sickly and obsessive mother. Describing the duke's deforming childhood, Browning twice invokes "red Berold" as the better but neglected alternative. Berold is described as "Mad with pride, like fire to manage! . . . With the red eye slow consuming in fire, / And the thin stiff ear like an abbey spire!" Lowell's Berold may have had some of this feistiness originally, but after surviving the West Woods at Antietam, he never recovered his calm and became useless: "so foolish about bullets" and "entirely uncontrollable" under shellfire. Still, Effie had formed a deep affection for him.

became badly "corked," meaning unserviceable. "I have had my usual bad luck with horses," he wrote Effie. (He begged her not to tell others about it: "It seems foolish." What he perhaps really meant was that his superstition was foolish.)[12]

For two and a half years he had been spending what money he had on horses. At the end of August he had written Charlie Perkins to sell the farm he had bought in Illinois, because he needed money for more horses. But even if he'd had the money good horses were scarce. When Lieutenant Alvord rejoined the regiment just after the battle of Winchester, he brought two horses with him, one of which, a mare, Lowell coveted and determinedly set about trying to buy. The young lieutenant idolized Lowell and was much conflicted, but he refused to give up his mount.

Because of these difficulties with Ruksh and the gray, Lowell had begun to ride Forbes's horses. At first Lowell rode Dick despite his skittishness under fire. But Dick soon was shot in the hind leg, a bad break, and was "abandoned." Lowell then turned to Billy and continued to ride him, although he had been twice wounded. Two days before Winchester he had rather defensively told Effie that there was nothing cavalier in his use of the horse and insisted that he rode Billy only when he absolutely had to. But now Billy was dead. Yet another horse had been killed under Lowell in the afternoon charge on the artillery guns, and two more horses wounded.

Before Winchester Lowell had had eight horses shot from under him. Not all were his own, and not all had he paid for. Many men were taken prisoner when their horses were wounded or killed. But Lowell escaped injury and capture. He was light and agile enough to be able to jump clear, and as long as he had an orderly nearby, he had help changing horses as well as a fresh mount at the ready. When he lacked an orderly, his horsemanship stood him in good stead, for he was able to approach any loose horse on the field and gain control of it. As a colonel, he could commandeer any mount in his regiment if necessary, but he most likely never tested his men's devotion in this fashion.

The men kept count of the horses Lowell lost as a way of tallying his luck, and they believed him lucky. The more intimately a man worked with Lowell, the more he believed this. Lowell's orderly, Frank Robbins, became obsessed with it. His memoir of the war is essentially a list of Lowell's lucky moments. Dr. DeWolf said of Lowell, "I dared not look at him for I knew he would fall, & yet he came back steadily & all right—his horse always wounded or killed & himself never, *until I began to feel that he was safe,* but how, God alone knew." Lowell's luck made the men feel lucky, too. Sergeant Williams, on Lowell's staff, wrote that he had been forced to be where "there was the most danger for I must keep with the Colonel & He was always in the front when we were moving toward the enemy & in the rear when moving from them there were several solid shot & shell passed between us when not more than 20 ft. apart, but we were lucky."[13]

"My luck carried me through safe," wrote home a member of Company F. "I was lucky," many explained. "My usual luck" was another common comment. This confidence in their own survival was allied with recognition of themselves as "duty men." The more a man had this sense of himself, and the more he recognized his company as "a fighting lot," the more he admitted to a belief in luck. A soldier could describe examining a board of wood he had once hidden behind and although it was full of bullet holes not one had hit home. "Very lucky indeed" was how Private John Passage from Company F put it, noting that he had spent the last fifteen days and nights in the saddle.[14]

Private George W. Towle regularly served as Lowell's orderly. On one occasion he was sent to herd in some straggling prisoners who were winded and moving slowly. Towle, who was mounted, became the focus of artillery fire, and one shell burst at his horse's heels. Initially he assumed his horse's rump had been cut off, but in fact after the dirt and sand blown up by the explosion had settled, it was clear that both rider and horse were uninjured. Another piece of luck. Almost all the duty men duly noted the losses and near-deaths: "3 men [were] shot right beside me & [I] have never even received a scratch yet."[15] They knew that the distinction between life and death was but a matter of a yard or two at most, sometimes only a whisker's breadth or a split-second's timing.

In recounting these adventures both men remarked on the seemingly miraculous nature of their survival and also expressed the seeds of a kind of guilt about having survived. No one could explain the randomness of survival. But they were expressing a great truism: one did not need to be safe to survive. This was key. They learned they could ride through artillery fire and not be hit. The men learned they could charge an entrenched enemy and be over the barricades before the enemy fire had an effect. This knowledge was potent, and it led men to believe in themselves—not that they were invulnerable but that their fate lay, not in their own power or the power of their officers or of the enemy, but rather in some version of a divine power. They were kept safe by their own fate or by the power of prayer, usually not their own.

One man believed it was his sweetheart's prayers that protected him. Another was convinced that God had appointed the time and place of his death, and nothing he did could affect that moment. Backus told his father, "The ruler of all things controls my destiny," and he was not "destined to be taken off by any reb bullet." Such faith permitted him to fight without any regard for his own survival. Many spoke simply of how the bullet that would kill them "had not found them yet." Lowell led everyone to believe that "death would not touch him." A few recognized that some of this luck was also skill, that the odds of survival were better for the duty men than for those who did not keep their heads. A man like Backus understood this. He recognized that Lowell's capacity for clarity and quick thinking—for seeing the situation and seeing, in Lowell's words, "what needs to be done"—had repeatedly saved himself and his men.[16]

In describing how Lowell's courage inspired his men, Dr. DeWolf wrote that they "were ashamed to do anything less than their full duty under his eyes." They had "great confidence in him, wanted to see him among them, and wished for nothing so much as to show him what they dared to do." Sergeant Porter passionately claimed, "There wasn't a man who wouldn't have died for Lowell."[17] This was the expected power of an officer's leadership, of his example and inspiration fusing. The men needed to know their officers' worth, which could not be faked. Bravery was measurable. But the measure was a matter not merely of prowess in combat but of how an officer took risks. Essentially it became a matter of honor—in good comportment, exposure to risk, and acceptance of death—of evincing an officer's "moral worth," his self-knowledge and self-control. Men and boys who believed they needed to experience battle believed they would not know themselves until they had been tested in this way. The men were applying to their officers the same criteria by which they operated themselves. Few of them wanted to be heroes—glory seekers were rare—but most men did want to do their duty and their officer was key in establishing what that duty might be. This was why it was so important that Lowell took risks like leading the charge following the death of Eigenbrodt. Every time he took a risk, he renewed and deepened the bond between himself and his men.

It could be said that what his men saw was Lowell's "mask of command,"[18] of which his cool nerves, quick thinking, and philosophical or fatalistic mentality were vital ingredients. But in Lowell's case the mask was worn not just for purposes of command. As shown in his letters, he made a true confidant of no one. In essence, Lowell had developed his mask long before he joined the army.

The effect on the officers of their men's obedience to them is not well documented. But Dr. DeWolf described how Lowell would watch his men in action "with tears in his eyes."[19] Probably only DeWolf, as Lowell's tent-mate and a noncombatant, was in a position to have glimpsed behind the mask and noticed this show of feeling. And doubtless Lowell would have attributed the tears to the effect of a strong wind or the smoke of battle. But the small detail is important. So many of the men whom Lowell had respected and counted on were dead. He had grieved over the deaths of Willy Putnam and his brother, Jim, and Perkins, Savage, and Shaw—personal and most intimate losses, but not ones for which Lowell felt personal responsibility. The dead of his own command were another matter: men such as Dearborn and Eigenbrodt and Reed. Lowell knew little enough of the personal circumstances of his officers, nothing of his privates, but he knew that they had given all they had to give. He had asked it of them. True, he had gone there with them: they had all ridden into danger together, and however well protected they were by the guiding hand, Providence, the Fates, God, or some divine presence, bullets did find a great many of them. His luck had not protected them.

The battlefield was a place of overwhelming stimulation that quickly became a fantastic chaos. It was a place of deepest confusion, an unknown landscape baffled by the smoke of guns and noise of battle. No participant could have any idea of what the larger action was. Men moved en masse but quickly found a terrible aloneness. Within each individual there was an inner struggle to gain courage or simply to take action. Brutality was everywhere. Combat, while appearing completely impersonal, was actually intensely personal. Each man on the battlefield was waging his own lonely struggle to survive.

However little he showed it, the viciousness of battle disturbed Lowell greatly, we know, and yet just as some men became crazed with fear, some were possessed with fury. For a man like Lowell, rage had always been a motivating force. He had, from his infancy, had a supreme egotism, dominating his siblings and turning a deaf ear to his mother's chastisements. By the time he was seven or eight, he made his bow to what Anna had called the "sharp ring of necessity," but he remained a bluff child who loved hard sport and was brusque and ungracious, conceding turf to niceties only grudgingly. He was defensive and proud but most of all angry. He carried his sullenness with him onto the playground, learning to fight and to throw himself relentlessly into sport. When he came home with a black eye, he thought nothing of his injury. In the shame of his father's bankruptcy and the pain of his mother's sacrifice in "saving" the family, the emotional conditions were hatched for Lowell to develop the soul of a reformer. As he matured, he gained an articulate intellectuality that eventually tamed, or appeared to tame, his surliness. His brilliance permitted him to get most of what he wanted, and his powers of rational thought harnessed his rampant desires. Through sheer brainpower he gained self-control, creating a mask of indifference and ultimate coolness—which channeled his anger and outrage into a reformer's zeal—wanting to change the world, to bring greater justice to his society.

Once he was in the war, many believed that he was immune to fear and fatalistic. But indifference and coolness, fearlessness and fatalism did not motivate one to charge entrenched infantry or to gallop among enemy soldiers, whacking at their muskets with a saber. Perhaps the best clue to his motives lies in his retort to Custer. The reformer, the avenger, the man angry at injustice went after artillery, not battle flags. As he told Custer, artillery kills.

TWENTY

SCORCHED EARTH

In the final phases of the battle of Winchester, Union cavalry had chased the Confederates some twenty miles south of Winchester, and on September 20 they were once again at Strasburg, where the Massanutten Mountains split the Shenandoah Valley, creating two parallel valleys fraught with the possibilities of ambush and fighting on two fronts. The Confederates had taken the North Fork, following the western, broader valley. Sheridan now attempted to turn the potential trickiness of the geography to his advantage. He divided his army: Lowell, part of Merritt's First Division, was sent to join General Wilson's Third Division in the narrow, more mountainous eastern Luray Valley. Their purpose was to shoot up—that is, south—to Harrisonburg, where the Massanutten Mountains ended and the Shenandoah Valley once again opened up. Moving quickly, they would block the top of the North Fork, and when Sheridan's infantry drove Early's forces up the valley, they would become trapped between the two Union forces, creating the opportunity to destroy them.

Once in the Luray Valley, however, the cavalry found that the Confederates had anticipated them. Confederate General William C. Wickham (who had replaced Fitzhugh Lee after his wounding at Winchester) was well lodged at Snake Hill and held a steep pass blocking their way south. Wilson had spent the last twenty-nine hours attempting to dislodge them. General Torbert attacked this position. The fight was almost exclusively against artillery, and, as one rebel artillerist put it, "All hell will never move me from this position." After an initial attack to test the Confederate position, Torbert decided it was impregnable, the cost of a further attack too high, and he pulled back to Front Royal, at the northern entrance to the Luray Valley.[1]

The route of their retreat lay along a narrow road with steep embankments heavily wooded on both sides. With the ambulance trains leading, they approached the head of the valley and the outskirts of Front Royal when about fifty of Mosby's Rangers descended on the wagons and pitched into the advance guard, which was a portion of Lowell's Reserve Brigade, the Second U.S. Cavalry under the command of Lieutenant Charles McMaster. The Rangers drove them back, and when the Second Cavalry regrouped and charged, McMaster's bridle reins were clipped by gunshot. His unreined horse ran ahead and carried him into the middle of a group of Rangers, who immediately took him prisoner. As some Rangers liberated his possessions, others began to rob the wounded men in the ambulances, a move reminiscent of their actions in the Wilderness months before.

Only when the federal cavalrymen "came up like a flock of birds when a stone is cast into it,"[2] as one Ranger recalled, did they realize that two divisions of federal cavalry rode behind the wagons. All thoughts of prisoners and plunder were abandoned in the rush to escape. Whether McMaster's captors deliberately shot him or whether they simply abandoned him and he was randomly gunned down by fleeing Rangers riding past cannot be proved, but as the Second U.S. Cavalry rallied and charged, they found their lieutenant lying in the road riddled with bullets. Though badly wounded, he was able to explain that he had been shot after surrendering.

Meanwhile, alerted by the regulars that the ambulances had been ambushed, Lowell sent an order back through the column: "Colonel Lowell wants a California company."[3] The call was answered by a group of about twenty-five California men, largely from Company L. Because the road was narrow and clogged with men and horses, it took some time for them to get to the head of the line. They all had to pass the attacked ambulance trains and the stricken bodies of Lieutenant McMaster and the men around him. In one fashion or another they all learned something about what had occurred. Attacking an ambulance train put the Rangers on a low moral ground from the first, and shooting a prisoner who had surrendered was an outrage. The Californians were reminded of their own men whom Mosby had shot in similar fashion.

We do not know what order Lowell gave the Californians then. Presumably he had called for them because they would know what to do without great explanation. This supposes that speed was of the essence: here was a chance to chase the Rangers down. Just the week before, General Halleck had complained to Grant, "The two small regiments under General Augur [Sixteenth and Thirteenth New York Cavalries] have been so often cut up by Mosby's band that they are cowed and useless for that purpose."[4] Without effective opposition, Mosby had reemerged as a persistent, successful gadfly.

Rangers had impeded Sheridan's lines of supply, robbed supply trains and paymasters headed for Sheridan's army, raided wagon trains, and murdered commissaries. On August 13 Mosby had attacked a wagon train at Berryville; on August 20 a special detail of one hundred men under an old Indian fighter named Blazer armed with Spencers was sent to "clean out Mosby's gang," but daily attacks continued until September 14, when Lieutenant Henry Gansevoort's men succeeded in wounding Mosby, although that did not stop the action. On September 16 Rangers attacked a wagon train, captured a commissary wagon, and murdered a detail of the Eighth New York Cavalry. On September 21 they ambushed five Union soldiers and captured four of them. The next day they captured two of Custer's messengers. Now came this attack on an ambulance train. The Californians were eager to pursue the Rangers, and to show the rest of their division what experienced men could do against Mosby.

Private Sam Corbett from Company A recorded in his diary that evening how the Californians took off "like a swarm of bees," joining the Second Cavalry in pursuit of the Rangers. Not without some pride, he recounted how they chased them down, killed seventeen, and took four prisoners. He claimed to have captured one himself. George Buhrer in Company E, a survivor of the Dranesville disaster, described pursuing the Rangers "hotly and taking seventeen prisoners," and he recorded the grimmest sort of satisfaction in the murder of these men. "Their fat was tough," he wrote; "they had to suffer death." The macabre tone was doubtless intensified by the fact that his own regiment had run out of rations two days before. The men were, in the words of one of them, "hungry and ugly."[5]

A member of Company L writing in 1911, forty-seven years after the event, recalled nine prisoners captured, all of whom, he claimed, were turned over to Custer's brigade. Custer's men had a grievance against the Rangers, who on August 18 had run up against a picket post of the Fifth Michigan Cavalry, wounding and capturing most of them. In retaliation Custer's men had gone on a burning binge for two days, ruthlessly destroying homes and looting as they torched. On August 20 the Rangers counterattacked, with yells of "No quarter! Take no prisoners!"[6] They swooped down and killed fifteen of Custer's men.

It is doubtful that one brigade would have handed over prisoners to another, particularly when only three days earlier Custer had taunted and teased Lowell, flaunting his high numbers of captured flags and prisoners. On the other hand, these nine supposedly turned over to Custer, together with the four mentioned by Corbett, would explain the figure of thirteen killed that Lowell reported, a figure that also accords with that given by the Second U.S. Cavalry's regimental historian. Newspaper accounts at the time claimed that General Merritt had shot and hanged twelve of Mosby's men; other reports gave slightly different figures, one as high as eighteen. An exact figure was never established. In most engagements the number killed is substantially less than those wounded and captured, and yet in the Front Royal affair the numbers were reversed. It seems clear that the intention was to take "no prisoners" or give "no quarter." Robert C. Wallace, a member of General Torbert's staff, wrote that some of the captured men "were told to run and as they ran were fired upon until they fell,"[7] but he did not make it clear who the executioners were, although they were believed to be members of Custer's Michigan Cavalry. Yet logic would assume they were the Second U.S. or the Second Massachusetts Cavalry, who had swarmed after the Rangers. Thomas Anderson might very well have been the last of these victims. Eyewitnesses saw him running from his captors, who shot him at almost the same location where McMaster's body had been found. This suggests that the Second U.S. Cavalry was subjecting their prisoners to the same treatment the Rangers had doled out to McMaster.

Of the four prisoners brought in to Front Royal, Henry Rhodes was not even a Ranger. A local seventeen-year-old who dreamed of joining the Partisans, he had gone along that day on a borrowed horse, hoping to capture one he could call his own. (Mosby would accept no Ranger without a horse.) Instead he was dragged into town tied between two horses. His mother ran out and hysterically begged for his life. But her pleas may have helped to seal her son's death: civilians found in arms against the Union were not entitled to be treated like prisoners of war but instead were termed "enemies of mankind" and had "the rights due to pirates," by which was meant none at all.[8] Rhodes was shot at the far edge of town, his body was put in a wheelbarrow with a rubber coat draped over it, and he was dumped at his mother's door. Regardless of official sanction, the viciousness and needless cruelty of his death indicate men out of control.

No one in the Second Massachusetts Cavalry admitted involvement in the murder of Anderson or Rhodes. But the other four prisoners who made it to Front Royal were claimed as theirs. Private Corbett's diary describes their fate: "two of whom we shot and the other two we hung in retaliation for shooting two of our men that they had captured." The first two were David Jones and Lucian Love, both longtime Rangers, who were marched to Front Royal, turned over to the divisional provost guard, and questioned by General Torbert, who had been a friend of McMaster's and was upset by his mortal wounding. A member of his escort, Samuel C. Willis, recalled that, "satisfied that they were from Mosby's command, he [Torbert] ordered them shot." Love and Jones were taken out to the graveyard behind the Methodist church and dispatched, perhaps by the men of the Second Massachusetts Cavalry who captured them but more likely by a detail under the provost-marshal of General Merritt, Captain Theodore Bean of the Seventeenth Pennsylvania Cavalry. The second pair of men, William Overby and a man identified only as Carter, arrived just after these executions. Torbert had by now calmed enough to make at least a stab at interrogation. He asked them to reveal Mosby's hideout. He promised that if they did, they would be treated as prisoners of war; if they did not, they too would be shot. Overby, as spokesman for both, refused. Torbert was enraged by their lack of cooperation. All his passions were reexcited, and he told Bean, "Take those men up to that tree and hang them."[9]

Bean was loath to hang the men. He gave them many chances to give information in the hopes that he wouldn't have to do the job, but they refused to betray Mosby. Custer's band played the funeral dirge as the two men were marched to their hanging. Some accounts claim that Custer's men managed the hanging; others say only his band participated and that the Second U.S. Cavalry did the hanging. Carter, the smaller of the two, who seemed genuinely humbled at the thought of death, asked for time to pray. But Overby, a tall, proud Georgian, maintained a contemptuous disdain and assured his captors that Mosby would revenge the hangings tenfold. Custer's band struck up "Love Not, the One You Love May Die." Ropes were put around Overby's and Carter's necks, their horses' flanks pounded. As the horses took off, the bodies dropped. On Overby's swinging body a placard was placed: "This will be the fate of Mosby and all his men." Or perhaps it said, "Hung in retaliation for the murder of United States soldiers." Or simply, "Such is the fate of Mosby's men." The people of Front Royal were told not to cut down the bodies, and for days they remained as grisly reminders.[10]

These atrocities took less than two hours. Most of the Union command drew a veil of silence over the events at Front Royal. Custer, who was instantly held responsible, never spoke of it. Merritt and Torbert were also silent. Crowninshield claimed that the Second Massachusetts Cavalry had "nothing to do with this,"[11] no doubt drawing a distinction between the capture, then killing, of the Rangers in the field and the murder of the four prisoners after they had been turned in to the division provost-marshal in town.

Lowell knew that thirteen killed, the number he reported, was too high in relation to the number of prisoners taken. His only comment on the take-no-prisoners attitude of his men was to tell Effie he was "sorry enough his brigade" had had "a part in the hanging and shooting" of the four executed men, but "it was all by order of the Division Commander." He believed that "some punishment was deserved—but I hardly think we were within the laws of war, and any violation of them opens the door for all sorts of barbarity."[12] What did he mean in this case? Would he have been better pleased with the sort of drumhead court-martial and summary execution that he had used to handle William Ormsby? That had not been strictly within the laws of war either. Also there was the problem of the culprit: no one knew which of the Rangers had shot McMaster, much less whether that individual had been killed or even captured.

Temporarily things had gotten completely out of control. The challenge was to return the men to the command structure and the rules of war, to close the door on the possibilities for barbarity. Much of what had occured could not possibly be explained or understood, for it had taken place in that murky border region of moral ambiguity so frequent in war. Mosby had always teased these boundaries. Could one even call any of the incidents involving him subject to the rules of warfare? Many in the army thought not. Lowell had commanded the regular regiments for less than two weeks and earlier had spoken of the challenge he faced in winning their acceptance. Had he failed to control his men?

In the Second Massachusetts Cavalry the mood was strongly supportive of the executions. The men remembered the defilement of Reed's body after his death, the attacks on lone pickets, the times when Mosby's men had worn blue overcoats and passed as Union soldiers only to attack viciously, the humiliation at Coyle's Tavern, the times when Rangers had picked off troopers from the safety of woods and then run instead of standing and fighting, and the times they'd sworn loyalty oaths wearing the overalls of honest farmers, only to slip out and ride off with rifles that very evening. Still, it is worth noting that the only prisoners turned over to the provost-marshal in something that approximated the correct fashion were those delivered by the Second Massachusetts Cavalry.

For a year and a half general orders had sanctioned reprisals against guerrillas, encouraging their swift and merciless suppression. On August 16 Grant had reinforced this policy, telling Sheridan, "Where any of Mosby's men are caught hang them without trial." In another telegram of the same day, he had wanted Sheridan to send cavalry into Loudoun County to "destroy and carry off crops, animals, [and] Negroes" and all its male residents under fifty. On August 17 Sheridan wrote back, "Mosby has annoyed me and captured a few wagons. We hung one and shot six of his men yesterday." (In fact these were not Rangers but local bushwhackers or perhaps just suspicious locals.) On August 19 general circulars were issued implementing Grant's orders. The next day Sheridan assigned a party of one hundred men, the Blazers, to capture or kill Mosby. By the end of that week Grant was reminding General Augur to burn all wheat, hay, and fodder in Loudoun County. If he could not catch Mosby, he would starve him out. "So long as the war lasts they must be prevented from raising another crop."[13]

We can thus begin to appreciate the depth of the challenge that Lowell's men had faced earlier at Vienna, why they were so unhappy when Lowell denied them the satisfaction of retaliation, and the power of Lowell's leadership in requiring this unpopular and difficult discipline. After Front Royal his men could perhaps see that not only had they been effective in containing Mosby, but their forbearance had prevented an untenable escalation of violence so near the capital. In less than two months, the violence was profound. Front Royal to this day is a community for whom the trauma of September 23, 1864, continues.

But for the Union army, the door closed on the Front Royal affair as soon as it was over. Sheridan, livid that the cavalry had backed away from Wickham, sent them back into the Luray Valley, and on the very next day they found Wickham halfway up the valley, just outside the town of Luray, for which the narrow valley is named. The morning fog was very dense, and the men could not see more than thirty yards. They did not know the topography. After some hard and not very successful fighting, General James H. Wilson, Lowell's former colleague on McClellan's staff and superior at the Cavalry Bureau, who was now commanding the Third Division, ordered all the buglers of both divisions, some 250, to blow. Through the fog the hills echoed and reechoed, and the air filled with a swelling sound that seemed to come from all directions. The enemy, spooked and overwhelmed, "broke and ran in all directions."[14] Lowell's men captured the battle flag of the Sixth Virginia Cavalry. That evening the men roasted mutton and corn foraged from the local farmers. It was their first square meal in days.

As the brigade recouped, Lowell adopted into his retinue a "small black boy" named James. Since there were two Jameses already attached to the brigade, Lowell renamed him Luray, which he thought had an aristocratic ring. He wrote to Effie that he hoped she would teach him to read and write during the winter. But what most impressed Lowell was the countryside, "the loveliest mountain scenery you can imagine," he wrote. And he sent her a "little purple Gerardia" picked by General Wilson, which, he explained, "he had just handed . . . to me, when my unfortunate Adjutant-General was shot right behind us (not fatal, though we feared so for some time), so it has not very pleasant associations." It was a curious letter. A year earlier Lowell had crushed and thrown away the flowers he had picked for Effie at Manassas, merely mentioning with an uneasy and tentative optimism that flowers could bloom where battles were fought. Now he sent the flower and told the tale, as if any kind thought or beautiful thing, however entangled with misery, death, and misfortune, were worth preserving. "I used to look forward to things somehow—now I don't look forward, but all the old pleasure of looking forward seems to be stirred in with things as they come along. I can't explain what I mean, but the difference is immense."[15]

On September 25 the much-delayed cavalry, having finally routed Wickham, hurried down the Luray Valley to join the main army. Their progress was slowed by the fact that the Confederates had burned bridges behind them. The federals were forced into long delays, following hairpin turns that snaked down the steep ravines. After the long dusty march, Lowell wrote Effie, "I'm glad you can't see the handkerchief I just pulled out. [It was] quite unpresentable even for me."[16] But they were too late to trap Early's army, and Sheridan had to decide whether to pursue Early up the valley. Despite much pressure from Grant, Sheridan, for a variety of reasons, decided not to do so.

Although of great strategic importance to the Confederacy, the Shenandoah Valley was of no practical use to the Union army, since its southwesterly direction took them away from Richmond. Its occupation would be hard work for little reward, but as it was of no use to the Union, it made sense to render it useless to the Confederacy as well. Sheridan wanted to end the campaign with a retreat back north down the valley, "desolating" the countryside as he went. This involved not only driving out the Confederate army but also, by destroying its crops, preventing or rendering pointless the valley's reoccupation. Fed up with the half-solutions that had been tried previously, Grant had earlier told Sheridan that once he had beaten Early's forces, "it is desirable that nothing should be left to invite the enemy to return. Take all provisions, forage and stock wanted for the use of your command; such as cannot be consumed, destroy . . . crows flying over it [Virginia] for the balance of the season will have to carry their provender with them."[17] This was his scorched-earth policy, and its implementation was largely the task of the cavalry. The first taste of this job had come in mid-August, during the retreat from Strasburg.

Now on September 29 Sheridan sent both Merritt's and Custer's divisions into the upper valley. The weather was turning crisp, and the leaves were beginning to color. In his letters Lowell repeatedly mentioned the beauty of the countryside, as did almost every other letter writer. The farms were big, less charming or quaint but more impressive than in the lower valley, and Harrisonburg and Staunton reflected their wealth and solidity. The rebels had fled in a hurry, leaving behind a wealth of matériel. The cavalry destroyed Staunton's flour mills, military supplies, boot factory, and storehouses of Confederate supplies.

At Waynesboro the cavalry fired the railroad bridge that connected Waynesboro with Richmond and formed the central route by which the wealth of the valley was shipped to the rest of the Confederacy. The Confederate cavalry rallied to protect the bridge, and the Union's Reserve Brigade, forming the rear guard, took the brunt of its attack. Badly outnumbered, they were flanked and had to retreat. Captain George Bliss of the First Rhode Island Cavalry, a member of Torbert's staff, described Lowell as "the last man to fall back," taking his horse at a walk. "Bullets were whistling about him and frequent puffs of dust in the road showed where they struck." In the village itself, women stationed at their upper-story windows threw whatever came to hand at the troopers in the street, along with curses. "Their vocabulary was truly astounding," recalled one soldier.[18]

Conferring with Captain Bliss, Lowell said, "We must check their advance with a saber charge. Isn't that the best we can do?" Bliss agreed. Lowell turned to the major of a New Jersey regiment and told him, "Let your first squadron sling their carbines, draw their sabers and charge." The order was given, but the men did nothing. They had seen other troops driven back and were unwilling to take the risk. Their major was also unequal to the task.

The troops were not under Lowell's command, and he did not know them, or they he. There was, however, no time to consider the nuances of the situation. Riding up close along the line of the recalcitrant squadron, Lowell shouted, "Give a cheer boys and go at them." Spurring his horse, he took off at a gallop toward the enemy. The horses worked their magic. The officers and men followed, everyone cheering and galloping. Once the men were on the move, Lowell fell back to gather more troops and bring on additional support. This left Bliss in the lead. The Confederates were retreating in the face of the charge, but Bliss's horse was shot and he was captured. (He saw out the war in Libby Prison.) The fighting continued for the rest of the day, as Lowell's men held the Confederates back from flanking the cavalry and even driving them "some distance back into the mountains."[19]

By late afternoon, however, the Confederates were heavily reinforced and fighting back viciously. According to one private, "Our General Lowell and a few of us were nearly captured. We took desperate chances but were forced back."[20] In this skirmish, Lowell's horse was shot out from under him. As he searched for another mount, a Confederate lunged at him; a sergeant from the Second U.S. Cavalry stepped in and took a mortal saber wound. Crowninshield's favorite horse, Jim, was hit by a shell that broke his hind leg. He fell, got up, jumped a rail fence, and then collapsed, screaming terribly. Crowninshield could do nothing but shoot him.

When night fell, the brigade managed to get away under cover of darkness, losing pack mules and a good portion of their supplies. Lowell told Effie only that he left Waynesboro "in a hurry," confessing that the Confederates had come near "doing us a mischief." He listed casualties, horses, and men interchangeably, and about himself he said only that a sergeant "claims to have saved my life."[21]

As Sheridan retreated north down the valley, Lowell's men once again formed the rear guard. They bore witness to every barrel of flour, bale of hay, and bushel of wheat destroyed. Sheridan belonged to the school of hard war. Three years of fighting had taught him that "the loss of property weighs heavy with most of mankind; heavier often, than the sacrifices made on the field of battle." After the war, he wrote: "Death is popularly considered the maximum of punishment in war, but it is not; reduction to poverty brings prayers for peace more surely and more quickly than does the destruction of human life, as the selfishness of man has demonstrated in more than one great conflict."[22]

Sheridan's harsh words were the considered reflections of an experienced general. Nevertheless his orders were very specific: he did not want the destruction to get out of control. Both Grant and Sheridan stated clearly that buildings were not to be burned; Sheridan wanted a rational policy of strategic burning of crops but nothing that would appear as vengefully selective destruction; "no villages or private houses will be burned." He did not want

the troops to lose discipline or to settle private scores. On August 16 he repeated Grant's orders: "officers in charge of this delicate, but necessary, duty
must" be sure to obtain "regular vouchers for such as will be taken from
loyal citizens in the country through which you march."[23] July's experience
with Jubal Early's retaliatory burning of Chambersburg had revealed the
foolishness of overprovoking the enemy; creating implacable hatred among
the citizens of Virginia was not a goal.

Yet ironically, it was Sheridan and not his men who lost his head and began to use burning for vengeance. Early in October a favorite of Sheridan's,
a young topographer named Lieutenant John Meigs, the only son of the
Union army's brilliant quartermaster general Montgomery Meigs, was shot
and killed by three men in blue uniforms within Union lines. One of young
Meigs's assistants got away and rode into headquarters with this tale of deception and murder. Sheridan was "incensed." He ordered that everything
within a five-mile radius be burned—houses, barns, and storehouses. This
included the village of Dayton. On October 4 the citizens were ordered to
pack their belongings and leave. That evening "the heavens were lit up for
miles with the glare of burning buildings, houses, and barns alike destroyed." As the sky blazed with fires from the surrounding farms, the towns-
people became hysterical in their pleas for clemency. The Union officer
whose duty it was to torch the village begged Sheridan to rescind his orders,
and finally Sheridan, to his credit, did so. Lowell felt huge relief that his
brigade had not been the one to carry out those orders, that "my Brigade had
no hand in it."[24]

That night, October 4, the new moon was "within a quarter of an inch of
the evening star, and turning her back on him," or so Lowell wrote Effie.
The moon was the third eye, the symbol of divine blessing Lowell had used
in his Commencement Day oration as part of his final depiction of ideal
youth. And the evening star was timeless, reaching back to the inexorable
amoral wisdom of Greek myth that Lowell had once found so comforting.
He noted that both moon and star looked calm, peaceful, and "reproach-
ful." For three nights the sky reflected the flames. By day "clouds of smoke
marked the passage of the Federal army." One officer described "great
columns of smoke which almost shut out the sun." As darkness fell "the
whole horizon in the line of Sheridan's retreat was one bright sheet of
flames."[25]

At some point during these weeks Frederick Quant, one of the California
Hundred's tough Indian fighters, recorded in his diary the words to the song

"Rock Me to Sleep, Mother," in which the singer wishes to ease "the furrows of care." "Weary of flinging my soul's wealth away," the song's chorus asks "make me a child again, just for tonight . . . take me again to your heart." Lowell, in a letter to Effie, opined that divine judgment could hardly approve of the U.S. Cavalry. "The war in this part of the country is becoming very unpleasant to an officer's feelings," he wrote stiffly. After a few more lines he ended with an outburst: "I do wish this war was over! . . . Never mind. I'm doing all I can to end it."[26]

But the war wasn't ending quickly enough. That day, October 5, Sheridan ordered "a full-scale retrograde movement down the valley. He intended to leave in his wake an ashen ruin." And yet Lowell hoped it would end bushwhacking, and even approved of "making this whole Valley a desert from Staunton northward." What Lowell objected to was *partial* burning," the justice or propriety of which he did not understand. Presumably he had in mind the policy General Hunter had pursued in the summer of selectively destroying plantations and buildings without regard to their strategic value. The purpose of wholesale destruction was to hinder or prevent the Confederacy's capacity to launch a spring campaign. He wanted the hideous task of burning, like that of battle, to have a positive concrete effect on ending the war.[27]

Two days later their turn came. Matches were issued, and the Reserve Brigade was told to burn "everything in the shape of forage that could be found." These orders were carried out. Crowninshield, as he oversaw the work, turned to drinking applejack. It was quite unlike him to be manifestly drunk on duty. Women protested in much the way they had in Loudoun County. When Lowell refused the pleas of one woman whose cow he was driving off, she turned on him, screaming, "Take her god damn you and go to hell with her!"[28]

This work was even worse than the detail against Mosby because of the scale: the entire Cavalry Corps was acting in unison. Sheridan reported to Grant that he had "destroyed over 2,000 barns filled with wheat, hay and farming implements; over 70 mills, filled with flour and wheat; have driven in front of the army over 4,000 head of stock and have killed and issued to the troops not less than 3,000 sheep." In ten days Merritt's division alone burned 630 barns, 47 flour mills, four sawmills, one woolen mill, three iron furnaces, two tanneries, one railroad depot, one locomotive, three boxcars, 4,000 tons of hay, straw, and fodder, half a million bushels of wheat and oats, 515 acres of corn, and 560 barrels of flour, and it drove off 3,300 livestock, amounting to $3,304,672 worth of damage. Destruction on this scale was eroding the spirit of the Virginians. Sheridan told Grant, "The people here are getting sick of the war." One resident wrote,

> The women, children and old men looked on in blank submission. Some denounced and some deplored, but most of the people said but very little. The punishment was justly merited no doubt, but when I saw women and children looking hopelessly on while everything that they needed for comfort and sustenance the coming winter was being destroyed, and not uttering a word of complaint or showing any malice towards the destroyers, I thought if there was not real martyr-like heroism shown by this people.

Yet another put aside her diary for six months, explaining that her heart was "too sad . . . I had not the spirit to write."[29]

There were more green fields of unharvested crops to destroy, more rails to burn. Lowell and others believed that the draconian burning shortened the war and was, as a result, a mercy. But to many the prolonged destruction had become unbearable. With the night sky aglow and the surrounding fields ablaze, federal troops were awestruck by their actions. Long before armies existed or wars as we know them were fought, rival tribes burned one another's crops. Few among the troopers may have known that the Peloponnesian War ended with the burning of the Attic plain, but they responded instinctively with awe, horror, and self-disgust.

TWENTY-ONE

THE WOODSTOCK RACES

October 9, 1864

When Major-General Thomas Rosser and his veterans, the Laurel Brigade, arrived in the Shenandoah Valley on October 5 as reinforcements for Early's battered and demoralized army, they were enraged to see, as one Confederate officer, Henry Kyd Douglas, described, "mothers and maidens tearing their hair and shrieking to Heaven in their fright and despair." Even more alarming, many people were shocked into numbness, "voiceless and tearless in their pitiable terror." Rosser, who hoped to be "the Savior of the Valley," was brought "to the highest pitch of fury"[1] when, on October 8, part of the town of Woodstock was accidentally burned, and he flung his men at the Union cavalry. What had been fitful skirmishing now turned into nasty fighting, and by the evening, the federal cavalry was lagging behind the rest of the army and delayed in its burning schedule. General Sheridan lost his temper.

It had been two weeks since the federal cavalry was meant to demolish General Early's cavalry after Fisher's Hill, the battle following up Winchester. For reasons that remained opaque to Sheridan, General Torbert had lost his vigor in the Luray Valley and never really recovered. In the plain speaking for which he was widely recognized, Sheridan now told him to "whip the rebel cavalry, or get whipped [him]self." Sheridan was a man, in the words of another subordinate, "*who would be obeyed.*" Here was the decisiveness Lowell so admired, and Torbert was galvanized; he well understood that his fate hung in the balance, and he communicated this to the entire Cavalry Corps. The next morning they would turn and take on the Confederates.

When October 9 dawned, Lowell had to shake off a sense of foreboding; instinct told him the day would go badly. What Custer's chief of staff called the "steady old Reserve Brigade—the regulars under Lowell" formed the eastern end of the federal line north of Woodstock, opposing the infantry of

William Jackson and the cavalry of Bradley Johnson. There were few towns in this section of the Shenandoah Valley (settled by Germans: Strasburg had once been called Staufferstadt; and Woodstock, Muellerstadt), and the farmland, treed only on knolls that added undulation to the open valley floor, was "a magnificent place for a cavalry fight."[2]

The Confederates and their artillery batteries occupied these knolls of trees. Lowell deployed the Second Massachusetts Cavalry as skirmishers in the advance, behind which came the First and Second U.S. Cavalry in double rank and, finally, the brigade commander's staff. For a brief time the scene was picturesque. The thunder and smoke of the Confederate artillery added depth to the sharper cracks of the carbines as skirmishers trotted along somewhat unevenly, halting to aim and fire, then trotting on. Across the open ground, a strong breeze quickly pulled the puffs of white smoke from the skirmishers and the larger clouds from the cannons clear. However, about 9 a.m. Jackson's infantry began to offer stout resistance. Bullets kicked up dirt and whizzed overhead, sounding like rain on a tin roof. Horses and men began to fall. Lowell's Reserve Brigade was forced back about half a mile and then had to re-form, for half of the first line of men were killed or wounded. Before the battle it had been reduced, and now it was heavily outnumbered. Lowell sent word to Merritt that he needed support and, not satisfied with a place in the rear, rode up along with the Second Massachusetts Cavalry. The men crouched behind rocks, trees, and fences, anything to shelter them, but they were overwhelmed by their task. The three officers in charge of this skirmish line had all been wounded, and Lowell ordered his aide, Lieutenant Alvord, to take command of the line.

In short order the Fifth U.S. Cavalry and the First New York Dragoons arrived with orders from Merritt that the reinforced brigade must charge the center of the Confederate line and lead the frontal assault up the pike. A small pocket of Confederates had to be cleared before Lowell was ready. He sent orders that a portion of the skirmish line should advance on them. Alvord came riding back to advise Lowell that since the men were low on ammunition, he thought it unwise to advance. Lowell brushed the objection aside, saying, "That makes no difference; advance."[3] Alvord rode back to his position.

Alvord had only just arrived the day before from provost-marshal duty in Washington. Having missed out on much of the action, he was keen to prove himself, and despite his lack of experience he moved forward to take his place among the skirmishers. Like all men describing their first battle, he wrote in his account of that action that "bullets struck all around me thickly." Another veteran recalled that "it almost rained lead."[4] One bullet ricocheted off a rock and as it bounced into the air Alvord caught it in his hand. To catch in one's hand, harmlessly, like a child's ball, a bullet that might have killed one—nothing so effectively taught the lesson that one did not have to be safe to survive; all that was required was not to be killed.

Lowell briskly rode among them and came to a full stop, catching their attention. Bullets whizzed around him, and Alvord noted that a bullet striking the pummel of Lowell's saddle glanced through his coat.[5] But he walked his horse back and forth before them. They steadied, watching this show of assurance. Then again he gave the order, and the men, understanding better than Alvord, went forward with alacrity as the Confederates, tired out and low on ammunition themselves, retreated.

Over the course of the last month's fighting, Lowell and his men had learned that beyond physical courage was moral courage, and that trusting it was their best weapon. By "moral" they meant something close to psychological, something that had to do with observation, common sense, and instinct. Lowell had used his time in the front walking back and forth to judge his opponents. He had, in the words of Private Backus, seen the enemy growing "a little tremulous"[6]: they were firing high, and Lowell exploited that hesitancy. Just as he had taught his men the mechanics of safety and risk taking, he had also shown them the power of taking the psychological upper hand. Alvord now learned that the reality of low ammunition was superseded by the confidence that the enemy was, too.

Lowell ordered the bugles to sound the charge. The rest of the cavalry, Devin's brigade and Custer's division farther west, responded with bugle calls of their own. From the dark mass of uniforms and horses came the glint of the sun sparkling off four thousand sabers as they were drawn. The Reserve Brigade gave a whoop and took off. At first the Confederates retreated strategically, using the undulations in the land to protect themselves. Soon, however, the federal troopers passed the point of no return: galloping now, their only option was to outrun the guns as the hail of bullets intensified. The horses too become crazed with excitement, no longer galloping but leaping at breakneck speed. Then both Lowell's men and Custer's at the other end of the battlefield succeeded in driving around the side of General Lunsford Lomax's army: the Confederates had been flanked. From a military point of view, these three well-coordinated, well-executed charges had an almost ideal poetic quality. Realizing their situation, Jackson's ranks broke, and Johnson's crumbled. Panic quickly overtook them, and their only concern was to escape the old-fashioned saber, which the Confederates feared. Union troops used the Spencers for its seven rounds, then slung them and used revolvers, and finally, when charging, drew sabers. The Confederate cavalry, especially under Rosser, did not value or in some cases even use the saber. Thus once the Union cavalry had passed through Confederate fire and come in close, their use of the saber gave them a huge advantage, and the Confederate panic can be better appreciated. The Confederate cavalry evaporated across the board, and then even the Confederate artillery fell silent. "When the Rebels got started they ran like sheep," Sam Corbett recorded in his diary. The Union pursued them for some twenty-six miles, and the outcome had nothing to do with battle and everything to do with "the endurance of horseflesh." The engagement ended when the horses on both sides collapsed from exhaustion in the fading light. Even among the Confederates, the defeat at the "Woodstock Races" drew the ridicule of the Laurel Brigade. Early commented drily, "The laurel is a running vine." So much Confederate artillery was captured that the Union men joked that it was ordnance shipped from Richmond labeled "P.H. Sheridan, care of General Early." Casualties were negligible, confidence was brimming. That evening the Union troopers joked about whose horses had reached the finish line and how it would take two days for their baggage wagons to catch up with them.[7]

After the battle the army camped on the banks of the Shenandoah, drew rations, and rested. Lowell and the men bathed and attended to neglected chores—mended what they could, polished what there was to polish, and spruced themselves up. Lowell wrote home, but his letter to Effie gives little sense of the Union achievement that day, simply that the Reserve Brigade had chased two Confederate brigades, taken a battle flag, four guns, caissons, three artillery guns, nineteen wagons, eight ambulances, and about two hundred prisoners. Mostly Lowell was relieved to learn that his instincts had been wrong: he had feared the action would go badly, but instead it had been almost too easy. He told Effie, "My disinclination for 'fight' yesterday was a presentiment that came to naught."[8]

Lowell had begun to be quite nervous. When Effie wrote that she was sure he would be made a general, he cast this comment aside, repeating that he was "perfectly satisfied . . . now I have this Brigade; it has only been commanded before by Buford and Merritt." As he watched the exultation of the cavalry, he may have felt they were too confident, too cocky. And he knew that after all the army, at least his own brigade, was deeply flawed. That very evening he dismounted the Twenty-fifth New York Cavalry, a regiment that had joined the army on August 25 initially under Custer but was now attached to the Reserve Brigade. It had performed so poorly that its horses were more valuable than its men. Several days later, on October 12, Lowell ordered his men out for drill. Sam Corbett complained that he was "too ambitious," but the drilling was an expression of caution and anxiety.[9]

Effie, too, was nervous. To the world she presented a brave front, appearing "calm and hopeful," giving the impression that Lowell lived "a charmed life" and that "no ball could reach him." But her equanimity was an act. Indeed, ever since Rob's death her powerful romance of the soldier's heroism had been tempered by deep anguish at its price. In June 1863 Lowell had promised her he would not be rash, and throughout his time at Vienna, he had led very few scouts and been careful not to expose himself. But Effie, whose eyes had been opened to at least some of the realities of war thanks to seven months of living with Lowell's brigade, understood what such a promise was worth. And she knew her husband well enough to know that without her there his caution would leave him. After they parted at the end of July, Effie had returned home, and there, with little to do and much to brood on, her first letters had expressed her hope for any honorable means of Lowell's leaving the field. Nine months of marriage had given them both an experience of domestic contentment—no longer a speculation or a hope but certain knowledge—on which to build dreams and convictions of their future life together. Her pregnancy would make such dreams manifest. Her appreciation for the romance of battle, with its sublime and noble aspects, was now offset by the sentiments of a woman who preferred the man she loved to be safe. One of her mother's friends observed that when she went down to the post office to collect her letters, her hand trembled as she snatched them, and only on recognizing his writing did her face relax.[10]

After August 18, when General Grant announced that henceforth he would refuse all prisoner exchanges, Effie had written that if Lowell were captured, she hoped that he might take advantage of Grant's "special exchanges" of prisoners of war under exceptional circumstances. But on October 10 he quickly vetoed that idea, telling her that he had repeatedly stated to all the relevant people, "I didn't want any special exchange, and wanted that understood." Most important, he wanted the same treatment as his men.[11]

Lowell may not have clearly understood what life in a Confederate prison was like. He believed that if he were captured, he would not be ill in prison or "suffer even my share," but this was implausible, even though officers were treated better than enlisted men. All prisoners suffered, and the health of much stouter men than he was broken by the experience. In the spring of 1863, after five months at home, Lowell had been described as "stringy as a partridge." In the only photograph of him taken during the Shenandoah Valley campaign under the stress of daily skirmishing, little sleep, and poor meals, he looks gaunt, even skeletal. His tuberculosis, in remission, would surely have once again ravaged his body under the duress of imprisonment, poor diet, and the diseases of bad sanitation. Already lack of sleep and the cold nights had brought on a nasty cough.[12]

His belief that there was not "one chance in a great many" that he would be captured was equally irrational. He had had many narrow escapes. Ever since the heavy skirmishing in August, he was teased about his boldness on the battlefield and his tendency never to be satisfied. Just when everyone else was ready to exult in their success, Lowell would say, "A little more pluck and . . ." The response of both his superiors and of Caspar Crowninshield was to retort, "A little more pluck and you would have gone to Richmond!" by which they meant as a prisoner.[13]

Lowell believed it was necessary to minimize the likelihood and danger of capture for himself and his men because he felt responsible for keeping up morale, and many of his soldiers had been taken prisoner. Death in prison—or perhaps permanent physical deterioration, which was almost as bad—was considered a fate far worse than wounding or death in battle. Lowell did not want the fear of capture to affect his men's performance in the field. As for his own performance, he knew that his own coolness under fire helped to keep his men calm. It had worked over and over again. He wanted nothing to threaten this capacity.

At the end of his explanation for his refusal of special treatment, he wrote to Effie, "I guess that's the way you feel too, in spite of your 'concluding' that you did approve of special exchanges."[14] This careful, firm steering of her "conclusion" on a subject vital to both of them shows that Lowell did not want his duty to Effie to conflict with his duty to his men. He adroitly prevented a head-on confrontation, but he must also have wanted to free himself of the double bind that had dogged him all his adult life: the dichotomy between what he wanted to do and the obligations or duty he felt toward those he loved: women all—his mother, his sisters, his wife.

With the daily skirmishes and daily toll on his men that the Shenandoah

Valley campaign was taking, Lowell put away his personal longings and stopped writing informative, descriptive letters to Effie. Shortly after Eigenbrodt's death on August 25, he wrote, "I don't think it's pleasant telling you about our work, and I think I shan't tell any more."[15] It was a significant withdrawal. He had never liked recounting battle exploits, indeed seemed to want to forget them as fast as he could, and taking risks and commanding his men as he saw fit were easier if Effie did not know about those risks.

Yet he felt an undertow, as did she. Now that Effie was not with him, he wrote to her almost daily. His letters imagined her "looking in" on his camp or "stepping in here" to see him "snugly ensconced," lying upon their red blankets, "and I should get up and we'd go and see Berold together." He described pastoral scenes—beautiful morning views, evenings around a fire with the band playing and "darkies" dancing—that would have been improved for him by her presence. He was full of dreams for their child. Convinced that the baby would be a boy, Lowell wrote to his mother, "I hope Father won't mind our naming him after Rob Shaw instead of any of our names." Yet ambivalently mindful of his dead brother, he continued, "I daresay Jim could never have done more for the country, had he lived to suffer these years out, than he did by his death, dying as he did . . . Effie's little boy will certainly be a dear good fellow, if he takes after his Uncle." But the question was, which uncle?[16]

His letters contained elaborate if unpersuasive arguments that his separation from Effie had a fortuitous element to it. He wanted to convince her that "just as long as the war lasts," whatever it brought them, she would always be leading "just the best theoretic life." In a feat of circular logic, he explained that "we are bound, if anyone is, to do our all to see the war well finished, for without the war . . . we mightn't have come together—and then I'm sure I shouldn't have cared so about leaving the army." It is an interesting Panglossian desire to imagine that whatever their circumstances they were for the best, and that whatever their actual sentiments they could take comfort or solace in knowing that theoretically their life was "the best." Both the moon and the band, whose choice of music had grown increasingly sentimental, combined to make him "as homesick as possible."[17]

Among men discharged from the Union army for reasons of mental health, "homesickness or nostalgia" was, after insanity, the reason most frequently cited. It was considered a form of depression or melancholia that in its most extreme form caused men to lose their will to live and in milder form beset many soldiers after reading letters from home or returning to camp from leave. Despite his deep desire to be with Effie, Lowell was somewhat contradictory on the subject of applying for leave. He didn't want to take a leave before winter, "especially with a new command." After October 9 he was sorely tempted to get her to come to Winchester or to dash home himself, but he knew both were "out of the question." He flirted with the idea of "parading New York" in his government-issue army outfit, but he knew that his uniform, while acceptable in the context of a campaign, was less so in a drawing room or on the streets of Manhattan. His banter on the subject expressed his anxiety about the conduct of the war and his awareness that he was now steeped in death and destruction. He wondered about life and how a man might return to civilized life "after the war." He told Effie, "Keep your eyes open for opportunities for both of us after the war,—I mean, be thinking about the matter."[18]

Throughout the week following the Woodstock Races, the destruction of the Shenandoah Valley continued. But the campaign was drawing to a close. Lowell teased, "I went into winter-quarters yesterday," then turned his mind to where they would next be sent, recognizing that this was entirely dependent on "Grant's success before Richmond." On October 15 Lowell had orders to join General Torbert's cavalry on a raid. They were all to ride down the Luray Valley, cross the Blue Ridge at Chester Gap, find the Virginia Central Railroad at Charlottesville, and destroy it—thereby preventing any crop that escaped the torch from being shipped east to Lee's armies. Lowell thought he would be gone for about ten days, during which he was sure there would be one more battle in the Shenandoah Valley. "I am sorry to miss it . . . You will know that I am safe, at any rate—so safe do I feel tonight that I am riding Berold." He told Effie he wanted longer letters, and in asking for them he told her his first word as an infant had been "more. It was with reference to crackers, I think after eating several dozen."[19]

On October 16 Lowell broke camp at Cedar Creek and began the first leg of the raid, escorting Sheridan, who was headed for Washington, as far as Front Royal, where they camped for the night. That evening Sheridan was given an intercepted message, supposedly from Longstreet to Early, proposing an attack on the Union forces once the two joined forces in the valley. The message was a fake, but Sheridan believed it. In the morning Lowell's cavalry was ordered to rejoin the main army under the command of General Wright outside Middletown, along Cedar Creek, while Sheridan continued on to Washington.

Early's ruse served a confused purpose, for it actually returned troops to the army that he wished to attack, but his purpose had been to keep yet more Union troops from joining Grant. He also needed to take advantage of the Union forces' overconfidence and encourage them to believe that the Confederate troops were exhausted. In this he was successful. The Union forces presumed that Early was too weak to attack them and that they had the initiative, but they would not take it until Sheridan returned from Washington in a few days.

Lowell used these free days for sleep. For two months he'd been living on catnaps. Now he slept for ten hours at a stretch. He had time to read the newspapers and consider the election. He wrote to friends. To Charlie Perkins, who was still in Iowa, he wrote to congratulate him on his engagement, explaining that "mothers are excellent but wives are better." He also wanted to find out how the sale of his farm was progressing—a practical inquiry, given his chronic need for more horses. He added, "I believe McClellan's election would send this country to where Mexico and South America are. Do what you can to prevent it."[20]

And he wrote to John Murray Forbes, saying frankly that he hoped Will would not be returned to the regiment "till we are safely in winter-quarters," for he was sure Forbes's anxiety would be greater if Will were part of the campaign. He thanked Forbes for being understanding about the loss of Will's horse and repeated his hesitation about riding it, but acknowledged, "I had three orderlies' horses killed or disabled under me that day." He noted that the *Army and Navy Journal*'s report on the Shenandoah Valley campaign was flawed both in fact and analysis. "I am very glad we have not a handy writer among us," he wrote. "The reputation of regiments is made and is known in the Army,—the comparative merits are *well* known there."[21]

Finally he wrote his mother a tender teasing letter, complaining that she did not write often enough. "It's always the business of the fellow that's at home to write often," he began. "If you won't write, I shall have to make Father, or perhaps Ned." Both were unlikely correspondents. "It's too bad of you," he chided. "I'll warrant you write to Anna two or three times a week." But he had little to tell his mother. "There's really nothing to tell here. I never have any thing to tell even to Effie." He only wrote "to make you write to me. I have done my share, I think—but there's nothing to make a letter of." He spoke of his anticipated leave in December or January after the birth of the baby, when they would see each other.[22]

"Isn't it lucky that I keep always well and hearty?" he continued. "My friends never feel any anxiety on *that* account and I never have to write letters to tell them how I am. Effie is a strong girl too. I never have to feel anxious about her." The homesickness is almost palpable, the tone similar to that of a letter to Effie written five days earlier, asking for longer letters. "I don't want to be shot till I've had a chance to come home," he confessed. "I have no idea that I shall be hit, but I *want* so much not to now that it sometimes frightens me."[23]

Were Lowell's nerves beginning to go? At the time prevailing opinion was that "green troops" were all but useless because of their fear and lack of experience. It was believed that both "duty men" and "shirkers" were made that way. But modern studies have established that combat troops begin to lose their effectiveness after one hundred days of "intermittent exposure to battle." After two hundred days men will start to break down or burn out, a tendency exponentially more likely the older the soldier, explaining why it was called "old sergeant's syndrome." The execution of William Ormsby had occurred 264 days after Lowell had taken the field, a period interrupted only by the ten-day whirlwind leave in which he married. By mid-October 1864 Lowell had been in the field almost exactly two hundred days since his two months with the Cavalry Bureau at Giesboro. He was approaching his thirtieth birthday.

However thrilled the Second Massachusetts Cavalry was to have joined a campaign, it was also taking far greater casualties now. In both the battle of Winchester and the Woodstock Races, the initial dislodging of Confederate infantry had been grueling, and the daily heavy skirmishing against infantry of the past two months was taking a toll: the ranks of the Second Massachusetts Cavalry were reduced by half. The entire Reserve Brigade totaled less than a thousand men, the size of a full regiment. These were bald facts, and under his favorite Harvard professor, the mathematician Benjamin Peirce, Lowell had learned to work the probabilities of surviving till war's end.

A third consideration was his instinct, or intuition. Lowell always made light of the possibility of being captured or wounded. But his circle of Boston friends were mostly either dead or disabled. Willy, Jim, and Cabot were dead. Wendell Holmes, thrice wounded, had the good fortune of the Twentieth's being disbanded in July 1864. Pat Jackson was wounded. Sumner Paine was dead, and so were the Russell brothers. Of his friends, too many to count were dead: Jim Savage, Stephen Perkins, Rob Shaw, Wilder Dwight, William Sedgwick, Richard Cary, Richard Goodwin, the Revere brothers. The rest—Barlow, Higginson, Adams, Curtis—were on extended leave or resigned. Did Lowell sense Fortuna's gaze turning onto him? Certainly his life seemed to be running on two divergent tracks. When he had first conceived his ambitions for the war, it had been as a young man with no responsibilities. He had had no conception of the happiness he would find in his relationship with Effie, but a happy marriage and a child on the way opened huge vistas that he had not previously considered. He had become a rising star in the cavalry just as his personal life became truly fulfilling. He ended his letter to his mother, "This is only a reminder to you, remember your loving son, Charley."[24]

The next morning, October 18, Lowell was directed to move his camp to the west side of the main army, reinforcing its right flank; in fact, all the cavalry were massed on this western flank. Lowell chose a site near a ford on the north side of Cedar Creek. The Union infantry lay just south of the town of Middletown and across the Valley Pike. The Confederate army was ten miles southwest, at Fisher's Hill, commanding the entrance to the North Fork of the Shenandoah Valley. That evening a patrol of Second Massachusetts Cavalry stumbled on its own pickets and was caught in friendly fire. No damage was done, but loud curses were heard. For two days the entire army, which amounted to somewhere between 28,000 and 35,000 infantry and artillery and 6,000 to 8,000 cavalry, had been up and armed at 3 a.m. expecting an attack, but tomorrow they would sleep in. Eager not to repeat his men's encounter with friendly fire, Lowell requested that the other divisions be reminded that the next morning his men would be making a predawn scout to Fisher's Hill, where Early's Army of the Valley—amounting to 13,000 or 14,000 men, of which 9,000 were infantry, 4,000 cavalry, and 800 artillery—were camped.

Many of the Union officers, like the men, were cocky with the expectation of victory. They did not believe that the army they had trounced so spectacularly ten days earlier would attack them. But Lowell was not among them. Hoping to counteract the false confidence, he had told his staff there would soon be action. To naysayers who believed that action would come only when Union troops initiated it, Lowell put forward this argument: the federals had destroyed the valley, and the Confederate army would soon run out of provisions or perhaps already had; that meant Early had three choices: to starve, to leave the valley, or to fight. As Lowell saw it, the waiting game was close to an end.

TWENTY-TWO

THE BATTLE OF CEDAR CREEK

October 19, 1864

A great victory—a victory won from disaster by the gallantry of our officers and
men.   —Philip H. Sheridan to Ulysses S. Grant, October 20, 1864

Lowell was already up when reveille sounded at 4 a.m. on October 19.[1] The
weather had turned cold at night, and each morning the hollows of the valley were filled with a thick mist and fog, which reduced visibility and muf-
fled sound. Once the fog burned off as the day warmed up, all would
become obvious, but in these early hours of the day nothing was. As the
men of the Reserve Brigade finished their breakfast, they heard sporadic firing from distant pickets. Half an hour later they mounted and rode south.
Just as they reached Cedar Creek, they heard the bugles of Custer's division
on their extreme right signaling that they were under attack. Lowell hesitated. Rather than proceed with his scout, he decided to send out a detail to
investigate. This mounted party crossed the ford at Cedar Creek and disappeared into the fog. Soon Lowell heard the sound of more firing directly in
front of them, and the advance detail clattered back over the ford to report
that a greatly superior force had driven them back and now held the ford.

Lowell took a strong position and threw out a line of dismounted skirmishers, who soon engaged the enemy, which appeared to be cavalry aided
by artillery. The action was "quite brisk," recalled Lieutenant Alvord, who
was riding alongside Lowell as he personally directed the skirmishers. Alvord
noted that Lowell had "several very narrow escapes."[2] Even before the ford
was retaken, the Confederate opposition vanished. The firing stopped, and
Lowell's men took control of the ford. At about seven-thirty orders came
from General Merritt to retire slowly, to draw in skirmishers and pickets, and
to support Colonel James H. Kidd (who had taken command of the First
Brigade in the last week of September, when Custer had moved to the Third

Division). Lowell sent a courier back to camp with orders to break camp and prepare for battle. He pulled his men back from the ford and rode to Colonel Kidd's headquarters on a hill behind the original camp of the Reserve Brigade. The two men conferred. Kidd explained that he needed no help, for he had already driven the Confederates back and his men were only occasionally being shelled. As they listened to the distant sounds of infantry fire, the boom of artillery, and the yip-yelling of the Confederate infantry, they realized that the main thrust of the battle was in the infantry camps to their left, south of Middletown and across the Valley Pike. Pickets reported they could see men from the Eighth Corps moving to the rear, some in considerable haste. Three-quarters of an hour later, firing on the extreme left became very rapid and heavy. It seemed that the fighting was on the turnpike, where Union forces were being pushed back toward Middletown.

For almost an hour Lowell and Kidd waited, increasingly aware that their only orders were irrelevant to the situation. On October 18 the Confederate army had been at Fisher's Hill. Lowell's predawn scout had intended to monitor their position. General Wright had massed the cavalry on the west to deter Early from attacking by the most direct route. But the attack on the massed cavalry had evaporated—had proved a feint. As Lowell figured it, the bulk of the Confederate army must have used the night of October 18 to march from Fisher's Hill, using a circuitous route to the east, since now the Union infantry was most definitely under attack—a daring, courageous, perhaps desperate attack. The more Lowell considered it, the more likely it was that the Union army had been surprised; the lack of orders might not be deliberate.

Lowell told Kidd that he intended to follow the sound of gunfire and join the battle. He prepared to leave. Colonel Kidd, who was new to his command, asked Lowell for advice: without orders should he remain, or should he join the battle? "I think you ought to go too," Lowell said. Realizing he was the senior officer present, he added, "I will take the responsibility."[3] He ordered Kidd to join him.

Lowell explained if their two brigades could move quickly enough, they might prevent the infantry from losing Middletown. The two brigades set off, and as they reached a ridge just north of the town, the morning fog lifted and they had a full view of the scene. Colonel Kidd recalled that spread out across the landscape were Union infantry in clumps, large and small, most of them fleeing to the rear, "a disorganized mass" that, caught completely by surprise, "had simply lost the power of cohesion."[4] Men in the Nineteenth Corps had been roused from their tents half dressed and unarmed. They panicked and fled. The Eighth Corps had been hit next. They too had panicked, but their speedy retreat under artillery fire had some coherence. Lowell could see some soldiers spiriting the few wagons and artillery they had managed to save to the rear. The Sixth Corps, also retreating, was fighting in some semblance of order. Originally on the extreme right, it had spread itself east toward the pike trying to cover as much of the field as it could. But it was only a thin line of resistance. The rest of the scene was chaos.

With utter precision and calm, Lowell formed his two brigades, as if they were on dress parade, into a column some three-quarters of a mile long. Battle flags flying, gaudy swallow-tailed guidons snapping like a jib unfurling in the morning breeze, they paraded across the entire front of broken and crazed Union infantry. The sun glistened on the drawn sabers and sweaty horse flanks. They marched some three miles across the front between the line of battle and the skirmishers' line. As they did so, the Confederate artillery shifted fire to them. One round knocked out a set of four men, but the column closed ranks and moved on. Shells continued to fall.

For the badly demoralized infantry, Lowell's parade gained them time, drawing artillery fire away from them. It gave them a chance to recapture some of their old confidence or whatever shreds of courage remained. "They moved past me, that splendid cavalry," General William Dwight, a division commander of the Nineteenth Corps, tried to explain. "Lowell got by me before I could speak, but I looked after him for a long distance. Exquisitely mounted, the picture of a soldier, erect, confident, defiant, he moved at the head of the finest body of cavalry that today scorns the earth it treads." The prose is overblown, but it perhaps accurately gives the feeling these desperate men had. Another witness more analytically explained: "This bold and aggressive stand checked the ardor of the rapid though now disordered onslaught of the enemy."[5]

Lowell's object was Middletown, on the far side of the battlefield, but when an orderly from General Merritt arrived, he learned to his considerable disappointment that he was too late. The enemy had just occupied the village. Merritt directed Lowell to the north and east of the town along the pike, where all the cavalry were massing. (This order had been delayed because General Torbert, chief of cavalry, resisted exposing the western flank. Only when a compromise was worked out, leaving a detachment of three regiments on the left to cover that flank, was the order given.) Lowell had been right to move when he did. In the crisis, orders throughout the Union army were delayed if they arrived at all.

When Lowell reached the pike just north of Middletown, he met General Devin, commanding Merritt's Second Brigade. Devin had moved up the Valley Pike from the north trying to halt the fleeing infantry, firing on the men and whacking them with the flat of his saber. One of his troopers recalled this as "the most difficult and most distasteful duty." Devin shouted at one soldier leading a squad to halt. "I'll be hanged if I'll halt for any damned cavalrymen" came the reply.[6] Devin shot the soldier dead in his tracks. And only then did the squad, understanding that death would come faster if they continued to flee, turn around and take their place in the skirmish line. Lowell had last seen this sort of action at Antietam. He positioned his troops in front of this chaos. It was entirely unclear how much of the infantry was truly lost and what portion could be rallied and made to stand: the cavalry would have to function as a brake on the Confederate advance.

The gap between the Sixth Corps' "weak infantry skirmish line" to the west and, to the east, Merritt's First Brigade needed to be filled. But as Lowell began to take up this position, General Devin asked for help. He was trying to post men from the Second Division under Colonel Alpheus Moore in a forward position controlling the road north out of Middletown. Moore was a volunteer colonel; his men were armed with a smattering of weapons, not Spencer carbines; and they did not have the experience of regular cavalry or of the volunteer regiments commanded by regular officers. They flatly refused to dismount and fight like infantry, and Moore did not seem inclined to make them. Yet skirmishers were needed to keep the Confederates in Middletown. Orders from Merritt directed Lowell to hold the pike "at all hazards."[7]

Lowell ordered Company C, a Boston regiment commanded by Lieutenant William H. H. Hussey of the California Hundred, to dismount and seize the forward position, which amounted to a few stone walls. To give the men the cover they needed, he created a diversionary charge with the rest of his brigade against the east flank of the village. As they approached the garden fences and outbuildings, the well-protected enemy fired on them until they were forced back. Captain Rufus Smith, a Californian, was shot in the stomach and left beyond the skirmish line. Lieutenant Henry Kuhls was also wounded but managed to stay on his horse and return to federal lines. But the objective had been achieved: the skirmishers were now posted behind the stone walls, though hideously exposed, being within rifle shot of the northernmost houses of Middletown. Lieutenant Hussey was wounded in the shoulder, the bullet breaking his collarbone and lodging near his left shoulder blade, but he continued to command. Hussey was made of strong stuff: as an eighteen-year-old, six years earlier, he had tried mining in the Sierra goldfields, been caught for five days in a blizzard, and survived by eating his dog with the unfortunate name of Poison.[8] Crowninshield sent in another company to support him and his men. This made about fifty to seventy skirmishers, since neither company was up to full strength. The Reserve Brigade now controlled the road out of Middletown.

Shortly the Confederates positioned two sections of light artillery to shell the Reserve's skirmish line and its regiments. It was now 9 a.m. The Reserve Brigade would hold this position seven hours, until 4 p.m. Returning from division headquarters, Lieutenant Alvord rode up to his colonel and recognized that Lowell was riding an orderly's horse. He commented on this. Lowell explained that his own had just been shot. "How many does that make, Colonel?" "Thirteen, I believe."[9] And they returned to business.

Lowell rode from one portion of his command to another along the skirmish line, accompanied by his staff, brigade colors, and orderlies. Confederate sharpshooters stationed in the upper stories and on the roofs of Middletown's houses soon trained their fire on them. To frustrate the sharpshooters, Lowell occasionally sent the brigade colors a short distance away, which drew off their fire until the sharpshooters caught on to the ruse. Whenever the firing became too well directed and heavy, he shifted his position. Only when he was sure the brigade was positioned correctly and the line established did he ride back to the main body of the regiment and out of range of the sharpshooters. At 10 a.m. Lowell sent Alvord to Merritt's headquarters to report and to receive orders.

The situation on the field was that Lowell's Second Massachusetts Cavalry held the advance position, with skirmishers at the stone walls on the outskirts of the town and the rest of the regiment massed behind. Fanning out behind them, the First Cavalry connected with the Sixth Corps, and on the left the Second Cavalry connected with Devin's brigade and with Kidd (the rest of the First Division). Flying artillery were positioned with equal boldness on open ground. Custer's division, except three regiments detaining Rosser's cavalry in the old position on Cedar Creek, was massed in the rear. All these men, almost two full divisions constituting some three or four thousand cavalry, were a formidable sight. Moreover, they appeared as if poised to attack.

General Early responded exactly as the federals wished. Fearing a massed cavalry charge of the kind that had twice proved so effective, he reinforced his right, which meant that he drew power away from his intended aggressive rush on the federal infantry.[10] But in fact the momentum of the Confederate advance had already been checked by the Confederate infantry itself. Thomas Merry, more than twenty years later, recalled that sutler wagons loaded with whiskey had arrived at the Nineteenth Corps's camp the day before, and he surmised that an evening with sutlers' whiskey liberally imbibed by both officers and men explained the corps's poor performance in the predawn hours of October 19. He claimed it also explained the Confederate halt at the Union camps. Kingdoms have been lost for want of a nail: that whiskey should be the cause of the Confederates' losing a critical battle was also possible, but it is unlikely to have been the sole reason.

Confederate soldiers had been living lives of such privation that shoes, one suspects, had more allure. Most of the men had been on the march since 8 p.m. the night before, October 18. When, in the early morning hours, they overran the Union camps and stopped to eat breakfasts still hot in the pan, they discovered tents filled with clothes, rations, and essential amenities, things that for months now these Confederate soldiers had only dreamed about—boots, warm woolen shirts—and the men plundered, beyond the control of their officers.

Yet the straggling and plundering might have amounted to nothing if General Early had used his cavalry more effectively. A Confederate cavalry charge at this point would have been unstoppable, and the Union cavalry knew this, because it was what they would have done: dislodge the infantry and then charge. It could be argued that once Lowell brought two brigades into full view on the battlefield, Early's chance was lost. Nevertheless, the Union command wanted to know: Where was the Confederate cavalry? And was an attack imminent? Merritt ordered the Second Massachusetts Cavalry to attack. He wanted prisoners to interrogate.

Around ten-thirty or eleven, Major James A. Forsyth, one of Sheridan's aides, came charging up to Lowell, who thereby became one of the first to know that Sheridan was on the field. Sheridan had heard the artillery fire as he ate breakfast in Winchester, some ten miles away, where he had spent the night on his return journey from Washington. He had ridden over directly, receiving on the way reports of the surprise attack and the overrun of the Union camps. His first priority was to establish the strength and status of his extended army. Recognizing that Lowell's men formed the core of the

Union resistance and that the strength left in these troops would determine how much time he had to regroup and mobilize his infantry, Sheridan's first action was to send Forsyth to Lowell. According to Forsyth, Sheridan knew "that there was no cooler head or better brain in all the the army, nor one to be more absolutely relied upon."

The two men conferred briefly. "Can you hold on here for forty minutes?"

"Yes," Lowell replied. Forsyth asked for sixty minutes.

"It depends" was Lowell's response. He led Forsyth along the line to a point where they could both see the Confederate infantry using a line of trees to form for an attack. "I will if I can," Lowell promised. And Forsyth sped off.[11]

As Forsyth left, lines of Confederate skirmishers appeared across Lowell's front, and firing began. At about 1 p.m. the Confederates attacked, swarming out of Middletown on the east, but the power of the Second Massachusetts Cavalry's Spencer carbines was too much, and that portion of the Confederate line fell back, creating a gap in the line. To compensate, the neighboring Confederate brigade turned to face the gap and began to wheel eastward. From Lowell's position, it was obvious that the Confederate line would eventually find itself stretched too thin, at which point his cavalry might attack and flank it. He sent orders down the line to watch for this opportunity.

But rather than leave themselves vulnerable, the Confederates halted, clearly intending to renew their attack on Lowell's men. Lowell's options were limited. The houses of Middletown gave shelter for Confederate sharpshooters, and the federal cavalry, exposed on the fields, were easy targets. Under other circumstances he might easily have used one cavalry charge to distract the Confederates while his skirmishers retreated and remounted and the entire brigade withdrew to a more secure location. He would have encouraged the Confederates to pursue them, luring them out onto the open fields beyond Middletown, where he would have room to maneuver. But that was just what could not be done. Any Confederate advance had to be checked as firmly as possible. Ironically, the caution that Sheridan had shown earlier in the campaign had not prevented what he most feared: the likelihood of a Union defeat.

The election was just over two weeks away. The thought that after the victories of the past fortnight Sheridan's army might be ruined in the Shenandoah Valley and cost Lincoln the election, riding McClellan into the White House, now presented itself as all too likely. Sheridan's arrival on the battlefield had given new hope, and the disaster stood a chance of being reversed if the cavalry could hold back the Confederates long enough for Sheridan to gather his men. Lowell had to sustain his men in what was essentially an untenable position.

He held his dismounted men steady behind their stone walls and used the mounted cavalry to charge. This seemed remarkable to the infantry officers in both armies, though it was a maneuver that the Second Massachusetts Cavalry had perfected over the last several months. The combination of speed and firepower gave the men an edge, although their earlier experiences were quite different from what Lowell now attempted. With each repeated attack the surprise effect was reduced, and the Confederates were better prepared to sustain the assault. Nevertheless, the troopers charged the stone walls and rode up to the guns, and each time they were repulsed.

Company E had most consistently shown an eagerness for combat, and so it did this day. Lieutenant Crocker, commanding the picket reserve, volunteered to clear out the rebels who had advanced from the woods toward Lowell's front, taking a position behind a fence, from where they were doing a lot of damage. Crocker recalled, "My mind was immediately set upon checking those fellows, so I rode up to Colonel Crowninshield and asked permission to charge them." Having secured permission from Crowninshield with the request that he come back with a few prisoners, Crocker returned to his company with the news, which was "very much to their satisfaction," he wrote later. The half-hearted had long since found their way out of the company. Born in 1839 in Connecticut, Crocker had been a barkeeper in Oakland before the war. Among his men he had the reputation for being the "kind that is willing to be as near the war as possible." One of his sergeants explained to his sweetheart that "he gives me a chance to be shot at every opportunity that he possibly can." Whether this was a boast or a complaint is unclear.[12]

Once Crocker's men had teased their opponent into firing a volley, the men spurred and charged as they had learned to do. Leaning forward low over their horses' necks with their carbines alongside, they raced for the enemy lines firing willy-nilly at the Confederate infantry. When their seven shots were gone, the men slung their carbines onto their backs and drew their revolvers, waiting to fire until at closer range. Meanwhile the Confederates fired another round. "Saddles were emptied and horses went down," but Crocker's men kept going. Within seconds they were in the Confederate line and had broken it. The men of Company E made sure they captured fourteen rebels, knowing that once they had prisoners they were safe from fire, since the Confederates would not fire on their own men.

Early in the charge Crocker was hit below his knee—he felt the *ping* but kept on. Despite his wound Crocker stopped to rescue an unhorsed lieutenant. The two men rode safely back within the lines. For this Crocker would walk with a limp and in his old age receive a medal of honor.

Questioning the prisoners, Lowell learned that they were from General Joseph B. Kershaw's division of General James Longstreet's old corps, massed in Middletown at the extreme left of the rebel battle line. They did not know what had become of Rosser's cavalry. This was the intelligence Merritt had been seeking: Early had not been reinforced. Lowell ordered Alvord to escort the prisoners to Generals Merritt and Torbert in the rear.

It was now early afternoon. General Wright and the Union infantry officers had managed to rally and reorganize the men, but they had no spirit: morale was gone. This was not surprising. The men had just experienced an extreme version of panic. Panic has an almost physical presence; it is visceral and contagious; even brave men become demoralized by it; even men who do not flee lose their initiative. Even their officers who had witnessed the panic, and checked it, were thinking wholly defensively.

At this point Sheridan set off along the line of battle, riding before and among the infantry, waving his hat. The further they got from the event, the more those involved recalled that Sheridan's presence caused an instantaneous lift to morale. As one of Lowell's troopers recalled, "The boys began to cheer as he rode down the line and new courage seemed to inspire all." It eventually came to be believed that Sheridan almost single-handedly had rallied his men.

The month before, at Winchester, Sheridan had given a display of how he handled wavering troops, indeed the same Nineteenth Corps. Then he had "treated the infantrymen to a taste of the tallest swearing they had ever heard . . . He threw himself among the fugitives and fairly cursed them back into the lines, raving in such a manner that they feared him more than the enemy." One veteran claimed that Sheridan showed his temper only when "troops were breaking." Memories of him at Cedar Creek were less of his temper than of his spirit. Cheering or cursing, he inspired the men to believe in themselves again. Remembering their victories, they rallied behind him. It was the confidence to attack that Sheridan restored to the troops.[13]

He now positioned his men for a countercharge, though he was not yet ready to advance. Rumor had it that another Confederate army was momentarily to join Early; perhaps the intercepted message of October 16 was true and Longstreet would arrive. Sheridan feared an attack on two fronts, which, with his broken army, would mean defeat. He wanted more information. A fast rider was sent east down the road to Front Royal to look for any sign of Confederate reinforcements arriving. Other of his generals saw only a Confederate army tenuously positioned, with much of its infantry disorganized and distracted by the relative wealth of the Union camps.

At this juncture Lowell stopped to consult with Colonel Hastings of the Michigan cavalry (Kidd's brigade). The fire was very heavy and an orderly was killed; another had his horse shot from under him. Lowell was in the saddle with his right hand on his thigh, his elbow jutting out, as was his habit. A minié ball ricocheted off a stone wall, exactly as Lieutenant Alvord had described one doing ten days earlier. Then Alvord had caught it harmlessly in his hand. Now the ball pierced Lowell's coat just above his elbow, whizzed up his sleeve and across the armhole of his coat, and struck him forcefully in the right breast, hard enough that he reeled back on his horse. Immediately he went pale and felt faint, his voice very low and husky. Hastings helped him dismount. Lowell was sure he was mortally wounded and exclaimed, "My poor wife!" Unbuttoning his coat, the men found a hole in both shirts Lowell was wearing: an Enfield rifle minié ball had embedded itself in the muscle above his right lung without breaking the skin, creating a kind of pocket in his chest where it had settled. Lowell threw the ball away. Hastings, surprised, asked why. Lowell replied that it was "unlucky." Hastings pocketed the minié ball.[14]

Lowell's orderly wanted to move him to the rear, where Dr. DeWolf could look after him: DeWolf had had a special arrangement with the aides, orderlies, and officers on Lowell's staff to ensure that if the colonel were wounded, he would be whisked to the rear with all speed. Lowell scoffed at the idea. He asked for some whiskey and sent his orderly to borrow General Merritt's flask. Rather quickly, Alvord returned with General Merritt himself, and shortly after that General Torbert and his staff rode up.

Both Torbert and Merritt wanted Lowell to go to the rear, but Lowell would have none of it. He drank a little whiskey, which improved his voice, and said he wanted to "wait until blood was drawn upon him." This bit of bravado was brushed aside, but he said he was sure that the force of the ball had merely stunned him; he would get over it shortly. After more discussion, Lowell explained that his right lung was no good anyway, since it had been infected with tuberculosis. Perhaps the bruising from the ball had "caused the right lung to close entirely and temporarily cease operation."[15]

Very likely the lung had indeed "closed entirely." His breathing was labored and remained so. Some among the eyewitnesses thought he began to cough up blood. In addition to the collapsed lung, Lowell may have cracked a rib or his sternum; the loss of his voice suggests that something had disturbed his larynx or windpipe. He could not speak above a whisper.

Uppermost in Lowell's mind was whether, without his leadership, his regiment would stay at its post. They had been in position for five hours, and while the skirmishers had been rotated among the companies of the regiment, they had nevertheless been holding an outrageously exposed position for a long time. Rumor had it that a federal counterattack was imminent.

All this was occurring within range of enemy guns and sharpshooters. Balls were striking thick and fast, and it was clear that Lowell would not go to the rear. Torbert moved on, and Merritt too was called away, but before he went, he told Lowell to lead the countercharge. He could not have offered Lowell a better parting gift.

Since the death of Rob Shaw, Lowell had understood that he wanted to die "at the head of his regiment: that is the time to die when one is happiest." Now he understood that even if the wound was not mortal, the collapsed lung would ruin his health, and if he lived, it would be an invalid's life and a slow death from consumption. His luck had changed.

His men built up a dirt bank, on the far side of which he would be sheltered from fire. Lowell felt cold. He borrowed Alvord's overcoat and lay on the ground with his head in his lieutenant's lap. The *Baltimore American* for October 17 was being hawked by newspaper boys, who were turning the lull in the fighting to their advantage. Lowell had Alvord read it to him. For two hours they lay so, Lowell's mood improving when he learned that Colonel Gansevoort had captured Mosby's artillery piece.[16]

Shortly before 3 p.m., when the general advance would start, Lowell ordered his dismounted skirmishers to fall back in line and remount. As they fell back, the neighboring Union infantry, still jittery, began to retreat. But as troopers reappeared on their horses, the infantry rallied and surged forward. In the meantime, Lowell was lifted onto a horse, his fourteenth. He was so weak that he had Alvord strap him into the saddle. The line moved forward. Just as the line started to draw enemy fire, orders arrived to fall back. For about half an hour everyone waited in their saddles. The delay was caused by a second report that General Longstreet was advancing from Front Royal to Winchester. Only when another courier returned about three-thirty with the good news that the rumor was false did the word come to form for the counterattack.

Three thousand cavalrymen formed a line some five hundred yards long two ranks deep between the Valley Pike and Cedar Creek. Officers throughout the brigades moved to the front; the nerves of the men were still in question. Throughout the army virtually every officer was as close to the men he commanded as possible. They had overcome panic and near defeat. Now they would be tested by hard fighting. It would be no easy task to drive the Confederates from Middletown. The success of this countercharge would depend entirely on the army's moral resolve. The strongest influence on the men would be not discipline so much as the power of their officers to inspire them and rekindle their old confidence.

In the center was the Second Massachusetts Cavalry. Lowell might have taken up a position in the line. Instead, he and his staff rode to the front to stand with the flags: the red, white, and blue of the national flag, the white silk of the regimental flag, and the guidons of the brigade. Between them and Middletown were three dips in the landscape that offered some cover. Meanwhile the Confederates had plenty of time to dig in and entrench themselves. A series of stone walls offered shelter to several batteries and considerable infantry. Rails and logs had been piled strategically to create cover. Every sharpshooter in every tree and on every roof and in all the top-story windows facing north and east from Middletown were taking their aim, knowing that the greatest effect their firepower might have would be to bring down that small group of men at the front.

Finally, at four-fifteen, Lowell, who could only whisper, had his orders called out by his aides. The cavalrymen drew their sabers. Their guidons fluttered, and everyone awaited the bugle call. Wasting no time, Lowell gave the nod. His bugler blew. The call was picked up on the flanks and swelled. Three thousand horses responded. They started forward at a trot with Lowell at their head.

As the Union line crested the first of the three ravines, the Confederates began to fire: the infantry sent off a volley, and the artillery guns opened. Smoke began to obscure the field. The troopers slowed to a walk. Lowell's aides barked his commands. The cavalry began to trot again, then to gallop, and quickly came the order to charge. There was no time to waste. The fire against them was devastating. A "living wall of the enemy . . . emitted a leaden sheet of fire": grape, canister, and musket balls fell "in perfect showers," Crowninshield recalled. "I never expected to succeed or get out alive . . . Compared with it Ball's Bluff was child's play . . . I charged and said 'God just take my soul!' "[17]

With the entire line surging forward, Sergeant Russell of Company E, the bearer of the regimental colors, was shot dead. Almost immediately afterward Lowell was shot. "The Colonel is hit!"[18] someone shouted. Alvord was already on the ground with Sergeant Russell. He turned in time to catch Lowell as he was flung from his horse.

But the momentum was now unstoppable. Already a trooper had surged forward to take the flag as the brigade went forward. Alvord was barely able to dismount four men. Lowell was whisked into a sling made from a blanket, and they carried him to the rear. A member of his staff raced back to find Dr. DeWolf, who then ran forward to meet them. Lowell gave DeWolf a smile and teasingly told him there was no hurry, as the wound was mortal.

DeWolf quickly examined him. Lowell explained that he could not move his body or his legs or even his chest. Finding that he was not bleeding and that his pulse was strong, DeWolf ventured to suggest that the situation might not be as bad as Lowell feared. Most men were given to thinking a wound was the equivalent of death, but it was not always so. Lowell was not interested in false hope. He said that "there could be no doubt about it." He knew what DeWolf had not yet realized: that the first hit with the minié ball had been fatal. He was therefore prepared. However, he could not bear thinking of Effie: "My poor wife. I am afraid it will kill her."[19]

Lowell was carried farther back to the brigade field hospital to await the results of this counterattack. It took three charges, one for each ravine, before the Confederates finally gave way and the Union cavalry surged forward to reoccupy Middletown and the infantry to reclaim their old camps. As his men chased the Confederates for miles beyond the town, capturing and killing as many rebels as they could, Lowell and the other wounded were brought into town, to houses that were requisitioned as hospitals. He was laid on the dining-room table of a modest white house in the center of town. Within seconds of examining him again, Dr. DeWolf confirmed what Lowell had known since his first wounding: he was dying. The ball had "entered in the right shoulder, passed between the second and third vertebrae severing his spine and exited through his left shoulder blade taking with it a piece of bone." His paralysis meant, however, that he was free of pain. The only pain he had felt was when the first ball hit him, which was "like a shock of electricity," he said. As Lowell lay on the table with the other wounded officers of the Second Massachusetts Cavalry on the floor around him, Dr. DeWolf cut his clothes from him. Upset that Alvord's overcoat was being destroyed, Lowell told DeWolf to give both of his to Alvord. This led to a general discussion of all his things and their disposal. He wanted Crownin-shield to have his pistol: "I was very fond of him."[20]

In the same room, the distress of the wounded Captain Rufus Smith was now at its peak. Smith, twelve years Lowell's senior, was born in Maine and had immigrated to California and settled in San Francisco. When the war started, he resigned from the California Light Guard and enlisted in the Union army. Disappointed when these troops were not shipped east, he joined Company F, serving as second lieutenant to Captain DeMerritt. After DeMerritt's insanity following Coyle's Tavern in August 1863, Smith com-manded F Company. After Dranesville he had taken over Company A, re-placing Captain Reed. He had had ambitions to become a colonel.

Smith had been wounded at about 10 a.m. in the first charge at Cedar Creek, when the skirmishers were first taking position behind the stone walls. Smith and his lieutenant, Henry Kuhls, leading their men, had jumped the stone walls to get in among the Confederates and instead had been shot themselves, Smith through the stomach. They had lain for some time on the battlefield, and now nothing could be done for Smith except to give him morphine. This eased the pain but did not calm him. He was deeply agitated by the thought of his imminent death.

Lowell spoke quietly to calm him. He reminded him that his wound had come at a pivotal moment, and that the taking of that advance skirmish line had proved invaluable. They had held the Confederates in check long enough to secure the army time to recover. The battle had been entirely de-cisive: ending the campaign, destroying Early's army. With such a resound-ing victory Lincoln's reelection was assured. Lowell kept talking calmly: "I have always been able to count on you; you were the bravest of the brave, now you must be strong, you must meet this as you have other trials. Be steady, I count on you."[21]

When Smith died, Lowell told DeWolf that he "was very sorry for him but glad he left no family." The talk turned again to Effie and their unborn child. Lowell confessed that he had often thought of his possible death but had never talked to Effie about it; nor had he ever reckoned his possible death in terms of its effect on her. Now that he was dying, he was almost baf-fled that he had not attended to this. But after they talked a bit, Lowell calmed. He smiled and said, "She will bear it, Doctor, better than you & I think."

He talked about his parents, then returned to Effie. Once again he broke down. DeWolf reminded him of his own thoughts earlier, that Effie had reserves of courage not yet tapped. Once again Lowell calmed. DeWolf insisted that he write to Effie, but Lowell thought it could not be done, and he wanted the doctor to take notes. But despite his paralysis, he did retain some motor control, and DeWolf propped a pencil in his hands, and a piece of paper on a board of wood, and arranged them all, holding the hand against the paper. Lowell was able to scrawl something—"a word or two"—that the doctor could send to Effie. Lowell then dictated a longer letter.

Afterward Lowell turned his mind to his command. Through the evening he remained lucid. Several times he called for an aide, usually Alvord, and continued to issue orders and to dictate messages and directions regarding the disposal of his brigade. He ran through the requirements of his command, trying to think of everything he needed to pass on, as if to leave undone not one detail. This was interrupted only when the groans of the rebel prisoners outside became so distressing that Lowell, anxious "to see that everyone was taken care of about the house," sent DeWolf outside to tend them. Each time this happened, Sergeant Thayer stayed with Lowell, DeWolf leaving a vial of morphine in his care. And although DeWolf later told both Effie and Forbes that Lowell had been without pain, he was given morphine.

By 10 p.m. his pulse and voice were weak. He could no longer take in even tea. He complained that the morphine kept him awake. He spoke of his desire for Will Forbes's safe return and expressed how thankful he was that Will had not been part of the Shenandoah Valley campaign. He spoke of Will's father, John Murray Forbes, and of his own mother, Anna. DeWolf lay down next to him. The two men drifted off. About 5 a.m. Lowell put his hand on DeWolf's head and woke him: "Well, Doctor, you and I have had a little nap."

His breathing was now shallow, and he was becoming "a little insensible to [his] condition." Near dawn he told the doctor to feel his side "and feel it rattle." He wanted to know how much longer it would be.

"I could not tell," DeWolf replied.[22]

Lowell remarked to DeWolf that he did not know what he would find in the afterlife: "If there is another world after this I am prepared to meet it: if not, I am still willing to leave this one." DeWolf, who was not a religious man, thought it was a blessing that he was not suffering; it was unlikely that there would be any pain at the end.

"It is all right—all right—I am ready," Lowell answered.

In the early morning his officers appeared, and Lowell told them he was glad they had come. "I am not very presentable this morning but I should like to see you all."[23]

DeWolf allowed in only one officer at a time, so they took turns filing past. Quite a few took Lowell's hand but could not speak. His face had been washed, and he had been made as comfortable as possible. All the energy had gone from him, and it was disarming to realize how little there was to him, lying on the dining table, propped up with pillows, his small, gaunt body barely evident beneath the blanket. Crowninshield and he spoke for some time, Lowell giving him last-minute directions. By way of parting he added, "My only regret is that I cannot do something more for our cause." Crowninshield was overcome.[24]

After the officers bade farewell, what was left of the men of the regiment filed past, company by company. Once each company had been one hundred men strong. Now most had no more than twenty-five to forty men. It was hard to know which was more pitiful: their dying colonel or their own depleted ranks. When Company E passed by, Lowell spoke to them. They had a long history: the men had warmed to Lowell slowly. Almost exactly a year ago, many of them had petitioned to leave the regiment, so great was their discontent, which had peaked with Ormsby's execution. But at Rockville they had bonded, and after that they had been the first company of the regiment, despite their official letter. They had plumbed the depths both of betrayal and of loyalty. He could hardly speak, but he told them, "You did well."

After this Lowell lay with his eyes closed. His breath was increasingly labored. DeWolf left the room to gulp down some breakfast.

Within minutes Sergeant Thayer came to the door: "The Colonel does not breathe."[25]

Dr. DeWolf rushed to his bedside. It was nine o'clock.

EPILOGUE

—⟡⟡⟡—

Apollonius of Tyana tells us in his Travels that he saw "a youth, one of the blackest of the Indians, who had between his eyebrows a shining moon . . . but as he approached to man's estate, its light grew fainter and fainter and finally vanished." The world should see with reverence on each youth's brow, as a shining moon, his fresh ideal. It should remember that he is already in the hands of a sophist more dangerous than Herodes, for that sophist is himself. It should watch lest, from too early or exclusive action, the moon on his brow, growing fainter and fainter, should finally vanish, and sadder than all, should leave in vanishing no sense of loss.

      —Charles Russell Lowell, Commencement Day oration, 1854

AFTERMATH

In the days that followed the Union victory at Cedar Creek, all the cavalry generals paid Lowell tribute. General Merritt's report, as one might expect from his superior officer, gave full credit to Lowell's importance in the battle and to his high caliber as an officer. General Torbert called him "the beau ideal of a cavalry officer." General Sheridan described him as "the perfection of a man and a soldier" and claimed that if Lowell had lived, he would have commanded the Cavalry Corps and "done better with it than I could have done."[1] This recognition had not come in life: hierarchies, prejudices, and petty jealousies had gotten in the way.

A week after the battle Colonel George B. Sanford, an aide to General Torbert, was delivering the promotions that arrived from Washington. He handed Merritt his promotion to major-general and also gave him Lowell's promotion to brigadier-general. Taking the two pieces of paper, the hard-bitten warrior, known for his cool ambition, broke down. He recalled that Lowell had tried to hide the nature of his first wound. In the silence that followed, Sanford volunteered that Lowell had had an "unusually fine appearance" and the "most courteous manners." Merritt held up the two letters, waving one and then the other, and said, "I would gladly give up *this*, if only he could take *that*."[2]

A similar scene was played out in Washington. On October 21 the twelve battle flags captured at Cedar Creek were carried into Washington by General Custer. At Willard's Hotel William Schouler, Governor Andrew's adjutant general, introduced himself and offered him congratulations on the recent victory. Only then did Schouler learn of Lowell's death. Custer gave him the particulars of the battle, Lowell's role in it, his wounding, and his final charge, then explained that the honor of delivering the battle flags would have been Lowell's if he had lived. He invited Schouler to the flag ceremony at the War Department the next day. That evening Schouler wrote to Governor Andrew, "This news saddened my heart. Colonel Lowell was my *beau ideal* of an officer and a gentleman."[3]

The day before, October 20, Charlie Lowell's father had been summoned to the statehouse in Boston and given a telegram from Secretary Stanton himself with the news of his son's death. Family, friends, and community had immediately rallied around. Anna accepted the news immediately. For months now she had told herself and others that "he is where he wants to be," and she had knitted socks instead of worrying: the truth was, she had confronted his mortality years before. But the others were in shock. George Putnam, disbelieving the telegrams, set off for Washington immediately. The younger Anna, in Washington, was so swamped with nursing work at Armory Hospital that it wasn't until October 22 that she learned of her brother's fate. She rushed up to the War Department for confirmation and ran into General Custer, delivering the battle flags to Secretary Stanton. On meeting her, Custer broke down in tears and told her all he could of Lowell's last days and his role in the battle.[4]

Into this scene walked George Putnam, fresh from Boston, and he too spoke with Custer. Meanwhile Stanton, in whose office this scene occurred, received a telegram from John Murray Forbes making further inquiries about Lowell's death. Forbes had been devastated by the news: Lowell's death was his "hardest personal loss of the war."[5] He was not sure Stanton recalled Lowell and apologized for troubling him.

Stanton remembered Lowell very well, of course. And here in his office were Lowell's sister, his brother-in-law, and his former comrade-in-arms sharing information and consoling one another. He made the exceptional gesture of now telegraphing Forbes with the news that although Lowell had not lived to sign his commission and therefore it was not technically valid, Stanton waived the technicality and directed that Lowell be buried with the honors of a brigadier-general.

This telegram reached Boston on October 23, and with this news the decision was made to bring Lowell's body to Boston. (Previously the thought had been to take it to New York, out of consideration for Effie. Her father had been telegraphed on October 20 and had the heartbreaking job of conveying the news to her. "I cannot think of any thing but Effie," Anna Lowell had written and insisted the body stop at New York.) Massachusetts wanted to give Lowell full military honors, and on October 24 Lowell's body arrived in Boston, accompanied by Lieutenant Alvord. Ever since Lowell had rested his head on Alvord's lap in the midst of the battle on October 19, the two men had barely been separated. Alvord, who had joined the regiment at nineteen as a second lieutenant, came from a politically prominent abolitionist family in western Massachusetts. His father had tried to use his political clout to get his son a better commission, but Lowell had insisted Alvord be judged on his merits, and Governor Andrew had backed him. Alvord had knuckled down and done good work. "With Colonel Lowell I found a true and very dear friend and almost a second home," Alvord wrote. "Now he is gone I feel alone again—like a stranger in a strange land. I lost my dearest friend . . . I loved, I honored and admired—I almost worshipped him."[6]

Alvord also knew more about the battle of Cedar Creek than anyone else. Newspapers were already full of detailed accounts, but with Alvord in Boston and ready to talk, a new crop of stories were published. For a man who had zealously kept himself out of the newspapers, Lowell was now having every detail of his life printed, every virtue sung, every glory trumpeted. LAMENT FOR A TRUE KNIGHT ran one headline. NOBLE DEATH stated another.

His immediate family, never having had a very clear picture of Lowell's army life, was only slowly recognizing the role he had played there. From George Putnam's trip to Washington, from Lieutenant Alvord, and from Stanton, the Lowell family was learning, if not understanding, the glory of his military service and most particularly the part he had played at Cedar Creek to bring about "the closing victory." They were told that "he had borne a part second to none, except Sheridan." They were assured that he was reconciled to his death and "knew of the victory."[7] In many respects they did not need to know more for the moment.

More affecting for them was the receipt of his last letters. Lowell's last sad, lonely, homesick letter to his mother was the more devastating because of all the glorious things she had learned of. It recalled most vividly the primacy of their relationship, revealing that underneath all his accomplishments, talents, and remarkable skills was the same boyish child she had known so well who had always, as she had predicted "needed to feel close to one special person."[8]

The day after Shaw told his daughter Effie of Lowell's death, she received his last letter, telling her that he was to be sent out of the valley and that he was now feeling so "safe" he was riding Berold. And several days after that came the last scribble he had made as he was dying, included with the letter he had dictated to Dr. DeWolf and a long account by DeWolf giving Effie the vital assurances that Lowell had been well cared for, free from pain, and at peace. Dr. DeWolf was at pains to repeat and underline Lowell's comment: "She will bear it better than you or I think." But for the moment Effie was desolated and in shock.[9]

Lowell's father a week later was still disbelieving. "I always felt that he would go through the war, and have a long time to enjoy life." To some degree, the military hero the family buried on October 28 was not the man they had known. Brigadier-General Charles Russell Lowell was a stranger whom they were only just beginning to learn about. The man they mourned had been a boy who cried so piteously on his first day of school that Aunt Catherine had had to stay with him, a rude adolescent who "said things that no one should ever say," and a student with "a mind as clear as a diamond." His sister recalled the one Christmas of the war he had spent at home, in 1863, when he fell asleep on the sofa and the entire family sat and watched him. Smaller, more personal, and inconsequential moments were recalled: how he stretched himself when content like a cat, the lightning-quick twist of his head when he became impatient, the sound of his voice, the thrust of his jaw, the knowingness in his eyes. Still, his father was pleased to remark on the "extravagant" praise of his namesake, and the family took solace in the glory of his death.[10]

For some time after the war, Lowell's memory was kept alive in various ways. In July 1865 Harvard held a Commemoration Day to honor all its graduates who had participated in the war. James Russell Lowell recited his "Commemoration Ode." "In these brave ranks I only see the gaps, / Thinking of dear ones whom the dumb turf wraps." And it was perhaps fitting that Uncle James, who had a decade before told Charlie that "the victory's in believing," should now write of him as one who loved truth and that true to himself, "what [he] dare[d] to dream of, dare[d] to do." The next year Harvard published the *Harvard Memorial Biographies* compiled by Thomas Wentworth Higginson, two large volumes about all the graduates who had been killed in the Civil War. And by 1878 Harvard had built Memorial Hall, which literally engraved in stone what the *Memorial Biographies* had done in print. Down its main hall are plaques of all those sons of Harvard killed in the war. In the dining hall, portraits and busts display a smaller number, one of them a bust of Charles Russell Lowell by Daniel Chester French, the sculptor of the Lincoln Memorial.[11]

Over the years the Harvard Class of 1854 paid tribute in poetry and gifts to the man who had been "the genius of the class." Among his friends, babies were named after him; in the army, forts. In 1890 Henry Lee Higginson gave to Harvard the land on the opposite bank of the Charles River that is known today as Soldiers Field, principally the site of the Harvard football stadium. Soldiers Field was dedicated to six men: Charles and Jim Lowell, Rob Shaw, Stephen Perkins, Jim Savage, and an older surgeon, Edward Dalton. In his dedication of the field Higginson said he did not want it to be used for the aggrandizing of war. Instead, he hoped it would be used for pleasure and all the virtues of peace, one being that the horrors of war would be forgotten. Privately Higginson explained, "To these friends I tried to give everything, because my belief was that one cannot do or give or take too much from a friend."[12] It is known to Bostonians as the place to go on a beautiful summer's day to eat a picnic and watch the sculls go by on the river, to throw a football, to run or walk, or simply to waste the day in simple pleasure, to loaf as Higginson and Lowell and Stephen Perkins had done in the *campagna* outside Rome.

Justice Oliver Wendell Holmes, in his many speeches on the Civil War, struggled to provide a philosophy that reconciled the deep overpowering desire to live with the soldier's readiness to risk life. He spoke of the need "to believe in something" and to "want something with all your might." He spoke of a commitment to an unforeseeable outcome. For Holmes, living was an intense process. He believed in testing oneself to the limit, since "the measure of power is obstacles overcome." He believed that "the doubts of civil life" were "harder to overcome than all the misgivings of the battlefield." In these speeches, Holmes used Lowell and his friends as examples of what he called the "soldier's faith." Lowell was an example of one whose heart was touched with fire and for whom life was a profound and passionate thing. Indeed that much-quoted passage of Holmes's is preceded by a reference to Lowell and to Shaw: "one may fall at the beginning of a charge or at the top of the earthworks; but in no other way can he reach the rewards of victory."[13]

Holmes did not mention *what* it was that had touched their hearts with fire. That would have been too controversial in the postwar years. But the unspoken would have been implied: the abolition of slavery, its removal from both the Constitution and American life. Perhaps it is not surprising that the United States, despite being a relentlessly progressive nation, had stalled on this moral question. Down the millennia, human life had been profoundly transformed, but the moral state of humanity had evolved much more slowly. Since before the days of the ancient Greeks, men have owned other men, and the American South was only one of several places where slavery survived into the nineteenth century. When Lowell and his friends spoke of fighting for humanity and for civilization, they meant they wanted to see their world fundamentally transformed and the eradication of the idea that one man might own another.

Willy Putnam, Jim Lowell, Stephen Perkins, Jim Savage, and Rob Shaw had all died in this cause. Charlie Lowell distinguished himself from them in two ways. First, he had shown true military talent. Despite all the martial splendor of the state and all its many martyrs, only a handful of Massachusetts men had proved to have any military ability. Lowell was assuredly one of them. More important, he lived long enough to experience the dark side of war, not only the relentless destructiveness of battle after battle, and the intensely divisive fissures that war created among the American people, but also the horrendous price of victory. Not only did he witness the burning, the atrocities, and the laying waste, but he was complicit in it. His hand had, as he foretold in his Commencement Day oration, become steeped in that it worked in. With each promotion the stakes had risen higher. During three years in uniform he had progressed from butcher, murderer, executioner, and finally destroyer. To achieve the goal, he had, of necessity, become the kind of person he did not much like and was ashamed of being. The challenge, as Lowell saw it, was to survive his own shame and guilt. This was the challenge behind looking "strangers in the face, particularly Southern strangers."[14]

Yet however disgusted Lowell was by the moral stain of war, he found an intense and deep pleasure in battle. He achieved a clarity of action there that he had never enjoyed in civilian life. The clarity of mind, the singleness of purpose, that a crisis aroused in him functioned as a stimulant. His deepest realization of self came in battle, where he could "see what needed to be done" and did it. In the last hours of his life Lowell faced the full weight of this duty, of all he had sacrificed. Perhaps when he confessed to Dr. DeWolf that he had given little thought to the subject and had had no conversation with Effie about his possible death, he was acknowledging that he still had not taken a measure of its full price. Only Effie would come to know this. Anna Lowell described how all the young women of Boston envied Effie as the widow of such a hero, but she drily commented, "I think of her long life."[15]

Effie Shaw Lowell struggled through the funeral and burial on October 28, putting on a brave face. Her mother had assured her that the child would be a consolation. The baby was born November 30, a beautiful, healthy little girl, and they were all disappointed that she was not a boy. Effie took a long time in naming her because "nothing will be really his name." Finally she settled on Carlotta. But the child did not much resemble Lowell, at least not at first, and Effie confided to Anna that she did not believe it was "the baby." That is to say, none of them could find the spirit of Charlie Lowell in this infant.[16]

After the birth of her daughter, Effie "grew sadder and sadder." She became reclusive, "going about the house with her little girl in her arms . . . with a quiet look as if she were living in another world," Clover Hooper, the future Mrs. Henry Adams, noted in a letter. Anna Lowell reported to her daughter, "Effie says she no longer wants to live." Mrs. Shaw wrote that her nineteen-year-old daughter had "no wish to live or to be well while she does live." Others, too, reported her depression. She arranged her room to resemble a camp. The bare floor was spread with a blanket. She had Lowell's bookshelves and pictures of him everywhere. She liked to talk of him and did so at length. She attempted to find the wife of William Pendergast, the man Lowell had shot in the School Street Mutiny, but failed. She helped out many veterans from the regiment and throughout her life received letters and pleas from them. Everyone hoped that the baby would eventually break in upon her grief and recall her to life.[17]

Slowly Effie rallied. She visited her parents-in-law and summered in Kittery, Maine, with her sister-in-law, Harriet Putnam. In 1869, traveling in Europe, she was introduced to Thomas Carlyle. In their conversation Carlyle spoke of the "Nigger Agony," and of what so many on his side of the Atlantic felt about the needlessness and stupidity of the American Civil War. Carlyle could not have chosen a worse audience than Josephine Shaw Lowell. She sent the eminent philosopher the full two volumes of the *Harvard Memorial Biographies*, and after receiving this sobering dose of martyrdom, Carlyle wrote her a contrite apology. Speaking of "the sorrowful and noble tragedy each of their lives is," he assured her, "I would strew flowers on their graves along with you, and piously bid them rest in Hope! It is not doubtful to me that they also have added their mite to what is the eternal cause of God and man; or that, in circuitous but sure ways, all men, Black and White, will infallibly get their profit of the same."[18]

Although neither Carlyle nor Effie lived long enough to appreciate it, the final homage paid to Lowell was a small publication issued in 1920 entitled *Memoirs of '61: General Charles Russell Lowell and his Friends*, dedicated to the officers and soldiers of the First World War. It gave short biographies of Charlie Lowell and six of his cousins and close friends killed in the Civil War. The book was prepared by Lowell's cousin Elizabeth Cabot Putnam, who had been in love with James Savage and who, after his death, had remained a spinster. The book very delicately linked the devastations of the American Civil War with the slaughter that became standard in the Great War: the wholesale destruction of a nation's young men.

Something in her exchange with Carlyle served as a catalyst, and Effie did emerge from her malaise. Although she never rejoined society, never remarried, and wore black for the rest of her life, living with her mother and daughter, who also never married, she began to devote herself to "doing the work for two." She joined the New York State Charities Aid Association (an outgrowth of the Sanitary Commission). She did not want to perpetuate charity in its traditional form of "Lady Bountiful" handing out turkeys to the poor for their Christmas dinner. Instead she took a more scientific approach, analyzing the factors behind chronic poverty, and she became one of the proto-social scientists who inspired and directed the reform of the public welfare system of New York. Her reports on New York jails and almshouses earned her recognition. In 1875 she was asked to run a statewide study of paupers, and on the basis of that report she became the first woman appointed to the New York State Board of Charities. As Commissioner Lowell, Effie continued to inspect and report on hospitals, asylums, orphanages, and jails. By the 1880s she was an advocate for the working class generally. In 1890 she founded the Consumers League of the City of New York, which used boycotts to force employers to provide better working conditions for their women employees. Because of her intimate knowledge of the state system for dealing with the poor and incapacitated, she realized the rampant corruption within the political system. In alliance with Frank Barlow, who had married her younger sister and was briefly attorney general for the State of New York, she attempted to combat Tammany Hall. She founded the Women's Municipal League in 1894.[19]

But Effie's largest influence came from founding and overseeing the New York City Charity Organization. This institution expressed her commitment to scientific charity and her great faith in the disinterested philanthropist. She had one foot in the old world of Christian ministry of the sort Reverend Lowell had offered on the west side of Beacon Hill, and the other pointed toward the professional social scientist. Not coincidentally the American Social Science Association, founded in 1865, had as its president Frank Sanborn. Her service on behalf of the poor and disadvantaged of New York is a remarkable and complex story in itself. Admired for her idealism

and for her practical realism, she was an inspiration for a generation of reformers and, several generations later, feminists.[20]

One of her closest associates was Jacob Riis, the Danish immigrant, reporter, and photographer. His book *How the Other Half Lives* remains one
of the most powerful documentations of poverty in America. It earned him
the friendship of Theodore Roosevelt, then New York's commissioner of police, and it earned him Effie Lowell's mentorship. Under her guidance and
with her help, he too became a tireless advocate for social reform. Through
the late 1880s and 1890s Riis and Effie met almost daily. In 1905, when she
was dying of cancer, Riis came to say good-bye. She dismissed his praise of
her eminent career, her work as a "useful citizen." Taking his hand and
stroking it, she said, "Yes, yes; I know. But think of my waiting for my husband forty-one long years, forty-one years."[21]

Riis described her gentle smile, which hovered in his memory. Effie's
had been a long life. She had lived at Lowell's camp. She had understood
not only her husband's heroism and personal courage but also the darker—
to many, unspeakable—realities. She had almost been broken by this
strange and bitter knowledge. Hers was a final, less dramatic sacrifice, a long
labor of love by a tough and courageous woman of unshakable faith. She became the "useful citizen" Lowell had wanted to be. The duty that Lowell
had found so much easier to perform on the field of battle, Effie learned to
perform as a civilian.

NOTES

All the letters of Charles Russell Lowell found in Edward Waldo Emerson, *Life and Letters of Charles Russell Lowell* (1907), are so cited. Most letters not included in that publication are found in the three-volume set of Lowell-Putnam Family Papers compiled by Elizabeth Cabot Putnam in the 1920s, which include letters from other family members. I have donated a copy to the Houghton Library. Finally, I discovered a cache of uncatalogued (MS 235) Lowell Family Letters at the Houghton Library, which include transcriptions of Lowell's letters to his family made by his sister, Harriet Putnam, as well as Effie Lowell's transcriptions of his letters to her. From notations in these transcriptions, it is now clear that Elizabeth Cabot Putnam used these transcriptions for her Lowell-Putnam Family Papers. Except for a scant handful of letters in the author's possession (photocopies have been donated to the Houghton), it would appear that the original letters of Charles Russell Lowell are lost.

The Forbes family has been very generous in sharing the Ralph Emerson Forbes Collection of William Hathaway Forbes's letters to his parents and his sister, Alice Forbes, and also the letters of Edith Emerson Forbes in the Forbes/Emerson Letters.

I had done a fair bit of research on the Californians in the Second Massachusetts Cavalry when I discovered *Their Horses Climbed Trees: A Chronicle of the California 100 and Battalion in the Civil War, from San Francisco to Appomattox* (2001), by Larry Rogers and Keith Rogers, which gathers together most of the primary source material pertaining to the California Hundred and the California Battalion. Since much of this material is privately held or hard to access, I cite this book whenever possible.

LIST OF ABBREVIATIONS

SOURCES

BL	Bancroft Library, University of California, Berkeley, Calif.
SL	Arthur and Elizabeth Schlesinger Library on the History of Women in America, Radcliffe Institute, Harvard University, Cambridge, Mass.
BL-HBS	Baker Business Library, Harvard Business School, Harvard University, Cambridge, Mass.
F/EFL	Forbes/Emerson Family Letters, privately held by the Forbes family.
HL	Houghton Library, Harvard University, Cambridge, Mass.
HMB	*Harvard Memorial Biographies*, ed. Thomas Wentworth Higginson, 2 vols. (Cambridge, Mass.: Sever and Francis, 1866).

HUA   Harvard University Archives, Harvard University, Cambridge, Mass.
LFP   Lowell Family Papers (uncatalogued MS 235), HL.
LPFP   Lowell-Putnam Family Papers, Author's Collection.
MHS   Massachusetts Historical Society, Boston.
NA   National Archives, Washington, D.C.
NYPL   Manuscripts and Archives Division, New York Public Library, Astor, Lenox and Tilden Foundations, New York.
OR   *War of the Rebellion: A Compilation of the Official Records of the Union and Confederate Armies*, 70 vols. (Washington, D.C.: Government Printing Office, 1880–1901).
PJLFP   Putnam-Jackson-Lowell Family Papers, MHS.
REFC   Ralph Emerson Forbes Collection, privately held by the Forbes family.
THCT   Larry Rogers and Keith Rogers, *Their Horses Climbed Trees: A Chronicle of the California 100 and Battalion in the Civil War, from San Francisco to Appomattox* (Afglen, Pa.: Schiffer Military History Books, 2001).

PEOPLE

EWE   Edward Waldo Emerson
JMF   John Murray Forbes
HLH   Henry Lee Higginson
ACJL   Anna Cabot Jackson Lowell
CRL   Charles Russell Lowell, Jr.
JRL   James Russell Lowell
JSL   Josephine Shaw Lowell

INTRODUCTION: THE FUNERAL, OCTOBER 28, 1864

1. Henry I. Bowditch, "Brief Memoranda of Our Martyr Soldiers Who Fell during the Great Rebellion of the 19th Century," Nathaniel Bowditch memorial collection, 1851–86, MHS.
2. Caroline H. Dall to Lizzie Putnam, 10.29.64, JRL Papers, MHS. Other sources about the funeral are Elizabeth Cabot Putnam to Ella Lowell Lyman, 10.28.64, PJLFP; EWE, *Life and Letters of Charles Russell Lowell, captain Sixth United States Cavalry, colonel Second Massachusetts Cavalry, brigadier-general United States Volunteers* (Boston, New York: Houghton Mifflin, 1907), 370; HMB, 435–36.
3. Cyrus A. Bartol, *The Purchase of Blood: A Sermon Preached in the West Church* (Boston: J. Wilson & Son, 1864), 1, 5, 21. His text was Psalms 72:14: "He shall redeem their soul from deceit and violence: and precious shall their blood be in his sight," King David's prayer for Solomon.
4. George Putnam, *An Address Spoken in the College Chapel, Cambridge, October 28th 1864, at the Funeral of Brig.-Gen. Charles Russell Lowell, Who Fell at the Battle of Cedar Creek, October 19th 1864* (Cambridge, Mass.: Welch, Bigelow, 1864).
5. Ibid.
6. Sheridan, quoted in Bliss Perry, ed., *Life and Letters of Henry Lee Higginson* (Boston: Atlantic Monthly Press, 1921), 232.
7. Charles Russell Lowell, Sr. to Anna Lowell, 11.1.64, LPFP, vol. 2, 213.
8. Putnam, *Address*, 13.

9. Caroline H. Dall to Lizzie Putnam, 10.29.64, JRL Papers, MHS. The actual text reads, " . . . painful misgivings as to the price we are paying for our country's salvation, and whether it is not paying too much." Putnam, *Address*, 15.

10. Unattributed comment in John Mills Peirce, "Charles Russell Lowell," in *HMB*, 298.

11. Caroline H. Dall to Lizzie Putnam, 10.29.64, JRL Papers, MHS. The actual text reads, "But no, not too much! Think it not! If ever we might be permitted to think it, it would be here and now." Putnam, *Address*, 15.

12. Caroline H. Dall to Lizzie Putnam, 10.29.64, JRL Papers, MHS.

1. THE LOWELL-JACKSON FAMILY

1. James J. Putnam, A *Memoir of Dr. James Jackson* (Boston, New York: Houghton Mifflin, Riverside Press, 1905), 72.

2. For details of Patrick Tracy and a history of Tracy, Tracy & Jackson, see Kenneth Porter, *The Jacksons and the Lees*, 2 vols. (Cambridge, Mass.: Harvard University Press, 1937), and Ferris Greenslett, *The Lowells and Their Seven Worlds* (Boston: Houghton Mifflin, 1946), 52.

3. Harrison Gray Otis as quoted in Greenslett, *Lowells*, 67.

4. Putnam, *Dr. James Jackson*, 29.

5. Ibid., 98.

6. Samuel Eliot Morison, *Harrison Gray Otis, 1765–1848; The Urbane Federalist* (Boston: Houghton Mifflin, 1969), 88.

7. Ibid.

8. Putnam, *Dr. James Jackson*, 132; *Yankee Drover: Being the Unpretending Life of Asa Sheldon, Farmer, Trader, and Working Man, 1788–1870* (Hanover, N.H.: University Press of New England, 1988), 85.

9. Charles Warren, *Jacobin and Junto or Early American Politics, as Viewed in the Diary of Dr. Nathaniel Ames (1758–1822)* (Cambridge, Mass.: Harvard University Press, 1931), 8.

10. Boston Manufacturing's policy of employing female operatives and providing them with lodging, social activities, and paternal guidance represented the first time women were paid in hard cash for mill work. More important, it defied at least initially the common belief that industrial life degraded those whom it employed. But within twenty years circumstances for textile workers declined rapidly. See John Coolidge, *Mill and Mansion: Architecture and Society in Lowell, Massachusetts, 1820–1865* (New York: Russell & Russell, 1942).

11. For further information on Lycoming Coal, see Israel Rupp, *History and Topography of Northumberland, Huntingdon, Mifflin, Centre, Union, Columbia, Juniata and Clinton Counties, Pa. embracing local and general events, leading incidents, descriptions of the principal boroughs, towns, villages, etc., etc.,: with a copious appendix, embellished by engravings/compiled from authentic sources* (Lancaster City, Pa.: G. Hill, 1847), 358–59; John Blair Linn, *History of Centre and Clinton Counties, Pennsylvania* (Philadelphia: Louis H. Everts, 1883), 602–4; Sherman Day, "Historical Collections," in D. S. Maynard, *Historical View of Clinton County: from its earliest settlement to the present time: comprising a complete sketch and topographical description of each township in the county* (Lock Haven, Pa.: Enterprise Print House, 1875), 130–31; Lycoming Coal Co. Collection, BL-HBS.

12. Hannah Lowell Jackson Cabot to Sarah Jackson Russel, 5.26.35, Almy Family Papers, SL.

13. Elizabeth Cabot Jackson to James Jackson, Jr., 7.17.[31], PJLFP.
14. Patrick Tracy Jackson to Sarah Jackson Russel, as part of Hannah Lowell Jackson Cabot to Sarah Jackson Russel, 5.26.35, Almy Family Papers, SL.
15. ACJL Diary, LPFP, 1:83–115. Except where otherwise indicated, quoted material in this chapter comes from this diary.
16. ACJL to Mme. de Gerando, 4.8.53, PJLFP; Horace Scudder, *James Russell Lowell: A Biography*, 2 vols. (Boston, New York: Houghton Mifflin, 1901), 1:11.
17. Esther Lowell Cunningham, *The Three Houses* (Boston: Thomas Todd, 1955), 60.
18. JRL to George B. Loring, 12.23.38, in *New Letters of James Russell Lowell*, ed. Mark A. DeWolfe Howe (New York: Harper & Bros., 1932), 4.
19. Hannah Lowell Jackson Cabot to Sarah Jackson Russel, 1.38, Almy Family Papers, SL.
20. Mrs. William G. Farlow, "Quincy Street in the Fifties," *Cambridge Historical Society Proceedings* (1926), 18:38.
21. JRL to George B. Loring, 12.22.37 in Scudder, *James Russell Lowell*, 1:46.
22. Emerson, *Life*, 370.

2. MRS. LOWELL TAKES OVER, 1840–50

1. ACJL to Charles Russell Lowell, Sr., in ACJL Diary, vol. 2, LFP.
2. J. Milton Furey, *Historical and Biographical Work: or Past and Present of Clinton County [Pa. comprising a sketch of every town and township . . . biographical sketches of many prominent citizens . . . and a complete history of all murders, floods, and other important events that have occurred in Clinton County]* (Williamsport, Pa.: Pennsylvania Grit Publishing House, 1892), 359.
3. Ibid., Patrick Tracy Jackson to proprietors, 2.8.38, and "Historical Sketch of the Lycoming Coal Company," Lycoming Coal Company Records, BL-HBS.
4. For a more complete discussion, see "Anthracite Coal and the Beginning of the Industrial Revolution in the United States," in *The Essential Alfred Chandler: Essays Toward a Historical Theory of Big Business*, ed. Thomas K. McCraw (Boston: Harvard Business School Press, 1988), 307–42.
5. At the final reckoning, the proprietors of Lycoming Coal had paid in some $432,000 in stock. The partners of Franklin Nail Works had invested a further $250,000. See Lycoming Coal Company Records, BL-HBS.
6. JRL to Nathan Hale, 6.15.40, Edward Everett Hale Collection, New York State Library: "The Col lost 4/5 of father's property, & in addition the notes he sent him [in Europe] were protested so that he has about $9000 to pay abroad." See also JRL to Charles F. Briggs, n.d., in Greenslett, *Lowells*, 239; Henry W. Longfellow to Stephen Longfellow, 3.8.40 (425a), Henry Wadsworth Longfellow Letters to Various Correspondents (MS Am 1340.1), HL; Hannah Lowell Jackson Cabot Diary, 2.21.40, Almy Family Papers, SL.
7. "The Darkened Mind," in *The Writings of James Russell Lowell* (Boston: Houghton Mifflin, 1895), 3:243.
8. ACJL to Sarah Jackson Russel, 1.30.38, LPFP; ACJL to Sarah Jackson Russel, March 1838, LPFP, 1:121.
9. See Charles F. Briggs, "James Russell Lowell," in *Homes of American Authors* (New York: Putnam, 1853), 139.
10. Henry W. Longfellow to Stephen Longfellow, 9.11.38 (354), 3.13.40 (425), and 3.8.40 (425a), Henry Wadsworth Longfellow Letters to Various Correspondents (MS Am 1340.1), HL.

11. John Corry, *The History of Bristol, Civil and Ecclesiastical; Including Biographical No-tices of Eminent and Distinguished Natives* (Bristol: W. Sheppard, 1816), 1:400–1.
12. Edward Pessen, *Riches, Class and Power: America Before the Civil War* (New Brunswick, N.J.: Transaction Publishers, 1990), 139. Pessen worked from Boston tax records, which did not reflect Jackson's wealth outside the city. Nevertheless the scale of his losses is corroborated by various accounts. See John A. Lowell, *A Memoir of Patrick Tracy Jackson: written for the Merchants' magazine and Commercial review* (New York: Press of Hunt's Merchants' Magazine, 1848); Dr. James Jackson, *Notes on the Life & Character of the late P. T. Jackson*, PJLFP, MHS.
13. ACJL to Sarah Jackson Russel, 1.30.38, LPFP, 1:117.
14. LPFP, 1:128–29; *Dial*, January 1842.
15. LPFP, 1:129; Edna D. Cheney, "The Women of Boston," in Justin Winsor, ed., *Memorial History of Boston* (Boston: Ticknor, 1880–81), 4:344.
16. What remains of this collection is still in the author's possession.
17. ACJL to Sarah Jackson Russel, 12.17.43, LPFP, 1:132. In the spring of 1842 her sister Hannah stayed with them for several months, during which she "enjoyed and suffered much. Suffered in seeing Anna miserable, enjoyed being able to contribute somewhat to the comfort of the family." Hannah Lowell Jackson Cabot Diary, 5.26.42, Almy Family Papers, SL.
18. See receipt, Lowell & Hinckley, 4.25.49 (61), Series II: Business Papers, E. receipts, JRL Additional Papers (MS Am 1484.1), HL.
19. Harriet Lowell to Lucy Russel, 6.3.55, LPFP, 1:163–64.
20. Sarah Cabot Wheelwright Memoir in L. Vernon Briggs, *History and Genealogy of the Cabot Family, 1475–1927* (Boston: C. E. Goodspeed, 1927), 1:228, 291–92, 383. Originally Turnagain Alley, it was called Temple Court after the Masonic Temple was built, then Temple Place. Much of the land around "the Court" had been bought by Thomas Lee. As the Lees had intermarried with the Lowells, Jacksons, Cabots, and Perkins families, the area was populated with many of Charlie Lowell's cousins. Patrick Jackson's development of Pemberton Square was beginning to take some of the family into that newer, more luxurious area. And over the next ten years many fled the city altogether. Nevertheless, during Charlie's childhood many in the family still lived in the old neighborhood.
21. Perry, ed., *Higginson*, 7. Their first correspondence was a letter Charlie wrote in November 1844, when Higgy was ill. "Dear and Honoured Sir," it began, "I have marked the forenoon and evening lesson in your book. School does not keep tomorrow, and I hope you will be well enough to go out and play." Emerson, *Life*, 381.
22. Accounts of Boston in the 1840s include: Harriet Lowell to Lucy Russel, 1.7.48, LPFP, 1:135; John Carver Palfrey to Francis Winthrop Palfrey, 1.28.49 (195), Palfrey Family Papers (bMS Am 1704.2), HL; Sarah Cabot Wheelwright in Briggs, *Cabot Family*, 288, 291–92, 380, 383; Maud Howe Elliot, "The Old Rosewood Desk," in William S. Rossiter, ed., *Days and Ways in Old Boston* (Boston: R. H. Stearns, 1915); Elizabeth Cabot Putnam, "Brigadier-General Charles Russell Lowell and Josephine Shaw Lowell," PJLFP; Perry, ed., *Higginson*, 1921; HMB.
23. ACJL to Sarah Jackson Russel, 12.17.43, LPFP, 1:134.
24. *Charles Francis Adams, 1835–95; An Autobiography: With a Memorial Address Delivered November 17, 1916, by Henry Cabot Lodge* (Boston: Houghton Mifflin, 1916), 22–23.
25. Henry F. Jenks, *Catalogue of the Boston Latin School* (Boston: Boston Latin School Association, 1886); Perry, ed., *Higginson*, 6.

26. *The Education of Henry Adams* (New York: Modern Library, 1996), 41.

27. *More than Common Powers of Perception: The Diary of Elizabeth Rogers Mason Cabot* (Boston: Beacon Press, 1991), 322; Cheney, "Women of Boston," in Winsor, ed., *Memorial History*, 4:345.

28. JRL to CRL, 6.11.49, JRL Papers, MHS. He taught Charlie that punning was a social grace and wit was social capital; a quotation was a souvenir to be shown to acquaintances as evidence of one's literary voyages. One of Uncle James's whist partners was John Bartlett, who was compiling what would become *Bartlett's Familiar Quotations*. In his pantheon of "indispensable authors," Uncle James included Homer, "the greatest classical writer," Dante, Cervantes, Goethe, and Shakespeare. But James also turned Charlie toward modern visions of personal liberty, to Byron, Shelley, Coleridge, and Keats most of all. He admired Emerson, loved Longfellow, believed Hawthorne "the rarest creative imagination of the century," and liked Poe but did not understand Thoreau. His interests were wide, his enthusiasms changing, but it was the lyric, the Romantic, and the inspiration of the natural world that were his enduring preoccupations.

29. LPFP, 1:125–27. A sea monster was believed to inhabit the waters. The rumor was given credibility by its having been sighted by a variety of respectable and prominent men with seagoing backgrounds. Harriet swore that she had once seen it, but no one quite believed her. See Katharine Peabody Loring, "The Earliest Summer Residents of the North Shore and Their Houses," *Essex Institute Historical Collections* (Salem, Mass.: Essex Institute Press) 68, no. 3 (July 1932): 193–208; Kathleen Motes Bennewitz, "John F. Kensett at Beverly, Massachusetts," in *American Art Journal* 21, no. 4 (1989): 47–65.

30. Edwin Bacon, *King's Dictionary of Boston* (Cambridge, Mass.: Moses King, 1883), 165.

3. HARVARD, 1850-52

1. Records of the Harvard College Class of 1854, General Folder: news clippings (HUD 254), HUA. Lowell's years at Harvard, described in Chapters 3 and 4, draw heavily on holdings at HUA, in particular the biographical material on Charles Russell Lowell, Records of the Harvard College Class of 1854, Records of the Faculty of Arts and Sciences on Student Life for the period 1850–1854, Final Returns, Class Rank Scales, Class Records, Prizes, and Scales of Merit.

2. Samuel Eliot Morison, *Three Centuries of Harvard, 1636–1936* (Cambridge, Mass.: Oxford University Press, 1936), 273. The phrase is used as the title for his chapter on this period. See also Lord Acton, "American Diaries," *Fortnightly Review* (London: Chapman and Hall, December 1921), 54:932–33; Ronald Story, *The Forging of an Aristocracy* (Middletown, Conn.: Wesleyan University Press, 1980), 157; Van Wyck Brooks, *The Flowering of New England, 1815–1865* (New York: Dutton, 1940), 34; Harvard Class Book of 1854, HUA; Donald Fleming, "Eliot's New Broom," in *Glimpses of the Harvard Past*, ed. Bernard Bailyn (Cambridge, Mass.: Harvard University Press, 1986), 68.

3. Morison, *Harvard*, 281.

4. HMB, 1:297; Emerson, *Life*, 6.

5. Acton, "American Diaries," 930.

6. Records of the Harvard College Class of 1853, 12.19.51, 12.20.51, 12.31.51, 4.17.52, 10.7.52; James C. White, "An Undergraduate's Diary," *Harvard Graduates Magazine*, June 1913 (HUD 853.94A) HUA; Morison, *Harvard*, 300.

7. James M. McPherson, *Battle Cry of Freedom: The Civil War Era* (New York: Ballantine, 1989), 71.
8. Ibid., 73.
9. Elizabeth Cabot Putnam, "Reminiscences," *Christian Register*, July 8, 1915, 4.
10. Charles F. Adams, *Richard Henry Dana: A Biography* (Boston, New York: Houghton Mifflin, 1891), 1:127.
11. Andrew Preston Peabody, *Harvard Graduates Whom I Have Known* (Boston, New York: Houghton Mifflin, 1890), 106. Theodore Parker was well known to the African American community, but his relationship with it was not of such long standing.
12. Gary Collison, "Anti-Slavery, Blacks, and the Boston Elite: Notes on the Reverend Charles Lowell and the West Church," *New England Quarterly* 61 (September 1988): 420.
13. Ibid., 423.
14. Ibid.
15. Leonard Levy, "Sim's Case: The Fugitive Slave Law in Boston in 1851," *Journal of Negro History* 35 (January 1950): 41–42, 68.
16. Faculty of Arts and Sciences, Student Life, Clippings, etc. 1853 (HUD 853.2), HUA.
17. Charles F. Adams quoted in Kirkland, *Charles Francis Adams, Jr.*, 10.
18. Morison, *Harvard*, 295. College expenses are estimated to have been $75 tuition, $15 rent, $100 board, and $12 books, for a total of $202 per term or $404 per year, $1,616 for four years. These estimates are perhaps half what the actual costs were, as the students were acquiring fairly high living standards. Yet Lowell's actual costs were much less: $87 per term, further reduced by prizes to around $50, or $400 for his entire education.
19. Joseph Brent, *Charles Sanders Peirce: A Life* (Bloomington: Indiana University Press, 1993), 33; EWE, *The Early Years of the Saturday Club, 1855–1870* (Boston: Houghton Mifflin, 1918), 103.
20. *HMB*, 1:298.
21. Unattributed quotation, ibid., 1:297.
22. Horace Furness to William Furness, 6.5.52, *Letters of Horace Howard Furness*, ed. Horace Howard Furness Jayne, 2 vols. (Boston: Houghton Mifflin, Riverside, 1922), 1:7–8.
23. *The Autobiography of Thomas Jefferson Coolidge, 1831–1920* (Cambridge, Mass.: Riverside, 1923), 7; Records of the Harvard College Class of 1854, Class Book: HUD 254.70, HUA. A few were singular. Robert A. Renshaw had a Venezuelan mother and had been educated at Baltimore, where, he explained, "under the veil of religion, bigotry and narrow prejudices were instilled into the tender minds of inexperienced youth." Theodore Lang, the son of a Kershaw planter, was a highly unstable young man who eventually went mad. Alfred Hampton Preston was the nephew of Wade Hampton and the son of a very wealthy Louisiana plantation owner and state legislator; he lived largely in Europe and was a patron of numerous young artists.
24. ACJL to Maria White Lowell, 4.2.52, JRL Additional Papers, MS Am 1483 (207), HL; Faculty of Arts and Sciences, Student Life, The Institute Papers (HUD 3461.150–HUD 3461.153), HUA.
25. Records of the Harvard College Class of 1853, Clippings, etc., 1853: John L. Swift, "Political and Personal Reminiscences," *The State*, December 19, 1885, HUD 853.2, HUA. Tensions among the students rose and ebbed. Many of the southern students were easily shocked. In a lecture, one asked Louis Agassiz whether he considered the African "a

member of the human race." To which Agassiz replied, "Yes, gentlemen, from all that science teaches us, the negro is a man, and a pretty good man too." This struck the southerners as heretical and the height of radicalism. To the radicalized northern students who considered Harvard "frigid with conservatism" and believed Harvard to "frown with majestic scorn upon every phase of the anti-slavery agitation," it was only common sense.

26. Charles Lowell to Theodore Parker, 6.29.54; Parker Papers, 11:256, 8:352, MHS, quoted in Collison, "Anti-Slavery, Blacks," 427. See also Reverend Charles Lowell to Wendell Phillips, 12.23.54 (837), Wendell Phillips Papers, MS Am 1953, HL.

27. *Kossuth in New England* (Boston: John P. Jewett, 1852), 147. The following articles constitute the core of the debate between Francis Bowen, conservative history tutor, and Mary Lowell Putnam over the significance and meaning of the Hungarian uprising of 1848 and its failure: Francis Bowen, "The War of Races," *North American Review*, January 1850; "The Politics of Europe," *North American Review*, April 1850; "The Rebellion Against the Magyars," *North American Review*, January 1851; Mary Lowell Putnam, "Reviewing *De L'Esprit*," *Christian Examiner*, May 1850; Mary Lowell Putnam, "The North American Review on Hungary," *Christian Examiner*, November 1850. Bowen was denied tenure over the matter.

28. Mrs. William G. Farlow, "Quincy Street," 38; Harriet Lowell to Lucy Russel, LPFP, 1:132–57.

29. Ferencz Aurelius Pulszky, *White, Red, Black: Sketches of American Society in the United States, during the Visit of Their Guest [Louis Kossuth]*, 2 vols. (London: Trübner, 1853), 2:306, 309, 313, 316, 320, 292.

30. Edward Wagenknecht, *James Russell Lowell: Portrait of a Many-Sided Man* (New York: Oxford University Press, 1971), 49–50. He "looked forward with agony to the time when she may become a memory instead of a constant presence." For the first time he felt old, as if he were a man with a past, "something, I mean, quite alien to my present life, and from which I am exiled." Although Maria had promised to come to him in spirit, if that were possible, he found that this demanded too much "energy of the soul to believe without sight" and more simplicity of faith than he had to distinguish between fact and fantasy. In the end, he found that "I cannot see her, I cannot feel her," and he was left only with the hope of finding her again on his own death. This conclusion he came to with a sense of resignation, of failure on his part, forced to recognize the limits of his faith and perhaps of his love. JRL to Charles F. Briggs, 11.25.53, Norton, ed., *Letters of James Russell Lowell*, 1:205–6.

31. JRL, "A Moosehead Journal," in *Cambridge Thirty Years Ago, 1854: A Memoir Addressed to the Edelmann Storg in Rome* (Boston: Houghton Mifflin, 1910), 151.

32. JRL, "To ACL," in *Complete Poetical Works of James Russell Lowell*, ed. Horace E. Scudder (Boston: Houghton Mifflin, 1896), 19–20.

33. JRL, "To _____," ibid., 97.

34. CRL to HLH, 9.12.52, in Emerson, *Life*, 77.

35. Unattributed quotation in *HMB*, 1:298; Furness quoted in *HMB*, 1:297.

4. THE AMERICAN SCHOLAR, 1854

1. Record of the Harvard College Class of 1854, Class Book: autobiographical essay of Charles Russell Lowell, 187 (HUD 254.714), HUA; Morison, *Harvard*, 294.

2. Dale Baum, *The Civil War Party System: The Case of Massachusetts, 1848–1876* (Chapel Hill: University of North Carolina Press, 1984), 75.

3. Fleming, "Eliot's," 68.

4. John Van der Zee Sears, *My Friends at Brook Farm* (New York: D. Fitzgerald, 1912), 39; Edwin Abbot, "Francis Channing Barlow," in *Sons of the Puritans* (Boston: American Unitarian Association, 1908), 142–43. It has been suggested that Almira Barlow contributed to Hawthorne's central character in *The Blithedale Romance*, his novel about Brook Farm.

5. Ora Sedgewick, "A Girl of 16 at Brook Farm," *Atlantic Monthly* 85 (1900), 397.

6. Record of the Harvard College Class of 1854, HUA.

7. *Reflections of Seventy Years by F. B. Sanborn, of Concord* (Boston: R. G. Badger, 1909), 2:314.

8. Ibid., 2:316. Alcott was a peculiar educationalist and philosopher whose impracticalities were legion. His utopian experiment Fruitlands had proved a very short-lived venture, and his other efforts, mostly educational, had consistently failed as his exacting ideals and philosophies crashed into the wall of conventional reality. But Alcott, among liberals, had the status of visionary, an otherworldly dreamer.

9. *HMB*, 1:300.

10. CRL to ACJL, 8.16.57, in Emerson, *Life*, 142.

11. Harold Schwartz, "Fugitive Slave Days in Boston," *New England Quarterly* 27 (June 1954): 205; "Some Events of Boston and Its Neighbors," *State Street Events: A Brief Account of Divers Notable Persons and Sundry Stirring Events Having to Do with the History of This Ancient Street* (Boston: Imprint for the State Street Trust Co. of Boston, 1916), 51.

12. James Horton and Lois Horton, *Black Bostonians: Family Life and Community Struggle in the Antebellum North* (New York: Holmes & Meier, 1999), 108–9.

13. Schwartz, "Fugitive Slave Days," 207; Frank Sanborn, "Reflections on Col. Charles Lowell," in *Transcendental Youth and Age: Chapters in Biography and Autobiography* (Hartford, Conn.: Transcendental Books, 1981), 124.

14. "Some Events of Boston," 46, 47, 49, 53.

15. Emerson, *Life*, 8. For accounts of the Anthony Burns arrest, trial, and deportation, see also Perry, ed., *Higginson*, 82–83; Wilbur Siebert, "The Vigilance Committee of Boston," *Proceedings of the Bostonian Society* (1953): 38–40; Wilbur Siebert, "Underground Railroad in Massachusetts," *Proceedings of the American Antiquarian Society* 45 (April 1935): 82–83.

16. Records of the Harvard College Class of 1854, Class Day, General Folder (HUD 254), HUA.

17. Records of the Harvard College Class of 1854, Charles Russell Lowell, Jr., "Oration at Commencement 1854" (HUC 6853.76.2), HUA.

18. For Lowell's sources, see William Wordsworth, "Intimations of Immortality," *The Oxford Book of English Verse*, ed. Christopher Ricks (Oxford and New York: Oxford University Press, 1999), 349–55; Thomas Carlyle, *On Heroes, Hero-Worship and the Heroic in History* (New York, 1852); and "Nature; Addresses and Lectures," in *Ralph Waldo Emerson*, ed. Richard Poirier, The Oxford Authors (Oxford and New York: Oxford University Press, 1990), 3. He conceded that heroes come but once a century while "young men are always at hand"; nevertheless he argued that "young-man-worship should stand by the side of hero-worship."

19. King Minos of Crete compelled the city of Thebes to offer a yearly sacrifice of seven virgins and seven youths to assuage the appetite of the Minotaur, a bull-like monster who lived in the Labyrinth (built by Daedalus). The beast was eventually slain by Theseus.

20. Ralph Waldo Emerson, "The Transcendentalist," in *Ralph Waldo Emerson*, ed. Richard Poirier (Oxford and New York: Oxford University Press, 1990), 104.

5. FINDING A CAREER, 1854–56

1. Larkin & Stackpole, Collection, BL-HBS; see also Frank H. Forbes, "The Old Boston Water Front," in *Days and Ways in Old Boston*, ed. Wm. S. Rossiter (Boston: R. H. Stearns, 1915), 45–59.

2. Records of the Harvard College Class of 1854, Class Book, HUA.

3. *HMB*, 1:301.

4. Emerson, *Life*, 13; *HMB*, 1:371; Records of the Harvard College Class of 1854, Class Book, HUA; Sanborn, "Col. Charles Lowell," 124. Sanborn insisted that Lowell's participation in the Civil War was not for the Union "as it was . . . but for an ideal form of freedom and the uplifting of the downtrodden." He also compared Lowell's business ambitions with what had been said of John Brown's sheep keeping: that "he kept sheep with a royal mind."

5. "Report of the Committee on the Machinery of the United States," in *The American System of Manufactures: The Report of the Committee on the Machinery of the United States, before 1855, and the Special Reports of George Wallis and Joseph Whitworth, 1854*, ed. Nathan Rosenberg (Edinburgh: University Press of Edinburgh, 1969). The use of gun-stocking machines (lathes capable of turning a block of wood into the irregular shape of a gunstock), and milling machines that fabricated crude versions of a gun barrel and its firing mechanism but required copious hand filing, was widely known and understood. Their advantage, however, was speed of production rather than uniformity. They had been designed and refined in a partnership between the Springfield Armory's chief engineer, Cyrus Buckland, and the Ames Company, one of many such connections the armory had with manufacturers in the Connecticut Valley. See also David A. Hounshell, *From the American System to Mass Production, 1800–1932: The Development of Manufacturing Technology in the United States* (Baltimore: Johns Hopkins University Press, 1984), 64; Charles Fitch, "The Rise of a Mechanical Ideal," *Magazine of American History* 11 (January–June 1884): 526–27; Eugene S. Ferguson, "The American-ness of American Technology," *Technology and Culture* 20, no. 1 (January 1979); Oliver Warner, *Statistical Information Relating to Certain Branches of Industry in Massachusetts for the Year Ending May 1, 1865: Prepared from Official Returns, by Francis De Witt, Secretary of the Commonwealth* (Boston: W. White, printer to the state, 1856).

6. CRL to ACJL, 6.24.55, in Emerson, *Life*, 88. The manager of the Novelty Iron Works was the elder brother of Elmwood lodger William James Stillman.

7. CRL to ACJL, 4.1.55, ibid., 78; ibid.; CRL to ACJL, 9.30.55, ibid., 95; CRL to William James Potter, 5.20.55, ibid., 83; CRL to ACJL, 9.30.55, ibid., 95.

8. CRL to William James Potter, 5.20.55, ibid., 15; also see Thomas Carlyle, *Past and Present* (Boston: Estes and Lauriat, n.d.), 155.

9. CRL to William James Potter, 5.20.55, in Emerson, *Life*, 84; Ralph Waldo Emerson,

"Representative Men," in ed. Poirer, *Emerson*, 291; Carlyle, *Heroes*, 165; CRL to ACJL, 4.1.55 in Emerson, *Life*, 78; CRL to Franklin B. Sanborn, 1.15.55, ibid., 80; CRL to William James Potter, 5.20.55, ibid., 85; CRL to Franklin B. Sanborn, 1.15.55, ibid., 80; ibid. See also CRL to William James Potter, 5.20.55, ibid., 81–82: "You [Potter] and Sanborn and I are by nature reformers, we have hands given us, the age and the country furnish stuff enough, the only thing is to improve the tool . . . three old toads perched on the corner of a doorstep [or] three good fellows who have hopped together *instinctively*, who can *enjoy* one another's company even in silence, . . . even here the highest height is not reached till one of the three goes to sleep, *then* we have two active poles and between them a centre of rest, and as Coleridge would say, *then* the club has *Life*."

10. Harriet Lowell to Lucy Ellery Russel, 6.3.[55], LPFP, 1:164, 163–64.

11. Harriet Lowell to CRL, 7.15.55, LPFP, 1:178.

12. CRL to ACJL, 6.24.55, in Emerson, *Life*, 86–87; Harriet Lowell to CRL, 7.15.55, LPFP, 1:177. Harriet told Charlie, "I am determined no longer to abuse Mother, that she was mistaken may be and is, but there is so much more to love and respect than to blame and the reason was so good that we ought not to say anything against her, and that is one reason why A[nna] won't talk with me because I defend her." Harriet Lowell to CRL, 7.7.56, LPFP, 1:188.

13. CRL to ACJL, 6.24.55 in Emerson, *Life*, 87; Carlyle, *Past*, 9. "Even the Gods worked," Carlyle explained, "battling the Sublime sadness and applying Godlike earnestness in Infinite Battle against Infinite Labour. The Modern Worker," in Carlyle, *Past*, 149. CRL to ACJL, 6.25.55, *Life*, 87.

14. CRL to ACJL, 6.24.55, in Emerson, *Life*, 87. "Chicopee, it is true, is not 'a distant Grecian sky,' — but sons of Agamemnon may be nursed here." *Matthew Arnold*, ed. Miriam Allott and Robert H. Super (Oxford and New York: Oxford University Press, 1986), 8.

15. CRL to ACJL, 9.30.55, in Emerson, *Life*, 94–95.

16. CRL to ACJL, Sunday, ibid., 99–100; *HMB*, 1:303.

17. For further information on tuberculosis see Frank Ryan, *The Greatest Story Never Told: The Human Story of the Search for the Cure for Tuberculosis and the New Global Threat* (Refuge Assurance House, Market Street, Bromsgrove, Worcestershire, England: Swift Publishers, 1992), and Sheila M. Rothman, *Living in the Shadow of Death: Tuberculosis and the Social Experience of Illness in American History* (New York: Basic Books, 1994).

18. JMF to George Ashburner, 1.12.64, *Letters and Recollections of John Murray Forbes*, ed. Sarah Forbes Hughes (Boston: Houghton Mifflin, 1899), 2:398–99.

19. *Reminiscences of John Murray Forbes*, ed. Sarah Forbes Hughes, 3 vols. (Boston: Houghton Mifflin, 1902), 1:145–47, in the Boston Athenaeum.

20. CRL to ACJL, 9.28.56, in Emerson, *Life*, 121; LPFP, 1:197.

21. JMF to Mary and Sarah Forbes, 3.4.56, in Forbes, *Reminiscences*, 2:15; William H. Hurlbert, *Pictures of Cuba* (London: Longman, Brown, Green, & Longmans, 1855), 7; Richard H. Dana, *To Cuba and Back: A Vacation Voyage* (London: Smith, Elder & Co., 1859), 55; Hurlbert, *Pictures*, 21; JMF to Mary and Sarah Forbes, 3.7.56, in Forbes, *Reminiscences*, 2:16.

22. James Hamilton Couper to JMF, 11.6.56, in Hughes, ed., *Letters of Forbes*, 1:149. Couper was an accomplished man. His plantations were considered models for the cultivation of rice and sugar. Forbes understood Couper's opinions as signs of "the very worst indication of the coming storm."

23. JMF to Sarah Forbes, 3.28.56 and 3.11.56, in Forbes, *Reminiscences*, 2:20, 17, 18.
24. CRL to ACJL, 4.6.56, in Emerson, *Life*, 101.

6. EUROPE, 1856–58

1. CRL to ACJL, 5.27.56, in Emerson, *Life*, 103; CRL to Anna Lowell, 5.28.56, ibid., 106.
2. CRL to ACJL, 6.16.56, ibid., 109, 111, 115, 107.
3. Allott and Super, eds., "The Scholar-Gipsy," in *Matthew Arnold*, 208–15.
4. Greenslett, *Lowells*, 216; Georgina Lowell Diary, 9.20.56 and 9.10.56, Francis Cabot Lowell Collection II, MHS.
5. Ernest Samuels, *The Young Henry Adams* (Cambridge, Mass.: Harvard University Press, 1948), 53; Horace H. Furness to JRL, 10.3.66, JRL Papers, MHS. Also see Helen Haseltine Plowden, *William Stanley Haseltine* (London: Frederick Muller, 1947).
6. *New York Evening Post*, 5.23.56, quoted in William E. Gienapp, "The Crime Against Sumner: The Caning of Charles Sumner and the Rise of the Republican Party," in *Civil War History* 25 (1979): 232.
7. Jeffrey Rossbach, *Ambivalent Conspirators: John Brown, the Secret Six and a Theory of Slave Violence* (Philadelphia: University of Pennsylvania Press, 1982), 52–53.
8. Ibid.; CRL to HLH, 9.10.56, in Emerson, *Life*, 118.
9. HLH to George Higginson, 1.27.57, in Perry, ed., *Higginson*, 96.
10. CRL to ACJL, 5.27.56, in Emerson, *Life*, 104–5. The Emerson quote is from Ralph Waldo Emerson, *Journals and Miscellaneous Notes*, 16 vols. (Cambridge, Mass.: Belknap Press of Harvard University Press, 1960–82), 5:445; Allott and Super, eds., "The Scholar-Gipsy," in *Matthew Arnold*, 208–15.
11. CRL to ACJL, 9.28.56, LPFP, 1:196–98.
12. *Letters of Charles Eliot Norton, with Biographical Comment*, eds. Sara Norton and M. A. DeWolfe Howe (Boston and New York: Houghton Mifflin, 1913), 2:155, 163–64. For more information on Americans in Europe see Theodore E. Stebbins, Jr., *The Lure of Italy: American Artists and the Italian Experience, 1760–1914* (New York: Harry N. Abrams, 1992).
13. CRL to ACJL, 1.15.57, in Emerson, *Life*, 128, 129; CRL to ACJL, 10.20.56, ibid., 125.
14. Ibid., 124.
15. CRL to John C. Bancroft, 5.7.57, ibid., 133.
16. Perry, ed., *Higginson*, 101.
17. CRL to ACJL, 6.25.57, in Emerson, *Life*, 137–38.
18. Ibid., 139; Perry, ed., *Higginson*, 103.
19. Ibid., 95.
20. CRL to ACJL, 9.3.57, in Emerson, *Life*, 144.
21. CRL to ACJL, 9.16.57, ibid.
22. CRL to ACJL, 4.2.57, ibid., 130.
23. CRL to ACJL, 11.24.57, ibid., 146, 148.
24. CRL to John C. Bancroft, 12.5.57, ibid, 149–50; CRL to HLH, 3.13.58, ibid., 155.
25. CRL to ACJL, 4.9.57, ibid., 157.
26. David Ekserdjian and the late Richard Godfrey were able to identify these paintings for me. See also Mrs. [Sophia] Hawthorne, *Notes on England and Italy* (New York: G. P. Putnam & Son; London: S. Low & Co., 1872), 369; *Passages from the French and*

Italian Note-books of Nathaniel Hawthorne, 2 vols. (Boston and New York: Houghton Mifflin, 1883), 2:60; CRL to ACJL, 1.27.58, in Emerson, *Life*, 128–29.

27. CRL to ACJL, 9.28.56 and, 4.2.57, ibid., 119–21 and 131; CRL to John C. Bancroft, 5.7.57, ibid., 132; CRL to ACJL, 6.25.57 and 5.27.58, ibid., 139 and 158–60.

28. CRL to Charles Russell Lowell, Sr., 5.6.57, ibid., 131; CRL to John C. Bancroft, 5.7.57, ibid., 132.

29. CRL to ACJL, 6.4.57, 7.8.57, ibid., 135, 141.

30. CRL to ACJL, 7.8.57, ibid., 141; CRL to ACJL, 6.4.57, ibid., 135; CRL to ACJL, 5.1.58, ibid., 158. Once again Lowell was thinking of going to Kansas. He put out feelers to Thomas Wentworth Higginson and Frank Sanborn inquiring what use he might be there, and once again he sounded out both Henry Higginson and Stephen Perkins on their plans. To Henry he wrote, "By the Spring we ought to know if it [Kansas] would be a free place for a 'free man' to settle." Increasingly Charlie was convinced that he would need to spend a year in the West taking up John Murray Forbes's offer of a job on a railroad, but he was reluctant to commit himself quickly. Partly he longed to stay in Boston.

31. CRL to HLH, 4.8.58, in Emerson, *Life*, 156–57.

32. CRL to HLH, 7.2.58, ibid., 162.

7. LIFE IN THE WEST, 1858–60

1. CRL to HLH, 8.23.58, in Emerson, *Life*, 165, 164.

2. CRL to John C. Bancroft, 8.15.63, ibid., 163.

3. Ralph Waldo Emerson quoted in Arthur Stanwood Pier, *William Hathaway Forbes: Telephone Pioneer* (New York: Dodd, Mead, 1953), 7.

4. For information on Naushon Island, I am indebted to the Forbes family.

5. CRL to HLH, 4.8.57 and 8.23.58, in Emerson, *Life*, 157, 164–65; for more information on John Murray Forbes's railroad business, see the various editions of Forbes's letters edited by Sarah Forbes Hughes and Henry Greenleaf Pearson, *An American Railroad Builder, John Murray Forbes* (Boston, New York: Houghton Mifflin, 1904).

6. CRL to ACJL, 9.13.58, in Emerson, *Life*, 169.

7. CRL to ACJL, 4.15.59, ibid., 175; Cyrenus Cole, *A History of the People of Iowa* (Cedar Rapids, Ia.: Torch Press, 1921), 267.

8. United States, Works Projects Administration, *A Guide to Burlington, Iowa, Compiled and Written by the Federal Writers' Project* (Burlington, Ia.: Acres-Blackmar, 1938), 8, 16.

9. Bernhardt Henn to J. G. Read, 9.6.58, in Richard Cleghorn Overton, *Burlington West: A Colonization History of the Burlington Railroad* (New York: Russell & Russell, 1967), 104. See also Richard Cleghorn Overton, *Burlington Route: A History of the Burlington Lines* (New York: Alfred A. Knopf, 1965).

10. CRL to ACJL, 11.22.58, in Emerson, *Life*, 172.

11. CRL to HLH, 10.11.59, ibid., 179.

12. These pictures mentioned in CRL to HLH, 10.11.59, ibid., 180, remain unidentified.

13. CRL to Anna Lowell, 10.29.59, ibid., 183; CRL to ACJL, 4.15.59, ibid., 174.

14. CRL to HLH, 10.11.59, ibid., 180–82.

15. Ibid., 181.

16. CRL to Hans Thielsen, 10.6.59, in Overton, *Burlington West*, 143, 142.

17. CRL to Hans Thielsen, 12.8.59, ibid., 146.

18. Ibid., 150.

19. CRL to Hans Thielsen, 10.21.59, ibid., 143.

20. CRL to Charles Mason, 10.20.59, ibid., 159.

21. McPherson, *Battle Cry*, 209, and Belle Becker Sideman and Lillian Friedman, eds., *Europe Looks at the Civil War: An Anthology* (New York: Orion Press, 1960), 9; for more information on John Brown, the raid on Harpers Ferry, the involvement of the Secret Six, and the New England Emigrant Aid Society, see Otto J. Scott, *The Secret Six: John Brown and the Abolitionist Movement* (New York: Times Books, 1979); Jeffrey Rossbach, *Ambivalent Conspirators: John Brown, the Secret Six and a Theory of Slave Violence* (Philadelphia: University of Pennsylvania Press, 1982); E. J. Renehan, Jr., *The Secret Six: The True Tale of the Men Who Conspired with John Brown* (New York: Crown Publishers, 1995); Tilden Edelstein, *Strange Enthusiasm: A Life of Thomas Wentworth Higginson* (New Haven: Yale University Press, 1968).

22. CRL to ACJL, 1.31.60, Letters of Charles Russell Lowell, vol. 2, LFP; ibid., 4.29.60.

23. CRL to ACJL, 12.25.59, Letters of Charles Russell Lowell, vol. 2, LFP.

24. CRL to to George Ashburner, 12.23.59, in Emerson, *Life*, 184–85; CRL to JMF, 12.23.59, and CRL to ACJL, 12.25.59, ibid., 185–86.

25. CRL to George Ashburner, 12.23.59, ibid., 185; CRL to ACJL, 11.22.58, ibid., 172; CRL to ACJL, 11.12.58, ibid., 170.

26. Ibid., 170–71.

27. CRL to ACJL, 12.25.59, ibid., 187; CRL to HLH, 10.11.59, ibid., 182; CRL to ACJL, 4.29.60, Letters of Charles Russell Lowell, vol. 2, LFP; CRL to HLH, 6.13.60, in Emerson, *Life*, 188.

28. Ibid., 189; CRL to HLH, 8.23.58, 6.13.60, 10.11.59, ibid., 163–64, 188, 182; CRL to ACJL, 9.28.56, ibid., 120; CRL to George Ashburner, 12.23.59, ibid., 184.

29. CRL to ACJL, 3.27.59, ibid., 174; CRL to George Ashburner, EWE Papers.

30. CRL to J. N. Denison, 10.25.60, quoted in Overton, *Burlington West*, 163.

31. Ibid. Charles Eliot Perkins rose through the administration of the railroad to become the president of the Chicago, Burlington & Quincy Railroad, and it was under his leadership that that railroad was formed.

8. THE BORDER STATE OF MARYLAND, 1860–61

1. James M. Swank, *History of the Manufacture of Iron in All Ages, and Particularly in the United States for Three Hundred Years, from 1585 to 1885* (Philadelphia: James M. Swank, 1884), 256.

2. CRL to George Putnam, 5.24.60, in Emerson, *Life*, 188; Forbes, *Reminiscences*, 1:183–84.

3. CRL to ACJL, 1.27.61, in Emerson, *Life*, 192.

4. Mayer in McPherson, *Battle Cry*, 245.

5. CRL to ACJL, 12.28.60, in Emerson, *Life*, 400.

6. CRL, 12.28.60, in *HMB*, 1:306.

7. Quoted in McPherson, *Battle Cry*, 100.

8. Quoted in "Henry Varnum Poor: Business Analyst," in McCraw, *Chandler*, 41.

9. CRL to HLH, 12.28.60, in Emerson, *Life*, 191–92.

10. CRL to ACJL, 1.27.61, ibid, 193.

11. CRL to JMF, 2.11.61, ibid., 194–95.
12. CRL to ACJL, 3.28.61, in Emerson, *Life*, 196–97; JRL, "E Pluribus Unum," quoted in Edith Ellen Ware, *Political Opinion in Massachusetts during the Civil War* (New York, 1916), 43; CRL to ACJL, 4.15.61, in Emerson, *Life*, 197.
13. CRL to JMF, 2.11.61, ibid., 195; CRL to ACJL, 4.15.61, ibid., 197.
14. Ralph Waldo Emerson, unpublished lecture in James E. Cabot, *A Memoir of Ralph Waldo Emerson* (Boston, New York, 1887), 2:600, quoted in George M. Fredrickson, *The Inner Civil War: Northern Intellectuals and the Crisis of the Union* (New York: Harper & Row, 1965), 66, 69; Charles Eliot Norton in the "Christian Inquirer," 8.10.61, Charles Eliot Norton papers, HUA, quoted ibid., 69; Baron de Streckl to Prince Gortchakov, quoted in Albert Woldman, *Lincoln and the Russians* (Cleveland: World Publishing Co., 1952); quoted in Sideman and Friedman, eds., *Europe Looks*, 42.
15. William J. Evitts, *A Matter of Allegiances: Maryland from 1850 to 1861* (Baltimore: Johns Hopkins University Press, 1974), 180–82.
16. Franklin B. Sanborn to Benjamin Lyman, 9.16.60 and 9.18.60, in *Correspondence of Franklin Benjamin Sanborn, the Transcendentalist: A Checklist of Twenty-three Hundred Letters Supplementing Those in Clarkson's Inventory of 1971*, ed. Kenneth Walker Cameron (Hartford, Conn.: Transcendental Books, 1978), 27.
17. CRL to ACJL, 5.13.61, in Emerson, *Life*, 207–8.

9. A REGULAR COMMISSION, 1861–62

1. CRL to ACJL, 5.13.61, in Emerson, *Life*, 206–7.
2. CRL to Charles Sumner, 4.23.61, ibid., 201–2.
3. CRL to Edward Jackson, 4.24.61, and CRL to ACJL, 4.24.61, ibid., 203; Oliver Wendell Holmes, "Bread and Newspapers," in *Soundings from "The Atlantic"* (Boston: Ticknor & Fields, 1866), 4; CRL to Charles Sumner, 4.23.61 in Emerson, *Life*, 203.
4. LPFP, 2:50.
5. William Howard Russell, *My Diary, North and South* (New York: Harper, 1863), 46.
6. Robert Gould Shaw to Sarah Blake Sturgis Shaw, 6.9.61, Russell Duncan, ed., *Blue-Eyed Child of Fortune: The Civil War Letters of Robert Gould Shaw* (Athens, London: University of Georgia Press, 1992), 107. Sarah Blake Sturgis Shaw to JRL, 6.5.61, James Russell Lowell Papers, MHS.
7. CRL to ACJL, 4.15.61, in Emerson, *Life*, 197; Count Adam G. de Gurowski, *Diary* (Boston: Lee & Shepard, 1862–66), 40–41.
8. Eliza Amelia White Dwight, *Life and Letters of Wilder Dwight, Lieut.-Col. Second Mass. Inf. Vols.* (Boston: Ticknor & Fields, 1868), 39.
9. Ebenezer Rockwood Hoar to JMF, 5.7.61, in Forbes, *Reminiscences*, 2:132; CRL to JMF, 5.10.61, in Emerson, *Life*, 205.
10. Henry Greenleaf Pearson, *The Life of John A. Andrew, Governor of Massachusetts, 1861–1865* (Boston and New York: Houghton Mifflin, 1904), 1:221; also John A. Andrew, 5.11.61–5.17.61, Executive Department, Commonwealth of Massachusetts, Military Archives, Worcester, Mass.
11. CRL to JMF, 5.10.61, in Emerson, *Life*, 206; Charles Russell Lowell, Sr. to CRL, 5.17.61, LPFP, 64. (The Union Hall Association bore a remarkable resemblance to the sorts of associations formed for the wives of seamen and sailors that their grandparents supported fifty years before.)

12. CRL to JMF, 5.10.61, in Emerson, *Life*, 206; CRL to ACJL, 5.13.61, ibid., 207; Charles Russell Lowell, Sr. to CRL, 5.17.63, LPFP, 63; CRL to JMF, 5.21.61, in Emerson, *Life*, 209; ibid; LPFP, 2:50–51.

13. *OR*, ser. 3, 1:77, quoted in Stephen Z. Starr, *The Union Cavalry in the Civil War*, 3 vols. (Baton Rouge: Louisiana State University Press, 1979–85), 1:65; CRL to ACJL, 6.9.61, in Emerson, *Life*, 211.

14. Richard Taylor quoted in Starr, *Union Cavalry*, 1:54.

15. *HMB*, 1:354.

16. Emerson quoted in Fredrickson, *Inner Civil War*, 66; Perry, ed., *Higginson*, 146.

17. Perry, ed., *Higginson*, 150.

18. CRL to James Jackson Lowell, 4.29.61, in Emerson, *Life*, 204; CRL to ACJL, 5.13.61, ibid., 207; CRL to ACJL, 7.1.61, ibid., 213.

19. Kirkland, *Charles Francis Adams, Jr.*, 124.

20. CRL to Charles Eliot Perkins, 6.7.61, in *HMB*, 1:308–9; CRL to ACJL, 5.13.61, in Emerson, *Life*, 207.

21. CRL to ACJL, 7.1.61, ibid., 213; CRL to Charles Eliot Perkins, 7.21.61, ibid., 215; CRL to ACJL, 7.22.61, ibid., 216.

22. Adna R. Chaffee to EWE, 8.26.06, quoted ibid., 405; CRL to ACJL, 7.22.61, ibid., 216.

23. CRL to ACJL, 8.5.61, ibid., 217; CRL to Charles Sumner, 4.23.61, ibid., 201; CRL to James Jackson Lowell, 4.29.61, ibid., 204; CRL to ACJL, 8.5.61, ibid., 217.

24. For more information on General McClellan, see Stephen W. Sears, *The Civil War Papers of General George B. McClellan: Selected Correspondence, 1860–1865* (New York: Ticknor & Fields, 1989), and Stephen W. Sears, *George B. McClellan: The Young Napoleon* (New York: Ticknor & Fields, 1988).

25. Edward P. Tobie, quoted in Starr, *Union Cavalry*, 1:138.

26. CRL to Charles Russell Lowell, Sr., 1.23.61, in Emerson, *Life*, 220.

27. Henry L. Abbott to father, 10.22.64, in *Fallen Leaves: The Civil War Letters of Major Henry Livermore Abbott*, ed. Robert Garth Scott (Kent, Oh.: Kent State University Press, 1991), 60; Captain William F. Bartlett, quoted in Sheldon M. Novick, *Honorable Justice: The Life of Oliver Wendell Holmes* (Boston: Little, Brown, 1989), 45; *Touched with Fire, Civil War Letters and Diary of Oliver Wendell Holmes, Jr., 1861–1864*, ed. Mark De Wolfe Howe (Cambridge, Mass.: Harvard University Press, 1946), 13.

28. Captain William F. Bartlett, quoted in Novick, *Honorable Justice*, 46, 47.

29. Howe, ed., *Touched with Fire*, 26.

30. Dwight, ed., *Letters of Dwight*, 126.

31. Robert Gould Shaw to Sarah Blake Sturgis Shaw, 10.22.61, in Duncan, ed., *Child of Fortune*, 155; Perry, ed., *Higginson*, 154; Dwight, ed., *Letters of Dwight*, 121; Howe, ed., *Touched with Fire*, 31.

32. CRL to ACJL, 12.25.61, LPFP, 2:93.

33. Ibid., 2:34. CRL to Charles Eliot Perkins, 12.7.61, in Emerson, *Life*, 219.

34. Scudder, *James Russell Lowell*, 2:30; ACJL to Elizabeth Cabot Putnam, 12.11.61, PJLFP.

35. Pearson, *Life of Andrew*, 278; Sarah H. Southwick, *Reminiscences of Early Anti-slavery Days* (Cambridge, Mass.: Riverside Press, 1893), 208; ACJL to Elizabeth Cabot Putnam, 12.11.61, PJLFP.

36. WLP, n.d., Putnam cigar box, LFP; McPherson, *Battle Cry*, 357.

37. WLP, n.d., Putnam cigar box, LFP.

38. G. Anson Bruce, *The Twentieth Regiment of Massachusetts Volunteer Infantry*,

1861–1865 (Boston, New York: Houghton, Mifflin, 1906), 74–75; Gerald F. Linderman, *Embattled Courage: The Experience of Combat in the American Civil War* (New York: Free Press, 1987), 63.

39. Lucy Ellery Russel to Harriet Lowell, 11.24.61, LPFP, 2:92; Cabot Jackson Russel to William Channing Russel, 11.24.61, Cabot Jackson Russel Papers, NYPL; Ellen Tucker Emerson to William Emerson, 10.28.61, in *The Letters of Ellen Tucker Emerson*, ed. Edith E. W. Gregg (Kent, Oh.: Kent State University, 1982), 1:262.

40. CRL to ACJL, 5.13.61, in Emerson, *Life*, 206–7; CRL to Charles Eliot Perkins, 6.7.61, ibid., 211.

10. THE PENINSULA CAMPAIGN, 1862

1. Charles Russell Lowell, Sr., to James Jackson Lowell, 2.62, LPFP, 2:98.
2. Sears, *McClellan Papers*, 74–75, quoted in Mark Grimsley, *The Hard Hand of War: Union Military Policy toward Southern Civilians, 1861–1865* (New York and Cambridge: Cambridge University Press, 1995), 33.
3. James Jackson Lowell to Anna Lowell, 4.3.62, LPFP, 2:109.
4. Frank Robbins, Memoir, n.d., 3, JRL Papers, MHS.
5. Ibid.
6. *HMB*, 1:301; Emerson, *Life*, 373.
7. Starr, *Union Cavalry*, 1:274; attributed to Hooker and quoted ibid., 1:260. For an account of the Sixth U.S. Cavalry during the Peninsula campaign see William Giles Harding Carter, *From Yorktown to Santiago with the Sixth United States Cavalry* (Austin: State House Press, 1989), 23–50.
8. Charles Russell Lowell, Sr. to James Jackson Lowell, 2.62, LPFP, 2:98.
9. Henry Patten to Alfred S. Hartwell, 7.5.62; James Jackson Lowell to Charles Allen, 3.2.62; James Jackson Lowell to ACJL, 3.2.62; and James Jackson Lowell to Alfred S. Hartwell, 6.25.62, LPFP, 2:128, 104, 106, 123.
10. Oliver Wendell Holmes, Jr., Memorial Day Speech, in *Mind and Faith of Justice Holmes: His Speeches, Essays, Letters, and Judicial Opinions*, ed. Max Lerner (Boston: Little, Brown, 1943), 12.
11. LPFP, 2:132.
12. Henry Patten to Alfred S. Hartwell, 7.5.62, LPFP, 2:128.
13. James Jackson Lowell to ACJL, 6.14.62, and ACJL to Anna Lowell, 6.22.62, LPFP, 2:112, 120.
14. George Putnam to Harriet Lowell Putnam, 7.9.62, LPFP, 2:131; Oliver Wendell Holmes, Jr., to Amelia Jackson Holmes, 7.4.62, in Howe, ed., *Touched with Fire*, 56; Oliver Wendell Holmes, Jr., to his parents, 7.5.62; Howe, ed., *Touched with Fire*, 10. A curious incident, revealed only long after the war, occurred as Jim Lowell and the other wounded soldiers waited to fall into rebel hands. He apparently passed out. Major Christie, a rebel officer on the staff of General Jubal Early who had studied at Harvard, came upon the field hospital and inquired who the unconscious wounded officer was. Lowell, he was told. Christie recognized the name. He had been one of the many New Orleans boys whom Sally Lowell had befriended, offering them the comforts of a home away from home. As Major Christie remembered his college days and the pert little lady who had been so kind to him, he described himself as "completely overcome . . . for the first time since entering the service I bitterly regretted my position." Christie en-

sured that Jim was treated well and buried properly. From Vincent Bowditch, *Life and Correspondence of Henry Ingersoll Bowditch*, 2 vols. (Boston: Houghton Mifflin, 1902), 2:308–10.

15. Sears, *McClellan*, 237.

16. CRL to ACJL, 7.27.63, in Emerson, *Life*, 223.

17. ACJL to Anna Lowell, LPFP 2:138.

18. Richard Elliott Winslow, *General John Sedgwick: The Story of a Union Corps Commander* (Novato, Calif.: Presidio Press, 1982), 28; Francis Channing Barlow to Edward Barlow, 7.8.62, Francis Channing Barlow letters, 1861–65, MHS. See also Francis Channing Barlow to Edward Barlow, 7.12.62, Francis Channing Barlow letters, 1861–65, MHS: "We are surprised to learn from the New York papers that we gained a great victory. We thought here that he had made a disastrous retreat leaving all our dead and wounded and many prisoners and material and munitions of war in the hands of the enemy."

19. Hannah Lowell Jackson Cabot to Mary A. Bigelow, 7.9.62, Almy Family Papers, SL; CRL to ACJL, 7.18.62, in Emerson, *Life*, 221.

20. Ella Lowell Lyman to Frances A. Eliot, 8.10.62, in Ella Lyman Cabot, ed., *Arthur Theodore Lyman and Ella Lyman*, 3 vols. (Boston: privately printed, 1932), 2:118.

21. John Lothrop Motley to Oliver Wendell Holmes, 8.31.62, in *The Correspondence of John Lothrop Motley*, ed. George William Curtis, 2 vols. (New York: Harper & Bros., 1889), 2:89.

22. Perry, ed., *Higginson*, 164; Cabot Jackson Russel to William Channing Russel, 6.17.63, Cabot Jackson Russel Papers, NYPL; *HMB*, 2:483.

23. CRL to Henry Lee, 7.23.62, in Emerson, *Life*, 222–23.

24. Sears, *McClellan*, 233, 243, 235.

25. *HMB*, 2:171.

26. Richard Cary to Helen Cary, 1.16.62, quoted in Duncan, ed., *Child of Fortune*, 24.

27. *HMB*, 1:354; Kirkland, *Charles Francis Adams, Jr.*, 21.

28. Perry, ed., *Higginson*, 82, 95, 165.

29. Robert Gould Shaw to Annie Russell Agassiz, 8.13.62, in Duncan, ed., *Child of Fortune*, 234–35.

30. Worthington Chauncey Ford, ed., *A Cycle of Adams Letters, 1861–1865*, 2 vols. (Boston, New York: Houghton Mifflin, 1920), 1:177–78.

31. Stephen W. Sears, *Landscape Turned Red: The Battle of Antietam* (New Haven, Conn.: Ticknor & Fields, 1983), 17; HLH quoted in Emerson, *Life*, 421.

11. ANTIETAM, SEPTEMBER 17, 1862

1. Sears, *Landscape*, xi.

2. See Robert Gould Shaw to Charles F. Morse, 2.24.63, in Duncan, ed., *Child of Fortune*, 297, and Cabot, ed., *Arthur Lyman*, 2:157.

3. Winslow, *John Sedgwick*, 46. The following account of the battle of Antietam is drawn principally from Winslow, *John Sedgwick*; Sears, *Landscape*; and James A. Rawley, *Turning Points of the Civil War* (Lincoln, London: University of Nebraska Press, 1966).

4. General William Dwight, quoted in *HMB*, 1:311; William S. Abert to George Putnam, 11.15.64, LPFP.

5. Frank Robbins, Memoir, n.d., 6, JRL Papers, MHS.

6. HLH quoted in Emerson, *Life*, 422. See also Robert Gould Shaw to Charles F. Morse, 2.24.63, in Duncan, ed., *Child of Fortune*, 297 and Cabot, ed., *Arthur Lyman*, 2:157, and Henry Ropes, quoted in James H. Wilson, "The Cavalry of the Army of the Potomac," in *Papers of the Military Historical Society of Massachusetts* (Boston: Military Historical Society of Massachusetts, 1907), 6:43; CRL to JSL, 9.14.64, Letters to Josephine Shaw Lowell, LFP.
7. Sears, *Landscape*, 296.
8. Dwight, ed., *Letters of Dwight*, 292–99; HMB, 1:176.
9. CRL to ACJL, 9.19.62, in Emerson, *Life*, 225; CRL to JMF, 1.19.62, ibid., 225–26.
10. George McClellan to Henry Halleck, 9.19.62, in Sears, *Landscape*, 308; Sears, *McClellan*, 319; Sears, *Landscape*, 308; Sears, *McClellan Papers*, 379.
11. CRL to JMF, 1.19.62, in Emerson, *Life*, 226; CRL to ACJL, 9.19.62, ibid., 225; Sears, *Landscape*, 310, 298.
12. Sears, *McClellan*, 322, 233.
13. Sears, *Landscape*, 319; McPherson, *Battle Cry*, 559.
14. Sears, *Landscape*, 320.
15. Letter of James E. Howell, n.d., EWE Papers, MHS.
16. Sears, *Landscape*, 336.
17. Amos Adams Lawrence Papers, Letterpress Books, 1857–65, MHS.
18. Emerson, *Life*, 30.
19. CRL to JMF, 10.30.62, ibid., 229–31.
20. William Hathaway Forbes to Alice Forbes, 11.03.62, REFC; Caspar Crowninshield Diary, Crowninshield-Magnus Papers, MHS.
21. William Hathaway Forbes to Sarah Swain Hathaway Forbes, 11.04.62, REFC.
22. Robert Gould Shaw to Sarah Blake Sturgis Shaw, 11.17.62 and Robert Gould Shaw to JSL, 12.23.62, in Duncan, ed., *Child of Fortune*, 257, 271.

12. RAISING A REGIMENT, 1862–63

1. ACJL to Anna Lowell, 1.25.63, LPFP, 2:151.
2. Ralph Waldo Emerson to Rodman Family, 6.17.63, in *The Letters of Ralph Waldo Emerson*, ed. Ralph L. Rusk, 6 vols. (New York, London: Columbia University Press, 1966), 4:332.
3. ACJL to Anna Lowell, 1.25.63, and Anna Lowell to ACJL, 8.15.62, LPFP, 2:151, 144. In January 1863, when Anna caught a mild version of typhoid, her mother went to Washington, nursed her there for several weeks, and also did her job. She relished the work and the feeling of involvement and came home to Cambridge almost reluctantly.
4. CRL to HLH, 8.28.58, in Emerson, *Life*, 165; George S. Hillard quoted in *The Letters of Henry Adams, 1858–1891*, ed. Worthington Chauncey Ford (Boston, New York: Houghton Mifflin, 1930), 52; John Carver Palfrey quoted in Edward Chase Kirkland, "Boston during the Civil War," in *Proceedings of the Massachusetts Historical Society* (1953), 71:194–203.
5. Frank Otto Gatell, *John Gorham Palfrey and the New England Conscience* (Cambridge, Mass.: Harvard University Press, 1963), 252.
6. Oliver Wendell Holmes to Amelia Jackson Holmes, 11.16.62; Oliver Wendell Holmes, Jr., to "My dear Governor," 12.20.62, in Howe, ed., *Touched with Fire*, 73, 80, 79; Gatell, *John Gorham Palfrey*, 73.

7. Ibid., 78.

8. Perry, ed., *Higginson*, 179.

9. Lerner, ed., *Mind and Faith*, 10, 20.

10. ACJL to Anna Lowell, 12.10.62, LPFP, 2:148.

11. Thomas H. O'Connor, *Civil War Boston: Home Front and Battlefield* (Boston: Northeastern University Press, 1997), 115.

12. George B. Forgie, *Patricide in the House Divided: A Psychological Interpretation of Lincoln and His Age* (New York: Norton, 1979), 64.

13. Robert Gould Shaw to Sarah Blake Sturgis Shaw, 9.25.62, in Duncan, ed., *Child of Fortune*, 245; Francis Channing Barlow to Edward Barlow, 7.12.62, Francis Channing Barlow letters, 1861–65, MHS.

14. CRL to HLH, 1.21.63, in Emerson, *Life*, 232–33.

15. Ibid., CRL quoted in Robert Gould Shaw to Annie Kneeland Haggerty, 2.23.63, in Duncan, ed., *Child of Fortune*, 296; John A. Andrew to CRL, 3.14.63, Executive Department, Commonwealth of Massachusetts, Military Archives, Worcester, Mass.; CRL to HLH, 1.21.63, in Emerson, *Life*, 233.

16. John T. Morse, Jr., ed., *Memoir of Henry Lee with Selections from His Writings and Speeches* (Boston: Little, Brown, 1905), 63; O'Connor, *Civil War Boston*, 117; Ware, *Political Opinion*, 102.

17. The project had the support and patronage of Treasury Secretary Salmon Chase. For further information, see Grimsley, *Hard Hand of War*, 56, 127; McPherson, *Battle Cry*, 499.

18. The letter was from Ira P. Rankin, collector for the port of San Francisco as well as proprietor of the Pacific Iron Foundry.

19. Second Massachusetts Cavalry recruiting poster, Forbes family.

20. Samuel Corbett Diary, BL. Newspaper clipping tipped into inside front cover, no name, dated 1.16.63.

21. Amos Adams Lawrence to JMF, 12.1.63, in Ware, *Political Opinion*, 127.

22. Joseph T. Glatthaar, *Forged in Battle: The Civil War Alliance of Black Soldiers and White Officers* (New York: Free Press, 1990), 37.

23. CRL to ACJL, 2.9.63, in Emerson, *Life*, 234; CRL to HLH, 2.15.63, ibid., 235.

24. *Springfield Republican*, 2.9.63, quoted in Ware, *Political Opinion*, 121.

25. Charles Eliot Norton to George William Curtis, 1.30.63, in Norton and DeWolfe, *Letters of Charles Eliot Norton*, 1:259.

26. CRL to HLH, 2.15.63, in Emerson, *Life*, 234; Emerson, *Saturday Club*, 311; Sarah Forbes Hughes, ed., *Letters (Supplementary): John Murray Forbes*, 3 vols. (Boston: G. H. Ellis, 1905), 2:80.

13. ROMANCE AND MUTINY, SPRING 1863

1. ACJL to Anna Lowell, 1.18.63, LPFP, 2:150.

2. William James to HLH, quoted in Perry, ed., *Higginson*, 374; Elizabeth Cabot Putnam, "Brigadier-General Charles Russell Lowell and Josephine Shaw Lowell," 3, PJLFP.

3. JSL Diary, 7.23.61 and 7.4.62, quoted in William Rhinelander Stewart, *The Philanthropic Work of Josephine Shaw Lowell, Containing a Biographical Sketch of Her Life, Together with a Selection of Her Public Papers and Private Letters* (New York: Macmillan, 1911), 13, 30.

4. CRL to ACJL, 4.15.59 in Emerson, *Life*, 174; CRL to HLH, 10.11.59, ibid., 182; CRL to HLH, 6.13.60, ibid., 188.

5. CRL to ACJL, 2.22.63, LPFP.
6. CRL to Ellen Jackson, 3.7.63, LPFP, 2:160.
7. Robert Gould Shaw to JSL, 2.9.62, in Duncan, ed., *Child of Fortune*, 172; John C. Palfrey to Frank Palfrey, 4.28.63 (199) Palfrey Family Papers (bMS Am 1704.2), HL.
8. JRL to Sarah Blake Sturgis Shaw, 4.6.63, JRL Papers, MHS.
9. Robert Gould Shaw to Charles F. Morse, 3.12.63, in Duncan, ed., *Child of Fortune*, 306; CRL to ACJL, 3.10.63, LPFP, 2:161.
10. Sarah Blake Sturgis Shaw to JRL, 3.19.63, and JRL to CRL, 3.12.63, JRL Papers, MHS; ACJL to Anna Lowell, 3.29.63, LPFP, 2:164; Harriet Lowell Putnam to Anna Lowell, 3.15.63, LPFP.
11. HLH to JSL, 3.15.63, JRL Papers, MHS.
12. Sergeant Porter quoted in "Notes for book on Charles Russell Lowell," EWE Papers, MHS.
13. Arthur Stanwood Pier, "Major William Hathaway Forbes and Colonel John Singleton Mosby," in *Proceedings of the Massachusetts Historical Society* (Boston: The Society, 1957), 70:66.
14, CRL Report, Executive Correspondence, Military Archives, Worcester, Mass.
15. My account of the shooting is taken from two sources: "Report of the Inquest on the Body of William Pendergast," *Boston Journal*, 4.12.63, in Harriet Lowell Jackson Cabot to Dr. Samuel Cabot, Almy Family Papers, SL; and from newspaper cuttings in the JRL Papers, MHS.
16. John A. Andrew to ACJL, 2.13.66, John A. Andrew Papers, MHS.
17. Adams Hill quoted in ACJL to Anna Lowell, 1863, LPFP, 2:163; Emerson, *Life*, 31; Bowditch, "Brief Memoranda of Our Martyr Soldiers."
18. CRL to JSL, 6.18.63, Letters to Josephine Shaw Lowell, LFP.
19. Fredrickson, *Inner Civil War*, 115.
20. O'Connor, *Civil War Boston*, 24.
21. ACJL to Anna Lowell, 12.10.62, LPFP, 2:148–49; Fredrickson, *Inner Civil War*, 80, 75.
22. ACJL to Anna Lowell, 1863, LPFP, 2:163.
23. Thomas H. Merry, 5.4.63, in *Daily Alta California*, 5.30.63, in THCT, 133–34.
24. Joseph H. Choate quoted in Stewart, *Philanthropic Work*, 3.
25. JSL Diary, 10.25.62, 6.6.62, and 10.29.62, ibid., 36, 28.
26. JSL Diary, 6.6.62, ibid., 28–29.
27. JSL Diary, 10.29.62, ibid., 37.
28. Elizabeth Cabot Putnam, "Brigadier-General Charles Russell Lowell and Josephine Shaw Lowell," in PJLFP; ACJL to Anna Lowell, 5.1.63, LPFP.
29. Ellen Tucker Emerson to Haven, 5.5.63, in Gregg, ed., *Letters of Ellen Tucker Emerson*, 309; Edith Emerson to EWE, 9.13.63, F/EFL.
30. William James to Carlotta Lowell, n.d., JRL Papers, MHS.
31. ACJL to Anna Lowell, 1863, LPFP, 2:163.

14. DEFENDING THE CAPITAL, SUMMER 1863

1. CRL to JSL, 5.15.63, in Emerson, *Life*, 237–38; CRL to Henry Sturgis Russell, 5.16.63, ibid., 240.
2. CRL to JSL, 5.15.63, ibid., 238.
3. CRL to JSL, 5.20.63, ibid., 241.
4. CRL to Henry Sturgis Russell, 5.23.63, ibid., 244. Lowell's friend Charles Adams com-

plained that Hooker's headquarters were a "combination of barroom and brothel." Adams, *Autobiography*, 161.

5. CRL to JSL, 6.1.63, in Emerson, *Life*, 251; William Hathaway Forbes to Alice Forbes, 6.2.63, REFC.

6. CRL to JSL, 6.3.63, in Emerson, *Life*, 252.

7. CRL to JSL, 5.28.63, ibid., 249.

8. CRL to JSL, 5.24.63, ibid., 245–46.

9. CRL to JSL, 5.29.63, 5.21.63, 5.29.63, ibid., 250, 241–42, 250.

10. CRL to JSL, 5.24.63, ibid., 244.

11. CRL to JSL, 8.13.63, ibid., 296.

12. CRL to JSL, 6.23.63, ibid., 263.

13. Ibid., 264.

14. CRL to ACJL, 6.24.55, ibid., 86.

15. CRL to John C. Bancroft, 5.24.63, ibid., 247.

16. CRL to JSL, 6.10.63, ibid., 255–56.

17. Ibid., 256.

18. CRL to Robert Gould Shaw, 5.23.63, ibid., 242; Robert Gould Shaw to Annie Kneeland Haggerty, 6.1.63, in Duncan, ed., *Child of Fortune*, 335; CRL to JSL, 5.27.63, in Emerson, *Life*, 248.

19. CRL to JSL, 6.18.63, ibid., 261.

20. John A. Andrew to Edwin M. Stanton, 4.1.63, in Duncan, ed., *Child of Fortune*, 41.

21. Robert Gould Shaw to CRL, 6.20.63, ibid., 355.

22. Ibid.; Robert Gould Shaw to Annie Kneeland Haggerty, 6.9.63, ibid., 343.

23. Thomas H. Merry, 6.22.63, in *Daily Alta California*, 7.17.63, in *THCT*, 151.

24. CRL to ACJL, 2.9.63, in Emerson, *Life*, 234.

25. CRL to William Whiting, 6.26.63, ibid., 265.

26. CRL to JSL, 6.18.63, ibid., 260.

27. Ibid., 259, 261.

28. CRL to JSL, 6.17.63 and 6.21.63, ibid., 259.

29. CRL to Caspar Crowninshield, 6.20.63, in Emerson, *Life*, 262.

30. Perry, ed., *Higginson*, 207.

31. CRL to JSL, 7.1.63, in Emerson, *Life*, 268–70.

32. William Hathaway Forbes to Alice Forbes, 7.6.63, REFC; CRL to JSL, 7.7.63 and 7.5.63, in Emerson, *Life*, 273.

33. CRL to JSL, 7.7.63, ibid., 274.

34. *HMB*, 2:325.

35. CRL to ACJL, 6.5.63, in Emerson, *Life*, 254–55.

36. CRL to JSL, 7.24.63 and 7.7.63, ibid., 280, 274.

37. CRL to JSL, 7.24.63, in Emerson, *Life*, 280–81.

38. CRL to JSL, 7.1.63, ibid., 270.

39. J. H. Taylor to CRL, 7.15.63, Military Service Record for Charles Russell Lowell, RG94, NA.

40. CRL to JSL, 7.19.63, in Emerson, *Life*, 276; Thomas H. Merry, 9.6.63, in *Daily Alta California*, 10.4.63, in *THCT*, 186.

41. William Hathaway Forbes to Alice Forbes, 7.20.63, REFC; CRL to JSL, 7.9.63, in Emerson, *Life*, 275.

42. CRL to JSL, 7.23.63 and 7.24.63, ibid., 278, 282.

43. Grimsley, *Hard Hand of War*, 17.

44. Ibid., 17, 150.

45. William Hathaway Forbes to JMF, 8.14.63, REFC; CRL to JSL, 7.25.63, in Emerson, *Life*, 283.

46. Thomas H. Merry, 9.6.63, in *Daily Alta California*, 10.4.63, in THCT, 186, 187.

47. Henry E. Alvord, "A New England Boy in the Civil War," 1.24.64, ed. Caroline B. Sherman, *New England Quarterly* 5 (1932), 324–25.

48. CRL to JSL, 7.25.63, in Emerson, *Life*, 283.

49. Alvord, "New England Boy," 325; Grimsley, *Hard Hand of War*, 145; Thomas H. Merry, 9.6.63, in *Daily Alta California*, 10.4.63, in THCT, 188.

50. CRL to JSL, 10.9.63, in Emerson, *Life*, 312; Hughes, ed., *Letters of Forbes*, 2:285.

51. CRL to JSL, 7.25.63, 6.22.63, in Emerson, *Life*, 284, 263.

52. CRL to Henry Sturgis Russell, 7.26.63, ibid., 285.

53. Duncan, ed., *Child of Fortune*, 50–51.

54. CRL to JSL, 8.2.63, in Emerson, *Life*, 289; Francis G. Shaw quoted in Duncan, ed., *Child of Fortune*, 54.

55. Leon Edel, *Henry James: The Untried Years, 1843–1870* (London: Rupert Hart-Davis, 1953), 186.

56. Luis F. Emilio, *A Brave Black Regiment: History of the Fifty-fourth Regiment of Massachusetts Volunteer Infantry, 1863–1865* (Salem, N.H.: Ayer Co. Publishers, 1990), 29–30; William Wells Brown, *Negro in the American Rebellion; His Heroism and His Fidelity* (Boston: Lee & Shepard, 1867), 153–54.

57. Peter Burchard, *One Gallant Rush: Robert Gould Shaw and His Brave Black Regiment* (New York: St. Martin's Press, 1965), 93–94; Samuel Pickard, *Life and Letters of John Greenleaf Whittier*, 2 vols. (Boston: Houghton Mifflin, 1894), 2:362, quoted in Duncan, ed., *Child of Fortune*, 40; Lydia Maria Child to Sarah B. S. Shaw, July 1863, *Letters of Lydia Maria Child* (Boston, 1884), quoted in Fredrickson, *Inner Civil War*, 153.

58. O. B. Frothingham, quoted in Fredrickson, *Inner Civil War*, 83. Henry Lee spoke of the Boston officers as "young lambs," having observed the ardent eagerness with which they had sought their commissions. Lee had, of course, abetted the headlong rush of the Massachusetts men to the battlefield, having organized regiments, sorted out commissions, and done all he could to move men to the front. As they came home in coffins or never returned, these young men seemed to him to have "thrown away their lives like so many flowers." To glorify their self-sacrifice was to feel better about his own role.

59. CRL to JSL, 7.9.63, in Emerson, *Life*, 275; CRL to Henry Sturgis Russell, 7.26.63, ibid., 285; CRL to JSL, 7.27.63 and 7.26.63, Letters to Josephine Shaw Lowell, LFP.

60. CRL to ACJL, 7.26.63, in Emerson, *Life*, 284; CRL to JSL, 7.27.63, ibid., 286.

61. CRL to ACJL, 7.26.63, ibid., 284.

62. CRL to JSL, 7.28.63, ibid., 288; Robert Gould Shaw to CRL, 6.20.63, in Duncan, ed., *Child of Fortune*, 356.

63. CRL to JSL, 8.2.63 and 7.28.63, Letters to Josephine Shaw Lowell, LFP.

64. Burchard, *One Gallant Rush*, 135–36.

65. *Meade's Headquarters, 1863–1865: Letters of Colonel Theodore Lyman from the Wilderness to Appomattox*, ed. George R. Agassiz (Boston: Atlantic Monthly, 1922), 1.

66. CRL to JSL, 7.27.63 and 7.28.63, in Emerson, *Life*, 287, 289.

15. INGLORIOUS WARFARE, AUGUST–SEPTEMBER 1863

1. Mike Sorensen, "J. Sewall Reed," on "The Second Mass and Its Fighting Man," Website, http://2mass.omnica.com/Biographies/reed.htm.

2. Stanton Garner to author, 5.1.91.

3. Alexander Hunter quoted by Jeffry D. Wert, *Mosby's Rangers* (New York: Simon & Schuster, 1900), 77–78; Stanton Garner, "Melville's 'Scout Toward Aldie,'" in *Melville Society Extracts* 51 and 52 (September and November 1982), 3; Oscar DeWolf to James Mill Peirce, 4.23.66, JRL Papers, MHS.

4. CRL to JSL, 8.9.63, in Emerson, *Life*, 294; CRL to JMF, 8.12.63, EWE Papers, MHS; Samuel Hanscom to parents, 10.8.63, in Bruce MacAlpine, ed., "Corporal Samuel C. Hanscom's Letters Home," online at http://2mass.omnica.com/References/hanscom.htm; CRL to JSL, 8.9.63, in Emerson, *Life*, 294.

5. CRL to J. H. Taylor, 8.12.63, in *OR*, 29, pt. 1, 69.

6. William H. Moore, 8.9.63, in *Daily Alta California*, 9.9.63, in *THCT*, 172.

7. Alvord, "New England Boy," 322.

8. Thomas D. Barnstead, 11.28.63, in *Daily Alta California*, 12.29.63, in *THCT*, 208.

9. De Witt C. Thompson to L. C. Baker, 8.26.63, in *THCT*, 174.

10. CRL to JSL, 9.4.63, Letters to Josephine Shaw Lowell, LFP.

11. CRL to Henry Halleck, 8.22.63, in *THCT*, 175–76.

12. CRL to L. Thomas, 9.7.63, ibid., 191.

13. Thomas H. Merry, 9.6.63, in *Daily Alta California*, 10.4.63, ibid., 189.

14. David DeMerritt (compiled military service record), RG94, NA; CRL to JSL, 8.31.63, in Emerson, *Life*, 298–99.

15. Thomas D. Barnstead, 8.30.63, in *Daily Alta California*, 9.28.63, in *THCT*, 183; Thomas H. Merry, 9.6.63, in *Daily Alta California*, 10.4.63, ibid., 189; Caspar Crowninshield to Mammy, 8.25.63, Crowninshield-Magnus Papers, MHS; CRL to JSL, 10.8.63, in Emerson, *Life*, 311. On September 22 the court issued two findings. The first blamed Lowell for not having telegraphed to Lieutenant Pinkham the news that the regular escort would not meet the detachment, and for not ordering him to make other arrangements. Pinkham was secondarily blamed for not having had the sense to do so or to insist that Sergeant Varnum get an escort. However much Lowell might have resolved to "not care," he confessed that his reaction to this chastisement was shame.

16. William Channing Russel to Ellen Jackson, 8.3.63, Cabot Jackson Russel Papers, NYPL; CRL to JSL, 8.3.63, in Emerson, *Life*, 290.

17. CRL to JMF, 9.13.63, in Emerson, *Life*, 298; CRL to HLH, 9.14.63, ibid., 303.

18. CRL to JSL, 10.9.63, ibid., 311; CRL to J. H. Taylor, 8.24.63, in *OR*, 29, pt. 2, 113; H. B. Sargent quoted in Virgil Carrington Jones, *Gray Ghosts and Rebel Raiders* (McLean, Va.: EPM Publications, 1984), 196; CRL to JSL, 10.9.63, in Emerson, *Life*, 312.

19. CRL to JSL, 10.9.63, ibid., 313.

20. Nathaniel P. Banks to Sherman, 4.18.63, and Banks to Halleck, 3.27.63, in *OR* 15:703, 259; Halleck to Banks, 9.8.63, in *OR*, 26, pt. 1, 719–20.

21. William Hathaway Forbes to Alice Forbes, 9.15.63, REFC.

22. Samuel Backus, "Californians in the Field: Historical Sketch of the Organization and Services of the California 'Hundred' and 'Battalion,' 2nd Mass. Cav. A Paper Prepared and Read before California Commandery of the Military Order of the Loyal Legion of the United States, December 17, 1889," MOLLUS, no. 4 (1889).

23. CRL to HLH, 9.14.63, in Emerson, *Life*, 302.

24. CRL to JSL, 9.4.63, Letters to Josephine Shaw Lowell, LFP.
25. George Putnam, Jr. to Harriet Lowell Putnam, 8.8.63, LPFP, 2:169–70; CRL to JMF, 8.4.63, in Emerson, *Life*, 293.
26. CRL to JSL, 9.15.63, Letters to Josephine Shaw Lowell, LFP.
27. ACJL to Anna Lowell, 9.20.63, LPFP, 2:184.
28. CRL to JSL, 9.30.63, Letters to Josephine Shaw Lowell, LFP.
29. CRL to JSL, 10.13.63, in Emerson, *Life*, 313.
30. Thomas H. Merry, 9.6.63, in *Daily Alta California*, 10.4.63, in *THCT*, 189.
31. C. P. Briggs, 10.5.63, in *Napa Valley Register*, 11.7.63, ibid., 197.
32. JMF to Sarah Forbes, 11.20.63, REFC.
33. William Hathaway Forbes to Alice Forbes, 6.2.63, REFC.
34. James B. Randall to father, 10.29.63, in *THCT*, 204.
35. Samuel Backus, 10.25.63, ibid., 201.
36. CRL to J. H. Taylor, 10.20.63, Letters Received, Department and Defenses of Washington L-35, RG93, NA.
37. CRL to HLH, 10.1.63, in Emerson, *Life*, 309–10.
38. Perry, ed., *Higginson*, 212–13.
39. ACJL to Anna Lowell, 11.5.63, LPFP, 2:187.
40. Caspar Crowninshield to Mammy, 10.14.63, Crowninshield-Magnus Papers, MHS; William Hathaway Forbes to Alice Forbes, 11.3.63, and William Hathaway Forbes to EWE, 11.6.63, REFC.
41. CRL to ACJL, 11.19.63, LPFP, 2:189.
42. Ellen Tucker Emerson, 1.14.65, Ralph Waldo Emerson Additional Papers (bMS Am 1280.220), HL.
43. CRL to ACJL, 11.19.63, LPFP, 2:189.
44. CRL to HLH, 11.19.63, in Emerson, *Life*, 314; CRL to ACJL, 11.22.58, ibid., 172.

16. ALL QUIET ALONG THE POTOMAC, WINTER 1863–64

1. CRL to JSL, 8.4.63, in Emerson, *Life*, 291.
2. Thomas H. Merry, 9.6.63, in *Daily Alta California*, 10.4.63, in *THCT*, 190, 189.
3. De Witt C. Thompson to CRL, 12.3.63, ibid., 211.
4. CRL to Henry Sturgis Russell, 11.8.63, Letters of Charles Russell Lowell, vol. 4, LFP.
5. Caspar Crowninshield, 11.20.63, Letters Received, RG94, NA, in Thomas Parson, *Bear Flag and Bay State in the Civil War: The Californians of the Second Massachusetts Cavalry* (Jefferson, N.C.: McFarland, 2001), 97.
6. Samuel Backus to father, 10.25.63, in *Evening Bulletin* (San Francisco), 12.1.63, in *THCT*, 202.
7. Wert, *Mosby's Rangers*, 146.
8. Thomas D. Barnstead, 11.28.63, in *Daily Alta California*, 12.29.63, in *THCT*, 189; Louis Cabot to James Elliott Cabot, 11.26.63, Cabot Family Collection, SL.
9. Thomas D. Barnstead, 11.28.63, in *Daily Alta California*, 12.29.63, in *THCT*, 209.
10. CRL to J. H. Taylor, 11.26.63, OR 29, pt. 1, 658.
11. Thomas H. Merry, 12.22.63, in *Daily Alta California*, 1.31.64, in *THCT*, 220–24.
12. Ibid.
13. "Cadet," 11.25.63, in *Boston Journal*, 11.28.63, in *THCT*, 207.

14. Thomas H. Merry, 12.22.63, 12.7.63, and 12.22.63, in *Daily Alta California*, 1.31.64, 1.5.64, and 1.31.64, ibid., 220, 213, 221.
15. Charles A. Humphreys to Caspar Crowninshield, 1.8.64, in *Field, Camp, Hospital and Prison in the Civil War, 1863–1865; Charles A. Humphreys, Chaplain, Second Massachusetts Cavalry Volunteers* (Boston: G. H. Ellis, 1918), 388.
16. William Hathaway Forbes to JMF, 11.63, REFC; Caspar Crowninshield Diary, Crowninshield-Magnus Papers, MHS.
17. JMF to Sarah Forbes, 11.20.63, REFC.
18. William Hathaway Forbes to Alice Forbes, 9.6.63, REFC.
19. De Witt C. Thompson to CRL, 12.10.63, in *THCT*, 216. In his reports Lowell always mentioned when Mosby's effectiveness was enhanced by the help of "willing guides."
20. Thomas D. Barnstead, 4.30.63, in *Daily Alta California*, 6.10.63, in *THCT*, 130.
21. Ibid.
22. "Proceedings of a Drum-Head Court-Martial Convened at Head Quarters, Cavalry Camp, Vienna, Va., 2.6.64," M1523, Roll 7, Records of the Judge Advocate General, RG153, NA.
23. "Proceedings of a Court-Martial Convened at Head Quarters, Cavalry Camp, Vienna, Va., 11.14.63," Records of the Judge Advocate General, RG153, NA.
24. "Proceedings of a Drum-Head"; Humphreys, *Field, Camp, Hospital*, 19.
25. "Proceedings of a Drum-Head."
26. See Ella Lonn, *Desertion during the Civil War* (Lincoln: University of Nebraska Press, 1998).
27. "Proceedings of a Drum-Head"; Humphreys, *Field, Camp, Hospital*, 19.
28. Thomas H. Merry, 2.14.64, in *Daily Alta California*, 3.22.64, in *THCT*, 235; Humphreys, *Field, Camp, Hospital*, 20.
29. Pier, *Forbes*, 42.
30. Humphreys, *Field, Camp, Hospital*, 21.
31. Samuel Corbett Diary, 2.7.64, Samuel James Corbett Papers, BL.
32. Humphreys, *Field, Camp, Hospital*, 22; Pier, *Forbes*, 42; Valorus Dearborn Diary, 2.7.64, online at http://2mass.omnica.com/References/dearborn.htm.

17. FIGHTING THE GRAY GHOST, SPRING 1864

1. Wert, *Mosby's Rangers*, 146; William Hathaway Forbes to Alice Forbes, 2.24.64, REFC; Valorus Dearborn Diary, 2.22.64.
2. Humphreys, *Field, Camp, Hospital*, 392.
3. George W. Buhrer in E. E. Billings, "A California Soldier Writes Home," *Civil War Times*, May 1998; William Hathaway Forbes to Alice Forbes, 2.24.64, REFC; George A. Manning, 8.18.10, in *National Tribune*, online at http://2mass.omnica.com/References/Dranesville.htm.
4. Ibid.
5. *Memoirs of Colonel John S. Mosby*, ed. Charles Wells Russell (Boston: Little, Brown, 1917), 270–71.
6. Humphreys, *Field, Camp, Hospital*, 392.
7. Valorus Dearborn Diary, 2.24.64; *Washington Star*, 2.23.64; Humphreys, *Field, Camp, Hospital*, 392.

8. Charley Briggs, 2.26.64, in *Napa County Reporter*, 4.2.64, in *THCT*, 248; John Passage to Minnie Passage, 2.23.64, ibid., 244.

9. Caspar Crowninshield to Mammy, 2.27.64, Crowninshield-Magnus Papers, MHS.

10. CRL to JMF, 3.5.64, Letters of Charles Russell Lowell, vol. 4, LFP.

11. CRL to JMF, 2.24.64, in Emerson, *Life*, 316; Starr, *Union Cavalry*, 2:14–15, 69.

12. Starr, *Union Cavalry*, 2:69.

13. CRL to JMF, 2.24.64, Letters of Charles Russell Lowell, vol. 4, LFP.

14. Caspar Crowninshield to E. Y. Lansing, 3.12.64, in *THCT*, 253; CRL to JMF, 3.5.64, Letters of Charles Russell Lowell, vol. 4, LFP.

15. Thomas H. Merry, 3.25.64, in *Daily Alta California*, 4.28.64, in *THCT*, 261.

16. Valorus Dearborn Diary, 4.4.64.

17. Humphreys, *Field, Camp, Hospital*, 28.

18. Charles Russell Lowell Report, 4.20.64, in *OR*, 33, pt. 1, 306.

19. Herman Melville, *Billy Budd and Other Tales* (New York: Signet, 1961), 80.

20. Alvord, "New England Boy," 328; William Hathaway Forbes to Alice Forbes, 5.2.64, REFC; Caspar Crowninshield to Mammy, 5.2.64, Crowninshield-Magnus Papers, MHS.

21. Robert O. Tyler to Christopher C. Augur, 4.26.64, in *OR*, 33, pt. 1, 985; R. O. Tyler to C. C. Augur, 5.1.64, ibid., 316; C. C. Augur to John C. Kelton, 5.3.64, ibid., 315.

22. Charles Russell Lowell Report, 6.24.64, in *OR*, 37, pt. 1, 168; CRL to Taylor, 12.10.63, 1–54, Letters Received, Department and Defenses of Washington, RG13, NA; Lowell Report, 4.20.64, 306.

23. ACJL to Harriet Lowell Putnam, 5.19.64, LPFP, 2:193; Corbett Diary, 6.2.64; Louis Cabot to James E. Cabot, 12.09.63, Cabot Family Collection, SL.

24. William Hathaway Forbes to Alice Forbes, 6.5.64, REFC.

25. Valorus Dearborn Diary, 6.11.64; William Hathaway Forbes to Alice Forbes, 6.16.64, REFC; *HMB*, 2:328.

26. Samuel Hanscom, 6.18.64, in *THCT*, 276.

27. William Hathaway Forbes to Alice Forbes, 6.29.64, REFC.

28. Charles Russell Lowell Report, 7.8.64, *OR*, 37, pt. 1, 358–60.

29. CRL to JMF, 7.6.64, in Scott Schoenfeld, *The Fight at Aldie Gap* (Washington, D.C.: privately printed, 1992), 106–7.

30. Washington *Evening Star*, 7.9.64, quoted in Wert, *Mosby's Rangers*, 176.

31. *HMB*, 2:325–26.

32. Humphreys, *Field, Camp, Hospital*, 99–100; *HMB*, 2:331; Lowell Report, 7.8.64, 360.

33. CRL to JMF, 8.6.64, Letters of Charles Russell Lowell, vol. 4, LFP.

34. Pier, *Forbes*, 49.

18. REAL CAVALRY FIGHTING

1. Alvord, "New England Boy," 325–27.

2. Warren Cochran, Memoir, 2, EWE Papers, MHS.

3. Frank Robbins, Memoir, 7, JRL Papers, MHS.

4. Edward Thompson, CRL Miscellaneous Papers, NYPL.

5. Warren Cochran, 3, EWE Papers, MHS.

6. CRL to Christopher C. Augur, 7.13.64, in *OR*, 37, pt. 1, 252.

7. Edward Thompson, CRL Miscellaneous Papers, NYPL.

8. Backus, "Californians in the Field."
9. James M. Warner Report, 7.18.64, in *OR*, 37, pt. 1, 240; Martin D. Hardin, 7.19.64, ibid., 237; Robert O. Tyler to Christopher C. Augur, 4.26.64, in *OR*, 33, pt. 1, 985; Robert O. Tyler to Christopher C. Augur, 5.1.64, ibid., 316; Christopher C. Augur to John C. Kelton, 5.3.64, ibid., 315.
10. Jubal Early quoted in Grimsley, *Hard Hand of War*, 167.
11. Alvord, "New England Boy," 329; Caspar Crowninshield to Mammy, 8.2.64, Crowninshield-Magnus Papers, MHS; CRL to JSL, 8.2.64, Letters to Josephine Shaw Lowell, LFP.
12. Ulysses S. Grant to Henry Halleck, 8.1.64, quoted in *Personal Memoirs and Selected Letters of Ulysses S. Grant*, ed. Mary O. McFeely and William S. McFeely (New York: Library of America, 1990), 2:615.
13. CRL, Endorsement, 8.6.64, to De Witt C. Thompson to Caspar Crowninshield, 8.9.64, in *THCT*, 288.
14. CRL to JSL, 8.12.64, in Emerson, *Life*, 323.
15. Sheridan quoted in Jeffry D. Wert, *From Winchester to Cedar Creek* (Carlisle, Pa.: South Mountain Press, 1987), 37.
16. Philip H. Sheridan to Alfred A. Torbert, 8.16.64, in *OR*, 43, pt. 1, 816.
17. Ulysses S. Grant to David H. Hunter, 8.5.64, ibid., 698; Frank Robbins letter, n.d. 9, JRL Papers, MHS; CRL to JSL, 8.12.64, in Emerson, *Life*, 324.
18. Frank Robbins, Memoir, n.d., 10, JRL Papers, MHS.
19. Ibid., 12.
20. George W. Buhrer Diary, 8.25.64, in Billings, "A California Soldier Writes Home," 147.
21. Backus, "Californians in the Field," 13; Oscar DeWolf quoted in Forbes, *Reminiscences*, 2:312.
22. Frank Robbins, Memoir, n.d., 11, JRL Papers, MHS.
23. Oscar DeWolf to James M. Peirce, 4.23.66, JRL Papers, MHS.
24. George W. Towle, quoted in Parson, *Bear Flag*, 151.
25. Ibid.; EWE Papers, MHS; Edward Thompson, CRL Miscellaneous Papers, NYPL; Backus, "Californians in the Field," 17; Porter, EWE Papers, MHS.
26. CRL to JSL, 9.5.64, in Emerson, *Life*, 335; Caspar Crowninshield to Mammy, 9.8.64, Crowninshield-Magnus Papers, MHS; Oscar DeWolf to James M. Peirce, 4.23.66, JRL Papers, MHS.
27. Caspar Crowninshield to Mammy, 9.8.64, Crowninshield-Magnus Papers, MHS. When General Augur released Lowell to join Sheridan, he had given his permission on condition that Lowell command a brigade. It is an interesting endorsement, recalling Forbes's comments to Senator Sumner at the beginning of the war about Lowell being a "valuable man for everybody." JMF quoted in *LPFP*, 2:50–51.
28. Valorus Dearborn Diary, 8.26.64, quoted in Parson, *Bear Flag*, 149; Wert, *Winchester to Cedar Creek*, 71.
29. CRL to JSL, 9.5.64, in Emerson, *Life*, 336.
30. CRL to JMF, 9.10.64, ibid., 339; CRL to JSL, 9.5.64, ibid., 336.
31. George F. Price, *Across the Continent with the Fifth Cavalry* (New York: D. Van Nostrand, 1883), 224.
32. CRL to JSL, 9.9.64, in Emerson, *Life*, 338, 337.
33. CRL to JMF, 9.10.64, ibid., 339; CRL to JSL, 9.8.64, Letters to Josephine Shaw Lowell, LFL.

34. CRL to JSL, 9.9.64 and 9.1.64, in Emerson, *Life*, 338, 333; CRL to ACJL, 9.4.64, ibid., 334; CRL to JSL, 9.1.64, ibid., 333; CRL to HLH, 9.10.64, ibid., 340.

35. Charles Francis Adams, Jr. to HLH, 5.2.64, Henry Lee Higginson, Papers Relating to the Gift of Soldiers Field, HL; 8.17.64, Francis C. Barlow (compiled military service record), RG94, NA.

36. CRL to Francis C. Barlow, 9.10.64, in Emerson, *Life*, 343–44.

37. CRL to HLH, 9.10.64, ibid., 340–41.

38. Ibid., 342.

39. Ibid., 341.

40. CRL to JSL, 9.12.64, ibid., 346.

41. CRL to HLH, 9.10.64, ibid., 341; CRL to JSL, 9.8.64, ibid., 337.

19. WINCHESTER, SEPTEMBER 19, 1864

1. *Personal Memoirs of Philip H. Sheridan, General, United States Army* (1888; rpt. Cambridge, Mass.: DaCapo Press, 1992), 500.

2. Wesley Merritt, in *OR*, 43, pt. 1, 443.

3. Towle quoted in Parson, *Bear Flag*, 152; Smith quoted in Humphreys, *Field, Camp, Hospital*, 158; Backus, "Californians in the Field."

4. Wert, *Winchester to Cedar Creek*, 95.

5. Frederick Whittaker, *A Complete Life of General George A. Custer* (1876; rpt. Lincoln: University of Nebraska Press, 1993), 1:158.

6. Backus, "Californians in the Field."

7. Wert, *Winchester to Cedar Creek*, 95.

8. CRL to JSL, 7.24.63, in Emerson, *Life*, 281.

9. Towle quoted in Parson, *Bear Flag*, 154.

10. CRL to JSL, in Emerson, *Life*, 349.

11. CRL to Alice Forbes, 9.21.64, ibid., 348.

12. CRL to JSL, 8.24.64, ibid., 325–26.

13. Oscar DeWolf to JSL, JRL Papers, MHS; Robert H. Williams to parents, 8.26.64, in *THCT*, 296.

14. John Passage to Minnie Passage, 8.31.64, in *THCT*, 298; John Passage to Minnie Passage, 7.25.64, ibid., 285.

15. John Passage to Minnie Passage, 9.15.64, ibid., 303.

16. Samuel Backus to father, 10.25.63, ibid., 202; Greenslett, *Lowells*, 293.

17. Oscar DeWolf to JMF, 11.4.64, EWE Papers, MHS; Sergeant Porter, n.d., ibid.

18. See John Keegan, *The Mask of Command* (New York: Penguin, 1987). Keegan's book brilliantly develops the idea of the different masks that commanding officers have to wear.

19. Oscar DeWolf to JMF, 11.4.64, EWE Papers, MHS.

20. SCORCHED EARTH

1. Wert, *Winchester to Cedar Creek*, 131.

2. Samuel Corbett Diary, 9.22.64, BL.

3. F. E. Barron, in *National Tribune*, 5.18.11, quoted in *THCT*, 310.

4. Henry Halleck to Ulysses S. Grant, 9.4.63, *OR*, 43, pt. 2, 273.

5. Samuel Corbett Diary, 9.23.64, BL; George W. Buhrer Diary, 9.23.64, in Billings, "A California Soldier Writes Home"; Samuel Corbett Diary, 9.22.64, BL.

6. Horace Mewborn, *43rd Battalion, Virginia Cavalry, Mosby's Command* (Lynchburg, Va.: H. E. Howard, 1993), 163.

7. Robert C. Wallace, quoted in Roberta E. Fagan, "Custer at Front Royal: 'A Horror of the War'?" in Gregory Urwin, ed., *Custer and His Times* (Conway, Ark.: University of Central Arkansas Press, 1988).

8. Grimsley, *Hard Hand of War*, 113.

9. Samuel Corbett Diary, 9.23.64, BL; Samuel C. Willis, quoted in Fagan, "Custer at Front Royal," 41; ibid.

10. Ibid., 44; Laura Virginia Hale, *Four Valiant Years in the Lower Shenandoah Valley, 1861–1865* (Strasburg, Va.: Shenandoah Publishing, 1968), 431; Virgil Carrington Jones, *Ranger Mosby* (McLean, Va.: EPM Publications, 1987), 211; Denison quoted in Fagan, "Custer at Front Royal," 40; Bean quoted ibid., 43.

11. Caspar Crowninshield to Mammy, 10.2.64, Crowninshield-Magnus Papers, MHS.

12. CRL to JSL, 10.5.64, in Emerson, *Life*, 353.

13. Fagan, "Custer at Front Royal," 21.

14. James Harrison Wilson, *Under the Old Flag: Recollections of Military Operations in the War for the Union, the Spanish War, the Boxer Rebellion, etc.* (New York and London: D. Appleton, 1912), 559.

15. CRL to JSL, 9.27.64, 9.24.64, and 9.28.64, in Emerson, *Life*, 350, 349, 351.

16. CRL to JSL, 9.27.64, Letters to Josephine Shaw Lowell, LFP.

17. Grimsley, *Hard Hand of War*, 167.

18. Frederic Denison, *Sabres and Spurs: The First Regiment Rhode Island Cavalry in the Civil War, 1861–1865. Its Origin, Marches, Scouts, Skirmishes, Raids, Battles, Sufferings, Victories, and Appropriate Official Papers; with the Roll of Honor and Roll of the Regiment* (Central Falls, R.I.: The First Rhode Island Cavalry Veteran Association, 1876), 398–99.

19. Ibid.; George W. Buhrer Diary, 9.28.64., in Billings, "A California Soldier Writes Home."

20. Ibid.

21. CRL to JSL, 9.30.64, in Emerson, *Life*, 351–52.

22. *Memoirs of Sheridan*, 1:488; Denison, *Sabres*, 126.

23. Ulysses S. Grant to David H. Hunter, 8.5.64, in OR, 43, pt.1, 698.

24. Samuel Corbett Diary, 10.6.64, BL; CRL to JSL, 10.5.64, in Emerson, *Life*, 353.

25. Ibid.; Henry Kyd Douglas quoted in Hale, *Four Valiant Years*, 439.

26. "Rock Me to Sleep, Mother," on June-July Bills Payable, Frederick Quant Diary, 11–13, BL; CRL to JSL, 10.5.64, in Emerson, *Life*, 353–54.

27. Hale, *Four Valiant Years*, 433.

28. James McLean, *California Sabers: The 2nd Massachusetts Cavalry in the Civil War* (Bloomington: Indiana University Press, 2000), 151; Samuel Corbett Diary, 10.6.64, BL.

29. Wert, *Winchester to Cedar Creek*, 159; Philip Sheridan to Ulysses S. Grant, in OR, 43, pt. 2, 307–8; Wilbur Fiske quoted in Hale, *Four Valiant Years*, 434; Lucy Rebecca Buck, *Sad Earth, Sweet Heaven: The Diary of Lucy Rebecca Buck during the War Between the States, Front Royal, Virginia, December 25, 1861–April 15, 1865* (Birmingham, Ala.: Cornerstone, 1973), 287.

21. THE WOODSTOCK RACES, OCTOBER 9, 1864

1. Henry Kyd Douglas quoted in Hale, *Four Valiant Years*, 439; Whittaker, *George A. Custer*, 253.
2. Ibid., 256; Alfred Torbert quoted ibid., 1:255.
3. Towle quoted in Parson, *Bear Flag*, 22.
4. Alvord, "New England Boy," 332; Samuel Backus quoted in *HMB*, 2:320.
5. Alvord, "New England Boy," 330, 332.
6. Backus, "Californians in the Field."
7. Samuel Corbett Diary, 10.10.64, BL; Wesley Merritt Report, in *OR*, 43, pt. 1, 591; George E. Pond, *The Shenandoah Valley in 1864* (New York: Charles Scribner's Sons, 1883), 204.
8. CRL to JSL, 10.10.64, in Emerson, *Life*, 356.
9. CRL to JSL, 10.14.64, ibid., 359; Samuel Corbett Diary, 10.12.64, BL.
10. Mrs. B. Forbes to Rose Forbes, in *Family Letters, 1861–1869 of Charles Eliot Perkins and Edith Forbes Perkins*, ed. Edith Perkins Cunningham (Boston: privately printed, 1949), 208; Caroline H. Dall to Lizzie Putnam, 10.29.64, James Russell Lowell Papers, MHS.
11. CRL to JSL, 10.10.64, in Emerson, *Life*, 356.
12. Ibid.
13. Ibid.; Humphreys, *Field, Camp, Hospital*, 162.
14. CRL to JSL, 10.10.64, in Emerson, *Life*, 356.
15. Emerson, *Life*, 332.
16. CRL to ACJL, 9.4.64, LPFP, 2:202–3.
17. CRL to JSL, 8.12.64, 8.25.64, and 9.5.64, in Emerson, *Life*, 323, 328, 336.
18. CRL to JSL, 10.7.64, 10.12.64, 10.13.64, and 10.12.64, ibid., 354, 357, 359, 357.
19. CRL to JSL, 10.13.64 and 10.15.64, ibid., 358, 360.
20. CRL to Charles Eliot Perkins, 10.17.64, Letters of Charles Russell Lowell, vol. 4, LFP.
21. CRL to JMF, 10.17.64, in Emerson, *Life*, 363–64.
22. CRL to ACJL, 10.17.64, ibid., 364–65.
23. CRL to ACJL, 10.17.64, LPFP, 2:209–10; CRL to JSL, 10.64, in Emerson, *Life*, 357–58.
24. CRL to ACJL, 10.17.64, LPFP, 2:210.

22. THE BATTLE OF CEDAR CREEK, OCTOBER 19, 1864

1. Philip H. Sheridan to Ulysses S. Grant, 10.20.64, in *OR*, 43, pt. 2, 424. Although Emerson says three-thirty and that is usually the time given, DeWolf and Alvord, who were both there, say 4 a.m. Buhrer's diary says four.
2. Henry Alvord, "Notes from My Journal," 2, James Russell Lowell Papers, MHS; James H. Kidd, *Personal Recollections of a Cavalryman, with Custer's Michigan Cavalry Brigade in the Civil War* (Ionia, Mich.: Sentinel Printing Company, 1908), 412.
3. Kidd, ibid.; for the failure of orders see Benjamin W. Crowninshield, "Cedar Creek," Papers of the Military Historical Society (Boston: Military Historical Society of Massachusetts, 1907), 6:171.
4. Kidd, *Recollections*, 414.
5. William Dwight, quoted in Hazard Stevens, "The Battle of Cedar Creek," in *Shenandoah and Appomattox Campaigns*, Papers of the Military Historical Society of Massachusetts (Boston: Military Historical Society of Massachusetts, 1907), 6:112.
6. Wert, *Winchester to Cedar Creek*, 214.

7. Alvord, "Notes," 3; Kidd, *Recollections*, 412.
8. Mike Sorensen, "Captain Rufus Smith," online at http://2mass.omnica.com/Biographies/smith.htm; *History of Alameda County, California* (1883), quoted in Michael Fitzpatrick, *William Henry Harrison Hussey*, online at http://2mass.omnica.com/Biographies/hussey.htm.
9. Alvord, "Notes," 5.
10. See Stevens, "Battle of Cedar Creek," 123.
11. George A. Forsyth, *Thrilling Days in Army Life* (New York, London: Harper, 1900), 148.
12. Henry Crocker, quoted in Richard K. Tibbals, "An Act of Valor and a Medal of Honor: Thirty Years Later," in *Civil War Times Illustrated*, April 1986, 39–40; see Augustus C. Hamlin, "Who Recaptured the Guns at Cedar Creek?" in Papers of the Military Historical Society of Massachusetts (Boston: Military Historical Society of Massachusetts, 1907), 202; Crocker, in Tibbals, "An Act of Valor," 40–41; John Passage to Minnie Passage, 8.31.64, in THCT, 299, 298.
13. Samuel Corbett Diary, 10.19.64, BL; Whittaker, *George A. Custer*, 235.
14. Alvord, "Notes," 6–7; H. Hastings Smith to Harriet Lowell Putnam, 1890, in EWE Papers, MHS; Alvord, "Notes," 7.
15. Ibid.
16. Ibid.; William H. Thayer, JRL Papers, MHS.
17. Caspar Crowninshield to Mammy, 10.21.64, Crowninshield-Magnus papers, MHS.
18. Alvord, "Notes," 8.
19. Oscar DeWolf to JSL, 10.21.64, JRL Papers, MHS.
20. Records of the Harvard College Class of 1854, *Evening Transcript*, 10.26.64, in Charles Russell Lowell Biographical (HUG 300), HUA; Caspar Crowninshield to Mammy, 10.21.64, Crowninshield-Magnus Papers, MHS.
21. Oscar DeWolf to JMF, EWE Papers, MHS.
22. Oscar DeWolf to JSL, 10.21.64, JRL Papers, MHS.
23. Oscar DeWolf to JMF, EWE Papers, MHS; Oscar DeWolf to JSL, 10.21.64, JRL Papers, MHS.
24. Caspar Crowninshield to Mammy, 10.21.64, Crowninshield-Magnus Papers, MHS.
25. Oscar DeWolf to JSL, 10.21.64, JRL Papers, MHS.

EPILOGUE: AFTERMATH

1. Allan Nevins, ed., *A Diary of Battle: The Personal Journals of Colonel Charles S. Wainwright, 1861–1865* (New York: Harcourt, Brace & World, 1962), 475; HMB, 327; Philip Sheridan to JSL, n.d., quoted in Greenslett, *Lowells*, 298.
2. Col. George B. Sanford, LPFP, 2:220–21.
3. William Schouler, *A History of Massachusetts in the Civil War*, 2 vols. (Boston: E. P. Dutton & Co., 1868–71), 2:151–52.
4. ACJL to Anna Lowell, 8.21.64, LPFP, 2:200.
5. Hughes, ed., *Letters of Forbes*, 2:113.
6. ACJL to Anna Lowell, 10.23.64, LPFP, 2:211; Alvord, "New England Boy," 332–33.
7. George Putnam to Harriet Lowell Putnam, 10.23.64, LPFP, 2:212.
8. ACJL to Sarah Jackson Russel, 12.17.43, LPFP, 1:134.
9. CRL to JSL, 10.16.64, in Emerson, *Life*, 361; Oscar DeWolf to JSL, 10.21.64, JRL Papers, MHS.

10. Charles Russell Lowell, Sr. to Anna Lowell, 11.1.64, LPFP, 2:213; HLH to EWE, 11.15.06, EWE Papers, MHS.
11. JRL, "Commemoration Ode," quoted in LPFP, 2:238.
12. Perry, ed., *Higginson*, 299.
13. Ibid.; "Soldier's Faith," in Lerner, ed., *Mind and Faith*, 23, 24; "Memorial Day," ibid., 10.
14. CRL to HLH, 9.10.64, in Emerson, *Life*, 342.
15. ACJL to Anna Lowell, 12.6.64, LPFP, 2:227.
16. ACJL to Charles Russell Lowell, Sr., 1.12.65, LPFP, 2:232–33.
17. Elizabeth Cabot Putnam, "Brigadier-General Charles Russell Lowell and Josephine Shaw Lowell," 11, PJLFP; Stewart, *Philanthropic Work*, 43; ACJL to Anna Lowell, 11.1.66, LPFP, 2:257.
18. Stewart, *Philanthropic Work*, 51.
19. Elizabeth Cabot Putnam, "Brigadier-General Charles Russell Lowell and Josephine Shaw Lowell," PJLFP.
20. Some scholars have characterized Effie as an example of upper-class elitists using charity to mask their contempt for the masses. For a more balanced view see Joan Waugh, *Unsentimental Reformer: The Life of Josephine Shaw Lowell* (Cambridge, Mass.: Harvard University Press, 1997), and Joan Waugh, "From Charity to Politics: Josephine Shaw Lowell, Scientific Charity, and the Origins of Women's Political Activism in New York City, 1879–1890," Center for the Study of Philanthropy (New York: CUNY, 1992). And finally, I refer you to the correspondence of her biographer in the William Rhinelander Stewart collection at the New York Public Library. Weir Mitchell, writing to Stewart, 8.12.07, described her diary as expressing "extreme views." He wanted to omit "all extreme newspaper nonsense about the barbarities of the rebels and in fact of our own people." Worse, Robert Hill to Stewart, 9.3.09, gives his reaction on reading her journals (no longer extant): "It is somewhat amusing, however, to note the intensity with which she spoke of the evils of poverty, especially in connection with the views of Henry George. I doubt that it will be advisable to print the sentence in which she expresses a readiness for 'the revolution and cutting of throats.' "
21. Jacob Riis, quoted in "The Memorial Meeting, October 12, 1905, United Charities Building, New York," in "A Memorial Number: Josephine Shaw Lowell," in *Charities and the Commons: A Weekly Journal of Philanthropy and Social Advance*, Charity Organization Society of the City of New York 15, no. 9 (December 2, 1905): 317.

ACKNOWLEDGMENTS

I have incurred enormous debts of gratitude writing this book. Michael Musik at the National Archives introduced me to the late John Divine of Leesburg, Virginia. John shared with me his comprehensive knowledge of the Civil War history of northern Virginia and also referred me to Horace Mewborn, who took me on an extended tour of Mosby's Confederacy. David Gregg and Scott Schoenfeld of the Forbes family were very generous making available family archives. Scott also took me on a trip to Aldie, Virginia, and shared his knowledge of that skirmish. Mike Fitzpatrick, Mike Sorensen, Wayne Sherman, and most of all Larry Rogers helped on Californian aspects of the regiment. Tom Parson shared his knowledge and his invaluable insights into the Second Massachusetts Cavalry. For the supply of manuscript material I also thank the late Frances L. Burnett, Anna Lowell Tomlinson, Andy Harris, Lloyd Garrison, Ellen Shaw Kean, the late Dr. George Sturgis, and Mrs. Helen Almy Bradley. Also, Jeff Hull at the Veterans Administration Hospital in Dayton, Ohio. The Massachusetts Military Archives at Natick, the Massachusetts Historical Society, the Houghton Library, the Harvard University Archives, the New York Public Library, the Staten Island Institute of Arts and Sciences, and the Newberry Library have all provided valuable material. My entire family has been a source of great moral and practical support, and I thank them all. My brother Michael Bundy stands in a class all his own. For their care of my children, I thank Matt Szymankowski, Win Ruml, and most of all our beloved Manda Nichols. Of the many friends who have offered their support, advice, or faith, I would like to mention Nicholas Stogdon, Clare and Peter Libby, Valerie and Richard Constable, and the late Richard Godfrey; also, Heather Crocker, Parky and Lisa Shaw, Jackie Sohier and Jay Anania, Kemp Battle, George Pettinari, Belinda Rathbone, and, with extra gratitude, Hiller Zobel. My agent, Geri Thoma, has been the soul of patience. My editor, Elisabeth Sifton, I cannot praise too highly: her kindness and brilliance are unparalleled.

INDEX